LATIN AMERICAN
MILITARY HISTORY

MILITARY HISTORY BIBLIOGRAPHIES
(VOL. 12)

GARLAND REFERENCE LIBRARY
OF THE HUMANITIES
(VOL. 1024)

MILITARY HISTORY BIBLIOGRAPHIES

Advisory Editors:
Robin Higham
Jacob W. Kipp

1. *Israeli Military History: A Guide to the Sources*
   by Jehuda L. Wallach

2. *German Military Aviation: A Guide to the Literature*
   by Edward H. Homze

3. *German Military History: 1648–1982: A Critical Bibliography*
   by Dennis E. Showalter

4. *The Military in Imperial History: The French Connection*
   by Alf Andrew Heggoy and John M. Haar

5. *Japanese Military History: A Guide to the Literature*
   by Shinji Kondo

6. *French Military History, 1661–1799: A Guide to the Literature*
   by Steven T. Ross

7. *German Naval History: A Guide to the Literature*
   by Keith W. Bird

8. *Balkan Military History: A Bibliography*
   by John E. Jessup

9. *Napoleonic Military History: A Bibliography*
   edited by Donald D. Horward

10. *British Military History: A Supplement to Robin Higham's* Guide
    to the Sources
    by Gerald Jordan

11. *French Military Aviation: A Bibliographic Guide*
    by Charles Christienne, Patrick Facon, Patrice Buffotot, and
    Lee Kennett

12. *Latin American Military History: An Annotated Bibliography*
    edited by David G. LaFrance and Errol D. Jones

13. *British Naval History Since 1815: A Guide to the Literature*
    by Eugene L. Rasor

LATIN AMERICAN MILITARY HISTORY
An Annotated Bibliography

edited by
David G. LaFrance
and
Errol D. Jones

GARLAND PUBLISHING, INC. • NEW YORK & LONDON
1992

Library of Congress Cataloging–in–Publication Data

Latin American military history : an annotated bibliography / edited
by David G. LaFrance and Errol D. Jones.
    p.   cm. — (Military history bibliographies ; vol. 12)
(Garland reference library of the humanities ; vol. 1024)
   ISBN 0–8240–4634–X
   1. Latin American—History, Military—Bibliography. I. LaFrance,
David G. (David Gerald), 1948–   . II. Jones, Errol D., 1942–   .
III. Series. IV. Series: Garland reference library of the humanities ;
vol. 1024.
Z1621.L38   1992
[F1410.5]
016.355'0098—dc20   92–12606
                                    CIP

Printed on acid-free, 250-year-life paper
Manufactured in the United States of America

CONTENTS

General Editors' Introduction   vii
Preface   ix
Map   xii

I.   Introduction to Latin American Military History Research   1
David G. LaFrance and Errol D. Jones

II.   Latin American Colonial Era   8
Mark A. Burkholder

III.   The Latin American Independence Movements   43
Christon I. Archer

IV.   Nineteenth-Century Latin American Caudillismo   104
Guy P.C. Thomson

V.   Argentina   188
Errol D. Jones

VI.   Bolivia, Ecuador, and Peru   277
Thomas M. Davies, Jr.

VII.   Brazil   342
Errol D. Jones

VIII. The Caribbean   485
Bruce J. Calder

IX.   Central America   557
Stephen Webre

X.   Chile   587
Brian Loveman

XI.   Colombia and Venezuela   622
Winfield J. Burggraaff

XII.   Mexico   654
David G. LaFrance

XIII. Paraguay and Uruguay   718
John Hoyt Williams

THE GENERAL EDITORS' INTRODUCTION

Military history is a vast international field touching upon all aspects of society, yet guides to the immense literature it contains, essential for anyone writing in the field, have largely been conspicuous by their absence. Over twenty years ago an international start was made by Robin Higham with *Official Histories* (1970), which for the first time enabled even official historians to check what other offices had produced. That work established a pattern of historical essays, some by the original authors, followed by a checklist of the works published. While this was in process, *A Guide to the Sources of British Military History* (1971) was commenced along slightly different lines. In this each author was asked to provide a bibliographic essay over a segment of the military, naval or air history of one country, with a numbered alphabetical list by authors of those cited following. A further feature of each chapter was a short concluding section suggesting what research remained to be undertaken as well as what could profitably be reviewed. So successful was this volume, published simultaneously in the United States and in Britain, that not only did it become a standard library reference work, but also the editor was asked to undertake a similar compilation for U.S. military history. This latter guide was completed in 1975 on a more far-seeing scheme in which quinquennial supplements were planned to keep the work up to date (the first of these was issued in 1981). It was on the basis of these three successful volumes that the editors were approached by Garland in May 1978 to undertake the present series.

By that time both editors were involved in the United States and in the International Commissions for Military History, Dr. Higham being on the Editorial Advisory Board and Dr. Kipp on the Bibliographical Committee. They agreed with Garland that they would undertake to produce an international series of some thirty-odd volumes to provide scholars access to the vast collections in all the countries in the world other than the United States and the United Kingdom. Those authors whose native language was not English should also produce a volume in their own tongue so that scholars of at least two major languages concerned with the military history of that country should benefit. No limits were set on length, though as with the two previous *Guides* it was not expected that these works would be either totally comprehensive or exhaustive, if for no other than the two very good reasons that in most cases there is a lot of repetitive material and that inevitably bibliographies are dated from the moment their sections are completed.

The very existence of the International Commission on Military History and the vigorous programs of the various national commissions that compose it confirm the vitality of the field of military history. Both editors believe that this bibliographic series can render a valuable service by facilitating the study of military history across national lines and in a comparative context. It is hoped that each volume will make explicit the general and particular historiographic approaches associated with an individual nation's military institutions. In such a manner researchers will be able to consult a single volume that will outline the historiographic developments for a particular nation's military experience or, in the case of major powers, of that of one of its principal armed services. Such a guide, it is hoped, will serve as a compass for further research, both enumerating what has been done and suggesting what still needs to be done.

Essentially the authors have been asked to provide readable essays that will guide the readers through the labyrinth of the most important sources as though walking through a library and archives, mentioning authors and titles, but leaving the details to be acquired by taking the works from the shelves, in this case the numbered lists at the back of each chapter. Both authors and editors would be happy to have comments and suggestions from readers and users.

Jacob W. Kipp
Foreign Military Studies Office
U.S. Army Combined
Arms Center
Fort Leavenworth, KS   66027

Robin Higham
Department of History
Kansas State University
Manhattan, KS   66506, USA

PREFACE

A bibliography dealing with the history of the military in Latin America from the beginning days of the conquest in the late fifteenth century to the present is an overwhelming task for one or two historians to undertake. Therefore, when Robin Higham, one of the general editors for Garland Publishing's MILITARY HISTORY BIBLIOGRAPHIES series, approached us to do a bibliography on Latin America for that series, we immediately decided to enlist the aid of our colleagues in the field who were already familiar with the history of the military in a particular country or during a specific period. In this way, the joint effort of numerous experts in Latin American military history have enabled us to provide a bibliography that, while selective, is far more authoritative, comprehensive, and insightful than would have been possible otherwise.

The contributors to this bibliography have been free to select and comment on the works they thought most appropriate to include in their respective chapters. Nevertheless, we have adopted a general organizational format to which each chapter conforms. With few exceptions, following an introduction to their specific fields, each author includes sections on general works; bibliographies; archival guides and sources; published documents; memoirs, journals and eyewitness accounts; specialized works as well as periodicals and concludes with suggestions for future research. At the end of each bibliographic essay the author has listed the relevant works in alphabetical order. Each entry in the bibliography has a number which conforms to the one given it where it is mentioned in the essay. Not all citations listed in the bibliography are mentioned in the text owing to limitations of space. There are some duplicate citations, but these occur when several contributors considered the same work significant to their particular topics. Similarly, numerous authors listed many of the same periodicals because that particular publication carries articles pertinent to their respective areas, but for the most part the periodicals in each chapter are specific to that country's military history.

The works cited in this bibliography are mainly in English, Portuguese, and Spanish, with some citations in Dutch, French, German, and Russian. We have tried to be consistent in listing the entries in conformity with accepted practices common to each language. However, with the titles of books and periodicals we have employed capital letters rather than italics or underlinings and have dropped all diacritical markings. Thus: Comblin, Joseph. A ideologia da segurança nacional: o poder militar na América Latina, becomes; Comblin, Joseph. A IDEOLOGIA DA SEGURANCA NACIONAL: O PODER MILITAR NA AMERICA LATINA. Likewise, for simplicity's sake, we have opted for the shortest description possible of works that are contained in series or published by departments of various institutes or special programs, retaining only the essential data as to edition, volume number, place, publisher, and date.

Since this volume has been in the making for the past four years, each chapter has been revised and corrected several times and some have been updated as new literature has appeared in the field. For the most part, however, research was completed in 1990 and publications up to that year have been included. Scholarly interest in the history of the military in Latin America continues to grow at a rapid pace and new works appear almost daily, making today's bibliography out of date tomorrow. Despite this problem common to all bibliographies, we have made every effort to include the most recent materials published in each of the authors' fields.

To all our colleagues who contributed to this volume we express our appreciation and admiration for their excellent essays, their patience, and their words of encouragement and support. Not only did they give freely of their time and knowledge, but they graciously accepted our criticisms and corrections and expeditiously returned revised copies without complaint. We are also indebted to Robin Higham for his helpful comments and critical evaluation of each chapter. His experience and knowledge in the field of military history have benefited this work immensely.

Finally, we fall short of adequately being able to demonstrate our appreciation to the many people at Boise State University who have good-naturedly given their time and energy to enable us to complete this task. Robert Sims, Dean of the School of Social Sciences and Public Affairs, took serious interest in this project and found monies to aid in its completion. Marilyn Paterson of the Department of History typed most of the chapter on Brazil, making several corrections and revisions and not once condemning the Portuguese for inventing a language that made reading hand-written note cards and bibliographic citations an almost impossible chore. Liliana Angeles skillfully typed the lengthy bibliography on nineteenth-century caudillismo. Melanie Adams employed her mastery of computer technology in the Office of Research Administration, typing revision after corrected revision of the entire manuscript until we got it right. We tried her patience to the limit, but she saw the project through to the end with great tolerance. Susan Stacy and Juan Lemus, research assistants in the Department of History at Boise State University, checked citations and assisted in the research for the Brazil chapter. Russell Tremayne diligently aided in the research on the Argentine chapter and entered hundreds of bibliographic citations into the computer. Our thanks to all of these people and to the many researchers whose quest to understand the role of the military in Latin American society has made this bibliography possible. We hope that it serves as a useful guide to future students who will find it helpful in furthering our understanding of the armed forces in Latin America.

Latin American
Military History

CHAPTER I

INTRODUCTION TO LATIN AMERICAN MILITARY HISTORY RESEARCH

David G. LaFrance
Oregon State University

Errol D. Jones
Boise State University

INTRODUCTION

As we enter the decade of the 1990s few countries in Latin America find themselves under military control. This has not always been the case. Only ten years earlier the armed forces ruled directly in Argentina, Bolivia, Brazil, Chile, Guatemala, Honduras, Panama, Paraguay and Uruguay; moreover, in many other countries of the region they ruled indirectly or exerted tremendous pressure on civilian politicians.

Latin American military forces are small when compared to those of most other countries of commensurate size, but the military institution historically looms large in Latin America as a force of political and socio-economic influence and intervention. From the time Spanish and Portuguese military adventurers began to make their mark on the indigenous peoples of the Americas in the late fifteenth century, military forces, whether organized by the state and under its control, or armed bands controlled by those who were free from or in competition with the state, have played a significant historical role. Despite the historical importance of the military in Latin America no important analytical studies were published on the subject until the 1960s. Although the political and even the social roles of the Latin American armed forces certainly had not gone unnoticed by earlier social scientists and historians, Edwin Lieuwen pointed out in his pioneer work ARMS AND POLITICS IN LATIN AMERICA (1960) that no one had systematically studied these aspects of the region's armed forces. Instead, historians demonstrated a fascination with the individual military man, the caudillo on horseback and the cult of personalism; they focused on wars, campaigns, battles, and leaders. Political scientists, meanwhile, devoted themselves to an examination of laws, constitutions, political parties, and policy shifts. Few scholars studied the military as an institution with interests of its own and as a dynamic and changing actor on the complex socio-economic and political stage.

In the thirty years since Lieuwen published his work for the Council on Foreign Relations, a veritable avalanche of scholarly works on the Latin American armed forces has poured forth from the presses in Latin America, the United States, and Europe. The purpose of this bibliography is to serve as a selective guide to that body of literature as well as to relevant earlier studies and to the archival sources and other materials dealing with the military in Latin America from colonial times to the present. It discusses the most significant resource materials available in Europe, Latin America and in the United States and each chapter provides an analysis of the areas of military history that need to be probed. It is intended for students of the armed forces who wish to find information on the military at a certain period and in a specific country. Those individuals embarking upon a research project dealing with the Latin American armed forces for the purpose of writing seminar papers, M.A. theses, or Ph.D. dissertations will find this bibliography of value. This volume will be useful even to the specialist, especially as a finding aid for comparative analysis of the areas in which the researcher is not an expert.

It is not with the series of military takeovers of the 1960s and early 1970s that the armed forces' influence on the development of Latin American society first began, but much earlier with the coming of the Spanish and the Portuguese to the New World in the late fifteenth and early sixteenth centuries. However, as Mark Burkholder explains in his bibliographic essay on the Latin American colonial period, neither Spain nor Portugal sent many regular troops to the colonies. Rather, the crowns relied upon the bureaucracy and the Catholic Church to maintain control of their western empire. In order fully to understand the military during the colonial era, one must focus attention on such topics as frontier security, fleet protection, defense against pirates and foreign invasion, and the intermittent rivalry between the two Iberian powers over the disputed Río de la Plata region. Intensifying imperial stuggle in the last half of the eighteenth century, however, forced the Bourbon rulers of Spain to reorganize and to grant special privileges to the colonial militias and to create standing armies in the New World.

These steps further depleted scarce resources and shifted a measure of power from the church to the military.

For much of Latin America the protracted wars of independence in the early nineteenth century propelled the armed forces to a position of political power they had never before experienced. Christon Archer's essay weaves a complex and intricate tapestry from the diverse and disparate strands that emerged during the struggles to break free from the Iberian metropolises. Independence from Spain and Portugal may have meant political freedom for the newly emergent republics, but it did not necessarily bring peace and prosperity for their inhabitants. As historians moved away from biography and battle accounts, they directed their attention to social, economic, and political topics that are interrelated to the military events of independence. Despite what may appear on the surface as a well-worn road for researchers, Archer points out the many unknown twists and turns in the thoroughfare that still exist for the curious and resourceful investigator.

Certainly one of the results of the movements of independence was the growing strength and power of the military in the Latin American republics that led to its entrenchment in some of the new nations. During the half century following independence, won in the early 1820s, the region "fostered a political culture in which the armed route to power," as Guy Thomson notes in his chapter on nineteenth-century caudillismo, "became almost everywhere commonplace and even legitimate." In fact, the political role of the military in the nineteenth century was so extensive that the two countries free from armed forces control during this era, Brazil and Chile, are regarded as exceptions to the general rule. For most of Latin America this was the "Age of Caudillismo," a time during which there existed a political order characterized by rule not of laws and constitutions, but of powerful, charismatic men on horseback able to command the loyalty of armed bands and to impose their will on regions or upon nations. Thomson's essay, while pointing the way to sources on national caudillos, emphasizes materials that throw light on the conditions that brought these rulers to power. He is also concerned with those resources that indicate the existence and explain the nature of formal military institutions which began to form during the nineteenth century.

As civilian political forces gained control of the state in the latter part of the nineteenth century, they sought to rein in the caudillos and to make them subservient to civil authorities. This goal could be accomplished, it was believed, by creating a professional military institution modeled after those that existed in Europe at the time. Civilian and military leaders throughout Latin America busied themselves with establishing formal, professional military institutions subordinate to the legitimate powers as prescribed by their constitutions. French and German military missions trained their Latin American counterparts in modern military methods and infused them with a sense of pride, professionalism, and esprit de corps. At the end of the century evidence of military professionalism could be found in almost all of the region's armed forces. These modern institutions were to obtain their officers from military academies based upon an educational system that trained young men for a career in the armed forces. Upward mobility in this new profession would be based upon technical expertise and merit. The military, it was hoped, would be free from the meddling of civilian politicians and preoccupied with its newly developed professional duties, thus forgoing interference in national politics.

Therefore, an important aspect of twentieth-century Latin American military history is the account of growing European-style professionalism within the ranks, but as Frederick Nunn has so convincingly demonstrated, the goal of an apolitical institution failed to be realized. Instead, military professionalism came to mean in many countries professional militarism. This situation is perhaps nowhere better illustrated than in Argentina. Its military dominated the political life of that South American nation during much of the twentieth century. Consequently, historians attracted to studies of the Argentine military have tended almost exclusively to focus on the armed forces in politics. Errol Jones's chapter highlights the essential literature covering that involvement, but his bibliographic essay sketches the resources available for a multiplicity of research approaches to a deeper understanding of the professional armed forces and their political, economic and social role in Argentina.

In his review of the resources for study of the armed forces in the Andean countries of Bolivia, Ecuador, and Peru, Thomas M. Davies, Jr., notes that while there are similarities between the three nations' defense establishments, and their history of involvement in national political affairs, the Peruvian military's sophistication and unique institutional development, together with its importance as a "reformist/revolutionary" regime (1968-80), has attracted the lion's share of scholarly attention. For all three countries there is a serious need for research into virtually every aspect and period of the armed forces' history.

With its victory over Paraguay in the War of the Triple Alliance (1864-70), Brazil's armed forces began to intrude upon the political stage heretofore dominated by the monarchy. Ultimately they made an alliance with Republicans to unseat Dom Pedro II from his throne in 1889. With that, the Brazilian military embarked upon a journey through modern Brazilian history that has made it one of the most important and powerful institutions in that nation's evolution. In his chapter on the Brazilian armed forces, Errol D. Jones discusses the growing body of literature available for research into the complexities of military history in Brazil. While the student may be overwhelmed by the abundance of studies already done, there is a myriad of questions that remain as yet unanswered about the role of the armed forces in Brazilian society. With the return to civilian political control in 1990, an already open society has become even more accessible to the scholar thereby increasing the research opportunities that now abound. Jones's chapter indicates what has been done so far and where scholars need to direct attention for the future.

Owing to the important strategic location of the Caribbean islands, the military history of this region is of great complexity and significance. As Bruce Calder illustrates in his essay on the Caribbean, researchers must keep in mind the historical reality that this area has been a "zone of confrontation between larger outside powers." As a result the Caribbean policies of the United States and European countries must be taken into consideration and studied for an understanding of these important outside influences on Caribbean military history. While Cuba has begun to receive its deserved attention, the armed forces of other nations have been almost ignored, especially for the period from World War II to the present.

Like the Caribbean, Central America in the nineteenth and twentieth centuries has attracted the attention of outside powers whose commercial and strategic interests have led them to attempt to influence the internal development of the countries comprising the isthmus. The various military institutions of the Central American nations have been so central to their societies that, according to Stephen Webre, their influence affects "every aspect of life." Including Panama along with the five "historic" republics of Central America, Webre surveys the history of the region and analyzes the available resources for research into the armed forces of each of the nations. He concludes with numerous suggestions for future research including calling for more studies on the influence of foreign military missions in shaping the area's armed forces, as well as the need to challenge some of the prevailing assumptions about the Central American military.

Brian Loveman's bibliographic essay on Chile emphasizes the importance of the military in the development of the nation, its role in the extension of Chile's frontiers at the expense of neighboring republics and of indigenous peoples to the south. The armed forces helped mold Chilean nationalism and secured mineral rich regions upon which the economic foundation of the modern state is based. For much of the twentieth century Chile was noted for its professional, apolitical military; on the rare occasions that it intervened in the nation's political life, soldiers quickly withdrew to their barracks leaving such affairs to the civilians. This tradition came to an end in 1973 when the armed forces overthrew the elected Popular Unity government led by Salvador Allende and established a military dictatorship which lasted until 1990. After assessing the resources available on Chile's armed services and what has been written about them, Loveman calls for more "systematic empirical studies of the evolution, role, and performance" of the military and of civil-military relations.

The history of the armed forces in Colombia and Venezuela has been, as Winfield J. Burggraaff notes, "a study in contrasts." On the one hand, during most of the twentieth century the Colombian armed forces have been politically weak and subordinate to the country's powerful political elites. The Venezuelan army, on the other hand, totally dominated the country from 1899 to 1958 (with the exception of the three years, 1945-48, when Acción Democrática ruled). The bulk of the literature on the military of these two countries naturally favors Venezuela, but Colombia, as Burggraaff's essay shows, has not been ignored by historians. For an understanding of the military institution in both nations much remains to be researched even though significant accomplishments have been realized in the last quarter century.

David G. LaFrance in his chapter on Mexico shows that the Revolution of 1910 has had a great impact on both the military of that country and the historiography of the institution. Unlike most other Latin American nations where the armed forces have exhibited an overt tendency to interfere in civilian politics, in Mexico a complex set of factors emanating from the revolution (1910-1920) has meant a much reduced political role for the military. Scholars of the armed forces, in addition to the customary attention to battles, biographies, and the like, have also focused on why and how Mexico's experience is distinctive. LaFrance points out, however, that some recent works indicate that Mexico's polity may not be as free from military influence as observers have claimed. In addition to this important question, more emphasis must also be placed on the armed forces' role in the socio-economic development of the post-revolutionary state as well as on corruption, anti-drug and anti-guerrilla campaigns, and on the security issues involving the Caribbean Basin region in recent years.

Equal to the dissimilarities in the histories of Colombia and Venezuela are those that exist in the histories of two other South American countries: Paraguay and Uruguay. The army in Paraguay successfully defended that nation's claims in the Chaco against Bolivia (1932-1935); and one of the heroes of that conflict, General Alfredo Stroessner, took power in 1954 and held it until 1989. Uruguay, on the other hand, has had the reputation of possessing a highly professionalized, apolitical military institution which seldom became involved in affairs outside its role as defender of the nation against its external enemies. That all changed in the early 1970s, however, when the armed forces unleashed a brutal and savage war against its real and perceived internal enemies, establishing a military dictatorship that lasted for almost fifteen years. Pointing out the difficulty of doing research on the military in both these countries, John Hoyt Williams, nevertheless, outlines some of the areas where future studies are needed and are possible.

Historical research into the Latin American military prior to the 1960s was confined in Europe, Latin America and the United States to works that concentrated on wars, battles, campaigns, and the generals that led them. The historiography, with few exceptions, is descriptive, sometimes polemical, and lacks analysis. Beginning in the early 1960s, however, social scientists and historians began to view the military in Latin America in a different way; they sought to analyze the role the armed forces played in society and to understand the military's relationships with other institutions and organizations within the polity. They also applied sophisticated methods of analysis to determine the socio-economic composition of the military and to ascertain the existence of change over time. The result has been a proliferation of high quality literature that has subjected the institutions of the armed forces to searching examination. Nevertheless the extant historiography still reveals a great many holes, and it is hoped that this bibliography will stimulate students to continue research in this fascinating and important area.

CHAPTER II

LATIN AMERICAN COLONIAL ERA

Mark A. Burkholder
University of Missouri - St. Louis

INTRODUCTION

The Italian campaign in the 1490s inaugurated an era of European history in which Spanish armies became justly famous for their skill and success. Well into the seventeenth century *tercios* or infantry regiments composed of about 3000 arquebusiers and pikemen enjoyed an unequaled reputation. Given Spain's almost constant engagement in European wars in the sixteenth century, it is not surprising that in 1598 the famous Hispanophobe illustrator Théodore de Bry portrayed uniformed Spaniards in the New World armed with pikes, lances, swords, guns, and other instruments of death wreaking havoc on hapless natives.

Arms, however, are not armies. While the Spaniards brought an ample supply of weapons to the New World, no *tercio* crossed the Atlantic. Spain conquered the colonies with fighters, not trained soldiers, and maintained the possessions for nearly three centuries by relying on bureaucrats and clerics far more than armed might. Distance from Europe on the one hand and the immensity of the interior of the American mainlands on the other provided a measure of protection from foreign intruders, but at times such natural defenses were demonstrably insufficient as Francis Drake's raids in the 1580s revealed. Nonetheless, prior to the 1760s, few professional soldiers served in the empire.

The paucity of regular troops in the Spanish colonies means that, prior to the reforms of the 1760s, a discussion of military history must focus primarily on several specific issues. They include the protection

8

of the fleets that conveyed bullion from the Indies to Spain and brought trading goods to the New World, the efforts to secure the frontiers of Chile and of New Spain, responses to foreign incursions, notably those mounted by the Dutch West Indies Company in the 1620s, defense against attacks by pirates, and after 1680, the intermittent conflict between Spain and Portugal over the "debatable lands" adjoining the Río de la Plata.

While Brazil shared some of the characteristics of the Spanish Empire, particularly the natural defense offered by distance from Europe and an immense interior, the lack of significant bullion production until the close of the seventeenth century spared it the intensity of pressure experienced by Spain's possessions in and adjoining the Caribbean for most of the colonial era. Nonetheless, the Dutch occupation of northeastern Brazil from 1630 to 1654 was without parallel in the Spanish mainland colonies. In addition, the protracted campaigns of the *bandeirantes* in the Brazilian interior were unique in the annals of Latin American history.

The British capture and occupation of Havana in 1762 opened a new era in the military history of Spanish America. The creation of standing armies, the reorganization of militias, the dispatch of professional armed units from Spain, and the expanded reliance upon career military officers to serve high-ranking bureaucratic positions underscored the break with the past. Extending special judicial privileges (*fueros*) to the militiamen under certain circumstances created a new vested interest. At the same time, a conscious policy of reducing the prerogatives of the clergy revealed that the crown was shifting its historic reliance upon church and bureaucracy to the military and bureaucracy. Nonetheless, in no sense were the colonies militarized on the eve of independence. It required the wars of independence themselves to transform the military from a peripheral participant to a central actor on the stage of political power.

GENERAL WORKS

There is no general history of the military in colonial Latin America. Ambitious regional studies include Gutiérrez Santos (111), for Mexico and volume one of HISTORIA DO EXERCITO BRASILEIRO (122), for Brazil. The maritime history of Peru can be followed in Lohmann Villena (149).

ARCHIVAL GUIDES AND SOURCES

The Guerra Moderna section of the Archivo General de Simancas has nearly 8,000 bundles (*legajos*) containing documents that focus primarily on the colonies in the late eighteenth and early nineteenth centuries but date back as far as 1710. An indispensable guide to military personnel in the colonies is the Archive's CATALOGO XXII (16), which indicates the location of service records for soldiers in the New World in the late eighteenth and early nineteenth centuries. A limited amount of material dated before 1700 can be found in the section Guerra y Marina. The Archivo General de Indias contains numerous documents related to defense in the Gobierno section, itself subdivided for each major region of the empire. The section Capitanía General de la Isla de Cuba provides further material on this key strategic island. While the Archivo General Militar at Segovia also has material on the late colonial military, extremely difficult access to the collection severely limits its utility to scholars. National archives in Spanish America, described in Christon I. Archer's section in this volume, "Latin American Independence Movements," also house documentation related to the colonial military and defense.

PUBLISHED DOCUMENTS

Viceroys in colonial Spanish America were to compile a detailed report on their administration and the state of the viceroyalty upon leaving office. Since one of the viceroys' responsibilities (in their capacity as captains-general) was defense, their accounts (*relaciones*) regularly provide information on military activities and expenditures. The *relaciones* that have been published are frequently difficult to obtain outside of major research collections. Fortunately, modern editions are starting to appear as, for example, Moreno Cebrián (178).

Lewis Hanke and Celso Rodríguez's (113) multi-volume presentation of viceregal documents during Habsburg rule contains a limited amount of material related to the military. See also their guide to sources (112). Information on defensive expenditures is available in the reconstruction of colonial accounts presented by John J. TePaske and his collaborators (240, 241).

The recent publication by Thomas H. Naylor and Charles W. Polzer, S.J. (182), brings together published transcripts and English translations of archival manuscripts related to presidios and the northern frontier of New Spain, 1570-1700. Philip Wayne Powell (204), has published materials on the Chichimecan War. For late colonial Mexico, Alexander von Humboldt's (125), classic account of the viceroyalty just prior to independence is a rich source on the state of the military. See also the 1794 instruction of the Conde de Revillagigedo (212), to his successor. For Venezuela, see the numerous compilations by Santiago Gerardo Suárez (227, 228, 229, 230, 232).

Published contemporary accounts of the epic conquests of Mexico, Peru, and other regions of the Spanish Empire contain information of varying reliability about fighting, weaponry, numbers of participants, and strategy. An annotated introduction to this literature can be found in the Griffin (107), guide. The authoritative translation of Cortés's (68), letters by A.R. Pagden includes a valuable introduction written by J.H. Elliott.

SPECIALIZED WORKS

The Spanish conquest has attracted attention from numerous distinguished scholars. William Prescott (205, 206), wrote classic histories of the subjugation of Peru and Mexico. C. Harvey Gardiner (98), illuminated the military strategy of Cortés. Mario Góngora (103), examined groups of conquerors in Panama and northern South America. James Lockhart (145), emphasized the important distinction between soldiers and fighters in a prosopographical examination of the men present with Francisco Pizarro when the Inca Atahualpa was captured in 1533. The masterful examination by John Hemming (118), of the conquest of Peru includes a discussion of military tactics and equipment.

A useful survey of the borderlands frontier is John Francis Bannon (19). For the Pacific Northwest, see the monumental study by Warren L. Cook (66). The importance of military force in expanding the areas of settlement is developed by Philip Wayne Powell (200, 202). The presidio of northern New Spain is examined by Max L. Moorhead (176), and Naylor and Polzer (182). On the Chilean frontier and the unrelenting warfare there, the studies by Eugene Korth (133), and Alvaro Jara (127), are particularly useful. See also the brief article by Louis Armond (17). Weaponry employed after 1700 is illustrated in Sidney B. Brinckerhoff and Pierce A. Chamberlain (42).

The evolution of Spanish defensive policy in the Caribbean and the establishment of St. Augustine, Florida, as part of a system of defense are examined in Paul Hoffman's (123), sophisticated monograph and in the elegant study by Eugene Lyon (155), the latter is one of the best works to place developments in the borderlands into an imperial setting. The classic study of the Atlantic fleet system by C.H. Haring (115), must be supplemented by the massive work of Huguette and Pierre Chaunu (60).

The bibliography on pirates and Spanish efforts to defend against their attacks continues to grow. For the Pacific coast, the best examination is by Peter Gerhard (100). For the Caribbean, C.H. Haring's (114), still useful study should be read in conjunction with the more recent work by Kenneth R. Andrews (6).

Students of fortifications have added considerably to the military history of the colonial era. Especially important are the works by José A. Calderón Quijano (44, 45), Roberto Trigueros (249), Mariana Rodríguez del Valle (214), and L.A. Vigneras (257). Troy S. Floyd (94), treats Spanish military efforts to combat foreign intruders on the Mosquito Coast.

The Dutch invasion of northeastern Brazil and the activities of the *bandeirantes* as they undertook armed forays into the interior in pursuit of Indians to enslave are the two most important military developments prior to the conflict with Spain over the "debatable lands" adjoining the Río de la Plata. On the last topic, see Dauril Alden (3).

The British capture and occupation of Havana in 1762-63 spurred a stunned Spanish court to embark upon reform with unaccustomed vigor. Important works published in the 1950s by María del Carmen Velázquez (252), and Lyle N. McAlister (156), examined military reform in Mexico. McAlister's thoughtful thesis that the expansion of the special privileges of the enlarged military helped to explain the roots of the later emergence of praetorian government in Mexico stimulated some of the most important work on the subject that has been written subsequently. In the last two decades a substantial literature has illuminated efforts at administrative, economic, and commercial reform that would provide the financial resources necessary to support an unprecedented expansion of armed forces in the Spanish colonies. Particularly useful are the books by Jacques A. Barbier on Chile, D.A. Brading (34), on Mexico, John R. Fisher (90, 91, 92), on Peru, and the earlier work by John Lynch (154).

As a result of the archival labors of Christon I. Archer, Allan J. Kuethe, and Leon G. Campbell, the military reforms in Mexico, New Granada, Cuba, and Peru have received thorough examination. Archer's (7), monograph not only successfully challenges McAlister's thesis for Mexico but also is especially notable for its depiction of lower-class society, the group must vulnerable to the army's ongoing need for manpower. Both of Kuethe's (135, 139), major works relate military reform to local politics as well as political decision-making in Madrid. Campbell's (50), study of the army of Peru is a further challenge to

McAlister's thesis. Each of these authors examines the racial, social, and regional origins of the armies they studied; their findings further hone historians' understanding of creole-peninsular antagonism and the extent of discrimination against the former in the critical decades before independence. Looking at the New World military from an imperial perspective, Juan Marchena Fernández (162, 163, 164, 165, 166), has also added substantially to our knowledge of the military during Bourbon rule.

Biographies of military figures are few and tend to focus more on the professional life, times, and administrative and military actions of their protagonists than on their personal development and social ties. Among the more useful are Philip Wayne Powell's (200), study of Miguel Caldera's activities on New Spain's frontier in the sixteenth century; Bernard E. Bobb's (29), examination of Antonio María Bucareli as viceroy of late eighteenth-century New Spain; José Cruces Pozo's (69), consideration of Viceroy Manuel de Amat of Peru; Jaime Delgado's (71), review of the Conde de Ricla in Cuba (71); Bibiano Torres Ramírez's (246), work on Alejandro O'Reilly; and Iris W. Engstrand's (82), volume on Joaquín Velázquez de León, a royalist officer in Baja California in the late eighteenth century.

PERIODICALS

The HANDBOOK OF LATIN AMERICAN STUDIES (271), provides the most comprehensive ongoing compilation of books and articles related to the military during the colonial period. Since 1966 humanities listings appear in even years. No periodicals focus on the topic during the colonial era, but several occasionally publish relevant articles. Of particular note is the ANUARIO DE ESTUDIOS AMERICANOS (Spain), (272), the common outlet for studies undertaken in the General Archive of the Indies by faculty and advanced students of the University of Seville. REVISTA DE HISTORIA DE AMERICA (Mexico), (279), publishes works from scholars around the world in either Spanish or English. Similarly, two German publications JAHRBUCH FUR GESCHICHTE VON STAAT, WIRTSCHAFT UND GESELLSCHAFT LATEINAMERIKAS (Germany), (277), and IBERO-AMERIKANISCHES ARCHIV (Germany), (276), print materials in Spanish and English as well as German. Useful articles sometimes appear in HISTORIA MEXICANA (Mexico), (275), REVISTA DE INDIAS (Spain), (281), and REVISTA DE HISTORIA MILITAR (Spain), (280). For the student restricted to English, the HISPANIC AMERICAN HISTORICAL REVIEW (274), is valuable both for the high quality of its articles and for reviews of important works in other languages. THE AMERICAS (271), and the JOURNAL OF LATIN AMERICAN STUDIES (278), less frequently contain information concerning the colonial military.

FUTURE RESEARCH

Numerous aspects of military history during the colonial period have received little or no attention. This is especially true for the extended era before the British capture and occupation of Havana in 1762. With few exceptions, moreover, published studies focus on a single geographic region. Thus their description, analysis, and conclusion cannot be extended confidently beyond the region of focus to other colonies. Even the best-examined topic, military reform in the late eighteenth century, has not been fully studied for each colony, and a synthesis of this celebrated effort remains to be written. Among the many areas for future research, five warrant particular attention: the militia, military personnel, the cost of defense and warfare and the economic consequences of these expenditures, military involvement on colonial frontiers, and the origins of praetorian government in modern Latin America.

Colonial authorities repeatedly called upon militias to defend against enemy incursions and to suppress rebellious natives. Given their ubiquity, surprisingly little is known about militias before their reform beginning in the 1760s. How pervasive were militias? How frequently were they employed and for what purposes? How effective were they? Who served in them? When and to what extent did their composition change from exclusively white Spanish units to ones whose ranks included persons of mixed races?

The study of personnel offers the opportunity to combine military and social history. The geographic and social origins of officers and soldiers alike need elucidation for the pre-Bourbon reform centuries. To what degree did experienced people from Iberia direct or simply participate in military activities in the New World? To what degree did colonists oversee their own defense? When and where were professional soldiers to be found? How commonly did military personnel take over administrative positions once held by civilians? How important was prior armed service for an executive position in the colonies? How significant were the viceregal guards in Mexico City and Lima and who held their positions? Time consuming as they will be, prosopographical studies will help answer these and related questions.

Historians have long known that defensive measures in the New World devoured enormous amounts of revenue. The related reduction in bullion remissions to Spain has also been appreciated. The actual costs of defense, however, have not been systematically determined. What requires examination as well is the effects of military outlays on the colonial economies. Who was expending the funds and who was receiving them? Who were the defense contractors? Where did they fit into colonial society? What were the implications of these state expenditures on, for example, the cost of labor, the price of food, and the availability of other items needed by soldiers or employed as a means to pacify native populations.

The extensive literature on the use of the presidio in northern New Spain underscores the relative paucity of a similar historiography for other frontiers of the Spanish Empire. Before a synthetic account of this colonizing institution in the Americas can be written, detailed investigation into its use and evolution elsewhere is necessary.

Additional research is still needed on the origins of armed institutions in the independent countries of Latin America. A review of the literature on the colonial military reveals that recent research seriously has undermined McAlister's classic thesis about the importance of the extension of the *fuero militar* in the late colonial period for the expansion of military power. However, the question he asked, what were the roots of praetorian government, remains unanswered. Detailed examinations of the military during the wars of independence are required to resolve this important question.

In short, there is a need to explore the presence of the military from a variety of perspectives. Its ties with society, the economy, and administrative organization and modification require examination. The result will be an appreciation of the institution that goes far beyond recounting responses to foreign incursions, the onslaughts of buccaneers, and frontier conflicts.

BIBLIOGRAPHY: THE COLONIAL PERIOD

1. Abadíe-Aicardi, Aníbal. "La expedición del gobernador Cevallos al Plata." ANUARIO DE ESTUDIOS AMERICANOS 39 (1982): 159-216.

2. Albi de la Cuesta, Julio. LA DEFENSA DE LAS INDIAS, 1764-1799. Madrid: Ediciones Cultura Hispánica, 1987.

3. Alden, Dauril. ROYAL GOVERNMENT IN COLONIAL BRAZIL WITH SPECIAL REFERENCE TO THE ADMINISTRATION OF THE MARQUIS OF LAVRADIO, VICEROY, 1769-1779. Berkeley: University of California Press, 1968.

4. Allendesalazar Arrau, Jorge, ed. "Reconocimiento de las plazas, petrechos, y herramientas que se hallan en la frontera de este reino." REVISTA CHILENA DE HISTORIA Y GEOGRAFIA 109 (1965): 61-84.

5. ———. "Ejército y milicias del reino de Chile, 1737-1815." BOLETIN DE LA ACADEMIA CHILENA DE LA HISTORIA 66 (1962): 102-78.

6. Andrews, Kenneth R. THE SPANISH CARIBBEAN: TRADE AND PLUNDER, 1530-1630. New Haven: Yale University Press, 1978.

7. Archer, Christon I. THE ARMY IN BOURBON MEXICO, 1760-1810. Albuquerque: University of New Mexico Press, 1977.

8. ———. "Bourbon Finances and Military Policy in New Spain, 1759-1812." THE AMERICAS 37 (1981): 315-50.

9. ———. "Charles III and Defense Policy for New Spain, 1759-1788." In PAESI MEDITERRANEI E AMERICA LATINA, 190-200. Edited by Gaetano Masso. Rome: n.p., 1982.

10. ———. "The Deportation of Barbarian Indians from the Internal Provinces of New Spain, 1789-1810." THE AMERICAS 29 (1973): 376-85.

11. ——. "The Key to the Kingdom: The Defense of Veracruz, 1780-1810." THE AMERICAS 27 (1971): 426-49.

12. ——. "The Officer Corps in New Spain: The Martial Career, 1759-1821." JAHRBUCH FUR GESCHICHTE VON STAAT, WIRTSCHAFT UND GESELLSCHAFT LATEINAMERIKAS 19 (1982): 137-58.

13. ——. "Pardos, Indians, and the Army of New Spain: Inter-Relationships and Conflicts, 1780-1810." JOURNAL OF LATIN AMERICAN STUDIES 6 (1974): 231-44.

14. ——. "The Role of the Military in Colonial Latin America." THE HISTORY TEACHER 14 (1981): 413-21.

15. ——. "To Serve the King: Military Recruitment in Late Colonial Mexico." HISPANIC AMERICAN HISTORICAL REVIEW 55 (1975): 226-50.

16. Archivo General de Simancas. CATALOGO XXII: SECRETARIA DE GUERRA, SIGLO XVIII; HOJAS DE SERVICIOS DE AMERICA. Valladolid: Patronato Nacional de Archivos Históricos, 1958.

17. Armond, Louis. "Frontier Warfare in Colonial Chile." PACIFIC HISTORICAL REVIEW 23 (1954): 125-32.

18. Avila Martel, Alamiro de. "Régimen jurídico de la guerra de Arauco." In III CONGRESO DEL INSTITUTO INTERNACIONAL DE HISTORIA DEL DERECHO INDIANO, 325-37. Madrid: Instituto Nacional de Estudios Jurídicos, 1973.

19. Bannon, John Francis. THE SPANISH BORDERLANDS FRONTIER, 1513-1821. New York: Holt, Rinehart and Winston, 1970.

20. Barado, Francisco. MUSEO MILITAR: HISTORIA DEL EJERCITO ESPANOL. 3 vols. Barcelona: M. Soler, 1882-86.

21. Barbier, Jacques A. "Indies Revenues and Naval Spending: The Cost of Colonialism for the Spanish Bourbons, 1763-1805." JAHRBUCH FUR GESCHICHTE VON STAAT,

WIRTSCHAFT UND GESELLSCHAFT LATEINAMERIKAS 21 (1984): 171-88.

22. ——. REFORM AND POLITICS IN BOURBON CHILE, 1755-1796. Ottawa: University of Ottawa Press, 1980.

23. Bardwell, Ross Little. "The Governors of Portugal's South Atlantic Empire in the Seventeenth Century: Social Background, Qualifications, Selection, and Reward." Ph.D. dissertation, University of California, Santa Barbara, 1974.

24. Beerman, Eric. "Un bosquejo biográfico y genealógico del general Alejandro O'Reilly." HIDALGUIA: LA REVISTA DE GENEALOGIA, NOBLEZA, Y ARMAS 24 (1981): 225-44.

25. ——. "José de Ezpeleta." REVISTA DE HISTORIA MILITAR 21 (1977): 97-118.

26. Bellard Pietri, Eugenio de. "Las fortificaciones coloniales de Caracas y de la Guaira." In MEMORIA DEL TERCER CONGRESO VENEZOLANO DE HISTORIA, 1:173-202. Caracas: n.p., 1979.

27. Bensusan, Harold Guy. "The Spanish Struggle against Foreign Encroachment in the Caribbean, 1675-1697." Ph.D. dissertation, University of California, Los Angeles, 1970.

28. Beverina, Juan. EL VIRREINATO DE LAS PROVINCIAS DEL RIO DE LA PLATA: SU ORGANIZACION MILITAR. Buenos Aires: L. Bernard, 1935.

29. Bobb, Bernard E. THE VICEREGENCY OF ANTONIO MARIA BUCARELI IN NEW SPAIN, 1771-1779. Austin: University of Texas Press, 1962.

30. Borah, Woodrow. "La defensa fronteriza durante la gran rebelión tepehuana." HISTORIA MEXICANA 16 (1966): 15-29.

31. Borges, Analola. "Apuntes para la historia militar de la capitanía general de Venezuela." REVISTA DE HISTORIA MILITAR 7 (1963): 87-106.

32. Borja de Szaszdi, Dora León. "Guayaquil y la Real Armada de la Mar del Sur, 1579-1624." In MEMORIA DEL TERCER CONGRESO VENEZOLANO DE HISTORIA, 1: 239-98. Caracas: n.p., 1979.

33. Boyd-Bowman, Peter. "A Spanish Soldier's Estate in Northern Mexico, 1642." HISPANIC AMERICAN HISTORICAL REVIEW 53 (1973): 95-105.

34. Brading, D. A. MINERS AND MERCHANTS IN BOURBON MEXICO, 1763-1810. Cambridge: Cambridge University Press, 1971.

35. Bradley, Peter T. "The Cost of Defending a Viceroyalty: Crown Revenue and the Defence of Peru in the Seventeenth Century." IBERO-AMERIKANISCHES ARCHIV 10 (1984): 267-89.

36. ———. "The Defenders of Lima and Callao in the Seventeenth Century." REVISTA DE HISTORIA DE AMERICA 97 (1984): 87-113.

37. ———. "The Defense of Peru, 1600-1648." IBERO-AMERIKANISCHES ARCHIV 2 (1976): 79-111.

38. ———. "The Lessons of the Dutch Blockade of Callao, 1624 ." REVISTA DE HISTORIA DE AMERICA 83 (1977): 53-68.

39. ———. "Maritime Defence of the Viceroyalty of Peru, 1600-1700." THE AMERICAS 36 (1979): 155-75.

40. ———. "Some Considerations on Defence at Sea in the Viceroyalty of Peru during the Seventeenth Century." REVISTA DE HISTORIA DE AMERICA 79 (1975): 77-97.

41. Brinckerhoff, Sidney B., and Odie B. Faulk. LANCERS FOR THE KING: A STUDY OF THE FRONTIER MILITARY SYSTEM OF NEW SPAIN. Phoenix: Arizona History Foundation, 1965.

42. Brinckerhoff, Sidney B., and Pierce A. Chamberlain. SPANISH MILITARY WEAPONS IN COLONIAL AMERICA, 1700-1821. Harrisburg: Stackpole, 1972.

43. Cabrillana, Nicolás. "Las fortificaciones militares en Puerto Rico."
     REVISTA DE INDIAS 27 (1967): 157-87.

44. Calderón Quijano, José Antonio. "El fuerte de San Fernando de
     Omoa: Su historia e importancia que tuvo en la defensa del Golfo
     de Honduras." REVISTA DE INDIAS 3 (1942): 515-48 and 4
     (1943): 127-63.

45. ———. HISTORIA DE LAS FORTIFICACIONES DE LA
     NUEVA ESPANA. Seville: Escuela de Estudios
     Hispano-Americanos de Sevilla, 1953.

46. ———. "Ingenieros militares en Nueva España." ANUARIO DE
     ESTUDIOS AMERICANOS 6 (1949): 1-72.

47. Campbell, Leon G. "After the Fall: The Reformation of the Army
     of Peru, 1784-1816." IBERO-AMERIKANISCHES ARCHIV 3
     (1977): 1-28.

48. ———. "The Army of Peru and the Túpac Amaru Revolt,
     1780-1783." HISPANIC AMERICAN HISTORICAL REVIEW
     56 (1976): 31-57.

49. ———. "The Changing Racial and Administrative Structure of the
     Peruvian Military under the Later Bourbons." THE AMERICAS
     32 (1975): 117-33.

50. ———. THE MILITARY AND SOCIETY IN COLONIAL
     PERU, 1750-1810. Philadelphia: American Philosophical Society,
     1978.

51. ———. "Social Structure of the Túpac Amaru Army in Cuzco,
     1780-81." HISPANIC AMERICAN HISTORICAL REVIEW 61
     (1981): 675-94.

52. ———. "The Spanish Presidio in Alta California during the
     Mission Period, 1769-1785." JOURNAL OF THE WEST 16
     (1977): 63-77.

53. Campos, Alfredo R. "La organización defensiva de las fronteras
     coloniales de la que había de ser, en el tiempo, el Estado
     Oriental del Uruguay." REVISTA DEL INSTITUTO

HISTORICO Y GEOGRAFICO DEL URUGUAY 24 (1958-59): 3-98.

54. Cardozo, Manoel S. "The Guerra dos Emboabas: Civil War in Minas Gerais, 1708-1709." HISPANIC AMERICAN HISTORICAL REVIEW 22 (1942): 470-92.

55. ———. "The Last Adventure of Fernão Dias Pais, 1674-1681." HISPANIC AMERICAN HISTORICAL REVIEW 26 (1946): 467-79.

56. Castillero Calvo, Alfredo. "Estructuras funcionales del sistema defensivo del Istmo de Panamá durante el período colonial." In MEMORIA DEL TERCER CONGRESO VENEZOLANO DE HISTORIA, 1: 349-83. Caracas: n.p., 1979.

57. Castillo Lara, Lucas. "Las acciones militares del gobernador Ruy Fernández de Fuenmayor, 1637-1644." In MEMORIA DEL TERCER CONGRESO VENEZOLANO DE HISTORIA, 1: 385-440. Caracas: n.p., 1979.

58. Céspedes del Castillo, Guillermo. "La defensa militar del Istmo de Panamá a fines del siglo XVII y comienzos del XVIII." ANUARIO DE ESTUDIOS AMERICANOS 9 (1952): 235-75.

59. Chatelain, Verne E. THE DEFENSES OF SPANISH FLORIDA, 1565 to 1763. Washington: Carnegie Institution of Washington, 1941.

60. Chaunu, Huguette, and Pierre Chaunu. SEVILLE ET L'ATLANTIQUE, 1504-1650. 8 vols. Paris: A. Colin, 1955-59.

61. Christiansen, E. THE ORIGINS OF MILITARY POWER IN SPAIN, 1800-1854. Oxford: Oxford University Press, 1967.

62. Cidade, F. de Paula. LUTAS, AO SUL DO BRASIL, COM OS ESPANHOIS E SEUS DESCENDENTES, 1620-1828. Rio de Janeiro: Ministério de Guerra, 1948.

63. Clayton, Lawrence A. "Cañones en Cañete, 1615: La Armada del Sur y la defensa del Virreinato del Perú." In MEMORIA DEL TERCER CONGRESO VENEZOLANO DE HISTORIA, 1: 441-62. Caracas: n.p., 1979.

64. ———. "Local Initiative and Finance in Defense of the Viceroyalty of Peru: The Development of Self Reliance." HISPANIC AMERICAN HISTORICAL REVIEW 54 (1974): 284-304.

65. Colón y Larriátegui Ximénez de Embún, Félix. JUZGADOS MILITARES DE ESPANA Y SUS INDIAS . . . 4 vols. 2d ed. Madrid: n.p., 1786-96.

66. Cook, Warren L. FLOOD TIDE OF EMPIRE: SPAIN AND THE PACIFIC NORTHWEST, 1543-1819. New Haven: Yale University Press, 1973.

67. Cooney, Jerry W. "A Colonial Naval Industry: The Fábrica de Cables of Paraguay." REVISTA DE HISTORIA DE AMERICA 87 (1979): 105-26.

68. Cortés, Hernán. HERNAN CORTES: LETTERS FROM MEXICO. Translated and edited by A.R. Pagden. New York: Grossman, 1971.

69. Cruces Pozo, José. "Cualidades militares del virrey Amat." ANUARIO DE ESTUDIOS AMERICANOS 9 (1952): 327-45.

70. Cruz Hermosilla, Emilio de la. "Lorenzo Montalvo: Figura señera de la Armada." REVISTA GENERAL DE MARINA 202 (1982): 17-23.

71. Delgado, Jaime. "El Conde de Ricla: Capitán general de Cuba." REVISTA DE HISTORIA DE AMERICA 55-56 (1963): 41-138.

72. De Palo, William A. "The Establishment of the Nueva Vizcaya Militia during the Administration of Teodoro de Croix, 1766-1773." NEW MEXICO HISTORICAL REVIEW 48 (1973): 233-49.

73. Deschamps Chapeaux, Pedro. LOS BATALLONES DE PARDOS Y MORENOS LIBRES. Havana: n.p., 1976.

74. Destefani, Lauro H. "La defensa militar del Río de la Plata en la época hispana." In MEMORIA DEL TERCER CONGRESO VENEZOLANO DE HISTORIA, 1: 463-533. Caracas: n.p., 1979.

75. Díaz-Trechuelo Spínola, María Lourdes. "La defensa de Filipinas en el último cuarto del siglo XVIII." ANUARIO DE ESTUDIOS AMERICANOS 21 (1964): 145-209.

76. Domínguez Compañy, Francisco. "Obligaciones militares de los vecinos hispanoamericanos en el siglo XVI: según se desprende de las Actas Capitulares." REVISTA DE HISTORIA DE AMERICA 79 (1975): 37-61.

77. Dorenkott, Charles Joseph, Jr. "José da Silva Pais: The Defense and Expansion of Southern Brazil, 1735-1749." Ph.D. dissertation, University of New Mexico, 1972.

78. Dousdebes, Pedro Julio. CARTAGENA DE INDIAS: PLAZA FUERTE. Bogotá: Ejército, Estado Mayor General, Sección de Imprenta y Publicaciones, 1948.

79. Duarte Level, Lino. CUADROS DE HISTORIA MILITAR Y CIVIL DE VENEZUELA DESDE EL DESCUBRIMIENTO Y CONQUISTA DE GUAYANA HASTA LA BATALLA DE CARABOBO. Madrid: Editorial América, 1917.

80. Dutra, Francis Anthony. "Matias de Albuquerque: A Seventeenth-Century 'Capitão-Mor' of Pernambuco and Governor-General of Brazil." Ph.D. dissertation, New York University, 1968.

81. "El ejército de Nueva España a fines del siglo XVIII." BOLETIN DEL ARCHIVO GENERAL DE LA NACION 9 (1938): 236-75.

82. Engstrand, Iris W. ROYAL OFFICER IN BAJA CALIFORNIA, 1768-1777: JOAQUIN VELAZQUEZ DE LEON. Los Angeles: Dawsons, 1976.

83. Espinosa, J. Manuel. "The Recapture of Santa Fe, New Mexico, by the Spaniards, December 29-30, 1693." HISPANIC AMERICAN HISTORICAL REVIEW 19 (1939): 443-63.

84. ESTADO MILITAR DE ESPANA. Madrid: n.p., 1799.

85. Eyzaguirre, Jaime. BREVE HISTORIA DE LAS FRONTERAS DE CHILE. 2d ed. Santiago: Editorial Universitaria, 1968.

86. Faulk, Odie B. THE LAST YEARS OF SPANISH TEXAS, 1778-1821. The Hague: Mouton and Co., 1964.

87. ———. THE LEATHER JACKET SOLDIER: SPANISH MILITARY EQUIPMENT AND INSTITUTIONS OF THE LATE EIGHTEENTH CENTURY. Pasadena: Socio-Technical Publications, 1971.

88. Fernández Duro, Cesáreo. LA ARMADA ESPANOLA DESDE LA UNION DE LOS REINOS DE CASTILLA Y ARAGON. 9 vols. Madrid: n.p., 1895-1903.

89. Fireman, Janet R. THE SPANISH ROYAL CORPS OF ENGINEERS IN THE WESTERN BORDERLANDS: INSTRUMENT OF BOURBON REFORM, 1764 TO 1815. Glendale, CA: Arthur H. Clark Co., 1977.

90. Fisher, J.R. COMMERCIAL RELATIONS BETWEEN SPAIN AND SPANISH AMERICA IN THE ERA OF FREE TRADE, 1784-1814. Liverpool: University of Liverpool, 1985.

91. ———. GOVERNMENT AND SOCIETY IN COLONIAL PERU: THE INTENDANT SYSTEM, 1784-1814. London: Athlone Press, 1970.

92. ———. SILVER MINES AND SILVER MINERS IN COLONIAL PERU, 1776-1824. Liverpool: University of Liverpool, 1977.

93. Flickema, Thomas. "The Siege of Cuzco." REVISTA DE HISTORIA DE AMERICA 92 (1981): 17-47.

94. Floyd, Troy S. THE ANGLO-SPANISH STRUGGLE FOR MOSQUITIA. Albuquerque: University of New Mexico Press, 1967.

95. Folmer, Henry. FRANCO-SPANISH RIVALRY IN NORTH AMERICA, 1524-1673. Glendale, CA: Arthur H. Clark Co., 1953.

96. Fuentes Concha, Manuel. HISTORIA DE LA JUSTICIA MILITAR EN CHILE. Santiago: Imprenta de Carabineros de Chile, 1943.

97. García Gallo, Alfonso. "El servicio militar en Indias." ANUARIO DE HISTORIA DEL DERECHO ESPANOL 26 (1956): 447-515.

98. Gardiner, C. Harvey. NAVAL POWER IN THE CONQUEST OF MEXICO. Austin: University of Texas Press, 1956.

99. Gasparini, Graziano. "Las fortificaciones del Puerto de La Guaira durante el período colonial." In MEMORIA DEL TERCER CONGRESO VENEZOLANO DE HISTORIA, 2: 9-98. Caracas: n.p., 1979.

100. Gerhard, Peter. PIRATES ON THE WEST COAST OF NEW SPAIN, 1575-1742. Glendale, CA: Arthur H. Clark Co., 1960.

101. Gil Munilla, Octavio. MALVINAS: EL CONFLICTO ANGLO-ESPANOL DE 1770. Seville: Escuela de Estudios Hispano-Americanos de Sevilla, 1948.

102. Gómez, Carmen, and Juan Marchena. "Los señores de la guerra en la conquista." ANUARIO DE ESTUDIOS AMERICANOS 42 (1985): 127-215.

103. Góngora, Mario. LOS GRUPOS DE CONQUISTADORES EN TIERRA FIRME, 1509-1530: FISIONOMIA HISTORICO-SOCIAL DE UN TIPO DE CONQUISTA. Santiago: Universidad de Chile, 1962.

104. González, Asdrubal. "La fortificación de Puerto Cabello: Una empresa económico-militar." In MEMORIA DEL TERCER CONGRESO VENEZOLANO DE HISTORIA, 2:125-37. Caracas: n.p., 1979.

105. González González, Alfonso. "Las audiencias indianas y el mando militar, siglos XVI, XVII, y XVIII." In MEMORIA DEL SEGUNDO CONGRESO VENEZOLANO DE HISTORIA, 1: 487-518. Caracas: n.p., 1975.

106. González Lonziéme, Enrique. "La estrategia naval en la fundación del virreinato del Río de la Plata." REVISTA DE HISTORIA DE AMERICA 84 (1977): 219-34.

107. Griffin, Charles C., ed. LATIN AMERICA: A GUIDE TO THE HISTORICAL LITERATURE. Austin: University of Texas Press, 1971.

108. Guarda, Fernando. LAS DEFENSAS DE LA CIUDAD DE VALDIVIA. N.p.: n.p., n.d.

109. Guarda, Gabriel. INFLUENCIA MILITAR EN LAS CIUDADES DEL REINO DE CHILE. Santiago: Academia Chilena de la Historia, 1967.

110. Guiteras, Pedro J. HISTORIA DE LA CONQUISTA DE LA HABANA POR LOS INGLESES SEGUIDA DE CUBA Y SU GOBIERNO. Havana: Cultural, 1932.

111. Gutiérrez Santos, Daniel. HISTORIA MILITAR DE MEXICO, 1325-1810. 3 vols. Mexico City: Ediciones Ateneo, 1961.

112. Hanke, Lewis, and Celso Rodríguez. GUIA DE LAS FUENTES EN EL ARCHIVO GENERAL DE INDIAS PARA EL ESTUDIO DE LA ADMINISTRACION VIRREINAL ESPANOLA EN MEXICO Y EN EL PERU, 1535-1700. 3 vols. Cologne: Böhlau Verlag, 1977.

113. ———. LOS VIRREYES ESPANOLES EN AMERICA DURANTE EL GOBIERNO DE LA CASA DE AUSTRIA: MEXICO, 5 vols.; PERU, 7 vols. Madrid: Ediciones Atlas, 1976-80.

114. Haring, C.H. THE BUCCANEERS IN THE WEST INDIES IN THE XVII CENTURY. London: Methuen, 1910.

115. ———. TRADE AND NAVIGATION BETWEEN SPAIN AND THE INDIES IN THE TIME OF THE HAPSBURGS. Cambridge: Harvard University Press, 1918.

116. Hellwege, Johann. DIE SPANISCHEN PROVINZIALMILIZEN IM 18. JAHRHUNDERT. Boppard am Rhein: Harald Boldt Verlag, 1969.

117. ———. "Die Ubertragung des Provinzial-milizsystems auf Hispanoamerika im Rahmen der bourbonischen Militarreformen

in Ubersee und der Einfluss der Denkschrift des Grafen Aranda auf die Instruktion für Juan de Villalba y Angulo." JAHRBUCH FUR GESCHICHTE VON STAAT, WIRTSCHAFT UND GESELLSCHAFT LATEINAMERIKAS 6 (1960): 158-201.

118. Hemming, John. THE CONQUEST OF THE INCAS. New York: Harcourt Brace Jovanovich, 1970.

119. Heredia Herrera, Antonia M. "Las fortificaciones de la isla Margarita en los siglos XVI, XVII, y XVIII." ANUARIO DE ESTUDIOS AMERICANOS 15 (1958): 429-514.

120. Hernández y Sánchez-Barba, Mario. "Frontera, población, y milicia: Estudio estructural de la acción defensiva hispánica en Sonora durante el siglo XVIII." REVISTA DE INDIAS 63 (1956): 9-49.

121. Hewitt, Harry Paxton. "The Historical Development of Nueva Vizcaya's Defenses to 1646." Ph.D. dissertation, University of Utah, 1971.

122. HISTORIA DO EXERCITO BRASILEIRO: PERFIL MILITAR DE UM POVO. 3 vols. Rio de Janeiro: Estado-Maior do Exército, 1972.

123. Hoffman, Paul E. THE SPANISH CROWN AND THE DEFENSE OF THE CARIBBEAN, 1535-1585: PRECEDENT, PATRIMONIALISM, AND ROYAL PARSIMONY. Baton Rouge: Louisiana State University Press, 1980.

124. Holmes, Jack D. L. HONOR AND FIDELITY: THE LOUISIANA INFANTRY REGIMENT AND THE LOUISIANA MILITIA COMPANIES, 1766-1821. Birmingham, AL: n.p., 1965.

125. Humboldt, Alexander von. POLITICAL ESSAY ON THE KINGDOM OF NEW SPAIN. Translated by John Black. 4 vols. London: Longman, Hurst, Rees, Orme and Brown, 1811.

126. Inglis, G. Douglas. "The Spanish Naval Shipyard at Havana in the Eighteenth Century." In NEW ASPECTS OF NAVAL HISTORY. Edited by Department of History, U.S. Naval

Academy. Baltimore: Nautical & Aviation Publishing Company of
America, 1986.

127. Jara, Alvaro. GUERRA Y SOCIEDAD EN CHILE: LA
TRANSFORMACION DE LA GUERRA DE ARAUCO Y LA
ESCLAVITUD DE LOS INDIOS. Santiago: Editorial
Universitaria, 1971.

128. John, Elizabeth Ann Harper. "Spanish Relations with the *Indios
Bárbaros* on the Northernmost Frontier of New Spain in the
Eighteenth Century." Ph.D. dissertation, University of Oklahoma,
1957.

129. Kahle, Günter. "Die Encomienda als militärische Institution im
kolonialen Hispanoamérica." JAHRBUCH FUR GESCHICHTE
VON STAAT, WIRTSCHAFT UND GESELLSCHAFT
LATEINAMERIKAS 2 (1965): 88-105.

130. ——. MILITAR UND STAATSBILDUNG IN DEN
ANFANGEN DER UNABHANGIGKEIT MEXIKOS. Vienna:
Böhlau Verlag, 1969.

131. Klein, Herbert S. "The Colored Militia of Cuba, 1568-1868."
CARIBBEAN STUDIES 4 (1966): 17-27.

132. ——. "Structure and Profitability of Royal Finance in the
Viceroyalty of Río de la Plata in 1790." HISPANIC AMERICAN
HISTORICAL REVIEW 53 (1973): 440-89.

133. Korth, Eugene H. SPANISH POLICY IN COLONIAL CHILE:
THE STRUGGLE FOR SOCIAL JUSTICE, 1535-1700.
Stanford: Stanford University Press, 1968.

134. Kuethe, Allan J. "La batalla de Cartagena de 1741: Nuevas
perspectivas." HISTORIOGRAFIA Y BIBLIOGRAFIA
AMERICANISTAS 18 (1974): 19-38.

135. ——. CUBA, 1753-1815: CROWN, MILITARY, AND
SOCIETY. Knoxville: University of Tennessee Press, 1986.

136. ———. "The Development of the Cuban Military as a Sociopolitical Elite." HISPANIC AMERICAN HISTORICAL REVIEW 61 (1981): 695-704.

137. ———. "Guns, Subsidies, and Commercial Privilege: Some Historical Factors in the Emergence of the Cuban National Character, 1763-1815." CUBAN STUDIES 16 (1986): 123-28.

138. ———. "*Los Llorones Cubanos*: The Socio-Military Basis of Commercial Privilege in the American Trade under Charles IV." In THE NORTH AMERICAN ROLE IN THE SPANISH IMPERIAL ECONOMY, 1760-1819, 142-56. Edited by Jacques A. Barbier and Allan J. Kuethe. Manchester: Manchester University Press, 1984.

139. ———. MILITARY REFORM AND SOCIETY IN NEW GRANADA. Gainesville: University Presses of Florida, 1978.

140. ———. "The Pacification Campaign on the Riohacha Frontier, 1772-1779." HISPANIC AMERICAN HISTORICAL REVIEW 50 (1970): 467-81.

141. ———. "Reforma militar y control político en la Nueva Granada." MEMORIA DEL TERCER CONGRESO VENEZOLANO DE HISTORIA, 2: 139-60. Caracas: n.p., 1979.

142. ———. "Social Mobility in the Reformed Army of Colonial New Granada: A Historical Analysis." ARMED FORCES AND SOCIETY 5 (1979): 431-50.

143. Laviña, Javier. "El fijo de Cartagena de Indias en 1800: Un regimiento criollo." REVISTA LETRAS DE DEUSTO 6 (1976): 163-75.

144. Lewis, James Allen. "New Spain during the American Revolution, 1779-1783: A Viceroyalty at War." Ph.D. dissertation, Duke University, 1975.

145. Lockhart, James. THE MEN OF CAJAMARCA: A SOCIAL AND BIOGRAPHICAL STUDY OF THE FIRST CONQUERORS OF PERU. Austin: University of Texas Press, 1972.

146. Lohmann Villena, Guillermo. LOS AMERICANOS EN LAS ORDENES NOBILIARIAS, 1529-1900. 2 vols. Madrid: Consejo Superior de Investigaciones Científicas, 1947.

147. ——. "Las compañías de gentiles hombres, lanzas, y arcabuces de la guarda del Virreinato del Perú." ANUARIO DE ESTUDIOS AMERICANOS 13 (1956): 141-215.

148. ——. "Las defensas militares de Lima y Callao hasta 1746." ANUARIO DE ESTUDIOS AMERICANOS 20 (1963): 1-217.

149. ——. HISTORIA MARITIMA DEL PERU. Vol. 4, SIGLOS XVII Y XVIII. Lima: n.p., 1973.

150. ——. "Murallas y fortificaciónes en el Perú durante la época virreinal." In MEMORIA DEL TERCER CONGRESO VENEZOLANO DE HISTORIA, 1: 171-88. Caracas: n.p., 1979.

151. López Rivero, Raúl. LAS FORTIFICACIONES DE MARACAIBO, SIGLOS XVII, XVIII. Maracaibo: Universidad de Zulia, 1968.

152. Loreto, Aliatar. CAPITULOS DE HISTORIA MILITAR DO BRASIL: COLONIA-REINO. Rio de Janeiro: Ministério de Guerra, 1946.

153. Luengo Muñoz, Manuel. "Génesis de las expediciones militares al Darién en 1785-1786." ANUARIO DE ESTUDIOS AMERICANOS 18 (1961): 335-416.

154. Lynch, John. SPANISH COLONIAL ADMINISTRATION, 1782-1810: THE INTENDANT SYSTEM IN THE VICEROYALTY OF THE RIO DE LA PLATA. London: Athlone Press, 1958.

155. Lyon, Eugene. THE ENTERPRISE OF FLORIDA. Gainesville: University Presses of Florida, 1976.

156. McAlister, Lyle N. THE "FUERO MILITAR" IN NEW SPAIN, 1764-1800. Gainesville: University of Florida Press, 1957.

157. ———. "The Reorganization of the Army of New Spain, 1763-1766." HISPANIC AMERICAN HISTORICAL REVIEW 33 (1953): 1-32.

158. McNeill, John Robert. ATLANTIC EMPIRES OF FRANCE AND SPAIN: LOUISBOURG AND HAVANA, 1700-1763. Chapel Hill: University of North Carolina Press, 1985.

159. Magalhães, Joao Baptista. A EVOLUCAO MILITAR DO BRASIL: ANOTACOES PARA A HISTORIA. Rio de Janeiro: Biblioteca do Exército, 1958.

160. Manucy, Albert, and Ricardo Torres-Reyes. PUERTO RICO AND THE FORTS OF OLD SAN JUAN. Riverside, CT: Chatham Press, 1973.

161. March y Labores, José. HISTORIA DE LA MARINA REAL ESPANOLA DESDE EL DESCUBRIMIENTO DE LAS AMERICAS HASTA EL COMBATE DE TRAFALGAR. 2 vols. Madrid: J.M. Ducazal, 1854.

162. Marchena Fernández, Juan. "El ejército de América: El componente humano." REVISTA DE HISTORIA MILITAR 163-64 (1981): 121-54.

163. ———. "La financiación militar en Indias: Introducción a su estudio." ANUARIO DE ESTUDIOS AMERICANOS 36 (1979): 81-110.

164. ———. "Guarniciones y población militar en Florida oriental, 1700-1820." REVISTA DE INDIAS 163-64 (1981): 91-142.

165. ———. LA INSTITUCION MILITAR EN CARTAGENA DE INDIAS, 1700-1810. Seville: Escuela de Estudios Hispano-Americanos de Sevilla, 1982.

166. ———. OFICIALES Y SOLDADOS EN EL EJERCITO DE AMERICA. Seville: Escuela de Estudios Hispano-Americanos de Sevilla, 1983.

167. Marco Dorta, Enrique. CARTAGENA DE INDIAS: PUERTO Y PLAZA FUERTE. Cartagena: A. Amadó, 1960.

168. Mariluz Urquijo, José M. "La organización militar del virreinato en la época del Marqués de Avilés." TRABAJOS Y COMUNICACIONES 3 (1953): 117-51.

169. Matta, Enrique de la. LA PERDIDA DE CARTAGENA DE INDIAS, 1697. Seville: Escuela de Estudios Hispano-Americanos de Sevilla, 1979.

170. Medina, Francisco de Borja. "La reforma del ejército en Nueva España, 1785: Actuaciones y proyectos del inspector José de Ezpeleta." ANUARIO DE ESTUDIOS AMERICANOS 41 (1984): 315-95.

171. Meli, Rosa. "Los fueros militares en el derecho andino." In MEMORIA DEL TERCER CONGRESO VENEZOLANO DE HISTORIA, 2: 227-57. Caracas: n.p., 1979.

172. Mijares Pérez, Lucio. "La organización de las milicias venezolanas de la segunda mitad del siglo XVIII." In MEMORIA DEL TERCER CONGRESO VENEZOLANO DE HISTORIA 2: 259-82. Caracas: 1979.

173. Miller, Gary M. "Status and Loyalty in Colonial Spanish America: A Social History of Regular Army Officers in Venezuela, 1750-1810." Ph.D. dissertation, University of Florida, 1985.

174. ———. "Status and Loyalty of Regular Army Officers in Late Colonial Venezuela." HISPANIC AMERICAN HISTORICAL REVIEW 66 (1986): 667-96.

175. Moorhead, Max L. THE APACHE FRONTIER: JACOB UGARTE AND SPANISH INDIAN RELATIONS IN NORTHERN NEW SPAIN, 1769-1791. Norman: University of Oklahoma Press, 1968.

176. ———. THE PRESIDIO: BASTION OF THE SPANISH BORDERLANDS. Norman: University of Oklahoma Press, 1975.

177. ———. "The Private Contract System of Presidio Supply in Northern New Spain." HISPANIC AMERICAN HISTORICAL REVIEW 41 (1961): 31-54.

178. Moreno Cebrián, Alfredo, ed. RELACION Y DOCUMENTOS DE GOBIERNO DEL VIRREY DEL PERU, JOSE A. MANSO DE VELASCO, CONDE DE SUPERUNDA, 1745-1761. Madrid: Consejo Superior de Investigaciones Científicas, 1983.

179. Morton, F.W.O. "The Military and Society in Bahia, 1800-1821." JOURNAL OF LATIN AMERICAN STUDIES 7 (1975): 249-69.

180. Moya Pons, Frank. "Pobreza y militarismo en Santo Domingo en el siglo XVII, 1606-1648." In MEMORIA DEL TERCER CONGRESO VENEZOLANO DE HISTORIA, 2:309-32. Caracas: n.p., 1979.

181. Navarro García, Luis. DON JOSE DE GALVEZ Y LA COMANDANCIA GENERAL DE LAS PROVINCIAS INTERNAS DEL NORTE DE LA NUEVA ESPANA. Seville: Escuela de Estudios Hispano-Americanos de Sevilla, 1964.

182. Naylor, Thomas H., and Charles W. Polzer, S.J. THE PRESIDIO AND MILITIA ON THE NORTHERN FRONTIER OF NEW SPAIN: A DOCUMENTARY HISTORY. Vol. 1, 1570-1700. Tucson: University of Arizona Press, 1986.

183. Newton, Lowell W. "The Spanish Naval Officer Corps in the Eighteenth Century: Towards a Collective Biography." REVISTA DE HISTORIA DE AMERICA 103 (1987): 31-74.

184. Nowell, Charles E. "The Defense of Cartagena." HISPANIC AMERICAN HISTORICAL REVIEW 42 (1962): 477-501.

185. O'Dogherty, Angel. "La matrícula de mar en el reinado de Carlos III." ANUARIO DE ESTUDIOS AMERICANOS 9 (1952): 347-70.

186. Ogelsby, J.C.M. "Spain's Havana Squadron and the Preservation of the Balance of Power in the Caribbean, 1740-1748." HISPANIC AMERICAN HISTORICAL REVIEW 49 (1969): 473-88.

187. Oñat, Roberto, and Carlos Roa. REGIMEN LEGAL DEL EJERCITO EN EL REINO DE CHILE. Santiago: Universidad Católica de Chile, 1953.

188. ORDENANZAS DE S.M. PARA EL REGIMEN, DISCIPLINA, SUBORDINACION, Y SERVICIO DE SUS EXERCITOS. Madrid: A. Marín, 1768.

189. "La organización del ejército en Nueva España." BOLETIN DEL ARCHIVO GENERAL DE LA NACION 11 (1940): 617-63.

190. "La organización de milicias provinciales en Nueva España." BOLETIN DEL ARCHIVO GENERAL DE LA NACION 9 (1938): 408-34.

191. Pares, Richard. WAR AND TRADE IN THE WEST INDIES, 1739-1763. 2d ed. London: F. Cass, 1963.

192. Pérez Aparicio, Josefina. PERDIDA DE LA ISLA DE TRINIDAD. Seville: Escuela de Estudios Hispano-Americanos de Sevilla, 1966.

193. Pérez García, José. HISTORIA NATURAL, MILITAR, CIVIL, Y SAGRADA DEL REINO DE CHILE. Santiago: Imprenta Elzeviriana, 1900.

194. Pérez Martínez, Héctor. PIRATERIAS EN CAMPECHE, SIGLOS XVI, XVII, XVIII. Mexico City: Porrúa Hnos. y Cía., 1937.

195. Pike, Ruth. "Penal Servitude in the Spanish Empire: Presidio Labor in the Eighteenth Century." HISPANIC AMERICAN HISTORICAL REVIEW 58 (1978): 21-40.

196. Pizzurno Gelos, Patricia. "Ejército y fortificaciones en el Río de la Plata, 1700-1810." Doctoral thesis, Universidad de Sevilla, 1982.

197. Polich, John Leo. "Foreign Maritime Intrusion on Spain's Pacific Coast, 1786-1810." Ph.D. dissertation, University of New Mexico, 1968.

198. Porras Troconis, G. CARTAGENA HISPANICA, 1533-1810. Bogotá: Ministerio de Educación Nacional, 1954.

199. Powell, Philip Wayne. "The Chichimecas: Scourge of the Silver Frontier in Sixteenth-Century Mexico." HISPANIC AMERICAN HISTORICAL REVIEW 25 (1945): 315-38.

200. ———. MEXICO'S MIGUEL CALDERA: THE TAMING OF AMERICA'S FIRST FRONTIER, 1548-1597. Tucson: University of Arizona Press, 1977.

201. ———. "Presidios and Towns on the Silver Frontier of New Spain, 1550-1580." HISPANIC AMERICAN HISTORICAL REVIEW 24 (1944): 179-200.

202. ———. SOLDIERS, INDIANS, AND SILVER: THE NORTHWARD ADVANCE OF NEW SPAIN, 1550-1600. Berkeley: University of California Press, 1952.

203. ———. "Spanish Warfare against the Chichimecas in the 1570s." HISPANIC AMERICAN HISTORICAL REVIEW 24 (1944): 580-604.

204. ———, ed. WAR AND PEACE ON THE NORTH MEXICAN FRONTIER: A DOCUMENTARY RECORD. Madrid: José Porrúa Turanzas, 1971.

205. Prescott, William H. HISTORY OF THE CONQUEST OF MEXICO, WITH A PRELIMINARY VIEW OF THE ANCIENT MEXICAN CIVILIZATION; AND THE LIFE OF THE CONQUEROR, HERNANDO CORTES. 3 vols. New York: Harper and Brothers, 1843.

206. ———. HISTORY OF THE CONQUEST OF PERU. 2 vols. 3d ed. London: R. Bentley, 1848.

207. Priestley, Herbert I. JOSE DE GALVEZ: VISITADOR GENERAL OF NEW SPAIN, 1765-1771. Berkeley: University of California Press, 1916.

208. Ramos Pérez, Demetrio. "La bandera de recluta de Galicia para los regimientos del Plata, 1784-1800." In SEPARATA DEL BICENTENARIO DEL VIRREYNATO DEL RIO DE LA PLATA DE LA ACADEMIA NACIONAL DE LA HISTORIA, vol. 2. Buenos Aires: n.p., 1977.

209. Ramsey, Russell W. "The Defeat of Admiral Vernon at Cartagena in 1741." SOUTHERN QUARTERLY 1 (1963): 332-55.

210. REAL DECLARACION SOBRE PUNTAS ESENCIALES DE LA ORDENANZA DE MILICIAS PROVINCIALES DE ESPANA. Madrid: A. Marín, 1767.

211. REGLAMENTO PARA LAS MILICIAS DE INFANTERIA Y CABALLERIA DE LA ISLA DE CUBA, APROBADO POR S.M. Y MANDADO QUE SE OBSERVEN INVIOLABLEMENTE TODOS SUS ARTICULOS POR REAL CEDULA EXPEDIDA EN EL PARDO A 19 DE ENERO DE 1769. Madrid: J. de San Martín, 1769.

212. Revillagigedo, Conde de. INFORME SOBRE LAS MISIONES, 1793, E INSTRUCCION RESERVADA AL MARQUES DE BRANCIFORTE, 1794. Mexico City: Editorial Jus, 1966.

213. Rodríguez Casado, Vicente, and Florentino Pérez Embid. CONSTRUCCIONES MILITARES DEL VIRREY AMAT. Seville: Escuela de Estudios Hispano-Americanos de Sevilla, 1949.

214. Rodríguez del Valle, Mariana. "El Castillo de San Felipe del Golfo Dulce: Historia de las fortificaciones de Guatemala en la edad moderna." ANUARIO DE ESTUDIOS AMERICANOS 17 (1960): 1-103.

215. Rodulfo Cortés, Santos. "Las milicias de pardos de Venezuela durante el período hispánico." In MEMORIA DEL TERCER CONGRESO VENEZOLANO DE HISTORIA, 3: 9-85. Caracas: n.p., 1979.

216. Romero Cabot, Ramón. "La defensa de Florida en el segundo período español." Lic. thesis, Universidad de Sevilla, 1982.

217. Rubio Mañé, J. Ignacio. "Don Félix Calleja del Rey: Actividades anteriores a la guerra de independencia." Parts 1-4 BOLETIN DEL ARCHIVO GENERAL DE LA NACION (Mexico) 1 (1960): 57-86, 253-97, 553-81, and 2 (1961): 79-108.

218. Salas, Alberto Mario. LAS ARMAS DE LA CONQUISTA. Buenos Aires: Emecé, 1950.

219. Sánchez, Joseph Patrick. "The Catalonian Volunteers and the Defense of Northern New Spain, 1787-1803." Ph.D. dissertation, University of New Mexico, 1974.

220. Sanders, George Earl. "The Spanish Defense of America, 1700-1763." Ph.D. dissertation, University of Southern California, 1973.

221. Santoni, Pedro. "El cabildo de la ciudad de México ante las reformas militares en Nueva España, 1765-1771." HISTORIA MEXICANA 34 (1985): 389-434.

222. Sevilla Soler, María Rosario. SANTO DOMINGO: TIERRA DE FRONTERA, 1750-1800. Seville: Escuela de Estudios Hispano-Americanos de Sevilla, 1981.

223. Sluiter, Engel. "Dutch-Spanish Rivalry in the Caribbean Area, 1594-1609." HISPANIC AMERICAN HISTORICAL REVIEW 28 (1948): 165-96.

224. ———. "The Fortification of Acapulco, 1615-1616." HISPANIC AMERICAN HISTORICAL REVIEW 29 (1949): 69-80.

225. Sotto y Montes, Joaquín de. "Organización militar española de la Casa de Austria, siglo XVI." REVISTA DE HISTORIA MILITAR 9 (1965): 67-116.

226. ———. "Organización militar española de la Casa Borbón, siglo XVIII." REVISTA DE HISTORIA MILITAR 11 (1967): 113-77.

227. Suárez, Santiago Gerardo. FORTIFICACION Y DEFENSA. Caracas: Biblioteca de la Academia Nacional de la Historia, 1978.

228. ———. LAS INSTITUCIONES MILITARES VENEZOLANAS DEL PERIODO HISPANICO EN LOS ARCHIVOS. Caracas: Biblioteca de la Academia Nacional de la Historia, 1969.

229. ———. LAS MILICIAS: INSTITUCIONES MILITARES HISPANOAMERICANAS. Caracas: Biblioteca de la Academia Nacional de la Historia, 1984.

230. ———. EL ORDENAMIENTO MILITAR DE INDIAS. Caracas: Biblioteca de la Academia Nacional de la Historia, 1971.

231. ———. "El testamento militar." In MEMORIA DEL TERCER CONGRESO VENEZOLANO DE HISTORIA, 3: 125-63. Caracas: n.p., 1979.

232. ———, ed. LAS FUERZAS ARMADAS VENEZOLANAS EN LA COLONIA. Caracas: Biblioteca de la Academia Nacional de la Historia, 1979.

233. Tanzi, Héctor José. "El derecho de guerra en la América hispana." REVISTA DE HISTORIA DE AMERICA 75-76 (1973): 79-139.

234. ———. "La justicia militar en el derecho indiano." ANUARIO DE ESTUDIOS AMERICANOS 26 (1969): 175-277.

235. ———. "La justicia naval militar en el período hispano." REVISTA DE HISTORIA DE AMERICA 67-68 (1969): 65-102.

236. Tapson, Alfred J. "Indian Warfare on the Pampa during the Colonial Period." HISPANIC AMERICAN HISTORICAL REVIEW 42 (1962): 1-28.

237. Téllez, Indalicio. HISTORIA MILITAR DE CHILE, 1541-1883. 2 vols. 3d ed. Santiago: Prensas de la Fuerza Aérea de Chile, 1946.

238. Tengwall, David. "A study in Military Leadership: The *sargento Mor* in the Portuguese South Atlantic Empire." THE AMERICAS 40 (1983): 73-94.

239. TePaske, John J. THE GOVERNORSHIP OF SPANISH FLORIDA, 1700-1763. Durham: Duke University Press, 1964.

240. ———, with José Hernández Palomo and Mari Luz Hernández Palomo. LA REAL HACIENDA DE NUEVA ESPANA: LA REAL CAJA DE MEXICO, 1576-1816. Mexico City: Instituto Nacional de Antropología e Historia, 1976.

241. TePaske, John J., and Herbert S. Klein. THE ROYAL TREASURIES OF THE SPANISH EMPIRE IN AMERICA. 3 vols. Durham: Duke University Press, 1982.

242. Thomas, Alfred B. TEODORO DE CROIX AND THE NORTHERN FRONTIER OF NEW SPAIN, 1776-1783. Norman: University of Oklahoma Press, 1941.

243. Thurman, Michael E. "The Establishment of the Department of San Blas and Its Initial Naval Fleet, 1767-1770. HISPANIC AMERICAN HISTORICAL REVIEW 43 (1963): 65-77.

244. ———. THE NAVAL DEPARTMENT OF SAN BLAS: NEW SPAIN'S BASTION FOR ALTA CALIFORNIA AND NOOTKA, 1767-1798. Glendale, CA: Arthur H. Clark Co., 1967.

245. Toledo Sánchez, Pedro. ESQUEMA DEL DERECHO PENAL MILITAR INDIANO Y SU JURISPRUDENCIA CHILENA. Santiago: Editorial Jurídica de Chile, 1950.

246. Torres Ramírez, Bibiano. ALEJANDRO O'REILLY EN LAS INDIAS. Seville: Escuela de Estudios Hispano-Americanos de Sevilla, 1969.

247. ———. LA ARMADA DE BARLOVENTO. Seville: Escuela de Estudios Hispano-Americanos de Sevilla, 1981.

248. Torres Reyes, Ricardo. "El Mariscal O'Reilly y las defensas de San Juan, 1765-1777." HISTORIA (Puerto Rico) 4 (1954): 3-36.

249. Trigueros, Roberto. "Las defensas estratégicas del Río de San Juan de Nicaragua." ANUARIO DE ESTUDIOS AMERICANOS 9 (1954): 413-513.

250. Valera Marcos, Jesús. "El seminario de marinos: Un intento de formación de los marineros para las armadas y flotas de Indias." REVISTA DE HISTORIA DE AMERICA 87 (1979): 9-36.

251. Vega, Josefa. "Milicias y sociedad a finales del siglo XVIII: El caso de Michoacán." REVISTA DE INDIAS 45 (1985): 51-71.

252. Velázquez, María del Carmen. EL ESTADO DE GUERRA EN NUEVA ESPANA, 1700-1808. Mexico City: El Colegio de México, 1950.

253. ———. "Los indios flecheros." HISTORIA MEXICANA 13 (1963): 235-43.

254. ———. "La jurisdicción militar en la Nueva Galicia." HISTORIA MEXICANA 9 (1959): 15-34.

255. ———. "Una misión de la Armada de Barlovento." HISTORIA MEXICANA 8 (1959): 400-06.

256. Velázquez, Rafael Eladio. "Organización militar de la gobernación y capitanía general del Paraguay." In MEMORIA DEL TERCER CONGRESO VENEZOLANO DE HISTORIA, 3: 413-75. Caracas: n.p., 1979.

257. Vigneras, L.A. "Las fortificaciones de la Florida." ANUARIO DE ESTUDIOS AMERICANOS 16 (1959): 533-52.

258. Vigness, David M. "Don Hugo Oconor and New Spain's Northeastern Frontier, 1764-1776." JOURNAL OF THE WEST 6 (1967): 27-40.

259. Vigón, Jorge. EL EJERCITO DE LOS REYES CATOLICOS. Madrid: Editora Nacional, 1968.

260. ———. HISTORIA DE LA ARTILLERIA ESPANOLA. 3 vols. Madrid: Consejo Superior de Investigaciones Científicas, 1947.

261. Villalobos R., Sergio. "Tipos fronterizos en el ejército de Arauco." In MEMORIA DEL TERCER CONGRESO VENEZOLANO DE HISTORIA, 3: 517-37. Caracas: n.p., 1979.

262. Warner, Ted J. "The Career of Don Félix Martínez de Torrelaguna: Soldier, Presidio Commander, and Governor of New Mexico, 1693-1726." Ph.D. dissertation, University of New Mexico, 1964.

263. Williams, Lyle Wayne. "Struggle for Survival: The Hostile Frontier of New Spain, 1750-1800." Ph.D. dissertation, Texas Christian University, 1970.

264. Young, Duncan S. "The Eighteenth-Century Background for the Chilean Army's Royalist Posture during the Patria Vieja, 1810-1814." Ph.D. dissertation, Louisiana State University, 1976.

265. Zapatero, Juan Manuel. "Del Castillo de San Fernando de Omoa: Antigua Audiencia de Guatemala." REVISTA DE INDIAS 52-53 (1953): 277-306.

266. ———. "El castillo real Felipe del Callao." ANUARIO DE ESTUDIOS AMERICANOS 34 (1977): 707-33.

267. ———. LA GUERRA DEL CARIBE EN EL SIGLO XVIII. San Juan: Instituto de Cultura Puertorriqueña, 1964.

268. ———. HISTORIA DE LAS FORTIFICACIONES DE CARTAGENA DE INDIAS. Madrid: Ediciones Cultura Hispánica, 1979.

269. ———. "La plaza fortificada de Panamá." IBERO-AMERIKANISCHES ARCHIV 2 (1976): 227-56.

270. Zavala, Silvio. "Guerra de indios en Sonora en 1696." HISTORIA MEXICANA 17 (1967): 293-99.

PERIODICALS

271. THE AMERICAS, 1944-.

272. ANUARIO DE ESTUDIOS AMERICANOS, 1944-.

273. HANDBOOK OF LATIN AMERICAN STUDIES, 1935-.

274. HISPANIC AMERICAN HISTORICAL REVIEW, 1918-.

275. HISTORIA MEXICANA, 1951-.

276. IBERO-AMERIKANISCHES ARCHIV, 1975-.

277. JAHRBUCH FUR GESCHICHTE VON STAAT, WIRTSCHAFT UND GESELLSCHAFT LATEINAMERIKAS, 1964-.

278. JOURNAL OF LATIN AMERICAN STUDIES, 1969-.

279. REVISTA DE HISTORIA DE AMERICA, 1938-.

280. REVISTA DE HISTORIA MILITAR.

281. REVISTA DE INDIAS, 1940-.

CHAPTER III

THE LATIN AMERICAN INDEPENDENCE MOVEMENTS

Christon I. Archer
The University of Calgary

INTRODUCTION

Latin America entered a fifteen-year struggle for independence in 1810. Interpreting the revolutions, civil wars, campaigns, guerrilla conflicts, uprisings, insurgencies, counterinsurgencies, interventions, or in some cases the fairly peaceful transitions to nationhood offers a truly rich field for the military historian. It was clear from the outset of the separation movements that the military would play a much larger role in subsequent events. While creole discontent, incipient nationalism, the Napoleonic invasions of Spain and Portugal, and other themes offered universal causes for the independence movements, such explanations are clouded by a whole range of regional and local issues. Given the enormity of the continental landscapes and the differences in societies and economies, it should not be surprising that the military history of the Mexican independence movements shared only some similarities with events in La Plata, Venezuela, Chile, or elsewhere. After a slow start, Mexico's royalist armies drove patriot elements to adopt guerrilla warfare until 1821 when the royalist forces defected to support independence. In South America, the Gran Colombian forces commanded by Simón Bolívar eventually met the Southern Cone armies led by José de San Martín in a grand pincers movement to crush Spanish Peru. Often, however, major themes crucial to the military history of the period have been lost in sterile debates among partisan historians arguing the motivations of the great chieftains at the 1822 Guayaquil Conference. Despite the proliferation of heroic biographies and campaign accounts, there are still lacunae in the military history of all regions that remain to be researched.

Until recently, many patriotic Latin American historians viewed the military history of the independence period as an essential ingredient in nation building. The wars offered nineteenth-and twentieth-century historians a stage for epic struggles commanded by larger-than-life patriots imbued with the glorious cause to emancipate their lands from crushing servitude. Some royalist commanders enhanced this view by applying draconian counterinsurgency techniques and military solutions designed to preserve empire at any cost. Described as the butchers of patriots and with other negative epithets, the royalists appeared to deserve their eventual defeats. Ever since independence, nationalist historians employed centennials, sesquicentennials, or anniversaries of major events or important figures to publish series of printed documents, partisan campaign histories, or laudatory biographical studies that contributed to the epic of national liberation. In some countries, modern military regimes mobilized historians to prepare detailed military histories and to publish collections of documents. While the independence period in Peruvian history did not produce the panoply of martial heroes enshrined by some other countries, in 1971-72 the military government celebrated the sesquicentennial of independence with the publication of the massive COLECCION DOCUMENTAL DE LA INDEPENDENCIA DEL PERU (119), consisting of thirty tomes--some of which were multi-volume productions. Several nations publish ongoing series almost annually that expand the military history bibliography.

Much of the abundant biographical literature treating the lives and military careers of Bolívar, San Martín, Bernardo O'Higgins, José María Morelos, and other significant figures is so subjective in its favoritism that it does not merit scholarly attention. Less well known commanders, especially royalist officers who controlled large forces and territories, have not received similar attention. While Argentine, Chilean, and Venezuelan historians have produced many military biographies and well-researched studies, much less work has been published on Bolivia and Paraguay. Even where valuable printed documentary collections do exist, it should be kept in mind that the compilers often wished to glorify their heroes or simply neglected themes relevant to military history. In Mexico, for example, under-employed majors and colonels of the late nineteenth-century Porfirian army received the unenviable task of cataloging the massive documentation of the independence wars in the Operaciones de Guerra section of the Archivo General de la Nación. Because they were trained to think only in terms of patriot heroes, unless they saw the names of Miguel Hidalgo, José María Morelos, or other recognized insurgent leaders, they wrote in the inventory "sundry military correspondence of little significance." Often, the documents dismissed by these officers as irrelevant contain the most valuable insights about the nature of the independence struggles and clarify a variety of questions concerning guerrilla warfare, counterinsurgency, and the expansion of military power. Moreover, the royalist military commanders and officials of New Spain and other provinces kept the best archives. Notwithstanding this fact, many historians have tended to neglect archival collections in favor of repetitive studies based upon well-known published sources. As a result, the royalist side, its military commanders, and the anarchic nature of regional insurgencies remain relatively unknown. Even the most objective modern scholars writing on the independence period occasionally fall into the same traps. In an inventory of principal independence period personages published in THE SPANISH AMERICAN REVOLUTIONS, 1808-1826 (278), John Lynch neglected to mention the most outstanding royalist commander in Mexico, General and Viceroy Félix Calleja, or any of the other senior royalist military officers except Agustín de Iturbide. While his commanders were forgotten, a then unknown royalist lieutenant, Antonio López de Santa Anna, received an entry.

Historians have begun to move away from biography and the more traditional campaign and battle accounts of the independence period to investigate social, political, economic, and intellectual topics that are interrelated with military subjects. The studies of Brian R. Hamnett (216, 217), Eric Van Young (429, 431), Timothy Anna (14, 15), Tulio Halperin Donghi (203, 205), and Christon I. Archer (26, 29), offer new views of military themes that interrelate socio-economic aspects and explain much more about the real nature of the insurgencies and counterinsurgencies. These studies underscore the fragmented nature of the independence movements and the entrenchment of the military in many of the new nations. Unfortunately, there is not as much modern military-related research being done on the independence period in all areas of Latin America. The advent of bicentennial events, especially the independence movements beginning in 2010, will herald a new generation of historians who most certainly will add different dimensions to the military bibliography of the independence period.

GENERAL WORKS

Most often, the military history of the independence period has been treated in its parts by region rather than in all encompassing single or multi-volume general surveys. In order to explain the confusing diversity of independence movements, civil wars, and insurgencies, some historians, such as Charles Griffin (188, 189), adopted thematic approaches. The use of a metropolitan or imperial interpretation is difficult since the Napoleonic conquest of Iberia severed the links between the peninsula and the different regional revolutions in the Americas. Even after the defeat of the French and the restoration of Fernando VII in 1814, imperial war ministry authorities sometimes were many months, or even years, behind military events in the Americas. For historians wishing to write general military studies of the independence period, the complexity of insurgency and counterinsurgency and the shortcomings of existing published materials pose daunting difficulties. Most existing general works are of uneven quality as historians reach beyond their special research areas and regions of expertise to seek broad synthesis. Among the better studies, R.A. Humphreys and John Lynch (232), Joseph Pérez (344), and Jorge I. Domínguez (148), draw attention to precursor movements and the reasons for imperial decline. Other historians have studied independence through comparative examination of the major liberators or focused upon individual participants who served in different theaters of military activity. William Spence Robertson's RISE OF THE SPANISH AMERICAN REPUBLICS AS TOLD IN THE LIVES OF THEIR LIBERATORS (373), remains useful, and Irene Nicholson (319), followed a similar formula. Humphreys's study of James Paroissien (235), and Jaime Rodríguez's study of Vicente Rocafuerte (378), span the independence period and give background to military events. It should be noted that there are many memoirs and eyewitness accounts that are listed under a separate heading. Brian R. Hamnett (215), and Timothy E. Anna (18), have published comparative studies that shed light on major areas of interest for military history.

Several authors have written general studies on the Spanish American independence period, but none has produced an authoritative military history of the period. The best volume in English is by John Lynch (278), and is strongest on the South American revolutions. Lynch included a thorough bibliographical essay that identifies major works and published document collections on Spanish American independence by region. Short studies by Jay Kinsbruner (252), and Richard Graham (184), offer general introductions to the field. Recently, Leslie Bethell, ed., THE CAMBRIDGE HISTORY OF LATIN AMERICA, Vol. 3 FROM INDEPENDENCE TO C. 1870 (57), divided Latin America among regional and topical specialists who wrote excellent survey chapters supported by quite comprehensive bibliographies. Finally, special mention should be made of the contributions of David Bushnell who for years has edited the section on the South American independence movements for the HANDBOOK OF LATIN AMERICAN STUDIES (218).

Several historians have examined different aspects of Spain's response to the Spanish American independence wars and the loss of empire. Margaret L. Woodward published an important article on the role of the Spanish army (463), and Timothy E. Anna (21), Michael P. Costeloe (132, 133), L.H. Destefani (140), and Brian R. Hamnett (214), added works that clarify aspects of imperial policy and viewpoint. Allan Kuethe (254), studied the military in Cuba providing a useful bridge between the eighteenth- and nineteenth-century periods. Finally, José Luciano Franco (165), Edmundo A. Heredia (221), and José M. Mariluz Urquijo (286), examined aspects of Spain's futile plans to reconquer the lost American territories.

BIBLIOGRAPHIES

Information on the best guides to modern literature on Latin American independence military history can be found in recently published monographs and in the HANDBOOK OF LATIN AMERICAN STUDIES (218). Although somewhat dated, there are several general bibliographical works that remain useful as introductions to military topics and as catalogues of earlier works. For English language sources to 1958 and for contemporary accounts by travelers, Robin A. Humphreys, LATIN AMERICAN HISTORY: A GUIDE TO THE LITERATURE IN ENGLISH (234), gives good coverage to the independence movements in the different regions of Latin America. For additional accounts of the independence wars written by foreign observers, see Bernard Naylor (316). Comprehensive general and specific regional coverage of the military works may be found in Charles C. Griffin, ed., LATIN AMERICA: A GUIDE TO THE HISTORICAL LITERATURE (191). Griffin's article on social and economic aspects (188), Humphreys's historiographical essay (233), and a short co-authored study with John Lynch in LA EMANCIPACION LATINOAMERICANA: ESTUDIOS BIBLIOGRAFICOS (231), are good general introductions.

Each major Spanish American theater of independence warfare has bibliographical and historiographical works that introduce scholars to the wealth of available studies. For Mexico, military materials may be found in Jesús Guzmán y Raz Guzmán (197), Rogelio Orozco Farías (331), and in the older but still useful APUNTES PARA UNA BIBLIOGRAFIA MILITAR DE MEXICO (294). There are a number of useful studies for Gran Colombia beginning with an earlier work that remains useful for military figures by M. Leonídas Scarpetta and Saturnino Vergara (396,) which also covers Ecuador and Peru. Venezuela has general bibliographical works by Germán Carrera Damas (99), and John V. Lombardi, et al. (274). Pedro Grases (185), devotes comprehensive coverage to the independence movements. For Colombia, Robert H. Davis (137), offers a good introduction, and Javier Ocampo López (324), lists 2,000 printed works on the independence period. The Southern Cone nations have bibliographical works on many of the important liberation leaders: María J. Ardao and Aurora Capillas de Castellanos on José Artigas (32), Carlos I. Salas on José de San Martín (389), and José Zamudio Zamora on Bernardo O'Higgins (467). Guillermo Furlong Cárdiff and Abel R. Geoghegan prepared the comprehensive BIBLIOGRAFIA DE LA REVOLUCION DE MAYO 1810-1828 (168). For Peru, Leon G. Campbell surveyed recent literature concerning peasant revolts (94). Robert E. Norris has a chapter on Ecuadorian independence in the GUIA BIBLIOGRAFICA PARA EL ESTUDIO DE LA HISTORIA ECUADORIANA (320). Valentín Abecia Baldivieso's, HISTORIOGRAFIA BOLIVIANA (1), contains a chapter on Bolivian independence.

ARCHIVAL GUIDES AND SOURCES

There is a wealth of archival manuscript material available relating to the military history of Spanish American independence. In Spain, the Archivo de Indias (Seville), the Archivo Histórico Nacional (Madrid), the Museo Naval (Madrid), the Archivo General Militar de Segovia, and other archives contain royalist correspondence, service records, and other important documents. Although each depository has its own inventories and guides, works by Ricardo Donoso (150), Julio F. Guillén (195), and Pedro Torres Lanzas (399), remain useful.

In the Americas, national archives, national defense department archives, and other collections contain rich holdings of military documentation. In some cases inventories are poor or nonexistent, but barring fires, accidents, losses to repulping of old paper, and damages caused by later insurrections, the military documentation on the independence period can be extremely comprehensive. Both patriot and royalist army materials may be found. In some cases, royalist forces maintained quite complete records through much of the independence period continuing offices of military inspection and intendancy. Field dispatches, service and administrative files, hospital reports, and many other areas may be examined in remarkable detail. As might be expected, gaps in the documentation appear when major administrative centers came under military attack or when combat severed communications. Study of regional guerrilla and insurgent movements can be difficult since good records were seldom kept. Recently, many Latin American national archives have begun major projects to publish detailed inventories that will be of inestimable value for future studies.

Researchers should keep in mind that defense department archives often house current service dossiers and other national military records deemed to be delicate, confidential, or even secret. In some cases where a nation's prestige may be involved, accessibility to earlier service files and even independence documentation can be difficult. In order to follow correct application procedures, prospective scholars should check with military archives well in advance of research trips. This advice also pertains to the Archivo General Militar de Segovia in Spain since prior clearance must be obtained through the Ministerio de Defensa in Madrid.

Outside of the Archivo General de la Nación in Mexico City, some of the best archival collections on the Mexican independence period are to be found in the United States and elsewhere. For the University of Texas collection see Carlos E. Castañeda and Jack A. Dabbs (103), and Lota M. Spell (400). Both the California State Library, San Francisco (90), and the Bodleian Library, Oxford, have excellent pamphlet collections that refer in large part to the Independence Period (90, 402). For dated but still useful general works, see Agustín Millares Carlo (300), Manuel Carrera Stampa (102), and the more recent archival field guide compiled by Richard E. Greenleaf and Michael C. Meyer (187).

Many other Latin American nations have published and unpublished archival guides to sections relating to independence military history. John J. TePaske (409), recently edited a useful general guide to the archives of the Andean nations that introduces scholars to both national and regional collections. For studies related to Bolívar, see Casa Natal de Simón Bolívar (102). José María Ots Capdequí (336), has compiled a good guide to independence era topics in the Archivo Histórico Nacional in Bogotá, Colombia.

PUBLISHED DOCUMENTS

Probably no other area of Latin American history equals the independence period for published primary source documentation. National academics of history, defense departments, official archival *boletines*, and prolific scholars such as Vicente Lecuna of Venezuela, have made available remarkable collections. The desire to glorify great liberators, to seek the roots of Spanish American independence, and to explain the birth struggles of the new nations, have made bicentennial and sesquicentennial celebrations natural occasions for the launching of multi-volume works. While scholars must keep in mind that the compilers often avoided materials that would cast negative light upon their heroes and national origins, these collections offer researchers excellent sources prior to embarking upon archival fieldwork.

Mexican historians have experienced somewhat greater difficulties with the independence period than those of South America where many liberators played major roles following the victory of independence. Both Miguel Hidalgo and José María Morelos were long dead by 1821, and Agustín de Iturbide, never an easy figure for lionization, pursued the unfortunate direction of monarchy and set the stage for his exile and ignominious execution. The fragmented insurgencies proved difficult to study, detracted from nation building, and did not turn up the sort of heroic figures desired. Nevertheless, Hidalgo and especially Morelos became central figures crucial to the establishment of modern Mexican history. Two essential multi-volume collections compiled by Juan E. Hernández y Dávalos (224), and Genaro García (170), emphasize the patriot struggles and make available a wealth of military materials. Nicholás Rengel edited four volumes of DOCUMENTOS PARA LA HISTORIA DE LA GUERRA DE INDEPENDENCIA, 1810-1821, (293) published by the Archivo General de la Nación. Although it must be used with some care, the GAZETA DEL GOBIERNO DE MEXICO, 1810-1821 (176), printed excellent detail on the successful royalist army campaigns. As might be expected, there are numerous collections of Hidalgo and Morelos documents. See Luis Castillo Ledón (105), Ernesto Lemoine Villicaña (267), and Ernesto de la Torre Villar (416). On the royalist side, J. Ignacio Rubio Mañé (384), published some Calleja documents, and Iturbide has received attention (244, 245, 246).

Since independence, historians of Venezuela and Colombia have generated enormous compilations of documents on the military heroes. Collections of Bolivarian documents, campaign correspondence by his subordinates, and other major collections on the role of major military participants facilitate research on northern South America. The BIBLIOTECA DE HISTORIA NACIONAL, Columbia (123), and the BIBLIOTECA DE LA ACADEMIA NACIONAL DE LA HISTORIA Venezuela (438), have published many volumes containing primary sources on military history. In Venezuela, the first three volumes of the multi-volume LAS FUERZAS ARMADAS DE VENEZUELA EN EL SIGLO XIX: LA INDEPENDENCIA (440), treat military aspects of the independence period. Of the many compilations of published documents on Simón Bolívar, see José Félix Blanco, ed. (61), Felipe Larrazabal (256), and especially the collections of Vicente Lecuna (67, 68, 70, 260, 262). Two volumes of Bolívar's correspondence selected by Lecuna, edited by Harold Bierck (71), and translated into English, are quite useful. Care should be exercised with some of Lecuna's material on controversial issues such as the Guayaquil interview (264), in which he can be narrowly partisan. The Sociedad Bolivariana de Venezuela has been publishing the multi-volume ESCRITOS DEL LIBERTADOR (68), which should include almost all of Bolívar's correspondence. Also available are extensive collections on Francisco Miranda (31), Francisco de Paula Santander (130, 393, 394), Antonio José de Sucre (405), General Daniel Florencio O'Leary (322, 323), José Antonio Páez (337), General José María Córdova (310), and other participants. The facsimile reproduction of the GAZETA DE CARACAS (173), is a good reference work for the years 1808-18.

The Southern Cone nations have produced many excellent documentary collections. In Argentina, the Archivo General de la Nación published three volumes of DOCUMENTOS REFERENTES A LA GUERRA DE LA INDEPENDENCIA Y EMANCIPACION POLITICA DE LA REPUBLICA ARGENTINA (33). On the early independence stages, see MAYO DOCUMENTAL (35), and BIBLIOTECA DE MAYO (34). As might be expected, José de San Martín has received major attention (37, 39, 78). Published document collections provide comprehensive coverage of Manuel Belgrano (77, 156), Juan Facundo Quiroga (36), and other military figures. The facsimile reproduction of the GAZETA DE BUENOS AIRES, 1808-1821 (38), contains a great deal of material on the military history of the period. For Uruguay, there is the ARCHIVO ARTIGAS (422), and the facsimile reprinted GAZETA DE MONTEVIDEO (175), which covers the royalist period, 1810-11. Equally jealous of its glorious military history, the Academia Chilena de la Historia published the extensive ARCHIVO DE DON BERNARDO O'HIGGINS (2), and the COLECCION DE HISTORIADORES I DE DOCUMENTOS RELATIVOS A LA INDEPENDENCIA DE CHILE (3). This work includes volumes of patriot and royalist military materials, reports, and army dispatches.

Documentary collections for the Andean nations reflect the history of indigenous uprisings and the strength of the royalist side during the independence period. While some of the older collections have been surpassed, there are useful military sources compiled by M. de Odriozola (326), Fernando Valdés Torata (414), and José Manuel Valega (424). More recently, Jorge Cornejo Bouroncle (128), collected documents on revolutionary activity in southern Peru up to 1814, Javier Ortíz de Zevallos on San Martín (392), and Ruben Vargas Ugarte on the military campaigns of independence (434). Collections edited by Vicente Rodríguez Casado and J.A. Calderón Quijano (377), and Rodríguez Casado with C. Lohmann Villena (350), examine the role of Viceroys Abascal and Pezuela. To celebrate the sesquicentennial of Peruvian independence, the Comisión Nacional published the massive COLECCION DOCUMENTAL DE LA INDEPENDENCE DEL PERU (119). Of this collection, tomes V to VIII treat independence: LA ACCION PATRIOTICA DEL PUEBLO EN LA EMANCIPACION: GUERRILLAS Y MONTANERAS; ASUNTOS

MILITARES (nine separate volumes under tome VI compiled by Felipe de la Barra and others); LA MARINA 1780-1822; and LA EXPEDICION LIBERTADORA. Finally, the GAZETA DEL GOBIERNO DEL PERU: PERIODO DE SIMON BOLIVAR (177), is available in reprinted form.

There are fewer collections of published documents on Bolivian and Ecuadorian military activities during independence. Important compilations include Carlos Ponce Sanginés and Raúl Alfonso García (147), and Vicente Lecuna (263). For Ecuador, see Alfredo Ponce Ribadeneira (354), and, for the view that Ecuadorians played major roles in Peruvian battles, Luis A. Rodríguez S. (380).

For Brazil, parallel themes with Spanish America can be seen in the nine volumes of the REVOLUCAO DE 1817 (363).

MEMOIRS, JOURNALS, AND EYEWITNESS ACCOUNTS

There are numerous published journals and memoirs by participants and observers that cover the military history of the period. Unfortunately, many royalist accounts and dispatches that cast light upon military activities connected with guerrilla warfare, counterinsurgency, and army administration remain in manuscript form. On the other hand, foreigners who went to serve or observe Spanish American independence were anxious to write about their experiences. Many published accounts include information on the patriot commanders, battles, campaigns, and other interesting military topics. Bernard Naylor's bibliography (316), is useful in this regard, and Gerald S. Graham and R.A. Humphreys (183), cover Royal Navy commanders on the South American station during the period. Basil Hall (202), captain of H.M.S. *CONWAY* in the Pacific, published an excellent journal. Thomas Cochrane (117, 153), the most famous naval figure of Latin American Independence, wrote memoirs about his activities in the service of Chile, Peru, and Brazil. Alfred Hasbrouck (220), examined the role of foreign volunteers in Bolívar's armies. British officers of the 1817 expedition from England, Captain C. Brown (76), and James Hackett (198), left published accounts.

Because of the nature of Mexico's independence period, few major patriot commanders survived to leave memoirs. The apologia of Agustín de Iturbide (246), is only of moderate use. Fortunately, Lucas Alamán (5), Carlos María de Bustamante (86), and other contemporary participants listed under specialized works did write histories of independence that offer extensive information on military activities. On the royalist side, John S. Leiby (266), published the 1815 report of Colonel Juan Camargo y Cavallero. Of the foreign participants, William D. Robinson (375), offers military detail on the

Mina expedition, and Robert W. H. Hardy (219), George Francis Lyon (279), and especially Henry George Ward (455), were perceptive observers of military affairs.

Gran Colombia is particularly rich in memoirs and eyewitness accounts by military participants. Bolívar's use of foreign soldiers added a dimension that did not take place in New Spain. Officers and other travelers published extensively on military matters that were of interest to European readers. For useful works, see Charles S. Cochrane (116), William Duane (151), Gustavus Hippisley (226), Richard Longeville Vowell (454), Francisco B. O'Connor (321), Louis Peru de Lacroix (349), and the anonymous account by a British officer titled THE PRESENT STATE OF COLOMBIA (355). Of the major military leaders, José Antonio Páez (338), was one of the very few to leave a detailed, if somewhat self-serving, autobiography. Bolívar's Irish-born aide, Daniel Florencio O'Leary (323), produced the best memoirs--parts of which are available in English in R. A. Humphreys (237), and Robert F. McNerney (291). Another foreign officer, H.L.V. Ducoudray-Holstein (152), wrote a personal account that was highly critical of Bolívar. On the royalist side, see the memoirs of Captains General Juan Manuel de Cagigal (88), and Pablo Morillo (23), and the royalist official José F. Heredia y Mieses (222).

Travelers to the Southern Cone nations produced several memoirs if not the number of foreign soldiers' accounts as in Gran Colombia. The writing of General Gregorio Araoz de la Madrid (24), follows the career of an officer from Tucumán who fought in Argentina and Upper Peru. Other works are available in MAYO DOCUMENTAL (35). The British merchant Samuel Haigh (200), described Argentina, Chile, and Peru, observing the military and battlefield conditions. John Miers (296), traveled in La Plata and Chile. For Chile, María Callcott (91), and J.E. Coffin (118), described their experiences in a war torn country.

For Peru and Bolivia, the MEMORIAS of Viceroy Joaquín de la Pezuela (350), includes much military material. General John Miller's diary (301), describes campaign life under both San Martín and Bolívar, and the memoir of José Santos Vargas (395), presents an inside view of patriot guerrilla combat. General Andrés García Camba's (171), account traces the royalist side of the independence wars. One of the best works is by Robert Proctor (356), and covers the latter stages of Peruvian independence.

For Brazil, the journal of María Callcott (92), presents a contemporary view of the independence period, and Henry Koster (253), illustrates some of the themes that led to unrest.

SPECIALIZED WORKS: MEXICO

Mexico's first generation of post-colonial historians produced major studies on the military history of the independence wars that in many respects have not been superceded. While all of these writers employed history to advance their liberal, conservative, republican, federalist, or centralist ideological positions, their works also represent a combination of memoirs, contemporary histories, and solid archival research. Most of these histories focus upon the first years of the independence struggles to trace Miguel Hidalgo and José María Morelos through the military phases of their revolts. The period 1816-21 receives some attention, but regional guerrilla activities and a general decentralizing process were much more complex than these authors portrayed them. The idea that Mexico might fragment into a series of military chieftaincies and guerrilla strongholds was unattractive to later conservative and liberal historians. Moreover, the temporary empire of former royalist army officer, Agustín de Iturbide, presented few heroic themes comparable to those of Bolívar, San Martín, or O'Higgins.

Although they were completely at odds in terms of philosophy, Lucas Alamán (5), and Carlos María de Bustamante (85, 86, 87), should be the starting point for students of Mexican independence period military history. Still significant, but of secondary importance, are the writings of Servando Teresa de Mier (295), José María Luis Mora (307, 308), Lorenzo de Závala (469), Anastasio Zerecero (470), and José María de Liceaga (272). Generally speaking, these writers established themes that were continued by subsequent generations of Mexican historians through the nineteenth and sometimes well into the twentieth centuries. Among the major writers were Francisco de Paula de Arrangoiz y Berzábal (43), Francisco Bulnes (79), Emilio del Castillo Negrete (106), Luis Chávez Orozco (111, 112), Bernardo Reyes (363), and Julio Zárate's LA GUERRA DE INDEPENDENCIA in Vicente Riva Palacio, ed. (468). Recently, the official history of the Mexican army, edited by Jesús de León Toral, et al. (268), follows well-beaten paths of earlier historians.

Given the heroic themes and the martyrdom of many early patriot leaders, the literature on Hidalgo and Morelos is of mixed quality. By far the best work in English on Hidalgo, by Hugh M. Hamill (207), gives solid coverage to the military actions. Biographies by Luis Castillo Ledón (105), Juan N. Chavarri (108), Juan Hernández Luna (223), and others tend to be quite uncritical. For José María Morelos, the biography of Wilbert H. Timmons (413), is a basic introduction. For fuller detail see Ezequiel A. Chávez (110), Agustín Churruca Peláez (114), Virginia Guedea (192), Ernesto Lemoine Villicaña (267), and Alfonso Teja Zabre (408). José María Miguel i Vergés (298), and

Alejandro Villaseñor y Villaseñor (449), have compiled collections of sketches on insurgent leaders that are useful despite some errors and uncritical interpretations. Details on campaigns and battles may be found in Lorenzo Camacho Escamilla (93), Luis Chávez Orozco (111), and Carlos Garrocho Sandoval (172).

Other military and insurgent chiefs have received the attention of historians. Despite its limitations, the best work on Agustín de Iturbide in English remains William S. Robertson's (371). For other studies with a military focus on Iturbide, see Francisco Castellanos (104), Carlos Navarro y Rodrigo (315), and Rafael H. Valle (428). Recently, Timothy E. Anna wrote an article reappraising Iturbide's rule (20). Felipe Victoria Gómez (443), examined the insurgent career of Guadalupe Victoria, and William F. Sprague (401), provided some detail on Vicente Guerrero. On the less known insurgent commanders, see Jaime Olveda (329), on Gordiano Guzmán and Fernando Osorno Castro (334), on Albino García.

Recent studies have added important new dimensions to the military history of insurgency and counterinsurgency in Mexico during the independence era. Brian R. Hamnett's ROOTS OF INSURGENCY (216), is of seminal significance and should influence all future research on the period. Other studies by Hamnett (212, 213, 217), John Tutino (420, 421), Eric Van Young (429, 430, 431, 432), and Christon I. Archer (26), present new and important ideas. In Mexico, recent books by Luis Pérez Verdia (347), Carlos Herrejón Peredo (225), and Alvaro Ochoa S. (325), expand views on the nature of insurgency. For royalist army activities, see Timothy E. Anna (16, 17), Christon I. Archer (25, 27, 28, 29), Doris M. Ladd (255), Miguel Domínguez Loyo (149), Romeo Flores Caballero (164), Virginia Guedea (192), Hugh Hamill (208, 209), and Brian Hamnett (210). Jaime E. Rodríguez, (379), has assembled a volume that incorporates many of these recent views and points out directions for future research.

SPECIALIZED WORKS: THE GRAN COLOMBIAN NATIONS

The life, campaigns, and military career of Simón Bolívar and his subordinates dominate the military history of Venezuela, Colombia, and for that matter the Andean nations during the period of Bolivarian liberation. Much of the biographical literature on Bolívar is written in a rather tedious, heroic mold. In English, the biography by Gerhard Masur (289), remained for many years the standard work, but today it is out of date and appears somewhat pompous. Other useful volumes in English include Hildegarde Angell (12), Víctor Andrés Belaunde (54), David Bushnell, (84), Carlos Cortés Vargas (131), John J. Johnson and Doris M. Ladd (248), John Lynch (277), and Donald E. Worcester

(465). For a negative view of Bolívar, see Salvador de Madariaga (281). The Spanish language bibliography of Bolívar and his military campaigns is truly massive. A representative selection might include Germán Carrera Damas (100), Francisco A. Encina (155), Alirio Gómez Picón (182), Indalecio Lievano Aguirre (273), Augusto Mijares (299), and Francisco Rivas Vicuña (369). Vicente Lecuna's works on Bolívar demand the special attention of any student of the military history of the period. His detailed three-volume study, CRONICA RAZONADA DE LAS GUERRAS DE BOLIVAR (262), may be uncritical in some sections, but it remains a standard work on the military campaigns. Lecuna's other works with military significance on Bolívar include (259, 260), and (261).

For Bolívar's subordinate commanders and contemporaries, see David Bushnell (83), and Julio Hoenigsberg (228), on Santander, Pilar Moreno de Angel (311), on José María Córdova, Caracciolo Parra-Pérez (340), on Santiago Mariño, Manuel Pérez Vila (348), on Florencio O'Leary, and Alfonso Rumazo González (385), J.L. Salcedo-Bastardo, (391), and Laureano Villanueva (448), on Sucre. William Spence Robertson (372), and Joseph F. Thorning (411), while dated, present material in English on the military career of Francisco Miranda.

Both Venezuelan and Colombian historians have devoted considerable attention to the military and campaign histories of the independence period. For general military studies and other useful related works on Venezuela, see José de Austria (46), Rafael María Baralt and Ramón Díaz (48), Germán Carrera Damas (99), Miguel Izard (247), and Caracciolo Parra-Pérez (339). On the military history of Colombia during independence, see Camilo Riaño (366), Guillermo Plazas Olarte (353), and Luis Galvis Madero (169). Colombian participation in the liberation of Peru is treated by Carlos Cortés Vargas (131). Numerous battle accounts detail the campaigns of the patriots, royalists, and various insurgent groups. See Juan Friede (166), and Leonidas Peñuela Cayo (342), on the Battle of Boyacá, José Roberto Ibánez Sánchez (239, 240), on the Campaign of Bomboná-Pichincha in 1822 and the Battle of Carabobo, and Alberto Lozano Cleves (276), and Camilo Riaño (365), on the Boyacá Campaign of 1819. Alvaro Valencia Tovar (426), followed the career of General José María Córdova, and Astrúbal González (179), traced the activities of Bartolomé Salom.

On the royalist side in English, Stephen K. Stoan (403), examines the period of General Pablo Morillo. As might be expected, the sanguinary royalist caudillo of the llanos, José Tomás Boves, has received more than passing attention from Venezuelan historians Germán Carrera Damas (96), Manuel Fernández Avelló (160), and others. For Colombia, Oswaldo Díaz Díaz looks at savage royalist counterinsurgency warfare and patriot insurgency in his two-volume LA RECONQUISTA ESPANOLA (145). CONTRIBUCION DE LAS GUERRILLAS A LA CAMPANA LIBERTADORA, 1817-1819 (145).

SPECIALIZED WORKS:
THE SOUTHERN CONE NATIONS AND BRAZIL

The historians of many Spanish American nations focused special interest on the events that precipitated the independence movements. In Argentina, the Revolución de Mayo has received detailed attention from Ricardo Levene (270), Edberto Oscar Acevedo (4), Enrique C. Corbellini (127), Carlos A. Pueyrredón (358), Rodolfo Puiggrós (359), and other scholars. The classic work by Bartolomé Mitre (302), examines the role of Manuel Belgrano through the years of independence. Ricardo Piccirilli (351), studied Bernardino Rivadavia.

Argentine historians have lavished attention upon the military career of San Martín and defended his actions in the historical debates against Bolívar's partisans. Indeed, the work of Eduardo Colombres Mármol (125), fueled an outpouring of rather sterile research that might otherwise have been devoted to more useful topics. Of the rather poor biographies of San Martín available in English, Ricardo Rojas (383), presents a literary and highly positive view. For works on the revolutionary leader's military history, see Bartolomé Mitre's classic studies (303, 304), which retain much of their original value. For San Martín's early military activities, A.J. Pérez Amuchástegui (345), examined his role as commander of Argentina's northern front before his transfer to Mendoza. To follow San Martín's campaigns, see the study published by the Instituto Nacional Sanmartiano (37), the works by Fritz L. Hoffman (229), Carlos Ibarguren (238), José P. Otero (335), and Ricardo Piccirilli (352), and the detailed examination of his lieutenant, Juan G. Gregorio de las Heras in the Army of the Andes, Chile, and Peru by Fued Gabriel Nellar (317). For San Martín's role in Peru, see Benjamín Vicuña Mackenna (445), and Mariano de Vedia y Mitre (437), who covered the career of Mariano de Monteagudo from Argentina to his work with San Martín in the former country. For Argentine army and naval studies, see Augusto A. Maligné, HISTORIA MILITAR DE LA REPUBLICA ARGENTINA DURANTE EL SIGLO DE 1810 A 1910 (284), Angel J. Carranza, CAMPANAS NAVALES DE LA REPUBLICA ARGENTINA (95), and Héctor R. Ratto (360). Useful recent studies related to military matters during the independence period in the Río de la Plata region include Roger M. Haigh (199), and the works of Tulio Halperín Donghi (203, 204, 205). The best biography of Artigas of Uruguay is by John Street (404). For the separation of and military events in Paraguay, see Richard Alan White (461), and John Hoyt Williams (462).

As might be expected, the Chileans have devoted considerable attention to the origins of their independence movement and especially to the role of Bernardo O'Higgins. Standard works include older studies by Miguel Luis Amunátegui (10), Diego Barros Arana (51), and volumes six to ten of Francisco A. Encina, HISTORIA DE CHILE DESDE LA PREHISTORIA HASTA 1891 (155). More recently, Sergio R. Villalobos (447), examined the first stages of independence, and Simon Collier (121), surveyed the period from the political and intellectual perspectives. There are two studies in English on Bernardo O'Higgins by Stephen Clissold (115), and Jay Kinsbruner (251). In Spanish, the extensive bibliography includes Miguel Luis Amunátegui (9), Jaime Eyzaguirre (157), Sergio Fernández Larraín (161), Eugenio Orrego Vicuña (332), and Luis Valencia Avaria (425). The military campaigns have been examined in detail by Domingo Amunátegui Solar (11), Benjamín Vicuña Mackenna, LA GUERRA A MUERTE (444), and Guillermo Arroyo Alvarado (44).

The Chilean army has published general and specific works that devote attention to the wars of independence. Volume one of the HISTORIA MILITAR DE CHILE (113), examines the army. The recent HISTORIA DEL EJERCITO DE CHILE (227), devotes two volumes to the period. Military history syntheses by Indalicio Téllez Cárcamo (410), and, more recently, by Agustín Toro Dávila (415), have sections on independence. Specialized works with relevant chapters include Pablo Barrientos Gutiérrez (49, 50), on the Chilean artillery and staff, Edmundo González (180), on cavalry, and Alberto and Antonio Márquez (287), on uniforms. Biographies of important officers are to be found in Luis de la Cuadra (134). On the Chilean navy, Donald E. Worcester (466), and David J. Cubitt (135), examined the independence era. Recently, Alamiro de Avila Martel (47), wrote an excellent account of naval warfare during the period.

Often, Brazil's independence period has been viewed as a more or less non-violent affair that lacked much interest for the military historian. In fact, many themes present in Spanish America such as insurgency and counterinsurgency may be identified in Brazil. For general accounts and background, see John Armitage (41), A.J.R. Russell-Wood (386), Braz do Amaral (8), Manoel Oliveira Lima (327, 328), and Francisco Adolfo de Varnhagen (436). The pacific view of Brazil's independence period does not stand up in Bahia where fighting took place. See studies by John N. Kennedy (250), Luis Henrique Dias Tavares (407), Carlos Guilherme Mota (313), and Francisco Muniz Tavares (314). For works treating the history of the Brazilian armed forces that have sections on independence, see Nelson Werneck Sodré

(398), João Baptista Magalhães (283), and volume three of José Honório Rodrigues (376).

SPECIALIZED WORKS: THE ANDEAN NATIONS

As previously noted, the Viceroyalty of Peru was a bastion of royalist support for much of the independence period. The themes of outside intervention, insurgency, and counterinsurgency dominate the literature. A very good introduction to the military history is Rubén Vargas Ugarte, HISTORIA DEL PERU: EMANCIPACION, 1809-1825 (435). In English, Timothy E. Anna's recent book, THE FALL OF THE ROYAL GOVERNMENT IN PERU (15), provides an excellent introduction and includes up-to-date bibliographical material that covers the different interpretations. John Fisher's article (163), and the volume by Heraclio Bonilla, et al. (72), serve as important introductions to the complex movements. Carlos Dellepiane, HISTORIA MILITAR DEL PERU (139), devotes sections of his first volume to military aspects of the era.

Although distasteful to large numbers of Peru's nationalistic historians, armed interventions by the forces of San Martín and Bolívar took much of the initiative away from the Peruvian patriots. Many of the major works on the liberators discussed in other sections trace the course of their Peruvian military campaigns. On San Martín, see Timothy E. Anna (13), Gonzalo Bulncs (81), Germán Leguía y Martínez (265), and José A. de la Puente Candamo (357). Gonzalo Bulnes (80), also examined Bolívar's military campaigns in Peru, and Leonardo Altuve Carrillo (7), republished pamphlets and other materials relating to the Bolivarian interlude. The old debate over the famous or infamous Guayaquil Conference may be reviewed in articles by Vicente Lecuna (259), and Gerhard Masur (288). On Sucre, see John P. Hoover (230), and Luis Larrea Alba (257).

To counter the focus upon external military intervention, Peruvian historians have stressed their own insurgent movements. Some of these include Manuel Aparicio Vega (22), Ezequiel Beltrán Gallardo (55), Jorge Cornejo Bouroncle (128), Raúl Rivera Serna (370), and Gustavo Vergara Arias (441). On the royalist resistance and counterinsurgency campaigns, Fernando Díaz Venteo (146), and Carlos Corona Baratech (129), examined Viceroy Abascal's military activities.

Although the Bolivian bibliography remains thin, the survey by Charles W. Arnade (42), in English is still useful. Recently, René Arze Aguirre (45), examined the role of popular elements. Emilio A. Bidondo (59, 58), has published a highly interesting study on guerrilla warfare during the independence period and a biography of royalist Colonel Juan Guillermo de Marquiequi.

PERIODICALS

As might be expected, the major historical journals of the Latin American nations publish numerous articles on aspects of independence era military history. Examples are HISTORIA MEXICANA (478), and ESTUDIOS DE HISTORIA MODERNA Y CONTEMPORANEA DE MEXICO (475), Mexico; the BOLETIN DE LA ACADEMIA NACIONAL DE LA HISTORIA (474), and REVISTA DE HISTORIA (484), Venezuela; HISTORIA (477), Chile; and the BOLETIN DE HISTORIA Y ANTIGUEDADES, Colombia. In Spain, the REVISTA DE INDIAS and ANUARIO DE ESTUDIOS AMERICANOS (472), often contain works of interest. The major journals in English are the HISPANIC AMERICAN HISTORICAL REVIEW (476), JOURNAL OF LATIN AMERICAN STUDIES (481), THE AMERICAS (471), and MEXICAN STUDIES/ESTUDIOS MEXICANOS (482). Other periodicals such as the REVISTA DE HISTORIA DE AMERICA (485); PAST AND PRESENT (483); JAHRBUCH FUR GESCHICHTE VON STAAT, WIRTSCHAFT UND GESELLSCHAFT LATEINAMERIKAS (480); and IBERO-AMERIKANISCHES ARCHIV (479) publish occasional articles of interest to the military historian.

FUTURE RESEARCH

Although the military side of Latin American independence has been the subject of scholarly attention since the new nations emerged, further research is required. Even in the cases of the great liberators who have been idolized by nationalistic historians, there is room for reinterpretation and balance. Readers in English will search in vain for a single well-researched modern biography of Morelos, Bolívar, or San Martín, let alone the many less well known patriot and royalist commanders. In many instances, the traditional glorification of the patriot leaders masked more interesting and significant themes. Even where debates have occurred, national pride and defense of heroes result in little more than patriotic hyperbole.

The fragmented nature of many independence movements and the responses of the royalist regime make at least some of the revolts rank alongside better-known wars of national liberation. The counterinsurgent use of free-fire zones, flying columns, militia defended villages, concentrated civilian populations, natural resource destruction, and other tactics, underscore the parallels with twentieth-century guerrilla wars.

Fortunately, the archival documentation is very rich for at least some parts of Spanish America. The military history of independence for

Mexico and some other countries is being rewritten, but much basic work remains. Royalist documentation in Spain as well as in national archives should continue to yield important new interpretations. Setting aside somewhat the history of campaigns, battles, and generals, military historians will make contributions in social and economic areas. Often, the military records cast light upon a variety of significant questions. The relationships between urban centers and rural zones need further study. Few historians have examined the economic impact of insurgency, counterinsurgency, and the maintenance of large military structures. The role of women is evident from archival sources, but often absent in the published sources. The leadership of Spanish officers and of the peninsular expeditionary battalions needs to be examined. These new studies will cast light upon the entrenchment of armed forces and martial institutions in many parts of Spanish America. Destruction of the economy, loss of agriculture, and the polarization of societies left many men no other alternative than military service. Their leaders benefited from the anarchic conditions of insurgency to carve out military satrapies and in the process to decentralize the former political entities. With the bicentennials of independence on the horizon, the time is right for new military historical studies.

BIBLIOGRAPHY:

LATIN AMERICAN INDEPENDENCE MOVEMENTS

1. Abecia Baldivieso, Valentín. HISTORIOGRAFIA BOLIVIANA. La Paz: Editorial Letras, 1965.

2. Academia Chilena de la Historia. ARCHIVO DE DON BERNARDO O'HIGGINS. 30 vols. Santiago: Editorial Nascimento, 1946-68.

3. ———. COLECCION DE HISTORIADORES I DE DOCUMENTOS RELATIVOS A LA INDEPENDENCIA DE CHILE. 42 vols. Santiago: Academia Chilena, 1900-65.

4. Acevedo, Edberto Oscar. EL CICLO HISTORICO DE LA REVOLUCION DE MAYO. Seville: Escuela de Estudios Hispanoamericanos de Sevilla, 1957.

5. Alamán, Lucas. HISTORIA DE MEXICO DESDE LOS PRIMEROS MOVIMIENTOS QUE PREPARARON SU INDEPENDENCIA EN EL ANO DE 1808 HASTA LA EPOCA PRESENTE. 5 vols. Mexico City: Mariano Lara, 1850.

6. Alperovich, M.S. HISTORIA DE LA INDEPENDENCIA DE MEXICO, 1810-1824. Translated by Adolfo Sánchez Vázquez. Mexico City: Grijalba, 1967.

7. Altuve Carrillo, Leonardo. GENIO Y APOTEOSIS DE BOLIVAR EN LA CAMPANA DEL PERU. Barcelona: Herder, 1979.

8. Amaral, Braz do. HISTORIA DA INDEPENDENCIA NA BAHIA. Bahia: Impresa Oficial do Estado, 1923.

9. Amunátegui, Miguel Luis. LA CRONICA DE 1810. 3 vols. Santiago: Imprenta Barcelona, 1911.

10. ———. LA DICTADURA DE O'HIGGINS. Santiago: Rafael Jover, 1882.

11. Amunátegui Solar, Domingo. LA REVOLUCION DE LA INDEPENDENCIA. Santiago: Universidad de Chile, 1945.

12. Angell, Hildegarde. SIMON BOLIVAR: SOUTH AMERICAN LIBERATOR. New York: Norton, 1936.

13. Anna, Timothy E. "Economic Causes of San Martín's Failure in Lima." HISPANIC AMERICAN HISTORICAL REVIEW 54 (1974): 657-81.

14. ———. THE FALL OF THE ROYAL GOVERNMENT IN MEXICO CITY. Lincoln: University of Nebraska Press, 1978.

15. ———. THE FALL OF THE ROYAL GOVERNMENT OF PERU. Lincoln: University of Nebraska Press, 1979.

16. ———. "The Finances of Mexico City during the War of Independence." JOURNAL OF LATIN AMERICAN STUDIES 4 (1972): 55-75.

17. ———. "Francisco Novella and the Last Stand of the Royal Army in New Spain." HISPANIC AMERICAN HISTORICAL REVIEW 51 (1971): 92-111.

18. ———. "The Last Viceroys of New Spain and Peru: An Appraisal." AMERICAN HISTORICAL REVIEW 81 (1976): 38-65.

19. ———. "The Peruvian Declaration of Independence: Freedom by Coercion." JOURNAL OF LATIN AMERICAN STUDIES 7 (1975): 221-48.

20. ———. "The Rule of Agustín de Iturbide: A Reappraisal." JOURNAL OF LATIN AMERICAN STUDIES 17 (1985): 79-110.

21. ———. SPAIN AND THE LOSS OF AMERICA. Lincoln: University of Nebraska Press, 1983.

22. Aparicio Vega, Manuel. EL CLERO PATRIOTA EN LA REVOLUCIÓN DE 1814. Cuzco: n.p., 1974.

23. Arambarri, Francisco Javier. HECHOS DEL GENERAL PABLO MORILLO EN AMERICA. Madrid: Embajada de Venezuela, 1971.

24. Araoz de la Madrid, Gregorio. MEMORIA DEL GENERAL
    GREGORIO ARAOZ DE LA MADRID. 2 vols. Buenos Aires:
    G. Kraft, 1895.

25. Archer, Christon I. "The Army of New Spain and the Wars of
    Independence." HISPANIC AMERICAN HISTORICAL
    REVIEW 61 (1981): 705-14.

26. ———. "Banditry and Revolution in New Spain, 1790-1821."
    BIBLIOTHECA AMERICANA 1 (1982): 59-89.

27. ———. "The Officer Corps in New Spain: The Martial Career,
    1759-1821." JAHRBUCH FUR GESCHICHTE VON STAAT,
    WIRTSCHAFT UND GESELLSCHAFT LATEINAMERIKAS
    19 (1982): 137-58.

28. ———. "The Royalist Army in New Spain: Civil-Military
    Relationships, 1810-1821." JOURNAL OF LATIN AMERICAN
    STUDIES 13 (1981): 57-82.

29. ———. "Where did all of the Royalists Go? New Light on the
    Military Collapse of New Spain, 1810-22." In THE MEXICAN
    AND THE MEXICAN AMERICAN EXPERIENCE IN THE
    NINETEENTH CENTURY. Edited by Jaime Rodríguez 0.
    Tempe: Bilingual Press, 1988.

30. ARCHIVO DE SANTANDER. 24 vols. Bogotá: Aguila Negra
    Editorial, 1913-32.

31. ARCHIVO DEL GENERAL MIRANDA. 24 vols. Caracas:
    Editorial Sur-America, 1929-50.

32. Ardao, María J., and Aurora Capillas de Castellanos.
    BIBLIOGRAFIA DE ARTIGAS. 2 vols. Montevideo: Comisión
    Nacional Archivo Artigas, 1953-58.

33. Argentina. Archivo General de la Nación. DOCUMENTOS
    REFERENTES A LA GUERRA DE LA INDEPENDENCIA
    Y EMANCIPACION POLITICA DE LA REPUBLICA
    ARGENTINA. 3 vols. Buenos Aires: Archivo General, 1914-26.

34. Argentina. Congreso. Cámara de Senadores. BIBLIOTECA DE
    MAYO: COLECCION DE OBRAS Y DOCUMENTOS PARA

LA HISTORIA DE ARGENTINA. 17 vols. Buenos Aires: Congreso, 1960-63.

35. Argentina. Instituto de Historia Argentina "Doctor Emilio Ravignani." MAYO DOCUMENTAL. 12 vols. Buenos Aires: Universidad de Buenos Aires, 1962-65.

36. ———. ARCHIVO DEL BRIGADIER GENERAL DON FERNANDO QUIROGA. 2 vols. Buenos Aires: Universidad de Buenos Aires, 1957-60.

37. Argentina. Instituto Nacional Sanmartiano. CAMPANAS DEL LIBERTADOR DON JOSE DE SAN MARTIN. Buenos Aires: Talleres Gráficos del Instituto Geográfico Militar, 1978.

38. Argentina. Junta de Historia y Numismática Americana. GAZETA DE BUENOS AIRES, 1808-21. 6 vols. Buenos Aires: Compañía Sud-Americana de Billetes de Banco, 1910-15.

39. Argentina. Museo Histórico Nacional. DOCUMENTOS PARA LA HISTORIA DEL LIBERTADOR GENERAL SAN MARTIN. 8 vols. Buenos Aires: Instituto Nacional Sanmartiano, 1955-60.

40. Arias-Schreiber Pezet, Jorge. LOS MEDICOS EN LA INDEPENDENCIA DEL PERU. Lima: Editorial Universitaria, 1971.

41. Armitage, John. THE HISTORY OF BRAZIL FROM THE PERIOD OF THE ARRIVAL OF THE BRAGANZA FAMILY IN 1808, TO THE ABDICATION OF DOM PEDRO THE FIRST IN 1831. 2 vols. London: Smith Elder Co., 1836.

42. Arnade, Charles W. THE EMERGENCE OF THE REPUBLIC OF BOLIVIA. Gainesville: University of Florida Press, 1957.

43. Arrangoiz y Berzábal, Francisco de Paula de. MEJICO DESDE 1808 HASTA 1867. 4 vols. Madrid: A. Pérez Dubrill, 1871.

44. Arroyo Alvarado, Guillermo. HISTORIA DE CHILE: CAMPANA DE 1817-1818, GAVILAN, TALCAHUANO-CANCHA, RAYADA-MAIPO. Santiago: Imprenta Barcelona, 1918.

45. Arze Aguirre, René. PARTICIPACION POPULAR EN LA INDEPENDENCIA DE BOLIVIA. La Paz: Organización de los Estados Americanos, 1979.

46. Austria, José de. BOSQUEJO DE LA HISTORIA MILITAR DE VENEZUELA. 2 vols. Caracas: Academia Nacional de la Historia, 1960.

47. Avila Martel, Alamiro de. COCHRANE Y LA INDEPENDENCIA DEL PACIFICO. Santiago: Editora Universitaria, 1976.

48. Baralt, Rafael María, and Ramón Díaz. RESUMEN DE LA HISTORIA DE VENEZUELA DESDE EL ANO DE 1797 HASTA EL DE 1830. 2 vols. Paris: Desclee de Brower, 1939.

49. Barrientos Gutiérrez, Pablo. HISTORIA DE LA ARTILLERIA DE CHILE. Santiago: Biblioteca Oficial, 1948.

50. ———. HISTORIA DEL ESTADO MAYOR GENERAL DEL EJERCITO. Santiago: Biblioteca Oficial, 1947.

51. Barros Arana, Diego. HISTORIA DE LA INDEPENDENCIA DE CHILE. 4 vols. Santiago: Librería de Pedro Yuste, 1863.

52. Basadre, Jorge. EL AZAR EN LA HISTORIA Y SUS LIMITES. Lima: Ediciones P.L.V., 1973.

53. ———. HISTORIA DE LA REPUBLICA DEL PERU. 17 vols. Lima: Ediciones Historia, 1972.

54. Belaunde, Víctor Andrés. BOLIVAR AND THE POLITICAL THOUGHT OF THE SPANISH AMERICAN REVOLUTION. Baltimore: Johns Hopkins University Press, 1938.

55. Beltrán Gallardo, Ezequiel. LAS GUERRILLAS DE YUAYOS EN LA EMANCIPACION DEL PERU, 1820-1824. Lima: Editores Técnicos, 1977.

56. Benson, Nettie Lee, ed. MEXICO AND THE SPANISH CORTES: EIGHT ESSAYS. Austin: University of Texas Press, 1966.

57. Bethell, Leslie, ed. THE CAMBRIDGE HISTORY OF LATIN

AMERICA. Vol. 3, FROM INDEPENDENCE TO C. 1870. Cambridge: Cambridge University Press, 1985.

58. Bidondo, Emilio A. CORONEL JUAN GUILLERMO DE MARQUIEQUI: UN PERSONAJE AMERICANO AL SERVICIO DE ESPANA, 1777-1840. Madrid. Servicio Histórico Militar, 1982.

59. ———. LA GUERRA DE LA INDEPENDENCIA EN EL ALTO PERU. Buenos Aires: Círculo Militar, 1979.

60. Billingsley, Edward B. IN DEFENSE OF NEUTRAL RIGHTS: THE UNITED STATES NAVY AND THE WARS IN CHILE AND PERU. Chapel Hill: University of North Carolina Press, 1967.

61. Blanco, José Félix, ed. DOCUMENTOS PARA LA HISTORIA DE LA VIDA PUBLICA DEL LIBERTADOR DE COLOMBIA, PERU, Y BOLIVIA. 14 vols. Caracas: Imprenta de "La Opinión Nacional," 1875-77.

62. Blanco Moheno, Roberto. HISTORIA DE DOS CURAS REVOLUCIONARIOS. Mexico City: Editorial Diana, 1973.

63. Blossom, Thomas. NARINO: HERO OF COLOMBIAN INDEPENDENCE. Tucson: University of Arizona Press, 1967.

64. BOLETIN DE HISTORIA Y ANTIGUEDADES, Bogotá.

65. BOLETIN DE LA ACADEMIA NACIONAL DE LA HISTORIA. Caracas.

66. BOLETIN DEL ARCHIVO GENERAL DE LA NACION, Mexico City.

67. Bolívar, Simón. CARTAS DEL LIBERTADOR. 12 vols. Compiled by Vicente Lecuna. Caracas: Lit. y Tip. del Comercio, 1929-59.

68. ———. ESCRITOS DEL LIBERTADOR. Caracas: Sociedad Bolivariana de Venezuela, 1964-.

69. ———. OBRAS COMPLETAS. 3 vols. Havana: Editorial Lex, 1950.

70. ———. PROCLAMAS Y DISCURSOS DEL LIBERTADOR. Caracas: Lit. y Tip. del Comercio, 1939.

71. ———. SELECTED WRITINGS. 2 vols. Compiled by Vicente Lecuna. Edited by Harold A. Bierck. New York: Colonial Press, 1951.

72. Bonilla, Heraclio, et al. LA INDEPENDENCIA EN EL PERU. Lima: Campodonico Ediciones, 1972.

73. Brackenridge, H.M. VOYAGE TO SOUTH AMERICA PERFORMED BY ORDER OF THE AMERICAN GOVERNMENT IN THE YEARS 1817 AND 1818, ON THE FRIGATE CONGRESS. 2 vols. Baltimore: John Jay, 1819.

74. Brading, David A. HACIENDAS AND RANCHOS IN THE MEXICAN BAJIO: LEON, 1700-1860. Cambridge: Cambridge University Press, 1978.

75. ———. LOS ORIGENES DEL NACIONALISMO MEXICANO. Mexico City: Sep-Setentas, 1973.

76. Brown, Captain C. NARRATIVE OF THE EXPEDITION TO SOUTH AMERICA WHICH SAILED FROM ENGLAND AT THE CLOSE OF 1817, FOR THE SERVICE OF THE SPANISH PATRIOTS. London: J. Booth, 1819.

77. Buenos Aires. DOCUMENTOS DEL ARCHIVO DE BELGRANO. 7 vols. Buenos Aires: Imprenta de Coni Hermanos, 1913-17.

78. ———. Museo Mitre. DOCUMENTOS DEL ARCHIVO DE SAN MARTIN. 12 vols. Buenos Aires: Imprenta de Coni Hermanos, 1910-11.

79. Bulnes, Francisco. LA GUERRA DE INDEPENDENCIA: HIDALGO-ITURBIDE Mexico City: n.p., 1910.

80. Bulnes, Gonzalo. BOLIVAR EN EL PERU: ULTIMAS CAMPANAS DE LA INDEPENDENCIA DEL PERU. 2 vols. Madrid: Editorial América, 1919.

81. ———. HISTORIA DE LA EXPEDICION LIBERTADORA DEL PERU, 1817-1822. 2 vols. Santiago: R. Jover, 1887-88.

82. Bushnell, David. "The Last Dictatorship: Betrayal or Consummation?" HISPANIC AMERICAN HISTORICAL REVIEW 63 (1983): 65-105.

83. ———. THE SANTANDER REGIME IN GRAN COLOMBIA. Newark: University of Delaware Press, 1954.

84. ———, ed. THE LIBERATOR SIMON BOLIVAR: MAN AND IMAGE. New York: Knopf, 1970.

85. Bustamante, Carlos María de. CAMPANAS DEL GENERAL D. FELIX MARIA CALLEJA DEL REY, COMANDANTE EN GEFE DEL EJERCITO REAL DE OPERACIONES, LLAMADO DEL CENTRO. Mexico City: Aguila, 1826.

86. ———. CUADRO HISTORICO DE LA REVOLUCION MEXICANA. 3 Vols. Mexico City: Impr. de Lara, 1843.

87. ———. SUPLEMENTO A LA HISTORIA DE LOS TRES SIGLOS DE MEXICO DURANTE EL GOBIERNO ESPANOL ESCRITA POR EL PADRE ANDRES CAVO. 3 Vols. Mexico City: Imprenta de la Testamentaria de D. Alejandro Valdés, 1836.

88. Cagigal, Juan Manuel de. MEMORIAS SOBRE LA REVOLUCION DE VENEZUELA. Caracas: Ministerio de Justicia, 1960.

89. Caldcleugh, Alexander. TRAVELS IN SOUTH AMERICA DURING THE YEARS 1819-20-1821; CONTAINING AN ACCOUNT OF THE PRESENT STATE OF BRAZIL, BUENOS AIRES AND CHILE. 2 vols. London: J. Murray, 1825.

90. California State Library, San Francisco. CATALOGUE OF MEXICAN PAMPHLETS IN THE SUTRO COLLECTION. 14 vols. San Francisco: California State Library, 1939-40.

91. Callcott, María (Dundas) Graham. JOURNAL OF A RESIDENCE IN CHILE DURING THE YEAR 1822; AND A VOYAGE FROM CHILE TO BRAZIL IN 1823. London: Longman, 1824.

92. ——. JOURNAL OF A VOYAGE TO BRAZIL AND RESIDENCE THERE DURING PART OF THE YEARS 1821, 1822, 1823. LONDON: Longman, Hurst, Rees, Orme, Brown, and Green, 1824.

93. Camacho Escamilla, Lorenzo. LA BATALLA DEL MONTE DE LAS CRUCES. Toluca, México: Ed. Campañas, 1953.

94. Campbell, Leon G. "Recent Research on Andean Peasant Revolts, 1750-1820." LATIN AMERICAN RESEARCH REVIEW 14 (1979): 3-49.

95. Carranza, Angel J. CAMPANAS NAVALES DE LA REPUBLICA ARGENTINA: CUADROS HISTORICOS. 4 vols. Buenos Aires: n.p., 1914-16.

96. Carrera Damas, Germán. BOVES: ASPECTOS SOCIO-ECONOMICOS DE SU ACCION HISTORICA. Caracas: Ministerio de Educación, 1968.

97. ——. LA CRISIS DE LA SOCIEDAD COLONIAL VENEZOLANA. Caracas: Universidad Central de Venezuela, 1971.

98. ——. HISTORIA DE LA HISTORIOGRAFIA VENEZOLANA: TEXTOS PARA SU ESTUDIO. Caracas: Universidad Central de Venezuela, 1961.

99. MATERIALES PARA EL ESTUDIO DE LA CUESTION AGRARIA EN VENEZUELA, 1800-1830. Caracas: Universidad Central de Venezuela, 1964.

100. ——. "Simón Bolívar: El culto heróico y la nación." HISPANIC AMERICAN HISTORICAL REVIEW 63 (1983): 107-45.

101. Casa Natal de Simón Bolívar. EL ARCHIVO DEL LIBERTADOR: INDICE. Edited by Angel Grisanti. Caracas: Casa Natal de Simón Bolívar, 1956.

102. Carrera Stampa, Manuel. ARCHIVALIA MEXICANA. Mexico City: Instituto de Historia, 1952.

103. Castañeda, Carlos E., and Jack A. Dabbs. INDEPENDENT MEXICO IN DOCUMENTS: INDEPENDENCE, EMPIRE,

AND REPUBLIC; A CALENDAR OF THE JUAN E. HERNANDEZ Y DAVALOS MANUSCRIPT COLLECTION. Mexico City: Editorial Jus, 1954.

104. Castellanos, Francisco. EL TRUENO: GLORIA Y MARTIRIO DE AGUSTIN DE ITURBIDE. Mexico City: Editorial Diana, 1982.

105. Castillo Ledón, Luis. HIDALGO: LA VIDA DE HEROE. 2 vols. Mexico City: Talleres Gráficos de la Nación, 1948-49.

106. Castillo Negrete, Emilio del. HISTORIA MILITAR DE MEXICO EN EL SIGLO XIX. 2 vols. Mexico City: Imprenta de Rosas, 1883.

107. Cárdenas de la Peña, Enrique. HISTORIA MARITIMA DE MEXICO: GUERRA DE INDEPENDENCIA. 2 vols. Mexico City: Ediciones Olimpia, 1973.

108. Chavarri, Juan N. HIDALGO. Mexico City: Editorial Diana, 1971.

109. ———. HISTORIA DE LA GUERRA DE INDEPENDENCIA DE 1810 A 1821. Mexico City: Editorial Diana, 1973.

110. Chávez, Ezequiel A. MORELOS. Mexico City: Editorial Jus, 1957.

111. Chávez Orozco, Luis. EL SITIO DE CUAUTLA: LA EPOPEYA DE LA GUERRA DE INDEPENDENCIA. Mexico City: Costa-Amic, 1962.

112. ———. HISTORIA DE MEXICO, 1808-1836. Mexico City: Editorial Patria, 1947.

113. Chile. Ejército. Estado Mayor. HISTORIA MILITAR DE CHILE. 3 vols. Santiago: Círculo de Oficiales, 1969.

114. Churruca Peláez, Agustín. EL PENSAMIENTO INSURGENTE DE MORELOS. Mexico City: Editorial Porrúa, 1983.

115. Clissold, Stephen. BERNARDO O'HIGGINS AND THE INDEPENDENCE OF CHILE. London: Rupert Hart-Davis, 1968.

116. Cochrane, Charles Stuart. JOURNAL OF A RESIDENCE AND TRAVELS IN COLOMBIA DURING THE YEARS 1823 AND 1824. 2 vols. London: H. Colburn, 1825.

117. Cochrane, Thomas. MEMORIAS. Santiago: Editorial del Pacífico, 1954.

118. Coffin, J.E. DIARIO DE UN JOVEN NORTEAMERICANO DETENIDO EN CHILE DURANTE EL PERIODO REVOLUCIONARIO DE 1817-19. Santiago: Editorial Francisco de Aguirre, 1967.

119. COLECCION DOCUMENTAL DE LA INDEPENDENCIA DEL PERU. 30 vols. Lima: Comisión Nacional del Sesquicentenario de la Independencia del Peru, 1971-74.

120. Coll y Prat, Narciso. MEMORIALES SOBRE LA INDEPENDENCIA DE VENEZUELA. Caracas: Academia Nacional de la Historia, 1960.

121. Collier, Simon. IDEAS AND POLITICS OF CHILEAN INDEPENDENCE, 1808-33. Cambridge: Cambridge University Press, 1967.

122. ———. "Nationality, Nationalism, and Supranationalism in the Writings of Simón Bolívar." HISPANIC AMERICAN HISTORICAL REVIEW 63 (1983): 37-64.

123. Colombia. BIBLIOTECA DE HISTORIA NACIONAL. Bogotá: Editorial Kelly, 1910-.

124. Colombia. Ejército. Estado Mayor General. PARTICIPACION DE COLOMBIA EN LA LIBERTAD DEL PERU, 1824-1924. 3 vols. Compiled by Carlos Cortés Vargas. Bogotá: Talleres del Estado Mayor, 1945-47.

125. Colombres Mármol, Eduardo. LA ENTREVISTA DE GUAYAQUIL: HACIA SU ESCLARECIMIENTO. Buenos Aires: Editorial Universitaria, 1972.

126. Cooper, Donald B. EPIDEMIC DISEASE IN MEXICO CITY, 1761-1813: AN ADMINISTRATIVE, SOCIAL, AND MEDICAL STUDY. Austin: University of Texas Press, 1965.

127. Corbellini, Enrique C. LA REVOLUCION DE MAYO Y SUS ANTECEDENTES DESDE LAS INVASIONES INGLESAS. 2 vols. Buenos Aires: Lajouane, 1950.

128. Cornejo Bouroncle, Jorge. PUMACAHUA: LA REVOLUCION DEL CUZCO DE 1814; ESTUDIO DOCUMENTADO. Cuzco: Editorial Rozas, 1956.

129. Corona Baratech, Carlos. "Abascal: El virrey de la emancipación." ESTUDIOS AMERICANOS 3 (1951): 477-94.

130. Cortázar, Roberto. CORRESPONDENCIA DIRIGIDA AL GENERAL FRANCISCO DE PAULA SANTANDER. 6 vols. Bogotá: n.p., 1964-.

131. Cortés Vargas, Carlos. "Military Operations of Bolívar in New Granada: A Commentary of Lecuna; Crónica razonada de las guerras de Bolívar." HISPANIC AMERICAN HISTORICAL REVIEW 32 (1952): 615-33.

132. Costeloe, Michael P. RESPONSE TO REVOLUTION: IMPERIAL SPAIN AND THE SPANISH AMERICAN REVOLUTIONS, 1808-1840. Cambridge: Cambridge University Press, 1986.

133. ———. "Spain and the Spanish American Wars of Independence: The Comisión de Reemplazos, 1811-20." JOURNAL OF LATIN AMERICAN STUDIES 13 (1981): 223-37.

134. Cuadra, Luis de la. ALBUM DEL EJERCITO CHILENO. Valparaíso: Editorial del Mercurio, 1877.

135. Cubitt, David J. "The Manning of the Chilean Navy in the War of Independence." MARINERS MIRROR 63 (1977): 115-27.

136. Cuervo Márquez, Luis. INDEPENDENCIA DE LAS COLONIAS HISPANOAMERICANAS: PARTICIPACION DE LA GRAN BRETANA Y DE LOS ESTADOS UNIDOS; LEGION BRITANICA. Bogotá: Editorial Selecta, 1938.

137. Davis, Robert H. HISTORICAL DICTIONARY OF COLOMBIA. Metuchen, NJ: Scarecrow Press, 1977.

138. Dávila, Vicente. DICCIONARIO BIOGRAFICO DE ILUSTRES
      PROCERES DE LA INDEPENDENCIA SURAMERICANA.
      2 vols. Caracas: Imprenta Bolívar, 1924-26.

139. Dellepiane, Carlos. HISTORIA MILITAR DEL PERU. 2 vols.
      Buenos Aires: Librería e Imprenta Gil, 1931-36.

140. Destefani, L.H. "La real armada española y la guerra naval de
      emancipación hispanoamericana." In CUARTO CONGRESO
      INTERNACIONAL DE HISTORIA DE AMERICA, 4: 285-405.
      Edited by Academia de Historia. Buenos Aires: n.p., 1966.

141. Detweiler, Robert, and Ramón Eduardo Ruíz, eds.
      LIBERATION IN THE AMERICAS: COMPARATIVE
      ASPECTS OF THE INDEPENDENCE MOVEMENTS IN
      MEXICO AND THE UNITED STATES. San Diego: Campanile
      Press, 1978.

142. Di Tella, Torcuato S. "The Dangerous Classes in Early
      Nineteenth Century Mexico." JOURNAL OF LATIN
      AMERICAN STUDIES 5 (1973): 79-105.

143. Díaz Díaz, Fernando. CAUDILLOS Y CACIQUES: ANTONIO
      LOPEZ DE SANTA ANNA Y JUAN ALVAREZ. Mexico City:
      El Colegio de México, 1972.

144. Díaz Díaz, Oswaldo. LOS ALMEYDAS: EPISODIOS DE LA
      RESISTENCIA PATRIOTA CONTRA EL EJERCITO
      PACIFICADOR DE TIERRA FIRME. Bogotá: Editorial ABC,
      1962.

145. ———. LA RECONQUISTA ESPANOLA. 2 vols. Bogotá:
      Ediciones Lerner, 1964-67.

146. Díaz Venteo, Fernando. LAS CAMPANAS MILITARES DEL
      VIRREY ABASCAL. Seville: Escuela de Estudios
      Hispano-Americanos, 1948.

147. DOCUMENTOS PARA LA HISTORIA DE LA
      REVOLUCION DE 1809. 4 vols. Compiled by Carlos Ponce
      Sanginés and Raúl Alfonso García. La Paz: Biblioteca Paceña,
      1953-54.

148. Domínguez, Jorge I. INSURRECTION OR LOYALTY: THE BREAKDOWN OF THE SPANISH AMERICAN EMPIRE. Cambridge: Harvard University Press, 1980.

149. Domínguez Loyo, Miguel. EL BATALLON EXPEDICIONARIO ASTURIAS Y SU COMANDANTE DON JUAN DE CANDAMO: EPISODIOS DE LA GUERRA DE INDEPENDENCIA. Mexico City: Ed. Citlaltépetl, 1964.

150. Donoso, Ricardo. FUENTES DOCUMENTALES PARA LA HISTORIA DE LA INDEPENDENCIA DE AMERICA: MISION DE INVESTIGACION EN LOS ARCHIVOS EUROPEOS. Mexico City: Instituto Panamericano de Geografía e Historia, 1960.

151. Duane, William. A VISIT TO COLOMBIA, IN THE YEARS 1822 AND 1823, BY LAGUAYRA AND CARACAS, OVER THE CORDILLERA TO BOGOTA, AND THENCE BY THE MAGDALENA TO CARTAGENA. Philadelphia: T.H. Palmer, 1826.

152. Ducoudray-Holstein, H.L.V. MEMOIRS OF SIMON BOLIVAR, PRESIDENT LIBERATOR OF COLOMBIA; AND OF HIS PRINCIPAL GENERALS; COMPRISING A SECRET HISTORY OF THE REVOLUTON, AND THE EVENTS WHICH PRECEDED IT, FROM 1807 TO THE PRESENT TIME. 2 vols. London: H. Colburn, 1830.

153. Dundonald, Thomas Cochrane. 10th Earl of. NARRATIVES OF SERVICES IN THE LIBERATION OF CHILI, PERU, AND BRAZIL FROM SPANISH AND PORTUGUESE DOMINATION. 2 vols. London: J. Ridgeway, 1859.

154. Encina, Francisco A. BOLIVAR Y LA INDEPENDENCIA DE LA AMERICA LATINA. 8 vols. Santiago: Editorial Nascimento, 1965.

155. ———. HISTORIA DE CHILE DESDE LA PREHISTORIA HASTA 1891. 20 vols. Santiago: Editorial Nascimento, 1941-52.

156. Estrada, Marcos, ed. BELGRANO Y ANCHORENA EN SU CORRESPONDENCIA. Buenos Aires: Angel Estrada, 1966.

157. Eyzaguirre, Jaime. IDEARIO Y RUTA DE LA EMANCIPACION CHILENA. Santiago: Editorial Universitaria, 1957.

158. ———. O'HIGGINS. Santiago: Zig Zag, 1946.

159. Felsteiner, Mary L. "Kinship Politics in the Chilean Independence Movement." HISPANIC AMERICAN HISTORICAL REVIEW 56 (1976): 58-80.

160. Fernández Avelló, Manuel. BOBES: MARISCAL ASTURIANO PARA LA HISTORIA. Oviedo: Asturex, 1974.

161. Fernández Larraín, Sergio. O'HIGGINS. Santiago: Orbe, 1974.

162. Filisola, Vicente. LA COOPERACION DE MEXICO EN LA INDEPENDENCIA DE CENTRO AMERICA. 2 vols. Mexico City: C. Bourney, 1911.

163. Fisher, John. "Royalism, Regionalism, and Rebellion in Colonial Peru, 1808-1815." HISPANIC AMERICAN HISTORICAL REVIEW 59 (1979): 232-57.

164. Flores Caballero, Romeo. LA CONTRA-REVOLUCION EN LA INDEPENDENCIA: LOS ESPANOLES EN LA VIDA POLITICA, SOCIAL, Y ECONOMICA DE MEXICO, 1804-1838. Mexico City: El Colegio de México, 1969.

165. Franco, José Luciano. POLITICA CONTINENTAL AMERICANA DE ESPANA EN CUBA, 1812-1830. Havana: Archivo Nacional de Cuba, 1964.

166. Friede, Juan. LA BATALLA DE BOYACA, 7 DE AGOSTO DE 1819: A TRAVES DE LOS ARCHIVOS ESPANOLES. Bogotá: Banco de la República, 1969.

167. ———. LA OTRA VERDAD: LA INDEPENDENCIA AMERICANA VISTA POR LOS ESPANOLES. Bogotá: Ediciones Tercer Mundo, 1972.

168. Furlong Cárdiff, Guillermo, and Abel R. Geoghegan, eds. BIBLIOGRAFIA DE LA REVOLUCION DE MAYO, 1810-1828. Buenos Aires: Biblioteca del Congreso de la Nación, 1960.

169. Galvis Madero, Luis. LA GRAN COLOMBIA, 1819-1830. Bogotá: Ediciones Lerna, 1970.

170. García, Genaro, ed. DOCUMENTOS HISTORICOS MEXICANOS: OBRA CONMEMORATIVA DEL PRIMER CENTENARIO DE LA INDEPENDENCIA DE MEXICO. 7 vols. Mexico City: Museo Nacional de Arqueología, Historia y Etnología, 1910-12.

171. García Camba, Andrés. MEMORIAS DEL GENERAL GARCIA CAMBA PARA LA HISTORIA DE LAS ARMAS ESPANOLAS EN EL PERU, 1809-1825. 2 vols. Madrid: Editorial América, 1916.

172. Garrocho Sandoval, Carlos. LOS SOLDADOS POTOSINOS EN LA GUERRA DE LA INDEPENDENCIA. San Luis Potosí: Academia de la Historia Potosina, 1976.

173. GAZETA DE CARACAS. 6 vols. Paris: n.p., 1939.

174. GAZETA DE COLOMBIA. 5 vols. Bogotá: n.p., 1973-75.

175. GAZETA DE MONTEVIDEO. 2 vols. Montevideo: n.p., 1948-54.

176. GAZETA DEL GOBIERNO DE MEXICO, 1810-21.

177. GAZETA DEL GOBIERNO DEL PERU: PERIODO DE SIMON BOLIVAR. 3 vols. Caracas: Fundación Eugenio Mendoza, 1967.

178. Gilmore, Robert L. CAUDILLISMO AND MILITARISM IN VENEZUELA, 1819-1910. Athens: Ohio University Press, 1964.

179. González, Astrúbal. BARTOLOME SALOM O LA VIRTUD. Caracas: Corporación Universo, 1975.

180. González, Edmundo. HISTORIA Y GLORIA DE LA CABALLERIA CHILENA. Santiago: Biblioteca Oficial, 1953.

181. González García, Sebastián. "El aniquilamiento del ejército expedicionario de Costa Firme, 1815-23." REVISTA DE INDIAS 22 (1962): 129-50.

182. Gómez Picón, Alirio. BOLIVAR Y SANTANDER: HISTORIA DE UNA AMISTAD. Bogotá: Ediciones Kelly, 1971.

183. Graham, Gerald S., and R.A. Humphreys, eds. THE NAVY AND SOUTH AMERICA, 1807-1823: CORRESPONDENCE OF THE COMMANDERS-IN-CHIEF ON THE SOUTH AMERICAN STATION. London: Naval Records Society, 1962.

184. Graham, Richard. INDEPENDENCE IN LATIN AMERICA. New York: Knopf, 1972.

185. Grases, Pedro. "La bibliografía venezolana de la independencia y de los orígenes de la emancipación." In EL MOVIMIENTO EMANCIPADOR DE HISPANOAMERICA: ACTAS Y PONENCIAS, 273-316. Edited by Academia Nacional de la Historia. Caracas: Academia Nacional, 1961.

186. ———, ed. LA FORJA DE UN EJERCITO: DOCUMENTOS DE HISTORIA MILITAR, 1810-14. Caracas: Instituto Nacional Hipódromo, 1967.

187. Greenleaf, Richard E., and Michael C. Meyer, eds. RESEARCH IN MEXICAN HISTORY: TOPICS, METHODOLOGY, SOURCES, AND A PRACTICAL GUIDE TO FIELD RESEARCH. Lincoln: University of Nebraska Press, 1973.

188. Griffin, Charles C. "Economic and Social Aspects of the Era of Spanish American Independence." HISPANIC AMERICAN HISTORICAL REVIEW 29 (1949): 170-87.

189. ———. LOS TEMAS SOCIALES Y ECONOMICOS EN LA EPOCA DE LA INDEPENDENCIA. Caracas: Fundación John Bolton, 1962.

190. ———. THE UNITED STATES AND THE DISRUPTION OF THE SPANISH EMPIRE, 1810-22: A STUDY OF THE RELATIONS OF THE UNITED STATES WITH SPAIN AND WITH THE REBEL SPANISH COLONIES. New York: Columbia University Press, 1937.

191. ———, ed. LATIN AMERICA: A GUIDE TO THE HISTORICAL LITERATURE. Austin: University of Texas Press, 1971.

192. Guedea, Virginia. JOSE MARIA MORELOS Y PAVON: CRONOLOGIA. Mexico City: UNAM, 1981.

193. ———. "Los indios voluntarios de Fernando VII." ESTUDIOS DE HISTORIA MODERNA Y CONTEMPORANEA DE MEXICO 10 (1986): 11-83.

194. ———. "Mexico en 1812: Control político y bebidas prohibidas." ESTUDIOS DE HISTORIA MODERNA Y CONTEMPORANEA DE MEXICO 8 (1980): 25-66.

195. Guillén, Julio F., ed. INDEPENDENCIA DE AMERICA: INDICE DE LOS PAPELES DE EXPEDICIONES A INDIAS. 3 vols. Madrid: Archivo General de Marina Don Alvaro de Bazan, 1953.

196. Gutiérrez de Lafuente, Antonio. DIARIO Y DOCUMENTOS DE LA MISION SANMARTINIANA DE GUTIERREZ DE LA FUENTE, 1822. 2 vols. Buenos Aires: Academia Nacional de la Historia, 1978.

197. Guzmán y Raz Guzmán, Jesús. BIBLIOGRAFIA DE LA INDEPENDENCIA DE MEXICO. 2 vols. Mexico City: D.A.P.P., 1937-38.

198. Hackett, James. NARRATIVE OF THE EXPEDITION WHICH SAILED FROM ENGLAND IN 1817 TO JOIN THE SOUTH AMERICAN PATRIOTS. London: J. Murray, 1818.

199. Haigh, Roger. MARTIN GUEMES: TYRANT OR TOOL; A STUDY OF THE SOURCES OF POWER OF AN ARGENTINE CAUDILLO. Fort Worth: Texas Christian University Press, 1968.

200. Haigh, Samuel. SKETCHES OF BUENOS AIRES, CHILE, AND PERU. London: E. Wilson, 1831.

201. ———. VIAJE A CHILE DURANTE LA EPOCA DE LA INDEPENDENCIA. Santiago: Imprenta Universitaria, 1917.

202. Hall, Basil. EXTRACTS FROM A JOURNAL WRITTEN ON THE COASTS OF CHILI, PERU, AND MEXICO IN THE YEARS 1820, 1821, 1822. Edinburgh: A. Constable, 1824.

203. Halperín Donghi, Tulio. POLITICS, ECONOMICS AND SOCIETY IN ARGENTINA IN THE REVOLUTIONARY PERIOD. Cambridge: Cambridge University Press, 1975.

204. ———. REVOLUCION Y GUERRA: FORMACION DE UNA ELITE DIRIGENTE EN LA ARGENTINA CRIOLLA. Buenos Aires: Siglo XXI Editores, 1972.

205. ———. "Revolutionary Militarization in Buenos Aires, 1806-1815." PAST AND PRESENT 40 (1968): 84-107.

206. Hamill, Hugh M. "Early Psychological Warfare in the Hidalgo Revolt." HISPANIC AMERICAN HISTORICAL REVIEW 44 (1961): 206-35.

207. ———. THE HIDALGO REVOLT: PRELUDE TO MEXICAN INDEPENDENCE. Gainesville: University of Florida Press, 1966.

208. ———. "Royalist Counterinsurgency in the Mexican War for Independence: The Lesson of 1811." HISPANIC AMERICAN HISTORICAL REVIEW 53 (1973): 470-89.

209. ———. "Royalist Propaganda and 'La Porción Humilde del Pueblo' during Mexican Independence." THE AMERICAS 36 (1980): 423-44.

210. Hamnett, Brian R. "Anastasio Bustamante y la guerra de independencia, 1810-1821." HISTORIA MEXICANA 27 (1979): 515-45.

211. ———. "The Counter Revolution of Morillo and the Insurgent Clerics of New Granada, 1815-1820." THE AMERICAS 32 (1976): 597-617.

212. ———. "The Economic and Social Dimension of the Revolution of Independence, 1800-1824." IBEROAMERIKANISCHES ARCHIV 6 (1980): 1-27.

213. ———. "Mexico's Royalist Coalition: The Response to Revolution, 1808-1821." JOURNAL OF LATIN AMERICAN STUDIES 12 (1980): 55-86.

214. ———. LA POLITICA ESPANOLA EN UNA EPOCA REVOLUCIONARIA, 1790-1820. Mexico City: Fondo de Cultura Económica, 1985.

215. ———. REVOLUCION Y CONTRARREVOLUCION EN MEXICO Y EL PERU: LIBERALISMO, REALEZA, Y SEPARATISMO, 1800-1829. Mexico City: Fondo de Cultura Económica, 1978.

216. ———. ROOTS OF INSURGENCY: MEXICAN REGIONS, 1750-1824. Cambridge: Cambridge University Press, 1986.

217. ———. "Royalist Counterinsurgency and the Continuity of Rebellion: Guanajuato and Michoacán, 1813-1820." HISPANIC AMERICAN HISTORICAL REVIEW 62 (1982): 19-48.

218. HANDBOOK OF LATIN AMERICAN STUDIES. 1935-.

219. Hardy, Robert William Hale. TRAVELS IN THE INTERIOR OF MEXICO IN 1825, 1826, 1827, AND 1828. London: H. Colborn and R. Bentley, 1829.

220. Hasbrouck, Alfred. FOREIGN LEGIONAIRES IN THE LIBERATION OF SPANISH SOUTH AMERICA. New York: Columbia University Press, 1928.

221. Heredia, Edmundo A. PLANES ESPANOLES PARA RECONQUISTAR HISPANOAMERICA, 1810-1818. Buenos Aires: Editorial Universitaria, 1974.

222. Heredia y Mieses, José F. MEMORIAS SOBRE LAS REVOLUCIONES DE VENEZUELA. Paris: Garnier Hermanos, 1895.

223. Hernández Luna, Juan. IMAGENES HISTORICAS DE HIDALGO. Mexico City: UNAM, 1954.

224. Hernández y Dávalos, Juan E., ed. COLECCION DE DOCUMENTOS PARA HISTORIA DE LA GUERRA DE INDEPENDENCIA DE MEXICO DE 1808-1821. 6 vols. Mexico City: J.M. Sandoval, 1877-82.

225. Herrejón Peredo, Carlos, ed. REPASO DE LA INDEPENDENCIA. Zamora: El Colegio de Michoacán, 1985.

226. Hippisley, Gustavus. A NARRATIVE OF THE EXPEDITION TO THE RIVERS ORINOCO AND APURE, IN SOUTH AMERICA; WHICH SAILED FROM ENGLAND IN NOVEMBER, 1817, AND JOINED THE PATRIOTIC FORCES IN VENEZUELA AND CARACAS. London: J. Murray, 1819.

227. HISTORIA DEL EJERCITO DE CHILE. Santiago: Estado Mayor del Ejército, 1980.

228. Hoenigsberg, Julio. SANTANDER ANTE LA HISTORIA: ENSAYO HISTORICO-BIOGRAFICO. 3 vols. Baranquilla: Imprenta Departmental, 1969-70.

229. Hoffman, Fritz L. "The Financing of San Martín's Expeditions." HISPANIC AMERICAN HISTORICAL REVIEW 32 (1952): 634-38.

230. Hoover, John P. SUCRE: SOLDADO Y REVOLUCIONARIO. Cumaná, Venezuela: Universidad de Oriente, 1975.

231. Humphreys, R.A., and John Lynch. "The Emancipation of Latin America." In LA EMANCIPACION LATINOAMERICANA: ESTUDIOS BIBLIOGRAFICOS, 9-21. Instituto Panamericano de Geografía e Historia. Mexico City: Editorial Cultura, 1966.

232. ———. THE ORIGINS OF THE LATIN AMERICAN REVOLUTIONS, 1808-1826. New York: Knopf, 1965.

233. ———. "The Historiography of the Spanish American Revolutions." HISPANIC AMERICAN HISTORICAL REVIEW 36 (1956): 81-93.

234. ———. LATIN AMERICAN HISTORY: A GUIDE TO THE LITERATURE IN ENGLISH. London: Oxford University Press, 1958.

235. ———. LIBERATION IN SOUTH AMERICA, 1806-1827: THE CAREER OF JAMES PAROISSIEN. London: Athlone Press, 1952.

236. ———. TRADITION AND REVOLT IN LATIN AMERICA AND OTHER ESSAYS. New York: Columbia University Press, 1969.

237. Humphreys, R.A., ed. THE "DETACHED RECOLLECTIONS" OF GENERAL D.F. O'LEARY. London: Athlone Press, 1969.

238. Ibarguren, Carlos. SAN MARTIN INTIMO: EL HOMBRE EN SU LUCHA. Buenos Aires: Peuser, 1950.

239. Ibáñez Sánchez, José Roberto. CAMPANA DEL SUR, 1822: BOMBONA-PICHINCHA. Bogotá: Imprenta de las Fuerzas Militares, 1972.

240. ———. PRESENCIA GRANADINA EN CARABOBO. Bogotá: Depto. de Relaciones Públicas del Comando General de las Fuerzas Militares, 1971.

241. INDICE HISTORICO ESPANOL.

242. Instituto Panamericano de Geografía e Historia. Comisión de Historia. LA EMANCIPACION LATINOAMERICANA: ESTUDIOS BIBLIOGRAFICOS. Mexico City: Editorial Cultura, 1966.

243. Iturbide, Agustín de. LA CORRESPONDENCIA DE AGUSTIN DE ITURBIDE, DESPUES DE LA PROCLAMACION DEL PLAN DE IGUALA. Mexico City: Taller Autografía, 1945.

244. ———. "Documentos para la historia de la guerra de independencia." In PUBLICACIONES DEL ARCHIVO GENERAL DE LA NACION, vols. 9, 11, 16, 23. Mexico City: Talleres Gráficos de la Nación, 1923-33.

245. ———. EL LIBERTADOR: DOCUMENTOS SELECTOS COLECTADOS POR D. MARIANO CUEVAS. Mexico City: Editorial Patria, 1947.

246. ———. A STATEMENT OF SOME OF THE PRINCIPAL EVENTS IN THE PUBLIC LIFE OF AGUSTIN DE ITURBIDE. Washington: Documentary Publications, 1971.

247. Izard, Miguel. EL MIEDO A LA REVOLUCION: LA LUCHA POR LA LIBERTAD EN VENEZUELA, 1777-1830. Madrid: Editorial Tecnos, 1979.

248. Johnson, John J., and Doris M. Ladd. SIMON BOLIVAR AND SPANISH AMERICAN INDEPENDENCE, 1783-1830. Princeton: Van Nostrand, 1968.

249. Kaufman, William W. BRITISH POLICY AND THE INDEPENDENCE OF LATIN AMERICA, 1804-1828. New York: Yale Historical Publications, 1951.

250. Kennedy, John. N. "Bahian Elites, 1750-1822." HISPANIC AMERICAN HISTORICAL REVIEW 53 (1973): 415-39.

251. Kinsbruner, Jay. BERNARDO O'HIGGINS. New York: Twayne, 1968.

252. ———. THE SPANISH AMERICAN INDEPENDENCE MOVEMENT, 1806-1830. Hinsdale, IL: Dryden Press, 1973.

253. Koster, Henry. TRAVELS IN BRAZIL. London: Longman, Hurst, Rees, Orme, and Brown, 1816.

254. Kuethe, Allan J. CUBA, 1753-1815: CROWN, MILITARY, AND SOCIETY. Knoxville: University of Tennessee Press, 1986.

255. Ladd, Doris M. THE MEXICAN NOBILITY AT INDEPENDENCE, 1780-1826. Austin: University of Texas Press, 1976.

256. Larrazabal, Felipe. LA VIDA Y CORRESPONDENCIA GENERAL DEL LIBERTADOR SIMON BOLIVAR. 2 vols. New York: Imprenta del Espejo, 1878.

257. Larrea Alba, Luis. SUCRE: ALTO CONDUCTOR POLITICO Y MILITAR; LA CAMPANA DE 1821-22. Quito: Editorial Casa de la Cultura, 1975.

258. Lay, Bennett. THE LIVES OF ELLIS BEAN. Austin: University of Texas Press, 1960.

259. Lecuna, Vicente. "Bolívar and San Martín at Guayaquil." HISPANIC AMERICAN HISTORICAL REVIEW 31 (1951): 369-93.

260. ———. BOLIVAR Y EL ARTE MILITAR. New York: The Colonial Press, 1955.

261. ——. CATALOGO DE ERRORES Y CALUMNIAS EN LA HISTORIA DE BOLIVAR. 3 vols. New York: The Colonial Press, 1956-58.

262. ——. CRONICA RAZONADA DE LAS GUERRAS DE BOLIVAR. 3 vols. New York: The Colonial Press, 1950.

263. ——, ed. DOCUMENTOS REFERENTES A LA CREACION DE BOLIVIA. 2 vols. Caracas: Litografía del Comercio, 1924.

264. ——. LA ENTREVISTA DE GUAYAQUIL: RESTABLE-CIMIENTO DE LA VERDAD HISTORICA. Caracas: Academia Nacional de la Historia, 1948.

265. Leguía y Martínez, Germán. HISTORIA DE LA EMANCIPACION DEL PERU: EL PROTECTORADO. 7 vols. Lima: Comisión Nacional Sesquicentenario de la Independencia, 1972.

266. Leiby, John S., ed. REPORT TO THE KING: COLONEL JUAN CAMARGO Y CAVALLERO'S HISTORICAL ACCOUNT OF NEW SPAIN, 1815. New York: Peter Lang, 1984.

267. Lemoine Villicaña, Ernesto. MORELOS: SU VIDA REVOLUCIONARIA A TRAVES DE SUS ESCRITOS Y DE OTROS TESTIMONIOS DE LA EPOCA. Mexico City: UNAM, 1965.

268. León Toral, Jesús de, et al., eds. EL EJERCITO MEXICANO. Mexico City: Secretaría de Defensa Nacional, 1979.

269. Lerdo de Tejada, Miguel. APUNTES HISTORICOS DE LA HEROICA CIUDAD DE VERACRUZ. 2 vols. Mexico City: Secretaría de Educación Pública, 1940.

270. Levene, Ricardo. ENSAYO HISTORICO SOBRE LA REVOLUCION DE MAYO Y MARIANO MORENO. 2 vols. Buenos Aires: Universidad de Buenos Aires, 1920-21.

271. ——, ed. HISTORIA DE LA NACION ARGENTINA. 10 vols. Buenos Aires: Imprenta de la Universidad, 1936-42.

272. Liceaga, José María de. ADICIONES Y RECTIFICACIONES A LA HISTORIA DE MEXICO QUE ESCRIBIO D. LUCAS ALAMAN. Guanajuato: Imprenta de E. Serrano, 1868.

273. Lievano Aguirre, Indalecio. BOLIVAR. Medellín: Editorial la Oveja Negra, 1971.

274. Lombardi, John V., et al. VENEZUELAN HISTORY: A COMPREHENSIVE WORKING BIBLIOGRAPHY. Boston: G.K. Hall, 1977.

275. Lovett, Gabriel H. NAPOLEON AND THE BIRTH OF MODERN SPAIN. 2 vols. New York: New York University Press, 1965.

276. Lozano Cleves, Alberto. CAMPANA DE 1819. Bogotá: Editorial Kelly, 1977.

277. Lynch, John. "Bolívar and the Caudillos." HISPANIC AMERICAN HISTORICAL REVIEW 63 (1983): 3-35.

278. ———. THE SPANISH-AMERICAN REVOLUTIONS, 1808-1826. 2d ed. New York: Norton, 1986.

279. Lyon, George Francis. JOURNAL OF A RESIDENCE AND TOUR IN THE REPUBLIC OF MEXICO IN THE YEAR 1826. 2 vols. London: J. Murray, 1828.

280. Macías, Anna. GENESIS DEL GOBIERNO CONSTITUCIONAL EN MEXICO, 1808-1820. Mexico City: SepSetentas, 1973.

281. Madariaga, Salvador de. BOLIVAR. New York: Pelligrini, 1952.

282. Madrid. Museo Naval. CATALOGO DE LOS DOCUMENTOS REFERENTES A LA INDEPENDENCIA DE COLOMBIA EXISTENTES EN EL MUSEO NAVAL Y ARCHIVO DE MARINA "BAZAN." Madrid: Consejo Superior de Investigaciones Científicas, Instituto Histórico de Marina, 1969.

283. Magalhaes, Joao Baptista. A EVOLUCAO MILITAR DO BRASIL: ANOTACOES PARA A HISTORIA. Rio de Janerio: Biblioteca do Exército, 1958.

284. Maligné, Augusto A. HISTORIA MILITAR DE LA REPUBLICA ARGENTINA DURANTE EL SIGLO DE 1810 A 1910. Buenos Aires: La Nación, 1910.

285. Manning, William R., ed. DIPLOMATIC CORRESPONDENCE OF THE UNITED STATES CONCERNING THE INDEPENDENCE OF THE LATIN AMERICAN NATIONS. 3 vols. New York: Oxford University Press, 1925.

286. Mariluz Urquijo, José M. LOS PROYECTOS ESPANOLES PARA RECONQUISTAR EL RIO DE LA PLATA, 1820-1833. Buenos Aires: Editorial Perrot, 1958.

287. Márquez, Alberto, and Antonio Márquez. CUATRO SIGLOS DE UNIFORMES EN CHILE. Santiago: Editorial Andrés Bello, 1976.

288. Masur, Gerhard. "The Conference of Guayaquil." HISPANIC AMERICAN HISTORICAL REVIEW 31 (1951): 189-229.

289. ———. SIMON BOLIVAR. Albuquerque: University of New Mexico Press, 1948.

290. Matilla Tascón, A. "Las expediciones o reemplazos militares enviados desde Cádiz a reprimir el movimiento de independencia de Hispanoamérica." REVISTA DE ARCHIVOS, BIBLIOTECAS Y MUSEOS 57 (1951): 37-52.

291. McNerney, Robert F., ed. and trans. MEMORIAS DEL GENERAL DANIEL FLORENCIO O'LEARY: BOLIVAR AND THE WAR OF INDEPENDENCE. Austin: University of Texas Press, 1970.

292. Meléndez Chaverri, Carlos, comp. TEXTOS FUNDAMENTALES DE LA INDEPENDENCIA CENTROAMERICANA. San José: Editorial Universitaria Centroamericana, 1971.

293. Mexico. Archivo General de la Nación. PUBLICACIONES DEL ARCHIVO GENERAL DE LA NACION. 30 vols. Mexico City: AGN, 1910-36.

294. Mexico. Secretaría de Guerra y Marina. Comisión de Estudios Militares. APUNTES PARA UNA BIBLIOGRAFIA MILITAR

DE MEXICO, 1536-1936. Mexico City: Talleres Gráficos de la Nación, 1937.

295. Mier, Servando Teresa de. HISTORIA DE LA REVOLUCION DE NUEVA ESPANA. 2 vols. London: Impr. de G. Glindon, 1813.

296. Miers, John. TRAVELS IN CHILE AND LA PLATA. London: Baldwin, Cradock and Joy, 1826.

297. Miguel i Vergés, José María. DICCIONARIO DE INSURGENTES. Mexico City: Editorial Porrúa, 1969.

298. ——. LA INDEPENDENCIA MEXICANA Y LA PRENSA INSURGENTE. Mexico City: n.p., 1941.

299. Mijares, Augusto. EL LIBERTADOR. Caracas: Ministerio de Obras Públicas, 1969.

300. Millares Carlo, Agustín. REPERTORIO BIBLIOGRAFICO DE LOS ARCHIVOS MEXICANOS Y DE LOS EUROPEOS Y NORTEAMERICANOS DE INTERES PARA LA HISTORIA DE MEXICO. Mexico City: UNAM, 1959.

301. Miller, John. MEMOIRS OF GENERAL JOHN MILLER IN THE SERVICE OF THE REPUBLIC OF PERU. 2 vols. London: Longman, Rees, Orme, Brown and Green, 1829.

302. Mitre, Bartolomé. HISTORIA DE BELGRANO Y DE LA INDEPENDENCIA ARGENTINA. 4 vols. Buenos Aires: Editorial Universitaria, 1967.

303. ——. HISTORIA DE SAN MARTIN Y DE LA EMANCIPACION SUD-AMERICANA. 4 vols. Buenos Aires: F. Lajouane, 1889-90.

304. ——. OBRAS COMPLETAS. 18 vols. Buenos Aires: Congreso de la Nación, 1938.

305. Monteajano y Aguiñaga, Rafael. EL CLERO Y LA INDEPENDENCIA EN SAN LUIS POTOSI. San Luis Potosí: Academia de Historia Potosina, 1971.

306. ———. DOCUMENTOS PARA LA HISTORIA DE LA GUERRA DE INDEPENDENCIA EN SAN LUIS POTOSI. San Luis Potosí: Academia de la Historia, 1981.

307. Mora, José María Luis. MEJICO Y SUS REVOLUCIONES. 3 Vols. Mexico City: Editorial Porrúa, 1965.

308. ———. OBRAS SUELTAS. Mexico City: Editorial Porrúa, 1963.

309. MORELOS: DOCUMENTOS INEDITOS Y POCO CONOCIDOS. Compiled by Luis Castillo Ledón. 3 vols. Mexico City: Secretaría de Educación Pública, 1927.

310. Moreno de Angel, Pilar. CORRESPONDENCIA Y DOCUMENTOS DEL GENERAL JOSE MARIA CORDOVA. 4 vols. Bogotá: Editorial Kelly, 1974.

311. ———. JOSE MARIA CORDOVA. Bogotá: Editorial Kelly, 1977.

312. Morton, F.W.O. "The Military and Society in Bahia, 1800-1821." JOURNAL OF LATIN AMERICAN STUDIES 7 (1975): 249-69.

313. Mota, Carlos Guilherme. NORDESTE, 1817: ESTRUTURAS E ARGUMENTOS. Sao Paulo: Perspectiva, 1972.

314. Muniz Tavares, Francisco. HISTORIA DA REVOLUCAO DE PERNAMBUCO EM 1817. Recife: Impresa Industrial, 1917.

315. Navarro y Rodrigo, Carlos. VIDA DE AGUSTIN DE ITURBIDE: MEMORIAS DE AGUSTIN DE ITURBIDE. Madrid: Biblioteca Ayacucho, 1919.

316. Naylor, Bernard. ACCOUNTS OF NINETEENTH CENTURY SOUTH AMERICA: AN ANNOTATED CHECKLIST OF WORKS BY BRITISH AND UNITED STATES OBSERVERS. London: Athlone Press, 1969.

317. Nellar, Fued Gabriel. JUAN G. GREGORIO DE LAS HERAS: SU VIDA, SU OBRA. Buenos Aires: Círculo Militar, 1965.

318. Neumann, William L. "United States Aid to the Chilean Wars of Independence." HISPANIC AMERICAN HISTORICAL REVIEW 27 (1947): 204-19.

319. Nicholson, Irene. THE LIBERATORS: A STUDY OF INDEPENDENCE MOVEMENTS IN SPANISH AMERICA. London: Faber and Faber, 1969.

320. Norris, Robert E. GUIA BIBLIOGRAFICA PARA EL ESTUDIO DE LA HISTORIA ECUADORIANA Austin: Institute of Latin American Studies, University of Texas, 1978.

321. O'Connor, Francisco B. INDEPENDENCIA AMERICANA: RECUERDOS DE FRANCISCO O'CONNOR. Madrid: Biblioteca Ayacucho, 1915.

322. O'Leary, Daniel Florencio. MEMORIAS DEL GENERAL FRANCISCO O'LEARY: NARRACION. 3 vols. Caracas: Imprenta Nacional, 1952.

323. ———. MEMORIAS DEL GENERAL O'LEARY. 32 vols. Caracas: Imprenta de la Gazeta Oficial, 1879-1914.

324. Ocampo López, Javier. HISTORIOGRAFIA Y BIBLIOGRAFIA DE LA EMANCIPACION DEL NUEVO REINO DE GRANADA. Tunja, Colombia: n.p., 1969.

325. Ochoa S., Alvaro. LOS INSURGENTES DE MEZCALA. Zamora: El Colegio de Michoacán, 1985.

326. Odriozola, M. de. DOCUMENTOS HISTORICOS DEL PERU. 10 vols. Lima: Tip. de A., 1863-77.

327. Oliveira Lima, Manoel. DOM JOAO V NO BRASIL, 1808-21. 3 vols. 2d ed. Sao Paulo: José Olympio, 1945.

328. ———. O MOVIMENTO DA INDEPENDENCIA. Sao Paulo: Wieszenflog, 1922.

329. Olveda, Jaime. GORDIANO GUZMAN: UN CACIQUE DEL SIGLO XIX. Mexico City: Instituto Nacional de Antropología e Historia, 1980.

330. Ornstein, Leopoldo. LA CAMPANA DE LOS ANDES A LA LUZ DE LAS DOCTRINAS DE GUERRAS MODERNAS. Buenos Aires: Talleres Gráficos del Instituto Geográfico Militar, 1931.

331. Orozco Farías, Rogelio. FUENTES HISTORICAS DE LA INDEPENDENCIA DE MEXICO, 1808-1821. Mexico City: Editorial Jus, 1967.

332. Orrego Vicuña, Eugenio. O'HIGGINS: VIDA Y TIEMPO. Buenos Aires: Editorial Losada, 1941.

333. Ortíz, Sergio Elías. AGUSTIN AQUALONGO Y SU TIEMPO. Bogotá: Biblioteca Banco Popular, 1974.

334. Osorno Castro, Fernando. EL INSURGENTE ALBINO GARCIA. Mexico City: Editorial México Nuevo, 1940.

335. Otero, José P. HISTORIA DEL LIBERTADOR JOSE DE SAN MARTIN. Buenos Aires: Cabaut, 1932.

336. Ots Capdequí, José María. LAS INSTITUCIONES DEL NUEVO REINO DE GRANADA AL TIEMPO DE LA INDEPENDENCIA. Madrid: Consejo Superior de Investigaciones Ciéntíficas, 1958.

337. Páez, José Antonio. ARCHIVO DEL GENERAL JOSE ANTONIO PAEZ. Bogotá: Editorial El Gráfico, 1939.

338. ———. AUTOBIOGRAFIA. 2 vols. New York: Hallet and Brean, 1869.

339. Parra-Pérez, Caracciolo. HISTORIA DE LA PRIMERA REPUBLICA DE VENEZUELA. 2 vols. Caracas: Tipografía Americana, 1959.

340. ———. MARINO Y LA INDEPENDENCIA DE VENEZUELA. 5 vols. Madrid: Ediciones Cultura Hispánica, 1954-57.

341. Paz, José M. MEMORIAS POSTUMAS DEL GENERAL JOSE MARIA PAZ. 3 vols. Buenos Aires: Taller Gráfico de L. Bernard, 1924-26.

342. Peñuela Cayo, Leonidas. ALBUM DE BOYACA. 2 vols. Tunja, Colombia: Imprenta Departmental, 1969-70.

343. Peralta, H.G. AGUSTIN DE ITURBIDE Y COSTA RICA. San José: Editorial Costa Rica, 1968.

344. Pérez, Joseph. LOS MOVIMIENTOS PRECURSORES DE LA EMANCIPACION EN HISPANOAMERICA. Madrid: Ediciones Alhambra, 1977.

345. Pérez Amuchástegui, A.J. SAN MARTIN Y EL ALTO PERU, 1814. San Miguel de Tucumán, Argentina: Fundación Banco Comercial del Norte, 1976.

346. Pérez O., Eduardo. LA GUERRA IRREGULAR EN LA INDEPENDENCIA DE LA NUEVA GRANADA Y VENEZUELA, 1810-30. Tunja: Universidad Pedogógica y Tecnológica de Colombia, 1982.

347. Pérez Verdia, Luis. APUNTES HISTORICOS SOBRE LA GUERRA DE INDEPENDENCIA EN JALISCO. Guadalajara: Ediciones I.T.G., 1953.

348. Pérez Vila, Manuel. VIDA DE DANIEL FLORENCIO O'LEARY: PRIMER EDECAN DEL LIBERTADOR. Caracas: Imprenta Nacional, 1957.

349. Peru de Lacroix, Luis. DIARIO DE BUCARAMANGA. Caracas: Tipografía Americana, 1935.

350. Pezuela y Sánchez Muñoz de Velasco, Joaquín de la. MEMORIAS DE GOBIERNO. Seville: Escuela de Estudios Hispano Americanos, 1947.

351. Piccirilli, Ricardo. RIVADAVIA Y SU TIEMPO. 3 vols. Buenos Aires: Ediciones Peuser, 1960.

352. ———. SAN MARTIN Y LA POLITICA DE LOS PUEBLOS. Buenos Aires: Ediciones Gure, 1957.

353. Plazas Olarte, Guillermo. HISTORIA MILITAR: LA INDEPENDENCIA, 1819-1828. Bogotá: Ediciones Lerner, 1971.

354. Ponce Ribadeneira, Alfredo, ed. QUITO, 1809-1812: SEGUN LOS DOCUMENTOS DEL ARCHIVO NACIONAL DE MADRID. Madrid: n.p., 1960.

355. THE PRESENT STATE OF COLOMBIA; CONTAINING AN ACCOUNT OF THE PRINCIPAL EVENTS OF ITS

REVOLUTIONARY WAR. . . . BY AN OFFICER, LATE IN THE COLOMBIA SERVICE. London: J. Murray, 1827.

356. Proctor, Robert. NARRATIVE OF A JOURNEY ACROSS THE CORDILLERA OF THE ANDES AND OF A RESIDENCE IN LIMA AND OTHER PARTS OF PERU, IN THE YEARS 1823 AND 1824. London: Constable and Co., 1825.

357. Puente Candamo, José A. de la. SAN MARTIN Y EL PERU. Lima: Editorial Lumen, 1948.

358. Pueyrredón, Carlos A. 1810: LA REVOLUCION DE MAYO. Buenos Aires: Ediciones Peuser, 1953.

359. Puiggrós, Rodolfo. LOS CAUDILLOS DE LA REVOLUCION DE MAYO. Buenos Aires: Ediciones Corregidor, 1971.

360. Ratto, Héctor R. HISTORIA DE BROWN. 2 vols. Buenos Aires: Editorial "La Facultad," 1939.

361. Restrepo, José Manuel. DIARIO POLITICO Y MILITAR: MEMORIAS SOBRE LOS SUCESOS IMPORTANTES DE LA EPOCA PARA SERVIR A LA HISTORIA DE LA REVOLUCION DE COLOMBIA Y DE LA NUEVA GRANADA DESDE 1819 PARA ADELANTE. 4 vols. Bogotá: Biblioteca de la Presidencia de Colombia, 1954.

362. ———. HISTORIA DE LA REVOLUCION DE LA REPUBLICA DE COLOMBIA EN LA AMERICA MERIDIONAL. 8 vols. Bogotá: Ministerio de Educación Nacional, 1942-50.

363. REVOLUCAO DE 1817. 9 Vols. Rio de Janeiro: Biblioteca National, 1953-55.

364. Reyes, Bernardo. EL EJERCITO MEXICANO. Mexico City: J. Ballesca, 1901.

365. Riaño, Camilo. LA CAMPANA LIBERTADORA DE 1819. Bogotá: Editorial Andes, 1969.

366. ———. HISTORIA MILITAR: LA INDEPENDENCIA, 1810-1815. Bogotá: Ediciones Lerner, 1971.

367. ———. EL TENIENTE GENERAL DON ANTONIO NARINO. Bogotá: Imprenta de las Fuerzas Armadas, 1973.

368. Riva Palacio, Vicente, ed. MEXICO A TRAVES DE LOS SIGLOS. 4 vols. Barcelona: Espasa y Compañia, 1888-89.

369. Rivas Vicuña, Francisco. LAS GUERRAS DE BOLIVAR. 2 vols. Caracas: Editorial "Victoria," 1921-22.

370. Rivera Serna, Raúl. LOS GUERRILLEROS DEL CENTRO EN LA EMANCIPACION PERUANA. Lima: n.p., 1958.

371. Robertson, William Spence. ITURBIDE OF MEXICO. Durham: Duke University Press, 1952.

372. ———. THE LIFE OF MIRANDA. 2 vols. Chapel Hill: University of North Carolina Press, 1929.

373. ———. RISE OF THE SPANISH AMERICAN REPUBLICS AS TOLD IN THE LIVES OF THEIR LIBERATORS. New York: Appleton, 1918.

374. Robinson, John L. BARTOLOME MITRE: HISTORIAN OF THE AMERICAS. Washington: University Presses of America, 1982.

375. Robinson, William D. MEMOIRS OF THE MEXICAN REVOLUTION: INCLUDING A NARRATIVE OF THE EXPEDITION OF GENERAL XAVIER MINA . . . . Philadelphia: Lydia R. Bailey, 1820.

376. Rodrigues, José Honório. INDEPENDENCIA: REVOLUCAO E CONTRA-REVOLUCAO. 5 vols. Rio de Janeiro: Livraria Francisco Alves, 1975.

377. Rodríguez Casado, Vicente, and J.A. Calderón Quijano, eds. MEMORIA DE GOBIERNO DEL VIRREY ABASCAL. 2 vols. Seville: Escuela de Estudios Hispanoamericanos, 1944.

378. Rodríguez O., Jaime E. THE EMERGENCE OF SPANISH AMERICA: VICENTE ROCAFUERTE AND SPANISH AMERICANISM, 1808-1832. Berkeley: University of California Press, 1975.

379. ———. ed. THE INDEPENDENCE OF MEXICO AND THE CREATION OF THE NEW NATION. Los Angeles: Center for Latin American Studies, UCLA, 1989.

380. Rodríguez S., Luis A. AYACUCHO: LA BATALLA DE LA LIBERTAD AMERICANA. Quito: Casa de la Cultura Ecuadoriana, 1975.

381. Rodríguez Villa, Antonio. EL TENIENTE GENERAL DON PABLO MORILLO: PRIMER CONDE DE CARTAGENA, MARQUES DE LA PUERTA, 1778-1837. 4 vols. Madrid: Est. Tip. de Fortanet, 1908-10.

382. Roel Pineda, Virgilio. LOS LIBERTADORES. Lima: Editorial Gráfica Labor, 1971.

383. Rojas, Ricardo. SAN MARTIN: KNIGHT OF THE ANDES. Translated by Herschel Brickell. New York: Cooper Square, 1967.

384. Rubio Mañé, J. Ignacio. "La campaña de Calleja en la guerra de independencia." BOLETIN DEL ARCHIVO GENERAL DE LA NACION 19 (1948): 475-588.

385. Rumazo González, Alfonso. SUCRE: GRAN MARISCAL DE AYACUCHO; BIOGRAFIA. Madrid: Aguilar, 1963.

386. Russell-Wood, A.J.R., ed. FROM COLONY TO NATION: ESSAYS ON THE INDEPENDENCE OF BRAZIL. Baltimore: Johns Hopkins University Press, 1975.

387. Rydjord, J. FOREIGN INTEREST IN THE INDEPENDENCE OF NEW SPAIN. Durham: Duke University Press, 1935.

388. Sala de Touron, Lucía, Nelson de la Torre, and Julio C. Rodríguez. ARTIGAS Y SU REVOLUCION AGRARIA, 1811-1820. Mexico City: Siglo XXI Editores, 1978.

389. Salas, Carlos I. BIBLIOGRAFIA DEL GENERAL DON JOSE DE SAN MARTIN Y DE LA EMANCIPACION SUDAMERICANA. 5 vols. Buenos Aires: Compañía Sud Americana de Billetes de Banco, 1910.

390. Salazar, Ramón A. HISTORIA DE VEINTIUN ANOS: LA INDEPENDENCIA DE GUATEMALA. Guatemala: Secretaría de Educación Pública, 1928.

391. Salcedo-Bastardo, J.L., ed. ANTONIO JOSE DE SUCRE: DE MI PROPIA MANO. Caracas: Biblioteca Ayacucho, 1981.

392. San Martín, José de. CORRESPONDENCIA DE SAN MARTIN Y TORRE TAGLE. Compiled by Javier Ortíz de Zevallos. Lima: J. Mejía Baca, 1963.

393. ———. CARTAS DE SANTANDER. 3 vols. Compiled by Vicente Lecuna. Caracas: Lt. y Tip. del Comercio, 1942.

394. Santander, Francsico de Paula. CARTAS Y MENSAJES. 10 vols. Compiled by Roberto Cortázar. Bogotá: n.p., 1953-56.

395. Santos Vargas, José. DIARIO DE UN COMANDANTE DE LA INDEPENDENCIA AMERICANA, 1814-1825. Mexico City: Siglo XXI Editores, 1982.

396. Scarpetta, M. Leonídas, and Saturnino Vergara. DICCIONARIO BIOGRAFICO DE LOS CAMPEONES DE LA LIBERTAD DE NUEVA GRANADA, VENEZUELA, ECUADOR I PERU. Bogotá: Imprenta de Zalmea, 1879.

397. Sierra, Catalina. EL NACIMIENTO DE MEXICO. Mexico City: UNAM, 1960.

398. Sodré, Nelson Werneck. HISTORIA MILITAR DO BRASIL. Rio de Janeiro: Civilizaçao Brasileira, 1968.

399. Spain. Archivo General de Indias, Seville. LA INDEPENDENCIA DE AMERICA: FUENTES PARA SU ESTUDIO; CATALOGO DE DOCUMENTOS CONSERVADOS EN EL ARCHIVO GENERAL DE INDIAS DE SEVILLA. 8 vols. Compiled by Pedro Torres Lanzas. Madrid: Sociedad de Publicaciones Históricas, 1912-25.

400. Spell, Lota M. RESEARCH MATERIAL FOR THE STUDY OF LATIN AMERICA AT THE UNIVERSITY OF TEXAS. Austin: University of Texas Press, 1954.

401. Sprague, William Forrest. VICENTE GUERRERO: MEXICAN LIBERATOR; A STUDY IN PATRIOTISM. Chicago: R.R. Donnelley, 1939.

402. Steele, Colin, and Michael P. Costeloe. INDEPENDENT MEXICO: A COLLECTION OF MEXICAN PAMPHLETS IN THE BODLEIAN LIBRARY. Oxford: Mansell, 1973.

403. Stoan, Stephen K. PABLO MORILLO AND VENEZUELA, 1815-1820. Columbus: Ohio State University Press, 1974.

404. Street, John. ARTIGAS AND THE EMANCIPATION OF URUGUAY. Cambridge: Cambridge University Press, 1959.

405. Sucre, Antonio José de. ARCHIVO DE SUCRE. 4 vols. Caracas: Fundación Vicente Lecuna, 1973-.

406. ———. CARTAS DE SUCRE AL LIBERTADOR, 1826-1830. Compiled by Daniel Florencio O'Leary. Madrid: Editorial América, 1919.

407. Tavares, Luis Henrique Dias. A INDEPENDENCIA DO BRASIL NA BAHIA. Rio de Janeiro: Civilizaçao Brasileira, 1977.

408. Teja Zabre, Alfonso. VIDA DE MORELOS. Mexico City: UNAM, 1959.

409. TePaske, John J. RESEARCH GUIDE TO ANDEAN HISTORY: BOLIVIA, CHILE, ECUADOR, AND PERU. Durham: Duke University Press, 1981.

410. Téllez Cárcamo, Indalecio. HISTORIA MILITAR DE CHILE, 1520-1883. Santiago: Imprenta Balcells and Co., 1925.

411. Thorning, Joseph F. MIRANDA: WORLD CITIZEN. Gainesville: University of Florida Press, 1952.

412. Timmons, Wilbert H. "Los Guadalupes: A Secret Society in the Mexican Revolution for Independence." HISPANIC AMERICAN HISTORICAL REVIEW 30 (1950): 453-79.

413. ———. MORELOS: PRIEST, SOLDIER, STATESMAN OF MEXICO. El Paso: Texas Western College Press, 1963.

414. Torata, Fernando Valdés, ed. DOCUMENTOS PARA LA HISTORIA DE LA GUERRA SEPARATISTA DEL PERU. 4 vols. Madrid: Imprenta de la Viuda de M. Minuesa de los Ríos, 1894-98.

415. Toro Dávila, Agustín. SINTESIS HISTORICO MILITAR DE CHILE. Santiago: Editorial Universitaria, 1976.

416. Torre Villar, Ernesto de la, ed. LA CONSTITUCION DE APATZINGAN Y LOS CREADORES DEL ESTADO MEXICANO. Mexico City: UNAM, 1964.

417. ———. LA INDEPENDENCIA MEXICANA. 3 vols. Mexico City: UNAM, 1982.

418. ———, ed. LOS GUADALUPES Y LA INDEPENDENCIA CON UNA SELECCION DE DOCUMENTOS INEDITOS. Mexico City: Editorial Jus, 1966.

419. Torrente, Mariano. HISTORIA DE LA REVOLUCION HISPANOAMERICANA. 3 vols. Madrid: Impr. de L. Amarita, 1829-30.

420. Tutino, John. FROM INSURRECTION TO REVOLUTION IN MEXICO: SOCIAL BASES OF AGRARIAN VIOLENCE, 1750-1940. Princeton: Princeton University Press, 1986.

421. ———. "Hacienda Social Relations in Mexico: The Chalco Region in the Era of Independence." HISPANIC AMERICAN HISTORICAL REVIEW 55 (1975): 496-528.

422. Uruguay. Comisión Nacional Archivo Artigas. ARCHIVO ARTIGAS. 5 vols. Montevideo: Comisión Nacional, 1950-63.

423. Uslar Pietri, Juan. HISTORIA DE LA REBELION POPULAR DE 1814: CONTRIBUCION AL ESTUDIO DE LA HISTORIA DE VENEZUELA. Caracas: Edime, 1962.

424. Valega, José Manuel. LA GESTA EMANCIPADORA DEL PERU. 12 vols. Lima: Editora Peruana, 1940-44.

425. Valencia Avaria, Luis. BERNARDO O'HIGGINS: EL BUEN GENIO DE AMERICA. Santiago: Editorial Universitaria, 1980.

426. Valencia Tovar, Alvaro. GENERAL DE DIVISION JOSE MARIA CORDOVA. Bogotá: Imprenta y Litografía de las Fuerzas Militares, 1974.

427. Valle, José del. PENSAMIENTO VIVO DE JOSE CECILIO DEL VALLE. Compiled by Rafael Heliodoro Valle. San José: Editorial Universitaria Centroamericana, 1971.

428. Valle, Rafael H. ITURBIDE: VARON DE DIOS. Mexico City: Ediciones Xochitl, 1944.

429. Van Young, Eric. "Islands in the Storm: Quiet Cities and Violent Countrysides in the Mexican Independence Era." PAST AND PRESENT 118 (1988): 130-55.

430. ———. "Millenium on the Northern Marches: The Mad Messiah of Durango and Popular Rebellions in Mexico, 1800-1815." COMPARATIVE STUDIES IN SOCIETY AND HISTORY 28 (1986): 385-413.

431. ———. "Moving toward Revolt: Agrarian Origins of the Hidalgo Rebellion in the Guadalajara Region." In RIOT, REBELLION AND REVOLUTION: RURAL SOCIAL CONFLICT IN MEXICO, 176-204. Edited by Friedrich Katz. Princeton: Princeton University Press, 1988.

432. ———. "Who was that Masked Man Anyway?: Symbols and Popular Ideology in the Mexican Wars of Independence." In PROCEEDINGS OF THE 1984 MEETING OF THE ROCKY MOUNTAIN COUNCIL ON LATIN AMERICAN STUDIES, 18-35. Las Cruces: New Mexico State University Press, 1984.

433. Vargas. DIARIO DE UN SOLDADO DE LA INDEPENDENCIA ALTOPERUANA EN LOS VALLES DE SICSICA Y HAYOPAYA, 1816-1821, POR TAMBOR MAYOR VARGAS. Sucre: Universidad de San Francisco Xavier, 1953.

434. Vargas Ugarte, Rubén. DOCUMENTOS INEDITOS SOBRE LA CAMPANA DE LA INDEPENDENCIA DEL PERU, 1810-1824. Lima: n.p., 1971.

435. ———. HISTORIA DEL PERU: EMANCIPACION, 1809-1825. Buenos Aires: López, 1958.

436. Varnhagen, Francisco Adolfo de. HISTORIA DA INDEPENDENCIA DO BRASIL. Rio de Janeiro: Impresa Nacional, 1917.

437. Vedia y Mitre, Mariano de. LA VIDA DE MONTEAGUDO. 3 vols. Buenos Aires: G. Kraft, 1950.

438. Venezuela. Academia Nacional de la Historia. BIBLIOTECA DE LA ACADEMIA NACIONAL DE LA HISTORIA. 82 vols. Caracas: Academia Nacional, 1960-66.

439. ———. EL MOVIMIENTO EMANCIPADOR DE HISPANOAMERICA. 4 vols. Caracas: Academia Nacional, 1961.

440. Venezuela. Presidencia. LAS FUERZAS ARMADAS DE VENEZUELA EN EL SIGLO XIX: TEXTOS PARA SU ESTUDIO. 5 vols. Caracas: Presidencia, 1963.

441. Vergara Arias, Gustavo. MONTONEROS Y GUERRILLAS EN LA ETAPA DE LA EMANCIPACION DEL PERU, 1820-1825. Lima: Editorial Salesiana, 1973.

442. Vergara y Velasco, F.J. 1818: GUERRA DE INDEPENDENCIA. Bogotá: Editorial Kelly, 1960.

443. Victoria Gómez, Felipe. GUADALUPE VICTORIA: PRIMER PRESIDENTE DE MEXICO. Mexico City: Librería Botas, 1952.

444. Vicuña Mackenna, Benjamín. LA GUERRA A MUERTE. Buenos Aires: Ed. Francisco de Aguirre, 1972.

445. ———. SAN MARTIN: LA REVOLUCION DE INDEPENDENCIA DEL PERU. Santiago: Universidad de Chile, 1938.

446. ———. VIDA DE O'HIGGINS: LA CORONA DEL HEROE. Santiago: Universidad de Chile, 1936.

447. Villalobos, Sergio R. TRADICION Y REFORMA EN 1810. Santiago: Universidad de Chile, 1961.

448. Villanueva, Laureano. VIDA DE DON ANTONIO JOSE DE SUCRE: GRAN MARISCAL DE AYACUCHO. Caracas: Ediciones del Ministerio de Educación Nacional, 1945.

449. Villaseñor y Villaseñor, Alejandro. BIOGRAFIAS DE LOS HEROES Y CAUDILLOS DE LA INDEPENDENCIA. 2 vols. Mexico City: Editorial Jus, 1962.

450. Villoro, Luis. LA REVOLUCION DE INDEPENDENCIA: ENSAYO DE INTERPRETACION HISTORICA. Mexico City: UNAM, 1953.

451. Vizcaya Canales, Isidro. EN LOS ALBORES DE LA INDEPENDENCIA: LAS PROVINCIAS INTERNAS DE ORIENTE DURANTE LA INSURRECCION DE DON MIGUEL HIDALGO Y COSTILLA, 1810-1811. Monterrey: Instituto Tecnológico y de Estudios Superiores, 1976.

452. Víctor Amunátegui, Miguel. LA RECONQUISTA ESPANOLA. Santiago: Imprenta Barcelona, 1912.

453. Voss, Stuart F. ON THE PERIPHERY OF NINETEENTH-CENTURY MEXICO: SONORA AND SINALOA, 1810-1877. Tucson: University of Arizona Press, 1982.

454. Vowell, Richard Longeville. CAMPAIGNS AND CRUISES IN VENEZUELA AND NEW GRANADA, AND IN THE PACIFIC OCEAN: FROM 1817 TO 1830. London: Longman and Co., 1831.

455. Ward, Henry George. MEXICO IN 1827. 2 vols. London: n.p., 1828.

456. Warren, Harris G. "The Origin of General Mina's Invasion of Mexico." SOUTHWESTERN HISTORICAL QUARTERLY 42 (1938): 1-20.

457. ———. THE SWORD WAS THEIR PASSPORT: A HISTORY OF AMERICAN FILIBUSTERING IN THE MEXICAN REVOLUTION. Baton Rouge: Louisiana State University Press, 1943.

458. ———. "Xavier Mina's Invasion of Mexico." HISPANIC AMERICAN HISTORICAL REVIEW 23 (1943): 52-76.

459. Webster, Charles K. BRITAIN AND THE INDEPENDENCE OF LATIN AMERICA, 1812-1830: SELECT DOCUMENTS

FROM THE FOREIGN OFFICE ARCHIVES. 2 vols. London: Foreign Office Archives, 1938.

460. Whitaker, Arthur P. "Causes of the Spanish American Wars of Independence: Economic Factors." JOURNAL OF INTER-AMERICAN STUDIES 2 (1960): 132-39.

461. White, Richard Alan. PARAGUAY'S AUTONOMOUS REVOLUTION, 1810-1840. Albuquerque: University of New Mexico Press, 1978.

462. Williams, John Hoyt. THE RISE AND FALL OF THE PARAGUAYAN REPUBLIC, 1800-1870. Austin: University of Texas Press, 1978.

463. Woodward, Margaret L. "The Spanish Army and the Loss of America, 1810-1824." HISPANIC AMERICAN HISTORICAL REVIEW 48 (1968): 586-607.

464. Woodward, Ralph Lee, Jr. CENTRAL AMERICA: A NATION DIVIDED. 2d ed. New York: Oxford University Press, 1985.

465. Worcester, Donald E. BOLIVAR. Boston: Little Brown, 1977.

466. ———. SEA POWER AND CHILEAN INDEPENDENCE. Gainesville: University of Florida Press, 1962.

467. Zamudio Zamora, José. FUENTES BIBLIOGRAFICAS PARA EL ESTUDIO DE LA VIDA Y DE LA EPOCA DE BERNARDO O'HIGGINS. Santiago: Imprenta "El Esfuerzo," 1946.

468. Zárate, Julio. LA GUERRA DE INDEPENDENCIA. In MEXICO A TRAVES DE LOS SIGLOS, vol. 3. Edited by Vicente Riva Palacio. Barcelona: Espasa y Compañía, 1888-89.

469. Závala, Lorenzo de. ENSAYO CRITICO DE LAS REVOLUCIONES DE MEXICO DESDE 1808 HASTA 1830. Mexico City: N. de la Vega, 1845.

470. Zerecero, Anastasio. MEMORIAS PARA LA HISTORIA DE LAS REVOLUCIONES EN MEXICO. Mexico City: UNAM, 1975.

PERIODICALS

471. THE AMERICAS, 1944-.

472. ANUARIO DE ESTUDIOS AMERICANOS, 1944-.

473. BOLETIN DE HISTORIA Y ANTIGUEDADES, 1902-.

474. BOLETIN DE LA ACADEMIA NACIONAL DE LA HISTORIA.

475. ESTUDIOS DE HISTORIA MODERNA Y CONTEMPORANEA DE MEXICO, 1965-.

476. HISPANIC AMERICAN HISTORICAL REVIEW, 1918-.

477. HISTORIA, 1961-.

478. HISTORIA MEXICANA, 1951-.

479. IBERO-AMERICANISCHES ARCHIV, 1975-.

480. JAHRBUCH FUR GESCHICHTE VON STAAT, WIRTSCHAFT UND GESELLSCHAFT LATEINAMERIKAS, 1964-.

481. JOURNAL OF LATIN AMERICAN STUDIES, 1969-.

482. MEXICAN STUDIES/ESTUDIOS MEXICANOS, 1985-.

483. PAST AND PRESENT, 1952-.

484. REVISTA DE HISTORIA.

485. REVISTA DE HISTORIA DE AMERICAN, 1938-.

486. REVISTA DE INDIAS, 1940-.

CHAPTER IV

NINETEENTH-CENTURY LATIN AMERICAN CAUDILLISMO

Guy P. C. Thomson
University of Warwick

INTRODUCTION

Spanish and, to a lesser extent, Portuguese colonial governments were remarkable in the limited use made of formal military institutions for the securing of internal order or external defense. Only during the last half century of colonial rule were regular militia established to confront an external threat which never transpired. Indeed, the wars of independence provided the occasion for the continent's military apprenticeship. It is therefore paradoxical that this continent, during half a century following independence, should have fostered a political culture in which the armed route to power became almost everywhere commonplace and even legitimate. Yet, exploration of this paradox has attracted historians only sporadically.

The pervasiveness of political violence, prolonged regional rebellions, civil wars, coup d'états, and repression and the disordered picture that this presents of the past, has deterred historians during most of this century from studying nineteenth-century political and military history. The "Age of the Caudillos" is acknowledged as being colorful, but it is also perceived as being inaccessible, probably unstudiable, and best, perhaps, left to the novelist. Consequently, the countries that enjoyed the greatest stability and "order," Chile and Brazil, are predictably those that have received the most attention from historians. By contrast, the nineteenth-century historiographies of Mexico, Venezuela, Colombia, Peru, and Bolivia, fundamentally unstable countries for much of the century, are characterized by neglect. Military history has received the most cursory treatment of all. It is either given undue weight, with militarism presented as the fundamental "cause" of instability, or the military struggles are dismissed as mere "chaff," formless and meaningless bickerings which obscure understanding of the deeper disorders. Only recently have historians faced the challenge of exploring and explaining these "disorders" and of seeing military history as a potential key for understanding wider social, cultural, and political issues.

The newcomer to the nineteenth century by no means encounters a virgin land. It is evident, from the abundance of contemporary histories, collections of documents, and memoirs that, for nineteenth-century Latin Americans, the writing of history and the charting of military events had a central purpose in sanctifying rival liberal or conservative projects of nation-building. Military histories and memoirs legitimized the violence which frequently provided the only means for the pursuit or defense of these projects. These contemporary accounts provide the key to understanding the ideological struggles and broader mental world of the nineteenth century.

So pervasive was the political role of the military for much of the nineteenth century that it is often a difficult task to separate the "military" from the "political." Military power generally swiftly sought constitutional respectability just as constitutional authority was almost always bolstered by military force. In attempting to define the political space between formal constitutionalism and government by force alone, historians fall back on the imprecise and elastic concept of *caudillismo*. *Caudillismo* refers to rule by any kind of pre-eminent leader who derived authority more by an ability, through force of character and patronage, to command the loyalty of a substantial band of armed followers, than from adherence to the rule of law or the constitution. Frank Safford has recently drawn a loose distinction between three kinds of caudillo, based upon degrees of militarism:

> The caudillo is now generally thought of as one who used violence or the threat of violence for political ends -- whether as a professional officer commanding regular army units, or as a militia officer or civilian on horseback leading militia or irregular forces into battle, or (more broadly) as an essentially civilian leader who engaged in violent repression (as in the case or Dr. Francia in Paraguay or Diego Portales in Chile) (630).

This definition has been used as a general rule of thumb in the selection of works for inclusion in this bibliography.

Apart from references to national caudillos, the bibliography also lists a selection of works dealing with military events which were not directly concerned with the taking and holding of national power, but with challenges to national sovereignty and territorial integrity. These fall into two broad categories. The first are events which threatened the territorial integrity and sovereignty of the state such as wars between neighbors: the struggles in the River Plate region involving Brazil, Argentina, Uruguay, and Paraguay (1810-74); the War of the Pacific, involving Chile, Peru, and Bolivia (1879-83); and Mexico's war with the United States (1846-48); or, port blockades and armed interventions mounted by European powers against individual states, such as the French and British blockades of Juan Manuel de Rosas's Argentina during the 1840s, and the French, British, and Spanish intervention in Mexico in 1862. The second category of armed threat to territorial integrity includes secessionist movements, provincial rebellions, "Indian wars," armed popular or messianic movements, and banditry. Such local or regional events, often involving a high degree of militarization, have recently attracted considerable research and therefore deserve some space in this bibliography. They present the other side of the "order" which the caudillos sought to impose.

A further aim of the bibliography has been to list titles concerned with the history of the military, as such. Institutional history is the most neglected aspect of the nineteenth-century Latin American military. It is a convenient, but misleading, simplification to conclude that "military professionalization" in Latin America only really commenced in the twentieth century, and that what is found earlier resembles more the roving armed bands of the Dark Ages than the standing armies and "nations at arms" of nineteenth-century Europe. It can be too easily assumed that all that is necessary for understanding the nineteenth-century Latin American military is a knowledge of the hacienda/estancia and the man-on-horseback/*caudillo*, and that military institutions were mere cloaks for the exercise of private ("patrimonial") power. This view greatly underestimates the importance of formal military institutions, especially those on the regional level that emerged from the colonial tradition of militias, in the political life of most Latin American countries. It is also the case that, in most countries, military institutions represented wider social groupings than merely the elites. Unfortunately, little research has been done on national armies, let alone provincial militias and guards, to chart early professionalization or the social significance of military institutions.

GENERAL WORKS

The complexity and particularism of nineteenth-century Latin American political and military history do not lend themselves to easy general treatment. The 1910s and 1920s brought a crop of pathological studies of Latin American dictatorship, *caudillismo*, and *caciquismo* informed by positivism and the new science of psychoanalysis: Arguedas (41), Alvarez Suárez (22), Bray (109), Bunge (126), and Quevedo y Zubieta (584, 586). These tell us more about the elite mentality of the times in which they were written than of their subjects. Hugh Hamill has made a useful selection from these and other sources on caudillos in DICTATORSHIP IN SPANISH AMERICA (357). Less ambitiously theoretical works on dictatorship, written in the same period, and containing firmer data, are Wilgus (735), García Calderón (303), Fitzgibbon (277), and Jane (387).

There is a paucity of more recent general accounts of ninteenth-century Latin America. Halperín Donghi's AFTERMATH OF REVOLUTION (350), contains refreshing, and still largely untested ideas about the problems of early nationhood. His HISTORIA CONTEMPORANEA (353), and Carmen Velázquez Chávez's HISPANOAMERICA EN EL SIGLO XIX (720), are useful and still not superceded teaching texts. The recent, pathbreaking general work, THE EMERGENCE OF LATIN AMERICA IN THE NINETEENTH CENTURY by David Bushnell and Neil Macaulay (135) should also become a standard text for undergraduates. This is already true of E. Bradford Burns's POVERTY OF PROGRESS (131), an original, if not entirely satisfactory, attempt to give a broad cultural interpretation to *caudillismo* and the political changes of the nineteenth century. Robert Burr's BY REASON OR FORCE (132), remains a solitary, pioneering study of the neglected, but crucial, area of relations between Latin American states. Two recently published collections of conference papers, edited by Annino, et al. (27), and Buisson, König, and Pietschmann (119), contain useful and sometimes novel approaches to the study of the state and nation building in nineteenth-century Latin America. John Lynch's (437, 438), contributions to each collection hint at a forthcoming comparative study of caudillos, which will be welcomed by teachers of Latin American history. Safford (629, 630), gives the most complete and systematic explanation to date of the problems of early republican governments, a service which Colombianists, alert to infinitesimal provincial variations, seem adept at providing.

Interpretative essays on *caudillismo* and the problems of early republican government range from the now dated Chapman (181), and García Calderón (302), to the still useful Humphrey (377), Chevalier (184), Mörner (482), Graham (326), and Wolf and Hansen (746), to the more sophisticated and thought-provoking Dealy (227), Morse (491, 492), and Peter Smith (672).

BIBLIOGRAPHIES

Bibliographies dealing specifically with military matters, or even with the broader phenomenon of *caudillismo*, are few. There has been no attempt, as far as I know, to update Charles Chapman's (181, 182), pioneering articles written in the early 1930s at a time of intense interest in Latin America's *caudillo* tradition. The current, perhaps waning, vogue in the study of social, economic, and cultural history bypasses traditional political and military history which has yet to become infused and reinvigorated from its findings. Before *caudillismo* can be understood, the call of Eric Wolf's and Edward Hansen's (746), work on the political anthropology of the phenomenon has yet to be answered. Ironically, recent advances in our understanding of the "Age of Caudillos" have more often come from the study of political ideas, rather than from the scrutiny of social or economic structures. Charles Hale's article, "The Reconstruction of Nineteenth-Century Politics in Spanish America: A Case for the History of Ideas" (349), is richly suggestive of possibilities in this area. Recent fruits of this approach are to be found in his chapter in THE CAMBRIDGE HISTORY OF LATIN AMERICA (CHLA) (86), volume 4, pp. 367-441. E. Bradford Burns's (130, 131), "cultural" approach is also fresh and provocative, although marred by its over attachment to the crude paradigm of "the folk" versus "progress."

The best research guides are probably the bibliographical essays contained in general histories such as Woodward's CENTRAL AMERICA: A NATION DIVIDED (747), or Dobyns and Doughty, PERU: A CULTURAL HISTORY (250), in recent monographs, and in volumes three to five of THE CAMBRIDGE HISTORY OF LATIN AMERICAN (86), combined with the HANDBOOK OF LATIN AMERICAN STUDIES (361). Examples of recent monographs with comprehensive bibliographies are: John Lynch, ARGENTINE DICTATOR: JUAN MANUEL DE ROSAS (435), Jack Autrey Dabbs, THE FRENCH ARMY IN MEXICO, 1861-1867 (225), William Sater, CHILE AND THE WAR OF THE PACIFIC (651), Harris Gaylord Warren and Katherine F. Warren, PARAGUAY AND THE TRIPLE ALLIANCE (731), and John Hoyt Williams, THE RISE AND FALL OF THE PARAGUAYAN REPUBLIC (742). Useful starts may also be made from historiographical essays in journals: Benjamin and Ocasio-Meléndez (81), on Porfirian Mexico; Lozoya (434), on the nineteenth-century Mexican military; Griffith (332), and Lamadrid (400), on Central America; Corbitt (206), on Cuba's independence struggles; Fagen (266), on the mulatto leader Antonio Maceo; Szászdi (690), on Ecuador; Boehrer (99), and Stein (682), on Brazil; Barager (59), and Brown (117), on Argentina; and Blakemore (96), Collier (197), and Griffin (330), on Chile.

A selection of reputable general and more specialized national bibliographies, which include a substantial amount of military material, should be noted. Murray (496), is useful for Mexico's war with the United States. Good for the Reform Wars and European Intervention are Guzmán y Raz Guzmán (342), and Quirarte (587), for Maximilian's empire. For Cuba, see Pérez Cabrera's HISTORIOGRAFIA (555), and for Venezuela, the exhaustive Lombardi, et al. (422). Romero, et al. (623), and Laverde Amaya (406), cover Colombia, and for Ecuador consult Larrea (404), and Norris (510). For Brazil see Borba de Morães and Berrien (102, 103), and Costa (214), as well as Chiappini (185), for Rosas's Argentina, and Etchepareborda (263), for the Argentine military. Abecia Baldivieso (1), treats Bolivia and Aránguiz Donoso (28), deals with Chile. Porras Barrenchea (574), Basadre (74), and Moreyra y Paz Soldán (490), can be profitably consulted for Peru.

ARCHIVAL GUIDES AND SOURCES

If the Archivo Historico of the Mexican Secretaría de la Defensa Nacional is anything to go by, military archives are some of the best organized, meticulously catalogued, and the richest in Latin America. This archive has a staff running into the hundreds and complete card indexes of its holdings, as well as some printed catalogues (301, 591). Historians have been granted access to it during the past fifteen years without much difficulty, providing an appropriate protocol is followed. Foreign researchers should approach the ministry through their embassies' military attachés. Mexican scholars have gained access through the Colegio de México and the Universidad Iberoamericana. The problem for the researcher seeking access to military archives lies, of course, with the perceived political sensitivity of much of the material they contain. This obstacle varies between countries. The best guide to accessibility is to consult recent monographs dealing with military events, although direct approaches to defense ministries, in Mexico at least, will be met with unexpected courtesy and cooperation. Recent studies that have made extensive use of defense ministry archives are: Reina (599), Jean Meyer (471), and Vázquez (715), for Mexico; Bergquist (83), for Colombia's ministry; Dudley (253, 254), and Hahner (343, 344, 345, 346), in Brazil's; and Mallon (448), in Peru's Archivo Historico Militar (Lima).

Of course, national defense ministry archives have no monopoly upon military material, particularly for the nineteenth century, when so much of the "militarization" of power was local or semi-private. Government archives on every level, including municipal, yield abundant material on the funding and recruitment of forces, the conduct of campaigns, etc. The correspondence and personal archives of military men, held in public archives, in university libraries, or in private collections, are also an important source for the study of the nineteenth-century military. For Mexico, the library of the Institute of Latin American Studies at the University of Texas (164, 681), contains correspondence of Ignacio Comonfort (204), General Mariano Paredes y Arrillaga (539), Marshal Achille-François Bazaine (77), and General Manuel Doblado (249), to mention just four of the many important figures represented there. In Mexico itself, the vast correspondence of General Porfirio Díaz (572), is kept at the Universidad Iberoamericana in Mexico City, where it is in the process of being meticulously catalogued. A preliminary sketch of the content of the collection has been made by Perry (558), and a well chosen selection published by Carreño (157). Another important primary source on Díaz is discussed by Arnade (45). Further key sources for nineteenth-century Mexican military history are the manuscript collection of the Instituto Nacional de Antropología e Historia (INAH), containing the correspondence of Justo Benítez (Díaz's political agent) and the archive of General Felipe Berriozábal, and the following sections of the Archivo General de la Nacion: Ramo Militar, Ramo de Gobernacion, Ramo de Tranquilidad Publica, and the Ramo Archivo de Leyva, all in process of being catalogued. Figuring most prominently among the foreign archival sources on Mexican military history -- as for all other Latin American countries -- are the diplomatic consular reports of foreign powers. For the French Intervention and Empire consult Torre Villar (699), and Dabbs's bibliography (225).

Primary sources for military history and *caudillismo* in other Latin American countries are as varied and abundant as for Mexico. The Academia Colombiana de Historia (3),possesses an extensive collection of personal papers of leading nineteenth-century military men and politicians. The Archivo Histórico of Ecuador's Colegio Militar Eloy Alfaro (195), is cited as an important source for military history. For the military history of Brazil's Old Republic, Hahner acknowledges the importance of the Arquivo do Ministerio da Guerra (49), the Arquivo do Clube Militar (47), and the Arquivo do Instituto Historico e Geográfico Brasileiro (48). For Bolivia, Chile, Ecuador, and Peru, the recent guide to archives by John J. TePaske, et al. (695), is indispensible.

PUBLISHED DOCUMENTS

In contrast to the Independence period, which has spawned an abundance of collections of published documents, the remaining three quarters of the nineteenth century, perhaps with the exception of Colombia and Argentina, have so far yielded little. Mexico's two greatest compilations are Carreño's (157), thirty-volume selection of Porfirio Díaz's correspondence, and Tamayo's (691), fourteen volumes of Benito Juárez's papers, both published quite recently. Compiled at the beginning of this century, Genaro García's (297, 298, 299, 300), enormous works include several volumes dealing with military matters.

The Mexican Secretariá de la Defensa Nacional intermittently has published collections of documents from its abundant holdings (469). The Bolivarian nations have yielded a larger crop of published documents than has Mexico, even when the impressive collections corresponding to the Independence period are not included. The correspondence of General Francisco de Paula Santander, the creator of the Colombian state, collected by Cortázar (208, 209), fills twenty-four volumes. The *popayanejo* caudillo, General José María Obando, "The most popular soldier or politician Colombia produced in the last century" (Malcom Deas, CHLA 3, p. 527), also merits two collections (525, 616). "Liberals" appear to have been more often celebrated than "Conservatives" by collections of documents: Obando's fellow *popayanejo* caudillo, General Mosquera (367); Colombia's "Porfirio Díaz," Rafael Nuñez (411); Venezuela's federalist leaders, Generals Juan Crisóstomo Falcón (217), and Antonio Guzmán Blanco (340, 341); and Ecuador's Liberal caudillo, Eloy Alfaro (17, 18). Conservative figures have, nevertheless, inspired some documentary collections: Ecuador's theocratic Gabriel García Moreno (423), Venezuela's popular General José María "El Mocho" Hernández (42); and General Cipriano Castro (170, 566). Figures of lesser national renown have also inspired collections in this region: Colombia's generals José María Córdova (487), Juan José Nieto (410), and Domingo Caycedo (369), and Venezuela's Juan Francisco de León (475). The Venezuelan executive office is also publishing a collection documenting the country's almost incessant nineteenth-century civil wars (290).

Argentina's "Age of Caudillos" has inspired collections documenting the early history of *caudillismo* during the Independence and early republican periods (35, 36, 37, 93), the federalist leader of the interior, Juan Facundo Quiroga (588), and the caudillo-*máximo*, Juan Manuel de Rosas (65, 635). Argentina's providential vision of the nineteenth century has received ample documentation in the published works of the constitutional thinker, Juan Bautista Alberdi (12, 13, 14), the Liberal antagonist of Rosas, Domingo Faustino Sarmiento (649, 650), and his later nineteenth-century successor (as liberal thinker *cum* man of action), General Bartolomé Mitre (479, 480, 481). In the other Southern Cone and Andean countries, apart from Odriozola's (519), collection of Peruvian historical documents, the absence of a "grand" caudillo tradition, or of providential historical visions linked to "internal conquests" (Chile's sense of self-importance came from a foreign war), perhaps accounts for the paucity of published documentary material corresponding to the nineteenth century.

MEMOIRS, JOURNALS, AND EYEWITNESS ACCOUNTS

Military campaigning in Latin America's nineteeth-century civil wars was too commonplace and unsensational, and in foreign wars, too ignominious, to have inspired a fertile tradition of military memoirs, diaries, and eye-witness accounts. The modest production in this area may also be explained by low levels of literacy among combatants (including officers) as well as the inaccessibility of the printing press, for anything beyond the broadsheet and the newspaper. The considerable output of memoirs from United States and European combatants, contrasting with the paucity of Mexican and other Latin American military memoirs, bears out this point. Thus, the historian must turn to official state newspapers, and some of the national periodicals, where lengthy and detailed accounts of campaigns were reproduced, often dispatched directly from the field of battle, to be able to gain an idea of the character of warfare and a feeling for life *en campaña*.

Campaign and politico-military memoirs, recorded by Latin Americans (this bibliography lists only very few foreigners' accounts), do, nevertheless, exist. Early republican Mexican and Central American history has some useful memoirs: General Francisco Morazán (486), Rafael Carrera (159), Francisco Ortega Arancibia (524), Miguel García Granados (305), and Antonio López de Santa Anna (426). Mexico's military life and struggles were recorded by: Ferry (273), for the 1820s; Fisisola (276), for the war with Texas; Otero (527) and Carlos María de Bustamante (136), for the 1840s; Balbontín (57), Roa Bárcena (607), and Scott (665), for the war with the United States; Carreño (158), and Portilla (575, 576), for the Reform Wars; Blanchot (97), Cler (192), Galindo y Galindo (294), Gaulot (308), Hans (362), Huerta (376), Keratry (393, 394), and Salm Salm (636), for the French Intervention and Austrian Empire. Porfirio Díaz's rise to power through the *Ejército de Oriente* was recorded by the general himself (242), Ireneo Paz (548), and Santibáñez (645). Prieto (580), brilliantly records the view of the military events of the early 1850s from the capital. This last work should be read in conjunction with González Navarro's penetrating ANATOMIA DEL PODER (321). Contemporary accounts of Indian and peasant rebellions in Mexico are Molina (483), and Reina (599).

Memoirs and eyewitness accounts of Cuba's nineteenth-century "wars of liberation" are numerous. The Ten-Years' War (1868-78) is illuminated by Camps Felíu (150), Granda (327), Gutiérrez de la Concha (338), López Donato (427), Mauyanet (463), Navarro (498), Rosal y Vázquez de Mondragón (626), and Serra Orts (666). "Martí's War" (1895-98) is recorded in a collection of memoirs published by the Cuban Academia de la Historia (4), and by Bas (72), Boza (107), Llorens y Maceo (420), Miró (478), and Piedra Martel (563).

Reflections on military strategy and tactics for the suppression of Cuban insurrections are found in Almirante (19), Barrios (66), Jiménez Castellanos (389), Reparaz (600), and Velazco (718). The chief leader of Cuba's insurrections, the Dominican, General Máximo Gómez y Báez (314, 315), left scattered memoirs, letters, and pronouncements, and inspired others like Franco (288), to take up the pen.

More memoirs were written by Colombians than by any other nineteenth-century Latin Americans. Leading the field are works of outstanding quality: Restrepo (601), Samper (637), and Camacho Roldán (146). Concerned more specifically with military events are Masuera y Masuera (461), Briceño (112), Borda (104), Plazas Olarte (569), Ortiz (526), and Obando (514). The War of a Thousand Days inspired many memoirs: Arbeláez (30), Caballero (139), Florez Alvarez (281), Grillo (333), Latorre (405), París Lozano (541), Parra (546), Porras (573), and Posada Gutiérrez (577). Deas (230), offers an interesting demonstration of the historical use of Colombia's military memoirs. Only a few of Venezuela's numerous caudillos left their memoirs: José Antonio Páez (532), the *llanero* leader and "*caudillo máximo*" during the 1830s and 1840s, and Cipriano Castro, who was remembered by his principal general, Santiago Briceño Ayestarán (113), as well as by the historian, Vicente Lecuna (407), and by Parada (537).

Brazil has left us with the greatest classic of nineteenth-century military literature in Euclides da Cunha's (224), account of the suppression of the religious movement at Canudos. Argentina's early military struggles were recorded by Ferré (272), and José María Paz (549). The Paraguayan War, or The War of the Triple Alliance (1864-70), yielded a crop of memoirs: Cerqueira (178), Palleja (535), Aveiro (53), Centurión (177), and an eleven-volume collection of contemporary diaries and memoirs edited by Cardozo (154). So also did the War of the Pacific (1879-83): Campo (148), Canto (151), Cifuentes (190), Cáceres (140), Moreno de Cáceres (488), Subercaseaux (688), and Williams Rebolledo (743). For a useful selection of contemporary accounts of Argentina's Indian wars see Viñas (729). The ambivalent account of a journey among Argentina's Indians by one of their principal persecutors, General Lucio Mansilla (453), has been compared in its literary and historical significance to Da Cunha's work. For a contemporary account of an Indian rebellion in Peru during the 1860s, consult Juan Bustamante (137).

SPECIALIZED WORKS: MEXICO AND CENTRAL AMERICA

There are numerous, well-known, English language, general histories covering nineteenth-century Mexico, which have not been included for limitations of space. Henry Bamford Parkes (545), Michael C. Meyer and William L. Sherman (472), and Jan Bazant (79), are perhaps the most serviceable. In Spanish, the narrative histories by Arrangoiz y Berzábal (51), Zamacois (749), and the collection of essays by Riva Palacio (605), are still useful. Nineteenth-century Central America is admirably served in English by Woodward (747), and in Spanish, by the impressive, seven-volume contemporary work by Montúfar (484), and by Batres Jauregui (76). The chapters, and the corresponding bibliographical essays, by Jan Bazant, Ralph Lee Woodward, and Friedrich Katz in the CHLA (86), volumes three and five, are good introductions to the history of the region. More detailed studies of the very early republican period are Garza (307), Hamnett (360), and Marure (460). The 1830s and 1840s are examined by Hale (348), González Navarro (321), Carlos María de Bustamante (136), Kahle (391), Urias Hermosillo (703), Stevens (684), Vázquez Mantecón (716), and Marroquín Rojas (456). Tensions with France during this period, including the blockade and war in 1838-39 and culminating in the Intervention of 1861, are treated by Barker (61). Relations no less tense with Spain, in the early republican period, are studied by Flores Caballero (280), and Sánchez Lamego (642). Mexico's Reform Wars (1858-61) and European Intervention of 1862-67 are studied by Sinkin (669), Caldwell (143), Scholes (657), Galindo y Galindo (294), Francisco Bulnes (121, 122), Portilla (576), Iglesias (379), Dabbs (225), and Rivera Cambas (606). Mexico's República Restaurada and the Manuel González and Díaz presidencies have been studied by Perry (559), Coerver (193, 194), Quevedo y Zubieta (584, 585, 586), and by Daniel Cosío Villegas in his splendid and unsurpassed HISTORIA MODERNA DE MEXICIO (213). Guatemala's Liberal revolution is examined by McCreery (440, 441), Clegern (191), Herrick (372), and Zeceña (750).

Biographies and contextual histories of the region's national and regional caudillos and caciques are numerous, but are often outdated, and of uneven quality. The historiography of the nineteenth century is still too immature to be able to support good biographies. Antonio López de Santa Anna has always attracted attention but defied satisfactory explanation until the recent studies of Urias Hermosillo (703), Hamnett (360), Samponaro (638, 640), Díaz y Díaz (247), Vázquez Mantecón (716), Vázquez (714, 715), and Bazant (78), gave the cardboard figure created by Callcott (144), some depth. Guatemala's Conservative peasant caudillo, Rafael Carrera, has recently inspired considerable interest and debate among United States scholars: Woodward (748), Moorhead (485), Ingersoll (380), Miceli (473), and Burns (131). A full biography of Carrera in English is still awaited to join the Guatemalan biography by Coronado Aguilar (207), and the interesting study of Carrera's regional base by Tobar Cruz (698). Justo Rufino Barrios, Guatemala's Liberal caudillo, studied vividly by Burgess (128), is now much better understood as a result of McCreery's (440, 441), work on coffee, Barrios's obsession. Porfirio Díaz is still remarkably understudied and poorly understood. The biographies of Díaz written by Iturribarría (383), Quevedo y Zubieta (584, 586), López-Portillo y Rojas (428), and Beals (81), are quite outdated and add little to each other. Our understanding of Díaz is beginning to change, however, as a result of recent studies: Cosío Villegas (211, 212, 213), Perry (559), Falcone (268), Katz (392), David Miller (476), and Stevens (683). Professionalization of the military under Porfirio Díaz can be studied by using Gutiérrez Santos (339), Hardie (363), Javier (388), Kitchens (396), Reyes (602), Schiff (654), and Vanderwood (708, 709).

SPECIALIZED WORKS: CUBA

A complete bibliography of the Hispanic Caribbean would include references to Santo Domingo and Puerto Rico, together, of course, with material from metropolitan Spain. Regrettably, limitations of space permit this list to include only material on Cuba's nineteenth-century struggles for independence. The chapters and corresponding bibliographical articles on the Hispanic Caribbean in the CHLA (86), volumes three and five by Hugh Thomas, Frank Moya Pons, Luis Aguilar, Angel Quintero-Rivera, and Harry Hoetink are useful starting points for the study of the region. So also are Corbitt's (206), Fagen's (266), and Calder's (see below Chapter VIII), historiographical articles on Cuba's fight for independence.

Cuba's thirty-year independence struggle is studied by Ro6g de Leuchsenring (619), Centro de Estudios de Historia Militar (178), García Cañizares (304), and Varona Guerrero (713). The metropolitan political dimension is tackled in a classic of political history by Fernández Almagro (270). The "Ten-Years War" (1868-78) is studied by Guerra y Sánchez (336), Ponte Domínguez (571), and Figueredo Socarrás (274). Ignacio Agramonte, Cuba's first independence leader, is studied by his descendant, Betancourt Agramonte (85). The brilliant mulatto commander, Antonio Maceo, is idealized in Foner (283), Franco (288), and Roig de Leuchsenring (620). The "War of José Martí" (1895-98) is studied by Foner (284), Friedel (289), Pérez (553), Roig (617), Ramos Zúñiga (594), and Roig de Leuchsenring (618). A photographic portrait of the war was produced by Oñate Gómez (522). The great military caudillo of Cuba's struggle, General Máximo Gómez y Báez, is treated by Martí Pérez (457), Ramírez Sánchez (593), Benigno Souza (678), Centro de Estudios de Historia Militar (176), Saíz de la Mora (632), Santovenia y Echaide (647), and Falco (267).

SPECIALIZED WORKS:
VENEZUELA, COLOMBIA, AND ECUADOR

The three countries that emerged from the breakup of Bolívar's Federation of Gran Colombia, have intriguing, quite divergent, and largely unexplored nineteenth-century histories. There are few general studies of Venezuela, Colombia, and Ecuador during that period. Gilmore's (310), study of Venezuela is the only one directly to tackle *caudillismo*. Though packed with interesting sketches, the book is muddled. More useful and clear headed are Malcolm Deas's chapters in the CHLA (86), volumes three and five. These distill research achievements to date and suggest approaches for the future. Other useful general studies are Arcaya (31), Armas Chitty (43), González Guinán (320), and Valenilla Lanz (706), for Venezuela; Luis Robalino Dávila's (608), multi-volume history, Malo and Ayala (449), and Blanksten (98), for Ecuador; and an interesting collection of polemical essays on nineteenth-century Colombian politics by leading authorities edited by Martínez Carreño (458).

For the early republican period, Venezuela's José Antonio Páez (like Rosas and Santa Anna) has fascinated historians, although a good biography is still wanting. For this era see Gilmore (310), Castellanos V. (168), Cova (216), Cunningham Graham (223), and Michelena (474). On the *llanos*, whence Páez drew part of his following, one should study Mathews (462), Ovalles (529), José Antonio Páez (532), Mayer (464), and Izard (384, 385). The rise of Venezuela's Liberal party and the Federal Wars have attracted much attention, particularly the careers of the provincial caudillos, Juan Crisóstomo Falcón and Ezequiel Zamora. For insight on these subjects the researcher needs to start with Brito Figueroa (115), Alvarado (20), Díaz Sánchez (246), Landaeta Rosales (402), Pachano (530), Adolfo Rodríguez (614), J. S. Rodríguez (615), Laureano Villanueva (726), and Izard (386). Venezuela's great Liberal dictator, Antonio Guzmán Blanco, and his *llanero* successor, Joaquín Crespo, are examined in Briceño (111), Castellanos V. (167), Floyd (282), Rondón Márquez (624), Landaeta Rosales (401) and Wise (745). The rise of Cipriano Castro and *Los Andinos* at the turn of the century is the subject of the following studies: Ignacio Andrade (24), Cayama Martínez (174), Paredes (538), Picón Salas (562), Sullivan (689), Pérez Teneiro (557), and Rippy and Hewitt (604).

The politics and military events of early republican Colombia have been studied by Bushnell (134), Safford (631), Castellanos V. (166),

Colmenares (198), Duarte French (252), Grusin (334), Helguera (365, 366), Lemos Guzmán (412), Venancio Ortiz (526), Samper (637), and Rausch (595). For the rise of the Liberal Party and of Rafael Núñez, Butler (138), Delpar (236, 237, 238, 239), Park (542, 543), Palacio (534), and Deas (229), are useful. Child (189), and Galvis Salazar (296), have written about Uribe y Uribe, the radical Liberal from Antioquia. For the Colombia of Rafael Núñez see Liévano Aguirre (418), and Delpar (236, 237, 238, 239), while for Colombia's War of a Thousand Days consult Arbeláez (30), Bergquist (83), and Deas (231).

There is no good study of Ecuador's early republican caudillo, General Juan José Flores, though this period is covered well in Robalino Dávila's ORIGENES DEL ECUADOR DE HOY (608). Patee (547), Peter Smith (671), and Robalino Dávila (608), have studied Ecuador's Conservative, durable, dictator, Gabriel García Moreno, and Oscar Efraén Reyes (603), looks at Moreno's archenemy, Juan Montalvo. For Ecuador's harbinger of "progress," the Guayaquil Liberal caudillo, Eloy Alfaro, read Raúl Andrade (26), Calle (145), Guarderas (335), and Pareja y Diezcanseco (540).

In countries so plagued by civil war, and experiencing no important foreign wars, military history becomes indivisible from political history and is almost invisible as a separate discipline. The military history of nineteenth-century Venezuela is tackled, sketchily, by Austria (52), López Contreras (425), and Venezuela Presidencia de la República (721), and, for Colombia, see Plazas Olarte (569).

SPECIALIZED WORKS: BRAZIL

Brazil's nineteenth-century historiography is exceptional in Latin America for both quality and variety. This applies to both foreign scholarship and to indigenous production. For a general coverage, the newcomer can do no better than to consult the chapters, and the corresponding bibliographical essays, by Leslie Bethell, José Murilo de Carvalho, Emilia Viotti da Costa, and Boris Fausto in volumes three and five of the CHLA (86), which reflect this historiographical richness.

The Empire, calm on the surface, was turbulent underneath, as a fast growing body of political history is demonstrating. A sophisticated study of the imperial political elite is Carvalho (160). Independence and early national Bahia are examined perceptively and elegantly by Morton (493), and the Bahian revolt of 1837 is studied by Vianna Filho (722). Manuel Andrade (25), looks at the Guerra dos Cabanos (1832-35), and Filler (275), looks at the liberal rebellion of 1842. The "Ragamuffin War" (Guerra dos Farrapos, 1835-45) is intensively examined by Leitman (408, 409), Spalding (680), and Varela (710), while Naro (497), reviews the Praiera revolt of 1848. The "Quebra-Quilos" revolt of 1874-

75 is tackled lucidly by Barman (62), and is also studied by Joffley (390), and Souto Maior (676), while Amado (23), has given an account of the "Muckers Revolt" of Rio Grande do Sul (1868-78).

There is an ample literature on the Paraguayan War (1864-70), which had such important consequences for Brazil. Some of the more useful works are: Souza Docea (679), Box (106), Schneider (656), Tasso Fragoso (692), and Strauss (685). Ralph della Cava examines religious movements (233, 234), and Da Cunha (224), their ruthless suppression. The localized power structures, which held the country together and occasionally threatened to tear it apart during the Empire and the Old Republic, are studied by Lewin (417), Nunes Leal (513), Schwartzman (661), Uricoechea (704), and Queiroz (582). Brazilian regionalism during the Old Republic is now well documented by Levine (415), Love (430, 431), Pang (536), Wirth (744), and Cammack (147). Queiroz (581), Lewin (416), and Amaury de Souza (677), have contributed works on banditry, a ubiquitous and enduring Brazilian phenomenon.

Nineteenth-century military history has attracted more research in Brazil than elsewhere in Latin America. For narrative accounts of early campaigns of the imperial army, see Barroso (70). For traditional, institutional approaches consult Barroso (71), Fontoura Castellat (285), and Werneck Sodré (732). The national guard and localized military formations are studied by Uricoechea (704), Jeanne Berrance de Castro (171), and McCann (439). The role of the military in the fall of the Empire and during the First Republic, and Brazil's early military professionalization, are examined by Hahner (343, 344, 345, 346), Simmons (667), Carvalho (161), Ouro Prieto (528), Eduardo Prado (578), Dudley (253, 254), Schulz (660), and Magalhães (447).

SPECIALIZED STUDIES:
ARGENTINA, URUGUAY, PARAGUAY, AND BOLIVIA

For a general introduction to this region during the nineteenth century, the chapters and corresponding bibliographical essays by John Lynch, Heraclio Bonilla, Ezequiel Gallo, David Rock, Juan Oddone, Paul Lewis, and Herbert Klein in the CHLA (867), volumes three and five, provide good starting points.

Argentina's nineteenth-century historiography is almost as substantial as Brazil's. Alvarez (21), Quesada (583), Sommariva (673), and Best (845), have produced valuable general accounts of Argentina's civil wars, whose early economic background and international context is explained by Burgin (129), and Ferns (271). The early republican period of Argentine history has been studied more recently by two first-rate Argentine historians, Chiaramonte (187), and Halperín Donghi (351, 352, 354). Zorilla (752), makes an interesting social analysis of prominent caudillos, a task that Haigh (347), achieves brilliantly for the case of Martín Güemes. There is an outstanding recent biography of Argentina's *caudillo máximo*, Juan Manuel de Rosas, by John Lynch (435), to accompany the classic contemporary social portrait by Sarmiento (648), of the caudillo of La Rioja, Facundo Quiroga, a work long acknowledged as the greatest literary masterpiece of nineteenth-century Spanish America. Lynch considers the enormous and continually expanding literature on Rosas to be "a hindrance rather than a help to understanding." The following works on Rosas are frequently cited: Barba (60), Celesia (175), Etchepareborda (264), Ibarguren (378), Irazusta (381), and Saldías (634). Rosas's erstwhile ally, later rival, of the interior, Justo José de Urquiza, has also inspired several biographies, Bosch (105), Newton (509), and McLynn (446), to mention but three. Jorge Newton has drawn competent sketches of other caudillos: Francisco Reinafe (503), Francisco Ramírez (502), Estanislao López (500), Martín Güemes (505), Ricardo López Jordan (508), Manuel Taboaba (507), and Juan Felipe Ibarra (506). There is a large historiography dealing with Argentina's struggles for national unification, and with the role of General Bartolomé Mitre, scourge of Argentina's provinces. Some of the better works are Alberdi (11), Campobassi (149), McLynn (445), and Scobie (664). The chastiser of Argentina's Indians, General Julio Roca, also has attracted many biographers: Arce (32), Newton (504), Sánchez (641), Vedia y Mitre (717), and Hodge (373). The war with Paraguay has stimulated works by Alberdi (13), Cárcano (152), Cardozo (153, 154), Pomer (570), Fornos Penalba (286, 287), Kolinski (398), Thompson (696), and McLynn (443, 444). The "revolutions" (no longer civil wars) of the later nineteenth century (1880, 1890, 1893, 1905) have their historians: Balestra (58), Galíndez (293), Gallo (295), Etchepareborda (265), Sommi (674), and Zorraquín Becú (751). The various "desert" campaigns against the Indians are the subject of several studies; for example see Jorge Páez (531), Manuel Prado (579), Racedo (589), Schoo Lastra (659), Viñas (729), and Walther (730).

Military history, more narrowly conceived, is treated in Juan Beverina's (87, 88, 89, 90, 91, 92), account of the viceregal army and lively narratives of early republican campaigns, up to the Paraguayan War. Cady (142), Colli (196), and Rosa (625), tackle European and Brazilian intervention in Argentina during the 1840s and 1850s. Military professionalization in Argentina during the 1880s and 1890s is studied by Ramírez (590), Romay (622), Goldwert (313), and Schiff (655)

Uruguayan nineteenth-century military and political historiography is slender (a consequence perhaps of the concentration of research upon the country's remarkable early twentieth century). John Street (686), expertly tells the story of the birth of the Uruguayan state. A solid narrative of the nineteenth century is provided by Eduardo Acevedo (5). Sophisticated socio-economic interpretations of Uruguayan *caudillismo* are offered by Barrán (63), and Barrán and Nahum (64).

Paraguayan nineteenth-century historiography has more substance than Uruguayan, as a result of its extraordinary experiences during that century. Useful biographical material can be found in Bray (108). The period of isolation under Dr. José Gaspar Rodríguez de Francia is treated by Robertson and Robertson (610), Trías (701), White (733), Cháves (183), and Williams (738, 741). Pérez Acosta (554), and Bray (110), have studied his successors, Carlos Antonio López and Francisco Solano López. Varying interpretations of the origins of the War of the Triple Alliance are considered by Abente (2); its demographic consequences are explored by Reber (597), and its more general consequences are analyzed by Warren and Warren (731). Tate (693), assesses British influence upon Paraguay before 1870.

The political instability of nineteenth-century Bolivia presents problems for the historian; yet, some good work exists. Klein (397), offers a useful general coverage. Daniele Demelas's NATIONALISME SANS NATION? (240), is an interesting general interpretation of Bolivian history. James Dunkerley's (256, 257), work on the army and caudillismo breaks much new ground. Charles Arnade (44), and Lofstrom (421), explore the early years. O'Connor D'Arlach's biographical sketches in LOS PRESIDENTES DE BOLIVIA (517), are useful. The founder of the republic and creator of the short-lived Bolivian-Peruvian Confederation, Andrés de Santa Cruz, has inspired many biographies, among which are Crespo (220), Díaz Argüedas (244), Parkerson (544), and Oscar de Santa Cruz (644). His successor, José Ballivián is studied by Manuel Carrasco (155). Manuel José Cortés (210), and Crespo (219), have studied the popular mid-century caudillo, Manuel Isidoro Belzu. Bolivia's most notorious caudillo, Mariano Melgarejo, occupies much of O'Connor D'Arlach's (516, 518), work. Phillips (560), examines Bolivia's participation in the War of the Pacific (1879-83). The relationship of the Indian with the Bolivian state is the subject of Tristan Platt's (567, 568), highly original studies. Condarco Morales (205), examines the Indian revolt of 1899. Apart from Dunkerley's dissertation (256), there is the narrower study of the Bolivian army by Julio Díaz Arguedas (243), covering the same period.

SPECIALIZED WORKS: CHILE AND PERU

Chile possesses a strong tradition of historical writing, appropriate to a country whose elites acquired a providential sense of national purpose, the consequence of victory over, and territorial aggrandizement at the expense of, her northern neighbors in the War of the Pacific

(1879-83). The chapters by Simon Collier and Harold Blakemore in the CHLA (86), volumes three and five, with their accompanying bibliographical essays, provide a useful introduction to the study of Chile's nineteenth century. Loveman (432), offers a good general coverage and contains an excellent bibliography. Classic, somewhat outdated, but still serviceable general works on the nineteenth century are Donoso (251), Edwards (258), and Encina (260). A more recent general work is Marcella's (454),study of the oligarchy. Diego Portales, Chile's most renowned nineteenth-century conservative leader, is studied by Vicuña Mackenna (724), and Kinsbruner (395). Gonzalo Bulnes (123, 125), Galdámez Lastra (292), and Sotomayor y Valdés (675), cover military aspects of Chile's victorious conflict with the Bolivian-Peruvian Confederation in 1836-39. Grez Pérez (328), and Davis (226), study Chile's victorious participation in the war with Spain in the early 1860s. Chile's victorious participation in the War of the Pacific has, understandably, received much attention: see Ahumada Moreno (7), Bader (55), Bulnes (124), Sater (651, 652), Mayo (465), and Ortega (523). More narrowly military studies of the war are even more abundant: Bulnes (123), Caviano (173), Ekdahl (259), Machuca (442), and Vicuña Mackenna (723).

The "Prussia" of Latin America possesses a tradition of military historical writing, quite unmatched by other countries; for example, see Cuadra (221), Estado Mayor del Ejército (261), Langlois (403), López U. (429), Novoa de la Fuente (512), and Telles (694). Blakemore (95), tackles the economic and political consequences of Chile's victory in the War of the Pacific. The struggles on Chile's southern Araucanian frontier occupy León S. (413, 414).

Peru, like Bolivia, has an unsatisfactory nineteenth-century historiography, because of historians' unavoidable obsession with the coast. This "national and colonial problem" is evident in the chapters by Heraclio Bonilla and Peter Klaren in the CHLA (86), volumes three and five, which pay scant attention to the interior. This situation notwithstanding, these chapters and their accompanying bibliographical essays are necessary starting points. So also are Jorge Basadre's (73), Frederick Pike's (564), excellent general histories and the bibliographical essay in Dobyns's and Doughty's PERU: A CULTURAL HISTORY (250). The interpretative essays by Berg and Weaver (82), and Gormen (324), also provide useful orientations.

Gleason (312), Gootenberg (323), and Vargas Ugarte (711), (on General Ramón Castilla) examine early republican politics, while Wibel (734), looks at the provincial dimensions. Biographies of Peru's nineteenth-century leaders are too numerous to include but Dobyns and Doughty (250), list many works on Agustín Gamarra, Manuel Ignacio de Vivanco, Ramón Castilla, Francisco de Vidal, Juan Antonio Pezet,

Pedro Diez-Canseco, Mariano Ignacio Prado, Manuel Pardo, José Balta, Nicolás Pierola, etc., whose careers are briefly appraised in Manuel de Mendiburu's BIOGRAFIAS DE GENERALES REPUBLICANOS (466), and DICCIONARIO HISTORICO-BIOGRAFICO (467). Sources on the wars with Chile (1836-39) and with Spain (1866) are also listed in Dobyns and Doughty (250); the latter struggle is also treated by Davis (226), Diez-Canseco (248), and Novo y Colson (511).

Until the centenary, the War of the Pacific attracted little attention from Peruvian historians, as would be expected of the defeated party. Apart from the contemporary memoirs of generals Buendía (118), and Cáceres (140), and the narrative account by Paz Soldán (550), the war more often inspired foreign (especially, of course, Chilean) than Peruvian scholars: the British historian, Clements Markham (455), the Ecuadorian general, Francisco Salazar (633), and the Venezuelan, Jacinto López (424). Only in this century, with the wounds of the humiliation healed, have Peruvian historians explored the war: see Alayza Paz Soldán (9), who focuses on the Andean resistance organized by Andrés Cáceres; Arosemena Garland (47), on the naval dimension with a biography of Admiral Grau; Reátegui Chávez's (596), useful general account; and Delgado's (232), and Vargas Ugarte's (712), valuable collections of contemporary documents of the war. More recently, anticipating the centenary, Peruvian and foreign historians have explored the resistance of the Indian population to the Chilean army: Mallon (448), Manrique (450), Bonilla (101) and Favre (269). The centenary in 1979 brought a spate of new writing on the war, as well as editions of documents and renditions of memoirs and eyewitness accounts. Revisionism commenced with essays by Peru's leading historians, Jorge Basadre (75), and Heraclio Bonilla (100). A well-documented, official military history is being assembled by the Comisión Permanente de Historia del Ejército del Perú (200, 201, 202), a task accomplished in a briefer form by Grieve (329), and Mendoza Meléndez (468).

The post-war decades of Peru's prosperous "Aristocratic Republic" are studied by Burga and Flores Galindo (127), Rory Miller (477), and Peloso (551). For a general military history, see Dellepiane (235), and Víctor Villanueva (727, 728).

FUTURE RESEARCH

As pointed out earlier, the military history of the nineteenth century cannot simply be understood as the continuation of private, "patrimonial," and elite interests by means of force. Military history deserves a place of its own, and will undoubtedly undergo a recovery once the archives of national ministries of defense, often closed to the public, become more easily accessible. Research has scarcely begun on the organization of national armies, provincial forces, leadership, discipline, pay, military colonization, arms and equipment, martial music and armed forces bands, military medicine, or the development of tactics and strategy (particularly the importance of the guerrilla). For the moment, while national defense archives often remain off-limits to the researcher, provincial and district archives (generally more easily accessible) can furnish ample documentation on the organization of militias, national guards, police forces, provincial rebellions, etc.

The wider relationship between the military and society -- recruitment, social mobility through military service and promotion, the development of nationalism and patriotism, etc. -- must also be much more fully explored. It is now recognized that politics and war, especially their Latin American variant in *caudillismo*, cannot begin to be understood without an examination of underlying social and economic structures. It is not enough simply to place a particular caudillo among his presumed social class, linked to his putative economic base in an export commodity, in *auge* or decline: for example, Juan Manuel de Rosas, the *estancieros* of the province of Buenos Aires and the cattle industry. The relationship between politics, society, and economy was always more complicated. The strength and persistence of *caudillismo* rested on the close ties of kinship and clientelage between leader and follower, and drew sustenance from horizontal coalitions between "fractions" of elite groups (merchants and landowners, for example) as well from vertical ties between elite and popular sectors. For most of the nineteenth century, these networks of caudillo power were nearly always regional rather than national in scope. This was true even for successful national caudillos, such as Rosas, Paez, Santa Anna, or Porfirio Díaz, whose influence, however firm on their home patches, was unstable nationally, since it rested upon shifting personal allegiances and regional rivalries. Students of the nineteenth century, even in its purely military aspects, must therefore be alert to the great social and ethnic diversity and intense regionalism of countries which had emerged as states long before becoming nations. Recent studies, such as John Lynch's ground breaking study of Rosas, have dedicated as much space to these personal and structural factors as to conventional, politico-military narrative. Unfortunately, limitations of space preclude the inclusion in this bibliography of most of the recent advances in social, economic, or regional history, now considered the natural starting point of any study of politics and war in the "Age of *Caudillismo*."

BIBLIOGRAPHY: LATIN AMERICAN
NINETEENTH-CENTURY CAUDILLISMO

1. Abecia Baldivieso, Valentín. HISTORIOGRAFIA BOLIVIANA. La Paz: Editorial "Letras," 1965.

2. Abente, Diego. "The War of the Triple Alliance: Three Explanatory Models." LATIN AMERICAN RESEARCH REVIEW 22 (1987): 47-69.

3. Academia Colombiana de Historia. Bogotá. For the personal papers of Luis Martínes Delgado, Manuel A. Sanclemente, Jorge Holquín, Carlos Calderón, Juan E. Manrique, Aquileo Parra, Rafael Uribe Uribe, etc.

4. Academia de la Historia de Cuba. CRONICAS DE LA GUERRA DE CUBA. Havana: Imp. El Siglo XX, 1957.

5. Acevedo, Eduardo. ANALES HISTORICOS DEL URUGUAY. Vols. 2-3. Montevideo: Casa A. Barreiro y Ramos, 1933.

6. Acuña, Rodolfo. SONORAN STRONGMAN: IGNACIO PESQUEIRA AND HIS TIMES. Tucson: University of Arizona Press, 1974.

7. Ahumada Moreno, Pascual. LA GUERRA DEL PACIFICO. 8 vols. Valparaíso: Imp. del Progreso, 1884-92.

8. Alayza Paz Soldán, Luis. LA BRENA: GLORIA, SANGRE E INFAMIA DE LOS ANDES DEL PERU. Lima: Editorial Lumen, 1954.

9. ———. LA BRENA, 1882: CACERES EL CAMPEADOR. Lima: Editorial Lumen, 1954.

10. ———. LA BRENA, 1883. Lima: Editorial Lumen, 1954.

11. Alberdi, Juan Bautista. BASES Y PUNTOS DE PARTIDO PARA LA ORGANIZACION DE LA REPUBLICA DE ARGENTINA. Buenos Aires: Ed. Sudamericana, 1968. (Originally published 1852.)

12. ———. ESCRITOS POSTUMOS. 16 vols. Buenos Aires: Imp. Europea, 1895-1901.

124

13. ——. HISTORIA DE LA GUERRA DEL PARAGUAY. Buenos Aires: Ediciones de la Patria Grande, 1962.

14. ——. OBRAS COMPLETAS. 8 vols. Buenos Aires: n.p., 1876-86.

15. Alcaraz, Ramón, et al. APUNTES PARA LA HISTORIA DE LA GUERRA ENTRE MEXICO Y LOS ESTADOS UNIDOS. Mexico City: Siglo XXI Editores, 1970. (Facsimile of 1848 ed.)

16. Aldana Rendón, Mario Alfonso. REBELION AGRARIA DE MANUEL LOZADA, 1873. Mexico City: SEP/80, 1983.

17. Alfaro, Eloy. NARRACIONES HISTORICAS. Quito: n.p., 1983.

18. ——. OBRAS ESCOGIDAS. 2 vols. Guayaquil: Ediciones "Viento del Pueblo," 1959.

19. Almirante, José. GUIA DEL OFICIAL EN CAMPANA. Madrid: Imprenta y Fundición de Manuel Tello, 1881.

20. Alvarado, Lisandro. HISTORIA DE LA REVOLUCION FEDERAL EN VENEZUELA. Caracas: Comercio, 1909. (2d ed., Caracas: Ministerio de Educación, 1956.)

21. Alvarez, Juan. ESTUDIO SOBRE LAS GUERRAS CIVILES ARGENTINAS. Buenos Aires: Ed. Universitaria de Buenos Aires, 1966. (Originally published 1914.)

22. Alvarez Suárez, Agustín Enrique. SOUTH AMERICA: ENSAYO DE PSICOLOGIA POLITICA. Buenos Aires: "La Cultura Argentina," 1918.

23. Amado, Janaina. CONFLITO SOCIAL NO BRASIL: A REVOLTA DOS MUCKERS; RIO GRANDE DO SUL, 1868-1878. São Paulo: Edições Símbolo, 1978.

24. Andrade, Ignacio. POR QUE TRIUNFO LA REVOLUCION RESTAURADORA. Caracas: Ediciones Garrido, 1955.

25. Andrade, Manuel Correira de Oliveira. A GUERRA DOS CABANOS. Rio de Janeiro: Conquista, 1965.

26. Andrade, Raúl. VIDA Y MUERTA DE ELOY ALFARO. New York: n.p., 1916.

27. Annino, Antonio, et al., eds. AMERICA LATINA: DALLO STATO COLONIALE ALLO STATO NAZIONE, 1750-1940. 2 vols. Turin: Franco Angeli, 1987.

28. Aránguiz Donoso, Horacio, ed. BIBLIOGRAFIA HISTORICA, 1959-1967. Santiago: Instituto de Historia, Universidad Católica de Chile, 1967.

29. Aranzaes, Nicanor. LAS REVOLUCIONES DE BOLIVIA. La Paz: Librería Editorial Juventud, 1980. (Originally published 1918.)

30. Arbeláez, Tulio. EPISODIOS DE LA GUERRA DE 1889 A 1903: CAMPANAS DEL GENERAL CESAREO PULIDO. 2d ed. Bogotá: Imprenta Nacional, 1936.

31. Arcaya, Pedro Manuel. ESTUDIOS SOBRE PERSONAJE Y HECHOS DE LA HISTORIA VENEZOLANA. Caracas: Cosmos, 1911.

32. Arce, José. ROCA, 1843-1914: SU VIDA Y SU OBRA. Buenos Aires: Museo Roca, 1960.

33. Archivo del Ministerio de Defensa. DOCUMENTOS RELACIONADOS CON LA GUERRA DE LOS MIL DIAS. 170 vols. Bogotá: n.p., n.d.

34. Archivo del Ministerio de Defensa. Caracas.

35. Archivo General de la Nación. CORRESPONDENCIA DEL GENERAL JOSE ARTIGAS AL CABILDO DE MONTEVIDEO, 1814-1816. Montevideo: n.p., 1946.

36. Archivo Histórico de la Provincia de Buenos Aires. LA CAMPANA LIBERTADORA DEL GENERAL LAVALLE, 1838-1842. La Plata: n.p., 1944.

37. ———. MENSAJES DE LOS GOBERNADORES DE LA PROVINCIA DE BUENOS AIRES, 1822-1849. 2 vols. La Plata: n.p., 1976.

38. Argüedas, Alcides. LOS CAUDILLOS BARBAROS: HISTORIA-RESURRECCION; LA TRAGEDIA DE UN PUEBLO; MELGAREJO-MORALES, 1864-1972. Barcelona: Vda. de L. Tasso, 1929.

39. ———. HISTORIA DE BOLIVIA: LOS CAUDILLOS LETRADOS; LA CONFEDERACION PERU-BOLIVIANO, INGUI; O LA CONSOLIDACION DE LA NACIONALIDAD, 1828-1848. Barcelona: Sobs. de L. Robert y Cía., 1923.

40. ———. LA PLEBE EN ACCION, 1846-1847. Barcelona: Sobs. de L. Robert y Cía., 1924.

41. ———. PUEBLO ENFERMO: CONTRIBUCION A LA PSICOLOGIA DE LOS PUEBLOS HISPANO-AMERICANOS. La Paz: Ediciones Puerta del Sol, 1967. (Originally published 1909.)

42. Armas Chitty, José Antonio de, ed. 'EL MOCHO' HERNANDEZ: PAPELES DE SU ARCHIVO. Caracas: Universidad Central de Venezuela, 1978.

43. ———. VIDA POLITICA DE CARACAS EN EL SIGLO XIX. Caracas: n.p., 1976.

44. Arnade, Charles. THE EMERGENCE OF THE REPUBLIC OF BOLIVIA. Gainesville: University of Florida Press, 1957.

45. ———. "The Porfirio Díaz Papers of the William Clements Library." HISPANIC AMERICAN HISTORICAL REVIEW 33 (1953): 324-25.

46. Arosemena Garland, Geraldo. EL CONTRALMIRANTE MIGUEL GRAU. Lima: Sanmartí y Cía., 1946.

47. Arquivo do Clube Militar. Rio de Janeiro.

48. Arquivo do Instituto Histórico e Geográfico Brasileiro. Rio de Janeiro.

49. Arquivo do Ministerio da Guerra. Rio de Janeiro.

50. Arrangoiz y Berrizábal, Francisco de Paula de. APUNTES PARA LA HISTORIA DEL SEGUNDO IMPERIO MEXICANO. Madrid: Rivadeneyra, 1869.

51. ——. MEJICO DESDE 1808 HASTA 1867. 4 vols. Madrid: Pérez Dubrull, 1871-72.

52. Austria, José de. BOSQUEJO DE LA HISTORIA MILITAR DE VENEZUELA. 2 vols. Caracas: Academia Nacional de la História, 1960.

53. Aveiro, Colonel Silvestre. MEMORIAS MILITARES, 1864-1870. Asunción: Ediciones Comuneros, 1970.

54. Ayala, E. LUCHA POLITICA Y ORIGEN DE LOS PARTIDOS EN ECUADOR. Quito: Pontifícia Universidad Católica del Ecuador, 1978.

55. Bader, Thomas M. "A Willingness to War: A Portrait of the Republic of Chile during the Years Preceding the War of the Pacific." Ph.D. dissertation, University of California, Los Angeles, 1967.

56. Balbóntin, Manuel. APUNTES SOBRE UN SISTEMA MILITAR PARA LA REPUBLICA. Mexico City: I. Cumplido, 1867.

57. ——. MEMORIAS DEL CORONEL MANUEL BALBONTIN: LA INVASION MEXICANA, 1846 a 1848. Mexico City: n.p., 1883.

58. Balestra, Juan. EL NOVENTA: UNA EVOLUCION POLITICA ARGENTINA. 2d ed. Buenos Aires: J. Roldán, 1935.

59. Barager, Joseph R. "The Historiography of the Río de la Plata Area since 1930." HISPANIC AMERICAN HISTORICAL REVIEW 39 (1959): 588-642.

60. Barba, Enrique M. COMO LLEGO ROSAS AL PODER. Buenos Aires: Editorial Pleamar, 1972.

61. Barker, Nancy Nichols. THE FRENCH EXPERIENCE IN MEXICO, 1821-1861. Chapel Hill: University of North Carolina Press, 1979.

62. Barman, Roderick J. "The Brazilian Peasantry Reexamined: The Implications of the Quebra-Quilos Revolt, 1874-1875." HISPANIC AMERICAN HISTORICAL REVIEW 57 (1977): 401-24.

63. Barrán, José Pedro. APOGEO Y CRISIS DEL URUGUAY PASTORAL Y CAUDILLESCO, 1838-1875. Montevideo: Ediciones de la Banda Oriental, 1974.

64. Barrán, José Pedro, and Benjamín Nahum. "Proletariado ganadero, caudillismo y guerras civiles en el Uruguay del novecientos." NOVA AMERICANA 2 (1979): 169-94.

65. Barreto, Félix, ed. ARCHIVO HISTORICO DE SANTA FE: PAPELES DE ROSAS, 1821-1850. Santa Fé: n.p., 1928.

66. Barrios, Leopoldo. IMPORTANCIA DE LA HISTORIA DE LAS CAMPAÑAS IRREGULARES Y EN ESPECIAL DE LA GUERRA DE CUBA. Madrid: Imprenta El Correo Militar, 1893.

67. Barroso, Gustavo. A GUERRA DE ARTIGAS, 1816-1820. 2d ed. Rio de Janeiro: G.M. Costa, 1939.

68. ———. A GUERRA DE LOPEZ: CONTOS E EPISODIOS DA CAMPANHA DO PARAGUAY. São Paulo: Cía. Editôra Nacional, 1928.

69. ———. A GUERRA DE ROSAS: CONTOS E EPISODIOS RELATIVO A CAMPANHA DO URUGUAI Y DA ARGENTINA, 1851-1852. São Paulo: Cía. Editôra Nacional, 1929.

70. ———. A GUERRA DO VIDEO: CONTOS E EPISODIOS DA CAMPANHA DA CISPLATINA, 1825-1828. São Paulo: Cía. Editôra Nacional, 1930.

71. ———. HISTORIA MILITAR DO BRASIL. 2d ed. São Paulo: Cía. Editôra Nacional, 1938.

72. Bas, Pedro Pablo. FLORES DE VERDAD. Havana: Tip. F. AG., 1911.

73. Basadre, Jorge. HISTORIA DE LA REPUBLICA DEL PERU, 1822-1933. 17 vols. 6th ed. Lima: Editorial Universitaria, 1970.

74. ———. INTRODUCCION A LAS BASES DOCUMENTALES PARA LA HISTORIA DE LA REPUBLICA DEL PERU CON ALGUNAS REFLEXIONES. 2 vols. Lima: Ediciones P.L.V., 1971.

75. Basadre, Jorge, et al. REFLEXIONES EN TORNO A LA GUERRA DE 1879. Lima: F. Campodónico F., 1979.

76. Batres Jáuregui, Antonio. LA AMERICA CENTRAL ANTE LA HISTORIA. 3 vols. Guatemala: Tip. Sánchez y De Guise, 1920.

77. Bazaine Archive (University of Texas, Austin). 28 vols.

78. Bazant, Jan. ANTONIO HARO Y TAMARIZ Y SUS AVENTURAS POLITICAS. Mexico City: El Colegio de México, 1985.

79. ———. A CONCISE HISTORY OF MEXICO FROM HIDALGO TO CARDENAS. Cambridge: Cambridge University Press, 1977.

80. Beals, Carleton. PORFIRIO DIAZ: DICTATOR OF MEXICO. Philadelphia: J.B. Lippincott, Co., 1932.

81. Benjamin, Thomas, and Mario Ocasio-Meléndez. "Organizing the Memory of Modern Mexico: Porfirian Historiography in Perspective, 1880s-1980s." HISPANIC AMERICAN HISTORICAL REVIEW 64 (1984): 323-64.

82. Berg, Ronald, and Frederick Weaver. "Toward a Reinterpretation of Political Change in Peru during the First Century of Independence." JOURNAL OF INTERAMERICAN STUDIES AND WORLD AFFAIRS 20 (1978): 69-85.

83. Bergquist, Charles W. COFFEE AND CONFLICT IN COLOMBIA, 1886-1910. Durham: Duke University Press, 1978.

84. Best, Félix. HISTORIA DE LAS GUERRAS ARGENTINAS MAS IMPORTANTES REALIZADAS DESDE 1810 HASTA NUESTROS DIAS POR MAYOR DEL EJERCITO M. FELIX BEST. 2 vols. Buenos Aires: Ediciones Peuser, 1968-74.

85. Betancourt Agramonte, Eugenio. IGNACIO AGRAMONTE Y LA REVOLUCION CUBANA. Havana: Dorubecker, 1928.

86. Bethell, Leslie, ed. THE CAMBRIDGE HISTORY OF LATIN AMERICA. Vols. 3-5. London: Cambridge University Press, 1985-86.

87. Beverina, Juan. LAS CAMPANAS DE LOS EJERCITOS LIBERTADORES, 1838-1852. Buenos Aires: Ed. Ríoplatense, 1974.

88. ———. CASEROS, 3 DE FEBRERO DE 1852: ESTUDIO HISTORICO MILITAR DE LAS CAMPANAS DE 1851-1852. Varese, Italy: Cromo-Tip. de A. Nicola y Cía., 1911.

89. ———. EL GENERAL JOSE MARIA PAZ: SUS CAMPANAS Y SU DOCTRINA DE GUERRA. Buenos Aires: Biblioteca del Oficial, 1925.

90. ———. LA GUERRA CONTRA EL IMPERIO DEL BRASIL. 2 vols. Buenos Aires: L. Bernard, 1927-28.

91. ———. LA GUERRA DE PARAGUAY, 1865-1870: RESUMEN HISTORICO. Buenos Aires: Instituto Mitre, 1973.

92. ———. EL VIRREINATO DE LAS PROVINCIAS DEL RIO DE LA PLATA: SU ORGANIZACION MILITAR. Buenos Aires: Biblioteca del Oficial, 1935.

93. ———, ed. BIBLIOTECA DE MAYO. 17 vols. Buenos Aires: n.p., 1960-63.

94. Bidwell, Robert L. "The First Mexican Navy, 1821-1830." Ph.D. dissertation, University of Virginia, 1960.

95. Blakemore, Harold. BRITISH NITRATES AND CHILEAN POLITICS, 1886-1896. London: Athlone Press, 1974.

96. ———. "The Chilean Revolution of 1891 and Its Historiography." HISPANIC AMERICAN HISTORICAL REVIEW 45 (1965): 393-421.

97. Blanchot, Charles. MEMOIRES: L'INTERVENTION FRANCAISE AU MEXIQUE. 3 vols. Paris: Emile Nourry, 1911.

98. Blanksten, George I. ECUADOR: CONSTITUTIONS AND CAUDILLOS. Berkeley: University of California Press, 1951.

99. Boehrer, George C.A. "The Brazilian Republican Revolution: Old and New Views." LUSO-BRAZILIAN REVIEW 3 (1966): 43-57.

100. Bonilla, Heraclio. UN SIGLO A LA DERIVA: ENSAYOS SOBRE EL PERU, BOLIVIA Y LA GUERRA. Lima: Instituto de Estudios Peruanos, 1980.

101. ———. "The War of the Pacific and the National and Colonial Problem in Peru." PAST AND PRESENT 81 (1978): 92-118.

102. Borba de Morães, Rubens, and William Berrien. "Brazilian Historical Bibliography: Some Lacunae and Suggestions." REVISTA INTERAMERICANA DE BIBLIOGRAFIA/INTER-AMERICAN REVIEW OF BIBLIOGRAPHY 11 (1961): 137-49.

103. ———, eds. MANUAL BIBLIOGRAFICO DE ESTUDIOS BRASILEIROS. Rio de Janeiro: Gráfica Editô.ora Souza, 1949.

104. Borda, Francisco de Paula. CONVERSACIONES CON MIS HIJOS. 3 vols. Bogotá: Banco Popular, 1974.

105. Bosch, Beatriz. URQUIZA Y SU TIEMPO. Buenos Aires: Editorial Universitaria de Buenos Aires, 1971.

106. Box, Pelham Horton. THE ORIGINS OF THE PARAGUAYAN WAR. Urbana: University of Illinois Press, 1929.

107. Boza, Bernabé. MI DIARIO DE GUERRA. 2 vols. Havana: "La Propagandista," 1900-04.

108. Bray, Arturo. HOMBRES Y EPOCAS DEL PARAGUAY. 2 vols. Buenos Aires: Editorial Nizza, 1943-57.

109. ———. MILITARES Y CIVILES: ESTUDIO PSICO-PATOLOGICO DEL PRONUNCIAMIENTO. Buenos Aires: Editorial Nizza, 1958.

110. ———. SOLANO LOPEZ: SOLDADO DE LA GLORIA Y EL INFORTUNIO. 2d ed. Buenos Aires: Editorial Nizza, 1948.

111. Briceño, Manuel. LOS ILUSTRES: O LA ESTAFA DE LOS GUZMANES. Caracas: Ediciones Fé y Cultura, 1953. (Originally published 1884.)

112. ———. LA REVOLUCION, 1876-1877: RECUERDOS PARA LA HISTORIA. Bogotá: Academia Colombiana de Historia, 1947.

113. Briceño Ayestarán, Santiago. MEMORIAS DE SU VIDA MILITAR Y POLITICA. Caracas: Tip. Americana, 1948.

114. Bricker, Victoria Reifler. "The Caste War of Yucatán: The History of a Myth and the Myth of History." In ANTHROPOLOGY AND HISTORY IN YUCATAN, 251-58. Edited by Grant D. Jones. Austin: University of Texas Press, 1977.

115. Brito Figueroa, Federico. TIEMPO DE EZEQUIEL ZAMORA. Caracas: Centauro, 1975.

116. Broussard, Ray F. "Ignacio Comonfort: His Contribution to the Mexican Reform." Ph.D. dissertation, University of Texas, Austin, 1959.

117. Brown, Jonathan. "The Bondage of Old Habits in Nineteenth-Century Argentina." LATIN AMERICAN RESEARCH REVIEW 21 (1986): 3-31.

118. Buendía, Juan. GUERRA CON CHILE. Lima: Milla Bartres, 1973.

119. Buisson, Inge, Hans-Joachim König, and Horst Pietschmann, eds. PROBLEMAS DE LA FORMACION DEL ESTADO Y DE LA NACION EN HISPANOAMERICA. Cologne: Böhlau, 1984.

120. Bulnes, Francisco. LAS GRANDES MENTIRAS DE NUESTRA HISTORIA: LA NACION Y EL EJERCITO EN LAS GUERRAS EXTRANJERAS. Mexico City: Vda. de C. Bouret, 1904.

121. ———. JUAREZ Y LAS REVOLUCIONES DE AYUTLA Y DE LA REFORMA. 2d ed. Mexico City: H.T. Milenario, 1967. (Originally published 1905.)

122. ———. EL VERDADERO JUAREZ Y LA VERDAD SOBRE LA INTERVENCION Y EL IMPERIO. 2d ed. Mexico City: Editora Nacional, 1967.

123. Bulnes, Gonzalo. LAS CAUSAS DE LA GUERRA ENTRE CHILE Y EL PERU. Santiago: Soc. Imp. Litografía "Barcelona," 1918.

124. ———. LA GUERRA DEL PACIFICO. 3 vols. Santiago: Editorial Universo, 1911-19.

125. ———. HISTORIA DE LA CAMPANA DE PERU EN 1838. Santiago: Imp. de "Los Tiempos," 1878.

126. Bunge, Carlos Octavio. NUESTRA AMERICA: ENSAYO DE PSICOLOGIA SOCIAL. 6th ed. Buenos Aires: Casa Vaccaro, 1918.

127. Burga, Manuel, and Alberto Flores Galindo, eds. APOGEO Y CRISIS DE LA REPUBLICA ARISTOCRATICA. Lima: Ediciones Rikchay, 1980.

128. Burgess, Paul. JUSTO RUFINO BARRIOS: A BIOGRAPHY. Philadelphia: Dorrance, 1926.

129. Burgin, Miron. THE ECONOMIC ASPECT OF ARGENTINE FEDERALISM, 1820-1852. Cambridge: Harvard University Press, 1946.

130. Burns, E. Bradford. "Ideology in Nineteenth-Century Latin American Historiography." HISPANIC AMERICAN HISTORICAL REVIEW 58 (1978): 409-31.

131. ———. THE POVERTY OF PROGRESS: LATIN AMERICA IN THE NINETEENTH CENTURY. Berkeley: University of California Press, 1980.

132. Burr, Robert N. BY REASON OR FORCE: CHILE AND THE BALANCING OF POWER IN SOUTH AMERICA, 1830-1905. Berkeley: University of California Press, 1965.

133. Bushnell, Clyde Gilbert. "The Military and Political Career of Juan Alvarez, 1790-1867." Ph.D. dissertation, University of Texas, Austin, 1958.

134. Bushnell, David. THE SANTANDER REGIME IN GRAN COLOMBIA. Westport: Greenwood Press, 1954.

135. Bushnell, David, and Neill Macaulay. THE EMERGENCE OF LATIN AMERICA IN THE NINETEENTH CENTURY. New York: Oxford University Press, 1988.

136. Bustamante, Carlos María de. APUNTES PARA LA HISTORIA DEL GOBIERNO DEL GENERAL D. ANTONIO LOPEZ DE SANTA ANNA. Mexico City: Imp. de J.M. Lara, 1845.

137. Bustamante, Juan. LOS INDIOS DEL PERU. Lima: J.M. Monterola, 1867.

138. Butler, Robert W. "The Origins of the Liberal Party in Venezuela, 1830-1848." Ph.D. dissertation, University of Texas, Austin, 1972.

139. Caballero, Lucas. MEMORIAS DE LA GUERRA DE LOS MIL DIAS. Bogotá: "Aquila Negra" Editorial, 1939. (2d ed., 1980.)

140. Cáceres, Andrés. LA GUERRA DE '79: SUS CAMPANAS. Lima: Milla Bartres, 1973.

141. Cadenhead, Ivie E., Jr. JESUS GONZALEZ ORTEGA AND MEXICAN NATIONAL POLITICS. Fort Worth: Texas Christian University Press, 1972.

142. Cady, John Frank. FOREIGN INTERVENTION IN THE RIO DE LA PLATA, 1838-1850. Philadelphia: University of Pennsylvania Press, 1939.

143. Caldwell, Edward Maurice. "The War of 'La Reforma' in Mexico, 1858-1861." Ph.D. dissertation, University of Texas, Austin, 1935.

144. Callcott, Wilfred H. SANTA ANNA: THE STORY OF AN ENIGMA WHO ONCE WAS MEXICO. Norman: University of Oklahoma Press, 1936.

145. Calle, M. J. [Enrique de Rastignac]. HOMBRES DE LA REVUELTA. Guayaquil: Nueva Empresa Editorial de la Nación, 1906.

146. Camacho Roldán, Salvador. MEMORIAS. 2 vols. Bogotá: Librería Colombiana, Camacho, Roldán y Tamayo, 1945.

147. Cammack, Paul. "The Political Economy of the 'Politics of the States': Minas Gerais and the Brazilian Federation, 1889-1900." BULLETIN OF LATIN AMERICAN RESEARCH 2 (1982): 51-65.

148. Campo, José Rodolfo del. CAMPANA NAVAL: CORRESPONDENCIAS A "EL COMERCIO"; ANO DE 1879. Lima: Gil, 1920. (2d ed., 1979.)

149. Campobassi, José Salvador. MITRE Y SU EPOCA. Buenos Aires: Editorial Universitaria de Buenos Aires, 1980.

150. Camps Feliú, Francisco de. ESPANOLES E INSURRECTOS: RECUERDOS DE LA GUERRA DE CUBA. Havana: Tip. de A. Alvarez y Cía., 1890.

151. Canto, Estanislao del. MEMORIAS DE.... Santiago: Imp. la Tracción, 1927.

152. Cárcano, Ramón J. LA GUERRA DEL PARAGUAY: ORIGENES Y CAUSAS. Buenos Aires: Editorial Domingo Veau, 1939.

153. Cardozo, Efraín. VISPERAS DE LA GUERRA DEL PARAGUAY. Buenos Aires: Ateneo, 1954.

154. ———, ed. HACE 100 ANOS: CRONICAS DE LA GUERRA DE 1864-1870. 11 vols. Asunción: Editorial Emasa, 1967.

155. Carrasco, Manuel. JOSE BALLIVIAN, 1805-1852: ESTAMPAS HISTORICAS. Buenos Aires: Hachette, 1960.

156. Carreño, Alberto María. JEFES DEL EJERCITO MEXICANO EN 1847. Mexico City: Sec. de Fomento, 1914.

157. ———, ed. ARCHIVO DEL GENERAL PORFIRIO DIAZ: MEMORIAS Y DOCUMENTOS. 30 vols. Mexico City: Editorial Elede, 1947-61.

158. ———, ed. MEMORIAS DE LA GUERRA DE REFORMA: DIARIO DEL CORONEL MANUEL VALDES. Mexico City: Sec. de Fomento, 1913.

159. Carrera, Rafael. MEMORIAS DEL GENERAL CARRERA, 1837-1840. Guatemala City: Tip. Sánchez y De Guise, 1906.

160. Carvalho, José Murilo de. A CONSTRUCAO DA ORDEM: A ELITE POLITICA IMPERIAL. Rio de Janeiro: Editôra Campus, 1980.

161. ———. "As forças armadas na Primeira República: O poder desestabilizador." In HISTORIA GERAL DA CIVILIZACAO BRASILEIRA, 2:183-234. Edited by Boris Fausto. São Paulo: DIFEL, 1960-81.

162. ———. "Political Elites and State Building: The Case of Nineteenth-Century Brazil." COMPARATIVE STUDIES IN SOCIETY AND HISTORY 24 (1982): 378-99.

163. Castañeda, Carlos E., ed. LA GUERRA DE LA REFORMA SEGUN EL ARCHIVO DE GENERAL D. MANUEL DOBLADO, 1857-1860. San Antonio: n.p., 1930.

164. Castañeda, Carlos E., and Jack Autrey Dabbs. GUIDE TO THE LATIN AMERICAN MANUSCRIPTS IN THE UNIVERSITY OF TEXAS. Cambridge: Harvard University Press, 1939.

165. Castellanos García, Gerardo. LEGADO MAMBI: FORMACION, ODISEA Y AGONIA DEL ARCHIVO DEL GENERAL MAXIMO GOMEZ. Havana: Ucar García y Cía., 1940.

166. Castellanos V., Rafael Ramón. EL GENERAL MANUEL ANTONIO LOPEZ: ILUSTRE PROCER Y ESCRITOR PAYANES. Bogotá: Editorial Kelly, 1972.

167. ———. GUZMAN BLANCO INTIMO. Caracas: Ediciones Librería Historia, 1969.

168. ———. PAEZ: PEREGRINO Y PROSCRIPTO, 1848-1851. 2d ed. Caracas: Castellanos, 1975.

169. Castillo Negrete, Emilio del. HISTORIA MILITAR DE MEXICO EN EL SIGLO XIX. Mexico City: A. Rosas, 1883.

170. Castro, Cipriano. DOCUMENTOS DEL GENERAL CIPRIANO CASTRO. 6 vols. Caracas: Tip. J.M. Herrera Irigoyen y Cía., 1903-08.

171. Castro, Jeanne Berrance de. A MILICIA CIDADAO: A GUARDA NACIONAL DE 1831-1850. São Paulo: Cía. Editôra Nacional, 1977.

172. Cavazos Garza, Israel. MARIANO ESCOBEDO: EL GLORIOSO SOLDADO DE LA REPUBLICA. Monterrey: Gobierno del Estado de Nuevo León, 1949.

173. Caviano, Tomás. HISTORIA DE LA GUERRA DE AMERICA ENTRE CHILE, PERU Y BOLIVIA. N.p.: Librería Italiana, 1904.

174. Cayama Martínez, Rafael. EL GENERAL GREGORIO SEGUNDO RIERA: NOTAS BIOGRAFICAS. Caracas: Tip. La Nación, 1941.

175. Celesia, Ernesto H. ROSAS: APORTES PARA SU HISTORIA. 2 vols. 2d ed. Buenos Aires: Ediciones Peuser, 1968.

176. Centro de Estudios de Historia Militar. EL EJERCITO LIBERTADOR DE CUBA, 1868-1898. Havana: Imprenta de la Dirección Política de las Fuerzas Armadas Revolucionarias, 1985.

177. Centurión, Juan Crisóstomo. MEMORIAS DEL GENERAL...: O SEA REMINISCENCIAS HISTORICAS SOBRE LA GUERRA DEL PARAGUAY. 2 vols. Buenos Aires: Imprenta de J.A. Berra, 1894. (Republished, Asunción, 1976.)

178. Cerqueira, General Dionisio. REMINISCENCIAS DA CAMPANHA DO PARAGUAI, 1865-1870. 5th ed. Salvador: Prefeitura Municipal do Salvador, 1974. (Originally published 1910.)

179. Cerutti, Mario. ECONOMIA DE GUERRA Y PODER REGIONAL EN EL SIGLO XIX. Monterrey: Archivo General del Estado de Nuevo León, 1983.

180. ———. "Militares, terratenientes y empresarios en el noreste de México durante el porfiriato." ARGUMENTOS: ESTUDIOS

CRITICOS DE LA SOCIEDAD (Universidad Autónoma Metropolitana, Mexico City) 1 (1987): 43-74.

181. Chapman, Charles. "The Age of the Caudillos: A Chapter in Hispanic American History." HISPANIC AMERICAN HISTORICAL REVIEW 12 (1932): 281-300.

182. ———. "List of Books Referring to Caudillos: A Chapter in Hispanic American History." HISPANIC AMERICAN HISTORICAL REVIEW 13 (1933): 143-46.

183. Cháves, Julio César. EL SUPREMO DICTADOR: BIOGRAFIA DE JOSE GASPAR DE FRANCIA. Buenos Aires: Editorial Difusam, 1942.

184. Chevalier, François. "Caudilles et caciques en Amérique: Contribution al'etude des liens personnels." In MELANGES OFFERTS A MARCEL BATAILLON POUR LES HISPANISTES FRANCAIS, 30-47. Paris: Ferete Fils, 1962.

185. Chiappini, Julio O. BIBLIOGRAFIA SOBRE ROSAS. Rosario: Instituto de Investigaciones, Facultad de Humanidades de Rosario, 1973.

186. Chiaramonte, José Carlos. FORMAS DE SOCIEDAD Y ECONOMIA EN HISPANOAMERICA. Mexico City: Editorial Grijalbo, 1984.

187. ———. "Legalidad constitucional o caudillismo: El problema del orden social en el surgimiento de los estados autónomos del litoral argentino en la primera mitad del siglo XIX." In AMERICA LATINA: DALLO STATO COLONIALE ALLO STATO NAZIONE, 1750-1940, 2:536-56. Edited by Antonio Annino, et al. Turin: Franco Angeli, 1987.

188. ———. "Organización del estado y construcción del orden social: La política económica de la provincia de Corrientes hacia 1821-1840." ANUARIO DEL INSTITUTO DE INVESTIGACIONES HISTORICAS (Universidad Nacional de Rosario) (1985).

189. Child, Martha Cleveland. "Politics, Revolution and Reform: The Liberal Challenge to the Colombian Status Quo; Rafael Uribe Uribe, 1859-1914." M.A. thesis, Vanderbilt University, 1969.

190. Cifuentes, Abdón. MEMORIAS. 2 vols. Santiago: Editorial Nascimento, 1936.

191. Clegern, Wayne. "Transition from Conservatism to Liberalism in Guatemala, 1865-1880." In HISPANIC AMERICAN ESSAYS IN HONOR OF MAX LEON MOORHEAD. Edited by William S. Coker. Pensacola: Perdido Bay Press, 1979.

192. Cler, Jean-Joseph-Gustave. SOUVENIRS D'UN OFICIER DU 2ME DE ZOUAVES. Paris: Calmann Lévy, 1890.

193. Coerver, Don M. "Federal-State Relations during the Porfiriato: The Case of Sonora, 1879-1884." THE AMERICAS 33 (1977): 567-84.

194. ———. THE PORFIRIAN INTERREGNUM: THE PRESIDENCY OF MANUEL GONZALEZ OF MEXICO, 1880-1884. Fort Worth: Texas Christian University Press, 1979.

195. Colegio Militar Eloy Alfaro. Archivo Histórico. Quito.

196. Colli, Néstor S. LA POLITICA FRANCESA EN EL RIO DE LA PLATA: ROSAS Y EL BLOQUEO DE 1838-1840. Buenos Aires: n.p., 1963.

197. Collier, Simon. "The Historiography of the 'Portalian' Period (1830-1891) in Chile." HISPANIC AMERICAN HISTORICAL REVIEW 57 (1977): 660-90.

198. Colmenares, Germán. PARTIDOS POLITICOS Y CLASES SOCIALES. Bogotá: Ediciones Universidad de los Andes, 1968.

199. Comisión Permanente de la Historia del Ejército del Perú (CPHEP). LA GESTA DE LIMA, 1881-1981. Lima: Ministerio de Guerra, 1981.

200. ———. REFLEXIONES SOBRE LA RESISTENCIA DE LA BRENA: SIGNIFICADO Y PROYECCION HISTORICA. Lima: Ministerio de Guerra, 1982.

201. ———. LA RESISTENCIA DE LA BRENA: DE LOS REDUCTORES A JULCAMARCA, 16 ENERO 1881-22 FEBRERO 1882. Lima: Ministerio de Guerra, 1982.

202. ———. LA RESISTENCIA DE LA BRENA: HUAMACHUCO Y EL ALMA NACIONAL, 1882-1884. Lima: Ministerio de Guerra, 1983.

203. ———. SERIE BIOGRAFICA. Vol. 1, LOS HEROES DE LA BRENA. Lima: Ministerio de Guerra, 1982.

204. Comonfort Papers (University of Texas Library, Austin).

205. Condarco Morales, Ramiro. ZARATE 'EL TEMIBLE' WILLKA: HISTORIA DE LA REBELION INDIGENA DE 1899. La Paz: n.p., 1983.

206. Corbitt, Duvon C. "Cuba's Revisionist Interpretation of Cuba's Struggle for Independence." HISPANIC AMERICAN HISTORICAL REVIEW 43 (1963): 395-404.

207. Coronado Aguilar, Manuel. EL GENERAL RAFAEL CARRERA ANTE LA HISTORIA. Guatemala: Editorial del Ejército, 1965.

208. Cortázar, R., ed. CORRESPONDENCIA DIRIGIDA AL GENERAL FRANCISCO DE PAULA SANTANDER. 14 vols. Bogotá: n.p., 1964-67.

209. ———. CARTAS Y MENSAJES DEL GENERAL FRANCISCO DE PAULA SANTANDER. 10 vols. Bogotá: Academia Colombiana de Historia, 1953-56.

210. Cortés, Manuel José. ENSAYO SOBRE LA HISTORIA DE BOLIVIA. Sucre: Imp. de Breche, 1861.

211. Cosío Villegas, Daniel. "¿Dónde está el villano?" HISTORIA MEXICANA 1 (1952): 434-35.

212. ———. PORFIRIO DIAZ EN LA REVUELTA DE LA NORIA. Mexico City: Editorial Hermes, 1953.

213. ———, ed. HISTORIA MODERNA DE MEXICO. 10 vols. Mexico City: Editorial Hermes, 1959-72.

214. Costa, Emília Viotti da. "Sobre as origems da República." In DA MONARQUIA A REPUBLICA: MOMENTOS DECISIVOS, 243-90. São Paulo: n.p., 1977.

215. Cotner, Thomas E. THE MILITARY AND POLITICAL CAREER OF JOSE JOAQUIN DE HERRERA, 1792-1854. Austin: University of Texas Press, 1949.

216. Cova, Jesús Antonio. EL CENTAURO: VIDA DE GENERAL JOSE ANTONIO PAEZ; CAUDILLO VENEZOLANO Y BRIGADIER DEL EJERCITO ARGENTINO. Buenos Aires: Ediciones Venezuela, 1947.

217. ——, ed. ARCHIVO DEL MARISCAL JUAN CRISOSTOMO FALCON. 5 vols. Caracas: Imp. Nacional, 1957-60.

218. Cox, Patricia. BATALLON DE SAN PATRICIO. Mexico City: Stylo, 1954.

219. Crespo, Alfonso. MANUEL ISIDORO BELZU: HISTORIA DE UN CAUDILLO. La Paz: Colección Juvenil de Biografías Breves, 1980.

220. ——. SANTA CRUZ: EL CONDOR INDIO. Mexico City: Fondo de Cultura Económica, 1944.

221. Cuadra, Luis de. ALBUM DEL EJERCITO CHILENO. Valparaíso: Imp. del Mercurio, 1877.

222. Cuesta, Leonel Antonio de la, and Rolando Alum Linera, eds. CONSTITUCIONES CUBANAS, 1812-1962. New York: Ediciones Exilio, 1974.

223. Cunningham Graham, Robert B. JOSE ANTONIO PAEZ. New York: Macrae and Smith, 1929. (Reprint, Books for Libraries Press, 1971.)

224. Da Cunha, Euclides. REBELLION IN THE BACKLANDS. Chicago: University of Chicago Press, 1944.

225. Dabbs, Jack Autrey. THE FRENCH ARMY IN MEXICO, 1861-1867: A STUDY IN MILITARY GOVERNMENT. The Hague: Mouton and Co., 1963.

226. Davis, William Columbus. THE LAST CONQUISTADORES. Athens: University of Georgia Press, 1950.

227. Dealy, Glen. "Prolegomena on the Spanish American Political Tradition." HISPANIC AMERICAN HISTORICAL REVIEW 48 (1968): 37-58.

228. Dean, Warren. "Latin American Golpes and Economic Fluctuations, 1823-1966." SOCIAL SCIENCE QUARTERLY 51 (1970): 70-80.

229. Deas, Malcolm. "Algunas notas sobre la historia del caciquismo en Colombia." REVISTA DEL OCCIDENTE 63 (1973): 118-40.

230. ———. "Poverty, Civil War and Politics: Ricardo Gaitán Obeso and His Magdalena River Campaign in Colombia." NOVA AMERICANA (Turin) 2 (1979): 263-303.

231. ———. "La regeneración y la Guerra de los Mil Días." In ASPECTOS POLEMICOS DE LA HISTORIA COLOMBIANA DEL SIGLO XIX: MEMORIA DE UN SEMANARIO, 51-94. Edited by Aida Martínez Carreño. Bogotá: Fondo Cultural Cafetero, 1983.

232. Delgado, Luis Humberto. GUERRA ENTRE EL PERU Y CHILE, 1879: DE LA HISTORIA DEL GENERAL MARIANO IGNACIO PRADO; CON DOCUMENTOS ORIGINALES E INEDITOS POR.... Lima: Ariel Editores, 1965.

233. Della Cava, Ralph. "Brazilian Messianism and National Institutions: A Reappraisal of Canudos and Joaseiro." HISPANIC AMERICAN HISTORICAL REVIEW 48 (1968): 402-20.

234. ———. MIRACLE AT JOASEIRO. New York: Columbia University Press, 1970.

235. Dellepiane, Carlos. HISTORIA MILITAR DEL PERU. 2 vols. Buenos Aires: Círculo Militar, 1941.

236. Delpar, Helen V. "Aspects of Liberal Factionalism in Colombia, 1875-1885." HISPANIC AMERICAN HISTORICAL REVIEW 51 (1971): 250-74.

237. ———. "The Problem of Liberalism versus Conservatism in Colombia, 1849-1885." In LATIN AMERICAN HISTORY: SELECT PROBLEMS; SECURITY, INTEGRATION, AND

NATIONHOOD, 223-58. Edited by Fredrick B. Pike. New York: Harcourt, Brace and World, 1969.

238. ———. RED AGAINST BLUE: THE LIBERAL PARTY IN COLOMBIAN POLITICS, 1863-1899. Tuscaloosa: University of Alabama Press, 1981.

239. ———. "Road to Revolution: The Liberal Party of Colombia, 1886-1899." THE AMERICAS 32 (1976): 348-71.

240. Demelas, Daniele. NATIONALISM SANS NATION?: LA BOLIVIE AUX XIXE-XXE SIECLES. Paris: Editions du C.N.R.S., 1980.

241. DeVolder, Arthur L. GUADALUPE VICTORIA: HIS ROLE IN INDEPENDENCE. Albuquerque: Artcraft Studios, 1978.

242. Díaz, Porfirio. MEMORIAS DE PORFIRIO DIAZ, 1830-1867. 2 vols. 2d ed. Mexico City: El Libro Francés, 1923.

243. Díaz Argüedas, Julio. HISTORIA DEL EJERCITO DE BOLIVIA, 1825-1932. La Paz: n.p., 1940.

244. ———. EL MARISCAL SANTA CRUZ Y SUS GENERALES: SINTESIS BIOGRAFICAS. La Paz: n.p., 1965.

245. Díaz Ramírez, Fernando. LA VIDA HEROICA DEL GENERAL TOMAS MEJIA. Mexico City: Editorial Jus, 1968.

246. Díaz Sánchez, Ramón. GUZMAN: ECLIPSE DE UNA AMBICION DE PODER. 2 vols. Caracas: Ministerio de Educación, 1950.

247. Díaz y Díaz, Fernando. CAUDILLOS Y CACIQUES: ANTONIO LOPEZ DE SANTA ANNA Y JUAN ALVAREZ. Mexico City: El Colegio de Mexico, 1972.

248. Diez-Canseco, Ernesto. LOS GENERALES DIEZ-CANSECO: EPISODIOS HISTORICOS. Lima: Imp. Torres Aguirre, 1950.

249. Doblado Archive (University of Texas Library, Austin).

250. Dobyns, Henry E., and Paul L. Doughty. PERU: A CULTURAL HISTORY. New York: Oxford University Press, 1976.

251. Donoso, Ricardo. LAS IDEAS POLITICAS EN CHILE. 3d ed. Buenos Aires: Editorial Universitaria de Buenos Aires, 1975.

252. Duarte French, Jaime. PODER Y POLITICA: COLOMBIA, 1810-1827. Bogotá: E. Valencia Editores, 1980.

253. Dudley, William S. "Institutional Sources of Officer Discontent in the Brazilian Army, 1870-1889." HISPANIC AMERICAN HISTORICAL REVIEW 55 (1975): 44-65.

254. ———. "Professionalisation and Politicisation as Motivational Factors in the Brazilian Army Coup of 15 November 1889." JOURNAL OF LATIN AMERICAN STUDIES 8 (1976): 100-25.

255. Dumond, D. E. "Independent Maya of the Late Nineteenth Century: Chiefdoms and Power Politics." In ANTHROPOLOGY AND HISTORY IN YUCATAN, 103-38. Edited by Grant Jones. Austin: University of Texas Press, 1977.

256. Dunkerley, James. "The Politics of the Bolivian Army: Institutional Development, 1879-1935." Ph.D. dissertation, Oxford University, 1979.

257. ———. "Reassessing Caudillismo in Bolivia, 1825-1879." BULLETIN OF LATIN AMERICAN RESEARCH 1 (1981): 13-26.

258. Edwards, Alberto. LA FRONDA ARISTOCRATA. Santiago: Editorial Universitaria, 1982. (Originally published 1928.)

259. Ekdahl, Wilhelm. HISTORIA MILITAR DE LA GUERRA DEL PACIFICO ENTRE CHILE, PERU, Y BOLIVIA. 3 vols. Santiago: Imp. Universo and Imp. del Ministerio de Guerra, 1917-19.

260. Encina, Francisco Antonio. HISTORIA DE CHILE DESDE LA PREHISTORIA HASTA 1891. 20 vols. Santiago: Editorial Nascimento, 1942-52.

261. Estado Mayor del Ejército. HISTORIA DEL EJERCITO DE CHILE. 7 vols. Santiago: Estado Mayor, 1981-82.

262. ———. HISTORIA MILITAR DE CHILE. 3 vols. Santiago: Estado Mayor, 1969.

263. Etchepareborda, Roberto. HISTORIOGRAFIA MILITAR
      ARGENTINA. Buenos Aires: Círculo Militar, 1984.

264. ———. ROSAS: CONTROVERTIDA HISTORIOGRAFIA.
      Buenos Aires: Editorial Pleamar, 1972.

265. ———. TRES REVOLUCIONES, 1890-1893-1905. Buenos Aires:
      Editorial Pleamar, 1968.

266. Fagen, Particia W. "Antonio Maceo: Heroes, History and
      Historiography." LATIN AMERICAN RESEARCH REVIEW
      11 (1976): 69-93.

267. Falco, Francisco Federico. EL JEFE DE LOS MAMBISES.
      Havana: Imp. El Fígaro, 1898.

268. Falcone, Frank S. "Benito Juárez versus the Díaz Brothers:
      Politics in Oaxaca, 1867-1871." THE AMERICAS 33(1977): 630-
      51.

269. Favre, Henri. "Remarques sur la lutte des classes au Pérou
      pendant la Guerre du Pacifique." In LITTERATURE E
      SOCIETE AU PEROU DU XIXEME SIECLE A NOS JOURS.
      Edited by Association Francaise pour l'Etude et la Recherche sur
      les Pays Andins. Grénoble: Université de Langues et Lettres,
      1975.

270. Fernández Almagro, Melchor. HISTORIA POLITICA DE
      ESPANA CONTEMPORANEA. Madrid: Alizanza Editorial,
      1885-95.

271. Ferns, Henry S. BRITAIN AND ARGENTINA IN THE
      NINETEENTH CENTURY. Oxford: Clarendon, 1960.

272. Ferré, Pedro. MEMORIAS DEL BRIGADIER GENERAL...,
      OCTUBRE DE 1821 A DICIEMBRE DE 1842:
      CONTRIBUCION A LA HISTORIA DE LA PROVINCIA DE
      CORRIENTES EN SUS LUCHAS POR LA LIBERTAD Y
      CONTRA LA TIRANIA. Buenos Aires: "Coni," 1921.

273. Ferry, Gabriel [Louis de Bellemare]. SCENES DE LA VIE
      MILITAIRE AU MEXIQUE. Paris: L. Hachette et Cie., 1858.

274. Figueredo Socarrás, Fernando. LA REVOLUCION DE YARA, 1868-1878. Havana: Instituto del Libro, 1968.

275. Filler, Victor M. "Liberalism in Imperial Brazil: The Regional Rebellions of 1842." Ph.D. dissertation, Stanford University, 1976.

276. Fisisola, Vicente. MEMORIAS PARA LA HISTORIA DE LA GUERRA DE TEJAS. Mexico City: n.p., 1849.

277. Fitzgibbon, Russell H., ed. THE CONSTITUTIONS OF THE AMERICAS. Chicago: University of Chicago Press, 1948.

278. Flaccus, Elmer W. "Guadalupe Victoria: His Personality and the Cause of His Failure." THE AMERICAS 23(1967): 297-311.

279. Flores, Jorge. LA REVOLUCION DE OLARTE EN PAPANTLA, 1836-1838. Mexico City: Imp. Mundial, 1938.

280. Flores Caballero, Romeo. LA CONTRARREVOLUCION EN LA INDEPENDENCIA: LOS ESPANOLES EN LA VIDA POLITICA, SOCIAL Y ECONOMICA DE MEXICO, 1804-1838. Mexico City: El Colegio de México, 1969.

281. Florez Alvarez, Leonidas. CAMPANA EN SANTANDER, 1899-1900. 2 vols. Bogotá: Estado Mayor General, 1938.

282. Floyd, Mary B. "Antonio Guzmán Blanco: The Evolution of Septenio Politics." Ph.D. dissertation, Indiana University, Bloomington, 1981.

283. Foner, Phillip S. ANTONIO MACEO: THE BRONZE TITAN OF CUBA'S STRUGGLE FOR INDEPENDENCE. New York: Monthly Review Press, 1977.

284. ———. THE SPANISH-CUBAN-AMERICAN WAR AND THE BIRTH OF AMERICAN IMPERIALISM. 2 vols. New York: Monthly Review Press, 1972.

285. Fontoura Castellat, General Bibiano Sergio Machado da. "EXERCITO": LIBRO DE CENTENARIO, 1500-1900. 2 vols. Rio de Janeiro: n.p., 1901.

286. Fornos Peñalba, José Alfredo. "Draft Dodgers, War Resisters and Turbulent Gauchos: The War of the Triple Alliance against Paraguay." THE AMERICAS 38 (1982): 463-79.

287. ———. "The Fourth Ally: Great Britain and the War of the Triple Alliance." Ph.D. dissertation, University of California, Los Angeles, 1979.

288. Franco, José L. ANTONIO MACEO: APUNTES PARA UNA HISTORIA DE SU VIDA. 3 vols. Havana: Ediciones de Ciencias Sociales, 1975.

289. Freidel, Frank. THE SPLENDID LITTLE WAR. Boston: Little, Brown and Co., 1958.

290. LAS FUERZAS ARMADAS DE VENEZUELA EN EL SIGLO XIX: TEXTOS PARA SU ESTUDIO. 12 vols. Caracas: n.p., 1963-.

291. Galáviz de Capdevielle, María Elena. "Eleuterio Quiroz y la rebelión de 1847 en Xichú." ARCHIVOS DE HISTORIA POTOSINA 11 (1979): 5-27.

292. Galdámez Lastra, Fabio. HISTORIA MILITAR DE CHILE: ESTUDIO CRITICO DE LA CAMPANA DE 1838-1839. Santiago: Estado Mayor General, 1910.

293. Galíndez, Bartolomé. HISTORIA POLITICA ARGENTINA: LA REVOLUCION DEL 80. Buenos Aires: "Coni," 1945.

294. Galindo y Galindo, Miguel. LA GRAN DECADA NACIONAL, 1857-1867. 3 vols. Mexico City: Sec. de Fomento, 1904-06.

295. Gallo, E. FARMERS IN REVOLT: THE REVOLUTION OF 1893 IN THE PROVINCE OF SANTA FE. London: Athlone Press, 1976.

296. Galvis, Salazar, Fernando. RAFAEL URIBE URIBE. Medellín: n.p., 1968.

297. García, Genaro. LOS GOBIERNOS DE ALVAREZ Y COMONFORT SEGUN EL ARCHIVO DEL GENERAL DOBLADO. Mexico City: Vda. de C. Bouret, 1910.

298. ——. LA REVOLUCION DE AYUTLA SEGUN EL ARCHIVO DEL GENERAL DOBLADO. Mexico City: Vda. de C. Bouret, 1910.

299. ——, ed. DOCUMENTOS HISTORICOS MEXICANOS. 7 vols. Mexico City: Museo Nacional de Arqueología, Historia, y Etnología, 1910-12.

300. ——, ed. EL GENERAL PAREDES Y ARRILLAGA: SU GOBIERNO EN JALISCO; SUS MOVIMIENTOS REVOLUCIONARIOS; SUS RELACIONES CON EL GENERAL SANTA ANNA.... Mexico City: Vda. de C. Bouret, 1910.

301. García, General Rubén. GUIA DE LOS DOCUMENTOS MAS IMPORTANTES SOBRE EL PLAN Y LA REVOLUCION DE AYUTLA QUE EXISTEN EN EL ARCHIVO HISTORICO DE LA SECRETARIA DE LA DEFENSA NACIONAL. Mexico City: Sec. de Defensa Nacional, 1954.

302. García Calderón, Francisco. "Dictatorship and Democracy in Latin America." FOREIGN AFFAIRS 3 (1925): 459-77.

303. ——. LATIN AMERICA: ITS RISE AND PROGRESS. New York: Fisher Unwin, 1913.

304. García Cañizares, Santiago. LAS INVASIONES A OCCIDENTE EN LAS GUERRAS POR LA INDEPENDENCIA DE CUBA. Havana: Imp. Rambla y Bouza, 1937.

305. García Granados, General Miguel. MEMORIAS DEL.... 4 vols. 2d ed. Guatemala City: Ministerio de Educación Pública, 1952. (Originally published 1877-94 in 2 vols.)

306. García-Pérez, Antonio. ESTUDIO POLITICO-MILITAR DE LA CAMPANA DE MEJICO, 1861-67. Madrid: Imp. de Avriol, 1901.

307. Garza, Luis Alberto de la. "Algunos problemas en torno a la formación del Estado Mexicano en el siglo XIX." ESTUDIOS POLITICOS 2 (1983): 15-26.

308. Gaulot, Paul. REVE D'EMPIRE: L'EMPIRE DE MAXIMILIEN; FIN D'EMPIRE; LA VERITE SUR L'EXPEDITION DU MEXIQUE D'APRES LES DOCUMENTS INEDITS DE ERNEST LOUET, PAYEUR EN CHEF DU CORPS EXPEDITIONAIRES. 3 vols. Paris: Paul Olendorff, 1890.

309. Gill, Mario. "Heraclio Bernal: Caudillo Frustrado." HISTORIA MEXICANA 4 (1954): 138-58.

310. Gilmore, Robert L. CAUDILLISM AND MILITARISM IN VENEZUELA, 1810-1910. Athens: Ohio University Press, 1964.

311. Girón, Nicole. HERACLIO BERNAL: ¿BANDOLERO, CACIQUE O PRECURSOR DE LA REVOLUCION? Mexico City: Instituto Nacional de Antropología e Historia, 1976.

312. Gleason, Daniel Michael. "Ideological Cleavages in Early Republican Peru, 1821-1872." Ph.D. dissertation, University of Notre Dame, 1974.

313. Goldwert, Marvin. "The Rise of Modern Militarism in Argentina." HISPANIC AMERICAN HISTORICAL REVIEW 48 (1968): 189-205.

314. Gómez y Báez, General Máximo. CARTAS A FRANCISCO CARRILLO. Havana: Editorial de Ciencias Sociales, 1980.

315. ———. INVASION Y CAMPANA DE LA VILLAS, 1875-1876. Havana: Editora Militar, 1984.

316. Gómez Toro, Francisco. DIARIO DE CAMPANA. Havana: Instituto del Libro, 1968.

317. ———. LA INDEPENDENCIA DE CUBA O EL GENERAL MAXIMO GOMEZ Y SU POLITICA DE PAZ, UNION Y CONCORDIA. Havana: Tip. de los Niños Huérfanos, 1899.

318. ———. MI ESCOLTA: ULTIMA GUERRA DE INDE-PENDENCIA. Havana: Editorial Letras Cubanas, 1979.

319. ———. RECUERDOS DEDICADOS A LA FAMILIA Y A SUS AMIGOS. Havana: n.p., 1899.

320. González Guinán, Francisco. HISTORIA CONTEMPORANEA DE VENEZUELA. 15 vols. Caracas: Tip. Empresa el Cojo, 1909-25. (Reed., Caracas: Ed. España, 1954.)

321. González Navarro, Moisés. ANATOMIA DEL PODER EN MEXICO, 1848-1853. Mexico City: El Colegio de México, 1977.

322. González Simancas, Manuel. ESTUDIO GEOGRAFICO-MILITAR DE LA PROVINCIA DE SANTA CLARA. Madrid: Tip. de D. Pacheco, 1886.

323. Gootenberg, Paul. "The Social Origins of Protectionism and Free Trade in Nineteenth-Century Lima." JOURNAL OF LATIN AMERICAN STUDIES 14 (1982): 329-58.

324. Gormen, Stephen M. "The State, Elite and Exports in Nineteenth-Century Peru." JOURNAL OF LATIN AMERICAN STUDIES 21 (1979): 395-418.

325. Gossen, Gary H. "Translating Cuscat's War: Understanding Maya Oral History." JOURNAL OF LATIN AMERICAN LORE 3 (1977): 149-78.

326. Graham, Richard. "Political Power and Landownership in Nineteenth-Century Latin America." In NEW APPROACHES TO LATIN AMERICAN HISTORY, 112-36. Edited by Richard Graham and Peter Smith. Austin: University of Texas Press, 1974.

327. Granda, José de. REFLEXIONES SOBRE LA INSURRECCION DE CUBA. Madrid: Imp. de los Señores Rojas, 1876.

328. Grez Pérez, Carlos E. LOS INTENTOS DE UNION HISPANOAMERICANA Y LA GUERRA DE ESPANA EN EL PACIFICO. Santiago: Imp. Nascimento, 1928.

329. Grieve, Jorge. HISTORIA DE LA ARTILLERIA Y DE LA MARINA DE GUERRA EN LA CONTIENDA DEL 79. Lima: n.p., 1983.

330. Griffin, Charles C. "Francisco Encina and Revisionism in Chilean History." HISPANIC AMERICAN HISTORICAL REVIEW 37 (1957): 1-28.

331. ——, ed. LATIN AMERICA: A GUIDE TO THE HISTORICAL LITERATURE. Austin: University of Texas Press, 1971.

332. Griffith, William J. "The Historiography of Central America since 1830." HISPANIC AMERICAN HISTORICAL REVIEW 40 (1960): 549-69.

333. Grillo, Max. EMOCIONES DE LA GUERRA. Bogotá: n.p., 1903.

334. Grusin, Jay Robert. "The Revolution of 1848 in Colombia." Ph.D. dissertation, University of Arizona, 1978.

335. Guarderas, Francisco. EL VIEJO DE MONTECRISTI: BIOGRAFIA DE ALFARO. Quito: Editorial "La Union," 1953.

336. Guerra y Sánchez, Ramiro. GUERRA DE LOS DIEZ ANOS, 1868-1878. 2 vols. Havana: Cultural, 1950-52.

337. Guerrero, Mario Salcedo. "Vicente Guerrero's Struggle for Mexican Independence, 1810-1821." Ph.D. dissertation, University of California, Santa Barbara, 1977.

338. Gutiérrez de la Concha, José. MEMORIA SOBRE LA GUERRA DE LA ISLA DE CUBA Y SOBRE SU ESTADO POLITICO Y ECONOMICO DESDE ABRIL DE 1874 HASTA MARZO DE 1875. Madrid: Tip. de R. Labajos, 1875.

339. Gutiérrez Santos, Daniel. HISTORIA MILITAR DE MEXICO, 1876-1914. Mexico City: Ediciones Ateneo, 1955.

340. Guzmán Blanco, Antonio. EN DEFENSA DE LA CAUSA LIBERAL. Paris: Imp. de Lahure, 1894.

341. ——. DOCUMENTOS PARA LA HISTORIA. Caracas: Imp. de la "Opinión Nacional," 1876.

342. Guzmán y Raz Guzmán, Jesús. BIBLIOGRAFIA DE LA REFORMA, LA INTERVENCION Y EL IMPERIO. 2 vols. Mexico City: Sec. de Relaciones Exteriores, 1930-31.

343. Hahner, June E. "The Brazilian Armed Forces and the Overthrow of the Monarchy: Another Perspective." THE AMERICAS 26 (1969): 171-82.

344. ———. CIVIL-MILITARY RELATIONS IN BRAZIL, 1889-1898. Columbia: University of South Carolina Press, 1969.

345. ———. "Floriano Peixoto: Brazil's 'Iron Marshal'; A Re-Evaluation." THE AMERICAS 31 (1975): 252-71.

346. ———. "The Paulistas' Rise to Power: A Civilian Group Ends Military Rule." HISPANIC AMERICAN HISTORICAL REVIEW 47 (1967): 149-65.

347. Haigh, Roger. "The Creation and Control of a Caudillo." HISPANIC AMERICAN HISTORICAL REVIEW 44 (1964): 481-90.

348. Hale, Charles. MEXICAN LIBERALISM IN THE AGE OF MORA, 1821-1853. New Haven: Yale University Press, 1968.

349. ———. "The Reconstruction of Nineteenth-Century Politics in Spanish America: A Case for the History of Ideas." LATIN AMERICAN RESEARCH REVIEW 8 (1973): 53-73.

350. Halperín-Donghi, Tulio. THE AFTERMATH OF REVOLUTION IN LATIN AMERICA. New York: Harper and Row, 1973.

351. ———. ARGENTINA: DE LA REVOLUCION DE INDEPENDENCIA A LA CONFEDERACION ROSISTA. Buenos Aires: Editorial Paidós, 1972.

352. ———. GUERRAS Y FINANZAS EN LOS ORIGENES DEL ESTADO ARGENTINO, 1791-1850. Buenos Aires: Belgrano Colección Conflictos y Armonías, 1982.

353. ———. HISTORIA CONTEMPORANEA DE AMERICA LATINA. Madrid: Alianza Editorial, 1970.

354. ———. POLITICS, ECONOMICS AND SOCIETY IN ARGENTINA IN THE REVOLUTIONARY PERIOD. Cambridge: Cambridge University Press, 1975.

355. ———. PROYECTO Y CONSTRUCCION DE UNA NACION: ARGENTINA, 1846-1880. Caracas: Biblioteca Ayacucho, 1980.

356. ———. REVOLUCION Y GUERRA: FORMACION DE UNA ELITE DIRIGENTE EN LA ARGENTINA CRIOLLA. Buenos Aires: Siglo XXI Editores, 1972.

357. Hamill, Hugh M., Jr., ed. DICTATORSHIP IN SPANISH AMERICA. New York: Alfred A. Knopf, 1965.

358. Hamnett, Brian R. "Anastasio Bustamante y la guerra de independencia, 1810-1821." HISTORIA MEXICANA 28 (1979):515-45.

359. ———. "Factores regionales en la desintegración del régimen colonial en la Nueva España: El federalismo de 1823-1824." In LA FORMACION DEL ESTADO Y DE LA NACION EN HISPANOAMERICA, 305-18. Edited by Inge Buisson, Hans-Joachim König, and Horst Pietschmann. Cologne: Böhlau, 1984.

360. ———. "Partidos políticos mexicanos e intervención militar, 1823-1855." In AMERICA LATINA: DALLO STATO COLONIALE ALLO STATO NAZIONE, 1750-1940, 1:573-91. Edited by Antonio Annino, et al. Turin: Franco Angeli, 1987.

361. HANDBOOK OF LATIN AMERICAN STUDIES. 1935-.

362. Hans, Albert. LA GUERRE AU MEXIQUE SELON LES MEXICAINS: EDITION REVUE ET AUGMENTEE. Paris: Berger-Levrault et Cie., 1899.

363. Hardie, F. H. "The Mexican Army." JOURNAL OF THE MILITARY SERVICE INSTITUTION OF THE UNITED STATES 15 (1894): 1203-08.

364. Hart, John M. "Miguel Negrete: La epoyeya de un revolucionario." HISTORIA MEXICANA 2 4(1974): 70-93.

365. Helguera, J. León. "Antecedentes sociales de la Revolución de 1851 en el sur de Colombia, 1848-1849." ANUARIO COLOMBIANO DE HISTORIA SOCIAL Y DE LA CULTURA 5 (1979): 53-63.

366. ———. "The First Mosquera Administration in New Granada, 1845-1849." Ph.D. dissertation, University of North Carolina, 1958.

367. Helguera, J. León, and R.H. Davis, eds. ARCHIVO EPISTOLAR DEL GENERAL MOSQUERA. 3 vols. Bogotá: Editorial Kelly, 1966.

368. Hernández, Fortunato. LAS RAZAS INDIGENAS DE SONORA Y LA GUERRA DEL YAQUI. Mexico City: J. de Elizalde, 1902

369. Hernández de Alba, Guillermo, et al., eds. ARCHIVO EPISTOLAR DEL GENERAL DOMINGO CAYCEDO. 3 vols. Bogotá: Editorial ABC, 1943-47.

370. Hernández Rodríguez, Rosaura. "Comonfort y la intervención francesa." HISTORIA MEXICANA 13 (1963): 59-75.

371. ———. IGNACIO COMONFORT: TRAYECTORIA POLITICA; DOCUMENTOS. Mexico City: UNAM, 1967.

372. Herrick, Thomas. DESARROLLO ECONOMICO Y POLITICO DE GUATEMALA DURANTE EL PERIODO DE J.R. BARRIOS, 1871-1885. Guatemala City: Editora Universitaria, 1974.

373. Hodge, John E. "Julio Roca and Carlos Pellegrini: An Expedient Partnership." THE AMERICAS 32 (1976): 327-47.

374. Houdart-Morizot, Marie France. "Du bon usage des movements indiens: Rebelles et rebellions de la Sierra Gorda, Mexique, 1847-1849." CAHIERS DES AMERIQUES LATINES, no. 23 (1981): 47-100.

375. Hu-DeHart, Evelyn. YAQUI RESISTANCE AND SURVIVAL: THE STRUGGLE FOR LAND AND AUTONOMY. Madison: University of Wisconsin Press, 1984.

376. Huerta, Epitacio. APUNTES PARA SERVIR A LA HISTORIA DE LOS DEFENSORES DE PUEBLA QUE FUERON CONDUCIDOS PRISONEROS A FRANCIA. Mexico City: Imp. de Vicente G. Torres, 1868.

377. Humphreys, R. A. "Latin America: The Caudillo Tradition." In SOLDIERS AND GOVERNMENTS: NINE STUDIES IN CIVIL-MILITARY RELATIONS, 149-65. Edited by Michael Howard. Bloomington: Indiana University Press, 1959.

378. Ibarguren, Carlos. JUAN MANUEL DE ROSAS: SU VIDA, SU DRAMA, SU TIEMPO. Buenos Aires: Ediciones Theoria, 1961.

379. Iglesias, José María. REVISTAS HISTORICAS SOBRE LA INTERVENCION FRANCESA EN MEXICO. Mexico City: Editorial Porrúa, 1966. (Originally published 1867-69 in 3 vols.)

380. Ingersoll, Hazel. "The War of the Mountain: A Study of Reactionary Peasant Insurgency in Guatemala, 1837-1873." Ph.D. dissertation, University of Maryland, 1972.

381. Irazusta, Julio. VIDA POLITICA DE JUAN MANUEL DE ROSAS A TRAVES DE SU CORRESPONDENCIA. 8 vols. 2d ed. Buenos Aires: Editorial Huemul, 1970.

382. Islas García, Luis. MIRAMON: CABALLERO DEL INFORTUNIO. 2d ed. Mexico City: Editorial Jus, 1957.

383. Iturribarría, Jorge Fernando. PORFIRIO DIAZ ANTE LA HISTORIA. Mexico City: Carlos Villegas García, 1967.

384. Izard, Miguel. "Ni cuartreros ni montoneros: Llaneros." BOLETIN AMERICANISTA (Barcelona), 23 (1981): 83-142.

385. ———. "Oligarquías temblad, viva la libertad: Los llaneros del Apure y la Guerra Federal." BOLETIN AMERICANISTA (Barcelona), 32 (1982): 78-134.

386. ———. "Tanto pelear para terminar conversando: El caudillismo en Venezuela." NOVA AMERICANA (Turin) 2 (1979): 37-82.

387. Jane, Cecil. LIBERTY AND DESPOTISM IN SPANISH AMERICA. Oxford: Clarendon Press, 1929.

388. Javier, Thomas A. "The Mexican Army." HARPER'S NEW MONTHLY MAGAZINE 69 (1889): 813-27.

389. Jiménez Castellanos, Adolfo. SISTEMA PARA COMBATIR LAS INSURRECCIONES DE CUBA. Madrid: Establecimiento Tip., 1883.

390. Joffley, G. I. "Os quebraquilos: A revolta dos matutos contra os doutores." REVISTA DE HISTORIA 34 (1978): 69-145.

391. Kahle, Günter. MILITAR UND STAATSBILDUNG IN DEN ANFANGEN DER UNABHANIGKEIT MEXIKOS. Cologne: Böhlau, 1969.

392. Katz, Friedrich, ed. PORFIRIO DIAZ FRENTE AL DESCONTENTO POPULAR REGIONAL, 1891-1893. Mexico City: Universidad Iberoamericana, 1986.

393. Kératry, Emile de. CONTRAGUERRILLA FRANCESA EN MEXICO, 1864. Mexico City: SEP/80, 1981.

394. ———. LA CONTRE-GUERRILLA FRANCAISE AU MEXIQUE: SOUVENIRS DES TERRES CHAUDES. 2d ed. Paris: Librairie Internationale, 1869.

395. Kinsbruner, Jay. DIEGO PORTALES: INTERPRETATIVE ESSAYS ON THE MAN AND TIMES. The Hague: Mouton and Co., 1967.

396. Kitchens, John. "Some Considerations on the Rurales of Porfirian Mexico." JOURNAL OF LATIN AMERICAN STUDIES 9 (1967): 441-45.

397. Klein, Herbert S. BOLIVIA: THE EVOLUTION OF A MULTI-ETHNIC SOCIETY. New York: Oxford University Press, 1982.

398. Kolinski, Charles J. INDEPENDENCE OR DEATH!: THE STORY OF THE PARAGUAYAN WAR. Gainesville: University of Florida Press, 1965.

399. LaFrance, David G., and G. P. C. Thomson. "Juan Francisco Lucas: Patriarch of the Sierra Norte de Puebla." In THE HUMAN TRADITION IN LATIN AMERICA, 1-13. Edited by William H. Beezley and Judith Ewell. Wilmington: Scholarly Resources, 1987.

400. Lamadrid, Lázaro. "A Survey of the Historiography of Guatemala since 1821: Part 1, The Nineteenth Century." THE AMERICAS 8 (1951): 189-202.

401. Landaeta Rosales, Manuel. BIOGRAFIA DEL BENEMERITO GENERAL JOAQUIN CRESPO. Caracas: Imp. Bolívar, 1893.

402. ———. BIOGRAFIA DEL VALIENTE CIUDADANO GENERAL EZEQUIEL ZAMORA. Caracas: Ediciones Conmemorativas del Primer Centenario de la Revolución Federal (ECPCRF), 1961.

403. Langlois, Luis. INFLUENCIA DEL PODER NAVAL EN LA HISTORIA DE CHILE DESDE 1810 A 1910. Valparaíso: Imp. de la Armada, 1911.

404. Larrea, Carlos Manuel. BIBLIOGRAFIA CIENTIFICA DEL ECUADOR. Madrid: "Atlas," 1952.

405. Latorre, Benjamín. RECUERDOS DE CAMPANA, 1900-1902. Usaquén, Colombia: San Juan Eudes, 1938.

406. Laverde Amaya, Isidoro. APUNTES SOBRE LA BIOGRAFIA COLOMBIANA CON MUESTRAS ESCOGIDAS EN PROSA Y EN VERSO. Bogotá: Imp. de Zalamea Hermanos, 1882.

407. Lecuna, Vicente. LA REVOLUCION DE QUEIPA. Caracas: Ediciones Garrido, 1954.

408. Leitman, Spencer. RAIZES SOCIO-ECONOMICAS DA GUERRA DOS FARRAPOS. Rio de Janeiro: Graal, 1979.

409. ———. "Socio-Economic Roots of the Ragamuffin War: A Chapter in Early Brazilian History." Ph.D. dissertation, University of Texas, Austin, 1972.

410. Lemaitre Román, Eduardo. EL GENERAL JUAN JOSE NIETO Y SU EPOCA. Bogotá: C. Valencia Editores, 1983.

411. ———, ed. EPISTOLARIO DE RAFAEL NUNEZ CON MIGUEL ANTONIO CARO. Bogotá: n.p., 1977.

412. Lemos Guzmán, A.J. OBANDO, 1795-1861. Popayán: Instituto del Libro, 1959.

413. León S., Leonardo. "Alianzas militares entre los indios araucanos y los grupos indios de las pampas: La rebelión araucana de 1867-1872 en Argentina y Chile." NUEVA HISTORIA (London) 1 (1981): 3-49.

414. ——. "The Araucanian Rebellion of 1867-1872 in Argentina and Chile." M.A. thesis, University of London, 1979.

415. Levine, Robert M. PERNAMBUCO IN THE BRAZILIAN FEDERATION, 1889-1937. Stanford: Stanford University Press, 1978.

416. Lewin, Linda. "The Oligarchical Limitations of Social Banditry in Brazil: The Case of the 'Good' Thief Antonio Silvino." PAST AND PRESENT 82(1979): 116-46.

417. ——. "Politics and 'Parentela': A Case Study of Oligarchy in Brazil's Old Republic, 1889-1930." Ph.D. dissertation, Columbia University, 1976.

418. Liévano Aguirre, Indalecio. RAFAEL NUNEZ. Bogotá: Instituto Colombiano de Cultura, 1977.

419. Llanos y Alcarraz, Adolfo. TACTICA DEL GUERRILLERO. Mexico City: n.p., 1878.

420. Llorens y Maceo, José Silvino. CON MACEO EN LA INVASION. Havana: Duarte y Uriarte, 1928.

421. Lofstrom, William Lee. "The Promise and Problem of Reform: Attempted Social and Economic Change in the First Years of Bolivian Independence." Ph.D. dissertation, Cornell University, 1972.

422. Lombardi, John V., et al. VENEZUELAN HISTORY: A COMPREHENSIVE WORKING BIBLIOGRAPHY. Boston: G.K. Hall, 1977.

423. Loor, Wilfrido. CARTAS DE GABRIEL GARCIA MORENO. 4 vols. Quito: Prensa Católica, 1953-55.

424. López, Jacinto. HISTORIA DE LA GUERRA DEL GUANO Y EL SALITRE. New York: De Laisne and Rossboro, 1931. (2d ed., Lima, 1980.)

425. López Contreras, Eleazar. PAGINAS PARA LA HISTORIA MILITAR DE VENEZUELA. Caracas: Tip. Americana, 1944.

426. López de Santa Anna, Antonio. MI HISTORIA MILITAR Y POLITICA, 1810-1904. Mexico City: Vda. de C. Bouret, 1905.

427. López Donato, Indalecio. LA GUERRA ANTE LA OPINION PUBLICA: MUERTOS Y PRESENTADOS DEL INSURRECTO; FUERZA MORAL DE LA AUTORIDAD. Havana: Imp. Militar de la Vda. de Soler, 1873.

428. López-Portillo y Rojas, José. ELEVACION Y CAIDA DE PORFIRIO DIAZ. Mexico City: Librería Española, 1920.

429. López U., Carlos. LA HISTORIA DE LA MARINA DE CHILE. Santiago: Editorial Andrés Bello, 1969.

430. Love, Joseph. RIO GRANDE DO SUL AND BRAZILIAN REGIONALISM, 1882-1903. Stanford: Stanford University Press, 1971.

431. ———. SAO PAULO IN THE BRAZILIAN FEDERATION, 1889-1937. Stanford: Stanford University Press, 1980.

432. Loveman, Brian. CHILE: THE LEGACY OF HISPANIC CAPITALISM. 2d ed. New York: Oxford University Press, 1988.

433. Lozoya, Jorge Alberto. EL EJERCITO MEXICANO. 3d ed. Mexico City: El Colegio de México, 1984.

434. ———. "Un guión para el estudio de los ejércitos mexicanos en el siglo diecinueve." HISTORIA MEXICANA 17 (1968): 553-68.

435. Lynch, John. ARGENTINE DICTATOR: JUAN MANUEL DE ROSAS, 1829-1852. Oxford: Oxford University Press, 1981.

436. ———. "Bolívar and the Caudillos." HISPANIC AMERICAN HISTORICAL REVIEW 63 (1983): 2-35.

437. ———. "Los caudillos como agentes del orden social: Venezuela y Argentina, 1820-1850." In AMERICA LATINA: DALLO STATO COLONIALE ALLO STATO NAZIONE, 1750-1940, 1:483-500. Edited by Antonio Annino, et al. Turin: Franco Angeli, 1987.

438. ———. "Los caudillos de la independencia: Enemigos y agentes del estado-nación." PROBLEMAS DE LA FORMACION DEL ESTADO Y DE LA NACION EN HISPANOAMERICA, 197-218. Edited by Inge Buisson, Hans-Joachim König, and Horst Pietschmann. Cologne: Böhlau, 1984.

439. McCann, Frank D. "The Nation in Arms: Obligatory Military Service during the Old Republic." In ESSAYS CONCERNING THE SOCIO-ECONOMIC HISTORY OF BRAZIL AND PORTUGUESE INDIA, 211-43. Edited by Dauril Alden and Warren Dean. Gainesville: University Presses of Florida, 1977.

440. McCreery, David. "Coffee and Class: The Structure of Development in Liberal Guatemala." HISPANIC AMERICAN HISTORICAL REVIEW 56 (1976): 438-60.

441. ———. DEVELOPMENT AND THE STATE IN REFORMED GUATEMALA, 1871-1885. Athens: Ohio University Press, 1985.

442. Machuca, Francisco. LAS CUATRO CAMPANAS DE LA GUERRA DEL PACIFICO. Valparaíso: Imp. Victoria, 1926-30.

443. McLynn, Francis James. "The Causes of the War of the Triple Alliance: An Interpretation." INTER-AMERICAN ECONOMIC AFFAIRS 33 (1979): 21-43.

444. ———. "Consequences for Argentina of the War of the Triple Alliance, 1865-1870." THE AMERICAS 41 (1984): 81-98.

445. ———. "Political Instability in Córdoba Province during the 1860s." IBERO-AMERIKANISCHES ARCHIV 6(1980): 251-69.

446. ———. "Urquiza and the Montoneros: An Ambiguous Chapter in Argentine History." IBERO-AMERIKANISCHES ARCHIV 8 (1982): 283-95.

447. Magalhães, Raymundo de. DEODORO: A ESPADA CONTRA O IMPERIO. 2 vols. São Paulo: Companhia Editôra Nacional, 1957.

448. Mallon, Florencia. THE DEFENSE OF COMMUNITY IN PERU'S CENTRAL HIGHLANDS: PEASANT STRUGGLE AND CAPITALIST TRANSITION, 1860-1940. Princeton: Princeton University Press, 1983.

449. Malo, H., and E. Ayala, eds. ECUADOR, 1830-1980: POLITICA Y SOCIEDAD. Quito: n.p., 1980.

450. Manrique, Nelson. CAMPESINADO Y NACION: LAS GUERRILLAS INDIGENAS EN LA GUERRA CON CHILE. Lima: Editorial Ital, 1981.

451. ———. "La Guerra del Pacífico y los conflictos de clase: Los terratenientes de la sierra del Perú." ANALISIS 6 (1978): 56-71.

452. ———. "Los movimientos campesinos en la Guerra del Pacífico." ALLPANCHIS 11-12 (1978): 71-101.

453. Mansilla, Lucio Victorio. UNA EXCURSION A LOS INDIOS RANQUELES. 2 vols. Buenos Aires: Imp., Litografía y Fundición de Tipos, 1870.

454. Marcella, Gabriel. "The Structure of Politics in Nineteenth-Century Spanish America: The Chilean Oligarchy, 1833-1891." Ph.D. dissertation, University of Notre Dame, 1973.

455. Markham, Clements R. THE WAR BETWEEN PERU AND CHILE. London: Sampson, Low, 1883.

456. Marroquín Rojas, Clemente. MORAZAN Y CARRERA. Guatemala City: Editorial José de Pineda e Ibarra, 1971.

457. Martí Pérez, José. EL GENERAL GOMEZ. Havana: Ediciones Políticas, 1986.

458. Martínez Carreño, Aida, ed. ASPECTOS POLEMICOS DE LA HISTORIA COLOMBIANA DEL SIGLO XIX: MEMORIA DE UN SEMANARIO. Bogotá: Fondo Cultural Cafetero, 1983.

459. Martínez Sánchez, Antonio. NUESTRAS CONTIENDAS CIVILES. Caracas: Tip. Garrido, 1949.

460. Marure, Alejandro. BOSQUEJO HISTORICO DE LAS REVOLUCIONES DE CENTROAMERICA DESDE 1821 HASTA 1834. Guatemala City: Tip. de "El Progreso," 1877-78.

461. Masuera Y Masuera, Aurelio. MEMORIAS DE UN REVOLUCIONARIO. Bogotá: n.p., 1938.

462. Mathews, R.P. VIOLENCIA RURAL EN VENEZUELA, 1840-1858: ANTECEDENTES SOCIO-ECONOMICOS DE LA GUERRA FEDERAL. Caracas: Colección Temas Venezolanos, 1977.

463. Mauyanet, Santiago [Rubén Abel]. UN HEROE DEL EJERCITO LIBERTADOR DE CUBA: APUNTES PARA LA BIOGRAFIA DEL CORONEL CECILIO GONZALEZ. Puerto Plata: Imp. del Comercio, 1878.

464. Mayer, John. "El llanero." THE ATLANTIC MONTHLY 3 (1859): 174-88.

465. Mayo, John. "A Company War?: The Antofagasta Company and the Outbreak of the War of the Pacific." BOLETIN DE ESTUDIOS LATINOAMERICANOS Y DEL CARIBE 28 (1980): 3-11.

466. Mendiburu, Manuel de. BIOGRAFIAS DE GENERALES REPUBLICANOS. Lima: Instituto Histórico del Perú, Academia Nacional de la Historia, 1963.

467. ———. DICCIONARIO HISTORICO-BIOGRAFICO DEL PERU. 11 vols. Lima: Imp. "Enrique Palacios," 1931-34.

468. Mendoza Meléndez, Eduardo. HISTORIA DE LA CAMPANA DE BRENA. Lima: Editorial Milla Batres, 1981.

469. Mexico. Secretaría de Defensa Nacional. GUIA DEL ARCHIVO HISTORICO MILITAR DE MEXICO. Mexico City: Sec. de Defensa Nacional, 1949.

470. Meyer, Jean. ESPERANDO A LOZADA. Zamora: El Colegio de Michoacán, 1984.

471. ———. PROBLEMAS CAMPESINOS Y REVUELTAS AGRARIAS, 1821- 1910. Mexico City: SepSetentas, 1973.

472. Meyer, Michael C., and William L. Sherman. THE COURSE OF MEXICAN HISTORY. 3d ed. New York: Oxford University Press, 1987.

473. Miceli, Keith. "Rafael Carrera: Defender and Promoter of Peasant Interests in Guatemala, 1837-1848." THE AMERICAS 31 (1974): 72-95.

474. Michelena, Tomás. RESUMEN DE LA VIDA MILITAR Y POLITICA DEL CIUDADANO ESCLARECIDO GENERAL JOSE ANTONIO PAEZ. 2d ed. Caracas: Academia de Historia, 1973. (Originally published 1890.)

475. Mijares, Augusto. DOCUMENTOS RELATIVOS A LA INSURRECCION DE JUAN FRANCISCO DE LEON. Caracas: Instituto Panamericano de Geografía e Historia, 1949.

476. Miller, David Lynn. "Porfirio Díaz and the Army of the East." Ph.D. dissertation, University of Michigan, 1960.

477. Miller, Rory. "The Coastal Elite and Peruvian Politics, 1895-1919." JOURNAL OF LATIN AMERICAN STUDIES 14 (1982): 97-120.

478. Miró, José. CRONICAS DE LA GUERRA: LA CAMPANA DE LA INVASION. Havana: Editorial Lex, 1942.

479. Mitre, Bartolomé. ARCHIVO DEL GENERAL MITRE: DOCUMENTOS Y CORRESPONDENCIA. 28 vols. Buenos Aires: Biblioteca de "La Nación," 1911-14.

480. ———. CORRESPONDENCIA LITERARIA, HISTORICA Y POLITICA DEL GENERAL MITRE. 3 vols. Buenos Aires: Imp. de Coni Hermanos, 1912.

481. ———. CORRESPONDENCIA MITRE-ELIZALDE. Vol. 26, DOCUMENTOS PARA LA HISTORIA ARGENTINA. Buenos Aires: Universidad de Buenos Aires, 1960.

482. Mörner, Magnus. "Caudillos y militares en la evolución hispanoamericana." JOURNAL OF LATIN AMERICAN STUDIES 2 (1960): 295-310.

483. Molina, Cristóbal. WAR OF THE CASTES: INDIAN UPRISING IN CHIAPAS, 1867-1870. New Orleans: Dept. of Middle American Research, Tulane University, 1934.

484. Montúfar, Lorenzo. RESENA HISTORICA DE CENTRO AMERICA. 7 vols. Guatemala City: Tip. de "El Progreso," 1878-88.

485. Moorhead, Max Leon. "Rafael Carrera of Guatemala: His Life and Times." Ph.D. dissertation, University of California, Berkeley, 1942.

486. Morazán, General Francisco. MEMORIAS DEL BENEMERITO.... 2d ed. Tegucigalpa: Oficina de Relaciones Públicas, La Presidencia, 1971. (Originally published, Paris, 1870.)

487. Moreno de Angel, Pilar, ed. CORRESPONDENCIA Y DOCUMENTOS DEL GENERAL JOSE MARIA CORDOVA. 2 vols. Bogotá: Ed. Kelly, 1974.

488. Moreno de Cáceres, Antonia. RECUERDOS DE LA CAMPANA DE LA BRENA: MEMORIAS. Lima: Editorial C. Milla Batres, 1974.

489. Moreno Valle, L. CATALOGO DE LA COLECCION LAFRAGUA DE LA BIBLIOTECA NACIONAL DE MEXICO. Mexico City: UNAM, 1975.

490. Moreyra y Paz Soldán, Carlos. BIBLIOGRAFIA REGIONAL PERUANA. Lima: Librería Internacional del Perú, 1867.

491. Morse, Richard. "The Heritage of Latin America." In THE FOUNDING OF NEW SOCIETIES, 123-77. Edited by Louis Hartz. New York: Harcourt, Brace and World, 1964.

492. ———. "Toward a Theory of Spanish American Government." JOURNAL OF THE HISTORY OF IDEAS 15 (1954): 71-93.

493. Morton, F. W. O. "The Conservative Revolution of Independence: Economy, Society and Politics in Bahia, 1790-1840." Ph.D. dissertation, Oxford University, 1974.

494. Moya, Francisco Javier de. CONSIDERACIONES MILITARES SOBRE LA CAMPANA DE CUBA. Madrid: Imp. del Cuerpo de Artillería, 1901.

495. Muñoz y Pérez, Daniel. EL GENERAL DON JUAN ALVAREZ: ENSAYO BIOGRAFICO SEGUIDO EN UNA

SELECCION DE DOCUMENTOS. Mexico City: Editoral Academia Literaria, 1959.

496. Murray, Paul V. "La historiografía mexicana sobre la Guerra de 1847." REVISTA DE DERECHO Y CIENCIAS SOCIALES 21 (1948): 173-89.

497. Naro, Nancy Priscilla. "The 1848 Praiera Revolt in Brazil." Ph.D. dissertation, University of Chicago, 1981.

498. Navarro, Fabián. LA CUESTION DE CUBA: ORIGEN, CARACTER, VICISITUDES Y CAUSAS DE LA PROLONGACION DE AQUELLA GUERRA; MEMORIA POLITICO-MILITAR ESCRITA POR UN TESTIGO PRESENCIAL. Madrid: Tip. de A. Bacaycoa, 1878.

499. Naylor, Bernard. ACCOUNTS OF NINETEENTH-CENTURY SOUTH AMERICA: AN ANNOTATED CHECKLIST OF WORKS BY BRITISH AND UNITED STATES OBSERVERS. London: Athlone Press, 1969.

500. Newton, Jorge. ESTANISLAO LOPEZ: EL PATRIARCA DE LA FEDERACION. Buenos Aires: Colección Caudillo Argentino, 1964.

501. ———. FACUNDO QUIROGA: AVENTURA Y LEYENDA. Buenos Aires: Colección Caudillo Argentino, 1965.

502. ———. FRANCISCO RAMIREZ: EL SUPREMO ENTER-RIANO. Buenos Aires: Colección Caudillo Argentino, 1964.

503. ———. FRANCISCO REINAFE: EL PROMOTOR DE BARRANCA YACO. Buenos Aires: Plus Ultra, 1974.

504. ———. EL GENERAL ROCA: CONQUISTADOR DEL DESIERTO. Buenos Aires: Claridad, 1966.

505. ———. GUEMES: EL CAUDILLO DE LA GUERRA GAUCHA. Buenos Aires: Colección Caudillo Argentino, 1971.

506. ———. JUAN FELIPE IBARRA: EL CAUDILLO DE LA SELVA. Buenos Aires: Plus Ultra, 1972.

507. ———. MANUEL TABOABA: CAUDILLO UNITARIO. Buenos

Aires: Plus Ultra, 1972.

508. ———. RICARDO LOPEZ JORDAN: ULTIMO CAUDILLO EN ARMAS. Buenos Aires: Colección Caudillo Argentino, 1965.

509. ———. URQUIZA: EL VENCEDOR DE LA TIRANIA. Buenos Aires: Biblioteca de Grandes Biografías, 1961.

510. Norris, Robert E. GUIA BIBLIOGRAFICA PARA EL ESTUDIO DE LA HISTORIA ECUATORIANA. Austin: Institute of Latin American Studies, University of Texas, 1978.

511. Novo y Colson, Pedro de. HISTORIA DE LA GUERRA DE ESPAÑA EN EL PACIFICO. Madrid: Imp. de Fortanet, 1882.

512. Novoa de la Fuente, Luis. HISTORIA NAVAL DE CHILE. 3d ed. Valparaíso: Escuela Naval "Arturo Prat," 1958.

513. Nunes Leal, Víctor. CORONELISMO, MUNICIPALITY AND REPUBLICAN GOVERNMENT IN BRAZIL. London: Cambridge University Press, 1977.

514. Obando Espinosa, José María. APUNTAMIENTOS PARA LA HISTORIA. 2 vols. Bogotá: Ministerio de Educación, 1945. (Originally published 1842.)

515. ———. EPISODIOS DE LA VIDA DEL GENERAL JOSE MARIA OBANDO: SU VIAJE AL PERU POR EL PUTUMAYO Y MARANON, AMAZONAS. Bogotá: Biblioteca de Historia Nacional, 1973.

516. O'Connor D'Arlach, Tomás. EL GENERAL MELGAREJO: HECHOS Y DICHOS DE ESTE HOMBRE CELEBRE. La Paz: González y Medino, 1909. (Republished 1954, 1964.)

517. ———. LOS PRESIDENTES DE BOLIVIA DESDE 1825 HASTA 1912. La Paz: González y Medina, 1912.

518. ———. ROZAS, FRANCIA Y MELGAREJO. La Paz: González y Medina, 1914.

519. Odriozola, Manuel de, ed. DOCUMENTOS HISTORICOS DEL PERU. 10 vols. Lima: Tip. de A. Alfaro, 1863-77.

520. O'Gorman, Edmundo. GUIA BIBLIOGRAFICA DE CARLOS MARIA DE BUSTAMANTE. Mexico City: Fundación Cultural de Condumex, 1967.

521. Olveda, Jaime. GORDIANO GUZMAN: UN CACIQUE DEL SIGLO XIX. Mexico City: Instituto Nacional de Antropología e Historia, 1980.

522. Oñate Gómez, Enrique de. ALBUM DE LA GUERRA HISPANO-AMERICANA. Havana: n.p., 1925.

523. Ortega, Luis. "Nitrates, Chilean Entrepreneurs and the Origins of the War of the Pacific." JOURNAL OF LATIN AMERICAN STUDIES 16 (1984): 381-402.

524. Ortega Arancibia, Francisco. CUARENTA ANOS (1838-1878) DE HISTORIA DE NICARAGUA. 3d ed. Managua: Banco de América, 1975.

525. Ortiz, Sergio Elías, and Luis Martínez Delgado, eds. EPISTOLARIO Y DOCUMENTOS OFICIALES DEL GENERAL JOSE MARIA OBANDO. 4 vols. Bogotá: Editorial Kelly, 1973.

526. Ortiz, Venancio. HISTORIA DE LA REVOLUCION DEL 17 DE ABRIL DE 1854. Bogotá: Imp. Banco Popular, 1972.

527. Otero, Mariano. ENSAYO SOBRE EL VERDADERO ESTADO DE LA CUESTION SOCIAL Y POLITICA QUE SE AGITA EN LA REPUBLICA MEXICANA. Mexico City: I. Cumplido, 1842. (2d ed., Guadalajara: Ediciones I.T.G., 1952.)

528. Ouro Preto, Affonso Celso de Assis Figuereido, Visconde de. ADVENTO DA DITADURA MILITAR NO BRASIL. Paris: F. Pichon, 1891.

529. Ovalles, Víctor Manuel. LLANEROS AUTENTICOS. Caracas: Editorial Bolívar, 1935.

530. Pachano, Jacinto Regino. BIOGRAFIA DEL MARISCAL JUAN C. FALCON. Paris: E.D. Schmitz, 1876. (2d ed., Caracas: ECPCRF, 1960.)

531. Páez, Jorge. LA CONQUISTA DEL DESIERTO. Buenos Aires:
      Centro Editor de América Latina, 1970.

532. Páez, General José Antonio. AUTOBIOGRAFIA. 2d ed. New
      York: H.R. Elliot, 1941. [Reprinted 1971.]

533. Páez, Ramón. WILD SCENES IN SOUTH AMERICA: OR
      LIFE ON THE LLANOS OF VENEZUELA. New York: C.
      Scribner, 1862.

534. Palacio, Julio H. LA GUERRA DE 85. Bogotá: C. Roldán y
      Cía., 1936.

535. Palleja, Coronel León de. DIARIO DE LA CAMPANA DE LAS
      FUERZAS ARMADAS CONTRA EL PARAGUAY. 2 vols.
      Montevideo: Ministerio de Instrucción Pública y Previsión Social,
      1960.

536. Pang, Eul-Soo. BAHIA IN THE FIRST BRAZILIAN
      REPUBLIC: CORONELISMO AND OLIGARCHIES, 1889-
      1934. Gainesville: University Presses of Florida, 1979.

537. Parada, Nemecio. VISPERAS Y COMIENZOS DE LA
      REVOLUCION DE CIPRIANO CASTRO. 2d ed. Caracas: n.p.,
      1968.

538. Paredes, Antonio. COMO LLEGO CIPRIANO CASTRO AL
      PODER. 2d ed. Caracas: Garrido, 1954.

539. Paredes Y Arrillaga Archive (University of Texas Library,
      Austin).

540. Pareja y Diezcanseco, Alfredo. LA HOGUERA BARBARA:
      VIDA DE ELOY ALFARO. Mexico City: Cía. General Editora,
      1944.

541. París Lozano, Gonzalo. GUERRILLEROS DE TOLIMA.
      Manizales: n.p., 1937.

542. Park, James W. RAFAEL NUNEZ AND THE POLITICS OF
      COLOMBIAN REGIONALISM, 1863-1886. Baton Rouge:
      Louisiana State University Press, 1985.

543. ———. "Regionalism as a Factor in Colombia's 1875 Election." THE AMERICAS 42 (1986): 453-72.

544. Parkerson, Phillip T. "Sub-Regional Integration in Nineteenth-Century South America: Andrés Santa Cruz and the Peru-Bolivia Confederation, 1835-1839." Ph.D. dissertation, University of Florida, 1979.

545. Parkes, Henry B. A HISTORY OF MEXICO. Boston: Houghton Mifflin, 1938.

546. Parra, Aquileo. MEMORIAS. Bogotá: Librería Colombiana, 1912.

547. Patee, R. GABRIEL GARCIA MORENO Y EL ECUADOR DE SU TIEMPO. 3d ed. Mexico City: Editorial Jus, 1962.

548. Paz, Ireneo. ALGUNAS CAMPANAS: MEMORIAS. 3 vols. 2d ed. Mexico City: Imp. de I. Paz, 1884-85.

549. Paz, General José María. MEMORIAS POSTUMAS: CAMPANA CONTRA ROSAS. Madrid: Editorial América, 1917. (Republished, Buenos Aires: Ed. Almnueva, 1940.)

550. Paz Soldán, Mariano Felipe. NARRACION HISTORICA DE LA GUERRA DE CHILE CONTRA EL PERU Y BOLIVIA. Buenos Aires: Imp. de Mayo, 1884.

551. Peloso, Vincent C. "Cotton Planters, the State and Rural Labor Policy: Ideological Origins of the Peruvian *República Aristocrática*, 1895-1908." THE AMERICAS 40 (1983): 209-28.

552. Peña, Antonio de la, ed. LA PRIMERA GUERRA ENTRE MEXICO Y FRANCIA: ARCHIVO HISTORICO DIPLOMATICO MEXICANO. 2d ser. Vol. 23. Mexico City: Sec. de Relaciones Exteriores, 1927.

553. Pérez, Louis A. CUBA BETWEEN EMPIRES, 1878-1902. Pittsburgh: University of Pittsburgh Press, 1983.

554. Pérez Acosta, Juan Francisco. DON CARLOS ANTONIO LOPEZ: "OBRERO MAXIMO." Asunción: Editorial Guarnia, 1948.

555. Pérez Cabrera, José Manuel. HISTORIOGRAFIA DE CUBA. Mexico City: Instituto Panamericano de Geografía e Historia, 1962.

556. Pérez Gallardo, Basilio. MARTIROLOGIO DE LA DEFENSA DE LA INDEPENDENCIA DE MEXICO, 1863-1867. Mexico City: Imp. del Gobierno en Palacio, 1875.

557. Pérez Teneiro, Colonel Tomás. "Cipriano Castro: Ensayo de interpretación militar." FUERZAS ARMADAS DE VENEZUELA 158-159(1959): 14-22.

558. Perry, Laurens Ballard. INVENTARIO Y GUIA DE LA COLECCION GENERAL PORFIRIO DIAZ. Mexico City: University of the Americas Press, 1969.

559. ———. JUAREZ AND DIAZ: MACHINE POLITICS IN MEXICO. DeKalb: Northern Illinois University Press, 1978.

560. Phillips, Richard S. "Bolivia in the War of the Pacific, 1879-1884." Ph.D. dissertation, University of Virginia, 1973.

561. Pichardo Viñals, Hortensia. DOCUMENTOS PARA LA HISTORIA DE CUBA. 4 vols. Havana: Editorial de Ciencias Sociales, 1976.

562. Picón Salas, Mariano. LOS DIAS DE CIPRIANO CASTRO. Caracas: Ediciones Garrido, 1953.

563. Piedra Martel, Manuel. CAMPANAS DE MACEO EN LA ULTIMA GUERRA DE INDEPENDENCIA. Havana: Editorial Lex, 1946.

564. Pike, Fredrick B. THE MODERN HISTORY OF PERU. New York: Praeger Publisher, 1967.

565. Pino González, Juan José del. LAS SUBLEVACIONES INDIGENAS DE HUANTA, 1827-1896. Ayacucho: n.p., 1955.

566. Pino Iturrieta, Elías. CASTRO: EPISTOLARIO PRESIDENCIAL, 1899-1908. Caracas: Universidad Central de Venezuela, 1974.

567. Platt, Tristan. "Estado tributario y librecambio en Potosí durante el siglo XIX: Mercado indígena y lucha de ideologías monetarias" In AMERICA LATINA: DALLO STATO COLONIALE ALLO STATO NAZIONE, 1750-1940, 1:98-143. Edited by Antonio Annino, et al. Turin: Franco Angeli, 1987.

568. ———. "Liberalism and Ethnocide in the Southern Andes." HISTORY WORKSHOP 17 (1984): 3-18.

569. Plazas Olarte, Guillermo. CRONICAS MILITARES. Bogotá: Servicio Imp. y Publicaciones de las Fuerzas Armadas, 1963.

570. Pomer, León. LA GUERRA DE PARAGUAY: ¡GRAN NEGOCIO! Buenos Aires: Ediciones Calden, 1968.

571. Ponte Domínguez, Francisco. HISTORIA DE LA GUERRA DE LOS DIEZ ANOS. Havana: A. Muniz y Hno., 1944. (2d ed., 1972.)

572. Porfirio Díaz Archive (Universidad Iberoamericana, Mexico City).

573. Porras, Belisario. MEMORIAS DE LAS CAMPANAS DEL ISTMO, 1900. Panama City: Imp. Nacional, 1922.

574. Porras Barrenchea, Raúl. FUENTES HISTORICAS PERUANAS. Lima: n.p., 1963.

575. Portilla, Anselmo de la. HISTORIA DE LA REVOLUCION DE MEXICO CONTRA LA DICTADURA DEL GENERAL SANTA ANNA, 1853-1855. 2d ed. Puebla: Editorial Cajica, 1972. (Originally published 1856.)

576. ———. MEJICO EN 1856 Y 1857: GOBIERNO DEL GENERAL COMONFORT. New York: S. Hallet, 1858.

577. Posada Gutiérrez, Joaquín. MEMORIAS HISTORIO-POLITICAS. 4 vols. Bogotá: Biblioteca Popular de Cultura Colombiana, 1951. [Originally published 1929.]

578. Prado, Eduardo Paulo de Silva. FASTOS DA DITADURA MILITAR NO BRASIL. São Paulo: Escola Typ. Salesiana, 1902.

579. Prado, Manuel. LA CONQUISTA DE LA PAMPA. Buenos Aires: Librería Hachette, 1960.

580. Prieto, Guillermo. MEMORIAS DE MIS TIEMPOS, 1840 A 1853. Puebla: Editorial Patria, 1869.

581. Queiroz, María Isaura Pereira de. OS CANGACEIROS. São Paulo: Livraria Duas Cidades, 1977.

582. ———. O MANDONISMO LOCAL NA VIDA POLITICA BRASILEIRA. São Paulo: Editôra Alfa-Omega, 1976.

583. Quesada, Ernesto. LA EPOCA DE ROSAS: SU VERDADERO CARACTER HISTORICO. Buenos Aires: A. Moen, 1898.

584. Quevedo y Zubieta, Salvador. EL CAUDILLO: CONTINUACION DE PORFIRIO DIAZ; ENSAYO DE PSICOLOGIA HISTORICA, SEPTIEMBRE 1865- NOVIEMBRE 1876. Mexico City: Vda. de C. Bouret, 1909.

585. ———. EL GENERAL GONZALEZ Y SU GOBIERNO EN MEXICO. 2 vols. Mexico City: Patoni, 1884-85.

586. ———. PORFIRIO DIAZ, SEPTIEMBRE 1830-SEPTIEMBRE 1865: ENSAYO DE PSICOLOGIA HISTORICA. Mexico City: Vda. de C. Bouret, 1906.

587. Quirarte, Martín. HISTORIOGRAFIA SOBRE EL IMPERIO DE MAXIMILIANO. Mexico City: Instituto de Investigaciones Históricas, UNAM, 1970.

588. Quiroga, Juan Facundo. ARCHIVO DEL BRIGADIER GENERAL JUAN FACUNDO QUIROGA, 1815-1821. 2 Vols. Buenos Aires: Universidad de Buenos Aires, 1957-60.

589. Racedo, Eduardo. LA CONQUISTA DEL DESIERTO. Buenos Aires: n.p., 1921.

590. Ramírez, Gilberto, Jr. "The Reform of the Argentine Army, 1890-1904." Ph.D. dissertation, University of Texas, Austin, 1987.

591. Ramírez Fentanes, Luis. COLECCION DE LOS DOCUMENTOS MAS IMPORTANTES RELATIVOS AL C. GENERAL DE DIVISION VICENTE GUERRERO:

BENEMERITO DE LA PATRIA; QUE EXISTEN EN EL ARCHIVO HISTORICO MILITAR DE LA SECRETARIA DE LA DEFENSA NACIONAL. Mexico City: Sec. de Defensa Nacional, 1955.

592. ———. ZARAGOZA. Mexico City: Sec. de Defensa Nacional, 1962.

593. Ramírez Sánchez, Captain Francisco. MAYOR GENERAL MAXIMO GOMEZ: SUS CAMPANAS MILITARES, 1868-1898. Havana: Editora Política, 1986.

594. Ramos Zúniga, Antonio. LAS ARMAS DEL EJERCITO MAMBI. Havana: Editora Política, 1984.

595. Rausch, Jane M. "The Taming of a Colombian Caudillo: Juan Nepomuceno Moreno of Casanare." THE AMERICAS 42 (1986): 275-88.

596. Reátegui Chávez, Wilson. LA GUERRA DEL PACIFICO. Lima: Universidad Nacional Mayor de San Marcos, 1980.

597. Reber, Vera Blinn. "The Demographics of Paraguay: A Reinterpretation of the Great War, 1864-70." HISPANIC AMERICAN HISTORICAL REVIEW 68 (1988): 289-320.

598. Reed, Nelson. THE CASTE WAR OF YUCATAN. Stanford: Stanford University Press, 1964.

599. Reina, Leticia. LAS REBELIONES CAMPESINAS EN MEXICO, 1819-1906. Mexico City: Siglo XXI Editores, 1980.

600. Reparaz, Gonzalo de. LA GUERRA DE CUBA: ESTUDIO MILITAR. Madrid: La Espana, 1896.

601. Restrepo, José Manuel. DIARIO POLITICO Y MILITAR. 4 vols. Bogotá: Imp. Nacional, 1954.

602. Reyes, Bernardo. EL EJERCITO MEXICANO. Mexico City: J. Ballesca y Cía., 1901.

603. Reyes, Oscar Efraén. VIDA DE JUAN MONTALVO. Quito: Imp. Nacional, 1935.

604. Rippy, J. Fred, and Clyde E. Hewitt. "Cipriano Castro: 'Man without a Country.'" AMERICAN HISTORICAL REVIEW 55 (1949): 36-53.

605. Riva Palacio, Vicente. MEXICO A TRAVES DE LOS SIGLOS. 5 vols. Barcelona: Espasa, 1889.

606. Rivera Cambas, Manuel. HISTORIA DE LA INTERVENCION EUROPEA Y NORTEAMERICANA EN MEXICO Y DEL IMPERIO DE MAXIMILIANO DE HAPSBURGO. 5 vols. Mexico City: Aguilar, 1888.

607. Roa Bárcena, José María. RECUERDOS DE LA INVASION NORTEAMERICANA, 1846-1848. 3 vols. Mexico City: Editorial Porrúa, 1947.

608. Robalino Dávila, Luis. "García Moreno." In ORIGENES DEL ECUADOR DE HOY. vol. 4. Quito: Talleres Gráficos Nacionales, 1949.

609. Robertson, Frank Delbert. "The Military and Political Career of Mariano Paredes y Arrillaga, 1797-1849." Ph.D. dissertation, University of Texas, Austin, 1955.

610. Robertson, John Parish, and William Parish Robertson. FRANCIA'S REIGN OF TERROR. London: John Murray, 1839.

611. ———. LETTERS ON PARAGUAY. 3 vols. London: John Murray, 1838-39.

612. Robertson, William Spence. ITURBIDE OF MEXICO. Durham: Duke University Press, 1952.

613. Robles, Vito Alessio. LA CORRESPONDENCIA DE AGUSTIN DE ITURBIDE DESPUES DE LA PROCLAMACION DEL PLAN DE IGUALA. 2 vols. Mexico City: Sec. de Defensa Nacional, 1945.

614. Rodríguez, Adolfo. EZEQUIEL ZAMORA. Caracas: Ministerio de Educación Pública, 1977.

615. Rodríguez, J.S. CONTRIBUCION AL ESTUDIO DE LA GUERRA FEDERAL EN VENEZUELA. 2d ed. Caracas: ECPCRF, 1960. (Originally published 1933.)

616. Rodríguez Plata, H. JOSE MARIA OBANDO INTIMO: ARCHIVO, EPISTOLARIO, COMENTARIO. Bogotá: Academia Colombiana de Historia, 1958.

617. Roig, Pedro. LA GUERRA DE MARTI. Miami: Ediciones Universal, 1984.

618. Roig de Leuchsenring, Emilio. 1895 Y 1898: DOS GUERRAS CUBANAS; ENSAYO DE REVALORACION. Havana: Cultural S.A., 1945.

619. ———. LA GUERRA LIBERTADORA DE LOS TREINTA ANOS, 1868-1898. 2d ed. Havana: n.p., 1958.

620. ———. REVOLUCION Y REPUBLICA EN MACEO. Havana: Oficinas del Historiador de la Ciudad, 1961.

621. ———. WYLER IN CUBA: UN PRECURSOR DE LA BARBARIE FASCISTA. Havana: Página, 1947.

622. Romay, Francisco L. HISTORIA DE LA POLICIA FEDERAL ARGENTINA. 3 vols. Buenos Aires: Biblioteca Policial, 1963-65.

623. Romero, Mario Germán, et al. PAPELETAS BIBLIOGRAFICAS PARA EL ESTUDIO DE LA HISTORIA DE COLOMBIA. Bogotá: Banco de la República, 1961.

624. Rondón Márquez, Rafael Angel. GUZMAN BLANCO: EL ARISTOCRATICA CIVILIZADOR. 2 vols. Caracas: Tip. Garrido, 1944.

625. Rosa, José María. LA CAIDA DE ROSAS: EL IMPERIO DE BRASIL Y LA CONFEDERACION ARGENTINA, 1843-1851. 2d ed. Buenos Aires: Plus Ultra, 1968.

626. Rosal y Vázquez de Mondragón, Antonio. EN LA MANIGUA: DIARIO DE MI CAUTIVERIO. Madrid: Imp. de Bernardino y Cía., 1876.

627. Ruiz, Eduardo. HISTORIA DE LA GUERRA DE INTERVENCION EN MICHOACAN. Mexico City: Sec. de Fomento, 1896.

628. Rus, Jan. "Whose Caste War?: Indians, Ladinos and the 'Caste War' of 1869." In SPANIARDS AND INDIANS IN SOUTHEASTERN MESOAMERICA: ESSAYS ON THE HISTORY OF ETHNIC RELATIONS, 127-68. Edited by Murdo J. MacLeod and Robert Wasserstrom. Lincoln: University of Nebraska Press, 1983.

629. Safford, Frank R. "Bases of Political Alignment in Early Republican Spanish America." In NEW APPROACHES TO LATIN AMERICAN HISTORY, 71-111. Edited by Richard Graham and Peter H. Smith. Austin: University of Texas Press, 1974.

630. ———. "Politics, Ideology and Society in Post-Independence Spanish America." In CAMBRIDGE HISTORY OF LATIN AMERICA, 3:377-83. Edited by Leslie Bethell. London: Cambridge University Press, 1985-86.

631. ———. "Social Aspects of Politics in Nineteenth-Century Spanish America: New Granada, 1825-1850." JOURNAL OF SOCIAL HISTORY 5 (1972): 344-70.

632. Saíz de la Mora, Jesús. CONSIDERACIONES ALREDEDOR DEL GENERALISIMO MAXIMO GOMEZ. Havana: Imp. el Dante, 1927.

633. Salazar, Francisco Javier. LAS BATALLAS DE CHORRILLOS Y MIRAFLORES Y EL ARTE DE LA GUERRA. Lima: Imp. del Universo, 1882.

634. Saldías, Adolfo. HISTORIA DE LA CONFEDERACION ARGENTINA: ROSAS Y SU EPOCA. 9 vols. Buenos Aires: Orientación Cultural, 1958. (Originally published 1881-87.)

635. ———, ed. PAPELES DE ROSAS. 2 vols. La Plata: Talleres Gráficos Sesé y Larrañaga, 1904-07.

636. Salm Salm, Felix. MY DIARY IN MEXICO IN 1867: INCLUDING THE LAST DAYS OF THE EMPEROR MAXIMILIAN. 2 vols. London: Richard Bentley, 1868.

637. Samper, José María. ENSAYO SOBRE LAS REVOLUCIONES POLITICAS Y LA CONDICION SOCIAL DE LA

REPUBLICA COLOMBIANA. 3d ed. Bogotá: Ministerio de Educación Pública, 1984. (Originally published 1861.)

638. Samponaro, Frank N. "La alianza de Santa Anna y los federalistas, 1832-1834: Su formación y desintegración." HISTORIA MEXICANA 30 (1981): 358-90.

639. ———. "Mariano Paredes y el movimiento monarquista mexicano en 1846." HISTORIA MEXICANA 32 (1982): 39-54.

640. ———. "The Political Role of the Army in Mexico, 1821-1848." Ph.D. dissertation, State University of New York, Stony Brook, 1974.

641. Sánchez, Aurora Mónica. JULIO ARGENTINO ROCA. Buenos Aires: Círculo Militar, 1969.

642. Sánchez Lamego, General Miguel A. LA INVASION ESPANOLA DE 1829. Mexico City: Editorial Jus, 1971.

643. Sánchez Navarro y Peón, Carlos. MIRAMON: EL CAUDILLO CONSERVADOR. 2d ed. Mexico City: Editorial Patria, 1949.

644. Santa Cruz, Oscar de. EL GENERAL SANTA CRUZ: GRAN MARISCAL DE ZEPITA Y EL GRAN PERU. La Paz: Escuela Tip. Salesiana, 1924.

645. Santibáñez, Manuel. RESENA HISTORICA DEL CUERPO DEL EJERCITO DE ORIENTE. 2 vols. Mexico City: Tip. de la Oficina Imp. de Timbre, 1802-03.

646. Santoni, Pedro. "A Fear of the People: The Civic Militia of Mexico in 1845." HISPANIC AMERICAN HISTORICAL REVIEW 68 (1988): 269-88.

647. Santovenia y Echaide, Emeterio Santiago. GOMEZ: EL MAXIMO. Havana: Imp. el Siglo XX, 1936.

648. Sarmiento, Domingo Faustino. LIFE IN THE ARGENTINE REPUBLIC IN THE DAYS OF THE TYRANTS, OR CIVILIZATION AND BARBARISM. New York: Collier Books, 1961. (Originally published 1845.)

649. ———. OBRAS COMPLETAS. 52 vols. Santiago: n.p., 1887-1902.

650. ———. OBRAS DE.... 38 vols. Buenos Aires: Gobierno Nacional, 1900.

651. Sater, William F. CHILE AND THE WAR OF THE PACIFIC. Lincoln: University of Nebraska Press, 1986.

652. ———. "Chile during the First Months of the War of the Pacific." JOURNAL OF LATIN AMERICAN STUDIES 11 (1979): 67-99.

653. ———. THE HEROIC IMAGE IN CHILE: ARTURO PRAT, SECULAR SAINT. Berkeley: University of California Press, 1973.

654. Schiff, Warren. "German Military Penetration of Mexico during the Late Díaz Period." HISPANIC AMERICAN HISTORICAL REVIEW 39 (1959): 568-79.

655. ———. "The Influence of the German Armed Forces and War Industry in Argentina, 1880-1914." HISPANIC AMERICAN HISTORICAL REVIEW 52 (1972): 436-55.

656. Schneider, Louis. A GUERRA DA TRIPLICE ALIANCA. 4 vols. Rio de Janeiro: Imp. Militar, 1924. (Originally published 1868.)

657. Scholes, Walter V. MEXICAN POLITICS DURING THE JUAREZ REGIME, 1855-1872. Columbia: University of Missouri Press, 1957.

658. ———. "A Revolution Falters: Mexico, 1856-1857." HISPANIC AMERICAN HISTORICAL REVIEW 32 (1952): 1-21.

659. Schoo Lastra, Dionisio. EL INDIO DEL DESIERTO, 1537-1879. Buenos Aires: Agencia General de Librería y Publicaciones, 1928.

660. Schulz, John. "The Brazilian Army in Politics, 1850-1894." Ph.D. dissertation, Princeton University, 1973.

661. Schwartzman, Simon. "Regional Cleavages and Political Patriarchalism in Brazil." Ph.D. dissertation, University of California, Berkeley, 1973.

662. Scobie, James R. LA LUCHA POR LA CONSOLIDACION DE LA NACIONALIDAD ARGENTINA, 1852-1862. Buenos Aires: Librería Hachette, 1964.

663. ———. "The Significance of the September Revolution." HISPANIC AMERICAN HISTORICAL REVIEW 41 (1961): 236-58.

664. ———. "An Uneasy Triumvirate: Derqui, Mitre and Urquiza." HISPANIC AMERICAN HISTORICAL REVIEW 38 (1958): 327-52.

665. Scott, Winfield. MEMOIRS OF LIEUTENANT-GENERAL SCOTT LLD. 2 vols. New York: Sheldon, 1864.

666. Serra Orts, Antonio. RECUERDOS DE LA GUERRA DE CUBA, 1868-1898. Santa Cruz de Tenerife: n.p., 1906.

667. Simmons, Charles Willis. MARSHAL DEODORO AND THE FALL OF DOM PEDRO II. Durham: Duke University Press, 1966.

668. Singletary, Otis A. THE MEXICAN WAR. Chicago: University of Chicago Press, 1965.

669. Sinkin, Richard N. THE MEXICAN REFORM, 1855-1876. Austin: Institute of Latin American Studies, University of Texas, 1979.

670. Smith, Geoffrey A. "The Role of José Balmaceda in Preserving Argentine Neutrality in the War of the Pacific." HISPANIC AMERICAN HISTORICAL REVIEW 49 (1969): 254-67.

671. Smith, Peter H. "The Image of a Dictator: Gabriel García Moreno." HISPANIC AMERICAN HISTORICAL REVIEW 45 (1965): 1-24.

672. ———. "Political Legitimacy in Spanish America." In NEW APPROACHES TO LATIN AMERICAN HISTORY, 225-55. Edited by Richard Graham and Peter H. Smith. Austin: University of Texas Press, 1974.

673. Sommariva, Luis H. HISTORIA DE LAS INTERVENCIONES EN LAS PROVINCIAS. 2 vols. Buenos Aires: "El Ateneo," 1931.

674. Sommi, Luis Víctor. LA REVOLUCION DE 90. Buenos Aires: Ediciones Pueblos de América, 1957.

675. Sotomayor y Valdés, Ramón. CAMPANA DEL EJERCITO CHILENO CONTRA LA CONFEDERACION PERU-BOLIVIANA EN 1837. Santiago: Imp. Cervantes, 1896.

676. Souto Maior, Armando. QUEBRA-QUILOS: LUTAS SOCIAIS NO OUTONO DO IMPERIO. São Paulo: n.p., 1978.

677. Souza, Amaury de. "The *Cangaço* and the Politics of Violence in Northeast Brazil." In PROTEST AND RESISTANCE IN ANGOLA AND BRAZIL: COMPARATIVE STUDIES, 109-31. Edited by Ronald Chilcote. Berkeley: University of California Press, 1972.

678. Souza, Benigno. MAXIMO GOMEZ: EL GENERALISIMO. Havana: Editorial de Ciencias Sociales, 1986.

679. Souza Docea, Emilio Fernandes de. CAUSAS DE GUERRA COM O PARAGUAY. Porto Alegre: Cunha, Reutzsch y Cía., 1919.

680. Spalding, Walter. A REVOLUCAO FARROUPILHA. 2d ed. São Paulo: Cía. Editôra Nacional, 1980. (Originally published 1939.)

681. Spell, Lota. RESEARCH MATERIAL FOR THE STUDY OF LATIN AMERICAN HISTORY AT THE UNIVERSITY OF TEXAS. Austin: University of Texas Press, 1954.

682. Stein, Stanley J. "The Historiography of Brazil, 1808-1839." HISPANIC AMERICAN HISTORICAL REVIEW 40 (1960): 234-78.

683. Stevens, Donald F. "Agrarian Policy and Instability in Porfirian Mexico." THE AMERICAS 39 (1982): 153-66.

684. ———. "Instability in Mexico from Independence to the War of the Reform." Ph.D. dissertation, University of Chicago, 1983.

685. Strauss, Norman T. "Brazil after the Paraguayan War: Six Years of Conflict, 1870-6." JOURNAL OF LATIN AMERICAN STUDIES 10 (1978): 21-35.

686. Street, John. ARTIGAS AND THE EMANCIPATION OF URUGUAY. Cambridge: Cambridge University Press, 1959.

687. Suárez Suárez, Rosendo. BREVE HISTORIA DEL EJERCITO MEXICANO. Mexico City: Anáhuac, 1938.

688. Subercaseaux, Ramón. MEMORIAS DE OCHENTA ANOS. 2 vols. 2d ed. Santiago: Editorial Nascimento, 1936.

689. Sullivan, William M. "The Rise of Despotism in Venezuela: Cipriano Castro, 1899-1908." Ph.D. dissertation, University of New Mexico, 1974.

690. Szászdi, Adam. "The Historiography of the Republic of Ecuador." HISPANIC AMERICAN HISTORICAL REVIEW 44 (1964): 503-50.

691. Tamayo, Jorge L., ed. BENITO JUAREZ: DOCUMENTOS, DISCURSOS Y CORRESPONDENCIA. 14 vols. Mexico City: n.p., 1964-70.

692. Tasso Fragoso, Augusto. HISTORIA E GUERRA ENTRE A TRIPLICE ALIANCA E O PARAGUAI. 5 vols. Rio de Janeiro: Imp. do Estado-Maior do Exército, 1934.

693. Tate, Edward Nicholas. "Britain and Latin America in the Nineteenth Century: The Case of Paraguay, 1811-1870." IBERO-AMERIKANISCHES ARCHIV 5 (1979): 39-70.

694. Telles, Indalecio. HISTORIA MILITAR DE CHILE, 1541-1884. 2d ed. Santiago: Editorial Universitaria, 1917.

695. TePaske, John J., et al. RESEARCH GUIDE TO ANDEAN HISTORY: BOLIVIA, CHILE, ECUADOR, AND PERU. Durham: Duke University Press, 1981.

696. Thompson, George. THE WAR IN PARAGUAY. 2d ed. London: Longmans, Green and Co., 1869.

697. Thomson, Guy P. C. "Movilización conservador, insurrección liberal y rebeliones indígenas, 1854-1876." In AMERICA LATINA: DALLO STATO COLONIALE ALLO STATO NAZIONE, 1750-1940, 1:592-614. Edited by Antonio Annino, et al. Turin: Franco Angeli, 1987.

698. Tobar Cruz, Pedro. LOS MONTANESES. 2 vols. Guatemala City: Editorial Universitaria, 1959-71.

699. Torre Villar, Ernesto de la. LAS FUENTES FRANCESAS PARA LA HISTORIA DE MEXICO Y LA GUERRA DE LA INTERVENCION. Mexico City: Sociedad Mexicana de Geografía y Estadística, 1962.

700. Torrea, Juan Manuel. LA VIDA DE UNA INSTITUCION GLORIOSA: EL COLEGIO MILITAR, 1821-1930. Mexico City: Talleres Tip. Centenario, 1931.

701. Trías, Vivián. EL PARAGUAY: DE FRANCIA EL SUPREMO A LA GUERRA DE LA TRIPLE ALIANZA. Buenos Aires: Cuadernos de Crisis, 1975.

702. Tutino, John. FROM INSURRECTION TO REVOLUTION IN MEXICO: SOCIAL BASES OF AGRARIAN VIOLENCE, 1750-1940. Princeton: Princeton University Press, 1987.

703. Urias Hermosillo, Margarita. "Militares y comerciantes en México, 1828-1846: Las mercancías de la nacionalidad." HISTORIAS 6 (1984): 49-70.

704. Uricoechea, Fernando. THE PATRIMONIAL FOUNDATIONS OF THE BRAZILIAN BUREAUCRATIC STATE. Berkeley: University of California Press, 1980.

705. Valadés, José C. MEXICO, SANTA ANNA Y LA GUERRA DE TEXAS. 3d ed. Mexico City: Editores Mexicanos Unidos, 1965.

706. Valenilla Lanz, Laureano. CESARISMO DEMOCRATICO. Caracas: Universidad Santa María, 1961.

707. Vanderwood, Paul J. "El bandidaje en el sigo XIX: Una forma de subsistir." HISTORIA MEXICANA 34(1984): 41-75.

708. ———. DISORDER AND PROGRESS: BANDITS, POLICE, AND MEXICAN DEVELOPMENT. Lincoln: University of Nebraska Press, 1981.

709. ———. "Response to Revolt: The Counter-Guerrilla Strategy of Porfirio Díaz." HISPANIC AMERICAN HISTORICAL REVIEW 56 (1976): 551-79.

710. Varela, Alfredo. HISTORIA DA GRANDE REVOLUCAO: O CYCLO FARROUPILHA NO BRASIL. 6 vols. Porto Alegre: Barcellos, Bertaso y Cía., 1925.

711. Vargas Ugarte, Rubén. RAMON CASTILLA. Buenos Aires: Imp. López, 1962.

712. ———, ed. GUERRA CON CHILE: LA CAMPANA DEL SUR, ABRIL-DICIEMBRE 1879. Lima: C. Milla Batres, 1967.

713. Varona Guerrero, Miguel. LA GUERRA DE INDEPENDENCIA DE CUBA. 3 vols. Havana: Editorial Lex, 1946.

714. Vázquez, Josefina Z. "La crisis y los partidos políticos, 1833-1846." In AMERICA LATINA: DALLO STATO COLONIALE ALLO STATO NAZIONE, 1750-1940, 1:557-72. Edited by Antonio Annina, et al. Turin: Franco Angeli, 1987.

715. ———. "El ejército: Un dilema del gobierno mexicano, 1841-1864." In PROBLEMAS DE LA FORMACION DEL ESTADO Y DE LA NACION EN HISPANOAMERICA, 319-38. Edited by Inge Buisson, Hans-Joachim König, and Horst Pietschmann. Cologne: Bohlau, 1984.

716. Vázquez Mantecón, Carmen. "Santa Anna y la razón del estado." ESTUDIOS POLITICOS 3 (1977): 105-22.

717. Vedia y Mitre, Mariano. EL GENERAL ROCA Y SU TIEMPO. Buenos Aires: L.J. Rosso, 1962.

718. Velasco, José María. GUERRA DE CUBA: CAUSAS DE SU DURACION Y MEDIOS DE TERMINARLA Y ASEGURAR SU PACIFICACION. Madrid: J.J. Heras, 1872.

719. Velázquez, Ramón J. LA CAIDA DEL LIBERALISMO AMARILLO: TIEMPO Y DRAMA DE ANTONIO PAREDES. 2d ed. Caracas: Ediciones Venezuela, 1972.

720. Velázquez Chávez, María del Carmen. HISPANOAMERICA EN EL SIGLO XIX. Mexico City: Editorial Pormaca, 1965.

721. Venezuela. Presidencia. LAS FUERZAS ARMADAS DE VENEZUELA EN EL SIGLO XIX: LA INDEPENDENCIA. Caracas: n.p., 1960-66.

722. Vianna Filho, Luiz. A SABINADA: A REPUBLICA BAHIANA DE 1837. Rio de Janeiro: J. Olympio, 1938.

723. Vicuña Mackenna, Benjamín. EL ALBUM DE LA GLORIA DE CHILE: HOMENAJE AL EJERCITO I ARMADA DE CHILE EN LA MEMORIA DE SUS MAS ILUSTRES MARINOS I SOLDADOS MUERTOS POR LA PATRIA EN LA GUERRA DEL PACIFICO, 1879-1883. 2 vols. Santiago: Imp. Cervantes, 1883.

724. ———. DON DIEGO PORTALES. 2 vols. Valparaíso: Imp. y Librería del Mercurio de S. Tornero, 1863.

725. ———. HISTORIA DE LA CAMPANA DE LIMA. 2 vols. Santiago: Rafael Jouer, 1881.

726. Villanueva, Laureano. VIDA DEL VALIENTE CIUDADANO GENERAL EZEQUIEL ZAMORA. Caracas: Imp. Federación, 1898.

727. Villanueva, Víctor. CIEN ANOS DEL EJERCITO PERUANO: FRUSTRACIONES Y CAMBIOS. Lima: Juan Mejía Baca, 1972.

728. ———. EJERCITO PERUANO: DEL CAUDILLAJE ANARQUICO AL MILITARISMO REFORMISTA. Lima: Juan Mejía Baca, 1973.

729. Viñas, David. INDIOS, EJERCITO Y FRONTERA. Buenos Aires: Siglo XXI Editores, 1982.

730. Walther, Juan Carlos. LA CONQUISTA DEL DESIERTO. 2d ed. Buenos Aires: Círculo Militar, 1962.

731. Warren, Harris Gaylord, and Katherine F. Warren. PARAGUAY AND THE TRIPLE ALLIANCE: THE POST-WAR DECADE, 1869-1878. Austin: University of Texas Press, 1978.

732. Werneck Sodré, Nelson. HISTORIA MILITAR DO BRASIL. 2d ed. Rio de Janeiro: Civilizacão Brasileira, 1968.

733. White, Richard Alan. PARAGUAY'S AUTONOMOUS REVOLUTION, 1810-1840. Albuquerque: University of New Mexico Press, 1978.

734. Wibel, John Frederick. "The Evolution of a Regional Community within Spanish America and the Peruvian Nation: Arequipa, 1780-1845." Ph.D. dissertation, Stanford University, 1975.

735. Wilgus, A. Curtis, ed. SOUTH AMERICAN DICTATORS DURING THE FIRST CENTURY OF INDEPENDENCE. Washington: George Washington University Press, 1937.

736. Williams, John Hoyt. "The Archivo Nacional in Asunción, Paraguay." LATIN AMERICAN RESEARCH REVIEW 6 (1971): 101-18.

737. ———. "From the Barrel of a Gun: Some Notes on Dr. Francia and Paraguayan Militarism." PROCEEDINGS OF THE AMERICAN PHILOSOPHICAL SOCIETY 119 (1975): 73-86.

738. ———. EL DR. FRANCIA Y LA CREACION DE LA REPUBLICA DEL PARAGUAY. Asunción: n.p., 1977.

739. ———. "La guerra no-declarada entre el Paraguay y Corrientes." ESTUDIOS PARAGUAYOS 1 (1973): 35-43.

740. ———. "Paraguayan Historical Sources: Part 4, A Selective Paraguayan Historiography." THE AMERICAS 34 (1978): 537-52.

741. ———. "Paraguayan Isolation under Dr . Francia: A Reevaluation." HISPANIC AMERICAN HISTORICAL REVIEW 52(1972): 102-22.

742. ———. THE RISE AND FALL OF THE PARAGUAYAN REPUBLIC, 1800-1870. Austin: University of Texas Press, 1979.

743. Williams Rebolledo, Juan. OPERACIONES DE LA ESCUADRA CHILENA MIENTRAS ESTUVO A LAS ORDENES DE CONTRA-ALMIRANTE.... Valparaíso: Imp. Progreso, 1882.

744. Wirth, John D. MINAS GERAIS IN THE BRAZILIAN FEDERATION, 1889-1937. Stanford: Stanford University Press, 1977.

745. Wise, George S. CAUDILLO: A PORTRAIT OF ANTONIO GUZMAN BLANCO. New York: Columbia University Press, 1951.

746. Wolf, Eric R., and Edward C. Hansen. "Caudillo Politics: A Structural Analysis." COMPARATIVE STUDIES IN SOCIETY AND HISTORY 9 (1967): 168-79.

747. Woodward, Ralph Lee, Jr. CENTRAL AMERICA: A NATION DIVIDED. 2d ed. New York: Oxford University Press, 1985.

748. ———. "Liberalism, Conservatism and the Response of the Peasant of *La Montaña* to the Government of Guatemala, 1821-1850." PLANTATION SOCIETY 1 (1979): 109-29.

749. Zamacois, Niceto de. HISTORIA DE MEJICO DESDE SUS TIEMPOS MAS REMOTOS HASTA NUESTROS DIAS. 21 vols. Barcelona: J. F. Parres y Cía, 1878-1902.

750. Zecena, Mariano. ESTUDIOS POLITICOS: LA REVOLUCION DE 1871 Y SUS CAUDILLOS. Guatemala City: Tip. Sánchez and de Guise, 1898.

751. Zorraquín Becú, Horacio. LA REVOLUCION DEL NOVENTA: SU SENTIDO POLITICO. Buenos Aires: n.p., 1960.

752. Zorrilla, Rubén H. "Estructura social y caudillismo en la Argentina, 1810-1870." NOVA AMERICANA 2 (1979): 135-67.

753. ———. EXTRACCION SOCIAL DE LOS CAUDILLOS, 1810-1870. Buenos Aires: Editorial La Pleyade, 1972.

CHAPTER V

ARGENTINA

Errol D. Jones
Boise State University
(With the assistance of Russell Tremayne)

INTRODUCTION

For much of the twentieth century the armed forces in Argentina have had a significant impact on the nation's evolution. The military's presence in politics has attracted the attention of social scientists and historians who have endeavored to question, clarify, scrutinize, explain, and critique the institution's influence on the country. As a result, hundreds of articles, monographs, reports, memoirs, and eyewitness accounts have spilled from the presses attempting to justify or condemn the military's role in Argentina's modern history. The purpose of this chapter is to serve as a selective guide to that abundant literature and to suggest opportunities for future research.

The armed forces began to professionalize when President Domingo F. Sarmiento (1868-74) established the Colegio Militar in 1869 to train officers for the army. Sarmiento hoped that the Colegio would help create a professional force that could check the native and gaucho bands led by provincial strongmen who, since independence in 1816, challenged the president's authority during the long and bitter struggle between Buenos Aires and the provinces. But it was General Julio A. Roca who, during his two terms as president (1880-86, 1898-1904), pressed most ardently for military professionalization. Between 1880 and 1910 sucessive administrations fashioned a professional army that rested upon the foundations of modern weaponry and war materiel, an Escuela Superior de Guerra, organized and influenced by a German training mission, and obligatory military service.

As the military professionalization process advanced, a heightened corporate consciousness grew among the army officer corps. They sought to wrest institutional autonomy from civilian politicians, especially regarding promotions and to prevent them from using the armed forces for narrow political considerations. To ensure that the army controlled promotions of its officers it created the Tribunal de Clasificación in 1910. Ironically, this attempt to prevent civilian interference in its internal affairs propelled the army into the political arena in the 1920s.

When the Radical Party triumphed at the polls in 1916 and Hipólito Yrigoyen assumed the presidency, he attempted to reward through promotion those Radical sympathizers and adherents in the military who had joined the unsuccessful Radical revolts of 1890, 1893 and 1905. Yrigoyen's move to pay back these officers and to manipulate the army for his own political ends caused some officers like Generals José F. Uriburu and Agustín P. Justo, although bitter personal rivals, to unite their followers long enough to drive Yrigoyen from office two years after his reelection to the presidency in 1928. While Uriburu emerged as the leader of the rebellion, his anti-democratic, ultra-nationalist, fascist tendencies alienated a significant number of military men who rallied around General Justo. Throughout the decade of the 1920s Justo had carefully aligned himself with civilian leaders of the old conservative oligarchy while at the same time ingratiating himself with anti-personalist Radical notables. Faced with mounting civilian opposition, deep divisions in the military and dying of cancer, Uriburu was forced to step down as president in 1932. The fraudulent elections that followed brought General Justo to the presidency and with him a return of the old conservative oligarchy who held power during the "infamous decade" (1932-43).

In the course of that decade the political alliance that Justo had skillfully brought together soon fell apart, and he found himself increasingly dependent upon the conservative oligarchy for support. Election fraud and government corruption maintained the conservatives in power, but deepening economic dependency coupled with the regime's abuse of authority eroded Justo's influence among the Radical anti-personalistas (anti-Yrigoyen Radicals) within the officer corps. Uriburu's brand of ultra-nationalism now took root among the officer corps. Their faith in civilian politicians' ability to lead the nation and to meet its pressing needs, regardless of their political affiliation, evaporated. In less than a decade authoritarian ultra-nationalism had become the dominant force in the military.

World War II created still further division among the Argentine ruling elite and within the country's military. One group was intensely pro-Allied, while another hoped for an Axis victory; the navy inclined toward the British, while the army had a tendency to favor the Germans. While these splits served to maintain Argentine neutrality, the armed forces became increasingly uneasy as Brazil, long Argentina's principal South American rival, received military aid from the United States. When it became apparent that the unpopular, pro-Axis, reactionary president Ramón Castillo intended to bequeath the presidency to one of his wealthy cronies, the major military factions momentarily closed ranks again to depose the civilian government.

The June 1943 coup brought the armed forces back into the center of Argentine politics. Waiting for the opportune moment was Colonel Juan Domingo Perón who adroitly manipulated the factions within the military and skillfully took advantage of socio-economic changes in the country to build a political following. Perón was able to turn to his benefit United States charges published on the eve of the 1946 presidential elections in the infamous *Blue Book* that he and his military colleagues had collaborated with the Nazis during the recent war. Focusing his attacks on the United States Ambassador Spruille Braden, whom he accused of meddling in Argentina's internal affairs, Perón was able to wrap himself in the cloak of Argentine nationalism and easily won the presidency.

Although Perón ruled Argentina as a civilian "democratically" elected president from 1946 to 1955, the nation's armed forces watched him carefully and continued to influence his decisions and check his actions. Perón wanted to remove the military from the political arena by keeping the officer corps happy. At the same time, economic considerations caused him to trim the military budget by ending universal conscription and reducing the size of the armed forces. Still, inter-service and intra-service factionalism and rivalry persisted, and many officers distrusted Perón's manipulation of and growing control over labor. It was this rise of the lower classes and with them the increasing power of their champion and spokeswoman Evita Perón, the president's wife, which posed the major threat to the armed forces position.

Increasingly, some of the officer caste balked at Perón's directives, while labor made its demands. In 1951, military opponents blocked his attempts to make Evita his vice-president. Despite her death the following year, some of the officer corps stepped up pressure on Perón to reduce labor's power. In September 1955, a third and successful naval revolt, joined by elements of the army, air force and marines, forced Perón from power.

At the end of Perón's rule, Argentina's economy was in shambles. Hardline opponents to Perón, both within the military and outside it, shunted the moderates aside, installed General Pedro Aramburu as provisional president and vengefully went after the followers of Perón.

When the Peronists struck back in June 1956, the Aramburu government responded with an ominous spilling of blood; it rounded up and executed forty leaders, some of whom were in the armed forces.

Bound by promises to turn power over to civilians in 1958, the provisional Aramburu government was equally committed to preventing Peronists from participating in the new "democratic" order. The civilian party that won the presidential elections did so on the basis of openly campaigning for the Peronist vote, pledging to support labor unions and to restore Perón's followers to political legitimacy. Arturo Frondizi, leader of the Intransigent Radicals, rode into the Casa Rosada on a Peronist horse, but the anti-Peronists in the uniformed services made sure that Frondizi's mount never got untethered. His administration suffered thirty-five coup attempts, the last of which removed him from office in March 1962.

Argentina presented a sorry spectacle in the first couple of years after Frondizi's ouster. No less than thirty-nine different parties competed for political power, while none successfully exercised it. The armed forces, in spite of, or because of, their own lack of unity, and fearful that the Peronists or the left might become too powerful, refused to withdraw from the political arena. Even so, they were as fragmented and irresponsible as their civilian competitors, and frequent armed clashes erupted between several factions fighting for control of the military high command.

The newly legalized Peronist party registered significant victories in the 1965 congressional elections, making anti-Peronists in the military and in the middle and upper classes uneasy. Their discomfort did not last long; in June 1966 the combined forces of the army, navy and air force ejected the civilian president, Arturo Illia, closed congress and the provincial legislatures and disbanded political parties. Cavalry General Juan Carlos Onganía took command. A new day had dawned in Argentina; the military had tired of sharing power with civilians.

Onganía and his colleagues in uniform tried to resolve the country's pressing problems by proclaiming the advent of the "Argentine Revolution." Through the establishment of a bureaucratic-authoritarian state, Onganía sought to transform society. With the civilian politicians out of the way, military leaders forged alliances with foreign investors and technocrats. By repressing labor and keeping wages down, they thought profits would climb and be reinvested thereby attracting more investors and fueling economic growth. With some labor cooperation during the first two years of this economic stabilization program, Onganía's plan met with some success. But in 1969 strikes broke out in Córdoba that were met by military crackdowns resulting in numerous deaths of protestors and innocent bystanders. Soon the entire country was engulfed in political violence.

A military coup in 1970 removed Onganía and for the next three years two more generals tried to bring an end to the civil war while at the same time to keep the economy from collapsing. They were no more successful than their predecessors had been. As the violence mounted and the left became bolder and more powerful, the armed forces, in desperation, gambled on allowing Perón to return to run for reelection to the presidency. As a conservative, Perón, it was believed, could control the left, many of whom were attacking the government in his name.

Perón constructed a broad-based coalition which included a majority of the interest groups in the country. As expected, the conservative Perón gave the police and security forces the green light in their campaign agaist the left. Those who had hoped, however, that the returning hero could work miracles and heal the nation's wounds, saw their expectations dashed as the economy further deteriorated and political violence escalated. Perón's death in July 1974 placed the awful responsibility of governing Argentina squarely in the lap of his widow who, as vice-president, succeeded him in the presidency.

Military leaders stood by and watched as Isabel failed to hold the Peronists together. The economy careened out of control, political violence increased, and fear gripped the nation, but the men in uniform seemed determined to allow the widow Perón to finish her term of office. By March 1976, civilian rule in Argentina however, had proved such a failure that the armed forces undoubtedly had broader public support than ever before to intervene.

Convinced of the need to destroy its enemies and restructure society, the military, under the leadership of Jorge Rafael Videla, took over and unleashed a "holy war" against its opponents. Thousands of "subversives" were arrested, and thousands more simply "disappeared." Police and military terror provoked a similar response from the left, which struck back. Open warfare erupted producing an unprecedented unity and coherence within the armed forces. The middle and upper classes rallied behind the military's anti-guerrilla campaign, even though many of those who "disappeared" came from the ranks of the middle class and university student bodies.

General Videla and his fellow officers planned to alter Argentine society in such a way that they could eventually return to their barracks and stay there. Paradoxically, this led to a deeper military penetration into social organisms and institutions than in the past. It also meant that perceived opponents were to be eradicated and that the public would be reeducated to embrace the ideals and values that military men prized. Of course, to be successful in these areas, the officers had to resolve the perplexing economic difficulties. While their "neoliberal" economic tactics met with some successes, and they seemed to be winning the war against the guerrillas, by 1981 the generals still found themselves facing numerous anti-government demonstrations as Argentines blamed them for spiraling inflation, declining wages, bank failures, and recession.

In an apparent attempt to win public support for the regime, the junta, led by army General Leopoldo Galtieri, ordered the invasion of the British held Falkland Islands, 2 April 1982. While the move certainly stoked Argentine patriotism to fever pitch, it proved a disastrous tactic. The British sent a task force to the South Atlantic and humilated the Argentine military by retaking the islands without great difficulty. Faced with disaster, ugly internal demonstrations against them, and a worsening economy, military unity crumbled and the army found itself alone. The generals conceded defeat, called for elections, and went back to their barracks.

Since 1984, civilians have controlled the government in Argentina and with moderate success have tried to restore some semblance of normality to the war-ravished nation. They must tread lightly where issues directly involving the armed forces are concerned. Nevertheless, they have been able to hold the military and security forces accountable for crimes against civilians during the "dirty war," sending former President Videla and other high ranking military officers to prison. First the Radical Raúl Alfonsín and then the Peronist Carlos Menem governments have labored to restore Argentina to economic health and political sanity. But for all civilian rulers past and present the one factor that always needed to be taken into consideration was what role would the armed forces play. As Argentina entered the decade of the 1990s that was still an important question.

GENERAL WORKS

Owing to the integral political role the military has played in Argentine society since the inception of the twentieth century it is important for the student of that institution to become familiar with the broad sweep of the nation's past. Several excellent general histories exist that will allow researchers to place the armed forces in proper context. Robert J. Alexander's (5), older, but still useful work, emphasized the political causes for economic stagnation and covered the role of the military in the governmental process. Allub (10), in a more recent study, also concentrated on the peculiarities of the Argentine economy as one of the factors leading to political instability and to intervention by the armed forces. A popular, well written, essay based on archival research is Alonso (11), while Agozino (3), offered a fascinating new perspective on the formation and evolution of the country's political parties. Corradi's (132, 133), two fine studies did an excellent job, from a dependency point of view, of integrating the military into the broader trends of economic, political and social history.

Argentine journalist Eduardo Crawley (135), stimulated readers with a solid overview of Argentina from 1880 to 1980. McGann's (365), use of social psychology to interpret Argentine history challenged future scholars to follow up on some of the issues he raised. Polemical at times, but insightful and provocative, Ramos (499), offered a left, nationalist perspective of Argentine history which should be read in conjunction with Randall's (500), interesting economic history. Rennie (511), despite her obvious biases, can still be enlightening, while Rock's (524), impressive study is excellent on the relationship between militarism and the economy in Argentine history. One of the best syntheses of Argentina's past is Romero (531), compiled and updated posthumously, while Smith (578), stirred up controversy with his book on the failure of democracy in the Platine republic.

Carlos María Vilas (630), wrote a prize winning analysis of imperialist penetration into the Argentine economy; Whitaker (647), dealt with relations between the United States and the Southern Cone; Wynia (652), demonstrated a keen grasp of the major political and military trends shaping Argentina; and finally, Zuleta Alvarez (660), presented a monumental survey of Argentine nationalism from the nineteenth century to the 1970s.

General studies on the military fall into two catagories: those that treat the contemporary, informational aspect of the armed forces, and works that trace the historical evolution of the institution.

For basic statistical and institutional information on today's armed forces in Argentina one should refer to Brown (83), Dupuy (172), English (177), Heare (285), and Keegan (313). In addition, the STATISTICAL ABSTRACT OF LATIN AMERICA (591), is useful, as is the section on "National Security," in Rudolph's ARGENTINA, A COUNTRY STUDY (548).

Although outdated, Johnson's (304), and Lieuwen's (334, 335), pioneering syntheses should be read by anyone starting out in the field, especially for the comparative insights they offer. These have been updated by Alain Rouquié (541), and Augusto Varas (626), both of whom have written stimulating interpretations of Latin American militarism. These works, together with the excellent collections of readings edited by Loveman and Davies (349), and by Lowenthal (350), provide the Latin American context for the study of the Argentine military.

General studies on Argentine militarism are increasing in number and fortunately in quality as well. The CRONOLOGIA MILITAR ARGENTINA, 1806-1980 (136), documented military activities on a day-by-day, year-to-year basis. Darío Cantón (98), surveyed the armed forces since the beginning of this century and emphasized its conservative nature and its suspicion of popular movements. Imaz (298), explored the social origins and family background of the army officer crops, and Menéndez (388), described the use of armed force in Argentine territorial acquistions from 1810 to 1978. Orsolini's (427), general discussion is thoughtful and useful, as is the shorter paper by Perina (449). Potash's (479, 477), two books are outstanding; thoroughly and carefully researched, detailed, and complete, they examined political military relations from the process of professionalization at the turn of the century to the fall of Frondizi in 1962. He is currently completing a third volume covering the period from Frondizi's ouster to Perón's return (1962-73) (478). Ramos (498), considered the historical role of the armed forces as essentially reactionary; the productive Rouquié (544, 545), in his two-volume, cross-disciplinary approach identified the more permanent and notable features of military intervention in the political process and viewed that intervention as the result, rather than the cause, of the country's chronic political instability. Finally, Scenna (564), offered an objective, well-written and informative essay on the military as a socio-political group from 1806 to 1976, but emphasized the 1880-1932 era.

While the above works concentrated more on the army as the major political actor in the Argentine drama, there have been some general studies on other branches of the armed forces. Robert Scheina's (566), survey of Latin American naval history provided helpful information on the Argentine navy as well as devoted two chapters to the Malvinas/Falklands war. Humberto Burzio (88), wrote a significant summary of the navy's historical evolution through the 1960s, while Sequeira, Cal, and Calatayud (574), produced a well-illustrated history of the naval air force since 1910. Antonio Biedma (70), is the official historian for the air force, and Wahnish and French (635), provided a more up-to-date look at that branch of the armed services.

BIBLIOGRAPHIES

Bibliographies and other guides to sources for Argentine history are numerous but those dealing specifically with the military are limited to a handful. As it is our belief that the historian of the military must place that institution in its societal context the bibliographical aids discussed here are general as well as specific.

Arthur Gropp's (264, 266), two Latin American bibliographies of bibliographies includes those finding aids published to 1969. Follow-up works by Cordeiro (131), and Piedracueva (466), bring us down to the late 1970s. Gropp's (265), bibliography of bibliographies published in periodicals can be helpful through 1965. Nicolas Matijevic (382), has a bibliography of reference guides for Argentina which covers up to 1967.

No one can hope to do serious research on any Latin American topic without consulting the indispensible HANDBOOK OF LATIN AMERICAN STUDIES (282), now in its fifty-fifth year of publication. The HANDBOOK is broadly inclusive, but it should be used in conjunction with the HISPANIC AMERICAN PERIODICALS INDEX (HAPI) (289), which since 1970 has been an important source for articles on the Latin American military. One should also consult the BIBLIOGRAPHIC GUIDE TO LATIN AMERICAN STUDIES (69), an on-going compilation of the University of Texas's and the Library of Congress's acquisitions. The Argentine Ministry of Education (34), since 1949 has published sporadically bibliographies on Argentine history which are extremely useful in a broad general sense. Another valuable resource is the REVISTA INTERAMERICANA DE BIBLIOGRAFIA/INTER-AMERICAN REVIEW OF BIBLIOGRAPHY (708). The Instituto Bibliográfico Antonio Zinny (299), compiled an important index for the specialist which includes newspapers, magazines, and journals published provincially, nationally and internationally dealing with Argentina.

Focusing on a narrower chronological era, Roberto Etcheparreborda (184), produced a select, annotated bibliography for the period 1943-82. It is helpful for political, labor, and military history. For the same period Tanzi (599), presented a careful, intelligent historiographical review of the literature. Dissertations written in the United States on Argentine militarism can be located in DISSERTATION ABSTRACTS INTERNATIONAL (159), and Carl Deal (147), edited a bibliography of dissertations for Latin America and the Caribbean that has been supplemented by Walters (641), and University Microfilms International (617). For works on United States-Latin American relations Trask, Meyer, and Trask (613), supplemented by Meyer (390), compiled excellent bibliographies. Dias David (153), and Gooch (254), provided us with select bibliographies on military relations with the state in Latin America.

Turning to reference works on the armed forces in Argentina, a good place to start is with the Círculo Militar Argentina's CATALOGO (123). The bibliographical studies done by Roberto Etcheparreborda (186, 182, 183), greatly ease the researcher's burden in locating material on the military in general, and on the Revolution of 1930 and the Malvinas/Falklands controversy in particular. Einaudi and Goldhamer (176), rendered an invaluable service by bringing together an annotated list of Latin American military journals. For a select bibliography on the urban guerrillas in Argentina, consult Russel, Schinkel, and Miller (550). Hernández Ruigómez (286), added to

Etchepareborda's contribution on the Malvinas/Falklands controversy and placed particular emphasis on modern historians' treatment of Argentine historical claims on the islands. See also Yokota's (655), recent list of works on the Falklands war. Hoffmann's (292), two-part bibliographic essay on literature relating to Perón has useful material on the military. Lindenberg (366), contained a chapter on Argentina's armed forces citing many sources not mentioned elsewhere, and Ibarra, Leloir, and Mastrorilli (297), reviewed numerous books dealing with the country's security apparatus. McAlister's (362), older bibliographic essay on the Latin American armed forces cites some useful works on Argentina. And, for brief descriptions of military and political figures, see the historical dictionary by Wright and Nekhom (651), but the six-volume historical dictionary by Piccirilli, Romay, and Gianello (465), is more complete and detailed.

ARCHIVAL GUIDES AND SOURCES

Despite the fact that researchers of twentieth century Argentine military history confront frustrating obstacles and difficulties they can make headway with their investigations on a number of levels. First, Michael Grow (267), produced a guide to research depositories containing Latin American and Caribbean materials located in Washington, D.C. Confidential United States State Department Central Files, found in the National Archives in Washington, D.C., contain a wealth of data on Argentina's internal and foreign affairs. They are available to the public for the years 1945 to 1959. George S. Ulibarri's and John P. Harrison's (616), guide to the National Archives is of use here. The National Archives also hold United States Military Intelligence Reports on Argentina from 1918-41. University Publications of America (621), microfilmed a large number of United States government documents pertaining to Argentina and described these documents in their 1990 Research Collections Catalog. Also available from University Publications of America are CIA RESEARCH REPORTS, 1946-1976 (618), NATIONAL SECURITY FILES, 1961-1969 (619, 620), and PERON ERA POLITICAL PAMPHLETS AND MONOGRAPHS (622), edited by Joseph Criscenti.

Second, Robert Potash (479), discovered in his research that the German Foreign Office files, located in the United States National Archives, contained significant materials for his study of the military during the period 1920 to 1944. One should consult his bibliography, as well as the guide prepared by George O. Kent (316), for details as to location and microfilm roll numbers. Great Britain had significant interests in Argentina for much of the nineteenth and twentieth centuries, and Foreign Office Records, General Correspondence-Political-Argentina, found in the Public Record Office, London, should yield valuable information on Argentine military governments.

A major problem for the investigator of the Argentine armed forces is that their official files are usually closed to scholars. The papers of ex-presidents and cabinet ministers are generally regarded as their private property and therefore are not open to critical scrutiny. Potash (479), noted that only rarely have they "been turned over to public repositories." Thus, the Archivo General de la Nación, while rich in materials for the colonial era and the nineteenth century, has little to offer the student looking for twentieth-century data on the armed forces. But according to Potash, the heirs of General Augusto B. Justo and of ex-President General Julio Roca (1880-84, and 1898-1904), deposited the papers of these two men in the Archivo General and they are now available.

Research into social origins and family backgrounds recorded on officers' service records can be facilitated through the Ministerio de Guerra's Oficina de Estudios Históricos. However, researchers interested in going below the surface of published memoirs, documentary collections, and secondary sources will have to seek out collections of papers in private hands and trust to luck and be mindful of the uncertainty that they may be seeing only the things that interested parties wanted them to see. Potash's (279, 277), two-volume work lists the private archives he found most useful and the people with whom he was able to conduct interviews. He also made use of the Oral History Collection at Columbia University.

The 1983 return to democratic government led to the establishment of various foundations and research centers which are open to the public. One of these, the Fundación Centro de Estudios Nacionales located in Buenos Aires, contains former president Arturo Frondizi's presidential papers, much of his personal library, books, clippings file, magazines, etc. The Fundación Arturo Illia also located in Buenos Aires, publishes works on the military and maintains an archive of materials relating to the armed forces and its political role in Argentina. Labor organizations maintain archives and are generally open and accessible to responsible researchers.

PUBLISHED DOCUMENTS

Beyond governmental reports, collections of laws and decrees, congressional records, and reports from executive and legislative bodies, few published documentary collections specifically pertaining to the Argentine military exist.

Since the military exercised direct control of the nation for so many years government decrees and reports are essential sources. Some major governmental documentary collections are: the 33 volumes, bound in 70, of the ANALES DE LEGISLACION ARGENTINA, 1852-1973 (19); the DIARIO DE SESIONES DE LA CAMARA DE DIPUTADOS (24), in two sets, one for 1921-30, 1932-42, 123 volumes, and the other for the years 1946-55, 1958-66 in 117 volumes; Senate sessions (23), are similarly reported in two sets of 50 and 55 volumes corresponding closely to the years covered for the Chamber of Deputies; debates in the National Constituent Convention of 1957 (25), are recorded in two volumes; and a four-volume collection of executive decrees (26), for the military dictatorship of 4 June 1943 to 4 June 1946 is also available.

Reports from executive and legislative commissions provide a valuable resource. A commission established to study constitutional reform published a seven-volume report in 1957 (21). After Perón was pushed from the presidency the new military leaders created a commission (22), which busied itself with the collection of evidence showing, in five volumes, abuse of power and corruption in his government.

Essential documentary keys to the evolution of the Argentine armed forces are the annual reports of the Ministerio de Guerra (known also as the Ministerio de Ejército) (36), and the Ministerio de Marina (41). Collections of speeches and messages of presidents, military and otherwise, can be found for Yrigoyen (656), Alvear (15), Uriburu (623), Ortiz (428, 429), Farrell (195), and Perón (450, 456, 455, 459).

Numerous specialized documentary collections can be of valuable service to the researcher. For the government of General Agustín P. Justo (1932-38), there is a ten-volume set on National Executive Power (44); volumes 6 and 7 are on the army and the navy respectively. After the opening to the public of the Justo papers, Fernando García Molina and Carlos A. Mayo (226, 227), edited a selection of documents on both the Uriburu and Justo governments. The Ministerio del Interior (40), produced two volumes of documents on the elections which brought Juan Perón to power in 1946. The writings of socialist leader and Perón opponent Sánchez Viamonte (557), demonstrated the reasons why he and other socialists opposed the Perón regime. After his fall, Perón carried on an extensive correspondence with his representative John Cooke (454), in which they shared hopes of subverting and overthrowing the new military government. Enrique Pavón Pereyra (442), also published some of Perón's correspondence.

Perón's return to power in 1973 produced some important documentary collections. Selected statements and speeches given by the hero of the *descamisados* between the early 1940s and his death are collected in DOCTRINA PERONISTA (451), and in Perón, EL

GOBIERNO,... (453), as well as in PERON: EL REGRESO Y LA MUERTE (457). Marcelo Cavarozzi (113), collected presidential addresses, interviews, and other relevant political documents for the entire post-Perón period to 1983.

Guerrilla warfare erupted in Argentina in the 1960s and continued until the military surpressed it in the 1970s. Kohl and Litt (319), brought together documents published by guerrilla groups in Argentina, Brazil and Uruguay. Gutiérrez (277), collected excepts from documents from the Montoneros and from other Argentine guerrilla groups.

The military junta (309), that took the reigns of power from Perón's widow, Isabel, in 1976 justified its actions in a published set of documents. Civilian rule was restored in 1983, and that government investigated the charges of human rights abuses and state terrorism brought against the armed forces while they were in power. From this process has emerged an extraordinary series of documents: for example, the English language version of NUNCA MAS, THE REPORT OF THE ARGENTINE NATIONAL COMMISSION ON THE DISAPPEARED (410); ANEXOS DEL INFORME... (17); a report on the clandestine detention center at the navy's Escuela Mecánica (604); and the two sets compiled by López Saavedra (347, 348), containing interviews with prominent politicians, intellectuals, economists and historians made during the military's reign. Finally, two documentary collections cover the 1985 trial of the leaders of the armed forces who were held responsible for the disappearances of thousands of Argentines: TESTIMONIOS: "EL LIBRO DE JUICIO" (605), and EL LIBRO DE "EL DIARIO DEL JUICIO" (333). And, Alberto Quirós (493), together with friends and colleagues of Ricardo Balbín, leader of the "Popular Radicals" (UCR del Pueblo-UCRP) who died in 1981, collected and published his speeches and essays dating from the 1940s.

No doubt, as time goes by, more and more documents will emerge from the Malvinas/Falklands war. A good start is THE FALKLANDS WAR: THE OFFICIAL HISTORY (194), which provided official Argentine and British statements, and the multivolume British documentary, THE FALKLANDS WAR: THE DAY BY DAY RECORD FROM INVASION TO VICTORY (193). Consult as well Ethel and Price (189).

MEMOIRS, JOURNALS, AND EYEWITNESS ACCOUNTS

Like the Brazilian top brass, Argentine military leaders and their civilian counterparts tend to explain themselves to the public by publishing their memoirs or apologias. Certainly inadequate compensation for not leaving their papers in public archives, nevertheless, when used with great care, these accounts can serve the historian well.

Prior to the first quarter of the twentieth century few memoirs or eyewitness accounts of military life or of the armed forces' political activities exist. However, some notable actors in the Indian wars of the 1870s and 1880s published memoirs: Daza (146), Ramayón (494), and Prado (482). General José Ignacio Garmendia (228), besides his descriptions of Indian warfare, writes about an officer's duty, discipline, and civic virtue, among other themes. The memoirs of Colonel Manuel Baiggoria (52), should be consulted as well.

While the military institution underwent significant changes toward professionalization during the early 1900s, some officers, as Caballero (91), recalled, joined the Radicals in their abortive attempt to seize power. Cattáneo (111, 112), recounted activities and ideology of the secret Logia General San Martín during the 1920s, and he also remembered the Radical military revolts of the 1930s. Dr. Juan Carulla (105, 106, 107), a nationalist physician, newspaper publisher, and close associate to General Uriburu, left accounts of the Revolution of 1930 and after, as did Sarobe (562), who was a confidant of General Justo in his rivalry with Uriburu. See also in this regard the account given by the young Juan D. Perón (460). Pascual Vuotto (634), an anarchist jailed in 1931 along with two others, gave a personal account of life in the proletariat under military rule. Other important memoirs for the 1920s and 1930s are: Pinedo (468), Justo's voluble finance minister; Quebracho (488), pseudonym for Libório Justo, the president's son; Repetto (512, 513, 514), and de la Torre (608), both civilian opposition politicians.

Insight into conditions and activities in the Argentine armed forces during World War II and the 1943 coup can be gleaned from Carrill (104), Ghioldi (233), Hull (296), Korn (321), Lucero (351), Perón (459), and Ruiz-Guiñazú (549).

Perón's climb to power and eventual triumph as two-term president (1946-55) of Argentina have been eloquently described by the colonel himself (461). Plater (471), provided an insider's account of Perón's alliance building. Lanus (323), who opposed Perón, explained why and emphasized the pro-democracy faction in the army. Perón's sometime war minister, Lucero (351), offered his view of the era and revealed why he supported Perón, while Sumner Wells (642), and Spruille Braden (81), justified their opposition to Perón and explained United States policies toward Argentina. Güemes (269), provided important details about the secret military organization GOU, and David Kelly (314), who served as British ambassador during the events of 1945, cited civilian politicians' lack of political instinct for Perón's eventual triumph. From the vantage point of the navy ministry, Olivieri (419), made valuable observations about the Perón era.

Events surrounding the fall of Perón are described by Carril (104), while Lonardi (342), revealed the inner struggles of the opposition that eventually succeeded in overthrowing the former army colonel. Martínez (377), discussed the anti-clerical campaign and its alleged ties to the presidential succession as did Olivieri (419). Amadeo (16), related the details of the coalescence of military factions against Perón, and Lucero (351), remembered the steps taken to counter the plotters. Pavón Pereyra, in COLOQUIOS CON PERON (441), related Perón's side as he explained from exile the navy rebellion of 1955.

When the "Liberating Revolution" brought the military to power in 1955, many Peronists suffered exile or imprisonment or both. Others were executed. Antonio (18), remembered these events, including his internment in Tierra del Fuego. Barrios (62), a devoted follower of Perón, told of the times during and after the 1955 coup, and Vigo (629), wrote of his experiences while in prison. A former Peronist deputy, Eduardo M. Firpo (206), covered incidents after 1955, as did Colonel Juan F. Guevara (270), who participated in the political activities of the 1940s and 1950s. Perón's (452, 458), observations from exile make fascinating reading. Ramón Prieto (483, 484), a former Peronist who later joined the industrialist-journalist Rogelio Frigorio and Arturo Frondizi as they sought to build an alliance to oppose the military, provides an, at times, inaccurate and partisan account of these events. See also Díaz (154), Domínguez (164), Guardo (268), and Perina (447), all of whom describe the efforts to forge the anti-military alliance.

Frondizi's uneasy relationship with the armed forces is recounted by Gómez (244), while Luna's DIALOGOS CON FRONDIZI (355), allows the former president to make his own observations. Domínguez (164), Guardo (268), Guevara (270), and Toryho (611), helped us to glimpse the growing military opposition to Frondizi which put an end to his government in 1962.

The turbulent period between Frondizi's ouster and Perón's return (1962-1973) produced very few published memoirs or eyewitness accounts. Nevertheless, Roth (535), a close advisor to President General Onganía, wrote a provocative, revisionist assessment of the Onganiato, and Gregorio Selser (571, 572), well known Argentine journalist, published his critically insightful articles on two years (1966-67) of Onganía's regime in a useful two-volume work. General Lanusse (324), recounted his own administration in a brief, but crucial, memoir, and Mariano Castex (110), related how he witnessed it in a series of editorial pieces written in 1972. Those who fled the military repression in the 1960s told their stories to Alejandro Dorrego and

Victoria Azurduy (165). Urondo (624), and PRONTUARIO: TECNICA DEL INTERROGATORIO, LA REPRESION Y EL ASESINATO (485) described the circumstances surrounding the 1972 Trelew Massacre, in which sixteen guerrillas were gunned down after an unsuccessful prison escape.

Perón's return in 1973 was helped along through the efforts of Héctor J. Cámpora (93), who told of his role in this event and of his brief tenure as president. Newspaperman Rodolfo Terragno (602), remembered the 400 days of Perón's third and final presidency. Neustadt (408), provided a transcript of television interviews taped in 1975-76 with 132 people from government, the opposition, academia, business, labor, etc., who voiced their opinions on conditions in Argentina. And, finally, the Latin American Studies Association (LASA) (325), published testimonies from political prisoners and persons tortured by government and para-military forces.

A member of the military junta that removed Isabel Perón in 1976, Emilio E. Massera (381), justified his role in a memoir intended for his colleagues, business and agricultural leaders. Jacobo Timermann (606), founder and editor of the once prominent newspaper LA OPINION, authored what has become, perhaps, the best known inside story on the brutality and the torture committed by the military and police after 1976. General Ramón Camps (94, 95), in two different works, justified the arrest and torture of Timermann who, he claimed, worked with those who financed the Montonero guerrilla group. Unfortunately, Timermann's experience was not an isolated one. Marini (373), rendered an eyewitness account of the junta's anti-birth control policies and of the deteriorating status of working class women in 1976. MI HIJA DAGMAR (278), is the grim memoir of a father's futile search for his seventeen-year-old daughter seized by naval intelligence and never seen again. Zamorano (657), lived to tell the tale of his imprisonment from 1974 to 1979. Two foreign journalists, Frank Manitzas (372), and Mort Rosenblum (534), related intimate and chilling accounts of the terror that gripped Buenos Aires in 1976.

Argentina's war with Great Britain over the Falklands/Malvinas Islands was told from the soldiers' point of view in Kon (320); President General Galtieri justified his government's decision to invade the islands in "El interrogatorio...." (300); General Mario Benjamín Menéndez (387), commander in chief of the Argentine occupation forces, provided an invaluable account of the war from his vantage point; and Carballo (99) collected testimonies from Argentine air force pilots who described their experiences.

SPECIALIZED WORKS

Owing to the great strides made in the study of Argentine politico-military history in the last thirty years, this section will focus only on those works that the author considers to be the most useful. Furthermore, to aid the user this section is subdivided into the following areas: Early Professionalization, 1870-1910; Radicals and the Military, 1905-30; Army Rule and the "Infamous Decade," 1930-43; the Perón Era, 1943-55; "Liberating Revolution" and Civilian Rule, 1955-62; Military Intervention, 1962-73; The Restoration of Perón, 1973-76; the Military and National Reorganization, 1976-83; and Return to Civilian Government, 1983-90.

EARLY PROFESSIONALIZATION, 1870-1910

Historians examining the late nineteenth century will want to consult the Thomson chapter in this bibliography as well as Etchepareborda (187). In addition, McGann (336), offered an excellent historical background for military political activity, and Ferrari (204), pinned responsibility for successive military interventions on politicians' mistakes and inability to develop viable programs. Cuccorese (138), contended that confrontation with Chile in the 1890s increased military expenditures and forced the Pelligrini government to raise taxes. For other insights into border conflicts and Argentine expansionist goals at the turn of the century, consult Cuccorese (139), and Etchepareborda (185, 187).

Military professionalization and the development of the modern armed forces in Argentina are the subjects of works by Cantón (98), who provided a brief overview of early professional development; Grela (262), who has a good biography of General Pablo Riccheri; Atkins and Thompson (49), Nunn (411), Fritz Epstein (179), Schaefer (565), and Schiff (567), who studied German influence on professionalization and the dependency of Argentina on Germany for arms; Ramírez's dissertation (495), which analyzed the reforms of the army, 1890-1904; Romay (530), who studied in great detail the development of the federal police; and Piccinali (464), who examined the life of General Nicolás Lavalle, three-time minister of war and navy and founder of the Círculo Militar. From the facile pen of Félix Luna (360), emerged a best-selling biography of General Julio Roca. Lironi (337), researched the genesis of military and civilian aviation; Sanz (561), and Burzio (88, 89), explained the navy's role in conflicts with Uruguay and Brazil over use of the Río de la Plata, and the development of naval armaments, respectively.

RADICALS AND THE MILITARY, 1905-30

This crucial period in the rise of Argentine militarism has attracted the attention of numerous writers, some of whom are the most talented historians writing on Argentina since 1960.

Both Duval (174), a Brazilian military attaché in Buenos Aires 1916-20, and Maligné (369), an Argentine colonel, are reliable for information pertaining to military technical data for the era. Maligné (370), and Rodríguez (528), contributed useful historical surveys of the armed forces that cover this period. Arturo Torres's (609), biography of Elpídio González offered insights into the level of officer support for the 1905 revolution. Luna (353), produced a volume on the life of Radical leader, and Argentine President Marcelo T. de Alvear (1922-28), and Quiroga (492), showed the armed forces' desire for new weaponry after World War I. Rock (525), contributed an excellent survey of the rise and fall of the Radicals to 1930.

The coup that toppled Yrigoyen in 1930 and kept the Radicals from power for more than a quarter century has been well covered by Cantón (96), Ferrer (205), Goldwert (241, 243), Orona (423, 425), Potash (479), and Zorraquín Becú (659). Colonel Reyes (518, 519), analyzed military strategy and petroleum production, as well as industrialization, especially as it related to the arms industry. Mazo and Etchepareborda (386), Rottjer (536), and Valle (625), scrutinized the relationship between the armed forces and the Radical Civic Union, and Repetto (515), summarized the views of Socialist Party leaders. Bayer (64), contributed an excellent chronicle of the anarcho-syndicalist struggle in the south of the country during the 1920s. The breakdown of political legitimacy was the chief cause of the coup of 1930 according to Peter Smith (578, 580), while Deutsch (152), and Potter (481), placed heavy emphasis on the reaction of right-wing conservative groups who feared that a continuation of Radical rule would eventually destroy their power.

ARMY RULE AND THE "INFAMOUS DECADE," 1930-43

General Uriburu's provisional government,which lasted for seventeen months (6 September 1930 to 20 February 1932), was regarded by lawyer and publicist Colmo (127), as a military regime, whereas Sánchez Sorondo (554, 555), who served in it, believed it to have been essentially civilian. Orona's LA REVOLUCION DEL 6 DE SEPTIEMBRE (425), analyzed the reshuffling of army commands after Uriburu seized power; Quesada (489), recounted the wave of repression unleased against unions and anarchists; Goldwert (241), and Potash (479), briefly survey the regime.

The "Infamous Decade" began with the election to the presidency of General Agustín B. Justo, whose economic policies were reviewed critically by Palacio (435), and Scalabrini Ortíz (563), but less so by Rennie (511), and Whitaker (647). Potash (479), devoted three interesting chapters to the decade, which is the subject of Torres's (610), entire book. Carranza, Vinuales, and Ferrari (102), observed the political proposals and issues of the era. Sanguinetti (558, 559), found the Uriburu and Justo regimes a "fictive democracy" as he examined, through careful research and oral testimonies, the role played by two Socialist ministers in Justo's administration. Falcoff and Dolkart (192), provided a general account of the period, as did Ciria (124), whose Marxist analysis is thorough, interesting, and of great value. Hilton (287), studied Argentina's neutral stance in the first nine months of World War II, and Guglialmelli (275), Martínez (375), Panaia, Lesser, and Skupch (438), and Sadi (553), analyzed the problem of industrialization as it pertained to national defense.

PERON ERA, 1943-55

Military leaders put an end to the civilian rule of President Ramón Castillo, 4 June 1943, and created conditions that enabled Juan D. Perón to come to power in 1946. Potash's (477), three chapters on these epic events are essential reading as is Colonel Orona's (422), book on the GOU, the secret military society that led the coup against Castillo, which should be compared with Díaz Araujo's (155) work on the same topic. Caillet-Bois (92), explained the part taken in the coup by the Radical leader Emilio Ravignani, and Américo Ghioldi (233), examined the position of the German embassy toward the new military government. Ray Josephs' (308), journalistic account of the coup is enlightening, as is that of Ruth and Leonard Greenup (260).

Several excellent studies deal with the foreign relations conducted by the military regime once it assumed control. Frank (214), Conil Paz and Ferrari (128), MacDonald (363), Peterson (462), Rapoport (504, 505), and Whitaker's THE UNITED STATES AND ARGENTINA (647), all make solid contributions.

For an understanding of the new government's treatment of labor unions in particular and workers in general Alexander (7), and Baily (55), are still useful, but the student should also consult Belloni (68), Cerutti Costa (121), Durruty (173), Oddone (412), Stickell (593), and Torre (607).

Perón's triumph and the election of 1945 is given good coverage in Cantón (96), Llorente (340), Luna's EL 45 (354), Murmis, et al. (404), and the several works by Smith (578, 581, 582, 583). The role of the infamous *Blue Book* in Perón's victory is explained in Becke (67), and in Frank (213). For a collection of essays and a solid bibliography on the background of Perón's climb to power see Barager (57).

An avalanche of publications has cascaded from the printing presses since the mid-1960s treating one or another aspect of the Perón administrations. An essential place to start is with the relevant chapters in Potash's (477), second volume, as well as with Orona's (421, 422), two studies; LA DICTADURA DE PERON, is perhaps one of the most astute and polished syntheses of this era published to date. Robert J. Alexander (7, 6), wrote one of the first accounts in English of Perón's rise to power and his first administration; then he followed it up with a second, rather superficial account of Perón to his death in 1974. Both treated Perón in a negative manner. Blanksten's (74), early work is still of value; Ciria's (124, 125), studies looked at Perón's political philosophy and analyzed the various interpretations given it, and the formation of political organizations; see also Fayt (196), and Waldmann (637, 638), both of whom observed the nature of Peronism and the regime's relations with principal pressure groups. Halperín Donghi (281), Hodges (290), and Luna (358), all treated Perón in critical syntheses that covered the period from 1943 to 1973, while Rouquié's second volume of PODER MILITAR Y SOCIEDAD POLITICA EN LA ARGENTINA (545), concentrated on Perón's relationship with the military during the same time frame. Martínez's (376), two volumes is a treasure trove of information and is especially good on the complex nature of the times. Page (434), wrote an ambitious, scholarly, well documented biography of the dictator, and Crassweller (134), produced a superb life and times study. Turner and Miguens (614), provided a revisionist approach to Perón's place in Argentine history.

D'Amico (143), explained Perón's relations with the Catholic Church, as did Gambini (221), albeit in a journalistic fashion. Leonard (327), believed that the Perón/Church clash resulted from the government's attempts to interfere in education.

Perón's policies regarding the petroleum sector were critically analyzed by Kaplan (311, 312); Fador (191), with a revisionist's eye, looked at the government's policies on agricultural exports; Kenworthy (317), claimed that the new industrialists did not play a significant role in the formation of the Peronist alliance; Ranis (502, 503), challenged that view. Skidmore (577), compared populist economics in Argentina and Brazil; Teichman (601), found that in the textile and metallurgic sectors entrepreneurs supported the regime. Doyen (167), compared the labor disputes of the 1946-48 period with those that took place in 1953-54; Germani (231), Halperín Donghi (280), and Little (338, 339), differed over the character of Perón's labor support. Llorente (340, 341), examined the social composition of the Peronist movement, and with Mora y Araujo (397), edited a collection of electoral studies of the period. Smith (582, 583), quantatively studied the social base of Peronism and found that it cut across class lines. Stabb (590), explored the government's repressive measures, especially against intellectuals; and Mazo (384, 385), provided great detail in recounting Perón's relations with the Radicals.

Biographies of Eva Perón are increasing in quantity, but most are lacking in quality and objectivity. Barnes's (60), profile is useful, and Borroni and Vacca (76), provided a well documented, impartial study. Fraser and Navarro (215), ably demythefied and clarified many aspects of Eva's life, but the older work by Main (María Flores) (367), while sensationalistic and anecdotal, still contains useful insights. J. M. Taylor (600), imaginatively interpreted Eva's life from the varying ways in which she was perceived by Argentines.

"LIBERATING REVOLUTION" AND CIVILIAN RULE, 1955-62

For the era from the fall of Perón to the overthrow of Frondizi, Potash (477), devoted three authoritative chapters and concluded that "The democratic impulses that had underlain the uprising against Perón in 1955 and pressured the successor military regime to surrender power at the earliest opportunity proved insufficient to lay the bases for long-term political stability." Clara Celia Budeinsky (85), analyzed the era from a Peronist left perspective and found it to represent the return of the oligarchy to power. Cavarozzi in two excellent but brief studies, SINDICATOS Y POLITICAS EN ARGENTINA, 1955-1958 (114), argued that the country's political process was substantially changed during this time, and in UNIONS AND POLITICS, 1955-1962 (115), concentrated on worker militancy and ambivalence toward the military-civilian governments ruling in Perón's absence. In a third work, AUTORITARISMO Y DEMOCRACIA: (1955-1983) (113), he offered an able analysis of military thinking and the armed forces' relations with labor.

The prodigious Orona (424), focused on the antecedents of the rebellion against Perón and examined the provisional military government that replaced him. A leading Trotskyist, Nahuel Moreno (399), contended that only his faction understood the need to resist the coup of 1955 through force. On the other hand, Luis Ernesto Lonardi (342), and his sister Marta (343), wrote passionate, polemical accounts supporting the military government headed by their father Eduardo. Godio (239), chronicled Perón's last days from June to September 1955, and believed that it was his inability or unwillingness to rally popular support that led to his fall. Ferla (200), discussed at length the military uprising led by General Aramburu against fellow officer Lonardi on 9

June 1956 and condemned its brutality and the executions that followed. Gallo (220), recorded the split in the Radical party of the late 1950s and explained the response of each faction to the military government after 1955.

Arturo Frondizi and his efforts to bring Argentina back under civilian control were treated favorably by Nelly Casas (108). Barrera (61), examined his educational and ideological background, and Cuneo (141), and Florit (209), dealt with his foreign policy. Fayt's (197), highly informative work picked up with Frondizi, but stretched beyond to the early 1970s; Guevara (270), covered the same time period as did Selser (570), and Snow (584, 585). Odena (413), treated Frondizi favorably in his survey; Quinterno (490), recounted the era in journalistic style, and Bustos Fierro (90), reviewed the period from the Peronist perspective. Owing to Frondizi's weak government being composed of warring factions determined to overthrow it from the inception, Rodríguez Lamas (529), believed its policies of concessions and economic development cost him what support he had and doomed him to failure. O'Donnell (416), briefly surveyed the decade 1955-66 and offered thought provoking observations.

MILITARY INTERVENTION, 1962-73

With Frondizi's ouster in March 1962 factionalism within the armed forces intensified. Gregorich (261), investigated the Azul-Colorado conflict that divided the military and wrote the best account of it. Alberto Alvarez and Enrique Walter (14), published a brief, but useful review of the internal divisions. Orsolini (426), himself a military man, analyzed the internal conflicts, while Rattenbach (506), attempted a sociological inquiry into the armed forces to understand what differentiated them from the rest of society. Florit (208), a professor of law, raised essential questions about the causes and justifications for political intervention offered by the soldiers. He concluded that they had subjected society to constant psychological warfare. Baily (53, 54), and Whitaker (645, 646), chronicled the tumultuous period after the collapse of the Frondizi government.

Américo Ghioldi (232), a veteran Argentine political figure, collected 42 individual articles that he had written critical of the military coup of 28 June 1966 which brought General Onganía to the Casa Rosada. Similarly, an extremely useful source of information for the years 1966-1973 is the collection of editorials by Botana, Braun and Floria (80), in which they critiqued the military governments from a liberal, pluralist perspective. Rivera Echenique (522), saw the coup as part of an imperialist plan fostered by the United States to put friendly authoritarian governments in power throughout Latin America.

Unlike previous military interventions, the coup of 1966 demonstrated that the Argentine armed forces meant to hold power indefinitely. Buchanan (84), compared the government of Onganía with that of Perón, and Argentine journalist Gregorio Selser (571, 572), published a two-volume, highly detailed critical account of the Onganía regime. García Lupo's MERCENARIOS Y MONOPOLIOS EN LA ARGENTINA (223), was violently critical of Onganía and his successor, General Lanusse. Perina (448, 449), examined the military governments between 1966 and 1973 using the Huntington "developmentalist" model. Evers (190), produced a significant, solid monograph on the so-called "Argentine Revolution." Ceresole (117, 118), wondered if the officers in charge of the government were really up to the task before them. Michael Dodson (161, 162, 163), in three articles, outlined the rapid rise of the "Tercermundista" movement among the clergy during the Onganía regime.

Popular rebellion exploded against military rule in what has come to be known as the "Cordobazo" of 1969. Francisco Delich (150), produced an excellent socio-historical analysis of the events as they unfolded in Córdoba and took on national significance. Ramos, et al. (496), took the position that the masses spontaneously seized the revolutionary initiative against the regime. Massari (380), examined the circumstances that led to the uprising and emphasized the problems of regional economic devolopment.

The rise of radical guerrilla opposition to military repression and the regime's brutal reaction received serious scholarly examination from a number of investigators. Cirino (126), set the stage with a description and analysis of guerrilla warfare, but fell short of a solid explanation of the Argentine situation. Hodges (290), did an excellent job sympathetically treating resistance to the various regimes from 1943 to 1976. Gillespie (235), and Giussani (236), dissected the Montoneros, and Graham-Yooll (256), faulted armed forces involvement in public life for the rising level of political violence. Fernández Alvarino (201), focused on the kidnapping and execution of former president General Aramburu, calling it the "crime of the century." González Janzen (252), a radical Peronist, provided a passionate partisan view of political violence from 1955 to 1975, and the Buenos Aires Forum for the Promotion of Human Rights (210), depressingly recounted official misconduct of all kinds during the soldiers' control in 1972-73. See also Kenneth Johnson's GUERRILLA POLITICS IN ARGENTINA (305).

For an assessment of the events surrounding the collapse of the Onganía regime and the efforts of successor governments to rule, consult Gaignard (218), who wrote an excellent and well-documented article. López (344), evaluated the political and economic factors faced by Onganía's successors. Corradi (133), offered insight into the crisis of the early 1970s. Pandolfi (439), and Portes (474), briefly outlined the failures of the military governments after Onganía, but it is Rouquié's (545), work that is truly both a gold mine of information and a well documented analysis on this period. Dressl (168), and O'Donnell (414), theorized on the type of state system that emerged in Argentina between 1955 and 1976, while Quinterno (491), harshly condemned earlier populist attempts and advocated a strong, authoritarian system. Potash (478), promises a sequel to his two other fine studies of the army in politics with a third volume covering the era 1962-73.

THE RESTORATION OF PERON, 1973-76

Perón's return to power in 1973 was joyfully celebrated by the working people of Argentina who, according to Edward Epstein (178), believed that he would reverse the shabby treatment they had received at the hands of those who had ruled the country since his exile in 1955. Pablo's (432), astute analysis showed how Perón's economic program did not favor them as they hoped. Di Tella (160, in what is the most complete economic study of the period, concluded that despite Perón's failures, his death and his party's decline, Peronism will remain an important force in national politics for some time to come. Itzcovitz (302), in her able work, suggested that the Peronist government failed owing to the severe divisions in the ruling party. Tamarin (598), compared Perón's return to power with the second government of Yrigoyen and concluded that Argentine populism had come to an end. Policy making in a highly confrontational society lacking wide-spread political participation and a national consensus is the subject of Wynia's (652), excellent book on the period 1943 to 1976. An insightful overview of the tumultuous period is that published by the North American Congress on Latin America (NACLA) (406), which was critical of the increasing control of foreign capital in the Argentine economy. Landi (322), also analyzed the competing socio-economic forces and the opposing ideological bases that engendered a permanent political crisis.

A useful chronology of the events of January 1974 to the March 1976 military coup which removed Vice-President Isabel Perón from power can be found in "Argentine: Chronologie de la presidence de Perón..." (46), which also provided biographies of the new junta members and texts of their economic and political programs. The thinking behind the military actions in 1976 can be understood by consulting Díaz Loza (157), while the son-in-law of General Lonardi, José A. Deheza (148), passionately maintained that political intrigues inside the Justicialista Party aided the increasing military opposition to the floundering Isabel Perón regime. Rosendo Fraga (212), detailed the intrigues and factional alignments within the military during the Peróns' administration. The Latin American Studies Association (LASA) (325), sponsored a report researched and written by anonymous Argentine social scientists describing the increasing level of terror and repression unleashed against the left, labor, Peronist youth, and university and other dissidents during the Peróns' presidency.

THE MILITARY AND NATIONAL REORGANIZATION, 1976-83

Since the armed forces removed Isabel Perón from office in 1976 a staggering stream of articles and books have spewed forth from presses around the world covering events and topics through the Falklands/ Malvinas war and civilian resumption of political control in 1983. Space only permits a brief overview of some of the more significant literature.

In his IDEOLOGIA DE FASCISMO DEPENDIENTE: ESTADO Y SEGURIDAD NACIONAL, Alvaro Briones (82), focused primarily on Chile, but compared situations there to Argentina and concluded that the national and foreign business classes created the military governments in order to protect and consolidate their own interests. Riquet (520), a French Jesuit, briefly examined the military regime's relations with the Church in the context of the debate over liberation theology; Lernoux's (329, 330), two books have chapters on church/state relations under the armed forces government. Jordan (306), Rouquié (540, 542, 543), and Smith (579), provided straight forward reportage and analyses of the Videla regime through 1979. Most (401), explored changes in the "bureaucratic-authoritarian state" and how these changes have manifested themselves in Argentina. Munck (402), rejected the fascist characterization of the Argentine military government and called into question the bureaucratic-authoritarian model proposed by Guillermo O'Donnell (417). Peter Waldmann and Ernesto Garzón Valdés (640), edited a collection of diverse papers treating historical and socio-political aspects of the military regime, 1976-81.

The armed forces economic stabilization program attracted considerable attention. José María Rivera (521), critically evaluated Videla's stablization strategy and noted its short-term adverse effects. Mason Lugones (379), likewise found fault with the regime's economic performance and accused it of perpetuating long-term inequalities between Buenos Aires and the other provinces. Muñoz Grande (403), supported the military, not just in its economic goals, but in other respects as well. This work offers a good example of the logic used by the armed forces in justification of their actions. An economist at the World Bank, Colin Wogart (649), took a close look at the liberalization program in the late 1970s and provided, perhaps,the most informative account of it in English. The controversial minister of finance, José

Martínez de Hoz, drew the critical appraisal of Jorge Schvarzer (568, 569), who stressed the obstacles to economic liberalization and the mismanagement of financial policies. The same author also focused on the effects of the government's economic liberalization program and demonstrated the resulting indebtedness.

Organized labor's response to the military's repressive measures during this period was well documented by Alvaro Abos (1), and Santiago Senen González and Ricardo Gallo (573), provided a year-by-year account of the government's attempts to regulate and control the labor movement during the decade, 1973-83. "Nota de tapa: Los puntos sobre las íes." (409), is an informative and provocative description of the government's political objectives, pointing out the contradictions in its strategy. Political scientist Gary Wynia (654), noted the contradictions also as he reviewed the regime's economic policies during 1980.

Two interesting works coming from different directions offered insight into right-wing Argentine thought on the military during this era. Ricardo Zinn (658), wrote a personalized summary of the country's history applauding the nation's armed forces, especially those in power in 1979, for saving Argentina from decadence and "international Marxist conspiracy." Carlos Echague (175), however, criticized the Videla-Viola dictatorship for causing Argentina to become dependent on the USSR by stressing cereal production and exports to the Soviet Union. He feared that the Soviets would use Argentina to control the South Atlantic.

The reign of terror unleashed by security forces during the 1970s and early 1980s received a great deal of attention, and continues to do so, as it should. A recent and authoritative book is Hodges' ARGENTINA'S "DIRTY WAR," AN INTELLECTUAL BIOGRAPHY (291). Argentine journalist Eduardo Luis Duhalde (171), examined the ideas and objectives behind the state directed terror. Two BBC journalists, John Simpson and Jana Bennett (576), summarized the secret security operations in an excellent coverage of some of the most notorious cases. Mark Dowie of MOTHER JONES (166), gave a highly detailed report of official torture and murder as he looked at the experiences of the Santucho family of Santiago del Estero. Novelist V. S. Naipaul (407), left us a fascinating account of the terror from the left and from the right. He came to the chilling conclusion that both sides believed the country's political solutions would be realized only by "killing the right people." Andrew Graham-Yooll (256), fearing that he might be one of those killed, fled the country and later returned to investigate and write about the terror.

Emilio De Ipola and Liliana de Riz (149), by analyzing the material that appeared in the magazine CARTA POLITICA, drew interesting conclusions about the conservative ideology that spoke to the leaders in the armed forces, in the bureaucracy, and elsewhere in society during the period. Finally, David Pion-Berlin (470), after narrating the principal events that led to the demise of the military government in 1983, concluded that it brought about its own downfall.

Most will agree that the government's decision to invade the Falklands/Malvinas Islands and to push the British out of the South Atlantic was a foolish one, leading to disastrous and far reaching consequences for the armed forces. In SIGNALS OF WAR, Lawrence Freedman and Virginia Gamba-Stonehouse (216), presented an authoritative account of the origins, development and course of the war from both sides of the issue. Hoffman and Hoffman (293), effectively surveyed the history of the conflict from colonial times to the 1982 invasion and they were sympathetic to Argentine claims. Santos Martínez (560), provided an Argentine view of the issue, while Cardosa, Kirchbaum and Van der Kooy (100), in an excellent piece of investigative journalism, delved deep into the decisions behind the planning and waging of the war; it is essential reading for its insights into the behaviour of officials in the Galtieri regime. Based on photographs, official documents, and oral testimony from officers from both air forces, Romero Briaseo and Mafe Huertas (533), analyzed the tactics and equipment used by each side during the war. They faulted the Argentines for not establishing adequate air defenses for the islands. A superb retelling of the air war can be found in the book by Ethell and Price (189). Retired naval officer Charles W. Koburger (318), offered a technical evaluation of the war's naval operations; Gavshon and Rice (229), investigated the sinking of the *Belgrano* but stopped short of accusing the British of sinking the Argentine destroyer to thwart the peace process. Rozitchner (547), exemplified the view of Argentine leftists toward the country's defeat in the war and the subsequent collapse of the army's political control. Hastings and Jenkins (283), told an exciting tale about the war from the British point of view, but they blamed both governments for their failure effectively to communicate to each other the seriousness of their intentions.

Consequences of the war for Argentina's international relations, and especially its position in the inter-American community are considered by several experts who convened in a seminar in Lima in October 1982, and published their findings in REDEFINICION DE LAS RELACIONES INTRALATINOAMERICANAS... (510). Gordon Connell-Smith (129), emphasized growing fissures in the inter-American system as a result of the war. Mestre (389), intelligently critiqued the United States role in the conflict, and the Russian Goncharov (245), while ignoring the brutal nature of the Galtieri government, landed some telling blows on the body of British policies and actions.

Honeywell and Pearce (295), took into consideration the Argentine abuses, while skillfully exposing failures and blunders on both sides. Ossendorff (430), imaginatively analyzed how the enemy was depicted in the newspapers of the respective belligerent countries. Dabat and Lorenzano (142), from exile in Mexico, saw the conflict and the fall of the military regime in the context of Marxist analysis of class conflict.

RETURN TO CIVILIAN GOVERNMENT, 1983-90

The transition from military rule to civilian democracy at the end of 1983 has been of great interest to political scientists who have done the majority of the research on this topic to date. Alain Rouquié's "L'Argentine après les militaires" (538), is a thoughtful analysis of the problems confronting the Radical Alfonsín government in its first few months in power. Gary Wynia, writing in CURRENT HISTORY (653, 654), assessed the Radicals' performance in the renascent democracy and their relations with the military. Carlos J. Moneta (395), in an interesting article, discussed the institutional and ideological changes within the armed forces occasioned by the war with Britain and the return to civilian rule. Peter Ranis (501), analyzed the "dilemmas of democratization" in Argentina after the Radicals came to power, and Waisman and Peralta-Ramos (636), edited an important collection of views on the obstacles confronting the transition to democracy. Potash (476), produced an article on the military policies of Alfonsín and Menem and concluded that their reforms of the armed forces were rather limited.

PERIODICALS

Periodical literature on the Argentine armed services can be found in a variety of different journals specializing in history and the social sciences. In addition, there are a few magazines that concentrate specifically on military matters, most of which are published by the branches of the armed forces themselves. For the latter, the bibliography compiled by Einaudi and Goldhamer (176), is essential.

Searching for articles on Argentine military history can be facilitated by use of the HISPANIC AMERICAN PERIODICALS INDEX (HAPI) (289), which since 1977 has provided students with an accurate guide to the periodical literature. Most of the significant journals and magazines containing material on the Argentine military are listed at the end of this bibliography, but the list is selective and does not include publications found in the Soviet Union and Eastern Europe.

Valuable information and insights into various aspects of the Argentine armed services can be found in Argentine newspapers and news magazines such as LA NACION (692), LA PRENSA (696), PRIMEIRA PLANA (697), REVIEW OF THE RIVER PLATE (698), HECHOS E IDEAS (680), CARTA POLITICA (672), and LA VANGUARDIA (715), to name but a few. Major Latin American, North American, and Western European daily and weekly news sources provide good coverage of military and political affairs, especially if they have their own observers in the country. ARGENTINE OUTREACH (665), since 1976 monitored the human rights situation in Argentina, but also supplied excellent coverage of political events. Consult as well MILITARY AFFAIRS (686), for occasional articles on Argentine military history and the listing of doctoral dissertations dealing with military topics.

FUTURE RESEARCH

Although a great deal of basic informational research into the political history of the Argentine armed forces has been done, opportunities abound for research in specific areas. Of course, investigating an institution that is normally closed to public scrutiny can be frustrating and poses challenges to the researcher. Nevertheless, hard work, persistence, luck, and skillful diplomacy can bring forth significant results and produce valuable contributions to an understanding of the military and its role in society.

While the foregoing bibliographic essay discusses many of the excellent surveys of the the Argentine army in politics, it is notably silent on the history of the navy and the air force. While Scheina's (566), work on Latin American naval history is a good start, this is an area that is open to further investigation. Similarly, the air force needs thorough examination.

Some writers like Nunn (411), have brought their considerable skills to bear on comparative analyses of certain military history topics, such as the role of European influence in the development of professional armies in Latin America. Nevertheless, this is still an area that needs further exploration, and a comparative analysis of the history of the Argentine, Brazilian, and Chilean armed forces would make a valuable contribution to our understanding of the security institutions in these three countries.

Biographies of Argentine politicians abound as do studies of "men on horseback" from the nineteenth century, but thoughtful, carefully researched biographies of generals and admirals in the twentieth century would enhance our understanding of the individual leaders' impact on the institution and on the nation. General-presidents

Agustín P. Justo and Pedro E. Aramburu and admirals Isaac F. Rojas and Arturo Rial offer possiblities for interesting and important biographies. More work still needs to be done on Eva Perón and especially her tumultuous relationship with the military. Despite the numerous works already done on Perón there is still a need to explore his voluminous correspondence and make sense of his impact on the military and on Argentine society. We still do not have a clear understanding of Perón's influence in the army from the time of his overthrow in 1955 to his death in 1974. Indeed, the military's relationship with labor needs to be reassessed in light of the Pacto Sindical Militar which emerged after the Cordobazo.

There is a dearth of thorough studies on the General Directorate of Military Manufactures (Dirección General de Fabricaciones Militares-DGFM), the considerable military-industrial complex. In the mid 1980s Argentina figured second only to Brazil among Latin American nations producing and exporting military equipment, and Milenky (393), and Porth (475), discuss this industry. Owing to the size and importance of the complex, however, and the significant reorganization which it underwent during the Alfonsín administration, an in-depth monograph is badly needed here. Similarly, a thorough investigation of the Argentine nuclear programs, that until 1983 had been under the control of the navy, would be important.

Another significant area that lacks thorough examination is the historical relationship of the three traditional branches of the armed services to paramilitary organizations and to the federal police. The role played by the corps of engineers and its civic works programs in the development of the national infrastructure needs to be examined, as does the evolution of the military educational program and its influence on civilian education theory and practice and vice versa. Historians need to analyze the factors that influence officers to adopt particular political orientations and to see if these differ from those held by men in other professions. While several works explain the national security doctrine, the ramifications of that doctrine on the military and civil society need to be explored.

The nature of civil-military relations at the provincial level and the changing image of the military in the national psyche from early professionalization to the end of the Alfonsín government remain somewhat of an enigma. Historians also should examine the level and extent of the military governments' promotion of science and the extent of armed forces interference in the scientific community. Also, what has been the economic impact of armed forces on the nation, i.e., has Argentina been able to afford its armed forces? Another problem area is the question why did the military regime during the "Proceso" (1976-83) react to subversion in the manner which it did? A comparison of the thinking of the high command during that era with that of those in charge during the decade before would be of immense value to an understanding of the changes of philosophy over this period of time.

Most studies dealing with the armed forces concentrate on the high command and on the officer corps, and our understanding of the elite cadres is deepening, but we remain ignorant of the majority of those who make the military a career. There is a demand for research into the socio-economic history of those who make up the non-commissioned officer class and to understand where this group fits into Argentine society. In addition, studies on the role and place of the veterans would fill a gap in our knowledge.

Certainly, the above suggestions are only a partial list of the variety of topics that await historians interested in studying the Argentine military; there exist numerous others that no doubt will arise as researchers plunge into their respective fields of investigation.

BIBLIOGRAPHY: ARGENTINA

1. Abos, Alvaro. LAS ORGANIZACIONES SINDICALES Y EL PODER MILITAR, 1976-1983. Buenos Aires: Centro Editor de América Latina, 1984.

2. Acuña, Marcelo Luis. DE FRONDIZI A ALFONSIN: LA TRADICION POLITICA DEL RADICALISMO. 2 vols. Buenos Aires: Centro Editor de América Latina, 1984.

3. Agozino, Adalberto C. LOS ESTILOS POLITICOS EN LA ARGENTINA, 1853-1955. Buenos Aires: Editorial El Tiempo, 1985.

4. Alende, Oscar Eduardo. QUE ES EL PARTIDO INTRANSIGENTE? Buenos Aires: Editorial Sudamérica, 1983.

5. Alexander, Robert J. AN INTRODUCTION TO ARGENTINA. New York: Frederick A. Praeger, 1964.

6. ———. JUAN DOMINGO PERON: A HISTORY. Boulder: Westview Press, 1979.

7. ———. THE PERON ERA. New York: Columbia University Press, 1951.

8. Alfonsín, Raúl. AHORA, MI PROPUESTA POLITICA. Buenos Aires: Sudamericana Planeta, 1983.

9. ———. QUE ES EL RADICALISMO? Buenos Aires: Sudamericana Planeta, 1983.

10. Allub, Leopoldo. ORIGENES DEL AUTORITARISMO EN AMERICA LATINA. Mexico City: Editorial Katún, 1983.

11. Alonso Pineiro, Armando. LA HISTORIA QUE MUCHAS ARGENTINOS NO CONOCEN. 5th ed. Buenos Aires: Ediciones Depalma, 1984.

12. ———. JUAN JOSE VIAMONTE: HISTORIA DE UN PATRICIO. Buenos Aires: Jockey Club, 1980.

13. Alsogaray, Alvaro. "La democracia de masas y la crisis en paises del mundo libre." CUADERNOS (Chile) 4 (1976): 1-19.

14. Alvarez, Alberto, and Enrique Walter. "Azules y Colorados." TODO ES HISTORIA 65 (1972).

15. Alvear, Marcelo T. de. ACCION DEMOCRATICA: DISCURSOS PRONUNCIADOS EN LA COMPANA DE RENOVACION PRESIDENCIAL. Buenos Aires: Editorial Cultura, 1937.

16. Amadeo, Mario. AYER, HOY, MANANA. 3d. ed. Buenos Aires: Ediciones Guré, 1956.

17. ANEXOS DEL INFORME DE LA COMISION NACIONAL SOBRE LA DESAPARICION DE PERSONAS. Buenos Aires: Editorial Universitária de Buenos Aires, 1984.

18. Antonio, Jorge. ¿Y AHORA QUE? Buenos Aires: Ediciones Verum et Militia, 1966.

19. Argentina. ANALES DE LEGISLACION ARGENTINA, 1852-1973. 33 vols. Buenos Aires: 1942-73.

20. ———. ANTEPROYECTO DE LA LEY AERONAUTICA CIVIL DE LA REPUBLICA ARGENTINA. Buenos Aires: 1935.

21. Argentina. Comisión de Estudios Constitucionales. MATERIALES PARA LA REFORMA CONSTITUCIONAL. 7 vols. Buenos Aires: 1957.

22. Argentina. Comisión Nacional de Investigaciones. DOCUMENTATION, AUTORES Y COMPLICES DE LAS IRREGULARIDADES COMETIDAS DURANTE LA SEGUNDA TIRANIA. 5 vols. Buenos Aires: 1958.

23. Argentina. Congreso Nacional. DIARIO DE SESIONES DE LA CAMARA DE SENADORES. ANOS 1916-1930, 1932-1942. 50 vols. ANOS 1946-1955, 1958-1966. 55 vols.

24. ———. DIARIO DE SESIONES DE LA CAMARA DE DIPUTADOS. ANOS 1921-1930, 1932-1942. 123 vols. ANOS 1946-1955, 1958-1966. 117 vols.

25. Argentina. Convención Nacional Constituyente. DIARIO DE SESIONES ANO 1957. 2 vols. Buenos Aires: 1958.

26. Argentina. DECRETOS NACIONALES, 4 DE JUNIO DE 1943-
4 DE JUNIO DE 1946. 4 vols. Buenos Aires: 1944-46.

27. ———. DIGESTO MARITIMO Y FLUVIAL. Buenos Aires:
Talleres Gráficos Frigerio, n.d.

28. Argentina. Dirección General de Cultura. BOLETIN
BIBLIOGRAFICO NACIONAL, ANO 1952 Y 1953. Buenos
Aires: 1954.

29. Argentina. Dirección General de Navegación y Puertos.
ANUARIO DEL MOVIMIENTO DE LOS PUERTOS DE LA
REPUBLICA ARGENTINA CORRESPONDIENTE A 1939 Y
NOTICIA SUMARIA DEL PERIODO 1935-1939.

30. Argentina. Dirección Nacional de Turismo. ANTARTICA
ARGENTINA. Buenos Aires: Dirección Nacional de Turismo,
1979.

31. Argentina. DOCTRINA PERONISTA: FILOSOFICA,
POLITICA, SOCIAL. Buenos Aires: n.p., 1947.

32. Argentina. Ministerio de Economia. ONE YEAR OF
ARGENTINE ECONOMIC DEVELOPMENT, 1976-1977.
Buenos Aires: Ministerio de Economia, 1977.

33. ———. FIFTEEN MONTHS OF ARGENTINE ECONOMIC
DEVELOPMENT, APRIL 1976-JUNE 1977. Buenos Aires:
Ministerio de Economia, 1977.

34. Argentina. Ministerio de Educación, Dirección General de
Cultura. BOLETIN BIBLIOGRAFICO ARGENTINO. Buenos
Aires: Ministerio de Educación, 1950-.

35. Argentina. Ministerio de Guerra. ANUARIO DEL INSTITUTO
GEOGRAFICO MILITAR. Vol. 9, 1933-1943. Buenos Aires:
Ministerio de Guerra, 1947.

36. ———. MEMORIA DE.... Buenos Aires: Annual.

37. ------. RESENA HISTORICA DEL INSTITUTO
GEOGRAFICO MILITAR: SU MISION, SU OBRA. Buenos
Aires: Ministerio de Guerra, 1951.

38. Argentina. Ministerio de Guerra. Dirección General de Fabricaciones Militares. INCIDENCIAS DE LOS CONSUMOS ENERGETICOS EN INDUSTRIAS DE INTERES NACIONAL. Buenos Aires: Ministerio de Guerra, 1963.

39. ———. MEMORIA ANUAL CORRESPONDIENTE AL SEGUNDO EJERCITO. Buenos Aires: Ministerio de Guerra, 1943.

40. Argentina. Ministerio del Interior. LAS FUERZAS ARMADAS RESTITUYEN EL IMPERIO DE LA SOBERANIA POPULAR: LAS ELECCIONES GENERALES DE 1946. 2 vols. Buenos Aires: Imprenta de la Cámara de Diputados, 1946.

41. Argentina. Ministerio de Marina. MEMORIA DEL.... Buenos Aires: Annual.

42. Argentina. Ministerio de Marina, Administración General de la Flota Mercante del Estado. MEMORIA. Buenos Aires: Ministerio de Marina, 1942-. Annual.

43. Argentina. Ministerio de Marina. Servicio de Hidrografia Naval. ESCUELA DE CARTOGRAFOS. Buenos Aires: Servicio de Hidrografia Naval, 1965.

44. Argentina. Poder Ejecutivo Nacional. PERIODO 1932-1938: PRESIDENTE DE LA NACION AGUSTIN B. JUSTO. 10 vols. Buenos Aires: Kraft, n.d.

45. Argentina. Secretaría de la Presidencia. Sub-secretaría de Informaciones y Prensa. PERON: CUATRO ANOS DE SU GOBIERNO. Buenos Aires: Sec. de la Presidencia, n.d.

46. "Argentine: Chronologie des presidences de Perón; La prise du pouvoir par la Junte Militaire; Chronique du coup d'etat, 21-31 mars 1976; Le programme economique de la Junte Militaire; L'exposé du nouveau Ministre de l'Economie." NOTES ET ETUDES DOCUMENTAIRES 4292/4293 (1976): 23-80.

47. Arnaudo, Aldo A. "El nuevo régimen financiero argentino: Una perspectiva." ESTUDIOS 1 (1978): 203-11.

48. Asseff, Alberto Emilio. PROYECCION CONTINENTAL DE ARGENTINA: DE LA GEOHISTORIA A LA GEOPOLITICA NACIONAL. Buenos Aires: Editorial Pleamar, 1980.

49. Atkins, George Pope, and Larry V. Thompson. "German Military Influence in Argentina, 1921-1940." JOURNAL OF LATIN AMERICAN STUDIES 4 (1972): 257-74.

50. Auza, Nestór Tomás. EL EJERCITO EN LA EPOCA DE LA CONFEDERACION, 1852-1861. Buenos Aires: Círculo Militar, 1971.

51. Azaretto, Roberto. HISTORIA DE LAS FUERZAS CONSERVADORES. Buenos Aires: Centro Editor de América Latina, 1983.

52. Baigorria, Manuel. MEMORIAS DEL CORONEL MANUEL BAIGORRIA. 2d ed. Buenos Aires: EUDEBA, 1977.

53. Baily, Samuel L. "Argentina: Reconciliation with the Peronists." CURRENT HISTORY 50 (1965): 356-60, 368-69.

54. ———. "Argentina: Search for Consensus." CURRENT HISTORY 51 (1966): 301-06.

55. ———. LABOR, NATIONALISM, AND POLITICS IN ARGENTINA. New Brunswick: Rutgers University Press, 1967.

56. Baquerizas, José Manuel. POR QUE SE CREYO EN PERON: POLITICOS, MILITARES Y PERONISTAS. Buenos Aires, n.p., 1957.

57. Barager, Joseph R., ed. WHY PERON CAME TO POWER. New York: Knopf, 1968.

58. Barber, William F., and C. Neale Ronning. INTERNAL SECURITY AND MILITARY POWER: COUNTER-INSURGENCY AND CIVIC ACTION IN LATIN AMERICA. Columbus: Ohio State University Press, 1966.

59. Barco, Ricardo del., et al. 1943-1982, HISTORIA POLITICA ARGENTINA. Buenos Aires: Editorial de Belgrano, 1983.

60. Barnes, John. EVITA: FIRST LADY; A BIOGRAPHY OF EVA PERON. New York: Grove Press, 1978.

61. Barrera, Mario. INFORMATION AND IDEOLOGY: A CASE STUDY OF ARTURO FRONDIZI. Beverly Hills: Sage, 1973.

62. Barrios, Américo. CON PERON EN EL EXILIO: ¡LO QUE NADIE SABIA! Buenos Aires: Editorial Treinta Días, 1964.

63. Basílico, Ernesto. SOBRE EL CANAL BEAGLE Y LAS ISLAS LITIGIOSAS. Buenos Aires: Centro Naval, Instituto de Publicaciones Navales, 1974.

64. Bayer, Osvaldo. LA PATAGONIA REBELDE. Mexico City: Editorial Nueva Imagen, 1980.

65. Beck, Peter J. "Falklands or Malvinas: The View from Argentina." CONTEMPORARY REVIEW 247 (1985): 136-42.

66. ———. "The Future of the Falkland Islands: A Solution Made in Hong Kong?" INTERNATIONAL AFFAIRS 61 (1985): 643-60.

67. Becke, Carlos von der. DESTRUCCION DE UNA INFAMIA: FALSOS "DOCUMENTOS OFICIALES." Buenos Aires: n.p., 1956.

68. Belloni, Alberto. DEL ANARQUISMO AL PERONISMO. Buenos Aires: A. Pena Lillo 1960.

69. BIBLIOGRAPHIC GUIDE TO LATIN AMERICAN STUDIES. Boston: G.K. Hall, 1978-.

70. Biedma, Antonio. CRONICA HISTORICA DE LA AERONAUTICA ARGENTINA. Buenos Aires: Círculo de Aeronáutica, 1968.

71. Bielsa, Rafael. CARACTERES JURIDICOS Y POLITICOS DEL EJERCITO. Santa Fé: Universidad Nacional del Litoral, n.d.

72. Bittel, Deolindo F. PERONISM Y DICTADURA. Buenos Aires: Editora del Movimiento Nacional Justicialista, 1983.

73. ——. ¿QUE ES EL PERONISMO? Buenos Aires: Editorial Sudamericana, 1983.

74. Blanksten, George I. PERON'S ARGENTINA. Chicago: University of Chicago Press, 1953.

75. Borrini, Alberto. COMO SE HACE UN PRESIDENTE. Buenos Aires: Ediciones El Cronista Comercial, 1984.

76. Borroni, Otelo, and Roberto Vacca. LA VIDA DE EVA PERON. VOL I. TESTIMONIOS PARA SU HISTORIA. Buenos Aires: Editorial Galerna, 1970.

77. Bortnik, Ruben. EL EJERCITO ARGENTINO Y EL ANTE DE LO POSIBLE. Buenos Aires: Ediciones Güemes, 1967

78. Bosch, Felipe. HISTORIA NAVAL ARGENTINA. Buenos Aires: Editorial Alborada, 1962.

79. Botana, Natalio R., and Ezequiel Gallo. "La politica argentina entre las dos guerras mundiales." REVISTA DE OCCIDENTE 37 (1984): 45-58.

80. Botana, Natalio R., et al. EL REGIMEN MILITAR, 1966-1973. Buenos Aires: Ediciones La Bastilla, 1973.

81. Braden, Spruille. DIPLOMATS AND DEMOGOGUES: THE MEMOIRS OF SPRUILLE BRADEN. New Rochelle: Arlington House, 1971.

82. Briones, Alvaro. IDEOLOGIA DEL FASCISMO DEPENDIENTE: ESTADO Y SEGURIDAD NACIONAL. Mexico City: Editorial Edicol, 1978.

83. Brown, Michael P. AIR FORCES OF THE WORLD. Geneva: INTERAVIA, 1984.

84. Buchanan, Paul G. "State Corporatism in Argentina: Labor Administration under Perón and Onganía." LATIN AMERICAN RESEARCH REVIEW 20 (1985): 61-95.

85. Budeinsky, Clara Celia. EL RETORNISMO OLIGARQUICO. Buenos Aires: Schapire Editor, 1973.

86. Buenos Aires. POLICIA DE LA CAPITAL FEDERAL. MEMORIA CORRESPONDIENTE AL ANO 1936. Buenos Aires: Servicio de Aprovisionamiento, n.d.

87. ———. POLICIA DE LA CAPITAL FEDERAL. MEMORIA CORRESPONDIENTE AL ANO 1937. Buenos Aires: Servicio de Aprovisionamiento, n.d.

88. Burzio, Humberto F. ARMADA NACIONAL: RESENA HISTORICA DE SU ORIGEN Y DESARROLLO ORGANICO. Buenos Aires: Sec. de Estado de Marina, Depto. de Estudios Históricos Navales, 1960.

89. ———. HISTORIA DEL TORPEDO Y SUS BUQUES EN LA ARMADA ARGENTINA. Buenos Aires: Sec. de Estado de Marina, Depto. de Estudios Historicos Navales, 1968.

90. Bustos Fierro, Raúl. DESDE PERON HASTA ONGANIA: LA DEMOCRACIA JUSTICIALISTA, LA AUTOCRACIA SEPTEMBRINA, LA RESTAURACION DEL FRAUDE, LA MONARQUIA MILITAR. Buenos Aires: Ediciones Octubre, 1969.

91. Caballero, Ricardo. YRIGOYEN: LA CONSPIRACION CIVIL Y MILITAR DEL 4 DE FEBRERO DE 1905. Buenos Aires: Editorial Raigal, 1951.

92. Caillet-Bois, Ricardo. "Emilio Ravignani." BOLETIN DEL INSTITUTO DE HISTORIA ARGENTINA, Second Series, 2 (1957): 238-77.

93. Cámpora, Héctor J. EL MANDATO DE PERON. Buenos Aires: Ediciones Quehacer Nacional, 1975.

94. Camps, Ramón Juan Alberto. CASO TIMERMANN: PUNTO FINAL. Buenos Aires: Tribuna Abierta, 1982.

95. ———. EL PODER EN LA SOMBRA: EL AFFAIRE GRAIVER. Buenos Aires: RO. CA. Producciones, 1983.

96. Cantón, Darío. ELECCIONES Y PARTIDOS POLITICOS EN LA ARGENTINA: HISTORIA, INTERPRETACION Y BALANCE, 1910-1966. Buenos Aires: Siglo XXI Editores, 1973.

97. ———. "Notas sobre las Fuerzas Armadas Argentinas." REVISTA LATINOAMERICANA DE SOCIOLOGIA 1 (1965): 290-313.

98. ———. LA POLITICA DE LOS MILITARES ARGENTINOS, 1900-1971. Buenos Aires: Siglo XXI Editores, 1971.

99. Carballo, Pablo Marcos. DIOS Y LOS HALCONES: ILUSTRACIONES DE EXEQUIEL MARTINEZ. Buenos Aires: Editorial Abril, 1983.

100. Cardosa, Oscar R., R. Kirschbaum, and E. van der Kooy. MALVINAS: LA TRAMA SECRETA. Buenos Aires: Editorial Sudamericana-Planeta, 1983.

101. Carpi, Pier, and José Capparelli. LA P-2 SE DEFIENDE. Buenos Aires: El Cid Editor, 1984.

102. Carranza, María Ines, Ines María Vinuales, and Luis A. Ferrari. NOTAS SOBRE FUERZAS POLITICAS EN EL PERIODO 1930-1943. Buenos Aires: Fundación para el Estudio de los Problemas Argentinos, 1977-81.

103. Carranza, Mario Esteban. "The Role of Military Expenditure in the Development Process: The Argentine Case, 1946-1980." IBERO AMERICANA 12 (1983): 115-66.

104. Carril, Bonifacio del. CRONICA INTERNA DE LA REVOLUCION LIBERTADORA. Buenos Aires: n.p., 1959.

105. Carulla, Juan E. AL FILO DEL MEDIO SIGLO. Paraná, Argentina: Editorial Llanura, 1951.

106. ———. EL MEDIO SIGLO SE PROLONGA. Buenos Aires: n.p., 1965.

107. ———. VALOR ETICA DE LA REVOLUCION DEL SEIS DE SEPTIEMBRE. Buenos Aires: Impresora Belgrano, 1931.

108. Casas, Nelly. FRONDIZI: UNA HISTORIA DE POLITICA Y SOCIEDAD. Buenos Aires: Ediciones La Bastilla, 1973.

109. Casellas, Alberto O. EL TERRITORIO OLVIDADO. Buenos Aires: Centro Naval, Instituto de Publicaciones Navales, 1974.

110. Castex, Mariano N. UN AÑO DE LANUSSE: DEL ACUERDO INCREIBLE AL RETORNO IMPOSIBLE. Buenos Aires: Achával Solo Frabricante de Libros, 1973.

111. Cattaneo, Atilio E. "ENTRE REJAS" (MEMORIAS). Buenos Aires: Editorial "Chango," 1939.

112. ———. PLAN 1932: EL CONCURRENCISMO Y LA REVOLUCION. Buenos Aires: Proceso Ediciones, 1959.

113. Cavarozzi, Marcelo. AUTORITARISMO Y DEMOCRACIA, 1955-1983. Buenos Aires: Centro Editor de América Latina, 1983.

114. ———. SINDICATOS Y POLITICAS EN ARGENTINA, 1955-1958. Buenos Aires: Centro de Estudios de Estado y Sociedad, 1979.

115. ———. UNIONS AND POLITICS, 1955-1962. Washington: The Wilson Center, 1980.

116. Centro Naval. PRINCIPIOS POLITICOS UNIVERSALES; PATAGONIA: FRONTERAS Y SEGURIDAD; LAS FUERZAS ARMADAS Y LA POLICIA FRENTE A LAS ALTERACIONES DEL ORDEN PUBLICO. Buenos Aires: Instituto Naval de Conferencias y Publicaciones Navales, 1972.

117. Ceresole, Norberto. EL EJERCITO Y LA CRISIS POLITICA ARGENTINA. Buenos Aires: Editorial Política Internacional, 1970.

118. ———. EJERCITO Y POLITICA NACIONALISTA. Buenos Aires: Editorial Sudestada, 1968.

119. ———. LA VIABILIDAD ARGENTINA: UNA ALTERNATIVA DE SUPERVIVENCIA; LINEAMIENTO BASICOS DE UN PROYECTO NACIONAL ALTERNATIVO. Madrid: Altalena, 1983.

120. Cerón, Sergio. MALVINAS: ¿GESTA HEROICA O DERROTA VERGONZOSA? Buenos Aires: Editorial Sudamericana, 1984.

121. Cerutti Costa, Luis. EL SINDICALISMO: LAS MASAS Y EL PODER. Buenos Aires: n.p., 1957.

122. Chaffee, Lyman. "Coup Finishes Peronism Era." LATIN AMERICAN DIGEST. 10 (1976): 1-6.

123. Círculo Militar Argentina. CATALOGO DE MATERIAS MILITARES. Buenos Aires: Biblioteca Nacional Militar, 1957.

124. Ciria, Alberto. PARTIDO Y PODER EN LA ARGENTINA MODERNA, 1930-1946. Buenos Aires: Jorge Alvarez, 1964.

125. ———. POLITICA Y CULTURA POPULAR: LA ARGENTINA PERONISTA, 1946-1955. Buenos Aires: Ediciones de la Flor, 1983.

126. Cirino, Julio Alberto. ARGENTINA FRENTE A LA GUERRA MARXISTA: ANALISIS Y CAUSAS DE UN LARGO CONFLICTO. Buenos Aires: Editorial Rioplatense, 1974.

127. Colmo, Alfredo. LA REVOLUCION EN LA AMERICA LATINA. Buenos Aires: Editorial M. Gleizer, 1932.

128. Conil Paz, Alberto, and Gustavo Ferrari. ARGENTINA'S FOREIGN POLICY, 1930-1962. Notre Dame, IN: Notre Dame University Press, 1966.

129. Connell-Smith, Gordon. "Latin America and the Falklands Conflict." THE LONDON INSTITUTE OF WORLD AFFAIRS 38 (1984): 73-88.

130. Corbett, Charles D. THE LATIN AMERICAN MILITARY AS A SOCIO-POLITICAL FORCE: CASE STUDIES OF BOLIVIA AND ARGENTINA. Coral Gables: University of Miami Press, 1972.

131. Cordeiro, Danial Raposo, ed. A BIBLIOGRAPHY OF LATIN AMERICAN BIBLIOGRAPHIES: SOCIAL SCIENCES AND HUMANITIES. Metuchen, NJ: Scarecrow Press, 1979.

132. Corradi, Juan Engenio. "Argentina," In LATIN AMERICA: THE STRUGGLE WITH DEPENDENCY AND BEYOND, 305-408. Edited by Ronald H. Chilcote and Joel C. Edelstein. Cambridge, MA: Schenkman Publishers, 1974.

133. ———. "Argentina and Peronism: Fragments of the Puzzle." LATIN AMERICAN PERSPECTIVES 1 (1974): 3-20.

134. Crassweller, Robert D. PERON AND THE ENIGMAS OF ARGENTINA. New York: Norton, 1987.

135. Crawley, Eduardo. A HOUSE DIVIDED: ARGENTINA, 1880-1980. New York: St. Martin's Press, 1984.

136. CRONOLOGIA MILITAR ARGENTINA, 1806-1980. Buenos Aires: Editorial CLIO, 1983.

137. Cruces, Néstor. HACIA OTRO EJERCITO POSIBLE: INVITACION AL DEBATE SOBRE ASPECTOS INTIMOS DE LA PROFESION MILITAR. Buenos Aires: Grupo Editorial Planeta, 1988.

138. Cuccorese, Horacio Juan. "La cuestión limítrofe con Chile: Tiempo de agudización del conflicto, 1900-1901." INVESTIGACIONES Y ENSAYOS 19 (1975): 305-23.

139. ———. "El estanco de alcohol como recurso financiero: La practicidad económica de Carlos Pellegrini." TRABAJOS Y COMUNICACIONES 23 (1978): 41-60.

140. Cuenca, Eduardo. EL MILITARISMO EN LA ARGENTINA. Buenos Aires: Editorial Independencia, 1971.

141. Cuneo, Dardo. LAS NUEVAS FRONTERAS. Buenos Aires: Editorial Transición, 1963.

142. Dabat, Alejandro, and Luis Lorenzano. ARGENTINA, THE MALVINAS, AND THE END OF MILITARY RULE. London: Verso, 1984.

143. D'Amico, David F. "Religious Liberty in Argentina during the First Perón Regime, 1943-1955." CHURCH HISTORY 46 (1977): 490-503.

144. Damonte Taborda, Raúl. ¿A DONDE VA PERON?: DE BERLIN A WALL STREET. Montevideo: Ediciones de la Resistencia Revolucionaria Argentina, 1955.

145. Daneri, Alberto. CARTA ABIERTA DE UN PERONISTA A UN CONFUNDIDO. Buenos Aires: Ediciones Machacha, 1974.

146. Daza, José S. EPISODIOS MILITARES. Buenos Aires: EUDEBA, 1975.

147. Deal, Carl W., ed. LATIN AMERICA AND THE CARIBBEAN: A DISSERTATION BIBLIOGRAPHY. Ann Arbor: University Microfilms International, 1977.

148. Deheza, José A. ¿QUIENES DERROCARON A ISABEL PERON? Buenos Aires: Ediciones Cuenca del Plata, 1981.

149. De Ipola, Emilio, and Liliana de Riz. UN JUEGO DE CARTAS POLITICAS: INTELECTUALES Y DISCURSO AUTORITARIO EN LA ARGENTINA ACTUAL. Mexico City: Facultad Latinoamericana de Ciencias Sociales, Coordinación Académica, 1982-83.

150. Delich, Francisco Jose. CRISIS Y PROTESTA SOCIAL: CORDOBA, 1969-1973. 2d ed. Buenos Aires: Siglo XXI Editores, 1974.

151. DESPARECIDOS EN LA ARGENTINA. São Paulo: Comité de Defensa de Derechos Humanos en el Cono Sur, 1982.

152. Deutsch, Sandra McGee. COUNTERREVOLUTION IN ARGENTINA, 1900-1932: THE ARGENTINE PATRIOTIC LEAGUE. Lincoln: University of Nebraska Press, 1986.

153. Dias David, Mauricio. "El estado en América Latina y los militares en la política latinoamericana." IBERO AMERICANA 7 (1978): 133-60.

154. Díaz, Fanor. CONVERSACIONES CON ROGELIO SOBRE LA CRISIS POLITICA ARGENTINA. Buenos Aires: Colihue/Hachette, 1977.

155. Díaz Araujo, Enrique. LA CONSPIRACION DEL '43: EL G.O.U.: UNA EXPERIENCIA MILITARISTA EN LA ARGENTINA. Buenos Aires: Ediciones La Bastilla, 1971.

156. ———. EL G.O.U. EN LA REVOLUCION DE 1943: UNA EXPERIENCIA MILITARISTA EN LA ARGENTINA. Mendoza, Argentina: Universidad Nacional de Cuyo, 1970.

157. Díaz Loza, Florentino. DOCTRINA POLITICA DEL EJERCITO. Buenos Aires: A. Peña Lillo Editor, 1976.

158. Díaz Melian, Mafalda Victoria. LA REVOLUCION ARGENTINA DE 1890 EN LAS FUENTES ESPANOLES. Buenos Aires: Plus Ultra, 1978.

159. DISSERTATION ABSTRACTS INTERNATIONAL. Ann Arbor: University Microfilms International, 1938-.

160. Di Tella, Guido. ARGENTINA UNDER PERON, 1973-1976: THE NATION'S EXPERIENCE WITH A LABOUR-BASED GOVERNMENT. New York: St. Martin's Press, 1983.

161. Dodson, Michael. "The Catholic Church in Contemporary Argentina, 1962-1970." In NEW PERSPECTIVES IN MODERN ARGENTINA, 57-68. Edited by Alberto Ciria, et al. Bloomington: Indiana University Press, 1973.

162. ———. "Catholic Radicalism and Political Change in Argentina." In RELIGION IN LATIN AMERICA: LIFE AND LITERATURE, 317-30. Edited by Lyle G. Brown and William F. Cooper. Waco, TX: Markham Press Foundation, 1980.

163. ———. "Priests and Peronism: Radical Clergy in Argentine Politics." LATIN AMERICAN PERSPECTIVES 1 (1974): 58-72.

164. Domínguez, Nelson. CONVERSACIONES CON JUAN JOSE TACCONE SOBRE SINDICALISMO Y POLITICA. Buenos Aires: Colihue/Hachette 1977.

165. Dorrego, Alejandro, and Victoria Azurduy, eds. EL CASO ARGENTINO: HABLAN SUS PROTAGONISTAS. Buenos Aires: Editorial Prisma, 1977.

166. Dowie, Mark. "The General and the Children." MOTHER JONES 3:6 (1978): 37-40,42,46-48.

167. Doyen, Louise M. "Conflictos obreros durante el régimen peronista, 1946-1955." DESARROLLO ECONOMICO 76 (1977): 437-73.

168. Dressl, Klaus. "Argentinien: Politik und Parteien, 1955-1972." VIERTELJAHRESBERICHTE (Bonn) 49 (1972): 247-72.

169. Druretta, Gustavo Adolfo, et al. DEFENSA Y DEMOCRACIA: UN DEBATE ENTRE CIVILES Y MILITARES. Buenos Aires: Punto Sur, 1990.

170. Dubrovsky, Jorge, et al. ¿LAS MALVINAS: CONFLICTO AMERICANO? Lima: Centro de Investigaciones Económicas y Sociales, 1982.

171. Duhalde, Eduardo Luis. EL ESTADO TERRORISTA ARGENTINO. Barcelona: Argos Vergara, 1983.

172. Dupuy, Trevor N., et al. THE ALMANAC OF WORLD MILITARY POWER. San Rafael, CA: Presidio Press, 1980.

173. Durruty, Celia. CLASE OBRERA Y PERONISMO. Córdoba, Argentina: Ediciones Pasado y Presente, 1969.

174. Duval, Armando. A ARGENTINA: POTENCIA MILITAR. 2 vols. Rio de Janeiro: Imprensa Nacional, 1922.

175. Echague, Carlos. EL SOCIALIMPERIALISMO RUSO EN LA ARGENTINA. Buenos Aires: Ediciones Agora, 1984.

176. Einaudi, Luigi, and Herbert Goldhamer. "An Annotated Bibliography of Latin American Military Journals." LATIN AMERICAN RESEARCH REVIEW 2 (1967): 95-122.

177. English, Adrian J. THE ARMED FORCES OF LATIN AMERICA: THEIR HISTORIES, DEVELOPMENT, PRESENT STRENGTH, AND MILITARY POTENTIAL. London: Jane's, 1984.

178. Epstein, Edward C. "Politicization and Income Redistribution in Argentina: The Case of the Peronist Worker." ECONOMIC DEVELOPMENT AND CULTURAL CHANGE 23 (1975): 615-31.

179. Epstein, Fritz T. "European Military Influence in Latin America." Library of Congress Photoduplication Service. Washington: 1961.

180. Escude, Carlos, and Cristóbal Williams. LA ARGENTINA: ¿PATRIA INTERNACIONAL? Buenos Aires: Editorial de Belgrano, 1984.

181. Estep, Raymond. THE ARGENTINE ARMED FORCES AND
      GOVERNMENT. Maxwell Air Force Base, AL: Aerospace
      Studies Institute, 1970.

182. Etchepareborda, Roberto. "Bibliografía de la revolución de 1930."
      REVISTA DE HISTORIA 3 (1958): 156-73.

183. ———."La bibliografía reciente sobre la cuestión malvinas."
      REVISTA INTERAMERICANA DE BIBLIOGRAFIA 34
      (1984): 1-52, 227-88.

184. ———. "Elementos bibliográficos para una história argentina:
      1943-1982." CRITERIO 55 (1982): 22-54.

185. ———. "Estanislao S. Zeballos y los debates secretos de 1914 en
      la Cámara de Diputados." HISTORIA 1 (1981): 25-44.

186. ———. HISTORIOGRAFIA MILITAR ARGENTINA. Buenos
      Aires: Círculo Militar, 1984.

187. ———. ZEBALLOS Y LA POLITICA EXTERIOR
      ARGENTINA. Buenos Aires: Editorial Pleamar, 1982.

188. Etchepareborda, Roberto, Ricardo M. Ortíz, and Juan V. Orona.
      LA CRISIS DE 1930: ENSAYOS (I). Buenos Aires: Centro
      Editor de América Latina, 1983.

189. Ethell, Jeffery, and Alfred Price. AIR WAR SOUTH
      ATLANTIC. New York: Macmillan, 1983.

190. Evers, Tilman Tönnies. MILITARREGIERUNG IN
      ARGENTINIEN: DAS POLITISCHE SYSTEM DER
      "ARGENTINISCHEN REVOLUTION." Hamburg: Alfred
      Metzner Verlag, 1972.

191. Fador, Jorge. "Perón's Policies for Agricultural Exports, 1946-
      1948: Dogmatism or Common Sense?" In ARGENTINA IN
      THE TWENTIETH CENTURY, 135-61. Edited by David Rock.
      Pittsburgh: University of Pittsburgh Press, 1975.

192. Falcoff, Mark, and Ronald H. Dolkart, eds. PROLOGUE TO
      PERON: ARGENTINA IN DEPRESSION AND WAR, 1930-
      1943. Berkeley: University of California Press, 1975.

193. THE FALKLANDS WAR: THE DAY BY DAY RECORD FROM INVASION TO VICTORY. 14 vols. London: Marshall Cavendish Ltd., 1983-.

194. THE FALKLANDS WAR: THE OFFICIAL HISTORY. London: Latin American Newsletter, 1983.

195. Farrell, Edelmiro J. DISCURSOS PRONUNCIADOS POR EL EXCELENTISIMO SENOR PRESIDENTE DE LA NACION ARGENTINA DURANTE SU PERIODO PRESIDENCIAL, 1944-1946. Buenos Aires: n.p., 1946.

196. Fayt, Carlos. "Naturaleza del Peronismo." APORTES 1: (1966): 5-12.

197. ———. EL POLITICO ARMADO: DINAMICA DEL PROCESO POLITICO ARGENTINO. Buenos Aires: Editorial Pannedille, 1971.

198. Feinmann, José Pablo. ESTUDIOS SOBRE EL PERONISMO: HISTORIA, METODO, PROYECTO. Buenos Aires: Editorial Legasa, 1983.

199. Feldman, David Lewis. "The United States Role in the Malvinas Crisis, 1982: Misguidance and Misperception in Argentina's Decision to Go to War." JOURNAL OF INTER-AMERICAN STUDIES AND WORLD AFFAIRS 27 (1985): 1-12.

200. Ferla, Salvador. MARTIRES Y VERDUGOS: SENTIDO HISTORICO DEL 9 DE JUNIO DE 1956. Buenos Aires: Talleres Gráficos el Manantial, 1964.

201. Fernández Alvarino, Próspero Germán. ARGENTINA: EL CRIMEN DEL SIGLO, TENIENTE GENERAL PEDRO EUGENIO ARAMBURU. Buenos Aires: Published by author, 1973.

202. Fernández, Julio A. "Crisis in Argentina." CURRENT HISTORY 64 (1973): 49-52, 85.

203. Fernández, Roque B. "The Expectations Management Approach to Stabilization in Argentina during 1976-82." WORLD DEVELOPMENT 13 (1985): 871-92.

204. Ferrari, Gustavo. "Las ilusiones del Ochenta." CRITERIO 53 (1980): 84-98.

205. Ferrer, José. "The Armed Forces in Argentine Politics to 1930." Ph.D. dissertation, University of New Mexico, 1965.

206. Firpo, M. Eduardo. PERON Y LOS PERONISTAS. Buenos Aires: Talleres Gráficos Alberdi, 1965.

207. Floria, Carlos Alberto. "Dilemmas of the Consolidation of Democracy in Argentina." In COMPARING NEW DEMOCRACIES: TRANSITION AND CONSOLIDATION IN MEDITERRANEAN EUROPE AND THE SOUTHERN CONE, 179-240. Edited by Enrique Baloyra. Boulder: Westview Press, 1987.

208. Florit, Carlos A. LAS FUERZAS ARMADAS Y LA GUERRA PSICOLOGICA. Buenos Aires: Arayu, 1963.

209. ———. POLITICA EXTERIOR NACIONAL. Buenos Aires: Arayu, 1960.

210. Foro de Buenos Aires por la Vigencia de los Derechos Humanos, B.A. PROCESO A LA EXPLOTACION Y A LA REPRESION EN LA ARGENTINA, MAYO DE 1973. Buenos Aires: Foro de Buenos Aires por la Vigencia de los Derechos Humanos, 1973.

211. Foulkes, Haroldo. MALVINAS: 74 DIAS ALUCINANTES EN PUERTO ARGENTINO. Buenos Aires: Corregidor, 1984.

212. Fraga, Rosendo. EJERCITO: DEL ESCARNIO AL PODER, 1973-1976. Buenos Aires: Grupo Editorial Planeta, 1988.

213. Frank, Gary. JUAN PERON VS SPRUILLE BRADEN: THE STORY BEHIND THE BLUE BOOK. Lanham, MD: University Press of America, 1980.

214. ———. STRUGGLE FOR HEGEMONY: ARGENTINA, BRAZIL AND THE UNITED STATES DURING THE SECOND WORLD WAR. Coral Gables: University of Miami Press, 1979.

215. Fraser, Nicholas, and Marysa Navarro. EVA PERON. New York: W.W. Norton, 1981.

216. Freedman, Lawrence, and Virginia Gamba-Stonehouse. SIGNALS OF WAR: THE FALKLANDS CONFLICT OF 1982. Princeton: Princeton University Press, 1991.

217. Freijo, Adrián Enrique. LECCIONES DE NUESTRA HISTORIA RECIENTE: TREINTA ANOS DE VIDA ARGENTINA, 1945-1975. Buenos Aires: Editorial Sudamericana, 1977.

218. Gaignard, Romain. "L'evolution de la politique argentine en 1970 et 1971: Du Président Onganía au Président Lanusse." NOTES ET ETUDES DOCUMENTAIRES 3913/3914 (1972): 7-51.

219. Gallo, Ezequiel. FARMERS IN REVOLT: THE REVOLUTION OF 1893 IN THE PROVINCE OF SANTA FE, ARGENTINA. London: University of London, 1976.

220. Gallo, Ricardo. BALBIN, FRONDIZI Y LA DIVISION DEL RADICALISMO, 1956-1958. Buenos Aires: Editorial de Belgrano, 1983.

221. Gambini, Hugo. EL PERONISMO Y LA IGLESIA. Buenos Aires: Centro Editorial de la América Latina, 1971.

222. Gándara, Horacio F. YO ESPERO. Buenos Aires: A. Peña Lillo Editor, 1972.

223. García Lupo, Rogelio. MERCENARIOS Y MONOPOLIOS EN LA ARGENTINA: DE ONGANIA A LANUSSE, 1966-1977. Buenos Aires: Achával Solo, 1971.

224. ———. LA REBELION DE LOS GENERALES. 3d ed. Buenos Aires: Jamcana, 1963.

225. García Martínez, Carlos. LA GRANDEZA ARGENTINA. Buenos Aires: Editorial Sudamericana, 1983.

226. García Molina, Fernando, and Carlos Mayo, eds. ARCHIVO DEL GENERAL JUSTO: LA PRESIDENCIA. SELECCION DE DOCUMENTOS. 2 vols. Buenos Aires: Centro Editor de América Latina, 1987.

227. ———. ARCHIVO DEL GENERAL URIBURU: AUTORI-TARISMO Y EJERCITO. SELECCION DE DOCUMENTOS. 2 vols. Buenos Aires: Centro Editor de América Latina, 1986.

228. Garmendia, José Ignacio. LA CARTERA DE UN SOLDADO: BOCETOS SOBRE LA MARCHA. 6th ed. Buenos Aires: Círculo Militar, 1973.

229. Gavshon, Arthur L., and Desmond Rice. THE SINKING OF THE BELGRANO. London: Secker & Warburg, 1984.

230. Gazzoli, Luis. CUANDO LOS MILITARES TENEMOS RAZON. Buenos Aires: Editorial Plus Ultra, 1973.

231. Germani, Gino. "El surgimiento del peronismo: El rol de los obreros y los migrantes internos." DESARROLLO ECONOMICO 51 (1973): 435-88.

232. Ghioldi, Américo. EJERCITO Y POLITICA: EL GOLPE DEL 28 DE JUNIO DE 1966. Buenos Aires: n.p., 1967.

233. ———. HISTORIA CRITICA DE LA REVOLUCION DE 43. Buenos Aires: n.p., 1950.

234. Ghioldi, Rodolfo. ESCRITOS. 4 vols. Buenos Aires: Editorial Anteo, 1975-77.

235. Gillespie, Richard. SOLDIERS OF PERON: ARGENTINA'S MONTONEROS. Oxford: Clarendon Press, 1982.

236. Giussani, Pablo. MONTONEROS: LA SOBERBIA ARMADA. Buenos Aires: Sudamericana-Planeta, 1984.

237. Gize, Fragoise, and Alain Labrousse. ARGENTINA: REVOLUTION ET CONTRE-REVOLUTION. Paris: Editions du Seuil, 1975.

238. Glick, Edward B. PEACEFUL CONFLICT: THE NON-MILITARY USE OF THE MILITARY. Harrisburg, PA: Stackpole Books, 1967.

239. Godio, Julio. LA CAIDA DE PERON DE JUNIO A SEPTIEMBRE DE 1955. Buenos Aires: Editor Granica, 1973.

240. Goldstraj, Manuel. ANOS Y ERRORES: UN CUARTO DE
      SIGLO DE POLITICA ARGENTINA. Buenos Aires: Soplios,
      1957.

241. Goldwert, Marvin. DEMOCRACY, MILITARISM, AND
      NATIONALISM IN ARGENTINA, 1930-1966: AN
      INTERPRETATION. Austin: University of Texas Press, 1972.

242. ———. "Dichotomies of Militarism in Argentina." ORBIS 10
      (1966): 930-34.

243. ———. "The Rise of Modern Militarism in Argentina." HISPANIC
      AMERICAN HISTORICAL REVIEW 48 (1968): 189-205.

244. Gómez, Alejandro. POLITICA DE ENTREGA. Buenos Aires:
      A. Peña Lillo, 1963.

245. Goncharov, A., comp. THE MALVINAS (FALKLAND) CRISIS:
      THE CAUSES AND CONSEQUENCES. Moscow: Social
      Sciences, 1984.

246. Goni Garrido, Carlos M. CRONICA DEL CONFLICTO
      CHILENO-ARGENTINO. Buenos Aires: Ediar Editores, 1984.

247. González Arzac, Rodolfo A. "Nuestra marina mercante requiere
      leyes urgentes." ACCION ECONOMICA 3 (1942?): 14-17.

248. González Climent, Aurelio. LA COMPETENCIA EN EL MAR
      Y LA MARINA MERCANTE ARGENTINA. Buenos Aries:
      Facultad de Ciencias Económicas, 1951.

249. ———. "La Flota Mercante del Estado." REVISTA DE LA
      FACULTAD DE CIENCIAS ECONOMICAS 4 (1951): 1401-23.

250. González Guevara, Campo. LA GUERRA DE LAS ISLAS
      MALVINAS O FALKLANDS. Bogotá: Ediciones Tercer Mundo,
      1984.

251. González Hernández, Juan Carlos and Enrique Alvarez Cande.
      ARGENTINA EN EL SISTEMA INTERNACIONAL. Madrid:
      Instituto de Cuestiones Internacionales, 1984.

252. González Janzen, Ignacio. 20 ANOS DE LUCHAS PERONISTAS. Mexico City: Ediciones de la Patria Grande, 1975.

253. González Lonzieme, Enrique. LA ARMADA EN LA CONQUISTA DE DESIERTO. 2d ed. Buenos Aires: EUDEBA, 1977.

254. Gooch, Herbert E. THE MILITARY AND POLITICS IN LATIN AMERICA. Los Angeles: California State University, 1979.

255. Goodman, Luis, et al., comps. LOS MILITARES Y LA DEMOCRACIA: EL FUTURO DE LAS RELACIONES CIVICO-MILITARES EN AMERICA LATINA. Montevideo: Pleitho, 1990.

256. Graham-Yooll, Andrew. A STATE OF FEAR: MEMORIES OF ARGENTINA'S NIGHTMARE. London: Eland, 1986.

257. ———. TIEMPO DE VIOLENCIA: CRONOLOGIA DEL "GRAN ACUERDO NACIONAL." Buenos Aires: Gránica Editor, 1973.

258. Graves, Norman J. "The Falklands or Las Malvinas: An Issue in Political Geography." JOURNAL OF GEOGRAPHY 82 (1983): 123-26.

259. Green, Leslie C. "The Falklands, the Law, and the War." In THE YEAR BOOK OF WORLD AFFAIRS 1984. London: The London Institute of World Affairs, 38 (1984): 89-119.

260. Greenup, Ruth, and Leonard Greenup. REVOLUTION BEFORE BREAKFAST. Chapel Hill: University of North Carolina Press, 1947.

261. Gregorich, Luis. LA REPUBLICA PERDIDA. Buenos Aires: Sudamericana-Planeta, 1983.

262. Grela, Plácido. FUERZAS ARMADAS Y SOBERANIA NACIONAL: VIDA Y OBRA DEL TENIENTE GENERAL PABLO RICCHERI, FORJADOR DEL MODERNO EJERCITO ARGENTINO. Rosario, Argentina: Litoral Ediciones, 1973.

263. Grondona, Mariano C. "La estructura cívico-militar del nuevo estado Argentino." APORTES 6 (1967): 66-76.

264. Gropp, Arthur E., ed. A BIBLIOGRAPHY OF LATIN AMERICAN BIBLIOGRAPHIES. Metuchen, NJ: Scarecrow Press, 1968.

265. ———. A BIBLIOGRAPHY OF LATIN AMERICAN BIBLIOGRAPHIES PUBLISHED IN PERIODICALS. 2 vols. Metuchen, NJ: Scarecrow Press, 1976.

266. ———. A BIBLIOGRAPHY OF LATIN AMERICAN BIBLIOGRAPHIES: SUPPLEMENT. Metuchen, NJ: Scarecrow, 1971.

267. Grow, Michael. SCHOLAR'S GUIDE TO WASHINGTON, D.C., FOR LATIN AMERICAN AND CARIBBEAN STUDIES. Washington: Smithsonian Institute Press, 1979.

268. Guardo, Ricardo C. HORAS DIFICILES. Buenos Aires: n.p., 1963.

269. Güemes, Goutran de. ASI SE GESTO LA DICTADURA: "EL G.O.U." Buenos Aires: Ediciones Rex, 1956.

270. Guevara, Juan Francisco. ARGENTINA Y SU SOMBRA. 2d ed. Buenos Aires: Mauri Hermanos Impresores, 1973.

271. Guglialmelli, Juan Enrique. "Argentina, Brazil y la bomba atómica." ESTRATEGIA 30 (1974): 1-15.

272. ———. ARGENTINA, BRAZIL Y LA BOMBA ATOMICA. Buenos Aires: Tierra Nueva, 1976.

273. ———. "Argentina: Política nacional y política de fronteras; crisis nacional y problemas fronterizos." ESTRATEGIA 37/38 (1975-76): 5-21.

274. ———. "As forças armadas na América Latina." REVISTA BRASILEIRA DE POLITICA INTERNACIONAL 14 (1971): 81-90.

275. ———. "El General Savio: Industrias bélicas, poder militar y poder nacional." ESTRATEGIA 60 (1979): 5-36.

276. Guillén, F. "Militarismo y golpes de estado en América Latina."
     CUADERNOS AMERICANOS XXIV (1965): 7-19.

277. Gutiérrez, Guillermo. EXPLOTACION Y RESPUESTAS
     POPULARES. Buenos Aires: El Cid Editor, 1974.

278. Hagelin, Ragnar. MI HIJA DAGMAR. 2d ed. Buenos Aires:
     Sudamericana-Planeta, 1984.

279. Halperin, Ernst. TERRORISM IN LATIN AMERICA. Beverly
     Hills: Sage Publications for Georgetown University, 1976.

280. Halperín Donghi, Tulio. "Algunas observaciones sobre Germani:
     El surgimiento del peronismo y los migrantes internos."
     DESARROLLO ECONOMICO 56 (1975): 765-81.

281. ———. LA DEMOCRACIA DE MASAS. Buenos Aires: Paidós,
     1972.

282. HANDBOOK OF LATIN AMERICAN STUDIES. 1935-.

283. Hastings, Max, and Simon Jenkins. THE BATTLE FOR THE
     FALKLANDS. New York: Norton, 1983.

284. Hazard, John L. "Maritime Development in Argentina in the Past
     Decade." INTER-AMERICAN ECONOMIC AFFAIRS 4
     (1951): 48-72.

285. Heare, G.E. TRENDS IN LATIN AMERICAN MILITARY
     EXPENDITURES, 1940-1970. Washington: U.S. Department of
     State, 1971.

286. Hernández Ruigómez, Manual. "El diferendo anglo-argentino en
     el Atlántico Sur: Un acicate para la producción bibliográfica."
     REVISTA DE INDIAS 14 (1984): 293-307.

287. Hilton, Stanley. "Argentine Neutrality, September 1939-June 1940:
     A Re-Examination." THE AMERICAS 22 (1966):227-57.

288. ———. "Brazil and the Post-Versailles World: Elite Images and
     Foreign Policy Strategy, 1919-1929." JOURNAL OF LATIN
     AMERICAN STUDIES 12 (1980): 341-64.

289. HISPANIC AMERICAN PERIODICALS INDEX (HAPI). Los Angeles: Latin American Center, UCLA, 1970/74-.

290. Hodges, Donald C. ARGENTINA: 1943-1976; THE NATIONAL REVOLUTION AND RESISTANCE. Albuquerque: University of New Mexico Press, 1976.

291. ———. ARGENTINA'S "DIRTY WAR:" AN INTELLECTUAL BIOGRAPHY. Austin: University of Texas Press, 1991.

292. Hoffman, Fritz Leo. "Perón and after." HISPANIC AMERICAN HISTORICAL REVIEW 36 (1956): 510-28, and 39 (1959): 212-33.

293. Hoffman, Fritz Leo, and Olga Mingo Hoffman. SOVEREIGNTY IN DISPUTE: THE FALKLANDS/MALVINAS, 1493-1982. Boulder: Westview Press, 1984.

294. Hopple, Gerald W. "Intelligence and Warning: Implications and Lessons of the Falkland Island War." WORLD POLITICS 36 (1984): 339-61.

295. Honeywell, Martin, and Jenny Pearce. FALKLANDS/MALVINAS: WHOSE CRISIS? London: Latin American Bureau, 1982.

296. Hull, Cordell. MEMOIRS. 2 vols. New York: Macmillan, 1948.

297. Ibarra, Raquel, Alejandro Leloir, and Carlos Mastrorilli. "Política y fuerzas armadas en la República Argentina." ESTRATEGIA 3 (1972): 116-31.

298. Imaz, José Luis de. LOS QUE MANDAN. Buenos Aires: EUDEBA, 1964.

299. Instituto Bibliográfico Antonio Zinny. INDICE HISTORIOGRAFICO ARGENTINO, 1970. Buenos Aires: Biblioteca F.V., 1973.

300. "El Interrogatorio: Galtieri, Anaya, Menéndez y Costa Méndez." GENTE (8 December 1983): 4-34, 68-95.

301. INTER-AMERICAN REVIEW OF BIBLIOGRAPHY/
     REVISTA INTERAMERICANA DE BIBLIOGRAFIA, 1951-.

302. Itzcovitz, Victoria. ESTILO DE GOBIERNO Y CRISIS
     POLITICA, 1973-1976. Buenos Aires: Centro Editor de América
     Latina, 1985.

303. Jaureteche, Arturo. EJERCITO Y POLITICA. Buenos Aires: A.
     Peña Lillo Editor, 1976.

304. Johnson, John J. THE MILITARY AND SOCIETY IN LATIN
     AMERICA. Stanford: Stanford University Press, 1964.

305. Johnson, Kenneth. GUERRILLA POLITICS IN ARGENTINA.
     London: Institute for Studies of Conflict, 1975.

306. Jordan, David C. "Argentina's Military Commonwealth."
     CURRENT HISTORY 76 (1979): 66-69.

307. ———. "Authoritarianism and Anarchy in Argentina." CURRENT
     HISTORY 68 (1975): 1-4, 40.

308. Josephs, Ray. ARGENTINE DIARY: THE INSIDE STORY OF
     THE COMING OF FASCISM. New York: Random House, 1944.

309. Junta Militar. DOCUMENTOS BASICOS Y BASES
     POLITICAS DE LAS FUERZAS ARMADAS PARA EL
     PROCESO DE REORGANIZACION NACIONAL. Buenos
     Aires: La Junta, 1980.

310. Kaplan, Marcos. "50 años de história argentina, 1925-1975: El
     laberinto de la frustración." In AMERICA LATINA: HISTORIA
     DE MEDIO SIGLO. VOL 1, AMERICA DEL SUR, 1-73.
     Edited by Pablo González Casanova. Mexico City: Siglo XXI
     Editores, 1977.

311. ———. GOBIERNO PERONISTA Y POLITICA DE
     PETROLEO EN ARGENTINA, 1946-1955. Caracas: Editorial
     de la Biblioteca, Universidad Central, 1971.

312. ———. "La naturaleza del gobierno peronista, 1943-1955."
     PROBLEMAS DEL DESARROLLO (Mexico) 3 (1972): 77-94.

313. Keegan, John. WORLD ARMIES. 2d ed. Detroit: Gale Research Co., 1983.

314. Kelly, David Victor. THE RULING FEW. London: Hollis & Carter, 1952.

315. Kelly, Elsa. LAS MALVINAS Y EL DERECHO DE DESCOLONIZACION. Buenos Aires: Instituto de Estudios Latinoamericanos, 1984.

316. Kent, George O., comp. A CATALOGUE OF FILES AND MICROFILMS OF THE GERMAN FOREIGN MINISTRY ARCHIVES, 1920-1945. 3 vols. Stanford: Stanford University Press, 1962-66.

317. Kenworthy, Eldon. "Did the New Industrialists Play a Significant Role in the Formation of the Peronist Alliance?" In NEW PERSPECTIVES IN MODERN ARGENTINA, 15-28. Edited by Alberto Ciria, et al. Bloomington: Indiana University Press, 1973.

318. Koburger, Charles W. SEA POWER IN THE FALKLANDS. New York: Praeger Publishers, 1983.

319. Kohl, James, and John Litt, eds. URBAN GUERRILLA WARFARE IN LATIN AMERICA. Cambridge: MIT Press, 1974.

320. Kon, Daniel. LOS CHICOS DE LA GUERRA: HABLAN LOS SOLDADOS QUE ESTUVIERON EN MALVINAS. Buenos Aires: Editorial Galerna, 1982.

321. Korn, Guillermo. LA RESISTENCIA CIVIL. Montevideo: Editorial Ceibo, 1945.

322. Landi, Oscar. LA TERCERA PRESIDENCIA DE PERON: GOBIERNO DE EMERGENCIA Y CRISIS POLITICA. Buenos Aires: Centro de Estudios de Estado y Sociedad, 1978.

323. Lanus, Roque. AL SERVICIO DEL EJERCITO. Buenos Aires: n.p., 1946.

324. Lanusse, Alejandro A. MI TESTIMONIO. Buenos Aires: Lasserre Editores, 1977.

325. Latin American Studies Association. Committee on Academic Freedom and Human Rights. Subcommittee on Academic Freedom and Human Rights in Argentina. ARGENTINA DE HOY: UN REGIME DE TERROR; INFORME SOBRE LA REPRESION DESDE JULIO DE 1973 HASTA DICIEMBRE DE 1974; REPORT AND DOCUMENTARY SUPPLEMENT. Gainesville, FL: LASA, 1975.

326. Legon, Faustino J., and Samuel W. Medrano. LAS CONSTITUCIONES DE LA REPUBLICA. Madrid: Ediciones Cultura Hispánica, 1953.

327. Leonard, Virginia W. "Education and the Church-State Clash in Argentina." CHURCH HISTORY REVIEW 45 (1980): 34-52.

328. Lerner, Abel. EL PERONISMO Y NUESTRA TIEMPO. SU DOCTRINA A LA LUZ DE LAS IDEAS PROGRESISTAS DEL MUNDO. Buenos Aires: Editorial Nueva Libertad, 1945.

329. Lernoux, Penny. CRY OF THE PEOPLE: UNITED STATES INVOLVEMENT IN THE RISE OF FASCISM, TORTURE AND MURDER AND THE PERSECUTION OF THE CHURCH IN LATIN AMERICA. New York: Doubleday, 1980.

330. ———. PEOPLE OF GOD: THE STRUGGLE FOR WORLD CATHOLICISM. New York: Viking, 1989.

331. Levi, Nadia. GUIA DE PUBLICACIONES PERIODICAS DE UNIVERSIDADES LATINOAMERICANAS. Mexico City: UNAM, 1967.

332. Lewis, Paul H. "Was Perón a Fascist?: An Inquiry into the Nature of Fascism." THE JOURNAL OF POLITICS 42 (1980): 242-56.

333. EL LIBRO DE "EL DIARIO DEL JUICIO." Buenos Aires: Editorial Perfil, 1985.

334. Lieuwen, Edwin. ARMS AND POLITICS IN LATIN AMERICA. New York: Praeger Publishers, 1960.

335. ———. GENERALS VS. PRESIDENTS: NEOMILITARISM IN LATIN AMERICA. New York: Praeger Publishers, 1964.

336. Lindenberg, Klause. FUERZAS ARMADAS Y POLITICA EN AMERICA LATINA: BIBLIOGRAFIA SELECTA. Santiago, Chile: Instituto Latinoamericano de Investigaciones Sociales, 1972.

337. Lironi, Julio Víctor. GENESIS DE LA AVIACION ARGENTINA, 1910-1915: SU HISTORIA Y SUS HOMBRES. Buenos Aires: Artes Gráficas Congreso, 1971.

338. Little, Walter. "La Organización obrera y el estado peronista, 1943-1955." DESARROLLO ECONOMICO 75 (1979): 331-76.

339. ———. "The Popular Origin of Peronism." In ARGENTINA IN THE TWENTIETH CENTURY, 162-78. Edited by David Rock. Pittsburgh: University of Pittsburgh Press, 1975.

340. Llorente, Ignacio. "Alianzas políticas en el surgimiento del peronismo: El caso de la provincia de Buenos Aires." DESARROLLO ECONOMICO 17 (1977): 61-88.

341. ———. "La composición social del movimiento peronista hacia 1954." In EL VOTO PERONISTA: ESTUDIOS DE SOCIOLOGIA ELECTORAL ARGENTINA, 367-96. Edited by Manuel Mora y Araujo and Ignacio Llorente. Buenos Aires: Editorial Sudamericana, 1980.

342. Lonardi, Luis Ernesto. DIOS ES JUSTO. Buenos Aires: F. Colombo, 1958.

343. Lonardi, Marta. MI PADRE Y LA REVOLUCION DEL 55. Buenos Aires: Ediciones Cuenca de Plata, 1980.

344. López, Alvaro. El dilema de los militares argentinos. PENSAMIENTO CRITICO 45 (1970): 187-98.

345. López, Norberto A. EL PLEITO DE LA PATRIA. Buenos Aires: Círculo Militar, 1975.

346. López, Pablo. "El antisemitismo en Argentina." AREITO 5 (1979): 24-27.

347. López Saavedra, Emiliana. APELACION A LA DEMOCRACIA: ENTREVISTAS CON RAUL ALFONSÍN ET AL. Buenos Aires: Editorial Redacción, 1983.

348. ——. TESTIGOS DEL "PROCESO" MILITAR, 1966-1983. Buenos Aires: Centro Editor de América Latina, 1984.

349. Loveman, Brian, and Thomas M. Davies, eds. THE POLITICS OF ANTIPOLITICS: THE MILITARY IN LATIN AMERICA. 2d ed. Lincoln: University of Nebraska Press, 1989.

350. Lowenthal, Abraham F., ed. ARMIES AND POLITICS IN LATIN AMERICA. New York: Holmes & Meier, 1976.

351. Lucero, Franklin. EL PRECIO DE LA LEALTAD. Buenos Aires: Editorial Propulsión, 1959.

352. Lugones, Leopoldo. LOS ARGENTINOS Y SU HISTORIA INTERNA. Buenos Aires: Ediciones Centurón, 1962.

353. Luna, Félix. ALVEAR. Buenos Aires: Libros Argentinos, 1958.

354. ——. EL 45. Buenos Aires: Editorial Sudamericana, 1971.

355. ——. DIALAGOS CON FRONDIZI. Buenos Aires: Editorial Desarrollo, 1963.

356. ——. GOLPES MILITARES Y SALIDAS ELECTORALES. Buenos Aires: Editorial Sudamericana, 1983.

357. ——. DE PERON A LANUSSE, 1943-1973. Buenos Aires: Editorial Planeta Argentina, 1972.

358. ——. PERON Y SU TIEMPO: LA ARGENTINA ERA UNA FIESTA, 1946-1949. Buenos Aires: Editorial Sudamericana, 1984.

359. ——. "El 'Proceso,' 1976-1982." CRITERIO 55 (1982): 739-46.

360. ——. SOY ROCA. Buenos Aires: Editorial Sudamericana, 1989.

361. ——. YRIGOYEN: EL TEMPLARIO DE LA LIBERTAD. Buenos Aires: Editorial Raigal, 1956.

362. McAlister, Lyle. "Recent Research and Writing on the Role of the Military in Latin America." LATIN AMERICAN RESEARCH REVIEW 2 (1966): 5-36.

363. MacDonald, C.A. "The Politics of Intervention: The United States and Argentina, 1941-1946." JOURNAL OF LATIN AMERICAN STUDIES 12 (1980): 365-96.

364. Maceyra, Horacio. LA SEGUNDA PRESIDENCIA DE PERON. Buenos Aires: Centro Editor de América Latina, 1984.

365. McGann, Thomas F. ARGENTINA: THE DIVIDED LAND. New York: Van Nostrand, 1966.

366. ———. ARGENTINA, THE UNITED STATES AND THE INTER-AMERICAN SYSTEM, 1880-1914. Cambridge: Harvard University Press, 1957.

367. Main, Mary (María Flores). THE WOMAN WITH THE WHIP: EVA PERON. New York: Doubleday, 1952.

368. Malagarriga, Carlos C. EN FAVOR DEL RETORNO AL REGIMEN DE LA CONSTITUCION. Buenos Aires: Talleres Gráficos Gadda, n.d.

369. Maligné, Augusto. "El ejército argentino en 1910." REVISTA DE DERECHO, HISTORIA Y LETRAS 38 (1910): 306-12.

370. ———. HISTORIA MILITAR DE LA REPUBLICA ARGENTINA DURANTE EL SIGLO DE 1810 A 1910. Buenos Aires: La Nación, 1910.

371. Mandelli, Humberto A. TEMAS DE HISTORIA DE LAS INSTITUCIONES ARGENTINAS. Buenos Aires: Alcarios, 1967.

372. Manitzas, Frank N. "Argentina's Cold Season." HARPER'S 253 (1976): 14-21.

373. Marini, Ana María. "Women in Contemporary Argentina." LATIN AMERICAN PERSPECTIVES 4 (1977): 114-20.

374. Martínez, Carlos J. "El ejército ante el problema de la siderurgía nacional." INGENIERIA 46 (n.d.): 35-41.

375. Martínez, Edgar Argentino. DEFENSA NACIONAL POLITICO: UN ANALISIS DE SUS RELACIONES CON LAS FUERZAS ARMADAS Y EL PODER MILITAR. Buenos Aires: A. Peña Lillo Editor, 1974.

376. Martínez, Pedro Santos. LA NUEVA ARGENTINA, 1946-1955. 2 vols. Buenos Aires: Ediciones La Bastilla, 1976.

377. Martínez, Rodolfo. GRANDEZAS Y MISERIAS DE PERON. Mexico City: Distribuidor "Mexico Lee," 1957.

378. "Más allá de Videla." CARTA POLITICA, PERSONA A PERSONA 76 (1980): 30-39.

379. Mason Lugones, Raúl. "Argentina: El actual plan económico compromete el futuro del país, en particular la seguridad nacional." ESTRATEGIA 61/62 (1979-80): 64-75.

380. Massari, Roberto. "Le Cordobazo." SOCIOLOGIE DU TRAVAIL (Paris) 17 (1975): 403-19.

381. Massera, Emilio E. EL CAMINO A LA DEMOCRACIA. Caracas: El Cid Editor, 1979.

382. Matijevic, Nicolas. BIBLIOGRAFIA BIBLIOTECOLOGICA ARGENTINA. Bahia Blanca: Universidad Nacional del Sur Centro de Documentación Bibliotecológica, 1969.

383. Mayer, Jorge M. DE MONROE A LAS MALVINAS. Buenos Aires: Academia Nacional de Derecho y Ciencias Sociales de Buenos Aires, 1983.

384. Mazo, Gabriel del. EL RADICALISMO. EL MOVIMIENTO DE INTRANSIGENCIA Y RENOVACION, 1945-1957. Buenos Aires: Editorial Guré, 1957.

385. ———. EL RADICALISMO: NOTAS SOBRE SU HISTORIA Y DOCTRINA, 1922-1952. Buenos Aires: Editor Raigal, 1955.

386. Mazo, Gabriel del, and Roberto Etchepareborda. LA SEGUNDA PRESIDENCIA DE YRIGOYEN: ANTECEDENTES DE LA CRISIS DE 1930. Buenos Aires: Centro Editor de América Latina, 1984.

387. Menéndez, Mario Benjamín, and Carlos M. Turolo. MALVINAS: TESTIMONIO DE SU GOBERNADOR. Buenos Aires: Editorial Sudamericana, 1983.

388. Menéndez, Rómulo Félix. LAS CONQUISTAS TERRITORIALES ARGENTINAS. Buenos Aires: Círculo Militar, 1982.

389. Mestre, Tomás. EL SISTEMA INTERAMERICANO Y LA GUERRA DE LAS MALVINAS: SU MUTUO IMPACTO. Madrid: Instituto de Cuestiones Internacionales, 1984.

390. Meyer, Michael C. SUPPLEMENT TO A BIBLIOGRAPHY OF UNITED STATES-LATIN AMERICAN RELATIONS SINCE 1810. Lincoln: University of Nebraska Press, 1979.

391. Middlebrook, Martin. TASK FORCE: THE FALKLANDS WAR, 1982. London: Penguin, 1987.

392. Milenky, Edward S. ARGENTINA'S FOREIGN POLICY. Boulder: Westview Press, 1978.

393. ———. "Arms Production and National Security in Argentina." JOURNAL OF INTER-AMERICAN STUDIES AND WORLD AFFAIRS 22 (1980): 267-88.

394. Milia, Juan Guillermo. EL VALOR ESTRATEGICO ECONOMICO DEL ATLANTICO SUR Y LA GUERRA DE LAS MALVINAS. Buenos Aires: Publicaciones de Oikos Asociación para la Promoción de los Estudios Territorales y Ambientales, 1987.

395. Moneta, Carlos Juan. "Fuerzas armadas y gobierno constitucional después de las Malvinas: Hacía una nueva relación civil-militar." FORO INTERNACIONAL 26 (1985): 190-213.

396. ———. "La política exterior del peronismo, 1973-1976." FORO INTERNACIONAL 20 (1979): 220-76.

397. Mora y Araujo, Manuel, and Ignacio Llorente, eds. EL VOTO PERONISTA: ESTUDIOS DE SOCIOLOGIA ELECTORAL ARGENTINA. Buenos Aires: Editorial Sudamericana, 1980.

398. Morales, Loza Néstor. FRONDIZI Y LA VERDAD. Buenos Aires: Urania, 1957.

399. Moreno, Nahuel. EL GOLPE GORILA DE 1955: LAS POSICIONES DEL TROTSKISMO. Buenos Aires: Ediciones Pluma, 1974.

400. Moreno, Oscar. "Acerca del Peronismo." NUEVA SOCIEDAD 36 (1978): 105-16.

401. Most, Benjamin A. "Authoritarianism and the Growth of the State in Latin America: An Assessment of Their Impacts on Argentine Public Policy." COMPARATIVE POLITICAL STUDIES 13 (1980): 173-203.

402. Munck, Ronaldo. "The 'Modern' Military Dictatorship in Latin America: The Case of Argentina, 1976-1982." LATIN AMERICAN PERSPECTIVES 12 (1985): 41-74.

403. Muñoz Grande, Juan Ramón. "Argentina: Objectivo orgánico del ejército para el largo plazo." ESTRATEGIA 60 (1979): 37-43.

404. Murmis, Miguel, et al. ESTUDIOS SOBRE LOS ORIGINES DEL PERONISMO. 2 vols. Buenos Aires: Siglo XXI Editores, 1971-73.

405. NACLA. "Alfonsín's Argentina: The Ties That Bind." NACLA REPORT ON THE AMERICAS. 21:4 (1987): 13-39.

406. ———. ARGENTINA IN THE HOUR OF THE FURNACES. New York: NACLA, 1975.

407. Naipaul, V.S. "Argentine Terror: A Memoir." NEW YORK REVIEW OF BOOKS 26 (1979): 13-16.

408. Neustadt, Bernardo. LA ARGENTINA Y LOS ARGENTINOS. Buenos Aires: Emece Editores, 1976.

409. "Nota de tapa: los puntos sobre las íes." CARTA POLITICA, PERSONA A PERSONA 61 (1978): 32-37.

410. NUNCA MAS: THE REPORT OF THE ARGENTINE NATIONAL COMMISSION ON THE DISAPPEARED. New York: Farrar, Straus, and Giroux, 1986.

411. Nunn, Frederick M. "European Military Influence in South America: The Origins and Nature of Professional Militarism in

Argentina, Brazil, Chile, and Peru, 1890-1940." JAHRBUCH FUR GESCHICHTE VON STAAT, WIRTSCHAFT UND GESELLSCHAFT LATEINAMERIKAS 12 (1975): 230-52.

412. Oddone, Jacinto. GREMIALISMO PROLETARIO ARGENTINO. Buenos Aires: Editorial La Vanguardia, 1949.

413. Odena, Isidro J. LIBERTADORES Y DESARROLLISTAS, 1955-1963. Buenos Aires: Ediciones La Bastilla, 1977.

414. O'Donnell, Guillermo A. "Estado y alianza en la Argentina, 1956-1976." CENTRO DE ESTUDIOS DE ESTADO Y SOCIEDAD 5 (1976): 1-40.

415. ———. "Notas para el estudio de procesos de democratización política a partir del estado burocrático-autoritario." DESARROLLO ECONOMICO 22 (1982): 231-48.

416. ———. "Permanent Crisis and the Failure to Create a Democratic Regime: Argentina, 1955-1966." In THE BREAKDOWN OF DEMOCRATIC REGIMES: LATIN AMERICA, 138-77. Edited by Juan Linz and Alfred Stepan. Baltimore: Johns Hopkins University Press, 1978.

417. ———. "Reflections on the Patterns of Change in the Bureaucratic-Authoritarian State." LATIN AMERICAN RESEARCH REVIEW 13 (1978): 3-38.

418. Olascoaga, Manuel J. ESTUDIO TOPOGRAFICO DE LA PAMPA Y RIO NEGRO. 2d ed. Buenos Aires: EUDEBA, 1974.

419. Olivieri, Anibal O. DOS VECES REBELDE: MEMORIAS. Buenos Aires: Ediciones Siglo, 1958.

420. Olivieri, Mabel. "Peronismo e forze armate." MULINO 24 (1975): 706-28.

421. Orona, Juan V. LA DICTADURA DE PERON. Buenos Aires: n.p., 1970.

422. ———. LA LOGIA MILITAR QUE DERROCO A CASTILLO. Buenos Aires: Editorial Leonardo Impresora, 1967.

423. ———. LA LOGIA MILITAR QUE ENFRENTO HIPOLITO YRIGOYEN. Buenos Aires: Editorial Leonardo Impresora, 1965.

424. ———. LA REVOLUCION DEL 16 DE SEPTIEMBRE. Buenos Aires: Editorial del Autor, 1971.

425. ———. LA REVOLUCION DEL 6 DE SEPTIEMBRE. Buenos Aires: Editorial Leonardo Impresora, 1966.

426. Orsolini, Mario Horacio. LA CRISIS DEL EJERCITO. Buenos Aires: Ediciones Arayu, 1964.

427. ———. EJERCITO ARGENTINO Y CRECIMIENTO NACIONAL. Buenos Aires: Ediciones Arayu, 1965.

428. Ortiz, Roberto Marcelino. IDEARIO DEMOCRATICO (A TRAVES DE LA REPUBLICA). Buenos Aires: M. Gleizer, 1937.

429. ———. EL PRESIDENTE ORTIZ Y EL SENADO DE LA NACION. Buenos Aires: Impresora Argentina, 1941.

430. Ossendorff, Ingo. DER FALKLAND-MALWINEKONFLIKT 1982 UND SEINE RESONANZ IN DER NATIONALEN PRESSE: EINE STUDIE UBER FEINDBILDER IN DER REGIERUNGSKOMMUNIKATION. Frankfurt am Main: P. Lang, 1987.

431. Oved, Iaacov. EL ANARQUISMO Y EL MOVIMIENTO OBRERO EN ARGENTINA. Mexico City: Siglo XXI Editores, 1978.

432. Pablo, Juan Carlos de. ECONOMIA POLITICA DEL PERONISMO. Buenos Aires: El Cid Editor, 1980.

433. ———. POLITICA ECONOMICA ARGENTINA: MATERIALES PARA EL DESARROLLO DEL TEMA SEGUN EL METODO DE LOS CASOS. Buenos Aires: Ediciones Macchi, 1984.

434. Page, Joséph A. PERON: A BIOGRAPHY. New York: Random House, 1983.

435. Palacio, Ernesto. HISTORIA DE LA ARGENTINA, 1515-1976.

13th ed. Buenos Aires: Abeledo-Perrot, 1981.

436. Palacios, Alfredo Lorenzo. MENSAJE A LA JUVENTUD. Buenos Aires: Ediciones Populares Argentinas, 1956.

437. Palacios, Elena Julia, and Irma Verissimo. HISTORIA DE LAS INSTITUCIONES ARGENTINAS SOCIALES Y POLITICAS. Buenos Aires: Perrot, 1952.

438. Panaia, Marta, Ricardo Lesser, and Pedro Skupch. ESTUDIOS SOBRE LOS ORIGENES DEL PERONISMO. Vol. 2. Buenos Aires: Siglo XXI Editores, 1973.

439. Pandolfi, Rodolfo. "La caida de Lanusse." CONFIRMADO 19 (1973): 31-39.

440. Pardo, M. Sixto. "El estado militar argentino." OCCIDENTE 1:10 (1944?): 11-21.

441. Pavón Pereyra, Enrique. COLOQUIOS CON PERON: EL PENSAMIENTO DEL EX-PRESIDENTE ARGENTINO A TRAVES DE CONVERSACIONES MANTENIDAS CON EL DURANTE LOS TRES ULTIMOS ANOS. Buenos Aires: n.p., 1965.

442. ———. CONVERSACIONES CON JUAN DOMINGO PERON. Buenos Aires: Colihue, 1978.

443. ———. PERON TAL COMO ES. 2d ed. Buenos Aires: Editorial Macacha Güemes, 1973.

444. ———. LOS ULTIMOS DIAS DE PERON. Buenos Aires: Ediciones La Campaña, 1981.

445. Pendle, George. "Perón and Vargas." FORTNIGHTLY REVIEW 176 (1951): 723-28.

446. Peralta Ramos, Mónica. ACUMULACION DE CAPITAL Y CRISIS POLITICA EN ARGENTINA, 1930-1974. Mexico City: Siglo XXI Editores, 1978.

447. Perina, Emilio. DETRAS DE LA CRISIS. Buenos Aires: Editorial "Periplo", 1960.

448. Perina, Ruben M. ONGANIA, LEVINGSTON, LANUSSE: LOS
      MILITARES EN LA POLITICA ARGENTINA. Buenos Aires:
      Editorial de Belgrano, 1983.

449. ———. "Raices históricas de la participación política de los
      militares argentinos." MUNDO NUEVO 3 (1981): 35-67.

450. Perón, Juan Domingo. DISCURSOS DEL EXCMO. SENOR
      PRESIDENTE DE LA NACION . . . DIRIGIDOS A LAS
      FUERZAS ARMADAS, 1946-1951. Buenos Aires: Ministerio de
      Ejército, 1951?

451. ———. DOCTRINA PERONISTA. Buenos Aires: Editora Volver,
      1982.

452. ———. LA FUERZA ES EL DERECHO DE LAS BESTIAS.
      Havana: S. Tourino, 1956.

453. ———. EL GOBIERNO, EL ESTADO Y LAS ORGANI-
      ZACIONES LIBRES DEL PUEBLO [AND] LA COMUNIDAD
      ORGANIZADA: TRABAJOS, ALOCUCIONES Y ESCRITOS
      DEL GENERAL . . . QUE FUNDAMENTAN LA
      CONCEPCION JUSTICIALISTA DE LA COMUNIDAD.
      Buenos Aires: Editorial de la Reconstrucción, 1975.

454. ———. PERON-COOKE CORRESPONDENCIA. Buenos Aires:
      Ediciones Papiro, 1972.

455. ———. PERON EXPONE SU DOCTRINA. Buenos Aires:
      Presidencia de la Nacion, Subsec. de Información, 1951.

456. ———. PERON HABLA A LAS FUERZAS ARMADAS, 1946-
      1954. Buenos Aires: Presidencia de la Nación, Sec. de Prensa y
      Difusión, 1955.

457. ———. PERON, EL REGRESO Y LA MUERTA. Montevideo:
      Biblioteca de Marcha, 1974.

458. ———. DEL PODER AL EXILIO: COMO Y QUIENES ME
      DERROCARON. Buenos Aires: Ediciones Argentina, 1973.

459. ———. EL PUEBLO QUIERE SABER DE QUE SE TRATA.
      Buenos Aires: n.p., 1944.

460. ——. TRES REVOLUCIONES MILITARES. Buenos Aires: Ediciones Sintesis, 1963.

461. ——. YO, JUAN DOMINGO PERON: RELATO AUTOBIOGRAFICO. Barcelona: Editorial Planeta, 1976.

462. Peterson, Harold F. ARGENTINA AND THE UNITED STATES, 1810-1960. New York: University Publishers, 1964.

463. Piaggio, Mauricio Víctor. "The Argentine Marine Corps." MARINE CORPS GAZETTE 50 (1966): 21-24.

464. Piccinali, Héctor Juan. VIDA DEL TENIENTE GENERAL NICOLAS LEVALLE. Buenos Aires: Círculo Militar, 1982.

465. Piccirilli, Ricardo, Francisco L. Romay, and Leoncio Gianello. DICCIONARIO HISTORICO ARGENTINO. 6 vols. Buenos Aires: Ediciones Históricas Argentinas, 1953.

466. Piedracueva, Haydee. A BIBLIOGRAPHY OF LATIN AMERICAN BIBLIOGRAPHIES, 1975-1979: SOCIAL SCIENCES AND HUMANITIES. Metuchen, NJ: Scarecrow Press, 1982.

467. Pinedo, Federico. "La constitución vigente y el proceso económico y social." REVISTA DEL COLEGIO DE ABOGADOS DE BUENOS AIRES 26 (1947?): 323-74.

468. ——. EN TIEMPO DE LA REPUBLICA. 5 vols. Buenos Aires: Editorial Mundo Forense, 1946-48.

469. Piñeiro, Armando Alonso. "El equilibrio político sudamericano." ESTRATEGIA 30 (1974): 62-71.

470. Pion-Berlin, David. "The Fall of Military Rule in Argentina, 1976-1983." JOURNAL OF INTER-AMERICAN STUDIES AND WORLD AFFAIRS 27 (1985): 55-76.

471. Plater, Guillermo. UNA GRAN LECCION. La Plata, Argentina: Almafuerte, 1959.

472. "Políticos y militares: La di-con-vergencia." CARTA POLITICA, PERSONA A PERSONA 74 (1980): 26-33.

473. Poneman, David. "Nuclear Proliferation: Prospects for Argentina." ORBIS 27 (1984): 853-80.

474. Portes, Alejandro. PERON AND THE NATIONAL ELECTIONS. Austin: Institute of Latin American Studies Special Publication, University of Texas, 1973.

475. Porth Jacquelyn S. "Argentina." In ARMS PRODUCTION IN DEVELOPING COUNTRIES: AN ANALYSIS OF DECISION MAKING, 53-72. Edited by James Everett Katz. Lexington, MA: Lexington Books, 1984.

476. Potash, Robert A. "Alfonsín's Argentina in Historical Perspective." PROGRAM IN LATIN AMERICAN STUDIES OCCASIONAL PAPERS SERIES NO. 21. Amherst: University of Massachusetts, 1988.

477. ———. THE ARMY AND POLITICS IN ARGENTINA, 1945-1962: PERON TO FRONDIZI. Stanford: Stanford University Press, 1980.

478. ———. THE ARMY AND POLITICS IN ARGENTINA, 1962-1973. Forthcoming.

479. ———. THE ARMY AND POLITICS IN ARGENTINA, 1928-1945: YRIGOYEN TO PERON. Stanford: Stanford University Press, 1969.

480. ———. "The Military Policies of Alfonsín and Menem." Article to be published in a forthcoming book edited by Colin Lewis.

481. Potter, Anne L. "The Failure of Democracy in Argentina, 1916-1930: An Institutional Perspective." JOURNAL OF LATIN AMERICAN STUDIES 13 (1981): 83-109.

482. Prado, Manuel. LA GUERRA AL MALON. Buenos Aires: Editorial Xanadú, 1976.

483. Prieto, Ramón. CORRESPONDENCIA PERON-FRIGORIO, 1958-1973. Buenos Aires: Editorial Macacha Güemes, 1975.

484. ———. EL PACTO: 8 ANOS DE POLITICA ARGENTINA. Buenos Aires: Editorial "En Marcha," 1963.

485. PRONTUARIO: TECNICA DEL INTERROGATORIA; LA REPRESION Y EL ASESINATO. Santiago: Editora Nacional Quimantú, 1973.

486. Puiggros, Rodolfo. ¿ADONDE VAMOS ARGENTINOS? Buenos Aires: Ediciones Corregidor, 1972.

487. Putman, Robert. "Toward Explaining Military Intervention in Latin American Politics." WORLD POLITICS 20 (1967): 83-110.

488. Quebracho [pseud. for Liborio Justo]. PRONTUARIO: UNA AUTOBIOGRAFIA. Buenos Aires: Ediciones Guré, 1956.

489. Quesada, Fernando. EL PRIMER ANARQUISTA FUSILADO EN LA ARGENTINA. Buenos Aires: Editorial Destellos, 1974.

490. Quinterno, Carlos Alberto. HISTORIA RECIENTE: LA CRISIS POLITICA ARGENTINA ENTRE 1955 Y 1966. Buenos Aires: Librería Huemul, 1970.

491. ———. MILITARES Y POPULISMO: LA CRISIS ARGENTINA DESDE 1966 HASTA 1976. Buenos Aires: Editorial Temas Contemporáneos, 1978.

492. Quiroga, Abraham. "Las enseñanzas orgánicas de la guerra europea en el ejército francés y su adaptación a nuestro ejército." REVISTA MILITAR 37 (1921): 965-1018.

493. Quirós, Alberto. BALBIN: UN CAUDILLO, UN IDEAL. Buenos Aires: Editorial Abril, 1982.

494. Ramayón, Eduardo E. LAS CABALLADAS EN LA GUERRA DEL INDIO. Buenos Aires: EUDEBA, 1975.

495. Ramírez, Gilberto, Jr. "The Reform of the Argentine Army, 1890-1904." Ph.D. dissertation, University of Texas, Austin, 1987.

496. Ramos, Jorge Abelardo, et al. EL CORDOBAZO. Buenos Aires: Ediciones Octubre, 1974.

497. ———. LA ERA DEL PERONISMO, 1943-1976. Buenos Aires: Ediciones del Mar Dulce, 1981.

498. ———. HISTORIA POLITICA DEL EJERCITO ARGENTINO Y OTROS ESCRITOS SOBRE TEMAS MILITARES. Buenos Aires: Ediciones Rancagua, 1973.

499. ———. REVOLUCION Y CONTRARREVOLUCION EN LA ARGENTINA. 3 vols. 5th ed. Buenos Aires: Editorial Plus Ultra, 1973.

500. Randall, Laura. AN ECONOMIC HISTORY OF ARGENTINA IN THE TWENTIETH CENTURY. New York: Columbia University Press, 1978.

501. Ranis, Peter. "The Dilemmas of Democratization in Argentina." CURRENT HISTORY 85:507 (1986): 29-33,42.

502. ———. "Early Peronism and the Early Post-Liberal Argentine State." JOURNAL OF INTER-AMERICAN STUDIES AND WORLD AFFAIRS 21 (1979): 313-38.

503. ———. "En respuesta a Eldon Kenworthy: Interpretaciones ortodoxas revisionistas del apoyo inicial del Peronismo." DESARROLLO ECONOMICO 57 (1977): 163-82.

504. Rapoport, Mario. GRAN BRETANA, ESTADOS UNIDOS Y LAS CLASES DIRIGENTES ARGENTINAS, 1940-1945. Buenos Aires: Editorial de Belgrano, 1980.

505. ———. LAS RELACIONES ANGLO-ARGENTINAS: ASPECTOS POLITICOS Y ECONOMICOS; LA EXPERIENCIA DEL GOBIERNO MILITAR, 1943-1945. Buenos Aires: Fundación para el Estudio de los Problemas Argentinos, 1979.

506. Rattenbach, Benjamin. EL SECTOR MILITAR DE LA SOCIEDAD: PRINCIPIOS DE SOCIOLOGIA MILITAR. Buenos Aires: Círculo Militar, 1965.

507. ———. EL SISTEMA SOCIAL-MILITAR EN LA SOCIEDAD MODERNA. Buenos Aires: Editorial Pleamar, 1972.

508. Ratti, Horacio A. "Civic Action of the Argentine Armed Forces." AIR UNIVERSITY REVIEW 19 (1968): 53-58.

509. Ravenal, Eugenio A.L. ISLES OF DISCORD: A FILE ON THE FALKLANDS MALVINAS. Geneva: Siboney and Venture Books, 1983.

510. REDEFINICION DE LAS RELACIONES INTRALATINOAMERICANAS E INTER-AMERICANAS DESPUES DEL CONFLICTO DE LAS MALVINAS: SEMINARIO, LIMA, 27-28 DE OCTUBRE DE 1982. Lima: Instituto de Desarrollo Económico, Escuela de Administración de Negocios para Graduados, 1983.

511. Rennie, Ysabel F. THE ARGENTINE REPUBLIC. New York: Macmillan, 1945.

512. Repetto, Nicolás. CONTRA LA CORRUPCION Y LA INTRIGA: LOS PROCEDIMIENTOS DEL NAZISMO. Buenos Aires: Editorial Acción Argentina, n.d.

513. ———. MI PASO POR LA POLITICA. 2 vols. Buenos Aires: Santiago Rueda Editorial, 1957.

514. ———. MIS NOVENTA ANOS. Buenos Aires: Editorial Bases, 1962.

515. ———. LOS SOCIALISTAS Y EL EJERCITO. Buenos Aires: Editorial La Vanguardia, 1946.

516. Repetto, Robert. "Las Malvinas: Nuestros títulos históricos y juídicos." REVISTA DE LA JUNTA DE ESTUDIOS HISTORICOS DE MENDOZA 10 (1984): 443-48.

517. LA REPRESION EN ARGENTINA, 1973-74: DOCUMENTOS. Mexico City: UNAM, 1978.

518. Reyes, Franklin E. "Estrategia militar y petroleo." REVISTA DE INFORMACIONES 18 (1940).

519. ———. "La movilización industrial en lo referente a la fabricación de armas y municiones de guerra." REVISTA MILITAR 60 (1933): 201-28.

520. Riquet, Michel. "L'Argentine entre la dictature militaire et l'Eglise" LA NOUVELLE REVIEW DE DEUX MONDES 9 (1978): 526-37.

521. Rivera, José María. "Argentina: Programa económico y política financiera." ESTRATEGIA 52/53 (1978): 50-62.

522. Rivera Echenique, Silvia. MILITARISMO EN LA ARGENTINA: GOLPE DE ESTADO DE JUNIO 1966. Mexico City: UNAM, 1976.

523. Riz, Liliana de. RETORNO Y DERRUMBE. Mexico City: Folios Ediciones, 1981.

524. Rock, David. ARGENTINA, 1516-1982: FROM SPANISH COLONIZATION TO THE FALKLANDS WAR. Berkeley: University of California Press, 1985.

525. ———. POLITICS IN ARGENTINA, 1890-1930: THE RISE AND FALL OF RADICALISM. Cambridge: Cambridge University Press, 1975.

526. ———. "Repression and Revolt in Argentina." NEW SCHOLAR 7 (1978-1979): 105-120.

527. Rock, David. ed. ARGENTINA IN THE TWENTIETH CENTURY. Pittsburgh: University of Pittsburgh Press, 1975.

528. Rodríguez, Augusto. RESENA HISTORICA DEL EJERCITO ARGENTINO, 1862-1930. Buenos Aires: Dirección de Estudios Históricos, Secretaría de Guerra, 1964.

529. Rodríguez Lamas, Daniel. LA PRESIDENCIA DE FRONDIZI. Buenos Aires: Centro Editor de América Latina, 1984.

530. Romay, Francisco L. HISTORIA DE LA POLICIA FEDERAL ARGENTINA. 3 vols. Buenos Aires: Biblioteca Policial, 1963-65.

531. Romero, José Luis. LA EXPERIENCIA ARGENTINA Y OTROS ENSAYOS. Buenos Aires: Editorial de Belgrano, 1980.

532. Romero, Luis Alberto. LOS GOLPES MILITARES, 1812-1955. Buenos Aires: Carlos Pérez Editor, 1969.

533. Romero Briaseo, Jesús and Salvador Mafe Huertas. MALVINAS: TESTIGO DE BATALLAS. Valencia, Spain: F. Domenech, 1984.

534. Rosenblum, Mort. "Terror in Argentina." NEW YORK REVIEW OF BOOKS 23:17 (1976): 26-28.

535. Roth, Roberto. LOS ANOS DE ONGANIA: RELATOS DE UN TESTIGO. 3d ed. Buenos Aires: Ediciones La Campaña, 1981.

536. Rottjer, Enrique. "La revolución de 6 de septiembre desde el punto de vista militar." REVISTA MILITAR 55 (1930): 575-90.

537. Rouquié, Alain. "Adhesión militar y control político del ejército en el régimen peronista, 1946-55." APORTES 14 (1971): 74-93.

538. ———. "L'Argentine aprés les militares." POLITIQUE ETRANGERE (Paris) 49 (1984): 113-25.

539. ———. "Argentine: La fin du regime militaire et le retour du General Perón au pouvoir." NOTES ET ETUDES DOCUMENTAIRES 4110/4111 (1974): 1-70.

540. ———. "L'Argentine du General Videla: Deux ans de reorganisation national, 1976-78." NOTES ET ETUDES DOCUMENTAIRES 4499/4500 (1978): 10-43.

541. ———. EL ESTADO MILITAR EN AMERICA LATINA. Mexico City: Siglo XXI Editores, 1984.

542. ———. "Les eternels retours a la legalité consitutionnelle." NOTES ET ETUDES DOCUMENTAIRES 4545/4546 (1978): 110-29.

543. ———. "Groupes de pression et forces armies en Argentine: La logique de l'état pretorien." REVUE FRANCAISE D'HISTOIRE D'OUTREMER 66 (1979): 377-83.

544. ———. PODER MILITAR Y SOCIEDAD POLITICA EN LA ARGENTINA, HASTA 1943. Buenos Aires: EMECE, 1978.

545. ———. PODER MILITAR Y SOCIEDAD POLITICA EN LA ARGENTINA, 1943-1973. Buenos Aires: EMECE, 1982.

546. Rowe, James. "Argentina's Restless Military." AMERICAN UNIVERSITIES FIELD STAFF. East Coast South American Series. 11 (1964).

547. Rozitchner, Leon. LAS MALVINAS: DE LA GUERRA "SUCIA" A LA GUERRA "LIMPIA." Buenos Aires: Centro Editor de América Latina, 1985.

548. Rudolph, James D., ed. ARGENTINA: A COUNTRY STUDY. 3d ed. Washington: United States Government Printing Office, 1985.

549. Ruiz-Guiñazú, Enrique. LA POLITICA ARGENTINA Y EL FUTURO DE AMERICA. Buenos Aires: Librería Huemul, 1944.

550. Russel, Charles A., James F. Schinkel, and James A. Miller. "Urban Guerrillas in Argentina: A Select Bibliography." LATIN AMERICAN RESEARCH REVIEW 9 (1974):53-92.

551. Russell, Roberto. "La nueva política exterior argentina: Rupturas conceptuales." IDEAS EN CIENCIAS SOCIALES 1 (1984): 30-45.

552. Sabate Lichtschein, Domingo. PROBLEMAS ARGENTINOS DE SOBERANIA TERRITORIAL. Buenos Aires: Abeledo Perrot, 1985.

553. Sadi, José P. "La organización de nuestra industria bélica." ACCION ECONOMICA 2/17 (1942?): 17-19.

554. Sánchez Sorondo, Marcelo. LA REVOLUCION QUE ANUNCIAMOS. Buenos Aires: Ediciones Nueva Política, 1945.

555. ———. "6 de septiembre de 1930." REVISTA DE HISTORIA 3 (1958): 104-26.

556. Sánchez Viamonte, Carlos. HISTORIA INSTITUTIONAL ARGENTINA. 2d ed. Mexico City: Fondo de Cultura, 1957.

557. ———. UTILIDAD DE LAS DICTADURAS. Buenos Aires: La Vanguardia, 1947.

558. Sanguinetti, Horacio. LA DEMOCRACIA FICTA: 1930-1938. Buenos Aires: Editorial Astrea, 1975.

559. ———. LOS SOCIALISTAS INDEPENDIENTES. Buenos Aires: Editorial Sudamericana, 1981.

560. Santos Martínez, Pedro. "Pasado y presente de las Malvinas e islas del Atlántico Sur." BOLETIN DE LA ACADEMIA NACIONAL DE LA HISTORIA 66 (1983): 41-79.

561. Sanz, Luis Santiago. "El poder naval y la junta de notables de 1906." ESTRATEGIA 46/47 (1977): 47-95.

562. Sarobe, José M. MEMORIAS SOBRE LA REVOLUCION DEL 6 DE SEPTIEMBRE DE 1930. Buenos Aires: Ediciones Guré, 1957.

563. Scalabrini Ortíz, Raúl. POLITICA BRITANICA EN EL RIO DE LA PLATA. 3d ed. Buenos Aires: Ediciones Hechos e Ideas, 1950.

564. Scenna, Miguel Angel. LOS MILITARES. Buenos Aires: Editorial de Belgrano, 1980.

565. Schaefer, Jurgen. DEUTSCHE MILITARHILFE AN SUDAMERIKA: MILITAR UND RUSTUNGSINTERESSEN IN ARGENTINIEN, BOLIVIEN UND CHILE VOR 1914. Dusseldorf: Bertelsmann-Universitäts-Verlag, 1974.

566. Scheina, Robert L. LATIN AMERICA: A NAVAL HISTORY, 1810-1987. Annapolis, MD: Naval Institute Press, 1987.

567. Schiff, Warren. "The Influence of the German Armed Forces and War Industry in Argentina, 1880-1914." HISPANIC AMERICAN HISTORICAL REVIEW 52 (1972): 436-55.

568. Schvarzer, Jorge. ARGENTINA, 1976-81: EL ENDEUDAMIENTO EXTERNO COMO PIVOTE DE LA ESPECULACION FINANCIERA. Buenos Aires: Centro de Investigaciones Sociales sobre el Estado y la Administración, 1983.

569. ———. MARTINEZ DE HOZ: LA LOGICA POLITICA DE LA ECONOMICA. Buenos Aires: Centro de Investigaciones Sociales sobre el Estado y la Administración, 1983.

570. Selser, Gregorio. ARGENTINA A PRECIO DE COSTO: EL GOBIERNO DE FRONDIZI. Buenos Aires: Editorial Iguazú, 1965.

571. ———. EL ONGANIATO: LA ESPADA Y EL HISOPO. Buenos
      Aires: Carlos Samonta Editor, 1973.

572. ———. EL ONGANIATO: LA LLAMABAN REVOLUCION
      ARGENTINA. Buenos Aires: Carlos Samonta Editor, 1973.

573. Senen González, Santiago, and Ricardo Gallo. DIEZ ANOS DE
      SINDICALISMO ARGENTINO: DE PERON AL PROCESO.
      Buenos Aires: Corregidor, 1984.

574. Sequeira, Sebastián, Carlos Cal, and Cecilia Calatayud.
      AVIACION NAVAL ARGENTINA. Buenos Aires: SS & CC
      Ediciones, 1984.

575. Silenzi de Stagni, Adolfo. LAS MALVINAS Y EL PETROLEO.
      2 vols. Buenos Aires: El Cid Editor, 1982-83.

576. Simpson, John, and Jana Bennett. THE DISAPPEARED:
      VOICES FROM A SECRET WAR. London: Robson Books,
      1985.

577. Skidmore, Thomas E. "The Economic Dimension of Populism in
      Argentina and Brazil: A Case Study in Comparative Public
      Policy." NEW SCHOLAR 7 (1978): 129-66.

578. Smith, Peter H. ARGENTINA AND THE FAILURE OF
      DEMOCRACY: CONFLICT AMONG POLITICAL ELITES,
      1904-1955. Madison: University of Wisconsin Press, 1974.

579. ———. "Argentina: The Uncertain Warriors."   CURRENT
      HISTORY 78 (1980): 62-65, 85-86.

580. ———. "The Breakdown of Democracy in Argentina, 1916-30." In
      THE BREAKDOWN OF DEMOCRATIC REGIMES: CRISIS,
      BREAKDOWN AND REEQUILIBRATION, 3-27. Edited by
      Juan J. Linz and Alfred Stepan. Baltimore: John Hopkins
      University Press, 1978.

581. ———. "Las elecciones argentinas de 1946 y las inferencias
      ecológicas." DESARROLLO ECONOMICO 14 (1974) 385-98.

582. ———. "The Social Base of Peronism." HISPANIC AMERICAN
      HISTORICAL REVIEW 52 (1972) 55-73.

583. ———. "Social Mobilization, Political Participation and the Rise of Juan Perón." POLITICAL SCIENCE QUARTERLY 84(1969): 30-49.

584. Snow, Peter G. "Argentine Radicalism, 1957-1963." JOURNAL OF INTER-AMERICAN AFFAIRS 5 (1963): 507-31.

585. ———. "Parties and Politics in Argentina: The Elections of 1962 and 1963." MIDWEST JOURNAL OF POLITICAL SCIENCE 9 (1965): 1-36.

586. Sobel, Lester A., ed. ARGENTINA AND PERON, 1970-75. New York: Facts on File, 1975.

587. LOS SOFISTAS Y LA PRENSA CANALLA: EL CID EDITOR VS. EDITOR VIGILANTE. Córdoba: El Cid Editor Argentina, 1984.

588. Solberg, Carl E. OIL AND NATIONALISM IN ARGENTINA. Stanford: Stanford University Press, 1979.

589. Spector, Leonard. NUCLEAR PROLIFERATION TODAY. New York: Vintage Books, 1984.

590. Stabb, Martin S. "Argentine Letters and the Peronato." JOURNAL OF INTER-AMERICAN STUDIES AND WORLD AFFAIRS 13 (1971): 434-55.

591. STATISTICAL ABSTRACT OF LATIN AMERICA. Los Angeles: Latin American Center, UCLA, 1955-.

592. Steelstrag, Arturo. INFORME DE LA COMISION EXPLORADORA DEL CHACO. 2d ed. Buenos Aires: EUDEBA, 1977.

593. Stickell, A. Lawrence. "Peronist Politics in Labor." In NEW PERSPECTIVES ON MODERN ARGENTINA. Edited by Alberto Ciria, et al. Bloomington: Indiana University Press, 1972.

594. Stoetzer, O. Carlos. TWO STUDIES ON CONTEMPORARY ARGENTINE HISTORY: ON THE EVE OF THE 1976 CRISIS AND A REVIEW OF CURRENT U.S.-ARGENTINE RELATIONS. New York: Argentine Independent Review, 1980.

595. Strange, Ian J. THE FALKLAND ISLANDS. 3d ed. Newton Abbot, England: Davis & Charles, 1983.

596. Svencionis, Faustino. ARGENTINE FOREIGN POLICY AND THE WORLD EVENTS, 1958 TO 1982: A SURVEY. Washington: National Defense University, Fort Lesley J. McNair, 1984.

597. Tamarin, David. THE ARGENTINE LABOR MOVEMENT, 1930-1945: A STUDY IN THE ORIGINS OF PERONISM. Albuquerque: University of New Mexico Press, 1985.

598. ———. "Yrigoyen and Perón: The Limits of Argentine Populism." In LATIN AMERICA IN COMPARATIVE PERSPECTIVE, 31-46. Edited by Michael Conniff. Albuquerque: University of New Mexico Press, 1981.

599. Tanzi, Héctor José. HISTORIOGRAFIA ARGENTINA CONTEMPORANEA. Caracas: Instituto Panamericano de Geografía e História, 1976.

600. Taylor, Julie M. EVA PERON: THE MYTHS OF A WOMAN. Chicago: University of Chicago Press, 1979.

601. Teichman, Judith. "Interest Conflict and Entrepreneurial Support for Perón." LATIN AMERICAN RESEARCH REVIEW 16 (1981): 144-55.

602. Terragno, Rodolfo. LOS 400 DIAS DE PERON. Buenos Aires: Ediciones de la Flor, 1974.

603. "Terror in Argentina." NEW YORK REVIEW OF BOOKS 23 (1976): 26-28.

604. TESTIMONIO SOBRE EL CENTRO CLANDESTINO DE DETENCION DE LA ESCUELA DE MECANICA DE LA ARMADA ARGENTINA, ESMA. Buenos Aires: Centro de Estudios Legales y Sociales, 1984.

605. TESTIMONIOS: "EL LIBRO DE JUICIO." Buenos Aires: Editorial Testigo, 1985.

606. Timermann, Jacobo. PRISONER WITHOUT A NAME, CELL WITHOUT A NUMBER. New York: Knopf/Random House, 1981.

607. Torre, Juan Carlos. "La CGT y 17 de octubre de 1945." TODO ES HISTORIA 107 (1976): 70-90.

608. Torre, Lisandro de la. CARTAS INTIMAS. 2d ed. Avellaneda, Argentina: Editorial Futuro, 1959.

609. Torres, Arturo. ELPIDIO GONZALEZ: BIOGRAFIA DE UNA CONDUCTA. Buenos Aires: Editorial Raigal, 1951.

610. Torres, José Luis. LA DECADA INFAME. Buenos Aires: Editorial de Formación "Patria," 1945.

611. Toryho, Jacinto. ARAMBURU: CONFIDENCIAS, ACTITUDES, PROPOSITOS. Buenos Aires: Ediciones Libera, 1973.

612. Townsend, C.D. "The Future Of the Falkland Islands." CONTEMPORARY REVIEW 245 (1984): 289-93.

613. Trask, David F., Michael C. Meyer, and Roger R. Trask, eds. A BIBLIOGRAPHY OF UNITED STATES-LATIN AMERICAN RELATIONS SINCE 1810. Lincoln: University of Nebraska Press, 1968.

614. Turner, Frederick C., and José Enrique Miguens, eds. JUAN PERON AND THE RESHAPING OF ARGENTINA. Pittsburgh: University of Pittsburgh Press, 1983.

615. Ugalde, Alberto J. LAS EMPRESAS PUBLICAS EN LA ARGENTINA. Buenos Aires: Ediciones El Cronista Comercial, 1984.

616. Ulibarri, George S., and John P. Harrison, eds. GUIDE TO MATERIALS ON LATIN AMERICA IN THE NATIONAL ARCHIVES OF THE UNITED STATES. Washington: National Archives and Records Service, 1974.

617. University Microfilms International. LATIN AMERICA: A CATALOG OF SELECTED DOCTORAL DISSERTATION

RESEARCH. Ann Arbor: University Microfilms International, 1984.

618. University Publications of America. CIA RESEARCH REPORTS, LATIN AMERICA, 1946-1976. Bethesda, MD: University Publications of America, 1990. Microfilm.

619. ———. THE JOHN F. KENNEDY NATIONAL SECURITY FILES, LATIN AMERICA: NATIONAL SECURITY FILES, 1961-1963. Bethesda, MD: University Publications of America, 1990. Microfilm.

620. ———. THE LYNDON B. JOHNSON NATIONAL SECURITY FILES, LATIN AMERICA: NATIONAL SECURITY FILES, 1963-1969. Bethesda, MD: University Publications of America, 1990. Microfilm.

621. ———. 1990 RESEARCH COLLECTIONS. Bethesda, MD: University Publications of America, 1990.

622. ———. PERON ERA POLITICAL PAMPHLETS AND MONOGRAPHS. Bethesda, MD: University Publications of America, 1990. Microfilm.

623. Uriburu, José F. LA PALABRA DEL GENERAL URIBURU: DISCURSOS, MANIFIESTOS, DECLARACIONES Y CARTAS PUBLICADAS DURANTE SU GOBIERNO. Buenos Aires: Roldán, 1933.

624. Urondo, Francisco, ed. LA PATRIA FUSILADA: ENTREVISTAS, TESTIMONIOS DE MARIA ANTONIA BERGER, ALBERTO MIGUEL CAMPS, RICARDO RENE HAIDAR. 2d ed. Buenos Aires: Ediciones de Crisis, 1973.

625. Valle, Delfor del. "La unión cívica radical y el ejército." HECHOS E IDEAS 2 (1935): 122-28.

626. Varas, Augusto. MILITARIZATION AND THE INTERNATIONAL ARMS RACE IN LATIN AMERICA. Boulder: Westview Press, 1985.

627. Varas, Augusto, and Felipe Aguero. EL PROYECTO POLITICO MILITAR. Santiago, Chile: FLACSO, 1984.

628. Vernón, Horacio Luis. FUERZA MILITAR LATINO AMERICANA. Buenos Aires: Distribuidora Maipo, 1966.

629. Vigo, Juan M. ¡LA VIDA POR PERON!: MEMORIAS DE UN COMBATIENTE DE LA RESISTENCIA. Buenos Aires: A. Peña Lillo Editor, 1973.

630. Vilas, Carlos María. LA DOMINACION IMPERIALISTA EN ARGENTINA. Buenos Aires: EUDEBA, 1974.

631. Vilches, B. Ernesto. PERON VISTO DESDE CHILE. Santiago: Editorial Cultura, 1947.

632. Villegas, Osiris Guillermo. EN CONFLICTO CON CHILE EN LA REGION AUSTRAL. Buenos Aires: Editorial Pleamar, 1978.

633. Viñas, Alberto. CELDA 43: TREINTA Y DOS MESES DE CAUTIVERIO, 1951-1953. Buenos Aires: Ediciones Rex, 1956.

634. Vuotto, Pascual. VIDA DE UN PROLETARIO: EL PROCESO DE BRAGADO. 5th ed. Buenos Aires: R. Alonso Editor, 1975.

635. Wahnish, José A., and Carlos R. French. "Creación de la Fuerza Aérea Argentina y síntesis de la evolución del poder aéreo nacional." ESTRATEGIA 59/60 (1979): 107-12, 105-25.

636. Waisman, Carlos H., and Mónica Peralta-Ramos, eds. FROM MILITARY RULE TO LIBERAL DEMOCRACY. Boulder: Westview Press, 1986.

637. Waldmann, Peter. "Las cuatro fases del gobierno peronista." APORTES 19 (1971): 94-106.

638. ———. EL PERONISMO, 1943-1955. Buenos Aires: Editorial Sudamericana, 1981.

639. ———. "Terrororganizationen en Argentinien." BERICHTE ZUR ENTWICKLUNG IN SPANIEN, PORTUGAL, LATEINAMERIKA 2 (1977): 10-22.

640. Waldmann, Peter, and Ernesto Garzón Valdés, comps. EL PODER EN LA ARGENTINA, 1976-1981: ASPECTOS HISTORICOS Y SOCIOPOLITICOS. Frankfurt am Main: Vervuert, 1982.

641. Walters, Marian C., ed. LATIN AMERICA AND THE CARIBBEAN II: A DISSERTATION BIBLIOGRAPHY. Ann Arbor: University Microfilm International, 1980.

642. Wells, Sumner. WHERE ARE WE HEADING? New York: Harper and Bros., 1946.

643. Whitaker, Arthur P. ARGENTINA. Englewood Cliffs, N.J.: Prentice-Hall, 1964.

644. ———. ARGENTINE UPHEAVAL. New York: Praeger Publishers, 1956.

645. ———. "Left and Right Extremism in Argentina." CURRENT HISTORY 62 (1963): 84-88, 116.

646. ———. "Social and Economic Crisis in Argentina." CURRENT HISTORY 60 (1961): 208-13, 218.

647. ———. THE UNITED STATES AND ARGENTINA. Cambridge: Harvard University Press, 1954.

648. ———. THE UNITED STATES AND THE SOUTHERN CONE: ARGENTINA, CHILE, AND URUGUAY. Cambridge: Harvard University Press, 1976.

649. Wogart, Colin M. "Combining Price Stabilization Policies: The Argentine Experience, 1976-1981." JOURNAL OF INTER-AMERICAN STUDIES AND WORLD AFFAIRS 25 (1983): 445-76.

650. Wood, David. ARMED FORCES IN CENTRAL AND SOUTH AMERICA. London: Institute for Strategic Studies, 1967.

651. Wright, Ione S., and Lisa M. Nekhom. HISTORICAL DICTIONARY OF ARGENTINA. Metuchen, NJ: Scarecrow Press, 1978.

652. Wynia, Gary W. ARGENTINA AND THE POST-WAR ERA: POLITICS AND ECONOMIC POLICY MAKING IN A DIVIDED SOCIETY. Albuquerque: University of New Mexico Press, 1978.

653. ———. "Democracy in Argentina." CURRENT HISTORY 84 (1985): 53-56.

654. ———. "Illusion and Reality in Argentina." CURRENT HISTORY 80 (1981): 62-65.

655. Yokota, Marilyn B. BIBLIOGRAPHY ON THE 1982 FALKLANDS WAR. Santa Monica, CA: Rand Corporation, 1985.

656. Yrigoyen, Hipólito. PUEBLO Y GOBIERNO. 2d ed. 12 vols. Buenos Aires: n.p., 1956.

657. Zamorano, Carlos Mariano. PRISIONERO POLITICO: TESTIMONIO SOBRE LAS CARCELES POLITICAS ARGENTINAS. Buenos Aires: Ediciones Estudio, 1983.

658. Zinn, Ricardo. ARGENTINA: A NATION AT THE CROSSROADS OF MYTH AND REALITY. New York: Robert Speller & Sons, 1979.

659. Zorraquín Becú, Horacio, et al. CUATRO REVOLUCIONES ARGENTINAS, 1890-1930-1943-1955. Buenos Aires: Club Nicolás Avellaneda, 1960.

660. Zuleta Alvarez, Enrique. EL NACIONALISMO ARGENTINO. Buenos Aires: Ediciones La Bastilla, 1975.

PERIODICALS

661. AIR POWER HISTORY, 1988-. (Formerly AEROSPACE HISTORIAN, 1953-88.)

662. AHORA.

663. THE AMERICAS, 1944-.

664. APORTES.

665. ARGENTINE OUTREACH, 1976-.

666. ARMAS Y TIRO, 1910-. (Formerly REVISTA DE TIRO, and earlier TIRO NACIONAL ARGENTINO.)

667. AVIACION Y ASTRONAUTICA, 1958-.

668. BOLETIN DE ESTUDIOS LATINOAMERICANOS Y DEL CARIBE, 1965-.

669. BOLETIN DEL CENTRO NAVAL, 1881-.

670. BULLETIN OF LATIN AMERICAN RESEARCH, 1981-.

671. CAHIERS DU MONDE HISPANIQUE ET LUSO-BRASILIEN (CARAVELLE), 1963-.

672. CARTA POLITICA, PERSONA A PERSONA, 1977-.

673. CLARIN.

674. COMPARATIVE POLITICS.

675. CURRENT HISTORY.

676. DESARROLLO ECONOMICO.

677. ESTO ES.

678. ESTRATEGIA, 1969-82.

679. FORO INTERNACIONAL.

680. HECHOS E IDEAS.

681. HISPANIC AMERICAN HISTORICAL REVIEW, 1918-.

682. JAHRBUCH FUR GESCHICHTE VON STAAT, WIRTSCHAFT UND GESELLSCHAFT LATEINAMERIKAS, 1964-.

683. JANE'S DEFENCE WEEKLY.

684. JOURNAL OF INTERAMERICAN STUDIES AND WORLD AFFAIRS.

685. JOURNAL OF LATIN AMERICAN STUDIES, 1969-.

686. JOURNAL OF MILITARY HISTORY, 1989-. (Formerly MILITARY AFFAIRS, 1936-89.)

687. LATIN AMERICAN PERSPECTIVES, 1974-.

688. LATIN AMERICAN RESEARCH REVIEW, 1965-.

689. LATIN AMERICAN WEEKLY REPORT, 1967-.

690. MANUAL DE INFORMACIONES, 1958-. (Depto. de Acción Psicológica del Ejército.)

691. MARINA, 1955-.

692. LA NACION.

693. NACLA. REPORT ON THE AMERICAS, 1966-.

694. NAVAL WAR COLLEGE REVIEW.

695. NOTES ET ETUDES DOCUMENTAIRES.

696. LA PRENSA.

697. PRIMERA PLANA.

698. REVIEW OF THE RIVER PLATE.

699. REVISTA ARGENTINA DE ESTUDIOS ESTRATEGICOS, 1984-.

700. REVISTA DE HISTORIA.

701. REVISTA DE LA ESCUELA DE COMANDO Y ESTADO MAYOR.

702. REVISTA DE LA ESCUELA SUPERIOR DE GUERRA, 1922-.

703. REVISTA DE LA SANIDAD MILITAR ARGENTINA, 1891-.

704. REVISTA DE PUBLICACIONES NAVALES, 1869-.

705. REVISTA DEFENSA NACIONAL, 1962-.

706. REVISTA DEL CIRCULO MILITAR, 1904-.

707. REVISTA DEL SUBOFICIAL.

708. REVISTA INTERAMERICANA DE BIBLIOGRAFIA/
      INTER-AMERICAN REVIEW OF BIBLIOGRAPHY, 1951-.

709. REVISTA MEXICANA DE SOCIOLOGIA, 1939-.

710. REVISTA MILITAR DE VETERINARIA, 1953-.

711. REVISTA NACIONAL AERONAUTICA Y ESPACIAL, 1940-.

712. EL SOLDADO ARGENTINO, 1921-.

713. TODO ES HISTORIA.

714. UNIVERSITIES FIELD STAFF REPORTS.

715. LA VANGUARDIA.

716. WASHINGTON REPORT ON THE HEMISPHERE.

CHAPTER VI

BOLIVIA, ECUADOR, AND PERU

Thomas M. Davies, Jr.
San Diego State University
(With the assistance of Kirsten Barstad-Mulvey)

INTRODUCTION

It is axiomatic when writing about Latin American politics in the nineteenth and twentieth centuries to note that the area's most important political actor has been and remains the military establishment in each nation, but that axiom carries even greater weight when describing the Andean republics of Bolivia, Ecuador, and Peru. There, the incredible plethora of coups and counter coups, with military caudillos replacing both civilian politicians and other military strongmen, doomed to failure any attempt to install even a semblance of the liberal, democratic state.

Moreover, while almost every military leader asserted that he was acting in the name of the "Constitution" (as well as "La Patria"), the reality was that constitutions were violated, ignored, discarded, and "rewritten" so often that the "rule of law" in the three republics was usually nothing more than rule from the barracks covered with only the thinnest veneer of constitutionality.

To be sure, the military establishments in each country could point to the wars of independence and argue correctly that they, and not the civilians, had liberated their respective nations from Spanish domination. Military liberation from Spain took on even greater importance in the Andes due both to the length and bloodiness of the campaigns and to the fact that the final victories against the Spanish were indeed achieved there, first by Antonio José de Sucre in 1822 at Pichincha, near Quito, Ecuador, and then, definitively, by Sucre, in 1824, on the plains of Ayacucho in Peru. Since that date, the militaries of all three nations have pointed to the independence wars as definitive proof of their patriotism and have used them as the principal justification for intervening at will to protect or save the fatherland for which they had fought and died. Moreover, following the long wars of independence, all three nations were in the direst of economic and political straits, bankrupt in every respect, but the very military commanders who had created them saved them from ruin and dismemberment; the Age of the Caudillos had begun.

Interestingly, Bolivia, the country that suffered the greatest political instability over the next 150 years, actually enjoyed the most propitious beginning of the three Andean nations. Under the very able leadership of Andrés de Santa Cruz (1829-1839), Bolivia prospered economically, politically, culturally, and educationally. Moreover, Santa Cruz is held to be the father of both the Bolivian army and the national police force --the Carabineros. Thus, for modern Bolivian military leaders, Andrés de Santa Cruz is the model to be emulated today.

In Peru, the period immediately following independence was one of the most chaotic in the nation's history, with military caudillos treating the presidency as a type of door prize in the incessant civil wars which wreaked havoc on the nation. Finally, in 1845, the military "founding father" of Peru, Ramón Castilla (1797?-1867), assumed office for the first time. Castilla was so successful in his efforts to establish economic prosperity and political stability, as well as military preparedness, that he ranks first in the pantheon of Peruvian heroes and is revered by the military today for his honesty, patriotism, and firm commitment to national defense.

Ecuador, too, has its military founder, one of the greatest of the South American caudillos--Juan José Flores (1800-1864). Flores, like his counterparts to the south, succeeded in consolidating the republic, restoring relative economic and political stability and in building a national military establishment, the point of reference or "origin myth" for today's Ecuadorian military officers.

But the area's militaries did not just free their peoples and create their nation states, they also defended those nations from outside aggressors. Ecuador's military stood in opposition to Andrés de Santa Cruz's Peru-Bolivian Confederation (1836-1839), and again it resisted the 1859 invasion and blockade of Guayaquil by Ramón Castilla. All three nations' militaries successfully defended their coastal installations against Spanish attack in 1865.

Nevertheless, the most important military event of the nineteenth century was the War of the Pacific (1879-1883), during which both Bolivia and Peru suffered humiliating defeats to Chile and lost vital national territory (Bolivia lost its seacoast and Peru its southernmost province). The militaries of both nations look back on this event and swear that it will not only never happen again, but in fact, it will be avenged. Bolivian military officers assert that they have a "right to a seacoast and a duty to recover it," while all Peruvian military cadets are taught that they will, during their own lifetimes, "recuperar el Morro" (recover the bluff overlooking the bay of Arica). Finally, the War of the Pacific all but guaranteed the continued existence of the arms race involving Peru, Bolivia, and Chile which has proved so injurious to national development in the twentieth century. As Ramón Castilla said, "if Chile buys one ship, Peru should buy two."

The dawn of the twentieth century brought with it continued military presence/intervention in politics, albeit with a slightly different tone. The War of the Pacific interrupted a process which had begun in Peru in the 1870s--attempts by civilian politicians to "professionalize" the military and thereby remove it from politics. The Peruvians were the first among these three nations to act by contracting, in 1896, a French military mission headed by Capt. Paul Clément. Clément was to have an incredibly important impact on Peruvian military ideology and "professionalism" and civil-military relations. In a very real sense, the military regimes that ruled Peru after 1930 owed their professional and ideological formation to Clément and his fellow French officers.

The impact of foreign military advisers in Bolivia was even more pronounced than in Peru. In 1910, the Bolivians formally requested a military mission from the German government. It arrived one year later, headed by Col. Hans Kundt and composed of four captains and eight sergeants. Over the next twenty-five years, Kundt not only trained and armed the Bolivian army (with German weapons of course), but he succeeded in becoming Army Chief-of-Staff and led Bolivia into the disastrous Chaco War against Paraguay (1932-1935).

Initially, Ecuador did not contract directly with a foreign military mission, but rather sent officers to study at the Escuela Militar in Chile, while Chilean officers manned the Escuela Militar in Quito. Thus, German influence passed through Chilean officers directly into the Ecuadorian psyche. Then, in 1922, an Italian mission arrived in the country, instituted a number of reforms, and helped to found schools of aviation and military engineering. Nevertheless, the Italians left no lasting impact on Ecuadorian military thought.

Military dominance of political affairs in all three republics continued unabated throughout the twentieth century. In two cases, there were real wars which required the services of professional soldiers, but the resulting impact on civil-military relations was, in each instance, quite different. The bloody and senseless Chaco War devastated both Paraguay and Bolivia, but in the latter country it also served to awaken the masses and to politicize, even radicalize, young military officers. This process ultimately led to the Bolivian National

Revolution of 1952 with its concerted attempt to remove the military from national politics.

In Peru skirmishes with Colombia (1932-1933) and the short-lived war with Ecuador (1941), in which Peru obtained a substantial piece of Ecuadorian territory, served to demonstrate to Peruvian military officers the need for bigger and better armed forces. At the same time, this experience reinforced the horribly self-fulfilling prophesy that more arms were needed to fight the wars which were caused, in part, by the new arms.

Moreover, throughout this history there existed the basic tenet that because the military in each country created the nation, it was, therefore, directly responsible for the nation's protection and salvation. The armed forces also understood that civilians were corrupt, venal, and self-serving to the extent of betraying the very fatherland they had been elected to preserve.

All of these themes are treated in the bibliography which follows, but as is patently obvious from the distribution of entries, the number of works on the military in Bolivia and Ecuador pales when compared to the tremendous amount on Peru. This paucity of materials on the former two countries is, of course, no reflection of the important political role played by their armed forces (particularly Bolivia with its more than two hundred illegal regime changes since independence), but rather an indication of the sophistication of the Peruvian military and of its institutional development in contrast to that of Bolivia and Ecuador.

As outlined above, there are similarities between the three nations' defense establishments, such as an "origin myth," the importance of foreign military missions, the propensity to intervene in national politics to "save La Patria," and the dislike and disdain for the liberal democratic state and everything that even smells of "politics." Nevertheless, there is no Centro de Altos Estudios Militares (CAEM) in either Bolivia and Ecuador, and there certainly has been no military reformist/revolutionary regime in either country which even approaches in importance that of the Revolutionary Government of the Armed Forces (RGAF) (1968-1980) in Peru.

Whether few or many, however, the studies cited under each country also vary widely in terms of quality of research and sophistication of analysis. This is as true for the general and specialized works as it is for the memoirs and journals. Thus, because of this fact, as well as the space restraints in this volume, no attempt has been made in this short essay to discuss all the citations listed in the bibliography. A few of the entries have been annotated, but this was done only to clarify a vague or potentially misleading title or to point out the very best works on a given topic. Finally, the bibliography should in no way be considered exhaustive or definitive; rather it should be taken as merely a preliminary starting point for any serious study of the subject.

GENERAL WORKS

The only book that treats all three republics in the twentieth century is Pike (409), and while it is not focused specifically on the military, it is the best summary of Andean culture and socio-political development (including the armed forces) in any language. Loveman and Davies (279, 280, 281), treat both Bolivia and Peru in terms of military "antipolitics" and the response to Guevara-like guerrilla movements in the 1960s. Gott (217), also provides extensive treatment of guerrillas in Peru and Bolivia in the 1960s.

The best general accounts of the military in Bolivia are Dunkerley (167), Díaz Arguedas (154, 155), Bedregal (67), Corbett (131), Pozzo Medina (415), and Prado Salmón (416). Also valuable, though not focused specifically on the military, are Baptista Gumucio (51), Barton (62), Delgado González (150), Dunkerley (168), Fellman Delarde (190), Gallardo Lozada (205), Kelley and Klein (248), Klein (250, 253), Ladman (257), Lora (275, 276, 277), Malloy and Gamarra (298), Nash (348), and Weil (523).

As noted above, the literature on Ecuador is limited, but the reader is directed first to Fitch (197), and then to Corporación Editora Nacional (136), Drekonja Kornat (166), Martz (309), Orellana (365), Reyes (425), Schodt (449), Varas and Bustamante (493), and Weil (524).

In the vast literature on Peru, the basic starting point is Jorge Basadre's monumental HISTORIA DE LA REPUBLICA DEL PERU (63), but there are also a number of general studies on the military itself. Foremost on the list are the multi-volume works published by the military services themselves with the ones by the navy (240, 492), being the most important, followed by the army (130), and the air force (244).

Peru's best and most prolific military historian, Víctor Villanueva, began with his now classic EL MILITARISMO EN EL PERU (514), followed by several other volumes (508, 509, 510, 515); EJERCITO PERUANO (510), is his best effort. Villanueva's study of the CAEM (508), is the most important work on that crucial educational institution, but the reader should also consult Einaudi (181), Einaudi and Stepan (186), Rodríguez Beruff (432), and Stepan (463); the last is an outstanding general examination of Peru, the military, and the Revolutionary Government of the Armed Forces (1968-80).

Other general accounts of the military include Barra (54), Dellepiane (151, 152), García Rosell (210), and McAlister, Maingot, and Potash (285). Nunn (358) is, without doubt, the best study, in any language, of the influence of European military missions in South America. Gerlach (211), and Masterson (312), are both fine dissertations which, taken together, offer a cogent overview of the period 1914-63.

Finally, there are several more general works on Peru which merit serious attention. Bourricaud (91), is a fine study of the twentieth century, as is Cotler (137). Also very valuable are Astiz and García (42), Nyrop (359), Palmer (374), Pike (408), and Werlich (525). For accounts of military performance in the economic realm, see Fitzgerald (199), and Thorp and Bertram (475).

BIBLIOGRAPHIES

Like too many modern weapon systems, bibliographies (including this one) are obsolete before they even see print. Nevertheless, they still constitute fundamental tools for all researchers. With that caveat in mind, by far the most important bibliographic guide is TePaske, RESEARCH GUIDE TO ANDEAN HISTORY (469), whose fifty articles treat a wide range of bibliographic, historiographic, and archival topics. The footnotes in Pike (409), also contain a wealth of citations.

For Bolivia there are good bibliographies by Abecia Baldivieso (1), Arze (38), and Guttentag T. (228), as well as useful ones in Alexander (11), Klein (250, 253), and Weil (523). Those scholars interested in Ecuador should consult Drekonja Kornat (165), Benites Vinueza (78), Fitch (197), and Weil (524).

There are a number of excellent bibliographies for Peru, but, as with general works, one must begin with Basadre's HISTORIA DE LA REPUBLICA DEL PERU (63), specifically volume seventeen, and his incredibly valuable INTRODUCCION A LAS BASES DOCUMENTALES PARA LA HISTORIA DE LA REPUBLICA DEL PERU (64). Extremely important on the military are Barra (53), and Nunn (354, 358). There are many other Peruvian bibliographies of a general nature, but the ANUARIO BIBLIOGRAFICO PERUANO (395), is the most complete. Others include Herbold and Stein (233), Matos Mar and Ravines (315), Pease García G.Y. (385), Pérez-Rosas Cáceres (389), Pike (408), and Tauro (468).

ARCHIVAL GUIDES AND SOURCES

In many ways, the most important as well as accessible depository for the study of the military in the Andean region is the National Archive of the United States in Washington, D.C., which is well organized with material open through the year 1949. The most pertinent record groups are the Internal Affairs Serial Files for each country and the Military Intelligence Document Files. Scholars should also consult the Federal Records Center in Suitland, Maryland.

The most important library/archive in Bolivia is the Archivo y Biblioteca de Bolivia located in Sucre and brilliantly directed for many years by Gunnar Mendoza. There are others, but lack of funds has prevented their proper organization and development.

Ecuador boasts of a number of archives on the military which are accessible to researchers. There are several separate ones maintained in the Ministerio de Defensa, but the primary depository is the well-organized Archivo General del Ministerio de Defensa in Quito. In addition, each military service maintains its own archive which can be used with prior permission: the Archivo de la Comandancia General del Ejército, the Archivo de la Comandancia Naval, and the Archivo de la Comandancia de la Fuerza Aérea. Finally, two other indispensable repositories for the study of the military are those at the Colegio Militar Eloy Alfaro and the Centro de Historia y Geografía Militar, both of which are in Quito.

Two superb archival depositories in Peru are particularly apt for the study of the twentieth-century military. The first, and most important, is the Sala de Investigaciones in the Biblioteca Nacional. It and other parts of the library contain the Colección de Volantes, congressional debates, *memorias* and *informes* from all the military ministries, presidential addresses, and a major collection of newspapers and periodicals.

The military's own archive is the Centro de Estudios Histórico-Militares. It houses the Escalafones Generales, the Ordenes Generales del Ejército, Marina, Aeronáutica, and Guardia Civil y Policía, military codes and legislation, military journals, and other pertinent documents.

PUBLISHED DOCUMENTS

The most important and largest documentary collections are those of the annual *informes* and *memorias* from the various defense ministries. Also of great value are published congressional debates, presidential messages to Congress and/or the nation (many from military officers), *manifiestos* justifying this coup d'état or that "revolution," and the myriad of propaganda *folletos* and small books that were published in the 1970s and 1980s to justify long-term military rule. None of these sources have been cited below because of space limitations, but they are all readily available in national libraries or, oftentimes, in used book stores.

Another form of published documents can be found in the officer-authored articles printed in the various armed forces journals of the three countries. Although some are dry regurgitations of warmed over strategies, many provide valuable insight into the soldier's mind, what influenced it, and what impact that thinking has had or will have on civil-military relations. For a brilliant example of the use of these periodicals, see Nunn (358).

The published documents cited below in no way constitute even a preliminary list, let alone a definitive one, but they are good examples of the type of material one might expect to find in various time frames. For Bolivia there is Arze Quiroga's (39), three-volume set of documents on the Chaco War as well as Bolivian military government publications (83, 84, 85, 86, 87), from two very important yet quite distinct periods. The key documents on Ecuador (170, 171, 172, 173, 174, 175), provide insight into the junta of 1963-66.

The entries for Peru are even more varied. They encompass two works by Paul Clément (124, 125), commander of the first French military mission in Peru (1896-1911), and two volumes of heretofore secret documents on covert operations (including military ones) of the Alianza Popular Revolucionaria Americana (APRA) in the 1930s (144, 145). There are also navy papers (347), an official history of the Escuela Militar (391), several volumes of material on the 1941 war with Ecuador (396), counterinsurgency and civic action in the 1960s (399, 400), and a number of official publications of the Revolutionary Government of the Armed Forces (1968-80) (390, 392, 393, 397, 401, 402, 403).

MEMOIRS, JOURNALS, AND EYEWITNESS ACCOUNTS

There exists in all Latin American countries a plethora of personal memoirs and journals of important personages and military officers as well as eyewitness accounts of key historical events or periods, particularly of armed conflicts. Many are of poor quality and of dubious veracity, but even so, it would be impossible to list even a fraction of the good ones. Thus, what follows is merely a representative sample.

For Bolivia there is Ambassador Andrade's (26), account of his role in the diplomatic corps during the Bolivian National Revolution, and Díaz Machicao's (156), personal view of the 1930s and 1940s about which he wrote so well in earlier works. General Quiroga Ochoa (419), remembers his long and politically influential military career, while Lara (260), Sarmiento (446), and Toro Ruilova (478), reminisce about their participation in the Chaco War.

On the Peru-Ecuador war of 1941 there is Ureta (486), the commander of the Peruvian forces, and Rosero Revelo (435), from the Ecuadorian side. On Peru itself, there exist two works by Carlos Delgado (146, 147), who was the principal civilian architect of the first phase (1968-75) of the Revolutionary Government of the Armed Forces

(1968-80), as well as by Generals Martínez (307, 308), Montagne Markholz (337), and Mercado Jarrín (326), the sum of whose careers span the first eighty years of the century. Víctor Villanueva (505, 506, 507, 516), was an observer of or a key participant in the events he describes including the fall of Augusto B. Leguía in 1930 and the 1948 Aprista plot to overthrow President Manual Bustamante y Rivero.

SPECIALIZED WORKS

At the outset of this section, two general comments are in order. First, the topics chosen are, to a certain degree, arbitrary and should in no way be construed as definitive or as precluding others. Second, there are innumerable books on each of these themes which are not cited (e.g., the Bolivian National Revolution, human rights, guerrilla movements, etc.), both for reasons of space and because this bibliography is focused on the military, not on the topics themselves.

SPECIALIZED WORKS: BOLIVIA

The best overall account of the 1932-52 period remains Klein (253); his work on Colonel David Toro and Germán Busch (251, 252), likewise has stood the test of time. The literature on the Chaco War (1932-35) between Bolivia and Paraguay is literally overwhelming, but the reader should begin with Vergara Vicuña's (502), classic seven-volume work, Querejazu Calvo (418), and Zook (534). Sarmiento (446), Taborga T. (466), Saracho Calderón (445), and Urioste (488), are also valuable.

Díaz Machicao (157, 158, 159), covers the period 1931-43, while Guerrero (223, 224), offers two laudatory pieces on General Enrique Peñaranda. Barrero U. (58), is a fine study of the secret military lodge Razón de Patria which began during the Chaco War and then took power in 1943, while José Antonio Arze (37), González Torres and Iriarte Ontiveros (213), and Olmos (364), present differing views of the controversial military president, Gualberto Villarroel (1943-46).

Alexander (11), presents a highly favorable but now somewhat dated overview of the National Revolution (1952-64), while Andrade (26), offers a very personal account of his years as the Bolivian ambassador to the United States. Malloy (296), Malloy and Gamarra (298), and Malloy and Thorn (300), are much more critical of the revolution as is Dunkerley (168), who carries his account through the Luis García Meza regime (1980-82). Mitchell (333), views the revolution from the perspective of populism; General Seleme Vargas (453), recounts his personal involvement in the events of 1952; Ríos Reinaga (427), treats the interaction between civilians and military officers; and Ladman (257), looks back on the revolution from the vantage point of the 1980s.

The overthrow of Víctor Paz Estenssoro and the National Revolutionary Movement (MNR) in 1964 ended the National Revolution and thrust the military back to the forefront of national politics. Brill (94), is one of the better accounts of the coup itself. Diez de Medina (164), Llosa M. (272), Peña Bravo (386), and Salamanca Trujillo (440), offer favorable views of General René Barrientos Ortuño, the populist caudillo who led the 1964 revolt. Baptista Gumucio (50), discusses Barrientos and Che Guevara, and Vargas Valenzuela (497), seeks to explain the circumstances surrounding Barrientos's fatal accident in 1969.

The Juan José Torres regime (1970-71), with its popular assembly and seemingly sharp drift to the left, is a controversial period in Bolivian history. The most complete accounts are Gallardo Lozada (206), and Knudson (255), but Mendoza (319), and Sandoval Rodríguez (444), are also important.

The best overviews of the 1971-82 period are Dunkerley (168), and Malloy and Gamarra (298). The remaining citations are much more biased owing both to the recentness of the events and to the harshness with which Hugo Banzer (1971-78) and García Meza ruled. Echazú Alvarado (169), Lora (275), Morales Dávila (341), Quiroga Santa Cruz (420, 421), Sánchez (443), and Vargas Martínez (495), concentrate on the Banzer regime. Bedregal (68), emphasizes Banzer's foreign relations with Augusto Pinochet in Chile while Padilla Arancibia (372), discusses his role in the 1978 coup against Banzer. Alcaraz del Castillo (8), Ramos Sánchez (422, 423), and Selzer (454), focus their works on García Meza.

SPECIALIZED WORKS: ECUADOR

The best studied aspect of the military in twentieth-century Ecuador is the junta which ruled from 1963 to 1966. The earliest account of the coup d'état is Needler (349), which has been superceded by Fitch's fine work (197), and Egas R. (176). The junta's own justification for and analysis of its actions are to be found in (170, 172, 173, 174, 175).

SPECIALIZED WORKS: PERU

The literature on military intervention in Peru's domestic politics between 1909 and 1968 is vast indeed, but there are some key works that can provide the reader with a flavor of the different periods and personages involved. For the aborted yet highly colorful attempt to overthrow President Augusto B. Leguía in 1909, see Bontá Chávez (88), and Paz-Soldán (381). For Leguía's own successful coup in 1919, there is a favorable account by naval Captain Pinto Bazurco (413), while both López (274), and Solís (459), bitterly attack Leguía and his policies. A perfectly marvelous account of the 1914 coup against President Guillermo Billinghurst, written by an army officer who participated in the event, is Urdanivia Ginés (485). Matos (314), discusses the defeat of several anti-Leguía revolts in the mid-1920s.

There is a voluminous amount of literature on the 1930s (the Luis M. Sánchez Cerro and Oscar Raimundo Benavides regimes), but most of it focuses on the APRA movement. Works that cover both presidencies are Villanueva (505), and Davies and Villanueva (144, 145), while Ugarteche (484), Ciccarelli (122), and Eguiguren (179), concentrate on the former. Documentation for the Benavides presidency can be found in EL MARISCAL BENAVIDES (306), and a good opposition piece by Eguiguren (180), who looks at the cancellation of the 1936 elections. The best sources for the abortive early 1930's war between Peru and Colombia are Araujo Arana (31), Wood (529), and Jaramillo Ruíz (246).

The 1948 coup d'état of Manuel A. Odría was really directed against the APRA, and most of the literature reflects that fact. For a sense of the period, the reader is directed to deposed President Bustamante I. Rivero's (97), account, Odría's (362), own view and an APRA-slanted version by MacLean Estenós (293). Also of tremendous importance is the fascinating work by Villanueva (516), who served as the APRA's liaison between the army and APRA militants in the planning phases of the coup.

In retrospect, one can begin to discern elements of what would come to be termed the "new militarism" in the pronouncements and actions of the military junta which overthrew President Manuel Prado in 1962 and ruled until 1963. Given the importance of the period, it is particularly unfortunate that so little is available on it. Payne (380), is a rather perfunctory account of the coup itself while Castro Bastos (106), and Ledesma Izquieta (269), fell afoul of the junta and were jailed. The best analysis is Villanueva (504). The junta's own justification for its actions is in República Peruana (424).

The rise and fall of Che Guevara-like guerrilla movements in 1965 prompted a spate of works which continue to be published; Campbell (103), is an excellent beginning bibliography. Most of the Peruvian authors are pro-guerrilla, such as Béjar (70), one of the principal insurgent leaders. Others include Añi Castillo (28), Malpica (301), and Mercado (321). The Peruvian military's perspective on the guerrillas is found in Artola Azcárate (36), an army officer who participated in their destruction and then served in the cabinet during the first phase of the RGAF, and Peru (399, 400). More balanced accounts are contained in Gott (217), and Loveman and Davies (279).

No event or period in the history of Peru has generated as many books, articles, pamphlets, and broadsides as that of the Revolutionary Government of the Armed Forces, 1968-80. Indeed, there is a pressing need for a carefully written, book-length bibliography of this period alone, but that is obviously impossible here. Therefore, the citations listed below include a number of the most important works and are identified with the letters RGAF after the publication date. Two very good post-Docenio analyses are Gorman (216), and Handelman and Sanders (230).

Without doubt the most complex and fascinating guerrilla movement to emerge in the Andean region is the Sendero Luminoso or Shining Path. Sendero is messianic, millenarian, and neo-Inca, all wrapped in a cloak of neo-Maoism. Although Sendero has been operating openly since 1980, the group remains almost as shadowy and enigmatic as ever. The available literature is still in its infancy, but the reader is directed particularly to McClintock (288, 289, 290), Palmer (377), Mercado (320, 322), Ceresole (112), Anderson (25), and the background articles in INFORME DE LA COMISION INVESTIGADORA DE LOS SUCESOS DE UCHURACCAY (238). Also useful are Mercado Ibáñez (324), Salcedo (442), and Fernández Salvatteci (191, 192, 193).

SPECIALIZED WORKS: PERU-ECUADOR WAR

Although of extremely short-lived duration owing to the rapid and energetic intervention of the United States, the Peru-Ecuador war of 1941 offers a classic example of the senseless conflicts over ill-defined and generally worthless boundaries in post-independence Latin America. The conflict is also an example of the principal justification advanced by military officers who want their governments to purchase ever greater amounts of the newest and most modern weapon systems available.

From the Ecuadorian perspective, Muller (344), presents his nation's historical position on the delimitation of the boundary itself. Alvarado (13), Larrea Alba (261), Ochoa (360), and Urrutia Suárez (490), passionately attack Peru, as does Barrera Valverde (57), in his account of the outbreak of renewed hostilities in 1981. For his part, Gálvez (207), criticizes Peru's position on all of its boundary disputes with Colombia, Ecuador, and Chile.

Peruvian authors have responded just as fervently. The best overall account is Araujo Arana (30), while the best documentation is found in Peru (396), Eguiguren (177, 178), and Mariátegui y Cisneros (305). Mar Alcázar (302), and Mercado Jarrín (325), are also useful. The most balanced histories of the 1941 conflict are by Wood (529), and Zook (535). Hidalgo Morey (235), deals with the 1981 clash from the Peruvian perspective.

SPECIALIZED WORKS: HUMAN RIGHTS IN THE ANDES

As in the rest of Latin America (particularly in Uruguay, Argentina, Brazil, and Chile) military, paramilitary, and police forces in Bolivia, Ecuador, and Peru have been guilty of gross violations of basic human rights over the past two decades. Incidents in Peru have been better reported due to wide-spread public interest in and international organizations' concern for both the "dirty little war" against the Sendero Luminoso movement and the prison massacres of 1986. Americas Watch (18, 20), Amnesty International (23, 24), and the Washington Office on Latin America (521), have all expressed deep concern over events in Peru, while opposition members of the Peruvian Congress have also been active in exposing violations: Diez Canseco (162), and Diez Canseco and Echeandía (163), in general, and Ames (22), and Haya de la Torre (231), specifically on the massacres of prisoners in three Lima penitentiaries in 1986. The official version of the killing of seven journalists in Uchuraccay (Department of Ayacucho) is INFORME DE LA COMISION INVESTIGADORA DE LOS SUCESOS DE UCHURACCAY (238), drawn up by a commission headed by novelist Mario Vargas Llosa.

Although less publicized, human rights violations in Bolivia and Ecuador are a source of equally deep concern for many. Specific items on Bolivia include Asamblea Permanente de Derechos Humanos de Bolivia (40), Asociación Pro-Derechos Humanos (41), Central Obrera Boliviana (111), and Morales Dávila (341). Moreover, all works dealing with the military and its rule treat this topic in some detail, as does the highly personal account of the brutalized life of miners by Barrios de Chungara (60). For Ecuador the reader is directed to Americas Watch (19), and Armas et al. (34).

PERIODICALS

All professional journals and political magazines will, at times, publish articles on the military and militarism in Bolivia, Ecuador, and Peru--it is a matter of seeking them out. For this section on military periodicals, I have gratefully borrowed heavily from an extremely useful article by Einaudi and Goldhamer, "An Annotated Bibliography of Latin American Military Journals" (185).

For Bolivia, one should consult MENSAJERO AERONAUTICO (537), the official journal of the air force, REVISTA AEREA MILITAR (538), and the army's official organ, REVISTA MILITAR (539).

Ecuador boasts two journals, REVISTA DE LA FUERZA AEREA ECUATORIANA (540), which appears irregularly, and REVISTA MILITAR DE LAS FUERZAS ARMADAS ECUATORIANAS (541). The possibilities for Peru are much greater that for its two neighbors. ACTUALIDAD MILITAR (542), uses a newspaper format and reports on various activities both social and professional. AVIACION: REVISTA DE LA FUERZA AEREA DEL PERU (543), is the official publication of the air force. GACETA PRE MILITAR (544), in the words of the journal itself, "is the official organ of the Inspección General de Instrucción Pre Militar in the service of the nation's students. Its aim is to affirm the basic principles of the Puruvian nation, to disseminate healthy doctrines and to instruct young Peruvians attending primary and secondary schools and institutions of higher learning in those matters related to their preparation for the civil and military defense of the fatherland"; see Einaudi and Goldhamer (185). GUARDIA REPUBLICANA DEL PERU (545), is devoted almost exlusively to institutional news. REVISTA DE LA ESCUELA MILITAR DE CHORRILLOS (546), covers the activities of the students and faculty at the institution. Likewise, REVISTA DE LA ESCUELA SUPERIOR DE GUERRA (547), is confined almost exclusively to professional and school matters. REVISTA DE LA GUARDIA CIVIL DEL PERU (548), contains technical articles and institutional news and history. Medical issues are covered in REVISTA DE LA SANIDAD MILITAR DEL PERU (549). The official organ of the navy is REVISTA DE MARINA (550), and it deals with all topics of interest to naval personnel. REVISTA DEL CADETE (553), is the mouthpiece of the Escuela Nacional de Investigación Política. REVISTA DEL CENTRO DE ESTUDIOS HISTORICO-MILITARES DEL PERU (554), contains articles on Peruvian military history and related topics as well as news about the Centro itself. REVISTA DEL CENTRO DE INSTRUCCION MILITAR DEL PERU (CIMP) (555), focuses on such subjects as military technology and history, economic development, and civic action, as well as on the ceremonial activities of the CIMP. The most important organ of the Peruvian army is REVISTA MILITAR DEL PERU (556), and it contains articles on tactics, strategy, doctrine, and history in addition to extensive information on current military activities including retirements, promotions, and transfers. REVISTA PARA SUBOFICIALES Y CLASES (557), is published for the non-commissioned corps. Additional military periodicals on Peru can be found at the end of the bibliography.

FUTURE RESEARCH

Even a casual perusal of the seemingly endless number of titles in the bibliography below indicates that, with some notable exceptions, the study of the military in Bolivia, Ecuador, and Peru is in its infancy. There is really no time span in the history of any of the three countries in which the role of the armed forces has been studied definitively; indeed, for an amazing number of periods, little or nothing at all has been published. Most of the literature is heavily biased and/or based on very weak or non-existent research. This situation becomes increasingly true as one moves toward the present.

Clearly, space precludes mention of every possible research topic, but several major themes do emerge. First, and most importantly, we do desperately need solid institutional histories of the military in all three republics, particularly for Bolivia and Ecuador. Moreover, sound histories of each military service are also needed if we are to begin to understand inter- and intra-service rivalries and their impact on civil-military relations.

There is also a pressing need for comparative studies of the three nations. Why did the military in Peru develop more quickly and with greater sophistication than in Bolivia and Ecaudor? Why did personalism give way to professionalism so much later in some areas than in others? What was and is the socio-economic composition of the officer corps in various time frames in the three countries and how and why did it change, if it did? In a similar vein, why did the Centro de Altos Estudios Militares (CAEM) develop first in Peru? Is there a comparable movement developing in Ecuador and Bolivia? If so when, if not, why not?

Of equal importance is the entire question of enlisted personnel. Who were/are they; where were/are they from; what was/is their socio-economic orgin; what impact, if any, did military service have on them? Unlike Argentina or Chile with their relatively homogeneous populations, Ecuador, Peru and Bolivia all have huge, largely unassimilated Indian populations from which the enlisted personnel have been drawn since independence. Most military officers in the region argue that military service is the best and most efficient vehicle for assimilating Indians, both culturally and linguistically, while most non-military observers would disagree vehemently.

Moreover, how did the military as an institution deal with racism? Did the racial cleavages between Indian troops and white or mestizo officers affect military preparedness and efficiency? What problems arose when Indian soldiers were ordered to fire on Indian peasants? This is an incredibly relevant subject because it deals, albeit from a military perspective, with the most important issue in the economic, political and social development of the area.

Although armed conflicts in the Andean area have been better studied than in some parts of Latin America, there still remain vast lacunae in the literature on wars and other less formalized conflicts. Indeed, many military campaigns and battles have not been treated at all, while biographical data on even the most important military commanders is often missing. It goes without saying, of course, that the role of the enlisted man, the "grunt," has been totally neglected.

In addition to the traditional military services (army, navy, air force), there exist in the Andean region paramilitary forces which are of paramount importance to any discussion of civil-military relations. These national police forces (Policia Civil Nacional in Ecuador, Guardia Civil in Peru, and Carabineros in Bolivia) were often used (even created) by civilian politicians as a counterpoise to the regular military. We need detailed studies of these forces and their relationships to both civilian politicians and regular military officers.

In addition, the new responsibilities assigned to these forces in the war against drug traffickers and terrorists (e.g., the Peruvian Guardia Civil's special counterinsurgency unit, the Sinchis) have substantially altered their traditional mission and their place in civil-military relations. Moreover, their actions, and those of the regular military, have been severely criticized by most human rights organizations, not only for the use of torture and "disappearances," but also for wholesale corruption.

This leads to the whole question of military use of repression, torture, murder, coercion, etc., to stifle dissent or to achieve a desired ideological or political goal. How has this propensity developed over the past century and a half and why? Why is it worse in some countries (Argentina, Chile, Uruguay) than in Ecuador and Peru? What role did or does the military establishment play in death squad activity? Is there institutionalized torture in a given country?

Finally, there is the vast subject of military expenditures, their percentage of the GNP, and their impact (positive and negative) on national development. To what degree does the military rely upon foreign sources for its arms purchases, and what impact has that had on both domestic and foreign policy? Has the military truly served as a major modernizing force within their nations as many officers have argued, or is it one of the principal causes of underdevelopment?

These are but a few of the many topics which cry out for scholarly treatment. Indeed, without appearing to be too glib, one could offer the view that the opportunity for the study of the history of the military in the Andean region is wide open and waiting for scholars. So let us begin.

BIBLIOGRAPHY: BOLIVIA, ECUADOR, PERU

1. Abecia Baldivieso, Valentín. HISTORIOGRAFIA BOLIVIANA. 2d ed. La Paz: Editorial "Juventud," 1973.

2. Acha Monzón, Tomás. ANECDOTAS MILITARES. Lima: Editorial Jurídica, 1973.

3. Agreda V., Jorge, et al. EL SISTEMA POLITICO BOLIVIANO. Bogotá: Publicaciones Codex, 1974.

4. Aguirre Gamio, Hernando. EL PROCESO PERUANO: COMO, POR QUE, HACIA DONDE. Mexico City: Ediciones "El Caballito," 1974. RGAF. Henceforth all works dealing with the Revolutionary Government of the Armed Forces of Peru, 1968-80, will be labeled RGAF for easier reader identification.

5. ———. LA REVOLUCION: ¿TIENE FUTURO? Lima: Talleres de la Imprenta "Ormea," 1977. RGAF.

6. Alberti, Giorgio. "The Military and the 'Third Road' in Peru." POLITICA INTERNAZIONALE (Florence) 2 (1981-82): 14-25. RGAF.

7. Alberti, Giorgio, Jorge Santistevan, and Luis Pásara. ESTADO Y CLASE: LA COMUNIDAD INDUSTRIAL EN EL PERU. Lima: Instituto de Estudios Peruanos, 1977. RGAF.

8. Alcaraz del Castillo, Irving. EL PRISIONERO DE PALACIO. La Paz: Editorial Los Amigos del Libro, 1984.

9. Alcázar, José Luis. NACAHUASU: LA GUERRILLA DEL CHE EN BOLIVIA. La Paz: n.p., n.d.

10. Alcázar Mavila, Luis. HISTORIA MILITAR DEL PERU. Lima: Imprenta y Librería del Ministerio de Guerra, 1941.

11. Alexander, Robert J. THE BOLIVIAN NATIONAL REVOLUTION. New Brunswick: Rutgers University Press, 1958.

12. Alva Orlandini, Javier. RESPUESTA A LA DICTADURA. Lima: Librería Editorial "Minerva," 1978. RGAF.

13. Alvarado, Rafael. LA ELOCUENCIA DE LAS CIFRAS EN EL

PROBLEMA TERRITORIAL ECUATORIANO - PERUANO. Quito: Talleres Gráficos de Educacioñ, 1941.

14. Alvarado Sánchez, Jerónimo. REFLEXIONES SOBRE EL GOLPISMO, LA TIRANIA Y LA REVOLUCION: ANOTACIONES HISTORICAS Y FILOSOFICAS ACERCA DEL LIBRO "TESTIMONIO DE LUCHA"; DOCUMENTAL PARA LA HISTORIA DEL PERU DE JOSE MARIA DE LA JARA Y URETA. Lima: Editorial "Minerva," 1979. RGAF.

15. Alvarez, Elena. "Política agraria del gobierno militar y su posible impacto sobre la población, 1969-1979." Lima: Universidad Nacional Agraria La Molina, 1980. RGAF.

16. ———. POLITICA ECONOMICA Y AGRICULTURA EN EL PERU, 1969-1979. Lima: Instituto de Estudios Peruanos, 1983. RGAF.

17. Amat, Carlos, et al. REALIDAD DEL CAMPO PERUANO DESPUES DE LA REFORMA AGRARIA: 10 ENSAYOS CRITICOS. Lima: Centro de Investigación y Capacitación, 1980. RGAF.

18. Americas Watch. DERECHOS HUMANOS EN EL PERU: CIERTA PASIVIDAD FRENTE A LOS ABUSOS. Lima: Comisión Andina de Juristas, 1987.

19. ———. HUMAN RIGHTS IN ECUADOR. New York: Americas Watch, 1988.

20. ———. HUMAN RIGHTS IN PERU AFTER PRESIDENT GARCIA'S FIRST YEAR. New York: Americas Watch, 1986.

21. ———. A NEW OPPORTUNITY FOR DEMOCRATIC AUTHORITY: HUMAN RIGHTS IN PERU. New York: Americas Watch, 1985.

22. Ames, Rolando, ed. INFORME AL CONGRESO SOBRE LOS SUCESOS DE LOS PENALES. Lima: Talleres Gráficos OCISA, 1988.

23. Amnesty International. PERU: "DISAPPEARANCES," TORTURE, AND SUMMARY EXECUTIONS BY GOVERNMENT FORCES AFTER THE PRISON REVOLTS

OF JUNE 1986. New York: Amnesty International Publications, 1987.

24. ———. PERU BRIEFING. London: Amnesty International Publications, 1985.

25. Anderson, James. SENDERO LUMINOSO: A NEW REVOLUTIONARY MODEL? London: Institute for the Study of Terrorism, 1987.

26. Andrade, Víctor. MY MISSIONS FOR REVOLUTIONARY BOLIVIA, 1944-1962. Translated and edited by Cole Blasier. Pittsburgh: University of Pittsburgh Press, 1976.

27. Angell, Alan. "Classroom Maoists: The Politics of Peruvian Schoolteachers under Military Government." BULLETIN OF LATIN AMERICAN RESEARCH 1 (1982): 1-20.

28. Añi Castillo, Gonzalo. HISTORIA SECRETA DE LAS GUERRILLAS. Lima: Ediciones "Más Allá," 1967.

29. Araujo, Angel F. EPISODIOS DE CAMPANA Y RELATOS HISTORICOS. Quito: Imprenta Nacional, 1922.

30. Araujo Arana, Humberto. ANTECEDENTES Y CHOQUES FRONTERIZOS: OCUPACION Y DESOCUPACION PERUANA DE TERRITORIO ECUATORIANO EN 1941-1942. 4 vols. Lima: (various publishers), 1963-72.

31. ———. CONFLICTO FRONTERIZO PERU-COLOMBIA, 1932-1933. 4 vols. Lima: Litografía Huascarán, 1965.

32. Argones, Nelson. EL JUEGO DEL PODER: DE RODRIGUEZ LARA A FEBRES CORDERO. Quito: Corporación Editora Nacional, 1985.

33. Arizaga Vega, Rafael. LA MANO NEGRA Y LOS PALIDOS REFLEJOS: LAS ELECCIONES DE 1978. Quito: Impreseñal Cía., 1984.

34. Armas, Amparo, et al. LOS DERECHOS HUMANOS: EL CASO ECUATORIANO. Quito: Editorial El Conejo, 1985.

35. Artola Azcárate, Armando. PRESSURE GROUPS AND

POWER ELITES IN PERUVIAN POLITICS. Ithaca: Cornell University Press, 1969.

36. ———. ¡SUBVERSION! Lima: Editorial Jurídica, 1976.

37. Arze, José Antonio. BOLIVIA BAJO EL TERRORISMO NAZIFASCISTA. Lima: Editora Peruana, 1945.

38. Arze, José Roberto. ENSAYO DE UNA BIBLIOGRAFIA BIOGRAFICA BOLIVIANA. La Paz: Editorial Los Amigos del Libro, 1981.

39. Arze Quiroga, Eduardo, ed. DOCUMENTOS PARA UNA HISTORIA DE LA GUERRA DEL CHACO, SELECCIONADOS DEL ARCHIVO DE DANIEL SALAMANCA. 3 vols. La Paz: Editorial Don Bosco, 1951-60.

40. Asamblea Permanente de Derechos Humanos de Bolivia. LA MASACRE DE TODOS LOS SANTOS. La Paz: Asamblea Permanente de Derechos Humanos de Bolivia, 1980.

41. Asociación Pro-Derechos Humanos. BOLIVIA, 1971-1977: EL GOBIERNO DE BANZER Y LA VIOLACION DE LOS DERECHOS HUMANOS. Madrid: n.p., 1977.

42. Astiz, Carlos A., and José Z. García. "The Peruvian Military: Achievement Orientation, Training, and Political Tendencies." WESTERN POLITICAL QUARTERLY 25 (1972): 667-85.

43. Ayala Mora, Enrique. LUCHA POLITICA Y ORIGEN DE LOS PARTIDOS EN ECUADOR. Quito: Corporación Editora Nacional, 1985.

44. Baella Tuesta, Alfonso. EL MISERABLE. Lima: Editorial Andina, 1978. RGAF.

45. ———. EL PODER INVISIBLE. Lima: Editorial Andina, 1976. RGAF.

46. ———. SECUESTRO. Lima: Editorial Andina, 1978. RGAF.

47. ———. EL TIEMPO: ¿QUE PASA? Lima: Editorial Andina, 1977. RGAF.

48. Bahbah, B. "Israel's Military Relationship with Ecuador and Argentina." JOURNAL OF PALESTINE STUDIES 15 (1986): 76-101.

49. Baptista Gumucio, Mariano. "Bolivia: La noche de los generales." POLITICA 6 (1967): 67-78.

50. ———. GUERRILLEROS Y GENERALES SOBRE BOLIVIA. Buenos Aires: Editorial Jorge Alvarez, 1968.

51. ———. HISTORIA CONTEMPORANEA DE BOLIVIA, 1930-1978. 2d ed. La Paz: Gisbert & Cía., 1978.

52. Barra, Felipe de la. LA ESCUELA MILITAR Y SU PAPEL PROFESSIONAL Y SOCIAL. Chorrillos: Imprenta de la Escuela Militar, 1939.

53. ———. FICHERO BIBLIOGRAFICO HISTORICO-MILITAR PERUANO Y ANTOLOGIA DE ESCRITOS. Lima: Editorial Gráfica Industrial, 1970.

54. ———. OBJETIVO: PALACIO DE GOBIERNO; RESENA HISTORICO-CRONOLOGICA DE LOS PRONUN-CIAMIENTOS POLITICOS Y MILITARES DE LA CONQUISTA A LA REPUBLICA Y QUE PERMITIERON LA OCUPACION DEL PALACIO DE GOBIERNO. Lima: Librería-Editorial Juan Mejía Baca, 1967.

55. ———. PANORAMA HISTORICO-CRITICO MILITAR. Lima: Tipografía y Offset Peruana, 1974.

56. ———. PREFACIO A LA HISTORIA POLITICA Y MILITAR PERUANA. Lima: Editorial "Gráfica Industrial," 1972.

57. Barrera Valverde, Alfonso. HOMBRES DE PAZ EN LUCHA. 2d ed. Quito: Promotora Cultural Popular, 1985.

58. Barrero U., Francisco. RADEPA Y LA REVOLUCION NACIONAL. La Paz: Empresa Editora "Urquizo," 1976.

59. Barreto, Emilio G. PERU: LOS DESARROLLOS ECONOMICOS Y FINANCIEROS, 1970-1980. Lima: Editorial Andina, 1980. RGAF.

60. Barrios de Chungara, Domitila. LET ME SPEAK! New York: Monthly Review Press, 1978.

61. Barrón Coral, Marcial. EL COMPORTAMIENTO DE LAS CENTRALES SINDICALES FRENTE A LAS REFORMAS DEL GOBIERNO, 1968-1979. Lima: Editorial Pedagógica "Asencios," 1980. RGAF.

62. Barton, Robert. A SHORT HISTORY OF THE REPUBLIC OF BOLIVIA. La Paz: Editorial Los Amigos del Libro, 1968.

63. Basadre, Jorge. HISTORIA DE LA REPUBLICA DEL PERU, 1822-1933. 17 vols. 6th ed. Lima: Editorial Universitaria, 1968.

64. ———. INTRODUCCION A LAS BASES DOCUMENTALES PARA LA HISTORIA DE LA REPUBLICA DEL PERU CON ALGUNAS REFLEXIONES. 3 vols. Lima: Ediciones P.L. Villanueva, 1971.

65. Becker, David G. "Bonanza Development and the New Bourgeoisie: Peru under Military Rule." COMPARATIVE POLITICAL STUDIES 15 (1982): 243-88. RGAF.

66. ———. THE NEW BOURGEOISIE AND THE LIMITS OF DEPENDENCY: MINING, CLASS, AND POWER IN "REVOLUTIONARY" PERU. Princeton: Princeton University Press, 1983. RGAF.

67. Bedregal, Guillermo. LOS MILITARES EN BOLIVIA: ENSAYO DE INTERPRETACION SOCIOLOGICA. La Paz: Editorial Los Amigos del Libro, 1971.

68. ———. ENTRE EL MUTUN Y CHARANA: ANTIDE-SARROLLO, MASACRE CAMPESINA, Y SATELIZACION DE BOLIVIA. La Paz: n.p., 1975.

69. ———. "El problema militar en Bolivia." POLITICA 5 (1966): 24-41.

70. Béjar, Héctor. NOTES ON A GUERRILLA EXPERIENCE. Translated by William Rose. New York: Monthly Review Press, 1970.

71. ———. LA REVOLUCION EN LA TRAMPA. Lima: Ediciones Socialismo y Participación, 1976. RGAF.

72. ———. "Velasco: ¿Reformismo burgués?" SOCIALISMO Y PARTICIPACION 5 (1978): 73-86. RGAF.

73. ———. LA VERDAD SOBRE LOS DIARIOS. Lima: Ediciones Socialismo y Participación, 1977. RGAF.

74. Beltrán, Pedro G. LA VERDADERA REALIDAD PERUANA. Madrid: Librería Editorial San Martín, 1976. RGAF.

75. Benavides Correa, Alfonso. EL CASO PERUANO: ¿CONTRARREVOLUCION DENTRO DE LA REVOLUCION? Mexico City: n.p., 1975. RGAF.

76. ———. DESAFIANDO A LA CENSURA: TRES DOCUMENTOS PROHIBIDOS. Lima: Impresa Editorial Pedagógica "Asencios," 1978. RGAF.

77. ———. TRUE FREEDOM OF PRESS. Lima: Editorial Enterprise of the Official Newspaper "The Peruvian," 1970. RGAF.

78. Benites Vinueza, Leopoldo. ECUADOR: DRAMA Y PARADOJA. Mexico City: Fondo de Cultura Económica, 1950.

79. Bernales, Enrique. CRISIS POLITICA: ¿SOLUCION ELECTORAL?; ANALISIS DE LOS RESULTADOS DE LAS ELECCIONES PARA LA ASAMBLEA CONSTITUYENTE DE 1978. Lima: DESCO, 1980. RGAF.

80. Blanco Galindo, Carlos. RESUMEN DE LA HISTORIA MILITAR DE BOLIVIA. La Paz: Intendencia de Guerra, Talleres, 1922.

81. Blanksten, George I. ECUADOR: CONSTITUTIONS AND CAUDILLOS. Berkeley: University of California Press, 1951.

82. Bocco, Arnaldo. "Ecuador: Economic Policy and Styles of Development during the Oil Boom, 1972-78." DESARROLLO ECONOMICO (Buenos Aires) 22 (1983): 485-510.

83. Bolivia. EJERCITO Y REVOLUCION: BASES IDEOLOGICAS

DE LA TENDENCIA REVOLUCIONARIA DE LAS FF.AA. 2d ed. La Paz: Vivo Rojo, 1984.

84. ———. LIBRO BLANCO DE REALIZACIONES DEL GOBIERNO DE LAS FUERZAS ARMADAS: BOLIVIA, 1971-1978; INFORME DE LAS REALIZACIONES DEL GOBIERNO DE LAS FUERZAS ARMADAS PARA EL DESARROLLO ECONOMICO Y SOCIAL. La Paz: n.p., 1978.

85. ———. Departamento Nacional de Propaganda Socialista. INFORME PRESENTADO POR EL SEÑOR CORONEL PRESIDENTE DE LA JUNTA MILITAR SOCIALISTA DE GOBIERNO AL EJERCITO NACIONAL, DE 17 DE MAYO A 31 DE DICIEMBRE DE 1936. La Paz: Imprenta de la Intendencia General de Guerra, 1937.

86. Bolivia. Ministerio del Interior, Migración y Justicia. BOLIVIA: ELECCIONES, FRAUDE Y DEMOCRACIA = BOLIVIA: ELECTIONS, FRAUD AND DEMOCRACY. Translated by William R. Mendoza. La Paz: El Ministerio, 1980.

87. Bolivia. Sección del Prensa de Palacio de Gobierno. BAJO EL REGIMEN MILITAR SOCIALISTA: ¿HAY LABOR GOBERNATIVA? La Paz: Imprenta Intendencia General de Guerra, 1936.

88. Bontá Chávez, Fernando. EL "29 DE MAYO" PARA LA HISTORIA: FIESTA DEL CARACTER, 1909-1926. Lima: n.p., 1926.

89. Booth, David, and Bernardo Sorj, eds. MILITARY REFORMISM AND SOCIAL CLASSES: THE PERUVIAN EXPERIENCE, 1968-80. London: Macmillan, 1983. RGAF.

90. Bourricaud, François. "Perú: El círculo vicioso; O militares o políticos." In EL PAPEL POLITICO Y SOCIAL DE LAS FUERZAS ARMADAS EN AMERICA LATINA, 203-26. Edited by Virgilio Rafael Beltrán. Caracas: Monte Avila Editores, 1970. RGAF.

91. ———. POWER AND SOCIETY IN CONTEMPORARY PERU. Translated by Paul Stevenson. New York: Praeger Publishers, 1970.

92. Bravo Bresani, Jorge. "Dinámica y estructura del poder: Reflexiones preliminares." In PERU: HOY, 175-259. Edited by Fernando Fuenzalida Vollmar, et al. 3d ed. Mexico City: Siglo XXI Editores, 1975.

93. Brill, William H. "Military Civic Action in Bolivia." Ph.D. dissertation, University of Pennsylvania, 1965.

94. ———. MILITARY INTERVENTION IN BOLIVIA: THE OVERTHROW OF PAZ ESTENSSORO AND THE MNR. Washington: Institute for the Comparative Study of Political Systems, 1967.

95. Burneo, José, Adolfo Ciudad, and Luis Pásara. EMPLEO Y ESTABILIDAD LABORAL. Lima: DESCO, 1976. RGAF.

96. Bustamante, Alberto, et al. PROPIEDAD SOCIAL: MODELO Y REALIDAD. Lima: DESCO, 1977. RGAF.

97. Bustamante I. Rivero, José Luis. TRES ANOS DE LUCHA POR LA DEMOCRACIA EN EL PERU. Buenos Aires: Artes Gráficas Bartolomé U. Chiesino, 1949.

98. Caballero, José María. AGRICULTURA, REFORMA AGRARIA Y POBREZA CAMPESINA. Lima: Instituto de Estudios Peruanos, 1980. RGAF.

99. ———. FROM BELAUNDE TO BELAUNDE: PERU'S MILITARY EXPERIMENT IN THIRD-ROADISM. Cambridge: Centre of Latin American Studies, Cambridge University, 1981. RGAF.

100. Cabrera, Luis, et al. MISION MILITAR CHILENA EN EL ECUADOR. Quito: Imprenta del Ejército, 1902.

101. Calvo, Roberto. LA DOCTRINA MILITAR DE LA SEGURIDAD NACIONAL: AUTORITARISMO POLITICO Y NEOLIBERALISMO EN EL CONO SUR. Caracas: Universidad Católica Andrés Bello, 1979.

102. Camacho Peña, Alfonso. "Los militares en la política boliviana." APORTES 22 (1971): 41-95.

103. Campbell, Leon G. "The Historiography of the Peruvian Guerrilla

Movement." LATIN AMERICAN RESEARCH REVIEW 8 (1973): 45-70.

104. Cánepa Sardón, Alfredo. LA REVOLUCION PERUANA: ENSAYO POLEMICO. Buenos Aires: Editorial Paracas, 1971. RGAF.

105. Carrión, Alejandro. "Las fuerzas armadas y las instituciones democráticas." REVISTA DEL COLEGIO MILITAR "ELOY ALFARO" 25 (1962).

106. Castro Bastos, Leonidas. ¡GOLPISMO! Lima: Editorial Librería e Imprenta D. Miranda, 1964.

107. Castro de Mendoza, Mario. LA MARINA MERCANTE EN LA REPUBLICA, 1821-1968. 2 vols. Lima: Talleres de Artes Gráficas Martínez, 1980.

108. Castro Jijón, Ramón. "Breves apuntes sobre la historia de la escuela naval de Ecuador." REVISTA DEL COLEGIO MILITAR "ELOY ALFARO" 25 (1962).

109. Cavalla Rojas, Antonio. "Notas sobre un posible conflicto en el Cono Sur: Las hipótesis de guerra y la correlación de fuerzas militares en Argentina, Bolivia, Chile y Peru." ESTADOS UNIDOS: PERSPECTIVA LATINOAMERICANA 4 (1978): 227-54.

110. Cavanagh, Jonathan. REFLECTIONS ON CLASS THEORY SUGGESTED BY ANALYSES OF THE PERUVIAN MILITARY REGIME, 1968-1979. Göttingen: University of Göttingen, 1980. RGAF.

111. Central Obrera Boliviana. INFORME: VIOLACION DE LOS DERECHOS HUMANOS EN BOLIVIA. La Paz: n.p., 1976.

112. Ceresole, Norberto. PERU: SENDERO LUMINOSO, EJERCITO Y DEMOCRACIA. Madrid: Prensa y Ediciones Iberoamericana, 1987.

113. ———. PERU: UNA REVOLUCION NACIONALISTA. Buenos Aires: Editorial Sudestada, 1969. RGAF.

114. ———. PERU O EL NACIMIENTO DEL SISTEMA

LATINOAMERICANO. Buenos Aires: Editorial Galerna, 1971. RGAF.

115. Céspedes, Augusto. EL DICTADOR SUICIDA: 40 ANOS DE HISTORIA DE BOLIVIA. 2d ed. La Paz: Editorial "Juventud," 1968.

116. ———. EL PRESIDENTE COLGADO: HISTORIA BOLIVIANA. La Paz: Editorial Jorge Alvarez, 1966.

117. ———. SANGRE DE MESTIZOS: RELATOS DE LA GUERRA DEL CHACO. Santiago: Editorial Nascimento, 1936.

118. Céspedez Bedregal, J. Teófilo. LA REVOLUCION PERUANA. Lima: Editorial Nueva Constitución, 1973. RGAF.

119. Chaplin, David, ed. PERUVIAN NATIONALISM: A CORPORATIST REVOLUTION. New Brunswick: Transaction Books, 1976. RGAF.

120. Chirinos Lizares, Guido, and Enrique Chirinos Soto. EL SEPTENATO, 1968-75. Lima: Editorial "Alfa," 1977. RGAF.

121. Chirinos Soto, Enrique. PIDO LA PALABRA ANTE LA SEGUNDA FASE. Lima: Editorial Andina, 1978. RGAF.

122. Ciccarelli, Orazio A. "The Sánchez Cerro Regimes in Peru, 1930-1933." Ph.D. dissertation, University of Florida, 1969.

123. Cleaves, Peter S., and Martin J. Scurrah. AGRICULTURE, BUREAUCRACY, AND MILITARY GOVERNMENT IN PERU. Ithaca: Cornell University Press, 1980. RGAF.

124. Clément, Paul. CONFERENCIAS MILITARES DEL GENERAL P. CLEMENT. Lima: Imprenta del Estado Mayor General del Ejército, 1919.

125. ———, ed. LA ESCUELA MILITAR EN EL XXV ANIVERSARIO DE SU FUNDACION, 1898-1923. Chorrillos: Empresa Tipográfica La Unión, 1924.

126. Clinton, Richard Lee. "The Modernizing Military: The Case of Peru." INTER-AMERICAN ECONOMIC AFFAIRS 24 (1971): 43-66.

127. Cobas Corrales, Manuel Efraín. FUERZA ARMADA, MISIONES MILITARES Y DEPENDENCIA EN EL PERU. Lima: Editorial Horizonte, 1982.

128. Collier, David. SQUATTERS AND OLIGARCHS: AUTHORITARIAN RULE AND POLICY CHANGE IN PERU. Baltimore: Johns Hopkins University Press, 1976. RGAF.

129. Collings, Richard J. "Dependency and Military Rule: A Peruvian Case Study". ANNALS OF THE SOUTHEASTERN CONFERENCE ON LATIN AMERICAN STUDIES 10 (1979): 15-37. RFAG.

130. Comisión Permanente de Historia del Ejército del Perú. HISTORIA GENERAL DEL EJERCITO PERUANO. 4 vols. Lima: Imprenta del Ministerio de Guerra, 1980-84.

131. Corbett, Charles D. THE LATIN AMERICAN MILITARY AS A SOCIO-POLITICAL FORCE: CASE STUDIES OF BOLIVIA AND ARGENTINA. Coral Gables: Center for Advanced International Studies, University of Miami, 1972.

132. ———. "Military Institutional Development and Sociopolitical Change: The Bolivian Case." JOURNAL OF INTERAMERICAN STUDIES AND WORLD AFFAIRS 14 (1971): 399-435.

133. Cordera, Rolando, and Salvador Hernández. "Recent Developments in Peru: An Interview with Aníbal Quijano." FEDERAL RESERVE BANK OF NEW YORK/MONTHLY REVIEW 24 (1983): 53-61.

134. Corkill, David, and David Cubitt. ECUADOR: FRAGILE DEMOCRACY. London: Latin American Bureau, 1988.

135. Cornejo, Raúl Estuardo. VELASCO O EL PROCESO DE UNA REVOLUCION. Lima: Centro Peruano de Estudios, Investigaciones y Documentación, 1969. RGAF.

136. Corporación Editora Nacional. ECUADOR, 1830-1980. 4 vols. Quito: Corporación Editora Nacional, 1980-83.

137. Cotler, Julio. CLASES, ESTADO Y NACION EN EL PERU. Lima: Instituto de Estudios Peruanos, 1978.

138. ———. "Crisis política y populismo militar." In PERU: HOY, 87-174. Edited by Fernando Fuenzalida Vollmar, et al. 3d ed. Mexico City: Siglo XXI Editores, 1975. RGAF.

139. ———. DEMOCRACIA E INTEGRACION NACIONAL. Lima: Instituto de Estudios Peruanos, 1980.

140. ———. "Peru: Estado oligárquico y reformismo militar." In AMERICA LATINA: HISTORIA DE MEDIO SIGLO, 1: 373-423. Edited by Pablo González Casanova. Mexico City: Siglo XXI Editores, 1977. RGAF.

141. ———. "Political Crisis and Military Populism in Peru." In MILITARISM IN DEVELOPING COUNTRIES, 219-57. Edited by Kenneth Fidel. New Brunswick: Transaction Books, 1975. RGAF.

142. "Criterio económico del ejército." EL EJERCITO NACIONAL 11 (1932).

143. Cueva, Agustín. THE PROCESS OF POLITICAL DOMINATION IN ECUADOR. Translated by Danielle Salti. New Brunswick: Transaction Books, 1982.

144. Davies, Thomas M., Jr., and Víctor Villanueva, eds. SECRETOS ELECTORALES DEL APRA: CORRESPONDENCIA Y DOCUMENTOS DE 1939. Lima: Editorial Horizonte, 1982.

145. ———. 300 DOCUMENTOS PARA LA HISTORIA DEL APRA: CONSPIRACIONES APRISTAS DE 1935 A 1939. Lima: Editorial Horizonte, 1978.

146. Delgado, Carlos. EL PROCESO REVOLUCIONARIO PERUANO: TESTIMONIO DE LUCHA. Mexico City: Siglo XXI Editores, 1972. RGAF.

147. ———. REVOLUCION PERUANA: AUTONOMIA Y DESLINDES. Lima: Editorial Universo, 1975. RGAF.

148. Delgado, Luis Humberto. LA ESPADA EN EL PERU, 1821-1931. Lima: American Express, 1931.

149. ———. EL MILITARISMO EN EL PERU, 1821-1930: LA HORA SUPREMA DE SU ENCUMBRAMIENTO PARA SALVAR AL PAIS. Lima: Librería e Imprenta Gil, 1930.

150. Delgado González, Trifonio. 100 ANOS DE LUCHA OBRERA EN BOLIVIA. La Paz: Ediciones ISLA, 1984.

151. Dellepiane, Carlos. HISTORIA MILITAR DEL PERU. 2 vols. Lima: Librería e Imprenta Gil, 1931.

152. ———. HISTORIA MILITAR DEL PERU. 2 vols. 5th ed. Lima: Imprenta del Ministerio de Guerra, 1965.

153. Déniz, José. LA REVOLUCION POR LA FUERZA ARMADA: PERU, 1968-1977. Salamanca: Ediciones Sígueme, 1978. RGAF.

154. Díaz Arguedas, Julio. FASTOS MILITARES DE BOLIVIA. La Paz: Escuela Tip. Salesiana, 1943.

155. ———. HISTORIA DEL EJERCITO DE BOLIVIA, 1825-1932. La Paz: Imprenta Instituto Central del Ejército, 1940.

156. Díaz Machicao, Porfirio. LA BESTIA EMOCIONAL: AUTOBIOGRAFIA. La Paz: Editorial "Juventud," 1955.

157. ———. HISTORIA DE BOLIVIA: PENARANDA, 1940-1943. La Paz: Editorial "Juventud," 1958.

158. ———. HISTORIA DE BOLIVIA: SALAMANCA, LA GUERRA DEL CHACO, TEJADA SORZANO, 1931-1936. La Paz: Gisbert y Cía., 1955.

159. ———. HISTORIA DE BOLIVIA: TORO, BUSCH, QUINTANILLA. La Paz: Editorial "Juventud," 1957.

160. Dietz, Henry A. POVERTY AND PROBLEM-SOLVING UNDER MILITARY RULE: THE URBAN POOR IN LIMA, PERU. Austin: University of Texas Press, 1980. RGAF.

161. Dietz, Henry A., and David Scott Palmer. "Citizen Participation under Innovative Military Corporatism in Peru." In POLITICAL PARTICIPATION IN LATIN AMERICA, 1: 172-88. Edited by

John A. Booth and Mitchell A. Seligson. New York: Holmes and Meier, 1978. RGAF.

162. Diez Canseco, Javier. DEMOCRACIA, MILITARIZACION Y DERECHOS HUMANOS EN EL PERU, 1980-84. 2d ed. Lima: Servicios Populares, 1985.

163. Diez Canseco, Javier, and Miguel Echeandía. DICTADURA Y DERECHOS HUMANOS EN EL PERU: LO QUE NO DIJO "ACCION POPULAR." Lima: Perugraph Editores, 1981.

164. Diez de Medina, Fernando. EL GENERAL DEL PUEBLO: RENE BARRIENTOS ORTUNO; CAUDILLO MAYOR DE LA REVOLUCION BOLIVIANA. 3d ed. La Paz: Editorial Los Amigos del Libro, 1972.

165. Drekonja Kornat, Gerhard. "Ecuador: Ensayo bibliográfico." In ECUADOR HOY, 283-313. Edited by Gerhard Drekonja Kornat, et al. Bogotá: Siglo XXI Editores, 1981.

166. Drekonja Kornat, Gerhard, et al. ECUADOR HOY. Bogotá: Siglo XXI Editores, 1981.

167. Dunkerley, James. "Politics of the Bolivian Army: Institutional Development, 1879-1935." Ph.D. dissertation, Oxford University, 1979.

168. ———. REBELLION IN THE VEINS: POLITICAL STRUGGLE IN BOLIVIA, 1952-82. London: Verso Editions, 1984.

169. Echazú Alvarado, Jorge. EL FASCISMO EN BOLIVIA: TACTICA Y ESTRATEGIA REVOLUCIONARIAS. 2d ed. Oruro: Editorial Universitaria, 1984.

170. Ecuador. LA JUNTA MILITAR DE GOBIERNO AL PUEBLO DEL ECUADOR. Quito: Talleres Gráficos Nacionales, 1963.

171. ———. LEYES MILITARES DE LA REPUBLICA. Quito: Editorial "Fray Jodoco Ricke," 1961.

172. ———. Junta Militar de Gobierno. PAZ CREADORA Y TRABAJO FECUNDO: MENSAJE A LA NACION ECUATORIANA, JULIO DE 1964-JULIO DE 1965. Quito: Talleres Gráficos Nacionales, 1965.

173. ——. PAZ CREADORA Y TRABAJO FECUNDO: MENSAJE A LA NACION ECUATORIANA, JULIO DE 1963-JULIO DE 1964. Quito: Talleres Gráficos Nacionales, 1964.

174. ——. PLAN POLITICO DE LA JUNTA MILITAR DE GOBIERNO. Quito: Talleres Gráficos Nacionales, 1963.

175. Ecuador. Secretaría General del Consejo de Seguridad Nacional. Instituto de Altos Estudios Nacionales. SEGURIDAD Y DESARROLLO. Quito: Talleres Gráficos del Instituto de Altos Estudios Nacionales del Ecuador, 1983.

176. Egas R., José María. ECUADOR Y EL GOBIERNO DE LA JUNTA MILITAR. Buenos Aires: Tierra Nueva, 1975.

177. Eguiguren, Luis Antonio. INVINCIBLE JAEN: NOTES ON THE TERRITORIAL QUESTION BETWEEN PERU AND ECUADOR. Lima: n.p., 1943.

178. ——. MAYNAS: APUNTES SOBRE LA CUESTION INTERNACIONAL ENTRE EL PERU Y ECUADOR. Lima: n.p., 1941.

179. ——. EN LA SELVA POLITICA: PARA LA HISTORIA. Lima: Sanmartí y Cía. Editores, 1933.

180. ——. EL USURPADOR: PARA LA HISTORIA. Lima: n.p., 1939.

181. Einaudi, Luigi R. THE PERUVIAN MILITARY. Santa Monica: Rand Corporation, 1966.

182. ——. THE PERUVIAN MILITARY: A SUMMARY POLITICAL ANALYSIS. Santa Monica: Rand Corporation, 1969.

183. ——. PERUVIAN MILITARY RELATIONS WITH THE UNITED STATES. Santa Monica: Rand Corporation, 1970. RGAF.

184. ——. "Revolution from within: Military Rule in Peru since 1968." STUDIES IN COMPARATIVE INTERNATIONAL DEVELOPMENT 8 (1973): 1-87. RGAF.

185. Einaudi, Luigi R., and Herbert Goldhamer. "An Annotated Bibliography of Latin American Military Journals." LATIN AMERICAN RESEARCH REVIEW 2(1967): 95-122.

186. Einaudi, Luigi R., and Alfred C. Stepan. LATIN AMERICAN INSTITUTIONAL DEVELOPMENT: CHANGING MILITARY PERSPECTIVES IN PERU AND BRAZIL. Santa Monica: Rand Corporation, 1971.

187. Encinas del Pando, José A. "The Role of Military Expenditure in the Development Process: Peru; A Case Study, 1950-1980." IBERO AMERICANA (Stockholm) 12 (1983): 51-114.

188. Epstein, E.H. "Peasant Consciousness under Peruvian Military Rule." HARVARD EDUCATIONAL REVIEW 52 (1982): 280-300. RGAF.

189. Estrada, Jenny. PERSONAJES Y CIRCUNSTANCIAS: ENTREVISTAS Y REPORTAJES. Guayaquil: Editorial de la Casa de la Cultura Ecuatoriana Benjamín Carrión, Núcleo del Guayas, 1982.

190. Fellman Delarde, José. HISTORIA DE BOLIVIA. 3 vols. La Paz: Editorial Los Amigos del Libro, 1968-70.

191. Fernández Salvatteci, Major José A. GUERRILLAS Y CONTRAGUERRILLAS EN EL PERU: SENDERO LUMINOSO Y EL GOBIERNO DEL ARQ. F. BELAUNDE TERRY. Lima: n.p., n.d. Mimeographed.

192. ———. TERRORISMO: ¿DE QUIEN....? Lima: Editorial Venceremos E.I.R.L., 1982.

193. ———. TERRORISMO Y GUERRA SUCIA EN EL PERU. Lima: Punto Rojo, 1986.

194. ———. YO ACUSO: LA REVOLUCION PERUANA. Tacna: Editorial El Siglo, 1978. RGAF.

195. Fishel, John T. "Attitudes of Peruvian Highland Village Leaders toward Military Intervention." JOURNAL OF INTERAMERICAN STUDIES AND WORLD AFFAIRS 18 (1976): 155-78. RGAF.

196. Fitch, J. Samuel. "Class Structure, Populism, and the Armed Forces in Contemporary Ecuador." LATIN AMERICAN RESEARCH REVIEW 19 (1984): 270-74.

197. ———. THE MILITARY COUP D'ETAT AS A POLITICAL PROCESS: ECUADOR, 1948-1966. Baltimore: Johns Hopkins University Press, 1977.

198. Fitzgerald, E.V.K. "Peru: The Political Economy of an Intermediate Regime." JOURNAL OF LATIN AMERICAN STUDIES 8 (1976): 53-71. RGAF.

199. ———. THE POLITICAL ECONOMY OF PERU, 1956-78: ECONOMIC DEVELOPMENT AND THE RESTRUCTURING OF CAPITAL. Cambridge: Cambridge University Press, 1979.

200. Flores Caballero, Luis. SENTIDO HISTORICO DE LA REVOLUCION PERUANA. Lima: Editorial Ausonia, 1970. RGAF.

201. Franco, Carlos. LA REVOLUCION PARTICIPATORIA. Lima: Mosca Azul Editores, 1975. RGAF.

202. ———, ed. EL PERU DE VELASCO. 3 vols. Lima: Centro de Estudios para el Desarrollo y la Participación, 1983. RGAF.

203. Frías, Ismael. NACIONALISMO Y AUTOGESTION. Lima: Ediciones Inkarri, 1971. RGAF.

204. ———. LA REVOLUCION PERUANA Y LA VIA SOCIALISTA. Lima: Editorial Horizonte, 1970. RGAF.

205. Gallardo Lozada, Jorge. LA NACION POSTERGADA: CONTRIBUCION AL ESTUDIO DE LA HISTORIA DE BOLIVIA. La Paz: Editorial Los Amigos del Libro, 1984.

206. ———. DE TORRES A BANZER: DIEZ MESES DE EMERGENCIA EN BOLIVIA. Buenos Aires: Ediciones Periferia, 1972.

207. Gálvez, Juan Ignacio. INTERNATIONAL CONFLICTS: PERU AGAINST COLOMBIA, ECUADOR, AND CHILE. Santiago: Sociedad Imprenta y Litografía Universo, 1920.

208. Gambetta Bonatti, Néstor. DICCIONARIO MILITAR. Lima: Imprenta del Ministerio de Guerra, 1943.

209. Gándara Enríquez, Marcos. "Los militares y la política en el Ecuador, 1830-1980." In ECUADOR, 1830-1980, 1: 171-82. Edited by Corporación Editora Nacional. Quito: Corporación Editora Nacional, 1980-83.

210. García Rosell, César. HISTORIA DE LOS CUERPOS DE TROPA DEL EJERCITO. Lima: Ministerio de Guerra, 1951.

211. Gerlach, Allen. "Civil-Military Relations in Peru, 1914-1945." Ph.D dissertation, University of New Mexico, 1973.

212. Gilbert, Dennis. "Society, Politics, and the Press: An Interpretation of the Peruvian Press Reform of 1974." JOURNAL OF INTERAMERICAN STUDIES AND WORLD AFFAIRS 21 (1979): 369-94. RGAF.

213. González Torres, René, and Luis Iriarte Ontiveros. VILLARROEL: MARTIR DE SUS IDEALES Y EL ATISBO DE LA REVOLUCION NACIONAL. La Paz: Talleres-Escuela de Artes Gráficas del Colegio Don Bosco, 1983.

214. Goodfriend, Paul. "The Ecuadorian Army is Poor but Proud." INFANTRY JOURNAL 61 (1947): 23-25.

215. Gorman, Stephen M., "Peru before the Elections for the Constituent Assembly: Ten Years of Military Rule and the Quest for Social Justice." GOVERNMENT AND OPPOSITION 13 (1978): 288-306. RGAF.

216. ———, ed. POST-REVOLUTIONARY PERU: THE POLITICS OF TRANSFORMATION. Boulder: Westview Press, 1982. RGAF.

217. Gott, Richard. GUERRILLA MOVEMENTS IN LATIN AMERICA. Garden City, NY: Doubleday and Company, 1971.

218. Granda Aguilar, Víctor. LA MASACRE DE AZTRA: EL CRIMEN MAS ESPANTOSO DE LA DICTADURA DEL TRIUNVIRATO MILITAR. Cuenca: Facultad de Ciencias Económicas, Universidad de Cuenca, 1979.

219. Grayson, George. "Populism, Petroleum, and Politics in Ecuador." CURRENT HISTORY 68 (1975) 15-19, 39.

220. Guerra García, Francisco. EL PERUANO: UN PROCESO ABIERTO. Lima: Editorial Universo, 1975. RGAF.

221. ———. VELASCO: DEL ESTADO OLIGARQUICO AL CAPITALISMO DE ESTADO. Lima: Centro de Estudios para el Desarrollo y la Participación, 1983. RGAF.

222. Guerrero, Julio C. CIUDADANOS Y SOLDADOS. Lima: Lit. Tip. T. Scheuch, 1932.

223. ———. PENARANDA: ANTE LA HISTORIA. La Paz: Imprenta de la Intendencia General de Guerra, 1937.

224. ———. PENARANDA: SEMBLANZA DE UN HOMBRE EJEMPLAR. La Paz: Intendencia Central del Ejército, 1940.

225. Guerrero Martínez, Juan. CINCO ANOS DE REVOLUCION. Lima: Producciones del Perú, 1973. RGAF.

226. ———. SEIS ANOS DE REVOLUCION. Lima: Editorial Universo, 1974. RGAF.

227. ———. SIETE ANOS DE REVOLUCION. Lima: Talleres de Printcolors, 1975. RGAF.

228. Guttentag T., Werner. BIBLIOGRAFIA BOLIVIANA. La Paz: Editorial Los Amigos del Libro, 1963-.

229. Handelman, Howard, and Thomas G. Sanders. "Ecuador." In MILITARY GOVERNMENT AND THE MOVEMENT TOWARD DEMOCRACY IN SOUTH AMERICA, 3-74. Edited by Howard Handelman and Thomas G. Sanders. Bloomington: Indiana University Press, 1981.

230. ———. "Peru." In MILITARY GOVERNMENT AND THE MOVEMENT TOWARD DEMOCRACY IN SOUTH AMERICA, 77-141. Edited by Howard Handelman and Thomas G. Sanders. Bloomington: Indiana University Press, 1981.

231. Haya de la Torre, Agustín. EL RETORNO DE LA BARBARIE: LA MATANZA EN LOS PENALES DE LIMA EN 1986. Lima: Bahia Ediciones, 1987.

232. Heare, Gertrude E. TRENDS IN LATIN AMERICAN MILITARY EXPENDITURES, 1940-1970: ARGENTINA, BRAZIL, CHILE, COLOMBIA, PERU, AND VENEZUELA. Washington: U.S. Government Printing Office, 1971.

233. Herbold, Carl, Jr., and Steve Stein. GUIA BIBLIOGRAFICA PARA LA HISTORIA SOCIAL Y POLITICA DEL PERU EN EL SIGLO XX, 1895-1960. Lima: Instituto de Estudios Peruanos, 1971.

234. Hidalgo, Daniel. EL MILITARISMO: SUS CAUSAS Y REMEDIOS. Quito: R. Racines, 1913.

235. Hidalgo Morey, Teodoro. EL CONFLICTO DE LA CORDILLERA DEL CONDOR, 1981. Lima: Editorial Universo, 1984.

236. Howes Beas, Carlos. FUNDAMENTOS IDEOLOGICOS DE LA REVOLUCION PERUANA. Lima: Ediciones Debate, 1973. RGAF.

237. Hurtado, Oswaldo. POLITICAL POWER IN ECUADOR. Translated by Nick D. Mills, Jr. Albuquerque: University of New Mexico Press, 1980.

238. INFORME DE LA COMISION INVESTIGADORA DE LOS SUCESOS DE UCHURACCAY. Lima: Editora Perú, 1983.

239. "La institución armada y los partidos políticos." REVISTA MILITAR DE LAS FUERZAS ARMADAS ECUATORIANAS 3(1944).

240. Instituto de Estudios Histórico-Marítimos del Perú. HISTORIA MARITIMA DEL PERU. 15 vols. Lima: Editorial Ausonia Talleres-Gráficos, 1977-84.

241. Instituto de Estudios Regionales "José María Arguedas," and Universidad Nacional de San Cristóbal de Huamanga. LOS NINOS DE LA GUERRA. Lima: Condoreditores, 1987.

242. Instituto Moderno, Departamento de Extensión Cultural. LA II REPUBLICA: GENESIS, FINES Y PROYECCIONES DEL GOBIERNO REVOLUCIONARIO INSTITUIDO POR LA FUERZA ARMADA DEL PERU. Trujillo: Editorial Libros y Letras, 1968. RGAF.

243. Ismodes, Aníbal. "La conducta política de los militares." PANORAMAS 2 (1963): 61-70.

244. Jara, Carlos de la. HISTORIA AERONAUTICA DEL PERU. 2 vols. Lima: Comisión Encargada del Estudio, Revisión y Edición de la Historia Aeronáutica del Perú, 1975-77.

245. Jara y Ureta, José María de la. TESTIMONIO DE LUCHA, 1968-1978. Lima: Librería Editorial "Minerva," 1978. RGAF.

246. Jaramillo Ruíz, Augusto D. CONFLICTO PERUANO-COLOMBIANO: ¡PUCA-URCO!, 7 DE MAYO DE 1933. Lima: Imprenta "Gráfica Industrial," 1972.

247. Jiménez, César. PERU: REVOLUCION POPULAR O REFORMISMO BURGUES. Lima: Talleres de Editorial Gráfica Labor, 1980. RGAF.

248. Kelley, Jonathan, and Herbert S. Klein. REVOLUTION AND THE REBIRTH OF INEQUALITY: A THEORY APPLIED TO THE NATIONAL REVOLUTION IN BOLIVIA. Berkeley: University of California Press, 1981.

249. Kerbusch, Ernst J., ed. CAMBIOS ESTRUCTURALES EN EL PERU, 1968-1975. Lima: Fundación F. Ebert and Instituto Latinoamericano de Investigaciones Sociales, 1976. RGAF.

250. Klein, Herbert S. BOLIVIA: THE EVOLUTION OF A MULTI-ETHNIC SOCIETY. Cambridge: Cambridge University Press, 1982.

251. ———. "David Toro and the Establishment of 'Military Socialism' in Bolivia." HISPANIC AMERICAN HISTORICAL REVIEW 45 (1965): 25-52.

252. ———. "Germán Busch and the Era of 'Military Socialism' in Bolivia." HISPANIC AMERICAN HISTORICAL REVIEW 47 (1967): 166-84.

253. ———. PARTIES AND POLITICAL CHANGE IN BOLIVIA, 1880-1952. Cambridge: Cambridge University Press, 1969.

254. Knudson, Jerry W. BOLIVIA: PRESS AND REVOLUTION, 1932-1964. Lanham, MD.: University Press of America, 1986.

255. ———. BOLIVIA'S POPULAR ASSEMBLY AND THE OVERTHROW OF GENERAL JUAN JOSE TORRES. Buffalo: Council on International Studies, State University of New York, 1974.

256. Kohl, James V. "National Revolution to Revolution of Restoration: Arms and Factional Politics in Bolivia." INTER-AMERICAN ECONOMIC AFFAIRS 39 (1985): 3-30.

257. Ladman, Jerry R., ed. MODERN-DAY BOLIVIA: LEGACY OF THE REVOLUTION AND PROSPECTS FOR THE FUTURE. Tempe: Arizona State University, 1982.

258. Laidlaw, Karen A. "Civilian versus Military Rule as an Aid to Development: Peru, 1963-1974." INTERNATIONAL JOURNAL OF CONTEMPORARY SOCIOLOGY 17 (1980): 59-81. RGAF.

259. Langton, Kenneth P. "The Influence of Military Service on Social Consciousness and Protest Behavior: A Study of Peruvian Mine Workers." COMPARATIVE POLITICAL STUDIES 16 (1984): 479-504.

260. Lara, Jesús. REPETE: DIARIO DE UN HOMBRE QUE FUE A LA GUERRA DEL CHACO. 2d ed. Cochabamba: Editorial Canelas, 1938.

261. Larrea Alba, Luis. LA CAMPANA DE 1941: LA AGRESION PERUANA AL ECUADOR Y SUS ANTECEDENTES HISTORICOS, POLITICOS Y MILITARES. Quito: n.p., 1964.

262. ———. LA CAMPANA DE 1906: ANTECEDENTES DE LA REVOLUCION ALFARISTA; SU DESARROLLO Y SUS CONSECUENCIAS; EL CONFLICTO DE 1910. Quito: n.p., 1962.

263. ———. "El ejército y la política." El EJERCITO NACIONAL 10 (1931): 36-38.

264. Latin American Bureau. BOLIVIA: COUP D'ETAT. London: Latin American Bureau, 1980.

265. Latin American Bureau, and Instituto de Estudios Politícos para América Latina y Africa. NARCOTRAFICO Y POLITICA: MILITARISMO Y MAFIA EN BOLIVIA. Madrid: Instituto de Estudios Politícos para América Latina y Africa, 1982.

266. LATIN AMERICAN PERSPECTIVES 4 (1977). Special issue, "Peru: Revolution and Class Struggle." RGAF.

267. Lauer, Mirko, et al. EL REFORMISMO BURGUES, 1968-1976. Lima: Mosca Azul Editores, 1978. RGAF.

268. Lè Chàu. ROL DEL ESTADO: REFORMA ESTRUCTURAL Y CRISIS EN EL PERU, 1967-1977. Lima: Editorial Horizonte, 1982. RGAF.

269. Ledesma Izquieta, Genaro. COMPLOT: LIBRO ESCRITO EN EL FRONTON DURANTE LA REPRESION DE LA JUNTA MILITAR DE GOBIERNO, 1963. Lima: Editorial THESIS, 1964.

270. Lisigurski Pordominski, Rubén. LA REVOLUCION PERUANA: QUE ES Y DONDE VA. Lima: Editorial Santa Isabel, 1973. RGAF.

271. Listov, V.V. "The Wind of Change in the Land of the Incas: On the Peruvian Revolution." NOVAIA I NOVEISHAIA ISTORIIA (Moscow) 5 (1971): 84-98. RGAF.

272. Llosa M., José Antonio. RENE BARRIENTOS ORTUNO: PALADIN DE LA BOLIVIANIDAD. La Paz: Empresa Editora "Novedades," 1966.

273. Locker, Michael. "Perspective on the Peruvian Military." Parts 1, 2. NACLA NEWSLETTER 3 (1969). RGAF.

274. López, Jacinto. THE DOWNFALL OF THE CONSTITUTIONAL GOVERNMENT IN PERU: HISTORICAL ANALYSIS OF THE MILITARY REVOLUTION OF JULY 4TH, 1919, THAT ESTABLISHED THE DICTATORSHIP OF D. AUGUSTO B. LEGUIA IN PERU. New York: De Laisne and Rossboro, 1927.

275. Lora, Guillermo. ESTUDIOS HISTORICO-POLITICOS SOBRE BOLIVIA. La Paz: Ediciones El Amauta, 1978.

276. ———. HISTORY OF THE BOLIVIAN LABOUR MOVEMENT, 1848-1971. Cambridge: Cambridge University Press, 1977.

277. ———. EL PROLETARIADO EN EL PROCESO POLITICO, 1952-1980. La Paz: Ediciones Masas, 1980.

278. Lostaunau Rubio, Gabriel. FUENTES PARA EL ESTUDIO DEL PERU: BIBLIOGRAFIA DE BIBLIOGRAFIAS. Lima: n.p., 1980. Mimeographed.

279. Loveman, Brian, and Thomas M. Davies, Jr. CHE GUEVARA ON GUERRILLA WARFARE. Lincoln: University of Nebraska Press, 1985.

280. ———, eds. THE POLITICS OF ANTIPOLITICS: THE MILITARY IN LATIN AMERICA. Lincoln: University of Nebraska Press, 1978.

281. ———, eds. THE POLITICS OF ANTIPOLITICS: THE MILITARY IN LATIN AMERICA. 2d ed. Lincoln: University of Nebraska Press, 1989.

282. Lowenthal, Abraham F. "Dateline Peru: A Sagging Revolution." FOREIGN POLICY 38 (1980): 182-90. RGAF.

283. ———, ed. THE PERUVIAN EXPERIMENT: CONTINUITY AND CHANGE UNDER MILITARY RULE. Princeton: Princeton University Press, 1975. RGAF.

284. Lozada Uribe, Mario. EL NUEVO ROL SOCIAL DE LOS INSTITUTOS ARMADOS Y FUERZAS AUXILIARES: EJERCITO, MARINA, FUERZAS AEREAS, GUARDIA CIVIL Y REGIMIENTO GUARDIA REPUBLICANA. Lima: Imprenta LUX, 1957.

285. McAlister, Lyle N., Anthony P. Maingot, and Robert A. Potash. THE MILITARY IN LATIN AMERICAN SOCIOPOLITICAL EVOLUTION: FOUR CASE STUDIES. Washington: Center for Research in Social Systems, 1970.

286. McBride Espejo, Juan. ¿HACIA DONDE VA EL PERU?: 18
     MESES DE GOBIERNO REVOLUCIONARIO. Lima:
     Tipográfia Peruana, 1970. RGAF.

287. McClintock, Cynthia. PEASANT COOPERATIVES AND
     POLITICAL CHANGE IN PERU. Princeton: Princeton
     University Press, 1981. RGAF.

288. ———. "Peru's Sendero Luminoso Rebellion: Origins and
     Trajectory." In POWER AND POPULAR PROTEST: LATIN
     AMERICAN SOCIAL MOVEMENTS, 61-101. Edited by Susan
     Eckstein. Berkeley: University of California Press, 1989.

289. ———. "Sendero Luminoso: Peru's Maoist Guerrillas."
     PROBLEMS OF COMMUNISM 32 (1983): 19-34.

290. ———. "Why Peasants Rebel: The Case of Peru's Sendero
     Luminoso." WORLD POLITICS 37 (1984): 48-84.

291. McClintock, Cynthia, and Abraham F. Lowenthal, eds. THE
     PERUVIAN EXPERIMENT RECONSIDERED. Princeton:
     Princton University Press, 1983. RGAF.

292. Macha Bardales, Adolfo. LA DEFENSA EN LAS DIFERENTES
     ETAPAS HISTORICAS DEL PERU: APUNTES DE LAS
     CONFERENCIAS DICTADAS EN EL CAEM POR EL GRAL.
     DIV. ADOLFO MACHA BARDALES, 1984-85. Lima: Centro
     de Altos Estudios Militares, 1985.

293. MacLean Estenós, Percy. HISTORIA DE UNA REVOLUCION.
     Buenos Aires: Editorial Ediciones Argentinas para América
     Latina, 1953.

294. McNicoll, Robert E. PERU'S INSTITUTIONAL
     REVOLUTION. Pensacola: University of West Florida, 1973.
     RGAF.

295. Maldonado Donoso, Fernando. "Militares y política en el
     Ecuador de 1830 a 1980." In ECUADOR, 1830-1980, 1: 389-99.
     Edited by Corporación Editora Nacional. Quito: Corporación
     Editora Nacional, 1980-83.

296. Malloy, James M. BOLIVIA: THE UNCOMPLETED
     REVOLUTION. Pittsburgh: University of Pittsburgh Press, 1970.

297. ———. "Populismo militar en el Perú y Bolivia: Antecedentes y posibilidades futuras." ESTUDIOS ANDINOS 2 (1971-72): 113-35.

298. Malloy, James M., and Eduardo A. Gamarra. REVOLUTION AND REACTION: BOLIVIA, 1964-1985. New Brunswick: Transaction Books, 1988.

299. ———. "La transición a la democracia en Bolivia." APUNTES 17 (1985): 87-108.

300. Malloy, James M., and Richard S. Thorn, eds. BEYOND THE REVOLUTION: BOLIVIA SINCE 1952. Pittsburgh: University of Pittsburgh Press, 1971.

301. Malpica, Mario Antonio. BIOGRAFIA DE LA REVOLUCION. Lima: Ediciones Ensayos Sociales, 1967.

302. Mar Alcázar, Gerardo del. EL CONFLICTO MILITAR DEL PERU CON EL ECUADOR, 1941: EN EL TEATRO DE OPERACIONES DEL NOR-ORIENTE. Lima: Cenacape "Artes Gráficas," 1980.

303. Marcella, Gabriel. "Security Assistance Revisited: How to Win Friends and Not Lose Influence." PARAMETERS 12 (1982): 43-52.

304. Mares, Pompeyo. EL PROCESO REVOLUCIONARIO PERUANO: BALANCE Y PERSPECTIVAS. Lima: Imprenta Castillo, 1971. RGAF.

305. Mariátegui y Cisneros, Salvador. CONFLICTO PERUANO ECUATORIANO DE 1941. Lima: Librería Editorial "Minerva," 1968.

306. EL MARISCAL BENAVIDES: SU VIDA Y SU OBRA. 2 vols. Lima: Imprenta Editorial Atlántica, 1976-81.

307. Martínez, Pedro Pablo. HACIENDO HISTORIA. Lima: n.p., 1935.

308. ———. PAGINAS MILITARES. Lima: Imprenta Eduardo Rávago, 1924.

309. Martz, John D. ECUADOR: CONFLICTING POLITICAL CULTURE AND THE QUEST FOR PROGRESS. Boston: Allyn and Bacon, 1972.

310. ———. POLITICS AND PETROLEUM IN ECUADOR. New Brunswick: Transaction Books, 1987.

311. Masterson, Daniel M. "Caudillismo and Institutional Change: Manuel Odría and the Peruvian Armed Forces, 1948-1956." THE AMERICAS 40 (1984): 479-89.

312. ———. "The Peruvian Armed Forces in Transition, 1939-1963: The Impact of National Politics and Changing Professional Perspectives." Ph.D. dissertation, Michigan State University, 1976.

313. ———. "Soldiers, Sailors, and Apristas: Conspiracy and Power Politics in Peru, 1932-1984." In THE UNDERSIDE OF LATIN AMERICAN HISTORY, 24-42. Edited by John F. Bratzel and Daniel M. Masterson. East Lansing: Latin American Studies Center, Michigan State University, 1977.

314. Matos, Genaro. OPERACIONES IRREGULARES AL NORTE DE CAJAMARCA: CHOTA, CUTERVO, SANTA CRUZ, 1924-1925 A 1927. Lima: Imprenta del Ministerio de Guerra, 1968.

315. Matos Mar, José, and Roger Ravines. BIBLIOGRAFIA PERUANA DE CIENCIAS SOCIALES, 1957-1969. Lima: Instituto de Estudios Peruanos, 1971.

316. Mayorga, René Antonio. "National-Popular State, State Capitalism, and Military Dictatorship in Bolivia, 1952-1975." LATIN AMERICAN PERSPECTIVES 17 (1978): 89-119.

317. Medina Castro, Manuel. LA DOCTRINA Y LA LEY DE SEGURIDAD NACIONAL. Guayaquil: Departamento de Publicaciones de la Universidad de Guayaquil, 1979.

318. Mejía Scarneo, Julio. TEORIA Y PRACTICA DE LA REVOLUCION PERUANA. Lima: Ediciones Cooperativismo y Reforma Agraria Peruana, 1970. RGAF.

319. Mendoza, Samuel. ANARQUIA Y CAOS: LA NOCHE DE BOLIVIA. La Paz: Empresa Editora "Universo," 1973.

320. Mercado, Rogger. ALGO MAS SOBRE SENDERO. Lima: Ediciones de Cultura Popular, 1983.

321. ———. LAS GUERRILLAS DEL PERU: EL MIR; DE LA PREDICA IDEOLOGICA A LA ACCION ARMADA. Lima: Fondo de Cultura Popular, 1967.

322. ———. EL PARTIDO COMUNISTA DEL PERU: SENDERO LUMINOSO. 3d ed. Lima: Librerías "Studium"-"La Universidad," 1986.

323. ———. LA "REVOLUCION" FRACASADA: APUNTES CRITICOS SOBRE LA POLITICA DEL GOBIERNO MILITAR. Lima: Fondo de Cultura Popular, 1977. RGAF.

324. Mercado Ibáñez, Iván. EL GENOCIDIO APRISTA CONTRA SENDERO LUMINOSO. Lima: Ediciones Latinoamericanas, 1987.

325. Mercado Jarrín, Edgardo. EI CONFLICTO CON ECUADOR. Lima: Ediciones Rikchay Perú, 1981.

326. ———. ENSAYOS. Lima: Imprenta del Ministerio de Guerra, 1974. RGAF.

327. ———. SEGURIDAD, POLITICA Y ESTRATEGIA. Lima: Imprenta del Ministerio de Guerra, 1974.

328. Merino Arana, Rómulo. GUARDIA CIVIL. Lima: Imprenta "La Popular," 1951.

329. ———. HISTORIA POLICIAL DEL PERU EN LA REPUBLICA. Lima: Imprenta del Departamento de Prensa y Publicaciones de la Guardia Civil, n.d.

330. Middlebrook, Kevin, and David Scott Palmer. MILITARY GOVERNMENT AND POLITICAL DEVELOPMENT: LESSONS FROM PERU. Beverly Hills: Sage Publications, 1975. RGAF.

331. Mills, Nick D. CRISIS, CONFLICTO Y CONSENSO: ECUADOR, 1979-1984. Quito: Corporación Editora Nacional, 1984.

332. Miñano M., Carlos A. LAS MISIONES MILITARES FRANCESAS EN EL PERU. Lima: n.p., 1959.

333. Mitchell, Christopher. THE LEGACY OF POPULISM IN BOLIVIA: FROM THE MNR TO MILITARY RULE. New York: Praeger Publishers, 1977.

334. ———. "The New Authoritarianism in Bolivia." CURRENT HISTORY 80 (1981): 75-78, 89.

335. Moncayo, Pedro. BREVE HISTORIA DEL COLEGIO MILITAR. Quito: n.p., 1970. Typescript.

336. Moncloa, Francisco. PERU: ¿QUE PASO?, 1968-1976. Lima: Editorial Horizonte, 1977. RGAF.

337. Montagne Markholz, Ernesto. MEMORIAS DEL GENERAL DE BRIGADA E.P. ERNESTO MONTAGNE MARKHOLZ. Lima: n.p., 1962.

338. Monteforte Toledo, Mario. LA SOLUCION MILITAR A LA PERUANA, 1968-1970. Mexico City: UNAM, 1973. RGAF.

339. Morales, Waltraud Queiser. "Bolivia Moves toward Democracy." CURRENT HISTORY 78 (1980): 76-79, 86-88.

340. Morales Bermúdez, Francisco. EL PROYECTO NACIONAL. 2d ed. Lima: Centro de Documentación e Información Andina, 1984.

341. Morales Dávila, Manuel. LOS DERECHOS HUMANOS EN BOLIVIA, 1971-1977. N.p.: Confederación Nacional de Profesionales de Bolivia, 1978.

342. Moreira, Neiva. MODELO PERUANO. Lima: Ediciones La Linea, 1974. RGAF.

343. Morozov, Valeri. "Tras los acontecimientos de Bolivia." AMERICA LATINA (Moscow) 1-2 (1981): 52-75.

344. Muller, Richard. THE FRONTIER PROBLEM BETWEEN ECUADOR AND PERU AND THE OFFICIAL MAP OF PERU OF 1826. Guayaquil: Editorial Jouvin, 1937.

345. Muñoz, Julio. DOCTRINAS MILITARES APLICADAS EN EL ECUADOR: HISTORIA Y PEDAGOGIA MILITAR; EL EJERCITO QUE EL ECUADOR NECESITA. Quito: Imprenta del Estado Mayor General, 1949.

346. Murga, A. "Militarism in Peru or Revolution from Above." ESTUDIOS SOCIALES CENTROAMERICANOS 1 (1972): 184-88. RGAF.

347. Museo Naval del Perú. FUENTES PARA EL ESTUDIO DE LA HISTORIA NAVAL DEL PERU. 2 vols. Lima: Imprenta de la Marina, 1958-60.

348. Nash, June. WE EAT THE MINES AND THE MINES EAT US: DEPENDENCY AND EXPLOITATION IN BOLIVIAN TIN MINES. New York: Columbia University Press, 1979.

349. Needler, Martin C. ANATOMY OF A COUP D'ETAT: ECUADOR, 1963. Washington: Institute for the Comparative Study of Political Systems, 1964.

350. ———. "Military Withdrawal from Power in South America." ARMED FORCES AND SOCIETY 6 (1980): 614-24.

351. North, Liisa. CIVIL-MILITARY RELATIONS IN ARGENTINA, CHILE, AND PERU. Berkeley: Institute of International Studies, University of California, 1966.

352. North, Liisa, and Tanya Korovkin. THE PERUVIAN REVOLUTION AND THE OFFICERS IN POWER, 1967-1976. Montreal: Centre for Developing Area Studies, McGill University, 1981. RGAF.

353. Nunn, Frederick M. "European Military Influence in South America: The Origins and Nature of Professional Militarism in Argentina, Brazil, Chile, and Peru, 1890-1940." JAHRBUCH FUR GESCHICHTE VON STAAT, WIRTSCHAFT UND GESELLSCHAFT LATEINAMERIKAS 12 (1975): 230-52.

354. ———. "The Latin American Military Establishment: Some Thoughts on the Origins of Its Sociopolitical Role and an Illustrative Bibliographical Essay." THE AMERICAS 28 (1971): 135-51.

355. ———. "Latin American Militarylore: An Introduction and a Case Study." THE AMERICAS 35 (1979): 429-74.

356. ———. "Notes on the 'Junta Phenomenon' and the 'Military Regime' in Latin America with Special Reference to Peru, 1968-1972." THE AMERICAS 31 (1975): 237-51. RGAF.

357. ———. "Professional Militarism in Twentieth-Century Peru: Historical and Theoretical Background to the *golpe de estado* of 1968." HISPANIC AMERICAN HISTORICAL REVIEW 59 (1979): 391-417. RGAF.

358. ———. YESTERDAY'S SOLDIERS: EUROPEAN MILITARY PROFESSIONALISM IN SOUTH AMERICA, 1890-1940. Lincoln: University of Nebraska Press, 1983.

359. Nyrop, Richard F. PERU: A COUNTRY STUDY. 3d ed. Washington: Foreign Area Studies, The American University, 1981.

360. Ochoa, Octavio. TRAGEDIA ECUATORIANA, 1941. Quito: Gráf. "Chimborazo," 1976.

361. O'Donnell, Justin E. "The Political Role of the Bolivian Military." National Interdepartmental Seminar, Foreign Service Institute, Washington, July 1967.

362. Odría, Manuel A. PRINCIPIOS Y POSTULADOS DEL MOVIMIENTO RESTAURADOR DE AREQUIPA: EXTRACTO DE DISCURSOS Y MENSAJES DEL GENERAL DON MANUEL A. ODRIA, 1948-1955. Lima: n.p., 1956.

363. Olarte, A. "Función democrática de las fuerzas armadas." REVISTA MILITAR DE LAS FUERZAS ARMADAS ECUATORIANAS 2 (1943).

364. Olmos, Coronel Gualberto. CORONEL GUALBERTO VILLARROEL: SU VIDA, SU MARTIRIO. La Paz: S.P.I.C., n.d.

365. Orellana, J. Gonzalo, ed. RESUMEN HISTORICO DEL ECUADOR, 1830-1930, 1947-48. Quito: Editorial "Fray Jodoco Ricke," 1948.

366. Ortiz Acha, Gastón. DE LA INTERVENCION DE LAS FUERZAS ARMADAS EN LA POLITICA NACIONAL Y DE LAS CONSIGUIENTES REFORMAS LEGALES. Lima: Cía. Imprentas Unidas, CIUSAL, 1970. RGAF.

367. Ortiz Crespo, Gonzalo. LA HORA DEL GENERAL. Quito: Editorial El Conejo, 1986.

368. Ortiz de Zevallos Roedel, Gonzalo. ENTREGUISMO: LOS CONTRATOS PETROLEROS DE 1974. Lima: Talleres de Grafiser, 1978. RGAF.

369. Ortiz Sotelo, Jorge. ESCUELA NAVAL DEL PERU: HISTORIA ILUSTRADA. Callao: Escuela Naval del Perú, 1981.

370. ———. EX-CADETES NAVALES DEL PERU. Lima: Asociación de Ex-Cadetes Navales del Perú, 1982.

371. Ovando Candia, Alfredo. INFORME A LA NACION. La Paz: n.p., 1966.

372. Padilla Arancibia, David. DECISIONES Y RECUERDOS DE UN GENERAL. La Paz: n.p., 1980.

373. Palmer, David Scott. "The Changing Political Economy of Peru under Military and Civilian Rule." INTER-AMERICAN ECONOMIC AFFAIRS 37 (1984): 37-62. RGAF.

374. ———. PERU: THE AUTHORITARIAN TRADITION. New York: Praeger Publishers, 1980.

375. ———. "Reformist Military Rule in Peru, 1968-80." In NEW MILITARY POLITICS IN LATIN AMERICA, 131-49. Edited by Robert Wesson. New York: Praeger Publishers, 1982. RGAF.

376. ———. REVOLUTION FROM ABOVE: MILITARY GOVERNMENT AND POPULAR PARTICIPATION IN PERU, 1968-1972. Ithaca: Latin American Studies Program, Cornell University, 1973. RGAF.

377. ———. "The Sendero Luminoso Rebellion in Rural Peru." In LATIN AMERICAN INSURGENCIES, 67-96. Edited by Georges Fauriol. Washington: Center for Strategic and International Studies, Georgetown University, 1985.

378. Partido Liberal. LA POLITICA LIBERAL: FORMULADA POR EL JEFE DEL PARTIDO, GENERAL ELIODORO CAMACHO. La Paz: Imprenta Andina, 1916.

379. Pásara, Luis. "Diagnosing Peru." LATIN AMERICAN RESEARCH REVIEW 17 (1982): 235-43.

380. Payne, Arnold. THE PERUVIAN COUP D'ETAT OF 1962: THE OVERTHROW OF MANUEL PRADO. Washington: Institute for the Comparative Study of Political Systems, 1968.

381. Paz-Soldán, Juan Pedro. EL GOLPE DE ESTADO DEL 29 DE MAYO DE 1909. 2d ed. Lima: Imprenta del Estado, 1914.

382. Pease García, Henry. LOS CAMINOS DEL PODER: TRES ANOS DE CRISIS EN LA ESCENA POLITICA. Lima: DESCO, 1979. RGAF.

383. ———. EL OCASO DEL PODER OLIGARQUICO: LUCHA POLITICA EN LA ESCENA OFICIAL, 1968-1975. Lima: DESCO, 1977. RGAF.

384. Pease García, Henry, et al. PERU, 1968-1978: CRONOLOGIA POLITICA. 7 vols. Lima: DESCO, 1974-80. RGAF.

385. Pease García G.Y., Franklin. PERU: UNA APROXIMACION BIBLIOGRAFICA. Mexico City: Centro de Estudios Económicos y Sociales del Tercer Mundo, 1979.

386. Peña Bravo, Raúl. HECHOS Y DICHOS DEL GENERAL BARRIENTOS. La Paz: n.p., 1971.

387. Pennano, Guido, and Jürgen Schuldt. "Premisas y antecedentes para la evaluación del proyecto del Plan Túpac Amaru." APUNTES 3 (1977): 51-68. RGAF.

388. Pérez Reynoso, Ramiro. TRAYECTORIA DE UN SOLDADO. Santiago: Imprenta Nascimento, 1940.

389. Pérez-Rosas Cáceres, Augusto. FUENTES BIBLIOGRAFICAS PERUANAS EN LAS CIENCIAS SOCIALES, 1879-1979. Lima: DESCO, 1981.

390. Peru. BASES IDEOLOGICAS DE LA REVOLUCION PERUANA. Lima: Editorial Desarrollo, 1976. RGAF.

391. ———. HISTORIA DE LA ESCUELA MILITAR DEL PERU. 2 vols. Lima: Talleres Offset "Reprográfica" and Ministerio de Guerra, 1982.

392. ———. LINEAMIENTOS DE LA POLITICA ECONOMICO-SOCIAL DEL GOBIERNO REVOLUCIONARIO. Lima: Imprenta D.O. "El Peruano," 1968. RGAF.

393. ———. MANIFIESTO, ESTATUTO Y PLAN INCA DEL GOBIERNO REVOLUCIONARIO DE LA FUERZA ARMADA: ELABORADO ANTES DEL 3 DE OCTUBRE DE 1968. Lima: Editorial "Incarki," 1975. RGAF.

394. ———. LA MISION MILITAR FRANCESA EN EL PERU. Lima: Imprenta de la Intendencia General de Guerra, 1923.

395. ———. Biblioteca Nacional. ANUARIO BIBLIOGRAFICO PERUANO. 15 vols. Lima: [various publishers], 1945-78.

396. ———. Comisión Catalogadora del Centro de Estudios Histórico-Militares del Perú. COLECCION DOCUMENTAL DEL CONFLICTO Y CAMPANA MILITAR CON EL ECUADOR EN 1941. 7 vols. Lima: Talleres ITAL PERU, 1978-79.

397. ———. Comisión de la Fuerza Armada y Fuerzas Policiales. PLAN DE GOBIERNO "TUPAC AMARU": PERIODO, 1977-1980. Lima: Editorial "Inkari," n.d. RGAF.

398. ———. Estado Mayor General del Ejército del Perú, 5a Sección. MONOGRAFIA HISTORICA DEL EJERCITO PERUANO. Lima: Estado Mayor General del Ejército, 1930.

399. ———. Ministerio de Guerra. EL EJERCITO DEL PERU EN ACCION CIVICA: PARTICIPACION DEL EJERCITO PERUANO EN ACTIVIDADES ORIENTADAS AL DESARROLLO SOCIO-ECONOMICO NACIONAL. Lima: Ministerio de Guerra, 1965.

400. ———. LAS GUERRILLAS EN EL PERU Y SU REPRESION. Lima: Ministerio de Guerra, 1966.

401. ———. National Information Office. THE PHILOSOPHY OF THE PERUVIAN REVOLUTION. Lima: Editorial Enterprise of the Official Newspaper "The Peruvian," 1971. RGAF.

402. ———. Oficina Nacional de Información. LA REVOLUCION PERUANA NO SE DETENDRA: FUERZA ARMADA RATIFICO IDENTIFICACION CON EL GOBIERNO REVOLUCIONARIO. Lima: Oficina Nacional de Información, 1970. RGAF.

403. ———. Presidencia de la República. PLAN NACIONAL DE DESARROLLO PARA 1971-1975. 4 vols. Lima: Instituto Nacional de Planificación, 1971-72. RGAF.

404. Petras, James, and Robert LaPorte. PERU: ¿TRANSFORMACION REVOLUCIONARIA O MODERNIZACION? Buenos Aires: Amorrortu Editores, 1971. RGAF.

405. Petras, James, and Nelson Rimensnyder. "The Military and the Modernization of Peru." In POLITICS AND SOCIAL STRUCTURE IN LATIN AMERICA, 130-58. Edited by James Petras. New York: Fawcett Books, 1970. RGAF.

406. Philip, George D. THE RISE AND FALL OF THE PERUVIAN MILITARY RADICALS, 1968-1976. London: Athlone Press, 1978. RGAF.

407. ———. "Soldier as Radical: Peruvian Military Government, 1968-1975." JOURNAL OF LATIN AMERICAN STUDIES 8 (1976): 29-51. RGAF.

408. Pike, Fredrick B. THE MODERN HISTORY OF PERU. New York: Praeger Publishers, 1967.

409. ———. THE UNITED STATES AND THE ANDEAN REPUBLICS: PERU, BOLIVIA, AND ECUADOR. Cambridge: Harvard University Press, 1977.

410. Pillar Tello, María del. ¿GOLPE O REVOLUCION?: HABLAN LOS MILITARES DEL 68; ENTREVISTAS. 2 vols. Lima: Ediciones SAGSA, 1983. RGAF.

411. Pimental Obregón, Máximo. EL CONFLICTO PERU-ECUADOR: FRONTERA DEL NORTE; COMBATE DE PANUPALI, 18 DE SEPTIEMBRE DE 1941. Lima: Talleres Gráficos de ITAL PERU, 1985.

412. Pinoargote Cevallos, Alfredo. LA REPUBLICA DE PAPEL. Guayaquil: Talleres de Artes Gráficas Senefelder, 1982.

413. Pinto Bazurco, Moisés. EL 4 DE JULIO DE 1919 Y SU REPERCUSION EN EL CONTINENTE AMERICANO: ANOTACIONES PARA LA HISTORIA POR EL CAPITAN DE FRAGATA DR. MOISES PINTO BAZURCO. Lima: Sanmartí y Cía. Impresores, 1920.

414. LA POLITICA NACIONAL: DEMOCRACIA, CONTINUISMO, GOLPE DE ESTADO; OPINAN GUILLERMO BEDREGAL GUTIERREZ ET AL. La Paz: n.p., 1978.

415. Pozzo Medina, Julio. GEOPOLITICA Y GEOESTRATEGIA. La Paz: Editorial "Don Bosco," 1984.

416. Prado Salmón, Gary. PODER Y FUERZAS ARMADAS, 1949-1982. La Paz: Editorial Los Amigos del Libro, 1984.

417. Puma, Carlos E. PRISMAS MILITARES: ESCENAS DE CUARTEL. Quito: Talleres Gráficos del Colegio Militar, 1939.

418. Querejazu Calvo, Roberto. MASAMACLAY: HISTORIA POLITICA, DIPLOMATICA Y MILITAR DE LA GUERRA DEL CHACO. 3d ed. La Paz: Editorial Los Amigos del Libro, 1975.

419. Quiroga Ochoa, Ovidio. EN LA PAZ Y EN LA GUERRA AL SERVICIO DE LA PATRIA, 1916-1971. La Paz: Librería y Editorial Gisbert, 1974.

420. Quiroga Santa Cruz, Marcelo. BOLIVIA RECUPERA LA PALABRA: JUICIO A LA DICTADURA. La Paz: Ediciones M.E.P., 1982.

421. ———. EL SAQUEO DE BOLIVIA. 3d ed. La Paz: Ediciones Puerta del Sol, 1979.

422. Ramos Sánchez, Pablo. ANTECEDENTES Y MECANICA DEL
      GOLPE DEL 17 DE JULIO DE 1980. Mexico City: n.p., 1981.

423. ———. RADIOGRAFIA DE UN GOLPE DE ESTADO: OTRA
      VEZ LA DEMOCRACIA EN PELIGRO. La Paz: Ediciones
      Puerto del Sol, 1983.

424. República Peruana. LA FUERZA ARMADA Y EL PROCESO
      ELECTORAL DE 1962. Lima: Imprentas de la Fuerza Armada,
      1963.

425. Reyes, Oscar Efrén. BREVE HISTORIA GENERAL DEL
      ECUADOR. 3 vols. 6th ed. Quito: Editorial "Fray Jodoco Ricke,"
      1960.

426. Richards, Gordon. "Stabilization Crises and the Breakdown of
      Military Authoritarianism in Latin America." COMPARATIVE
      POLITICAL STUDIES 18 (1986): 449-85.

427. Ríos Reinaga, David. CIVILES Y MILITARES EN LA
      REVOLUCION BOLIVIANA. La Paz: Editorial y Librería
      Difusión, 1967.

428. Rocca Torres, Luis. CRITICA DE LA IDEOLOGIA DEL
      GOBIERNO DE LAS FUERZAS ARMADAS. Lima:
      Universidad "Ricardo Palma," 1975. RGAF.

429. ———. EL GOBIERNO MILITAR Y LAS COMUNICACIONES
      EN EL PERU. Lima: Fondo de Cultura Popular, 1975. RGAF.

430. ———. IMPERIALISMO EN EL PERU: VIEJAS ATADURAS
      CON NUEVOS NUDOS; APUNTES SOBRE EL
      CAPITALISMO MONOPOLICO Y LA POLITICA
      ECONOMICA DE LA JUNTA MILITAR. Lima: Fondo de
      Cultura Popular, 1974. RGAF.

431. Rodríguez, Angel. AUTOPSIA DE UNA GUERRA:
      CAMPANA DEL CHACO; CON OPINIONES TECNICAS DE
      CINCO GENERALES DE AMERICA. Santiago: Editorial
      Ercilla, 1940.

432. Rodríguez Beruff, Jorge. LOS MILITARES Y EL PODER: UN
      ENSAYO SOBRE LA DOCTRINA MILITAR EN EL PERU,
      1948-1968. Lima: Mosca Azul, 1983.

433. Romero, Emilio. POR EL NORTE: ECUADOR. Lima: Juan Mejía Baca and P.L. Villanueva Editores, 1955.

434. Romero Pintado, Fernando. IQUITOS Y LA FUERZA NAVAL DE LA AMAZONIA, 1830-1933. 3d ed. Lima: Ministerio de Marina, 1983. Originally titled NOTAS PARA UNA HISTORIA DE LA MARINA FLUVIAL DE GUERRA.

435. Rosero Revelo, Luis Alberto. MEMORIAS DE UN VETERANO DE LA GUERRA DEL 41. Quito: Editorial Casa de la Cultura Ecuatoriana, 1978.

436. Rozman, Stephen L. "The Evolution of the Political Role of the Peruvian Military." JOURNAL OF INTERAMERICAN STUDIES AND WORLD AFFAIRS 12 (1970): 539-64.

437. Rubio Correa, Marcial. "La actuación del poder ejecutivo y la estructura del orden jurídico." APUNTES 4 (1978): 81-98.

438. ———. "Las fuerzas armadas, la política y la doctrina de la contrainsurgencia." QUEHACER 31 (1984): 37-67.

439. Sacchi, Hugo M. CHILE, PERU, BOLIVIA: DOCUMENTOS DE TRES PROCESOS LATINOAMERICANOS. Buenos Aires: Centro Editor de América Latina, 1972.

440. Salamanca Trujillo, Daniel. SOCIOGRAFIA DE LA REVOLUCION DEL 4 DE NOVIEMBRE DE 1964: APUNTES PARA UNA BIOGRAFIA DEL GRAL. RENE BARRIENTOS ORTUNO. La Paz: Ediciones "Clio," 1969.

441. Salazar Larraín, Arturo. LA HERENCIA DE VELASCO, 1968-1975: EL PUEBLO QUEDO ATRAS. Lima: Editorial e Imprenta DESA, 1977. RGAF.

442. Salcedo, José María. LAS TUMBAS DE UCHURACCAY. Lima: Editora Humboldt, 1984.

443. Sánchez, Ramiro. BRAZIL EN BOLIVIA: LECCIONES DE UN MILITAR. Santiago: n.p., 1972.

444. Sandoval Rodríguez, Isaac. CULMINACION Y RUPTURA DEL MODELO NACIONAL-REVOLUCIONARIO: TORRES

EN EL ESCENARIO POLITICO BOLIVIANO. La Paz: Empresa Editora Urquizo, 1979.

445. Saracho Calderón, Julio C. UNA RAFAGA EN LA HISTORIA DE LA GUERRA DEL CHACO. Potosí: Empresa Editora Urquizo, 1980.

446. Sarmiento, Emilio. MEMORIAS DE UN SOLDADO DE LA GUERRA DEL CHACO. Buenos Aires: El Cid Editor, 1978.

447. Schaefer, Jürgen. DEUTSCHE MILITARHILFE AN SUDAMERIKA: MILITAR- UND RUSTUNGSINTERESSEN IN ARGENTINIEN, BOLIVIEN, UND CHILE VOR 1914. Düsseldorf: Bertelsmann Universitätsverlag, 1974.

448. Scheetz, Thomas. "Gastos militares en Chile, Perú y la Argentina." DESARROLLO ECONOMICO (Buenos Aires) 25 (1985): 315-27.

449. Schodt, David W. ECUADOR: AN ANDEAN ENIGMA. Boulder: Westview Press, 1987.

450. Schydlowsky, Daniel M., and Juan J. Wicht. ANATOMIA DE UN FRACASO ECONOMICO: PERU, 1968-1978. Lima: Universidad del Pacífico, 1979. RGAF.

451. Scurrah, Martín, and Abner Montalvo. CLASE SOCIAL Y VALORES SOCIALES EN PERU. Lima: Escuela de Administración de Negocios para Graduados (ESAN), 1975. RGAF.

452. ———. GOBIERNO REVOLUCIONARIO DEL PERU: BASES SOCIALES QUE LO APOYAN. Lima: Escuela de Administración de Negocios para Graduados (ESAN), 1975. RGAF.

453. Seleme Vargas, Antonio. MI ACTUACION EN LA JUNTA MILITAR DE GOBIERNO CON EI PRONUNCIAMIENTO REVOLUCIONARIO DEL 9 DE ABRIL DE 1952. La Paz: Imprenta Kollasuyo, 1969.

454. Selzer, Gregorio. BOLIVIA: EL CUARTELAZO DE LOS COCADOLARES. Mexico City: Mex-Sur Editorial, 1982.

455. Serrano Castrillón, Raúl. LA REVOLUCION Y LA SIESTA: CRONICAS DE PROPIEDAD SOCIAL. Lima: J. and R., 1980. RGAF.

456. Servicios Populares. DERECHOS HUMANOS Y LEY ANTITERRORISTA. Lima: LUGACE, 1982.

457. Silva Ruete, Javier. YO ASUMI EL ACTIVO Y EL PASIVO DE LA REVOLUCION. Lima: Centro de Documentación e Información Andina, 1981. RGAF.

458. Solar, Francisco José del. EL MILITARISMO EN EL PERU. Caracas: Tipografía "Principios," 1976. RGAF.

459. Solís, Abelardo. ONCE ANOS. Lima: Sanmartí y Cía. Editores, 1934.

460. Soto León Velarde, Enrique. MITO Y VERDAD DE LA "REVOLUCION MILITAR": EL PERU EN LAS LINEAS DE LA MANO. Lima: Ediciones "Nueva Era," 1977. RGAF.

461. Souza, Herbet de. THE WORLD CAPITALIST SYSTEM AND MILITARISM IN LATIN AMERICA: A COMPARATIVE ANALYSIS OF THE BRAZILIAN AND PERUVIAN MODELS. Toronto: Brazilian Studies, 1974. RGAF.

462. Stafford, Joseph D., III. "The Bolivian Military in Politics." ANNALS OF THE SOUTHEASTERN CONFERENCE ON LATIN AMERICAN STUDIES (SECOLAS) 10 (1979): 81-94.

463. Stepan, Alfred. THE STATE AND SOCIETY: PERU IN COMPARATIVE PERSPECTIVE. Princeton: Princeton University Press, 1978. RGAF.

464. Stephens, Evelyne Huber. "The Peruvian Military Government, Labor Mobilization, and the Political Strength of the Left." LATIN AMERICAN RESEARCH REVIEW 18 (1983): 57-93. RGAF.

465. ———. THE POLITICS OF WORKERS' PARTICIPATION: THE PERUVIAN APPROACH IN COMPARATIVE PERSPECTIVE. New York: Academic Press, 1980. RGAF.

466. Taborga T., Alberto. BOQUERON: DIARIO DE CAMPANA; GUERRA DEL CHACO. La Paz: Editorial Canata, 1956.

467. Tantaleán Vanini, Javier. YO RESPONDO. Lima: Talleres de Manturano-Gonzáles, S.C.R., 1978. RGAF.

468. Tauro, Alberto. BIBLIOGRAFIA PERUANA DE HISTORIA, 1940-1953. Lima: n.p., 1953.

469. TePaske, John, ed. RESEARCH GUIDE TO ANDEAN HISTORY: BOLIVIA, CHILE, ECUADOR, AND PERU. Durham: Duke University Press, 1981.

470. Terán Gómez, Luis. "¿Qué debe hacer el Ecuador para librarse de las dictaduras?" AMERICA (Havana) 8 (1940): 27-29.

471. Thorndike, Guillermo. EL ANO DE LA BARBARIE: PERU, 1932. Lima: Editorial Nueva América, 1969.

472. ———. NO, MI GENERAL. Lima: Mosca Azul Editores, 1976. RGAF.

473. ———. LA REPUBLICA MILITAR: 1930-PERU-1980. Lima: Guillermo Thorndike Editor, 1979.

474. ———. LA REVOLUCION IMPOSIBLE. Lima: Enrique Miranda Iturrino Editor, 1988.

475. Thorp, Rosemary, and Geoffrey Bertram. PERU, 1890-1977: GROWTH AND POLICY IN AN OPEN ECONOMY. New York: Columbia University Press, 1978.

476. Toranzo, Carlos. "Obreros y militares en Bolivia: Un golpe frustrado." CUADERNOS POLITICOS 23 (1980): 98-113.

477. Toro Ruilova, David. INFORME PRESENTADO POR EL SENOR CORONEL PRESIDENTE DE LA JUNTA MILITAR SOCIALISTA DE GOBIERNO AL EJERCITO NACIONAL, DE 17 DE MAYO A 31 DE DICIEMBRE DE 1936. La Paz: Imprenta de la Intendencia General de Guerra, 1936.

478. ———. MI ACTUACION EN LA GUERRA DEL CHACO: LA RETIRADA DE PICUIBA. La Paz: Ed. "Renacimiento," 1941.

479. Torre, Carlos H. de la. "La Escuela Militar de Quito en los cien años de la República." In RESUMEN HISTORICO DEL ECUADOR, 1830-1930. Edited by J. Gonzalo Orellana. Quito: Editorial "Fray Jodoco Ricke," 1947-48.

480. Tovar, Teresa. VELASQUISMO Y MOVIMIENTO POPULAR: OTRA HISTORIA PROHIBIDA. Lima: DESCO, 1985. RGAF.

481. Trias, Vivian. PERU: FUERZAS ARMADAS Y REVOLUCION. Montevideo: Ediciones de la Banda Oriental, 1971. RGAF.

482. Tufano, Vincent J. "Civil-Military Relations and the Peruvian Coup d' Etat of 1914." CENTERPOINT 2 (1979): 54-59.

483. Tyson, Brady. "The Emerging Role of the Military as National Modernizers and Managers in Latin America: The Cases of Brazil and Peru." In LATIN AMERICAN PROSPECTS FOR THE 1970S, 107-30. Edited by David Pollock and Arch Ritter. New York: Praeger Publishers, 1973. RGAF.

484. Ugarteche, Pedro, ed. SANCHEZ CERRO: PAPELES Y RECUERDOS DE UN PRESIDENTE DEL PERU. 4 vols. Lima: Editorial Universitaria, 1969-70.

485. Urdanivia Ginés, José. UNA REVOLUCION MODELO: EJERCITO PERUANO. Lima: Editorial Castrillón Silva, 1954.

486. Ureta, Eloy G. APUNTES SOBRE UNA CAMPANA, 1941. Madrid: Editorial Antorcha, 1953.

487. Ureta, Mario. ELOY G. URETA: TRAYECTORIA DE UNA VIDA. Lima: Editorial Jurídica, 1973.

488. Urioste, Ovidio. LA ENCRUCIJADA: ESTUDIO HISTORICO, POLITICO, SOCIOLOGICO Y MILITAR DE LA GUERRA DEL CHACO. Cochabamba: Editorial Canelas, 1940.

489. Urriza, Manuel. PERU CUANDO LOS MILITARES SE VAN. Caracas: Ediciones CIDAL, 1978. RGAF.

490. Urrutia Suárez, Francisco. APUNTES PARA LA HISTORIA: LA AGRESION PERUANA. Quito: Editorial Ecuatoriana, 1968.

491. Valderrama, Mariano. 7 ANOS DE REFORMA AGRARIA PERUANA, 1969-1976. Lima: Pontificia Universidad Católica del Perú, 1976. RGAF.

492. Valdizán Gamio, José. HISTORIA NAVAL DEL PERU. 4 vols. Lima: Ministerio de Marina, 1980-87.

493. Varas, Augusto, and Fernando Bustamante. FUERZAS ARMADAS Y POLITICA EN ECUADOR. Quito: Ediciones Latinoamérica, 1978.

494. Varga Valenzuela, José. NACIONALISMO CON DESARROLLO Y SEGURIDAD: CON REFLEXIONES SOBRE ALGUNOS TEMAS DE ANALISIS EN LA ESCUELA DE ALTOS ESTUDIOS MILITARES. La Paz: Editorial Los Amigos del Libro, 1977.

495. Vargas Martínez, Germán. RESPONSABILIDAD, JUICIO, O SAINETE?: JUICIO DE RESPONSABILIDADES CONTRA AL GRAL. HUGO BANZER SUAREZ Y OTROS. La Paz: Ediciones "MOXOS," 1982.

496. Vargas Prada, Julio. DESTIERRO: CARTAS A LOS PERUANOS. Lima: Imprenta Editora Atlántida, 1976. RGAF.

497. Vargas Valenzuela, Oscar. LA VERDAD SOBRE LA MUERTE DEL GENERAL BARRIENTOS A LA LUZ DE INVESTIGACIONES POLICIALES, TECNICAS Y ESOTERICAS. La Paz: Editorial Los Amigos del Libro, 1983.

498. Vásquez Benavides, José F. ESCRITOS Y DISCURSOS. Lima: Imprenta del Ministerio de Guerra, 1950.

499. Vegas G., Manuel I. HISTORIA DE LA MARINA DE GUERRA DEL PERU, 1821-1924. Lima: Museo Naval del Peru, 1978.

500. Velasco, Ramiro. LA DEMOCRACIA SUBVERSIVA. Buenos Aires: Consejo Latinoamericano de Ciencias Sociales, 1985.

501. Velasco Alvarado, Juan. VELASCO: LA VOZ DE LA REVOLUCION; DISCURSOS DEL PRESIDENTE DE LA REPUBLICA, GENERAL DE DIVISION JUAN VELASCO

ALVARADO, 1968-1972. 2 vols. Lima: Ediciones Participación, 1972. RGAF.

502. Vergara Vicuña, Aquiles. HISTORIA DE LA GUERRA DEL CHACO. 7 vols. La Paz: Imprenta Unidas, 1940-44.

503. Villacrez Riquelme, Captain Eloy. NUESTRA GUERRA CIVIL: AYACUCHO 80.... Lima: Graphos 100 Editores, 1985.

504. Villanueva, Víctor. UN ANO BAJO EL SABLE. Lima: Empresa Gráfica T. Scheuch, 1963.

505. ———. EL APRA EN BUSCA DEL PODER, 1930-1940. Lima: Editorial Horizonte, 1975.

506. ———. EL APRA Y EL EJERCITO, 1940-1950. Lima: Editorial Horizonte, 1977.

507. ———. ASI CAYO LEGUIA. Lima: Retama Editorial, 1977.

508. ———. EL CAEM Y LA REVOLUCION DE LA FUERZA ARMADA. Lima: Instituto de Estudios Peruanos, 1972. RGAF.

509. ———. CIEN ANOS DEL EJERCITO PERUANO: FRUSTRACIONES Y CAMBIOS. Lima: Librería Editorial Juan Mejía Baca, 1972.

510. ———. EJERCITO PERUANO: DEL CAUDILLAJE ANARQUICO AL MILITARISMO REFORMISTA. Lima: Librería Editorial Juan Mejía Baca, 1973.

511. ———. GOLPE EN EL PERU. Montevideo: Sandino, 1969.

512. ———. HUGO BLANCO Y LA REBELION CAMPESINA. Lima: Librería Editorial Juan Mejía Baca, 1967.

513. ———. MANUAL DEL CONSPIRADOR. Lima: Empresa Gráfica T. Scheuch, 1963.

514. ———. EL MILITARISMO EN EL PERU. Lima: Empresa Gráfica T. Scheuch, 1962.

515. ———. ¿NUEVA MENTALIDAD MILITAR EN EL PERU? 2d ed. Lima: Librería Editorial Juan Mejía Baca, 1969.

516. ———. LA TRAGEDIA DE UN PUEBLO Y UN PARTIDO: PAGINAS PARA LA HISTORIA DEL APRA. 2d ed. Lima: Talleres Gráficos "Victory," 1956.

517. Viteri, Telmo. "Legislación militar ecuatoriana: Su orígen, desarrollo y evolución." EL EJERCITO NACIONAL 3 (1924): 561-92.

518. Von Behring, Major. "Evolución cultural de nuestro ejército." REVISTA MILITAR DE LAS FUERZAS ARMADAS ECUATORIANAS 2 (1934).

519. Vorozhéikina, Tatiana. "Los militares en el poder: Experiencia peruana." AMERICA LATINA (Moscow) 4 (1978): 53-70. RGAF.

520. Waggener, John G. "Army Civic Action in Southeastern Peru: The Tambopata Valley and the Sandía-Tambopata Highway." ANDEAN AIR MAIL AND PERUVIAN TIMES, 5 March 1965 and 2 April 1965.

521. Washington Office on Latin America. PERU IN PERIL: THE ECONOMY AND HUMAN RIGHTS, 1985-1987. Washington: Washington Office on Latin America, 1987.

522. Webb, Richard Charles. GOVERNMENT POLICY AND DISTRIBUTION OF INCOME IN PERU, 1963-1973. Cambridge: Harvard University Press, 1977.

523. Weil, Thomas E., et al. AREA HANDBOOK FOR BOLIVIA. Washington: U.S. Government Printing Office, 1974.

524. ———. AREA HANDBOOK FOR ECUADOR. Washington: U.S. Government Printing Office, 1973.

525. Werlich, David P. PERU: A SHORT HISTORY. Carbondale: Southern Illinois University Press, 1978.

526. ———. "Peru: The Lame-duck 'Revolution.'" CURRENT HISTORY 76 (1979): 62-65. RGAF.

527. Whitehead, Laurence. "Banzer's Bolivia." CURRENT HISTORY 70 (1976): 61-64, 81.

528. Wilde Cavero, Manuel Fernando. HISTORIA MILITAR DE BOLIVIA. La Paz: n.p., 1963.

529. Wood, Bryce. THE UNITED STATES AND LATIN AMERICAN WARS, 1932-1942. New York: Columbia University Press, 1966.

530. Zapata Cesti, Víctor Armando. HISTORIA DE LA POLICIA DEL PERU: PRE-INCANTO, INCANTO, CONQUISTA, VIRREINATO, REPUBLICA. Lima: n.p., 1949.

531. Zimmermann Zavala, Augusto. CAMINO AL SOCIALISMO. Lima: Empresa Editora Humboldt, 1976. RGAF.

532. ———. EL PLAN INCA: OBJECTIVO; REVOLUCION PERUANA. Barcelona: Ediciones Grijalba, 1975. RGAF.

533. ———. LOS ULTIMOS DIAS DEL GENERAL VELASCO: ¿QUIEN RECOGE LA BANDERA? Lima: Empresa Editora Humboldt, 1978. RGAF.

534. Zook, David H., Jr. THE CONDUCT OF THE CHACO WAR. New York: Bookman Associates, 1960.

535. ———. ZARUMILLA-MARANON: THE ECUADOR-PERU DISPUTE. New York: Bookman Associates, 1964.

536. Zutter, Pierre de. CAMPESINADO Y REVOLUCION. Lima: Instituto Nacional de Cultura, 1975. RGAF.

PERIODICALS

Bolivia

537. MENSAJERO AERONAUTICO.

538. REVISTA AEREA MILITAR. 1950s-.

539. REVISTA MILITAR. 1885-.

Ecuador

540. REVISTA DE LA FUERZA AEREA ECUATORIANA.

541. REVISTA MILITAR DE LAS FUERZAS ARMADAS ECUATORIANAS. 1939-.

Peru

542. ACTUALIDAD MILITAR, 1962-.

543. AVIACION: REVISTA DE LA FUERZA AEREA DEL PERU. 1936-.

544. GACETA PRE MILITAR.

545. GUARDIA REPUBLICANA DEL PERU, 1961-.

546. REVISTA DE LA ESCUELA MILITAR DE CHORRILLOS. 1920s-.

547. REVISTA DE LA ESCUELA SUPERIOR DE GUERRA. 1953-.

548. REVISTA DE LA GUARDIA CIVIL DEL PERU. 1930s-.

549. REVISTA DE LA SANIDAD MILITAR DEL PERU. 1926-.

550. REVISTA DE MARINA. 1915-.

551. REVISTA DE POLICIA TECNICA.

552. REVISTA DE SANIDAD DE POLICIA.

553. REVISTA DEL CADETE.

554. REVISTA DEL CENTRO DE ESTUDIOS HISTORICO-MILITARES DEL PERU. 1948-.

555. REVISTA DEL CENTRO DE INSTRUCCION MILITAR DEL PERU. 1950s-.

556. REVISTA MILITAR DEL PERU. 1919-.

557. REVISTA PARA SUBOFICIALES Y CLASES. 1935-.

558. REVISTA POLICIAL DEL PERU.

559. TIRO NACIONAL DEL PERU.

CHAPTER VII

BRAZIL

Errol D. Jones
Boise State University

INTRODUCTION

On 15 March 1990 Brazilians inaugurated Fernando Collor de Mello their first popularly elected president since the military took over the country's government twenty-six years earlier. This important event closed another chapter in the long history of military intervention into the political rule of this nation of 145 million people. The history of the military in Brazil begins with the Portuguese conquest and colonization of that vast land. During the colonial experiment the armed forces were composed of officers and troops drawn mainly from the Iberian Peninsula, although colonials also held commissions. Early on, powerful landholders were made responsible for their own defense of life and property leading to the creation of private "armies." Some of these armies became quite large, especially if the land baron was also a slave-hunter. Theoretically, the crown controlled these forces and called upon them to defend the king's interests. In reality, the landlords commanded these private armies and used them to promote their own interests.

Independence from Portugal came to Brazil in 1822 without a protracted military struggle. This rather peaceful transition enabled the new nation to win its freedom comparatively free of a generation of military heroes and an aggressive martial spirit, unlike many of its Latin American neighbors. King Pedro I inherited and maintained a military organization composed primarily of Portuguese troops and officers guaranteed to arouse the jealousy and hostility of Brazilian officers. Such feelings toward the Portuguese military forces increased among the oligarchy when Pedro used them to disperse the legislature in

342

November 1823. The oligarchy became even more disaffected from the monarchy when Pedro intervened in the La Plata region (1825-28) using German and Irish mercenaries when Brazilians refused to serve under Portuguese officers. Brazil lost the war; Pedro abdicated to his five-year-old son and sailed away to Portugal.

An eleven-year regency followed which ruled in the name of the future Pedro II. It was a time of extreme agitation. Violent rebellions in several provinces threatened to divide the nation into numerous regional entities controlled by the private armies inherited from the colonial period. Furthermore, troops in revolt attempted to gain control of the government, while many of them followed their officers as they deserted to the regional revolutionaries. Powerful land barons with their private armed forces threatened the Regency as it countered with the creation of municipal militias controlled by the central government. The threat to national integrity only subsided when the regents declared Pedro's majority and the new king was able to win the loyalty of the army and the navy in putting down the last serious rebellion in 1845.

In the La Plata estuary Spain and Portugal had fought bitterly throughout the colonial era for dominance. With independence the struggle for control continued, pitting Brazil against Argentina. Brazilian military forces marched into Uruguay in 1851 backing local forces opposed to earlier Argentine intervention. Brazilian troops then joined Uruguayans and dissident Argentines to oust Juan Manuel de Rosas in 1852 who ruled Argentina from Buenos Aires.

Peace was shortlived in the area. In 1864 war erupted between Paraguay and Brazil and eventually involved Argentina and Uruguay as well in what came to be called the War of the Triple Alliance (1864-70). An important result of this conflict was the emergence of a new national military institution which soon came to play a significant role in shaping the political course of the nation. Always weak and inconsequential (it was not until a decree of 1839 that the army was systematically organized), the army numbered only 17,000 troops when the conflict with Paraguay broke out. At war's end that number had swelled to 100,000, and the army had borne the principal burden in the fighting against Paraguay.

Restless with the peace that had returned to South America after 1870 and annoyed by the lack of attention and rewards granted them by the monarchy, members of the officer class publicly entered the political arena in the 1880s. Encouraged by disaffected civilians and imbued with a spirit of republicanism, the military revolted against the monarchy in 1889 and sent an ailing King Pedro II into permanent exile.

Transition from monarchy to military rule to federal republic presided over by military men went smoothly and without violence or bloodshed, but peace was not to last for long. A naval revolt in 1893, joined by southern federalists, sought to overthrow the government of Marshal Floriano Peixoto. Nevertheless, the republic survived and an elected civilian administration took office in 1894. Civilians retained control of the executive branch of government until 1910. But civilian-military tensions persisted. The military had entered politics, an arena considered the privileged reserve of the civilian oligarchy. Through that experience the armed forces came to regard political power as an instrument that they too could wield for the promotion of their own institutional interests.

During the last decade of the nineteenth century coffee production rose spectacularly thus concentrating more and more economic power in the coffee growing regions of São Paulo, Rio de Janeiro, and Minas Gerais. With economic strength came political power. This new coffee elite carried out programs favoring its financial and regional interests. Economic progress and political stability characterized, with few exceptions, the heyday of the Old Republic.

One of those exceptions was the restlessness of the military during the Old Republic. In the presidential election of 1910 General Hermes da Fonseca, backed by young officers and civilian politicians from Minas Gerais and Rio Grande do Sul, clashed with Ruy Barbosa, the famous statesman and jurist from Bahia who had the support of his home state and that of São Paulo. Ruy quickly turned the campaign into a struggle against the military. His anti-military language was so intemperate and vitriolic that it alienated completely the armed forces and drove those officers who had opposed the candidacy of Hermes back into his camp. Hermes won the election and ruled until 1914 at which time the government was returned to the civilians; they maintained control until a military-civilian revolt ended the Old Republic in 1930.

The first quarter of the twentieth century was a period of intense ferment and institutional change for the Brazilian military. Ineffectiveness in handling the Canudos rebellion resulted in the total destruction of that backlands redoubt in 1897, and a similar encounter with "backlanders" in the Contestado (1912-15) embarrassed and discredited the army. Politicians utilized the armed forces for their own narrow, personal ends in Amazonas while several naval mutinies called attention to the terrible conditions in that branch of the armed services. This was also a period of growing militarism as Brazil and the rest of the world geared up for war in 1914. World War I caused the Brazilian military elite great consternation. As a key element in their drive to transform the army into a truly professional organization, aggressive officers had persuaded the government to arrange for a German military mission to train the Brazilian officer corps. As the conflict dragged on, civilian and government sympathy for the Allied cause grew. When German submarines began to attack Brazilian merchant ships the government declared war. While Brazil's participation in the conflict was primarily limited to furnishing supplies to the Allies, military leaders feared that confrontation with the enemy would spell disaster for a woefully unprepared army. As a result, they demanded that the government continue with the program of military professionalization, this time under the tutelage of a French mission.

The decade of the 1920s witnessed extraordinary changes in Brazil as elsewhere in Latin America. Accelerating industrialization, urbanization, and modernization stimulated a rich intellectual fermentation which produced an increasing nationalism and militarism. This process also created a fundamental problem; as Brazil underwent profound socio-economic change the political structure and those who benefited from it remained the same. Intellectuals, both within the military and outside it, became deeply involved in politics during the 1920s and thereafter. Divided internally, armed forces factions had participated in the political arena since the 1880s. Ironically, as the military became more professional, its political interventions grew in number. These professionals voiced their displeasure with the Old Republic and pointed out its faults: corruption, fraud, narrowly based political control, independently controlled state militias, appointment of civilians to the ministries of war and navy, and the general belief that Brazil was socially and economically backward. Some junior and middle-grade officers placed the blame squarely on the civilian controlled political system. For them, the Old Republic had to end. When the presidential elections did not go their way in 1922, a group of young lieutenants (*tenentes*) revolted in a vain attempt to overthrow the government. Like the society from whence it sprang, however, the Brazilian army lacked cohesion, and without the support of the senior officer corps the revolt was quickly quelled. While insignificant as an isolated incident, the *tenente* movement reflected a growing general dissatisfaction with the Republic, especially among young army officers. But *tenentismo* was more complex than just a rebellion of young, disaffected army officers. It represented both civilian and military discontent with the status quo symbolized by the political system of the Old Republic.

It took an international economic crisis and serious political errors on the part of the coffee oligarchy to touch off the revolution of 1930 which destroyed the Old Republic. Young military officers joined a coalition of politicians from Minas Gerais, Rio Grande do Sul, Paraíba, urban middle sectors, and assorted nationalists and intellectuals to form the Liberal Alliance. Led by *tenentes* of the earlier military revolts and with widespread civilian support even among the coffee elite of São Paulo, the rebels moved against the government of Washington Lúis. As unit after unit of the army adhered to their cause even the senior officers abandoned the regime.   They seized power on 24 October, established a junta of three officers, and less than two weeks later turned the presidency over to the civilian presidential candidate of the Liberal Alliance, Getúlio Vargas from Rio Grande do Sul. The armed forces had intervened in politics again, this time to destroy the Old Republic, just as they had intervened over forty years before to create it.

For almost a quarter century Getúlio Vargas wielded power in Brazil. But he did not do so alone. "The revolution of 1930," according to John J. Johnson (525), "propelled the armed forces into the center of Brazilian politics and the locus of power has resided in them ever since."   Strongly approving of the nationalistic authoritarianism of Vargas's Estado Nôvo, the professional army officer class joined forces with Vargas and served as his main political prop.   In return he appointed them to adminstrative posts and gave them a greater share of the national budget than ever before. The army almost doubled in size from 1920 to 1940, and by reducing the state militias to routine operations under the authority of the federal army, Vargas removed an old military fear of competitive state armed forces controlled by powerful political bosses.

With the outbreak of World War II, some of the officers close to Vargas hoped Brazil would align itself with the fascist powers. Vargas, however, took the country into the war on the side of the Western Alliance and committed Brazilian troops to the invasion of Italy. At war's end the military emerged with enormous prestige, and those officers with pro-United States and Western style democratic tendencies acquired the greatest power. United States influence grew considerably in military circles as it did in other areas of the society.

The two decades after the war (1945-64) were not years of order and progress. It was an era of political chaos, military intervention, confusion, and crisis. At the same time it was a period in which the armed forces' influence in the public sector grew enormously, with individual officers holding a wide array of elective and appointive positions at the federal, state, and municipal levels. Ex-armed forces officers, like their counterparts in the United States, entered the private sector and contributed to it with their superior education, administrative experience, and organizational skills.

The post-war Brazilian economy grew rapidly, even phenomenally. From 1947 to 1961 the Gross National Product increased at an impressive rate of over six and a half percent. Governments, especially that of Jucelino Kubitschek (1956-61), spent lavishly to build an infrastructure that would keep pace with the rapid industrialization process. Billions of *cruzeiros* poured from the printing presses fueling an inflationary trend that was further encouraged by the high investment rates, increasing wages, and mounting government deficits. Foreign capital flowed into the country in unprecedented amounts with the United States the single largest investor, accounting for about half the total foreign investment of over three billion dollars.

Economic nationalists, some of whom were high ranking military officers, argued that foreign capital was harmful to Brazil's security and should be curtailed, especially in primary industries and natural resources. Owing to the growing influence of North American capital, nationalists urged breaking economic ties with the United States and increasing trade with socialist countries. A political and economic crisis in 1954 compelled certain military officers to exert pressure on democratically-elected President Getúlio Vargas to resign. Rather than accede to their demands, Vargas took his own life and became a martyr for the nationalists and those who stood to the left of the political center.

In 1964, another political and economic crisis confronted the nation, and again certain members of the military hierarchy joined civilian opponents to the government to remove the president. João Goulart, a protege of Getúlio Vargas, assumed the presidency with the resignation of Jânio Quadros in 1961. As Vargas's Minister of Labor Goulart had made so many enemies among industrialists, military leaders, and the landed elite that Vargas was forced to remove him. Failing to block his succession to the presidency when Quadros resigned, some generals and their civilian allies succeeded in persuading congress to create a parliamentary system which severely limited presidential powers. In 1963, however, a national plebiscite terminated the parliamentary system.

Goulart's radical left, nationalistic solutions to Brazil's growing economic problems worried the more conservative elements of society. Many military and civilian leaders had graduated from the Escola Superior de Guerra, modeled on the United States National War College, which imbued its students with a strong anti-communist viewpoint. Reacting negatively to the Cuban Revolution and its implications for Latin America, they feared the growing militancy of Brazil's labor unions, peasant leagues, student organizations, and groups of clergy and intellectuals, and believed that Goulart was attempting to impose a socialistic state. When the president urged enlisted men to unionize, many officers saw this as a direct threat to the military institution itself. On 1 April 1964, telling the nation that they were saving it from civil war, the military, urged on by their civilian allies, revolted against "Jango" Goulart, and he went off to exile.

With Goulart gone and his supporters silenced through imprisonment or execution, civilian political leaders expected military officers to take their troops back to the barracks and turn power over to them, as they always had done in the past. But, as Leonardo Trevisan (965), wrote, when anti-Goulart civilians "woke up things were otherwise, there was another equation of power, a different 'natural order of things.'" As a concession to modern democratic institutions the Brazilian national legislature "would continue to function almost as by tradition, almost as the price to pay for [Brazil's] European heritage. As to power, this would be directly exercised by the military." This time the military did not go back to the *cuarteis*. A widespread belief among the officer corps held that continued civilian rule imperiled the military as an institution as well as threatened the nation's security. Therefore, armed forces leaders decided to rule the country themselves. General Artur da Costa e Silva seemed to express the view of those who seized power when he stated "I'm tired of seeing Brazilian revolutions wasted by politics" (483).

Army chief of staff General Humberto de Alencar Castello Branco assumed the presidency in 1964. Son of an army officer from the northeastern state of Ceará, Castello Branco represented that faction of the army known as the Sorbonne group of officers who were closely associated with the Escola Superior de Guerra. Known as the "softline," or moderates, this group was anti-communist, pro-free enterprise, pro-United States, authoritarian, and committed to the democratic idea, once they had set things straight through forceful, arbitrary control. These officers struggled with the "hardliners" who eventually came to power when General Costa e Silva took the presidency in March 1967. Much more militant in their nationalism, the hardliners had few ties to the United States and were intolerant of civilian politicians, a free press, academic freedom, and criticism of the military institution. Reverting to the arbitrary rule of the first months after the 1964 coup, Costa e Silva closed congress, centralized more and more power in the presidency, and stripped numerous Brazilians of their political rights. An incapacitating stroke removed Costa e Silva from the presidency in 1969, but another hardliner, General Emílio Garrastazú Médici, took his place. Médici moved Brazil farther to the right, unleashing a campaign of torture and state terrorism against the regime's enemies. Attempting to realize a long-held dream of national economic development and integration, the hardliners established state directed mega-projects for the purpose of creating an all-embracing infrastructure.

By 1974 the Castelistas (so named because they had been close to Castello Branco and favored the softline position) had fought their way back into power and placed General Ernesto Geisel in the presidency.

With Geisel came the *distensão*, or the lessening of tension, and a relaxation of the dictatorial aspect of the regime. The Geisel administration allowed for greater civilian participation within the political structure in response to the congressional elections of 1974 in which the opposition Movimento Democrático Brasileiro (MDB) candidates had won significant victories. Nevertheless, the military retained control of the presidency and another softliner, General João Batista de Oliveira Figueiredo, took command in 1979, despite intense opposition from both the MDB and military factions.

Figueiredo presided over the cautious transition to civilian political power and in 1985, for the first time in almost twenty years, the electoral college chose a civilian politician, Tancredo Neves, to be the next president. Before he could assume power, however, Neves died and his vice president, José Sarney, stepped into the presidency. While not popularly elected, it was clear that the Sarney administration would be the last in this transitional period not chosen by the Brazilian electorate as a whole. Before relinquishing power to civilian politicians, the military command made certain that civilians would not seek retribution against them for violation of human rights, as had occurred in Argentina when the military withdrew from power. It also appears that a tacit understanding was reached that the armed forces would return to the old moderating role they had exercised up to the coup of 1964.

It is now quite clear that the armed forces failed to accomplish the "military project" they had set out to establish in 1964. The officers had hoped to transform Brazil into a modern, industrial state organized along the same value system that governed the military: honesty, patriotism, moral rectitude, abstinence, hard work, physical fitness, strength of character, courage, and so on. Instead they found themselves unable to cope with the economic problems of the late 1970s and early 1980s; as a result they faced rebellion within the ranks of their own institution and within the political party they had created. In addition, corruption, violation of human rights, patronage politics, ecological destruction on a massive scale, and failure of the National Integration Program plagued military rule. It had become apparent by 1984 that the vices of the civilian political system had transformed the armed services. It was hard to tell a military politician from a civilian one. To protect the institution from increasing factionalism and to maintain its integrity, military leaders saw the wisdom of going back to their barracks. Just how long they will stay there only the future can tell.

This essay will concentrate on the bibliography dealing with the Brazilian armed forces from the time it helped overthrow the monarchy in 1889, to the present. Readers interested in colonial and nineteenth-century military history are encouraged to consult the two chapters in this book by Mark Burkholder and G.P.C. Thomson, respectively.

GENERAL WORKS

Since the military has been inextricably woven into the fabric of Brazilian history from the fall of the monarchy in 1889, historians striving for an understanding of the institution's history are urged to become acquainted with the broader sweep of the nation's past. There are a number of general histories that deal with the military establishment as it has interacted with and been affected by other institutions and events. E. Bradford Burns, A HISTORY OF BRAZIL (200), is an excellent place to start, and it also provides the reader with a good annotated bibliography. The same can be said of Rollie Poppino's work (783), while Nyrop's BRAZIL: A COUNTRY STUDY (730), places the military in historical context and has a separate chapter on the national security apparatus.

Numerous Brazilians have written general histories of their country, some of which appeared in English such as José Maria Bello's A HISTORY OF MODERN BRAZIL, 1889-1964 (93), with the concluding chapter, 1954 to 1964, written by Rollie Poppino. Unfortunately, it concentrates on the period 1889-1930, is difficult to read and digest, and there is no bibliography. Leôncio Basbaum's four-volume HISTORIA SINCERA DA REPUBLICA (87), provided a critical examination of the past from colonial times to the late 1960s. An impressive, multivolume, interdisciplinary work that examines politics, economics, society, the military, political elites and international relations, among other topics, is José Honório Rodrigues's five-volume INDEPENDENCIA, REVOLUCAO E CONTRA-REVOLUCAO (811). Celso Furtado (427), presented a valuable survey of economic history. Peter Flynn (401), produced a fine overview of the nation's political history. Other useful general studies are the works by Hélio Vianna (990), Lacombe (553), Aspasia Alcantara de Camargo (214), and Rodrigues's challenging, nationalistic THE BRAZILIANS: THEIR CHARACTER AND ASPIRATIONS (809). Finally, the appropriate chapters on Brazil from THE CAMBRIDGE HISTORY OF LATIN AMERICA (102), can be profitably utilized.

In the 1950s and 1960s a group of radical left, nationalists came forth to write systematic analyses of the period 1889 to 1945. See especially the works of Nelson Werneck Sodré (914), Basbaum (87), and Edgard Carone (238, 239, 240, 241). Representing the "dependency" model of social science research Theotonio Dos Santos (341), wrote a concise, interpretive overview which merits consideration, as does Sodré's BRASIL: RADIOGRAFIA DE UM MODELO (912).

General studies dealing specifically with the military institution can be divided into two catagories: references that treat the contemporary military and histories analyzing the armed forces over time.

For a basic understanding of the current Brazilian military institution (its position in government and society, its constitutional basis, and its personnel, administration, organization, training, equipment, and weapons), the following works should be consulted: Michael Brown (190), John Labayle Couhat (309), Trevor Dupuy, et al. (359), Gwynne Dyer (362), Adrian English (368), Kenneth Freed (415), Roy Ingleton (514), Eugene Keefe (531), John Keegan (532), Max Manwaring (641), John Moore (687), Eul Soo Pang (745), Eduardo Italo Pesce (768), the annually published STATISTICAL ABSTRACT OF LATIN AMERICA (1088), John Taylor (953), and John Hoyt Williams (1012).

Few scholars of the armed forces have written historical syntheses covering the period since the fall of the Empire. Most, instead, have concentrated on a single branch of the military establishment or on specific events, wars, or time periods. Works done prior to the 1940s have been, for the most part, uncritical and conceptually unsophisticated. With the emergence of formally organized universities in the 1930s, Brazil acquired the institutional structure for developing professional historians. See Skidmore's (892, 893), historiography. Nevertheless, there are a few general histories which are quite well done and can be useful to the researcher.

One of the first studies done in English on the Latin American military and which in that context provides interesting observations on Brazil is Edwin Lieuwen's ARMS AND POLITICS IN LATIN AMERICA (582). Written with the objective of influencing policy, Lieuwen argued against United States support of Latin American militaries. Another general study of the topic, but which contained chapters recounting the evolution of Brazil's armed forces, is John J. Johnson's insightful work (525). Johnson contrasted the historical role of the Brazilian military with that of other Latin American militaries and brought his account forward to the eve of the 1964 coup. The noted Brazilian sociologist, Gilberto Freyre in his NACAO E EXERCITO (420), recounted the role of the armed forces in the country's major events and praised them for their organizational abilities. Theodorico Lopes and Gentil Torres (595), biographically surveyed all of the ministers of war from 1808 to 1950.

A good place to start for an overview of the military's political role in Brazilian history is with João Batista Magalhães's work (626). Carlos Maul (655), gave much attention to the evolution of the institution in Brazil's development of nationalism. More critical treatments of the military's political role can be found in the Marxist historian Nelson

Werneck Sodré's work (915), which covers the colonial era to the *golpe* of 1964. Leonardo Trevisan (965), rendered a more concise political treatment covering the same chronology. A first-class, terse study with solid information and a penetrating analysis is Edmundo Campos Coelho's (285), work. Alexandre de Souza Costa Barros's (83), dissertation is an extremely important work for its systematic and comprehensive analysis of the armed forces as a factor in Brazilian political society. Grappling with what he calls the "military corporate mystique," Robert Hayes (483), surveyed the development of the idea, from colonial times to the mid-1980s, that the armed forces played a special role of savior of the Brazilian nation in times of crisis and need. Other helpful general sources are Bahiana (71), Carneiro (233), Costa (307), Fagundes (376), and Tavares (945).

General histories on the navy are growing in number and quality. Flores's (400), highly informative work on Brazilian naval power included data on port facilities, merchant marine, geography, security considerations, etc. Vidigal (995), traced the evolution of thought on naval strategy. A superbly illustrated work with excellent maps is the narrative history published by the Ministério da Marinha (179). Scavarda (850), sketched the history of the Naval Council from colonial times to the 1960s. Scheina (851), included material on the Brazilian navy in his general history of Latin American navies, and Ferreira (387), regarded the Brazilian navy as an emerging sea power.

A basic starting point for the history of the Brazilian air force, although poorly organized and uncritical, is Lavenère-Wanderly's (564), book. See as well his article on Brazilian thought regarding aerospace strategy (565). Bento (100), published a study of the military academy at Agulhas Negras, and the Brazilian army (163), published a general history of its quartermaster corps.

BIBLIOGRAPHIES

While there are few bibliographies that deal exclusively with the Brazilian military, there are numerous other bibliographic aids for Latin America and Brazil which are rich in material on the history of the armed forces in the country.

One should start with the standard bibliography of bibliographies of Latin America, Arthur Gropp's (460), 1971 volume which covered the period 1965-69. He also compiled a bibliography of Latin American bibliographies published in periodicals which included works through 1965 (461). Daniel Cordeiro, et al. (295), and Haydee Piedracueva (771), both produced bibliographies of Latin American bibiliographies for the social sciences and humanities. Exclusively for Brazil, see Bruno Basseches (88).

For anything published on Brazil one should consult the HANDBOOK OF LATIN AMERICAN STUDIES (478), which remains the best single general source for articles, books, and collections of documents. The HISPANIC AMERICAN PERIODICALS INDEX (HAPI) (504), is essential for articles only. A complilation of the Latin American holdings of the Library of Congress and the University of Texas can be found in the BIBLIOGRAPHIC GUIDE TO LATIN AMERICAN STUDIES (107). There is also a guide to Latin American materials in the United States National Archives (970). Robert Delorme compiled three volumes of bibliographies on the social sciences relating to Latin America (326,327,328). The last volume included works through 1987. Older, but still useful, bibliographic aids are Griffin and Warren (459), Humphreys (512), and Wilgus (1011). Since 1951, the REVISTA INTERAMERICANA DE BIBLIOGRAFIA/INTER-AMERICAN REVIEW OF BIBLIOGRAPHY (1083), has included bibliographic essays and lists of recently published articles, research in progress, completed doctoral dissertations, and publications of the United States Congress about Latin America. Quite often, the LATIN AMERICAN RESEARCH REVIEW (1060), will contain bibliographic essays on the Latin American military in general or on the armed services in Brazil specifically; see for example McAlister (606). Ronald Chilcote (277), organized a two-volume, 10,000-item, unannotated listing of materials un revolution and structural change in Latin America for the years 1930-65. For an annotated bibliography of Latin American military journals as of 1965, see Einaudi and Goldhamer (363). Herbert Gooch (447), provided an excellent bibliography on the political activity of the Latin American armed forces in general, with a specific section on Brazil. Cortés Conde's and Stein's LATIN AMERICA: A GUIDE TO ECONOMIC HISTORY, 1830-1930 (301), identified Brazilian economic history studies that contain materials relevant to the military.

Dissertations written on the Brazilian military in the United States can be found in DISSERTATION ABSTRACTS INTERNATIONAL (339). University Microfilms International also produced a dissertation bibliography specifically on the Caribbean and Latin America edited by Carl Deal (321). Two supplements have been printed, one in 1980 edited by Marian Walters (998), and another in 1984 (974). Carlos Humberto Correa provided researchers an invaluable service with his CATALOGO DAS DISSERTACOES E TESES DOS CURSOS DE POS-GRADUACAO EM HISTORIA, 1973-1985 (297). For the United States student of the Brazilian military who is unable to travel to Brazil, William Jackson prepared a LIBRARY GUIDE FOR BRAZILIAN STUDIES (519), which contains brief descriptions of the major United States library holdings of Braziliana. More recently,

Jackson (518), compiled a complete listing of publications on and from Brazil acquired and cataloged by the Library of Congress from 1964 to 1974. A more current, but general bibliography of Brazilian literature dealing with the humanities and the social sciences is that of Harmon and Chamberlain (481).

A number of valuable bibliographies and historiographical essays exist which are essential for finding works on or relating to the military in Brazilian history. Robert M. Levine's HISTORICAL DICTIONARY OF BRAZIL (578), contains extensive material on Brazilian terms, events, famous people, as well as a lengthy list of mostly English language works on the country. The periodical BOLETIM INFORMATIVO E BIBLIOGRAFICO CIENCIAS SOCIAIS (1037), publishes bibliographic essays on social science topics of interest to the student of Brazilian military history. An annual guide to the literature in the social sciences is published (since 1954) by the Instituto Brasileiro de Bibliografia e Documentação (1029). For materials prior to that time, Morães and Berrien (694), can still be useful, and Morães (693), has been updated in a two-volume edition published by the UCLA Latin American Center in conjunction with Livraria Kosmos in Rio de Janeiro. See also Sobrinho (911), and Blake (118). Sodré (918), covered the entire sweep of Brazilian history and has a short, annotated chapter on the military. Robert Levine compiled an annotated bibliography for social historians, the first volume of which covers the period 1822-1930 (576), and the second, since 1930 (577). E. Bradford Burns (202), provided a useful "working" bibliography of studies on Brazilian history in English. Stein (927), offered an analysis of sources on the Empire, Skidmore (892, 893), evaluated significant historiographical trends from 1889 to 1964, and Rodrigues (808), critically examined modern trends in Brazilian historiography, as did three more recent contributors: José Roberto do Amaral Lapa (563), Carlos Guilherme Mota (703), and Hélio Vianna (990). For government publications by ministry see Lombardi (593).

Several more specialized bibiliographic guides exist. They deal with periods during which the military played an active role in the political life of the nation or they treat topics that are related to military history. In his BRASIL: PERIODO NACIONAL, Américo Jacobina Lacombe (552), made invaluable bibliographical suggestions for studying the period between the fall of the Monarchy in 1889 and the end of World War II. Angela Pôrto, et al. (786), annotated over 2000 entries on the economic and social processes of modernization in Brazil from 1850 to 1930. Fausto (382), examined the literature of the Revolution of 1930, and Leite (570), did the same for the Paulista revolt of 1932. A 1981 study by Medeiros and Hirst (657), for the period 1930-45, lists 1337 books, articles, published memoirs, and documentary collections. The

Instituto Brasileiro de Geografia e Estatística (424), published a two-volume guide to its publications from the time of its establishment in 1936 to the mid-1980s. For the coup of 1964 Amaury de Souza (921), published an annotated bibliography. An essential bibliographical and biographical resource is the recent four-volume DICIONARIO HISTORICO-BIOGRAFICO BRASILEIRO, 1930-1983 (94). It contains almost 4500 entries of which 3741 are biographies of individuals influential mainly at the national level. This is a standard reference work for modern Brazilian history. For a bibliography on the radical left from 1922 to 1972, see Ronald Chilcote (275). Workers and labor unions have attracted the attention of numerous historians, and Leôncio Martins Rodrigues and Fabio Munhoz (814), have surveyed the literature to 1973. There is an extensive body of material on the last Vargas presidency in Medeiros and D'Araujo (658). One can find works by and about civilian and military political thinkers from 1870 to 1970 in Mendes (666). The Trask, Meyer, and Trask (963), volume, supplemented by Meyer (673), is an important bibliography for United States-Latin American relations.

After the military took power in 1964, historians began intensively studying the institution, but prior to the 1960s the military attracted enough attention to warrant a couple of bibliographies. For a useful guide published in 1960, see Franciso Ruas Santos, COLECAO BIBLIOGRAFICA MILITAR (843). Santos (844), also compiled a complete bibliography, to 1957, on the Brazilian Expeditionary Force (FEB) which fought in Italy during World War II. So much attention has been paid to the *tenentes* movement of the the 1920s that it has merited a fairly recent bibliography by Paulo Cesar Farah (378), while Boris Fausto (382), surveyed the historiography of the Revolution of 1930. A recent article by Edmundo Campos Coelho (286), provides a historiographical review of research on the Brazilian military. A selective, annotated bibliography on human rights in Latin America from 1964 to 1980 was compiled by the Hispanic Division of the Library of Congress (510), and contains a chapter on Brazil. For a guide to speeches, documents, articles, and books on the *abertura*, see Figueiredo and Cheibub (398). While most studies on the military and politics in Brazil contain guides to the sources, none quite compare with the annotated bibliographies that Thomas Skidmore (896, 897), included in his two books on this topic. The "notes" sections in each of these two monographs number close to one-hundred pages of references. E. Bradford Burns (200), Peter Flynn (401), June Hahner (472), Nelson Werneck Sodré (915), and Alfred Stepan (929, 931), included excellent notes and bibliographies on their respective military topics. Bartley (86), looked at Soviet scholarship for the decade 1958-68, and Le Doare

(569), examined the bibliography of frontier conflicts in the Southern Cone.

ARCHIVAL GUIDES AND SOURCES

Gaining access to materials on the military in an open society is oftentimes a frustrating and always a challenging task given the national security nature of the institution. In authoritarian countries this problem is compounded and in some instances becomes almost impossible. Even for the gathering of public information, to which the society at large has access, censorship and repression have distorted the record. This is especially the case when the military assumes direct political power and holds it as the Brazilian armed forces did from 1964 to 1985. Once in power the military is generally close-mouthed and blocks researchers' entry to certain sources. But in comparison to military governments in Argentina, Chile, and Uruguay, the Brazilian military has made itself far more accessible. This is partly because the repression in Brazil was less severe than in the other three states, and partly because since the end of World War II Brazil's political culture has been relatively open. That openness is reflected in the rich profusion of works published on the military and society after 1964.

A great deal of archival research on the Brazilian military can be done in Washington, D.C., and Michael Grow (462), produced a guide to research collections in the capital city of the United States relating to Latin America and the Caribbean. Collections housed in the National Archives in Washington, such as Records of the Department of State Relating to the Internal Affairs of Brazil; the Dispatches from United States Consuls; the Records of the Foreign Service Posts of the Department of State; and the United States Military Intelligence Reports, Brazil, are listed and discussed in Ulibarri's and Harrison's GUIDE... (970). Much of these materials can also be obtained on microfilm from Scholarly Resources of Wilmington, Delaware, and from University Publications of America, Frederick, Maryland. There is a wealth of information on the military, especially for the nineteenth century, in London's Public Record Office, Foreign Office Records, General Correspondence-Political-Brazil.

Europa Publications's WORLD OF LEARNING 1990 (1018), lists libraries, archives, academies, learned societies, and research institutes in Brazil, showing the holdings and emphasis of each, but it is not a complete guide. José Honório Rodrigues (812), produced an indispensible guide for the historical researcher in Brazil listing archives, libraries, and institutes and giving valuable suggestions for their use.

Several archives and libraries publish guides to their holdings that can save the researcher a great deal of time. The Biblioteca Nacional in Rio de Janeiro publishes its ANAIS (1026), and the quarterly BIBLIOGRAFIA BRASILEIRA (1029). The archive of the Centro de Pesquisa e Documentação de História Contemporânea do Brasil (CPDOC) in Rio de Janeiro is the depository for a growing body of oral histories, manuscripts, and documentary collections for the Vargas era, 1930-55, some of which will be discussed more fully below.

Many recent monographs on Brazilian political and military history contain sections on field techniques and descriptions of the archives that have yielded valuable information; see especially, Alfred Stepan, THE MILITARY IN POLITICS: CHANGING PATTERNS IN BRAZIL (929), June Hahner (472), and Thomas Skidmore (896, 897).

Rio de Janeiro is the home of many important archives and libraries. The Biblioteca Nacional houses an excellent collection of military and civilian memoirs, essays, books, newspapers, magazines, and congressional debates and laws pertinent to the armed forces. A great deal of useful information can be gathered in this one place alone. Also in Rio de Janeiro is the Biblioteca do Exército, the most valuable library for information on the army. Housed in the General Staff headquarters of the army, the library contains almost complete sets of all the army periodicals, bulletins, and registers.

The naval archives and library, the Serviço de Documentação Geral da Marinha, is located also in Rio de Janeiro at navy headquarters. Here, too, complete sets of naval periodicals such as the REVISTA MARITIMA BRASILEIRA (1084), and the NAVIGATOR (1066), can be found. This library, like that of the air force, also in its Rio headquarters, is smaller, less systematically organized, and not as research oriented as that of the army. Data on army, navy, air force, and state militia budgets can be located in the library of the Ministério da Fazenda, in Rio de Janeiro.

More restrictive to entrance is the archive of the Clube Militar in Rio de Janeiro. Special permission for certified scholars to work in the archive must be obtained from the club's presidency. The archive of this important military organization contains records relating to the organization and inner workings of the club, such as minutes of meetings, where important national political issues are debated, and election records.

Located also at army headquarters in Rio de Janeiro is the Arquivo do Exército. A letter of introduction from the qualified scholar's institution is necessary to gain entrance to the archive. This depository is a storehouse for historical data on the army going back into the colonial period. See June Hahner's (472), useful "Bibliographical Note," in her book on civilian-military relations at the end of the nineteenth

century for a useful guide to this archive and others which contain
source material for turn-of-the-century civil-military affairs.

Another excellent archival resource in Rio de Janeiro is the archive
of the newspaper JORNAL DO BRASIL. To gain access the
researcher's institution will need to write the publisher for permission.
Besides a rich collection of photographs, the archive contains news
clippings, background data, notes from interviews, biographical files,
etc., on Brazil's military and civilian leaders.

The library of the Army General Staff School (ECEME) in Rio de
Janeiro has opened a new archive named after ex-President and
General Castello Branco. Alfred Stepan writes of this archive:
"Procedures for access have not yet been established. I received
permission from the commandant of ECEME and was the first foreign
scholar to use this archive" (929). Nevertheless, the collection is mainly
comprised of materials relating to the life and times of Castello Branco
prior to his assumption of the presidency in 1964. It is a rich source of
material for political information relating to military-civilian relations.
Another archive that is limited and specific is that dedicated to José
America and the Revolution of 1930. A guide to its holdings, published
in 1985 (50), is available. For a guide to General Góes Monteiro's
papers, see Peter Seaborn Smith (905).

A small, private library-archive in Rio de Janeiro belonging to a
powerful business pressure group called Instituto de Pesquisas de
Estudos Sociais (IPES) holds all of the institute's publications on file.
These publications and documents are important for the period prior
to the overthrow of Goulart and the subsequent Castello Branco
regime.

In São Paulo the archive of the newspaper O ESTADO DE SAO
PAULO is accessible and offers the historian valuable information on
the military. The library staff will provide researchers with files of
clippings gathered on numerous topics reported in the press. There are
photographs, biographical files, government and military press releases,
and clippings from other newspapers. Stepan (929), reported that
through this archive researchers are able to gain access to the personal
archive of José Stacchini, a senior reporter for the newspaper who
collected taped interviews and typed manuscripts from the activists in
the military revolt of 1964. See also Stacchini's (924), account of the
coup which appeared in 1965.

Three other archives also will yield sources on the history of civil-
military relations in Brazil. The Biblioteca do Congresso, in Brasília,
has information pertaining to congressional relations with the military,
and the archive of the Ministério do Trabalho, contains data on unions
and their relationships with the state after the 1964 coup. Finally, the
library   at   the   non-governmental,   inter-union   research   office,

Departamento Intersindical de Estatística e Estudos Socio-Econômicos (DIEESE) maintains an excellent collection of materials relating to labor history.

Researchers have found Brazilian military officers open and accessible to interviews. More and more officers are willing to enter their histories and experiences into the public record through taped oral interviews which are being collected and filed by the Fundação Getúlio Vargas and CPDOC. Some of these have been published and will be discussed under the headings Documentary Collections, and Memoirs, Journals, and Eyewitness Accounts. See the guide to the Fundação Getúlio Vargas's publications (422).

DOCUMENTARY COLLECTIONS

Published documents that deal specifically with the Brazilian military are quite limited in number,but there are some good collections of general political material that, owing to military involvement in the political theater, can be useful to the historian of the armed forces.

For the period leading up to the military overthrow of the monarchy (1871-89) parliamentary debates on the pressing issues of the era reveal a great deal about the attitudes of the elite toward the monarchy, the military, and national institutions. The Brazilian Senate (147), in 1979 published a six-volume set of the most crucial debates, saving the historian the laborious and tedious task of wading through the ANAIS.

Artur Vieira Peixoto (756), collected and edited an important documentary set on the military dictatorship of Floriano Peixoto. The six volumes of documents tend to demonstrate that Peixoto was a "great man." Also, for the era of the military dictatorship and the Old Republic the works of Ruy Barbosa (79), which reveal his views on the military, are of use. A protege of Ruy, João Mangabeira (639), has had his speeches and writings collected in an important three-volume work that covers events from the Old Republic to after World War II. Olavo Bilac, the poet who urged universal military training in the 1910s, has had his speeches and poetry published in a work titled A DEFESA NACIONAL: DISCURSOS (111). The Ministry of the Navy collected the speeches and documents relating to the life of Pedro Max Fernando de Frontín (178), who played an important role in Brazil's marginal participation in World War I. The same ministry publishes an on-going series of documents relating to episodes in naval history called SUBSIDIOS PARA A HISTORIA MARITIMA DO BRASIL (179). Each volume contains various documents and, at times, monographs bolstered by material from the Ministry.

Another multi-volume collection of historical documents still under way is that compiled by Hélio Silva. This is a rather sprawling, unorganized, cut-and-paste series, but there is an impressive mass of material that can be profitably worked over by historians. Volume one begins with 1889 and the fall of the monarchy (875), while subsequent volumes are on the *tenentes* (872, 873, 874), the Revolution of 1930 (870), the Vargas years (870, 871, 872, 877), World War II and its aftermath (878, 879, 877), and (880), a volume on the events leading up to the coup of 1964. Similarly, Edgard Carone collected documents on the *tenentes* (243), the Old Republic (238), and the Vargas years (242, 244). Manoel Guimarães, et al. (469), organized documents on the background of the Revolution of 1930, but they added little to the volume Hélio Silva produced on that topic. Highlighting São Paulo's revolt against the Vargas regime in 1932, Antonio Carlos Pereira (762), edited a documentary collection which complements Silva's work. In addition the massive works of Plinio Salgado (838), the Brazilian Integralista leader, contain useful material on understanding the fascist movement of the 1930s. José Oliveira (736), edited a volume of Eurico Dutra's presidential speeches.

An important set of documents, most never before published, comes from the Vargas papers located in the Centro de Pesquiza e Documentação de História Contemporânea (CPDOC) at the Fundação Getúlio Vargas, and covers Vargas's last term in office, 1951-54. Judiciously selected and skillfully organized by Adelina Cruz, et al. (311), this volume is especially important for the debate within the military regarding presidential succession after Vargas's suicide and whether or not the military should intervene in the political process. See Lacerda's (550), congressional speeches for this period as well.

Castello Branco's DISCURSOS (132), and the volume edited by Viana Filho (987), of the testimonies of ten individuals who knew and worked with the 1964 coup leader, are useful instruments for examining the background to military intervention and the regime that emerged in the wake of the coup. Marcos Sá Correa (298), furnished a rather weak collection of documents from the Lyndon B. Johnson Library at the University of Texas which reveal the level of United States involvement in the coup of 1964. Two sets of speeches and personal documents, one from General Antonio Carlos da Silva Muricy (707), army chief of staff in 1970, and the other from labor and social welfare minister Julio de Carvalho Barata (1970-72) (78), can be useful for a study of the Médici dictatorship.

Published documents on guerrilla warfare and on the radical left after the coup of 1964 are available to the historian. Kohl's and Litt's (539), compilation of documents on urban guerrilla warfare in Latin America contains important materials on Brazil not easily accessible elsewhere. The Brazilian military police put together a four-volume work on communism (152), that was also meant to be a military manual for fighting the Communists. In 1971 the Escola Superior de Guerra (371), published an eleven-volume set of papers and documents drawn from a conference on national security and development. This is an excellent source for the study of the ideology of the post-1964 regime. The Brazilian Communist Party (PCB) (753), collected valuable documents for the period 1958 to 1979. Interviews with Communist Party leader Luis Carlos Prestes, collected by Morães and Viana (688), recount the intra-party disputes after 1964. Pro-Maoist dissidents from the PCB formed their own party in 1961, the Communist Party of Brazil (PC do B), (749, 750, 751), and published three collections of documents and manifestos explaining the direction of the party and critiquing the 1964 coup.

For useful documentary material on the oppression and the torture in Brazil based on Christian, revolutionary, governmental, and international sources see Brune (191). Texts and speeches of Miguel Arrães, the Northeastern leader who opposed the military government, were collected and edited by Antonio Callado, et al. (208). Church leaders from the Brazilian Northeast led by Dom Helder Câmara (213), produced a series of documents questioning the Brazilian economic miracle of the post-coup government. A collection of unedited statements by panelists at a 1978 conference discussing the direction that the military government was taking Brazil at the time comprises the three-volume set called ENCONTRO NACIONAL PELA DEMOCRACIA (367). Opposition viewpoints are amply represented. The economist Mario Henrique Simonsen (888), collected his speeches and lectures on government economic policy during the 1970s which contain interesting material.

An official biography together with selected speeches and documents on the armed forces can be found in UM HOMEN CHAMADO GEISEL:... (440). There is also a five-volume collection of Geisel's DISCURSOS (439), the second volume of which demonstrates his thinking on the creation of IMBEL, the Brazilian War Materials Industry. A startling batch of documents titled OS DEBATES DOS JORNALISTAS BRASILEIROSO, 1970-1982 (322), reveal how heavily regulated the press was in those years. A valuable compendium of documents and writings by Senator and Vice President Pedro Aleixo covering the 1970s was organized by Mauricio Brandi Aleixo, et al. (11). Reis Filho and Ferreira de Sá (802), compiled a useful bibliography and documentary collection on the left in the 1960s.

An important reference source of biographical data on virtually all federal deputies is the useful collection published by the Brazilian Chamber of Deputies titled PERFIS PARLAMENTARES (151), a multi-volume work with each tome done on an important congressman or senator and containing a brief biography, as well as important speeches and personal documents.

Last, but not least, the United States House of Representatives Committee on Foreign Affairs produced a useful report through its Sub-Committee on National Security Policy and Scientific Developments dealing with Military Assistance Training (971), with sections on Brazil.

MEMOIRS, JOURNALS, AND EYEWITNESS ACCOUNTS

From the fall of the empire in 1889 to the present, Brazilian military and political actors have shown little reluctance to express their point of view in writing memoirs or in granting interviews to those who would make their views public. No era in Brazilian history, however, has produced such a volume of eyewitness reports and memoirs as the period since the armed forces toppled the Goulart government in 1964 and then remained to rule the country directly for the next twenty years.

In the waning days of the empire General Couto de Magalhães (627), addressed the pertinent political-military issues with valuable, albiet brief, insights. Both Anfrisio Fialho (391), and Max Leclerc (568), left contemporary descriptions and commentary on military alienation from the imperial system after 1880 and described the revolt and the role of those who who directed it. Serzedello Correa (299), left an intimate view of the army revolt in 1889 which toppled the monarchy, and he also made valuable observations of Floriano Peixoto's government and the early years of the incipient republic. The Baron of Rio Branco (199), offered his opinion of Marshal Deodoro da Fonseca, and Zeca Netto (716), a military leader from Rio Grande do Sul with a reputation for bloodshed, recounted in great detail military life and events during the troubled times of the Old Republic (1889-1930). From insurgent naval commander Admiral Custódio José de Mello (662), came an excellent two-volume account of why the navy revolted in 1893. Using copious documentation, he spelled out the origins of problems, tendencies within the navy, and the formation of the revolt. Augusto Carlos de Souza e Silva (864), a participant in that revolt which weakened the military dictatorship of Floriano Peixoto and helped bring civilians to power the following year, graphically described the event.

A work that is both an eyewitness account of events and a remarkable, penetrating, psycho-socio analysis of Brazil's Northeast and the Brazilian military during the last decade of the nineteenth century is Euclides da Cunha's magnificent OS SERTOES. Originally published in 1902, Samuel Putnam masterfully translated it into English as REBELLION IN THE BACKLANDS (313), in 1944.

During the Old Republic, Vivaldo Coaracy (284), related his experiences in the military officers' school, the Escola Militar. He noted that many of those enrolled in the school had no real aspiration to become officers, but that owing to conditions of the era, it was a way for those not in the upper classes to obtain a free education. In his influential book first published in 1914 and reissued in 1933, Alberto Torres (960), lamented the deplorable conditions the majority of Brazilians lived in during the early part of the Old Republic. Enumerating the defects of the country, number one of which was a lack of nationhood, Torres's book had a profound impact on the *tenentes* movement of the 1920s and upon those who overthrew the Old Republic in 1930. Ruy Barbosa's speeches (79), made in his campaign for the presidency against General Hermes da Fonseca in 1910, reveal his distrust of military men in political power.

An excellent first-hand account of the Old Republic and the condition and role of the military after World War I is the memoirs of the civilian war minister João Pandía Calogeras (209, 210). Appointed minister of war in 1919 by President Epitacio Pessôa, Calogeras at first faced intense military opposition since officers thought the post should have gone to one of their own. Overcoming their opposition through his able dedication to military interests, Calogeras revealed in his works the terrible problems that beset the armed forces of this time. Calogeras's aide, Egydio Moreira de Costa e Silva (867), added interesting sidelights in his memoirs of the era. An artillery officer, Estevão Leitão de Carvalho (246), left his opinion of the Old Republic and the military's involvement in the political arena. His three-volume memoir contains important information on Brazil's participation in the disarmament negotiations after World War I and on the government's attempts to secure a permanent seat on the Council of the League of Nations. The League's refusal caused Brazil to withdraw from the world body in 1926. A leading Gaúcho politician of the period and intimate of Getúlio Vargas and Borges de Medeiros, João Neves da Fontoura (405), provided an excellent source for events in the South during the Old Republic.

The Old Republic witnessed the rise of military discontent and rebellion, especially among the younger army officers. One of those was Bertholdo Klinger, a key organizer and intellectual behind the *tenente* movement. Klinger (536), wrote a six-volume autobiographical description of his role in the *tenentes* crusade which offers rich detail on this era. See also his PARADA E DISFILE... (537), which is an overview of the first half of the twentieth century. Another *tenente*, Juarez Távora (951, 952), who masterminded the 1920s movement and played an important part in the Revolution of 1930, remembered his part in those events. João Alberto Lins de Barros (84), also a *tenente* and ex-member of the Prestes Column, provided a two-volume memoir of his part in the *tenente* revolts of the 1920s. Franco (411), and

Guillobel (467), wrote two other noteworthy memoirs on the same period.

For the Revolution of 1930, which ended the Old Republic and ushered in the Vargas era, an excellent published oral history is the reminiscences of General Cordeiro de Farias (215). As one of the leading military personages of the twentieth century, Cordeiro de Farias played an important and colorful role not only in the *tenentes* movement and in the Revolution of 1930, but also in the Estado Nôvo, in the army's participation in World War II, in the establishment of the Escola Superior de Guerra, in the overthrow of the Goulart government, and as first minister of the interior in the Castello Branco regime. He continued to take a part in the affairs of state up to his death in 1981. Added to this memoir are one hundred pages of supporting documents relating to Cordeiro de Farias's active life. Another first-rate, published, oral history is that of the former *tenente*-turned-civilian-politician Juracy Montenegro Magalhães (628). His memoir, like Cordeiro de Farias's, is a product of the oral history program at the Fundaçao Getúlio Vargas. Magalhães's memoir covers the period from the 1920s to his retirement from political life in 1967, and has especially good political material on the Vargas era. Another insightful, eyewitness account, particularly for the 1930s and for military-civilian relations, is the memoir of the army officer Pantaleão Pessôa (769). And, the politician and historian Aureliano Leite (571), focused his attention on what he remembered of his role in the Revolution of 1930 to Vargas's election to the presidency in 1950.

Several diarists recorded São Paulo's unsuccessful attempt to topple the Vargas government in 1932. Paulo Nogueira Filho's (721), memoir is of great significance for his emphasis on military affairs. The commander of the São Paulo insurrection, Euclydes Figueiredo (395), offered a complete narration of events, while Herbert Levy (581), a captain in the Paulista militia, wrote an interesting account of the revolt. A law student with no military training but who joined the Paulista forces, José de Assis Pacheco (741), published his diary of the war, and Didi Vasconcellos (981), a minor bureaucrat, radio announcer, druggist, and diarist, recounted the civil war and subsequent events which he witnessed.

Fortunately for historians, participants in the Vargas government and military leaders during that era left behind their recollections of those momentous times. One such diarist was Luiz Vergara (986), Vargas's personal secretary who remembered Vargas in an intimate and personal way from 1926 to the caudilho's death in 1954. Vargas's daughter Alzira in her GETULIO VARGAS, MEU PAI (755), while naturally adulatory toward her father, nevertheless, supplied us with useful and intimate details. Vargas, of course, had his enemies both within and outside of the military. The best known of them was the newspaper publisher-politician, Carlos Lacerda. Lacerda's DEPOIMENTO (549), is an indispensible and captivating autobiography. In thirty-four hours of taped interviews done in 1977, Lacerda, passionately and with great candor and lucidity, captured the essence of his activities from the 1930s to the 1960s. Leaving nothing to escape his censure, Affonso Henriques (489), leveled an unrestrained, three-volume attack on Vargas as a great betrayer of the Revolution of 1930, in which the author was an active participant. Góes Monteiro, upon whom Vargas relied heavily as his strong supporter within the military, penned his own account of those years; see his DEPOIMENTO (310). Four other memoirs are recommended for this period: the incomparable Nelson Werneck Sodré, historian and general, in his MEMORIAS DE UM SOLDADO (917), covered the era 1922 to 1964 with important indictments of the military, made all the more crucial because of his self-criticism and absence of rancor; Hamilton Leal (566), friend and associate of Eduardo Gomes in the 1940s, left an interesting analysis of civil-military relations from the 1920s to the fall of Vargas in 1945; General J. Justino Alves Bastos's memoir (90), unabashedly reveals the high level of intrigue in which he was involved from the 1920s to 1965 and also demonstrates a remarkable arrogance toward civilians; finally, another military man, Federico Mindello Carneiro Monteiro (686), scrutinized officer attitudes and events from the 1920s to 1970.

A few good memoirs came out of the Brazilian military experience in World War II. The commander of the Brazilian Expeditionary Force (FEB) Marshal João Baptista Mascarenhas de Morães (691), wrote an account and listed all the members. There is an English translation published in 1965 (690). Another useful synthesis of the FEB's experiences was written by amateur historian and participant José Juarez Bastos Pinheiro (774). Floriano de Lima Brayner (143, 144), in two different accounts, focused his attention on the experiences he had with the FEB during the Italian campaign. Especially useful material on the army covering the period 1935 to 1945 can be found in Marshal Eurico Gaspar Dutra's memoir (361). Dutra, who succeeded Vargas in the presidency in 1945, unfortunately ended his recollections with his own inauguration. A poorly written memoir, but one that sheds light on Dutra's activities as Vargas's minister of war, is the acerbic attack on Dutra by Miguel de Castro Ayers (60), whom Dutra forced into early retirement.

For the post-World War II years through the 1950s, some civilian politicians have recorded their experiences which cast light on civil-military relations. José Bento Teixeira de Salles (840), revealed details of his own activities from the 1940s to the coup of 1964 and close observations of other notables of the time, especially of Milton Campos. Vargas's vice president, João Café Filho (205), who became president upon Vargas's death in 1954 and was then removed by the military the next year, left an important and detailed two-volume account of his ordeal with Vargas and with the military. Jucelino Kubitschek (546), elected to the presidency after the military removed Café Filho, authored a three-volume memoir vividly recounting his political hegira from 1940 to 1964. As an important leader of the Brazilian Communist Party, Gregorio Bezerra (105), concentrated his two-volume autobiography on his party activities under Vargas to 1945 and reorganization efforts afterwards to 1969. The work contains significant material on the party's efforts to organize labor and the peasants in the Northeast. Paulo Cavalcanti (261), a left nationalist politician from Pernambuco, offered an excellent account of politics in the Northeast from the 1930s to the 1970s, and it is a useful complement to Bezerra's work. The leader of the Communist Party of Brazil and founder of the REVISTA BRASILIENSE, Elias Chaves Neto (712), wrote a series of descriptive and analytical articles on how he observed the political situation during the 1950s and early 1960s.

The tumultuous times of the Goulart government (1961-64), the coup that removed him, and the military dictatorships that followed, were described by numerous participants, both winners and losers. This period constitutes, perhaps, the richest era in Brazilian history for published, eyewitness accounts. As time goes by, more participants will undoubtedly come forward with their observations of those momentuous events. The works mentioned here are a selective sampling of that prodigious resource.

In his A GUERRA DAS ESTRELAS, 1964-1984: OS BASTIDORES DAS SUCESSOES PRESIDENCIAIS, journalist Carlos Chagas (272), crafted an interesting overview of the era based on his own observations. From his vantage point as commander of the fourth army (1963-64) J. Justino Alves Bastos (90), richly detailed the events leading up to the coup of 1964 and also discussed the army's internal political issues. Odylio Denys (330), a principal actor in the coup of 1964, kept a journal recording events back to the time of his involvement with the *tenentes* in the 1920s. His insights are especially important for an understanding of civil-military politics. Hernani D'Aguiar (314), served as a military history instructor at the Escola de Comando e Estado Maior do Exército (ECEME) during the early 1960s. His first-hand account, combined with the views of other ECEME instructors, students, and administrators, presented the ECEME as the "nerve center" in the war against "communism" and the military-led revolt against Goulart. Excellent, behind-the-scenes reporting of the last days of the Goulart regime and the takeover of the military can be found in Carlos Castello Branco's (131), three-volume work composed of his daily political observations which originally appeared in the JORNAL DO BRASIL. General Olympio Mourão Filho, commander of the fourth army in Minas Gerais who "jumped the gun" and led his troops against Goulart, explained his actions in his "Relatório..." (706), of May 1964. His MEMORIAS (705), not published until 1978, detail the military operations of 31 March 1964 against the incumbent regime. The work is also a caustic critique of the governments of Castello Branco and Costa e Silva. Much of the criticism emerges from Olympio's being passed over for important positions in either of the two military governments he reproaches. See also Guedes (463), in this connection. A reporter for O ESTADO DE São PAULO, José Stacchini, collected taped interviews and manuscripts from many of the coup's activists and published them in his MARCO 64: MOBILIZACAO DE AUDACIA (924).

In part, the coup of 1964 was the military high command's attempt to thwart Goulart's efforts to divide the non-commissioned officers from their superiors. Estanislau Fragoso Batista (91), a sergeant caught up in the military rebellion of 1963 and imprisoned and subsequently expelled from the armed forces, presented a riveting account of these events. French priest Paul Gallet (435), described conditions in Northeast Brazil in letters home and in his journal covering the years 1962 through 1967. His work should be read in conjunction with Antonio Callado (208), who related how armed forces leaders in 1964 considered the church to be deeply influenced by communists in Pernambuco. See also Dom Helder Câmara's (212), book in this regard. Paulo Cavalcanti recounted the coup's aftermath in Recife and elsewhere in the Northeast in his O CASO EU CONTO, COMO O CASO FOI (261). The governor of Goiás, Mauro Borges (127), sided with the 1964 *golpistas* and then published a defense of his actions.

Former president Jucelino Kubitschek (546), while in exile in Madrid, related his version of events leading up to the suspension of his political rights, known as cassation in Brazil. Another professional politician, Raul Pilla (772), judged the coup and its aftermath from his vantage point in the Chamber of Deputies, 1963-66, while his colleague, José Saldanha Coelho (287), wrote about the coup after he had gone into exile in Montevideo. Another exiled Brazilian, the journalist João Cândido Maia Netto (715), prior to his flight abroad, examined the coup and its aftermath and the role of the United States in those events. Mario Martins (651), another journalist, collected his articles from the JORNAL DO BRASIL covering the coup and published them in book form. Other interesting and important accounts of the coup of 1964 are: Georges M. Mattei (652), a collection of interviews of Brazilians living in exile who were willing to speak of their experiences; Carlos

Marighela (642), later killed by the police when he took up arms against the military regime, recounted his arrest and imprisonment for his political activities shortly after the coup; and Celso Frederico (414), who provided an eyewitness account of the coup's aftermath from the viewpoint of workers in São Paulo.

The military government that took power upon the ouster of "Jango" Goulart eventually came under the control of General Humberto Castello Branco. Castello Branco inclined toward purging the government of what he and his advisors considered to be "dangerous elements to democracy," so that the nation could be returned to its constitutional, democratic basis. His views are recorded in ENTREVISTAS, 1964-1965 (133). Castello Branco's press secretary, José Wamberto (1000), commented on the coup of 1964 and explored the views and personality of his boss in his published account. An economics professor from the Fundação Getúlio Vargas, Octavio Gouveia de Bulhões (196), became minister of finance under the new regime and in his work spelled out his economic philosophy. From his post he intended to reorganize the entire financial structure and to "sanitize" Brazil's public finances. Similarly, Roberto de Oliveira Campos (220, 221, 222), Castello Branco's minister of planning and economic coordination, in three separate works spelled out his philosophy and what he tried to accomplish during his three-year tenure. His comments go beyond economics to include his observations of his military bosses, the educational system, the church, foreign policy, labor, etc.

With the transfer of power from Castello Branco to Costa e Silva in 1964, the hardliners took command. Wanting a deeper transformation of Brazilian political society, they pushed the dictatorship to rigid extremes after the sudden death of Costa e Silva and Garrastazú Médici's assumption of the presidency. Carlos Chagas (271), a highly respected journalist who served as Costa e Silva's press secretary, in his, at first supressed, memoir which was not published until 1979, recounted the deepening crisis of Costa e Silva's government as hardliners demanded the elimination of guerrillas and radical opponents of the regime. Costa e Silva's chief of the military household, General Jayme Portella de Mello (663), regarded his boss's actions with sympathy and understanding. General Aurelio de Lyra Tavares (945), Costa e Silva's minister of war, saw the army as the great unifier and civilizer in Brazilian history. His discreet memoir published in 1977 (942), reveals the psychological and political outlook of the army officer corps during the Costa e Silva government. In O EXERCITO BRASILEIRO VISTO PELO SEU MINISTRO (944), he attempted to demonstrate a homogeneity of thought and action within the officer class. He also revealed the military's developmental plans for the

Amazon basin. The armed forces, he believed, were the only national institution capable of achieving success. Roberto de Oliveira Campos (220), always close to the political action, in a series of insightful and perceptive essays and speeches written from 1969 to 1974, observed the Brazil the military leaders had made and decided it was not to his liking.

Owing to the intense political repression of this period and to the abuse of human rights by the police and the armed forces, a depressingly large number of victims published accounts of torture and arbitrary confinement as the military relaxed its grip in the late 1970s. In his DAS CATACUMBAS: CARTAS DA PRISAO, 1969-1971, Carlos Christo (281), detailed the boring minutiae of life in prison and the agonizing delays in getting his case heard in the military tribunals. A courageous state attorney, Helio Pereira Bicudo (109), told a fascinating story of his efforts to identify and to prosecute members of São Paulo's death squads. He accused the police of being involved and the courts of cowardice in their failure to pursue the issue. For the memoirs and testimonials of members of leftist groups that experienced prison and torture at the hands of the political police, see Salles's (839), grim, but well-written diary of his nine years in prison, and Perrin's (766), chronicle of horrors as he described his arrest, imprisonment, torture, and exasperating efforts to defend himself before the military court system. Lawyers working for the Archdiocese of São Paulo on behalf of the military's victims smuggled court documents out of the military tribunals, copied them, and later published a report entitled BRASIL: NUNCA MAIS (49). There is an English translation edited by Joan Dassin (319). Certainly the most publicized and well-known capture, torture, and death engineered by the military police was that of the Paulista journalist Vladimir Herzog. Fernando Jordão (526), wrote an interesting account of Herzog's fellow journalists' attempts to publicize the case and to swing public opinion against the government's repressive methods. The memoirs of Jorge Fischer Nunes (725), articulately, and with a dose of black humor, testify to the torture, violation of human rights, and government repression during the early 1970s. And, in two different accounts, Fernando Gabeira (430, 431), one of the principal urban guerrillas, described the origins of the guerrilla movement, why he joined, how they recruited, their kidnapping of United States Ambassador Elbrick, and their hiding out, capture, and imprisonment. Both memoirs are important for their useful insights into the thinking and organization of the radical left. See as well the Dominican Frei Betto's (104), description of prison conditions and the systematic violation of human rights.

As the military eased back on its repressive controls under the Geisel government, an increasing number of those who had lost their civil and political rights came forth to testify against the former regime. In three separate works Marcos Freire (416, 417, 418), a well known senator from Pernambuco during the late 1960s and early 1970s, condemned the military regimes for their corruption, repression, and authoritarianism, and urged the armed forces to declare a general amnesty and move the country toward a democratic government. Former associates of Miguel Arrães, a leading leftist politician during the 1960s, taped interviews with him and published them as CONVERSACOES COM ARRAES (53). He recounted his experiences in 1964 and touched on several topics of importance during the subsequent military governments. See also his passionate BRAZIL: THE PEOPLE AND THE POWER (52). Federal deputy for the PMDB party, Marcello Cerqueira (268), published his observations on the military hardliners' attempts to intimidate government opponents as the Geisel and Figuereido *abertura* led to increased expression of opposition to government policies. He especially condemned the hardliners' promotion of right-wing terrorism. Caso (257), edited a collection of guerrillas' testimonies and other documents on the armed struggle. A witty, eyewitness account of the guerrilla movement by a youthful participant is that of Syrkis (937). See also Carlos Marighela's writings (642). Student leaders (505), recounted their militancy, misfortunes, and struggles during the ten years from 1961 to 1970, over half of which time their national organization had been disbanded by the armed forces governments.

Geisel's style of government and the selection process for his successor are recalled by Getúlio Bittencourt (112). João Paulo dos Reis Velloso (984), as minister of planning during the Médici and Geisel regimes, drew a favorable assessment of the economic achievements of those governments through the mid-1970s. As a journalist covering national politics since the 1950s, Portocarrero (787), compiled a series of interviews with senators and deputies who were in office during the Geisel and Médici era. The academician-turned-politician, Fernando Henrique Cardoso, offered his views on electoral politics and the military from 1978 to 1983 in a series of interviews with Eduardo P. Graeff (451). Alberto Goldman (445), MDB state deputy from São Paulo, reflected on his political activities of the period 1970 to 1977. He provided useful insights into the campaign of 1974 when the MDB made significant gains. Geisel's chief of the military household, Hugo Abreu (4, 5), who had seniority over Figueiredo and thought he was to be next in line for the presidency, published memoirs which reveal his anger at being passed over and his subsequent attempts to generate opposition to Figueiredo's candidacy. Both volumes reflect his self-righteousness, his sense of duty and self-importance, and make it very clear why Geisel chose Figueiredo. In two important books,

Hélio Beltrão (95, 96), chosen as Figueiredo's special minister for debureaucratization, explained the problems he faced as he tackled what he considered to be Brazil's most pressing problem, bureaucratic centralization. Last, but not least, is a work by General Golbery do Couto e Silva, one of the most significant and influential men in the military from the late 1950s to the time of his resignation from government service in 1981. This work, CONJUNTURA POLITICA NACIONAL: O PODER EXECUTIVO E GEOPOLITICA DO BRASIL (868), is a fundamental source on Golbery's thoughts, and therefore, it reflects the beliefs of a significant number of the military leadership during the 1960s and 1970s.

SPECIALIZED WORKS

Owing to the tremendous body of secondary sources published on Brazil since the fall of the empire in 1889, and because of the significant role the armed forces played in the course of that history, I have divided this section into the following sub-sections: the fall of the empire and subsequent military dictatorship, 1887-94; the Old Republic, 1894-1930; the Revolution of 1930 and the Estado Nôvo to 1945; post-World War II to the coup of 1964; and finally, the coup of 1964 and military government to 1985.

THE FALL OF THE EMPIRE AND SUBSEQUENT MILITARY DICTATORSHIP, 1887-94

A good place to start researching this period is with volume five of the CAMBRIDGE HISTORY OF LATIN AMERICA, edited by Leslie Bethell (102), which provides an overview of these years through the Old Republic. This work contains an excellent bibliography. Numerous authors have skillfully probed the origins of the collapse of the monarchy in Brazil. Boehrer's (121), older general study of the history of the Republican Party from 1870 to 1889 is still of value. José Carvalho's (250), sophisticated work on the imperial political elite establishes the importance of the military in politics from independence to the Revolution of 1930. His 1982 article (253), concentrates on the nineteenth century. According to João Dornas's account of the abolitionist Silva Jardim (340), popular agitation rather than a military conspiracy would have brought about the republic without the dangers of militarism. Colson (290), examined the coup's antecedents in great detail and concluded that powerful economic groups played the dominant role in the events leading to the crisis. Dudley's dissertation and two published articles (347, 348, 349), concentrate on the military reforms after the Paraguayan War. He noted that Dom Pedro II failed to heed legitimate complaints and alienated the moderate officers.

The traditional institutional approach to military history can be found in Castellet's (258), two-volume study; volume two covers the fall of the empire to 1900. In her two articles and book dealing with civil-military relations which developed after the fall of the monarchy, June Hahner (471, 472, 474), found that officers' attitudes were disdainful of civilian political leadership, but lack of unity within the armed forces enabled civilians to take control in 1894. See also her article in THE AMERICAS (473), on Marshal Floriano Peixoto. Note also Robert Hayes's article (485), and Miranda's enthusiastic biography of Peixoto (677).

In his two-volume, detailed, comprehensive, and scholarly work on the fall of the empire, the historian and diplomat, Heitor Lyra (604), regarded Benjamin Constant as the mastermind behind a military cabal which brought the Empire down. Magalhães Júnior's (629), richly illustrated work took a close look at Deodoro da Fonseca and other military personalities, while Raimundo Mendes (667), closely examined Benjamin Constant's activities in the army's overthrow of Dom Pedro II. Mercadante's (669), intellectual history of civil-military relations from colonial times to the 1920s offers good insights into the soldier's role. Morães's older work (689), is a competent review of the overthrow of the Empire in which he examined the "republicanization" of the armed forces long before 1889. Leda Rodrigues (813), showed how the Republican press influenced the military against the monarchy by blowing up minor incidents from 1886 to 1887 in order to create the "military question." In his 1973 dissertation on the Brazilian army and politics, John Henry Schulz (858), found that the military intervened in imperial politcs to encourage industrialization, abolish slavery, and end corruption. But the lack of a "clear ideology and consensus" enmeshed the military in corrupt politics, factionalized it, and forced it to hand power to the Paulista civilians in 1894. Consult also the works by Cyro Silva (865), and Charles Simmons (883, 884). An excellent study of the patrimonial foundations of the Brazilian bureaucratic state is that done by Uricochea (975). Based on the author's dissertation, he focused on the creation and role of the Guarda Nacional and its relationship to the patrimonial state. Other studies worth consulting for this era are: Francisco Vianna (989), on the fall of the Empire, and Wood (1017), on the establishment of military colonial settlements in Brazil's vast interior.

The role of diplomacy and the wide range of issues raised by the naval revolt of 1893 and subsequent foreign naval intervention is the focal point of Sergio Correa da Costa's book (308). In tomo two, volume four of their HISTORIA GERAL DA CIVILIZACAO

BRASILEIRA, Sergio Buarque de Holanda and Pedro Moacyr Campos (506), edited numerous contributions that deal with the military and society during this period. Pedro Lafayette (554), published a two-volume biography of Saldanha da Gama, the naval leader of the 1893 uprising against the army dictatorship. See also his earlier and shorter profiles on Saldanha da Gama, Barão de Penedo, and Silveira Martins (555), as well as the laudatory biography on Saldanha da Gama by Raul Rodrigues (815). Walter LaFeber (556), demonstrated that the United States role in the 1893-94 rebellion was to avoid hampering trade between the two nations. This study improved upon Michael McClosky's (619), earlier contribution on the same topic. Joaquim Nabuco (709), wrote a two-volume work on foreign intervention in the revolt of 1893, and Joseph Smith (901), used extensive British sources to reveal the role of the United Kingdom during that important event.

THE OLD REPUBLIC, 1894-1930

Recently, excellent studies have been published on the period referred to politically as the Old Republic. Many of these works have concentrated, however, on the *tenentes* movement of the 1920s and on the inception of the professionalization process within the armed forces which took place during this period. For general overviews of this era in which the military is placed in the context of the political, economic, and cultural events of the time there are a number of studies available. The social historian Gilberto Freyre's ORDER AND PROGRESS (421), covers the years 1889-1918 and contains interesting material. In tomo three of Holanda's and Campos's extensive HISTORIA GERAL DA CIVILIZACAO BRASILEIRA (506), two volumes are devoted to the Old Republic; volume two is the best for the army's role. As with the other volumes in this set, this work is a compilation of first-rate, in-depth articles by leading Brazilian and foreign historians who have examined this topic. A concise overview of the history of the Old Republic can be found by reading Leonardo Trevisan (966), while an apologetic, but nevertheless important source of information on the period is the biography of Epitacio Pessôa (1865-1942) written by his daughter Laureta Pessôa Raja Gabaglia (429). Epitacio played a major role in the struggle against the military dictatorship of Floriano Peixoto. He was also active in the *tenentes* rebellion, and Laureta covers these periods well, especially the revolt of the Copacabana fortress in 1922. Another work of filial piety, and poorly written at that, is Dulcina Bandeira's biography of her father Alipio (73). It is mentioned here only because her research illustrates that her father typified many men of the era who were born into families whose social status was on the wane and who joined the armed forces to obtain an education and perhaps improve their socio-economic position. Richard Graham (454), enlightened readers with an examination of governmental expenditures after the overthrow of the monarchy. Hayes's dissertation (484), assesses the historical factors present in the late colonial period and in the nineteenth century that contributed to the formation of the army, and José Carvalho's (252), worthy study sees the armed forces during the Old Republic as a destabilizing force.

The army's involvement in the Canudos uprising in the Northeast and the later Contestado affair in the South had, doubtlessly, far-reaching ramifications on the instititution. Orlando de Morães Rego (798), portrayed the role of the militias from Pará in the campaigns against Canudos, and Peregrino (761), analyzed Euclydes da Cunha's work, REBELLION IN THE BACKLANDS (313), on the Canudos rebellion for its value as a military history. Tocantins (958), wrote a first-class study of Euclydes da Cunha. The Italian historian Giorgio Marotti (646), reconstructed the origins of the rebellion, its impact on the nation's press and subsequent literature, and on the collective Brazilian psyche. His work is an intriguing analysis of how the event became a Brazilian legend and how it served the interests of the dominant elite. With sympathy for the folk of the Sertão, Edmundo Moniz (682), wrote a thoughtful, balanced synthesis concluding that the Canudos rebellion was an uprising against an unfair land-tenure system supported by a bourgeois government. See also José Silva's (881), insightful essays and superb bibliography on the war.

The fascinating story of military explorations into the Matto Grosso and the Amazon during the early part of the century can be followed in O'Reilly (738), whose dissertation is principally a biography of Cândido Mariano Rondôn, the founder of the Brazilian Indian Protection Service. One should also consult Stauffer (926), on the creation of this agency. Tambs (940), recorded the military action and diplomatic maneuvers in Brazil's quest for the Acre. Weinstein (1005), relived the Amazonian rubber boom and military involvement to 1920, and Abreu (3), recounted episodes of Indian warfare on the Paraná frontier during the first quarter of this century.

With regard to the Contestado uprising (1912-15), Walter Fernando Piazza's (770), history of Santa Catarina has a good chapter on it and places it in proper historical and geographical context. Queiroz's (791), truly excellent monograph on this messianic movement along the border between Santa Catarina and Paraná was unmatched until Duglas Monteiro (685), published his exciting, innovative reconstruction of the event a few years later. Both include information on the army's role in the affair that helps one to understand the disaffection of junior army officers the following decade.

The naval revolt in 1910 was analyzed by Paul Manor (640), in a detailed account of sailors' discontent and of Brazil's rivalry with Argentina for naval supremacy. An earlier work by Morel (700), covered the same event but it is undocumented. Bueno (195), evaluated the Brazilian-Argentine naval rivalry prior to the Brazilian 1910 naval revolt. João Pandía Calogeras's role as a civilian minister of war (1919-22) and the process of military professionalization are the subject of Hall's (476), 1984 dissertation. It is ironic that in Calogeras's attempts to depoliticize and professionalize the army he helped to create the new military/political group of junior officers that eventually forced its way onto the nation's political stage.

While professionalization started somewhat earlier, it rigorously got underway after World War I when a French military mission came to Brazil. Frank McCann (617), traced the professionalization process back to the nineteenth century and brought it forth to its fullest expression under the post-World War I government. His article (616), on obligatory military service during the Old Republic and his subsequent book A NACAO ARMADA (615), examine the deplorable conditions in the pre-1920 army and the strong pressures brought to bear by the emerging middle class for reform. See also his probing article on the formative period of army thought (614), in which he scrutinized the writings of officers in their official reports, journals, and books. In these writings he found present a strong doctrine of "development and security." This, he concluded, was the origin of the guiding principle for military governments after 1964. Likewise, in an article on European military influence in South America from 1890 to 1940, Frederick M. Nunn (726), examined French and German military influences on training officer corps in Argentina, Brazil, Chile, and Peru. He found that professionalization of the armed forces stimulated, rather than diminished their political interests. In his subsequent book (729), on the same topic, Nunn found that Brazilian army officers were more French than the French, and that these military men believed their institutions and training to be far superior to those of civilian society. Araripe's (45), article describes French influence in the army's staff college as it instilled originality and independence of thought among the officers. See also Cidade's (282), study of the French military mission.

The impact of World War I on Brazil and on other South American countries is the subject of Albert's and Henderson's (9), interesting comparative study. Stanley Hilton (496), did a competent job of documenting Brazil's continuing military and diplomatic rivalry with Argentina in the decade following the war. And Joseph Smith (900, 902), used United States diplomatic sources to review the relations between that country and Brazil from 1889 to 1930.

Increasing economic, social, and political problems during the 1920s and the breakdown in unity among members of the Brazilian oligarchy as they attempted to grapple with them affected the military during the decade. Elements of the armed forces expressed themselves in the movement known as *tenentismo*. In the first serious analysis of the movement Virginio Santa Rosa (822), saw the importance of *tenentismo* as a manifestation of middle-class values and their contradictions, incongruities that would eventually destroy the crusade. Since Santa Rosa's study appeared numerous scholars have turned their attention to the military during the 1920s. For example, Sães (834, 835), adhered to the view that *tenentes* did not speak for the middle classes and that the military frequently became the oligarchy's instrument of political repression. Henry H. Keith's dissertation (533), found that the young *tenentes* regarded themselves as the "saviours" of the republic. In another dissertation, Ilan Rachum (793), discovered that while early *tenente* political programs concentrated on achieving constitutional democracy and, to a lesser degree, economic and social justice, after 1927 ideological radicalization and division within the movement's leadership caused the dissolution of *tenentismo* as a coherent political force shortly before the Revolution of 1930. Still, many *tenentes* continued to exert influence and play an important role in national politics into the 1960s according to Rachum in a subsequent article (794). Luz's (603), brief, interpretive essay links the economic difficulties of manufacturers in the 1920s to the *tenentes's* ardent economic nationalism. Forjaz's (406), study on the *tenentes* shows them to have pursued urban, middle-class goals that the traditional oligarchy ignored and which put them in direct confrontation with the leaders of the Old Republic. Alexander's (13), older article on the role of army officers from 1922 to 1942 is still useful; José Dantas's (317), well-written, analytical account of *tenentismo* in Sergipe is a good socio-political reconstruction of that state and the factors that produced *tenentismo* there. The phenomenon in Sergipe, he concluded, lacked much social content.

For a detailed military account of the revolt of 1924 written by an army officer see Marshal Falção's article (377), as well as Duff (350). However, Anna Maria Martinez Correa's (296), analysis of the same revolt in São Paulo is doubtlessly the most thoughtful, perceptive, and well-documented study to date. From a wealth of raw data she concluded that *tenentes* were ideologically unprepared to take control of São Paulo and had no substantive reform program of their own. Nor did they oppose the existing relations of class and property. See also in this regard the articles by Jenkin (522), and Wirth (1015). Macaulay's (607) work on the Prestes Column offers good treatment of the complex warfare in the backlands, but is weak on socio-economic analysis. Amado (27), Lorenço Lima (587), and Sodré (913), have all contributed studies of Prestes.

THE REVOLUTION OF 1930 AND
THE ESTADO NOVO TO 1945

An excellent place to start digging for information on this period is with Skidmore's POLITICS IN BRAZIL, 1930-1964 (896); his detailed bibliographical notes provide a valuable research tool. Paulo Brandi and others (138), published a fine synthesis of national politics from the Revolution of 1930 to Vargas's death. The work is especially good on Vargas's relations with other political leaders and partisans, particularly after 1945. The Fundação Getúlio Vargas hosted an international seminar on the Revolution of 1930 and published the papers presented (423). Fausto's interesting essay (382), treats the *tenentes* role in the aftermath of the revolution. Young (1020), wrote a brief overview of the period and explored the military aspects of the 1930 coup which toppled the Old Republic. For a different view on the purges of the upper officer class after the revolution see Wirth (1015). Alexander (12), and Conniff (292) also took a look at the *tenentes* after Vargas assumed control. Tiller (957), regarded the 1930 revolution to be in imminent danger of failure had it not been for the assassination of João Pessôa, governor of Paraíba. See as well the two interesting studies on the Paraíba event by Inojosa (515), and Inêz Rodriguez (816). An impartial and penetrating study published in 1933 is the classic work by Alexandre José Barbosa Lima (586). Another important contemporary account, especially for the military preparations leading to the 1930 revolt, is Virgilio Mello Franco's OUTUBRO, 1930 (413). Calasans (206), recounted some local aspects from Bahia, as did Morães (695). Amora (33), sketched women's participation in several Brazilian revolts, one of which was that of 1930.

Valuable information on the military during this period can be found in the numerous biographies of Getúlio Vargas. Richard Bourne (129), contributed a significant study on the "Sphinx of the Pampas," as he called him. Dulles's (357), lengthy biography of Vargas examined the life of the Gaúcho leader. Levine (580), emphasized the period of Vargas's rule from 1934 to 1939, years that he considered critical. Affonso Henriques's (489), three-volume critical appraisal of Vargas and his era is a good antidote to the laudatory portrait left by Vargas's daughter Alzira (755). In volume two of his HISTORIA DA POLITICA REVOLUCIONARIA NO BRASIL, Abguar Bastos (89), summarized political events from 1933 to the 1945. Cortés (300), focused on politics in Rio Grande do Sul from the Revolution of 1930 to the coup of 1964. Conniff (293), turned his attention to the rise of the populist phenomenon in the cities during the Vargas era. Peter Seaborn Smith (906), analyzed the significant role that the military and Vargas played in the formulation of Brazil's petroleum policy prior to and after World War II, while Wirth (1014), delved into the politics of Brazilian industrial development in the Vargas epoch.

In volume two of his HISTORIA DAS REVOLUCOES BRASILEIRAS Glauco Carneiro (233), wrote, perhaps, the best brief account of the Paulista revolt of 1932. Clovis de Oliveira (734), investigated the Paulista industrial mobilization effort to support the revolt. Hélio Silva's documentary-cum-narrative (872), on the Paulista revolt is very good, as is Euclydes Figueiredo's (395).

The Communist revolt that erupted in 1935 is covered in detail by Dulles (352), in his work on Brazilian communism. See also his companion volume on anarchists and communists in Brazil (351), prior to the revolt. Chilcote's (276), study of the Brazilian Communist Party provides a broader overview with differing viewpoints. Levine's (580), earlier mentioned study is particularly helpful here as is his article (579), on the revolt in Rio Grande do Norte. See also the account by José Campos Aragão (43).

Secondary works on the Brazilian Integralistas are few, but the most thorough study is Hélio Henrique Trindade's (967). Among other things, this book explains the relationships between Integralismo and the Brazilian church, the military, and European fascism. Alistair Hennessy (488), made an important contribution in his general explanation of why fascism failed to take root in Brazil. Hilton (492), emphasized the Integralistas' relationships with labor, state governments, and the military, and McCann (618), narrated Vargas's campaign to destroy the party. See also Seitenfus (861), for Italian influence.

While many of the sources mentioned in this section cover military-political relations during this era, a few studies focus specifically on Vargas's relations with the armed forces from 1930 to 1945. One should consult Bento (99), who dealt with the evolution of military doctrine under Vargas; Carvalho (249), who found that the army was transformed into an "essential part of the state and an instrument of its policies;" Fagundes (376), who stressed the middle-class character of the army in 1945; and Peter Seaborn Smith (904), who surveyed the important activities of General Góes Monteiro.

Labor's relations with the armed forces and with the state became increasingly significant during the Vargas era, and a number of studies concentrate on this topic. Morães Filho's (696), older work is still one of the best. Luiz Vianna (993), did a detailed exploration of relations between the unions and the state, pointing out the limitations of liberal tenets. Weffort's (1004), work on populism is important, as is Harding's (479), on organized labor.

Several studies by Stanley Hilton analyze the role of military interests in the formulation of Brazilian foreign policy during the Vargas years. See especially his BRAZIL AND THE GREAT POWERS, 1930-1939: THE POLITICS OF TRADE RIVALRY (495). Other studies deal with German military espionage and allied attempts to counter it in Brazil (500), Brazilian diplomacy during World War II (494), the overthrow of Vargas (502), and Brazilian-Soviet relations, 1917-47 (497). R.A. Humphreys (511), investigated the response of Latin American nations to the crisis presented by World War II. McCann (610), in his study of the Brazilian-American alliance from 1937 to 1945, provided an understanding of the military position in this diplomacy, and he also looked at United States-Brazilian diplomacy as it related to aviation prior to Brazil's entry into the war (608). Seitenfus's (860), recent book investigates the process leading up to Brazil's involvement in the war.

The armed forces' venture into World War II has attracted some scholarly attention. Virginia Carneiro's (236), brief, journalistic account is a useful overview. Brayner's A VERDADE SOBRE FEB (144), criticized the United States for the poor military equipment sent to Brazil and for North American haughty attitudes toward Brazilians. Manoel Thomaz Castello Branco (135), competently narrated a history of the Brazilian Expeditionary Force. Paulo Duarte (346), concentrated on the war preparations in the Northeast, and his work is especially good on descriptions of training irregulars in the region. Granado-Díaz's (455), thesis retells Brazilian participation in the Battle of Monte Castello. Elber Henriques's (490), objective, forthright history of the FEB is a refreshing change from the passionate accounts of the commanders, as is the analysis by Lins (591). The role of the army in World War II and its philosophical transformation is the subject of McCann's (611), article; and in his work on the Brazilian general staff (613), he reviewed the military's thinking on strategic matters from 1900 to 1945. Paula (752), and Pinheiro (774), contributed two useful syntheses of the FEB. A.C. Gabaglia (428), and Gama (436), wrote works of rather limited value on the navy during the war. The Brazilian Medical Corps during the conflict is the subject of a study by Edgardo Moutinho dos Reis (799), and he included biographies of the principal participants. A well-written, sober account of the Brazilian Air Force during the war was published by Luis F. Perdigão (758), and Tavares (947), enlightened us on the role of the army corps of engineers during the Italian campaign.

POST-WORLD WAR II TO THE COUP OF 1964

Several good overviews for this twenty-year period provide students with a solid foundation in the era. Skidmore (896), mentioned above, devoted most of his book to a detailed examination of post-World War II Brazil. Chacon (270), interpreted the era from Vargas's 1937 coup to the 1964 military coup as an expression of the continuity of Vargas's far-reaching reforms. Flynn (401), gave a detailed review of political events for those years in his general survey. Hippólito (503), focused on the history of the Social Democratic Party (PSD) from 1945 to 1964, and Maria Souza (922), analyzed the history of political parties and the Brazilian state from 1930 to 1964.

General Dutra's climb to the presidency in 1945 is the subject of Vale's (977), unpretentious study. Cão (224), described Dutra's efforts to "discipline" the army after he assumed control of the government, and Mourão (704), found only political opportunism and financial mismanagement in the Dutra government.

A number of studies on the second Vargas government (1951-54) throw considerable light on the activities and political involvement of the armed forces. Sodré's HISTORIA MILITAR (915), provides an inside look at the political battles within the officer corps during this time. Haines's (475), study of Cold War diplomacy has a chapter on the relations between the United States and the Brazilian military from 1945 to 1954. Araujo's (47), recent book, based on extensive documentation from Vargas's files, is important. Oliveiros Ferreira (338), covered well the tumultuous second Vargas administration and is an important source for political currents among military officers, especially in the early 1960s. Afonso Ceasar (264), Machado (624), Manchester (638), Saunders (849), and Araken Tavora (949), all covered the political crisis which ended with Vargas's suicide. Volume one of John W.F. Dulles's biography of Vargas's arch enemy Carlos Lacerda (353), detailed the years 1914 to 1960.

For an examination of the era after the death of Vargas to the coup of 1964, Dulles's (356), encyclopedic chronology is a valuable reference tool. Alves (20), analyzed the role of the armed forces in the political turmoil that followed the Gáucho leader's death to the election of 1955. See also Loureiro Júnior (597), and Sodré's HISTORIA MILITAR (915), for the same period.

Ramos's (795), interesting analysis of the election of Quadros and the changes produced in Brazilian political institutions should be noted. Jânio Quadros's brief tenure in power can be understood by reading Cabral (204). Carli (232), concluded that there is no evidence to indicate that the military, foreign interests, or congressional leaders put pressure on Quadros to resign. Jaguaribe (520), probed deeply the events surrounding Quadros's renunciation, as did Luiz Bandeira (76). A number of works investigate the crisis leading to the military coup that deposed President João Goulart in 1964. For an analysis of the "crisis of populism" see Weffort (1003), who also examined the rise and fall of populist labor leaders from 1955 to 1964 (1002). Luiz Bandeira (75), wrote the most complete analysis of Goulart's presidency and drew upon a great store of unpublished archival material and interviews with key participants in the events. An excellent study of the National Democratic Union (UDN) was produced by Maria Victor de Mesquita Benevides (97), while Lucia Hippólito (503), produced an admirable study of the Social Democratic Party (PSD). Brazilian sociologist Octavio Ianni (513), explained the economic and political causes of the coup. In a book of collected essays, the Academy of Sciences of the USSR published EL EJERCITO Y LA SOCIEDAD (365), which includes an essay on the army in Brazil during the Goulart government. Lucifilia Neves (718), provided an analysis of the General Workers Command (CGT) during the Goulart crisis. A useful chronology of the crisis is found in Mario Victor (994). Alberto Dines, et al. (335), told the story of Goulart's fall from power, while Dulles (354), and Santos (845), concentrated on the career and military thought of General Castello Branco who led the coup against Goulart.

THE COUP OF 1964 AND MILITARY GOVERNMENT TO 1985

In his THE POLITICS OF MILITARY RULE IN BRAZIL, 1964-85, Thomas Skidmore (897), admirably reconstructed the political role of the armed forces for that period. His one hundred pages of notes are a gold mine of bibliographic information for those interested in pursuing research on the military after the coup. Other important studies that cover the period from the coup through the *abertura* in the late 1970s and early 1980s are: Maria Helena Moreira Alves (23, 25), whose works concentrate on the repression unleashed by the creation of the national security state, a question addressed as well by Marcio Moreira Alves (21, 22), Cavalcanti (261), Fiechter, (392), and Reis Filho, et al. (802). Luiz Pereira (763), addressed the growth of the politically conscious middle class and covered the period from 1930 to 1983; Bacchus's (62, 63), two works are brief, comprehensive surveys of the military in power; Faucher (380), saw the military regimes as quickening the denationalization of the Brazilian economy and meeting the opposition with severe repression. See also Peter Evans (373), and Stumpf and Pereira Filho (936).

In a copiously documented book Rene Armand Dreifuss (343), skillfully reconstructed the political alignments that took shape prior to the overthrow of the Goulart government. An important source on the movement of officers and the formation of opinions within the army is Fernando Pedreira (754). An excellent investigation into the Goulart administration, the coup, and the two military governments of Castello Branco and Costa e Silva is Schneider's (855). Rowe's (829, 830), two reports on the coup are particularly perceptive. See also the assessments by Horowitz (509), Harding (480), and Marini (644). Wallerstein (997), noted that the pre-coup governments' economic crises caused them to lose the support of the middle class bringing about the fall of Goulart in 1964. Santos, in his SESSENTA E QUATRO: ANATOMIA DA CRISE (848), provided a clear analysis of the deterioration of the Brazilian political system which led to paralysis in 1964. Starling (925), studied the conspirators in Minas Gerais, and Simões (885), portrayed the role of middle-class women in the anti-Goulart God, Fatherland, and Family organizations. For an analysis of the influence of the Escola Superior de Guerra and the national security doctrine on the coup planners, see Eliézer Oliveira (735).

The literature on the United States government's role in the 1964 coup is discussed in Alimonda's (15), brief review. A nationalistic journalist who lost his political rights after the April coup, Edmar Morel (699), believed that the United States engineered the ouster of Goulart. This is similar to the view taken by Carlos Nunes (724). Skidmore (896, 897), in his 1967 book, discussed the scant evidence showing the Lyndon Johnson regime's involvement and maintained that view in his 1988 study. In a carefully documented, well-balanced study, Parker (748), concluded that no proof existed to show that the United States planned, directed, or participated in the 1964 coup, but had contingency plans to intervene and to help the military if necessary. Brazilian historian Marcos Sá Correa (298), basically agreed with Parker's conclusions. Jan Knippers Black (117), and Luiz Alberto Moniz Bandeira (74), showed the extraordinary range of United States public and private influence in Brazil before and after the coup. Black's SENTINELS OF EMPIRE: THE UNITED STATES AND LATIN AMERICAN MILITARISM (116), is a passionate indictment of United States government policy from 1964 to 1984 of allying with Latin American military dictatorships to preserve and maintain North American economic hegemony in the region.

A useful chronology of the first military regime headed by General Castello Branco (1964-67) can be found in Gomes (446). Dulles's (356), second volume of his biography of Castello Branco focuses on the general's administration. It is a book rich in detail, well-researched, and essential reading for an understanding of the establishment of military control. Viana Filho (988), and José Wamberto (1000), both wrote favorable "insider" assessements of the regime and are valuable for the information they provide on individuals involved in the events of that time. Mendes (665), portrayed Castello Branco's government as a model for authoritarian regimes in Latin America. The journalist Carlos Castello Branco (131), distantly related to the general, commented on the regime's political activities. In a November/December 1966 issue of CADERNOS BRASILEIROS titled "Os militares" (677), several observers contributed informative essays on the military in power. James Rowe's (829, 830, 831), articles carefully analyzed political aspects of military rule, and Norman Blume (119), showed the influence of the Instituto de Pesquisas e Estudos Sociais (IPES) on the new government.

Works that have been highly critical of the Castello Branco regime abound. Basbaum's fourth volume of his HISTORIA SINCERA DA REPUBLICA (87), looked at the period from 1961 to 1967 and condemned the armed forces for destroying the democratic process. Alceu Lima (584), feared that the right-wing trend of the government would lead to the growth of communism. The journalist-politician Marcio Moreira Alves (21, 22), denounced the generals for unleashing a period of political repression, as did the radical Socialist governor of Pernambuco, Miguel Arrães (52). Maria Helena Moreira Alves (25), provided an indispensable overview of repression. Alvim (26), edited a collection of articles written in the Brazilian press critical of the government's arbitrary arrests, tortures, and political purges. Vieira in ESTADO E MISERIA SOCIAL NO BRASIL: DE GETULIO A GEISEL, 1951-1978 (996), analyzed the government's policies in education, health, housing, and social welfare, and Quartim (790), emphasized the harsh aspects of the dictatorship in his book. Student opposition to the government's educational policies is the subject of Poerner's (779), book, and Marcus Figueiredo (396), Rosenbaum (823), and Wedge (1001), directed attention to other aspects of student activism during the 1960s.

In an interesting analysis of Brazil's political parties and their relationship with the military Souza (922), argued that the political parties did not collapse after the 1964 coup, but underwent a process of realignment. Cammack (219), made a similar case in his study. Stepan's (929), work is an insightful probing of the institution of the military and the adjustments it had to undergo when it took power and held it. Markoff and Baretta (645), critiqued the logic behind Stepan's analysis. Skidmore's (895, 899), articles concentrated on the economic policies of the Castello Branco regime, as does the work of Syvrud (938), who favored the relatively orthodox stablization policy which it implemented.

The events surrounding the "coup" pulled off by Costa e Silva and the "hardliners" in 1967 are recounted in D'Aguiar (314), and Jayme Portella de Mello (663).   Sanders (841), wrote about the "institutionalization" of the "conservative revolution." Dimas Filho (333), painted a flattering portrait of Costa e Silva as soldier and war minister. Fiechter (392), Flynn (402), and Schneider (855), wrote penetrating analyses of the Costa e Silva regime.   Military changes brought about in the Brazilian system of higher education are discussed in Haussman and Haar (482), Douglas Graham (453), and Arapiraca (44).   For an understanding of the influence brought to bear by business groups see Souza (923).   Eliézer R. de Oliveira (735), analyzed the succession crisis triggered by Costa e Silva's sudden death, as did Schneider in his article "The Brazilian Military in Politics" (854).   Both authors strongly stressed the nature of military relationships with other major political groups. See also Pedreira (754).

A journalist with United Press International (UPI), Daniel Drosdoff (344), wrote a clear, direct, overview of the Médici government, with good background coverage of the period since the 1964 coup. Skidmore's article (894),   in O'Brien and Cammack   offered a comprehensive analysis of Médici's economic plans, while the Bank of London and South America (77), praised the government's policies and performance. See also in this regard Schneider (855), Fiechter (392), and Flynn (403).   In AUTHORITARIAN BRAZIL: ORIGINS, POLICIES, AND FUTURE, edited by Alfred Stepan (933), essayists dealt with various aspects of the Médici government. McDonough (620, 621), in two works, made good use of interviews with civilian politicians to conclude that power rested in the hands of a dictatorship controlled by the military and civilian technocrats for the benefit of foreign and domestic capitalist interests.

The debate over the Brazilian economic "*milagre*" of the late 1960s and early 1970s attracted the attention of numerous economists and historians.   Much can be learned of the ramifications of the armed forces' economic policies by consulting the work of Ames (31), who examined the effects of economic policy on education, salaries, and slums; Bacha (64), was critical of government economic policies; Fields (393), argued that despite growing inequality of income distribution in the 1960s, the income of the poorest groups improved; see the replies to his article in the March 1980 issue of the AMERICAN ECONOMIC REVIEW (29).   Morley (701), agreed that the poor benefited more from the economic growth than the statistics seem to indicate. Langoni (562), refuted the allegations that an increase of income concentration was a deliberate policy of the regime. Simonsen (887), later to become one of the top economic policy makers, analyzed changes in inflation rates, while the noted Brazilian economist Celso Furtado (426), passionately criticized the military regimes for the social and ecological costs of rapid growth. Barros and Graham (85), pointed out that the government opted for rapid economic growth rather than the more difficult, but sounder institutional restructuring necessary to insure the development of a vital and strong private sector. Camargo (217), Chalout (274), and Hewlett (491), provided well-documented and sweeping reviews of the economic situation and reached similar conclusions: the "*milagre*," enforced through severe political repression, enriched the few and impoverished the masses.

Catholic Church opposition to state repression emerged shortly after the 1964 coup. Charles Antoine (40), recounted the clergy's split over government dictatorial measures and Bruneau (192), showed the confrontation between church and state as the church fomented social and political change against the government's will. See also the works by Krischke (543), Luiz Lima (588), and Lernoux (574, 575). The struggle of Dom Helder Câmara to defend the poor and to confront the regime over human rights abuses is retold by Broucker (189).

Numerous writers recount the story of armed resistance to the post-coup governments. João Batista Berardo (101), wrote a valuable account of armed opposition movements in Latin America and emphasized the Brazilian events. Kohl and Litt (539), focused on the urban guerrillas in Brazil and elsewhere in Latin America to 1973. Quartim (790), described events from the guerrillas' perspective. Halperin (477), concentrated on Argentina, Brazil, and Uruguay and provided intriguing comparisons. See also Richard Gott (449), for the broader Latin American context. Langguth (561), covered events in Brazil as he followed the story of Dan Mitrione, executed by the Tupamaro guerrillas in Uruguay. TIRANDO O CAPUZ is the title of Alvaro Caldas's (207), book describing the influence of the Communist Party among college and university students. Frei Betto (103), a great admirer of Carlos Marighela, detailed the activities of the urban guerrilla leader, as did José and Miranda (529), for the army captain-turned-guerrilla, Carlos Lamarca. See Portela (784), for the best account of the Araguaia Guerrilla Front. Rebello (796), described the organization of former military men purged by Castello Branco into a guerrilla group that was defeated by the army, while Terra (956), reported on the guerrilla warfare in Pará state, 1972-73.

Military governments met the armed resistance with increased repression and torture. An excellent, authorative account is Fon (404), the best informed journalist on the subject, who had himself suffered torture. Venancio Filho (985), recorded the Brazilian equivalent to the American Bar Association's criticism of the government's illegal acts. Jakubs (521), looked at São Paulo's death squads, and Cavalcante, et al. (263), reconstructed the horrors suffered by a Dominican monk tortured and exiled by the military authorities. Amnesty International (32), published a report on the torture and showed the close relationship between military repression and rapid economic growth. Weschler (1006), compared the repressive systems of other Latin American countries with the situation in Brazil, and Nobrega (719), demonstrated the regime's reaction to the human rights policy of the United States. See also the works by Deckes (323), Elias José (528), Vargas (980), and the article "A tortura no Brasil," in VOZES (962).

With the governments of Ernesto Geisel (1974-79) and João Baptista Figueiredo (1979-84), the repression diminished and the process of a return to democracy began. An important result of the freedom gained during the *abertura* was the proliferation of high- quality literature from essayists, historians, political scientists, sociologists, and others, who observed and commented upon the transformation from military dictatorship to democracy. The body of literature is too vast to do justice in this bibliography, but a brief sample of some of these writings is in order.

An important journalistic overview of the political struggles characteristic of the 1974-80 period with good detail on intra-military conflicts is Kucinski (547). Wesson and Fleischer (1010), published a basic, general, political survey with useful observations on the changes that occurred in the 1970s. Skidmore (897), in his 1988 book, discussed in depth the politics of *abertura*. From a series of conferences and symposia held between 1983 and 1987, Stepan (934), organized a volume on the problems of transition from military dictatorship to a more democratic society. Contributions in this volume range from a historical overview of the period through economic problems, the role of the church, and the activities of grassroots movements. For a collection of articles on the ecclesiastical base communites during the transition, see Krischke and Mainwaring (545), while Bittencourt and Markum (113), painted a favorable portrait of Cardinal Evaristo Arns, champion of São Paulo's poor. Maria Alves's (24), article explored the challenges posed to "controlled" *abertura* by the church, labor unions, and grass-roots organizations. Prominent political sociologist and leftist politician Fernando Henrique Cardoso (225, 228), analyzed the procedure by which the government negotiated the process of *abertura*. One of the best studies dealing with the military's reasons for initiating the process of political liberalization is Stepan's OS MILITARES: DA ABERTURA A NOVA REPUBLICA (928). See also his RETHINKING MILITARY POLITICS: BRAZIL AND THE SOUTHERN CONE (931), and Selcher (863). Mainwaring and Viola (636), compared and contrasted Brazil's and Argentina's transition from armed forces rule. For the level of corruption under the military governments see the angry attack by Colonel Grael (452), and José Carlos de Assis's (58), widely-read book.

Several books and articles have been published on the government and style of Ernesto Geisel. Adirson de Barros (82), a Brazilian journalist, commented on the political reality of Geisel's climb to the presidency. Another journalist, Walder de Góes (441), provided an excellent overview of his government. Gaspari (437), published a penetrating discussion of the army's intelligence and internal security network during the Geisel years. In a first-rate article Schooyans (856), examined Geisel's foreign and domestic policies. Getúlio Bittencourt (112), captured Geisel's governing style and demonstrated how he and General Golbery de Couto e Silva manuevered to keep the presidency from falling into the hands of the hardliners. Stumpf and Pereira Filho (936), likewise provided good coverage on the crisis and struggle to keep the process of *abertura* on track. See also Anderson (34), and Gall (434), for background information on Figueiredo and the presidential selection process. Góes (442, 443), looked at the intrenchment of military officers in private and public sector bureaucracies as a principal cause for delaying the transition to civilian rule in 1984-85. Four recommended works deal with the national and Paulista bourgeoisie and their ambivalent relationship with their military governors from the time of the coup through the *abertura*: Boschi (128), Diniz and Boschi (338), Cardoso (229), and Pereira (763). For multinational corporations in Brazil see Arruda, Alfonso, and Souza (56).

There already exists an extensive and growing bibliography on labor's relationship with the armed forces regimes. Magano (630), published a brief description of the legal structure of Brazilian labor's relations with the state. A good, clear analysis of the system can be found in Erickson (369). Based upon his study of the chemical and pharmaceutical workers' union, Troyano (968), described the evolution of the union from the 1930s through the 1970s. Araujo (47), similarly recounted the history of the metalurgists from the Santos region (STIMMES) from 1933 to 1983. He devoted over two-thirds of the book to the years after the coup of 1964 when the military ousted the union's leadership and imprisoned its leading activists. Kenneth Mericle's (670, 671), dissertation and subsequent article examined the military regime's management of labor conflicts after the coup. Argelina Figueiredo (394), analyzed in detail the government's intervention in unions to purge them of recalcitrant leaders. Abranches (2), and Singer (890), faulted the government for not adopting policies which would be more favorable to the poor. Morley (701), investigated the relationship between government wage policies and social equity after the coup. Fernando Almeida (17), published a critical overview of the government's wage policies during the period 1964-81, as did

Livio de Carvalho (254). See also the Inter-Union Department of Statistics and Socio-Economic Studies (DIEESE) (331), and Bacha and Unger (66), for similar works. Green's (457), review of worker movements of the 1970s showed the government's need to take labor demands into consideration in its move toward liberalization.

Brazil's military governors' relations with the nation's political parties have attracted scholarly attention. In an excellent survey of legislation and party structures, Lima Júnior (589), argued that electoral participation increased after the 1964 coup as people found it the only legal way to demonstrate their dissatisfaction with the regime. Martins, et al. (648), agreed with that assessment. Jenks's (523, 524), works are important for an understanding of the political institutionalization. See Reis (800), for his conclusions about public opinion trends and the electoral process, and Krane (541), who analyzed the limits of vocal dissent and "interest articulation" under armed forces control. Diniz (336, 337), in two works, probed the machine politics of the MDB and its relationship with the military government. Kinzo (535), focusing on the MDB, explained the "disaggregation" of that party in the late 1980s, as a result of its being held together only by its disparate elements' opposition to military rule. Fleischer (399), provided reasons for the success of the military's program of a stable, gradual return to civilian control. See as well, Baretta and Markoff (80), and William C. Smith (907).

Some interesting examinations of the regime's control over the press have been published. Antonio Nunes (723), from a leftist perspective, covered the major struggles between the regime and journalists from 1969 to 1979. Comparing censorship around the world with the Brazilian experience, Coriolano Fagundes (375), included texts of the Brazilian orders and decrees. The highly respected columnist Carlos Chagas (273), reviewed the press's treatment under each military administration. Celina Duarte (345), showed how Geisel and Golbery do Couto e Silva courted the press against their military rivals, but used the government's powers to keep the press in check. Straubhaar (935), recounted the history of the state's use of television and showed how the military used it as a major propaganda tool. Bomeny (124), concluded that the military's use of educational television in Maranhão to transform the youth into passive supporters of an authoritarian regime was not very successful.

Several worthwhile investigations into the armed forces' preoccupation with national security have been made. The powerful National Information Service (SNI) from its origins to 1983 is the subject of Ana Lagoa's (558), book. Gurgel (470), presented a thorough and systematic discussion of national security doctrine. National security through industrial development is the topic of

Edmundo Silva's (866), article, while Durandin (360), reviewed Brazil's national security theory and policy and discussed the proposed South Atlantic Military Treaty with South Africa. Calvo (211), compared the impact of national security doctrines on Brazil and Chile and included an excellent one hundred-page bibliography on national security and the military in Latin America. Antonio de Arruda's (55), book critically recounted the history of the Superior War School (ESG). Burgess and Wolf (198), through a reading of ESG publications, explained the institution's concepts of power and national security. See also Augusto Fragoso (409), and Macedo (623). Moreira (698), advocated the development of a better merchant marine in order to strengthen Brazil's national security.

Military preoccupation with the Amazon region has a long history, but after the 1964 coup it intensified. Apesteguy (41), reviewed the government's programs for developing Amazonia from 1964 to 1979 and saw a shift from military definition of goals to federal manipulation by private interests. A well-researched and complete critique of the regime's programs for the Amazon is that of Mahar (632). Both Branford and Glock (139), and Cardoso and Müller (231), provided solid overviews of military Amazon policies. The government's position on Amazon development unleashed a debate over the question of whether the region should be developed or not. As an example of the pro-development argument see Rebelo (797), and Tocantins (959), while Denevan (329), Goodland and Irwin (448), and Monnet (684), sounded the alarm over the negative impact of opening Amazonia to development. Davis (320), attacked the armed forces' policies in the Amazon basin for their devastating effects on the indigenous population, and Nigel Smith (903), and Bunker (197), evaluated the planned colonization along the Transamazon Highway. Marianne Schmink (852), looked at the land conflicts that erupted in the Amazon as large agricultural enterprises purchased land occupied by untitled subsistence farmers. Rabben (792), noted the problems which developed over the huge gold diggings in forest areas of Roraima inhabited by the Yanomami people. Manuel Andrade (38), Cehelsky (266), and Marighela, et al. (643), showed how the military governments reversed plans for agrarian reform which fostered the continuation of latifundia development.

The military government's drive toward nuclear power as a solution to Brazil's energy problems is examined in Simon, et al. (886), and Meyers (674). Wonder (1016), discussed the issues in an excellent brief overview of Brazilian and German programs. Marini and Pellicer de Brody (644), analyzed the Costa e Silva government's opposition to the Nuclear Proliferation Treaty. Washington's opposition to the Brazilian-German nuclear accord is covered skillfully in a 1977 article in NOTES

ET ETUDES DOCUMENTAIRES (6), and in Luddeman (602). See
also a Brazilian scientist's opinions of the accord in Amarante (28), and
José Goldemberg (444), a leading nuclear physicist, criticized the
official policy. The president of the Brazilian state nuclear agency
(NUCLEBRAS), Paulo Batista (92), summarized events after the
signing of the accord, and Greno Velasco (458), examined the
implications of nuclear energy on socio-economic development in Brazil
and elsewhere in Latin America. Guglialmelli (464, 465, 466), analyzed
the politico-economic impact of nuclear energy in Brazil and Argentina
and the possible development of nuclear weapons. In a well-
documented study, Brazilian industrialist Kurt Mirow (678), rendered
a harsh attack on the government's nuclear policy, especially on the
accords with Germany.

Numerous scholars have written on the foreign affairs conducted by
the military governments since 1964. Grabendorff's and Nitsch's (450),
scholarly review of foreign policy interests of the post- coup regimes is
recommended. Wesson (1008), demonstrated how United States
influence over Brazil steadily waned from 1945 to 1980. See also
Robert Branco (136), for Brazil's relations with the United States.
Ralph Santos (846), reconstructed Brazil's participation in the United
States invasion of the Dominican Republic in 1965. Schneider (853),
took an insightful look into the military's world view, as did Perry (767),
and Selcher (862). Brazil's participation in international conferences
on the law and the sea came under Morris's (702), scrutiny, who
provided a valuable analysis of the navy and its place in national affairs.
See also Carvalho Filho (256). Moreira (697), traced the historic and
geostrategic importance of sea power and Brazil's place in the South
Atlantic. Bonturi (126), advocated that Brazil initiate the creation of a
South Atlantic Treaty Organization to insure the "security" of the region.
NACLA devoted an entire issue of its REPORT ON THE AMERICAS
(710), to Brazil's "continental strategy," which should be compared with
Jack Child (279). Osny Pereira (764), developed a good discussion of
Argentine-Brazilian points of view on the construction of the Itaipu
power complex. Penna (757), discussed the leadership's attempts to
reconcile foreign policy with internal security and order. General
Golbery do Couto e Silva (868, 869), addressed the army's geopolitical
concerns, as did Oliveiros S. Ferreira (389), and Mattos (653).

On the growing importance of the Brazilian arms industry Eul-Soo
Pang's 1989 paper (745), is an excellent overview. McCann (612),
reviewed the history of the Brazilian army's quest for arms
independence. Brigagão's work (186), and a comprehensive article
titled "Armas: O Brasil invade o mercado mundial" (48), provides
information on the weapons industry. See as well Freed (415), and
Varas (978).

State militias, military police, and the national guard have received attention from several investigators. Castro (259), compared the French and United States national guards to the Brazilian institution. Rego (798), reconstructed the role of the Pará state militia in the Canudos campaign. A significant study of blacks in the Brazilian national guard by Castro (260), reveals the extent and importance of the black in national defense and public order and sees the guard as a "democratizing force." Heloisa Fernandes (386), produced a well-researched study of the state police force of São Paulo from colonial times through the Old Republic. See as well the two works by Andrade and Câmara (37), and Dallari (315), on the Paulista state police. A rather dry chronology of the military police in Minas Gerais is Silveira (882). A good factual account of the role of the Mineiro military police in the revolts of 1924, 1930, and 1932 can be found in Andrade (39); see also Baggio (70), while Anatolio Assis (57), concentrated on the Third Battalion of the military police in Diamantina. For the military police in Paraíba see Naziazene (711), and for Piauí consult Pinheiro Filho and Pinheiro (775).

PERIODICALS

Information on the history of the Brazilian military is found in a wide range of periodical literature, and the researcher will be rewarded by searching through those that do not specifically treat Latin American topics as well as those that do. Much of value can be learned about the armed forces and their role in Brazilian society by reading the weekly news magazines cited below. Most materials on the Brazilian military, however, are located in two types of journal sources: those that deal with Latin American and Brazilian studies in general, and those exclusively focusing on the country's armed forces. Each branch of the Brazilian military publishes its own periodicals.

This bibliography of periodicals is not exhaustive, but serves to guide one in the direction of finding important information and leads for further research. Excellent articles on the military and society in Brazil have appeared in readily available, English-language, scholarly journals such as the HISPANIC AMERICAN HISTORICAL REVIEW (1051), LATIN AMERICAN RESEARCH REVIEW (1060), JOURNAL OF LATIN AMERICAN STUDIES (1056), LUSO-BRAZILIAN REVIEW (1062), and BRAZIL WATCH (1040), to name but a few. An excellent guide to English and foreign language periodical literature on Brazil is the HISPANIC AMERICAN PERIODICALS INDEX (HAPI) (504).

In Brazil there are numerous scholarly journals and newsweeklies which carry articles and stories on the armed forces and their activities in society. With no intention of being comprehensive, the following list will give the student of military history an idea of what is available. From time to time, good articles will appear on the topic in the pages of the REVISTA DO INSTITUTO HISTORICO E GEOGRAFICO BRASILEIRO (1081), published since 1839. Reflecting scholarly research carried on by historians in Brazilian universities, the REVISTA DE HISTORIA (São Paulo) (1074), yields some fine studies. After the coup in 1964, the REVISTA CIVILIZACAO BRASILEIRA (1072), emerged as a leftist newsmagazine which has been critical of the military government's authoritarian posture. From the field of economics, the National Association of Centers of Post-graduate Training in Economics took the government to task over its economic policies beginning in 1977 in the pages of ECONOMIA: REVISTA DA ANPEC (1044). Similarly, in the same year the BOLETIM DO INSTITUTO DOS ECONOMISTAS DO ESTADO DO RIO DE JANEIRO (IERP) (1035), appeared and debated the key economic questions in lay terminology. Excellent political studies of the armed forces can be found in the REVISTA BRASILEIRA DE ESTUDOS POLITICOS (1071), as well as in DADOS (1042). The high quality, analytical pieces that appear in the issues of ESTUDOS CEBRAP (1047), make this an essential resource for research into the military's impact on Brazilian society, especially since the 1964 coup. ESTUDOS SOCIOECONOMICOS (1048), also is a valuable source of interpretive analysis for the period since its inception in 1975.

Readily available newspapers and news magazines provide a rich resource for studies of the military. VEJA (1090), VISAO (1091), MANCHETE (1063), ISTO E (1052), OPINIAO (1069), JORNAL DO BRASIL (1054), O ESTADO DE SAO PAULO (1045), O GLOBO (1050), JORNAL DA TARDE (1053), and FOLHA DE SAO PAULO (1049), to name just a few, can be found in the Biblioteca Nacional.

The various branches of the armed services publish their own periodicals and these can reveal such things as: historical information; technical and personnel data relating to the branch; military doctrine; instruction and training; promotions; institutional news; articles on finances, administration, cultural and social activities; articles and opinions on political and economic affairs; necrologies; and institutional propaganda. Needless to say, these publications are of extreme importance to any historical analysis of the military. Frank McCann (614), Thomas Skidmore (897), and Alfred Stepan (929), have demonstrated in their excellent studies the significance of these periodicals for an inside glimpse of the armed forces. The following is a partial list of these publications: ALMANAQUE DO EXERCITO (1023), A ANCORA (1027), BOLETIM DO CLUBE NAVAL (1033), A DEFESA NACIONAL (1043), REVISTA DE AERONAUTICA (1073), REVISTA DO CLUBE MILITAR (1079), REVISTA DO

INSTITUTO DE GEOGRAFIA E HISTORIA MILITAR DO BRASIL (1080), REVISTA MARITIMA BRASILEIRA (1084), and REVISTA DE MEDICINA MILITAR (1077). These journals and newspapers can be located in the libraries and archives discussed above.

FUTURE RESEARCH

Despite the high volume and, at times, superior quality of the historical work done on the history of the armed forces in Brazil, there is room for the ambitious historian to make significant contributions to our understanding of the impact the military has had on Brazilian society. 15 March 1990 marked a watershed in Brazilian history with the nation-wide election of a civilian to the presidency and the return of the generals to their barracks. This would be a prime time to produce a general study of the history of the armed forces from the fall of the monarchy in 1889 to the return of the civilians in 1990. While access to materials in some cases will prove an obstacle to telling the "whole" story, there is still an abundance of data which needs to be sifted and analyzed and which should reveal a deeper insight than we now have into the evolutionary role of the military in society.

If a general overview is too ambitious an endeavor, then one could confine oneself to the systematic analysis of the numerous service publications mentioned in the "Periodicals" section of this essay, in order to arrive at some conclusions about the political, social, and economic attitudes of the men in uniform. Do officers in the navy think and behave differently than their colleagues in the other service branches? While there have been several important studies of how the army leadership views the military's mission in Brazilian society, especially during the first quarter of the twentieth century, it is not clear how officers in the other service branches think. A history of the relationships between the army, navy, and air force is lacking, and very little has been written on the state militias and their interactions with and ties to the national military forces.

Owing to the importance of the state militias up to the Estado Nôvo more studies similar to Dallari's on São Paulo's Força Pública (315), need to be undertaken. What happened to the various state militias after 1935 and what was their relationship to the federal armed forces? How important was regionalism after that period within the armed forces? To what extent did the high command after 1964 go toward further reducing the regional character of the various service branches and what is the level of conflict between local officialdom and federal commanders? Detailed studies of military regionalism might challenge the prevailing view that the armed forces served as important agents of national unification.

Alfred Stepan in his recent book RETHINKING MILITARY POLITICS: BRAZIL AND THE SOUTHERN CONE (931), has outlined some areas where research is badly needed and some of the reasons for Brazilians' neglect of the military as a topic of study worthy of their time and interest. While his own study and others recently have focused on the military during the period of *distensão* and *abertura*, more empirical analyses are needed. Taking into consideration the obstacles to researching the military, Brazil's armed forces publish a considerable amount of data which needs to be assessed and analyzed. Many retired officers have expressed a willingness to talk about their experiences to journalists and biographers, and there is every reason to exploit their openness. While some biographies have been done on leaders like Castello Branco, Luis Carlos Prestes, and Góes Monteiro, others would be welcome on officers such as Generals Golbery do Couta e Silva, Emílio Garrastazú Médici, and Ernesto Geisel.

While it is clear that the military gradually increased its economic power and its ties to the industrial elites in the era after World War II, the process by which this was accomplished and the extent to which it grew is still fuzzy and needs to be brought into clearer focus. Also, investigation on the new Brazilian political elite formed out of the Escola Superior da Guerra and its affiliated Asociação de Diplomados da Escola Superior da Guerra (ADESG) is need. Since 1962, the ADESG has conducted courses throughout the country for leaders in various sectors of Brazilian society who have been nominated to attend by members of the ADESG. An analysis of this process, who attends, what they learn, and how they put it into practice and how this affects Brazilian society would be an important contribution.

Despite the heavy cloak of secrecy in which it has wrapped itself, the Serviço Nacional da Informação (SNI), needs to be analyzed. While some studies such as Barros's (83), have revealed basic information on this important intelligence agency, much remains to be done. Denial of access to the SNI's archives notwithstanding, a great deal can be gleaned from the public record and from oral testimony that should be important and interesting. As a kind of government within a government, the Brazilian security apparatus wields considerable influence and power beyond merely gathering and controlling information. Like the United States Central Intelligence Agency, the SNI appears to reflect, since its inception, attitudes of virulent anti-communism and suspicion toward liberal democrats. In fact, a comparison of the two agencies would be most enlightening.

It is well known that the military in Brazil has a corps of engineers, but it is less well known what role it plays in civic action programs and what kind of power and influence it wields in the development of

Brazil's industrial infrastructure. An objective history of the engineers would make a valuable contribution to military historiography.

In addition, more comparative studies need to be made which will serve to put into perspective some of the many questions that emerge from a study of Brazilian history. For example, how much of Brazil's uniqueness and differing development can be attributed to the historic role of the military in the nation's evolution? As we enter the decade of the 1990s Brazil is still a country whose people have a weak sense of their rights as citizens and who suffer a level of inequality of income not experienced by other contemporary democracies in the world. While there are numerous historical reasons for this, it would be important to know to what degree the military is responsible for current conditions in Brazil. Comparative analyses will also throw light on explanations for the differences in the rapid return to democratic forms of government in Argentina, Chile, and Uruguay, and the long drawn out process of liberalization and democratization in Brazil which took place over the course of almost seventeen years, 1973-90.

Brazil's military-industrial complex and the participation of military men, either on active duty or in retirement, in the management of industries within this complex is another area in need of investigation. An important question is just how much are state enterprise and the military industrial complex a reflection of military power? This should be of special importance now that the military has turned political control over to the civilian politicians. In addition, a careful study of the armed forces' role in determining Brazilian foreign policy since the 1930s is an area in need of exploration.

Many other avenues of inquiry await the investigator of Brazilian armed forces' history, especially in the social field. While numerous studies have scrutinized the officer corps, few researchers have looked at the kinds of lives and opportunities experienced by recruits and the non-commissioned officers. What has been the collective historical experience of the common soldier or sailor and how have these people and their families been regarded in Brazilian society? With the return of civilian democratic government to Brazil this is a propitious time to deepen our understanding of the military institution.

BIBLIOGRAPHY: BRAZIL

1. Abramovay, Ricardo. "O velho poder dos barões da terra." In NOVA REPUBLICA: UM BALANCO, 204-26. Edited by Flavio Kontzii. São Paulo: L&PM Editores, 1986.

2. Abranches, Sergio Henrique. OS DESPOSSUIDOS: CRESCIMENTO E POBREZA NO PAIS DO MILAGRE. Rio de Janeiro: Zahar, 1985.

3. Abreu, Diores Santos. "O desbravamento da Alta-Sorocabana por um bandeirante moderno: Capitão Francisco Whitaker." REVISTA DE HISTORIA 31 (1965): 447-62.

4. Abreu, Hugo. O OUTRO LADO DO PODER. Rio de Janeiro: Editôra Nova Fronteira, 1979.

5. ———. TEMPO DE CRISE. Rio de Janeiro: Editôra Nova Fronteira, 1980.

6. "L'accord nucleaire germano-brésilien et Washington." NOTES ET ETUDES DOCUMENTAIRES 4391/4393 (1977): 19-36.

7. Aguiar, Neuma, ed. THE STRUCTURE OF BRAZILIAN DEVELOPMENT. New Brunswick, NJ: Transaction Books, 1979.

8. Akabane, Yoko. "La guerra de Canudos y el fanatismo religioso en Brasil del latifundismo a la guerra de Canudos." CUADERNOS HISPANOAMERICANOS 400 (1983): 151-56.

9. Albert, Bill, with Paul Henderson. SOUTH AMERICA AND THE FIRST WORLD WAR: THE IMPACT OF THE WAR ON BRAZIL, ARGENTINA, PERU, AND CHILE. Cambridge: Cambridge University Press, 1988.

10. Alcántara, Aspasia Brasileiro. O CRISTO DO POVO. Rio de Janeiro: Editôra Sabia, 1968.

11. Aleixo, Mauricio Brandi, et al., eds. PEDRO ALEIXO E SUA OBRA. Belo Horizonte: Senado Federal, Centro Gráfico, 1982.

12. Alexander, Robert J. "The Brazilian Tenentes after the Revolution of 1930." JOURNAL OF INTERAMERICAN STUDIES AND WORLD AFFAIRS 15 (1973): 221-48.

13. ——. "Brazilian 'Tenentismo.'" HISPANIC AMERICAN HISTORICAL REVIEW 36 (1956): 229-42.

14. Alimonda, Hector A. "'Paz y administracion-ordem e progresso': Notas para un estudio comparativo de los estados oligárquicos argentina y brasileño." REVISTA MEXICANA DE SOCIOLOGIA 44 (1982): 1323-50.

15. ——. "Reassessing the Literature of Military Intervention." LATIN AMERICAN PERSPECTIVES 11 (1984): 137-42.

16. Almeida, Antonio da Rocha. VULTOS DA PATRIA: OS BRASILEIROS MAIS ILUSTRES DE SEUS TEMPOS. 3 vols. Rio de Janeiro: Editôra Globo, 1965.

17. Almeida, Fernando Lopes de. POLITICA SALARIAL, EMPREGO E SINDICALISMO, 1964-1981. Petrópolis: Vozes, 1982.

18. Almeida, General Gil de. HOMENS E FACTOS DE UMA REVOLUCAO. Rio de Janeiro: Calvino Filho, 1934.

19. Almeida, José Americo de. OCASOS DE SANGUE. Rio de Janeiro: Livraria José Olympio, 1954.

20. Alves, Francisco M. Rodrigues. DEMOCRACIA CORROMPIDA, OU GOLPE DE ESTADO? São Paulo: Gea, 1955.

21. Alves, Marcio Moreira. A GRAIN OF MUSTARD SEED: THE AWAKENING OF THE BRAZILIAN REVOLUTION. Garden City, NY: Anchor Books, 1973.

22. ——. TORTURAS E TORTURADOS. Rio de Janeiro: Idade Nova, 1966.

23. Alves, Maria Helena Moreira. ESTADO E OPOSICAO NO BRASIL, 1964-1984. Petrópolis: Editôra Vozes, 1984.

24. ——. "Grassroots Organizations, Trade Unions, and the Church: A Challenge to the Controlled *Abertura* in Brazil." LATIN AMERICAN PERSPECTIVES 11 (1984): 73-102.

25. ———. STATE AND OPPOSITION IN MILITARY BRAZIL. Austin: University of Texas Press, 1988.

26. Alvim, Thereza Cesario, ed. O GOLPE DE 64: A IMPRENSA DISSE NAO. Rio de Janeiro: Civilização Brasileira, 1979.

27. Amado, Jorge. VIDA DE LUIZ CARLOS PRESTES: EL CABALLERO DE ESPERANZA. Buenos Aires: Ed. Claridad, 1942.

28. Amarante, José Alberto Albano do. "O Acordo Nuclear Brasil-Alemanha: Um reexame apos 21 meses." PROBLEMAS BRASILEIROS 15 (1977): 28-35.

29. AMERICAN ECONOMIC REVIEW, March 1980.

30. Ames, Barry Charles. "Bureaucratic Policy Making in a Militarized Regime: Brazil After 1964." Ph.D. dissertation, Stanford University, 1972.

31. ———. RHETORIC AND REALITY IN A MILITARIZED REGIME: BRAZIL SINCE 1964. Beverly Hills: Sage Publications, 1974.

32. Amnesty International. A REPORT OF ALLEGATIONS OF TORTURE IN BRAZIL. 3d ed. London: Amnesty International Publications, 1976.

33. Amora, Paulo. REBELIAO DAS MULHERES EM MINAS GERAIS. Rio de Janeiro: Edições GRD, 1968.

34. Anderson, Robin L. "Brazil's Military Regime under Fire." CURRENT HISTORY, February 1978, 61-65, 87.

35. Andrade, Auro Moura. UM CONGRESO CONTRA O ARBITRIO: DIARIOS E MEMORIAS, 1961-1967. Rio de Janeiro: Nôva Frontiera, 1985.

36. Andrade, Diva, and Alba Costa Maciel. DISSERTACOES E TESES DEFENDIDAS NA FFLCH/USP: 1939-1977. São Paulo: Universidade de São Paulo, 1977.

37. Andrade, Euclides, and Hely F. da Câmara. A FORCA PUBLICA DE SAO PAULO: ESBOCO HISTORICO, 1831-1931. São Paulo: Sociedade Impressora Paulista, 1931.

38. Andrade, Manuel Correia de Oliveira. LATIFUNDIO E REFORMA AGRARIA NO BRASIL. São Paulo: Livraria Duas Cidades, 1980.

39. Andrade, Paulo Rene de. TRES REVOLUCOES: A ATUACAO DA POLICIA MILITAR DE MINAS GERAIS, A ANTIGA FORCA PUBLICA, NOS MOVIMENTOS REVOLUCIONARIOS DE 1924, 1930 E 1932; ESBOCO HISTORICO. Belo Horizonte: Imprensa Oficial, 1976.

40. Antoine, Charles. CHURCH AND POWER IN BRAZIL. Mary Knoll, NY: Orbis Books, 1973.

41. Apesteguy, Christine. "L'intervention fédérale en Amazonie: Elements pour une définition de l'état militaire au Brésil." CAHIERS DES AMERIQUES LATINES 19 (1979): 89-100.

42. Aragão, José Campos de. HISTORIAS PARA SOLDADOS. Rio de Janeiro: Biblioteca do Exército, 1964.

43. ———. A INTENTONA COMUNISTA DE 1935. Rio de Janeiro: Biblioteca do Exército, 1973

44. Arapiraca, José Oliveira. A USAID E A EDUCACAO BRASILEIRA. São Paulo: Cortez, 1982.

45. Araripe, Tristão de Alencar. "A Escola de Estado Maior do Exército em un trecho de sua evolução." REVISTA MILITAR BRASILEIRA 71 (1960): 5-22.

46. ———. TASSO FRAGOSO: UM POUCO DE HISTORIA DO NOSSO EXERCITO. Rio de Janeiro: Biblioteca do Exército, 1960.

47. Araujo, Braz José de. OPERARIOS EM LUTA: METALURGICOS DA BAIXADA SANTISTA, 1933-1983. Rio de Janeiro: Paz e Terra, 1985.

48. "Armas: O Brasil invade o mercado mundial." SENHOR, September 1981, 37-61.

49. Arquidiocese de São Paulo. BRASIL: NUNCA MAIS. Petrópolis: Editôra Vozes, 1985.

50. O ARQUIVO JOSE AMERICO E A REVOLUCAO DE 30: REPRODUCAO DE COPIAS TELEGRAFICAS, CARTAS, OFICIOS E NOTAS DIVERSAS. Rio de Janeiro: Arquivo José Americo, 1985.

51. Arquivo Odilon Braga. MANIFESTO DOS MINEIROS E A REVOLUCAO DE 1930. Juiz de Fora, Minas Gerais: Universidade Federal de Juiz de Fora, 1979.

52. Arrães, Miguel. BRAZIL: THE PEOPLE AND THE POWER. London: Penguin Books, 1969.

53. ———. CONVERSACOES COM ARRAES. Belo Horizonte: Editôra Vega, 1979.

54. ———. PALAVRAS DE ARRAES: TEXTOS DE MIGUEL ARRAES; DEPOIMENTOS DE ANTONIO CALLADO, ET AL. Rio de Janeiro: Civilização Brasileira, 1966.

55. Arruda, Antonio de. ESG: HISTORIA DE SUA DOUTRINA. Rio de Janeiro: Edições GRD; Instituto Nacional do Livro; and Ministério da Educação e Cultura, 1980.

56. Arruda, Marcos, Carlos Alfonso, and Herbet de Souza. MULTINATIONALS AND BRAZIL: THE IMPACT OF MULTINATIONAL CORPORATIONS IN CONTEMPORARY BRAZIL. New York: NACLA, 1975.

57. Assis, Anatolio Alves de. HISTORIA DO 3o. BATALHAO. N.p.: n.p., 1972.

58. Assis, José Carlos de. A CHAVE DO TESOURO: ANATOMIA DOS ESCANDALOS FINANCEIROS; BRASIL, 1974-1983. Rio de Janeiro: Paz e Terra, 1983.

59. Aureli, Willy. BANDEIRANTES D'OESTE. 2d ed. São Paulo: Edições LEIA, 1962.

60. Ayers, Miguel de Castro. O EXERCITO QUE EU VI: MEMORIAS. Rio de Janeiro: A. Coelho Branco F. Editôra, 1965.

61. Azevedo, Pedro Cordolino de. HISTORIA MILITAR. 2 vols. Rio de Janeiro: Imprensa Nacional, 1950-52.

62. Bacchus, Wilfred. "Long-Term Military Rulership in Brazil: Ideologic Consensus and Dissensus, 1963-1983." JOURNAL OF POLITICAL AND MILITARY SOCIOLOGY 13 (1985): 99-123.

63. ———. MISSION IN MUFTI: BRAZIL'S MILITARY REGIMES, 1964-1985. Westport, CT: Greenwood Press, 1990.

64. Bacha, Edmar Lisboa. "Issues and Evidence on Recent Brazilian Economic Growth." WORLD DEVELOPMENT 5 (1977): 46-67.

65. ———. OS MITOS DE UMA DECADA. Rio de Janeiro: Paz e Terra, 1976.

66. Bacha, Edmar Lisboa, and Roberto Mangabeira Unger. PARTICIPACAO, SALARIO, E VOTO: UM PROJECTO DE DEMOCRACIA PARA O BRASIL. Rio de Janeiro: Paz e Terra, 1978.

67. Baer, Werner. THE BRAZILIAN ECONOMY: GROWTH AND DEVELOPMENT. New York: Praeger Publishers, 1989.

68. Baer, Werner, and Paul Beckerman. "The Decline and Fall of Brazil's Cruzado." LATIN AMERICAN RESEARCH REVIEW 24 (1989): 35-64.

69. Baer, Werner, and Isaac Kerstenetzky. "The Brazilian Economy in the Sixties." In BRAZIL IN THE SIXTIES, 105-45. Edited by Riordan Roett. Nashville: Vanderbilt University Press, 1972.

70. Baggio, Sheila Brandão. "A força pública de Minas na primeira república." REVISTA BRASILEIRA DE ESTUDOS POLITICOS 49 (1979): 201-32.

71. Bahiana, Paulo Henrique. AS FORCAS ARMADAS E O DESENVOLVIMENTO DO BRASIL. Rio de Janeiro: Bloch Editores, 1974.

72. Bandecchi, Brasil, et al. DICCIONARIO DE HISTORIA DO BRASIL: MORAL E CIVISMO. 4th ed. São Paulo: Edições Melhoramentos, 1976.

73. Bandeira, Dulcina. ANTES QUE SEJA TARDE: BIOGRAFIA DE ALIPIO BANDEIRA. Rio de Janeiro: n.p., 1979.

74. Bandeira, Luiz Alberto Moniz. CARTEIS E DESNACIONALIZACAO: A EXPERIENCIA BRASILEIRA, 1964-1974. Rio de Janeiro: Civilização Brasileira, 1975.

75. ———. O GOVERNO JOÃO GOULART: AS LUTAS SOCIAIS NO BRASIL, 1961-1964. 4th ed. Rio de Janeiro: Civilização Brasileira, 1978.

76. ———. A RENUNCIA DE JANIO QUADROS. Rio de Janeiro: Editôra Brasiliense, 1979.

77. Bank of London and South America. "Brazil: The Médici Administration; Performance and Prospects." QUARTERLY REVIEW 7 (1973): 152-63.

78. Barata, Julio de Carvalho. A POLITICA SOCIAL DA REVOLUCAO. Brasilia: Ministro do Trabalho e Previdencia Social, 1972.

79. Barbosa, Ruy. CONTRA O MILITARISMO: DISCURSOS POLITICOS. Rio de Janeiro: Companhia Eleitora, 1910.

80. Baretta, Silvio R. Duncan, and John Markoff. "Brazil's Abertura: A Transition from What to What?" In AUTHORITARIANS AND DEMOCRATS: REGIME TRANSITION AND LATIN AMERICA, 43-65. Edited by James M. Malloy and Mitchell A. Seligson. Pittsburgh: University of Pittsburgh Press, 1987.

81. Barreto, Anibal. FORTIFICACOES DO BRASIL: RESUMO HISTORICO. Rio de Janeiro: Biblioteca do Exército, 1958.

82. Barros, Adirson de. MARCO: GEISEL E A REVOLUCAO BRASILEIRA. Rio de Janeiro: Artenova, 1976.

83. Barros, Alexandre de Sousa Costa. "The Brazilian Military: Professional Socialization, Performance and State Building." Ph.D. dissertation, University of Chicago, 1978.

84. Barros, João Alberto Lins de. MEMORIAS DE UM REVOLUCIONARIO. 2 vols. Rio de Janeiro: Civilização Brasileira, 1953.

85. Barros, José Roberto Mendonça de, and Douglas H. Graham. "The Brazilian Economic Miracle Revisited: Private and Public Sector Initiative in a Market Economy." LATIN AMERICAN RESEARCH REVIEW 13 (1978): 5-38.

86. Bartley, Russell H. "A Decade of Soviet Scholarship in Brazilian History, 1958-1968." HISPANIC AMERICAN HISTORICAL REVIEW 50 (1970): 445-66.

87. Basbaum, Leôncio. HISTORIA SINCERA DA REPUBLICA. 4 vols. São Paulo: Editôra Alfa-Omega, 1975-77.

88. Basseches, Bruno. A BIBLIOGRAPHY OF BRAZILIAN BIBLIOGRAPHIES. Detroit: B. Ethridge Books, 1978.

89. Bastos, Abguar. HISTORIA DA POLITICA REVOLUCIONARIA NO BRASIL. 2 vols. Rio de Janeiro: Editôra Conquista, 1973.

90. Bastos, J. Justino Alves. ENCONTRO COM O TEMPO. Pôrto Alegre: Editôra Globo, 1965.

91. Batista, Estanislau Fragoso. CANTATA DE UM ANISTIADO-- PARA DEPOIS. São Paulo: Edições Loyola, 1981.

92. Batista, Paulo Nogueira. "A un año del Acuerdo Nuclear Brasileño-Alemán." ESTRATEGIA 42 (1976): 63-69.

93. Bello, José Maria. A HISTORY OF MODERN BRAZIL, 1889-1964. Stanford: Stanford University Press, 1966.

94. Beloch, Israel, and Alzira Alves de Abreu, eds. DICIONARIO HISTORICO-BIOGRAFICO BRASILEIRO, 1930-1983. 4 vols. Rio de Janeiro: Forense Universitaria, 1984.

95. Beltrão, Hélio. DESCENTRALIZACAO E LIBERDADE. Rio de Janeiro: Editôra Record, 1984.

96. Beltrão, Hélio, et al. DESBUROCRATIZACAO: IDEIAS FUNDAMENTAIS. Brasília: Presidencia da República, Programa Nacional de Desburocratização, 1982.

97.   Benevides, Maria Victoria de Mesquita. A UDN E O
      UDENISMO: AMBIGUIDADES DO LIBERALISMO
      BRASILEIRO, 1945-1965. Rio de Janeiro: Paz e Terra, 1981.

98.   Bento, Claudio Moreira. "Forte de S. Francisco Xavier de
      Piratininga ou Forte da Barra, 1702-1983." REVISTA DO
      INSTITUTO HISTORICO E GEOGRAFICA BRASILEIRO
      340 (1983): 7-14.

99.   ———. "Getúlio Vargas e a evolução da doutrina do exército,
      1930-1945." REVISTA DO INSTITUTO HISTORICO E
      GEOGRAFICO BRASILEIRO 339 (1983): 63-71.

100. ———. "História da Academia das Agulhas Negras." REVISTA
      DO   INSTITUTO   HISTORICO   E   GEOGRAFICO
      BRASILEIRO 336 (1982): 169-84.

101. Berardo, João Batista. GUERRILHAS E GUERRILHEROS
      NO DRAMA DA AMERICA LATINA. São Paulo: Edições
      Populares, 1981.

102. Bethell, Leslie, ed. THE CAMBRIDGE HISTORY OF LATIN
      AMERICA. Vols. 3-5. London: Cambridge University Press,
      1985-86.

103. Betto, Frei. BATISMO DE SANGUE: OS DOMINICANOS E
      A MORTE DE CARLOS MARIGHELA. Rio de Janeiro:
      Civilização Brasileira, 1982.

104. ———. CARTAS DE PRISAO. 4th ed. Rio de Janeiro:
      Civilização Brasileira, 1978.

105. Bezerra, Gregorio. MEMORIAS. 2 vols. Rio de Janeiro:
      Civilização Brasiliera, 1979.

106. "Bibliografia sobre a Revolução de 31 de Março." BOLETIM
      DA BIBLIOTECA DA CAMARA DOS DEPUTADOS 13
      (1964): 499-514.

107. BIBLIOGRAPHIC GUIDE TO LATIN AMERICAN STUDIES.
      Boston: G.K. Hall, 1978-.

108. BIBLIOGRAPHICA BRASILEIRA DE CIENCIAS SOCIAIS. Rio de Janeiro: Instituto Brasileiro de Bibliográphica e Documentação, 1955.

109. Bicudo, Hélio Pereira. MEU DEPOIMENTO SOBRE O ESQUADRAO DA MORTE. 6th ed. São Paulo: Pontificia Comissão de Justiça e Paz de São Paulo, 1977.

110. ———. SEGURANCA NACIONAL ON SUBMISSAO. Rio de Janeiro: Paz e Terra, 1984.

111. Bilac, Olavo. A DEFESA NACIONAL: DISCURSOS. Rio de Janeiro: Biblioteca do Exército, 1965.

112. Bittencourt, Getúlio. A QUINTA ESTRELA: COMO SE TENTA FAZER UM PRESIDENTE NO BRASIL. São Paulo: Editôra Ciencias Humanas, 1978.

113. Bittencourt, Getúlio, and Paulo Sergio Markum. O CARDEAL DO POVO: D. PAULO EVARISTO ARNS. São Paulo: Alfa-Omega, 1979.

114. Black, Jan Knippers. "Challenging the Divine Right of Generals in Latin America: Brazil, Bolivia, and Peru." COMPARATIVE SOCIAL RESEARCH 4 (1981): 319-52.

115. ———. "The Military and Political Decompression in Brazil." ARMED FORCES AND SOCIETY 6 (1980): 625-37.

116. ———. SENTINELS OF EMPIRE: THE UNITED STATES AND LATIN AMERICAN MILITARISM. Westport, CT: Greenwood Press, 1986.

117. ———. UNITED STATES PENETRATION OF BRAZIL. Philadelphia: University of Pennsylvania Press, 1977.

118. Blake, Augusto Victorino Alves Sacramento. DICCIONARIO BIBLIOGRAPHICO BRASILEIRO. Rio de Janeiro: n.p., 1883-1902.

119. Blume, Norman. "Pressure Groups and Decision-Making in Brazil." STUDIES IN COMPARATIVE INTERNATIONAL DEVELOPMENT 3 (1967-68): 204-23

120. Boal, Augusto. MILAGRE NO BRASIL. Rio de Janeiro: Civilização Brasileira, 1979.

121. Boehrer, George C.A. FROM MONARCHY TO REPUBLIC: A HISTORY OF THE REPUBLICAN PARTY OF BRAZIL, 1870-1889. Washington: Catholic University of America Press, 1951.

122. Boelcke, Willi A. "Die Waffengeschäfte des Dritten Reiches mit Brasilien." TRADITION (Munich) 16 (1971): 177-200, 280-87.

123. BOLETIM BIBLIOGRAFICO DA BIBLIOTECA NACIONAL. Rio de Janeiro: Biblioteca Nacional, 1978.

124. Bomeny, Helen Maria Bousquet. PARAISO TROPICAL: A IDEOLOGIA DO CIVISMO NA TVE DO MARANHAO. Rio de Janeiro: Achiame, 1981.

125. Bonavides, Paulo. "Las instituciones políticas en el Brasil antes y después de la Revolución de 1964." REVISTA DEL INSTITUTO DE CIENCIAS SOCIALES (Barcelona) 8 (1966): 220-34.

126. Bonturi, Orlando. BRAZIL AND THE VITAL SOUTH ATLANTIC. Washington: National Defense University Press, 1988.

127. Borges, Mauro. O GOLPE EM GOIAS: HISTORIA DE UMA GRANDE TRAICAO. Rio de Janeiro: Civilização Brasileira, 1965.

128. Boschi, Renato Raul. ELITES INDUSTRIAIS E DEMOCRACIA: HEGEMONIA BURGUESA E MUDANCA POLITICA NO BRASIL. Rio de Janeiro: Graal, 1979.

129. Bourne, Richard. GETULIO VARGAS OF BRAZIL, 1883-1954: SPHINX OF THE PAMPAS. London: Charles Knight, 1974.

130. Branco, Carlos Castello. INTRODUCAO A REVOLUCAO DE 1964. 2 vols. Rio de Janeiro: Editôra Artenova, 1975.

131. ———. OS MILITARES NO PODER. 3 vols. Rio de Janeiro: Editôra Nova Fronteira, 1976-77.

132. Branco, Humberto de Alencar Castello. DISCURSOS. 2 vols. Rio de Janeiro: Sec. de Imprensa, 1965-66.

133. ———. ENTREVISTAS, 1964-1965. Rio de Janeiro: Imprensa Nacional, 1966.

134. ———. "Papel do Estado-Maior do Exército." REVISTA DO INSTITUTO DE GEOGRAFIA E HISTORIA MILITAR DO BRASIL 31 (1963): 29-47.

135. Branco, Manoel Thomaz Castello. O BRASIL NA II GRANDE GUERRA. Rio de Janeiro: Biblioteca do Exército, 1960.

136. Branco, Robert J. THE UNITED STATES AND BRAZIL: OPENING A NEW DIALOGUE. Washington: National Defense University Press, 1984.

137. Brandão, Octavio. COMBATES E BATALHAS: MEMORIAS. São Paulo: Alfa-Omega, 1978.

138. Brandi, Paulo, with Mauro Malin and Plinio de Abreu Ramos. VARGAS: DA VIDA PARA A HISTORIA. Rio de Janeiro: Zahar Editôres, 1983.

139. Branford, Sue, and Oriel Glock. THE LAST FRONTIER: FIGHTING OVER LAND IN THE AMAZON. London: Zed, 1985.

140. Brasil, Francisco de Souza. "Segurança nacional: Caluniada, mas indispensável." REVISTA DE CIENCIA POLITICA 27 (1984): 35-43.

141. Brasil, Pedro (pseud.). LIVRO BRANCO SOBRE A GUERRA REVOLUCIONARIO NO BRASIL. Pôrto Alegre: O Globo, 1964.

142. Brayner, Floriano de Lima. LUZES SOBRE MEMORIAS. Rio de Janeiro: Livraria São José, 1973.

143. ———. RECORDANDO OS BRAVOS, EU CONVIVI COM ELES: CAMPANHA DA ITALIA. Rio de Janeiro: Civilização Brasileira, 1977.

144. ———. A VERDADE SOBRE FEB. Rio de Janeiro: Civilização Brasileira, 1969.

145. Brazil. COLECAO DAS LEIS.

146. ———. DIARIO OFICIAL.

147. Brazil, Congresso Nacional. O PARLAMENTO E A EVOLUCAO NACIONAL, 1871-1889 (3a SERIE). 6 vols. Brasília: Senado Federal, 1979.

148. Brazil. Congresso Nacional. Câmara dos Deputados. ANNAIS DE CONSTITUINTE DE 1891.

149. ———. DIARIO DA ASSEMBLEIA, 1946.

150. ———. DIARIO DO CONGRESSO.

151. ———. PERFIS PARLEMENTARES. Brasília: Câmara dos Deputados, 1976-. Multi-volume.

152. Brazil. Inquérito Policial Militar N° 709. O COMUNISMO NO BRASIL. 4 vols. Rio de Janeiro: Biblioteca do Exército, 1966-67.

153. Brazil. Instituto Brasileiro de Geografia e Estatística. ANUARIO ESTATISTICO DO BRASIL. Annual.

154. Brazil. Ministério de Aeronáutica. ALMANAQUE DOS OFICIAIS DA AERONAUTICA. Annual.

155. Brazil. Ministério do Exército. A ACAO DO EXERCITO NO PROGRAMA DO GOVERNO. General A. de Lyra Tavares. Rio de Janeiro: Imprensa do Exército, 1968.

156. ———. ALMANAQUE DO EXERCITO. Annual.

157. ———. OS CAMINHOS DA INTEGRACAO NACIONAL. Rio de Janeiro: Gráficos Block, 1967.

158. ———. EFETIVOS DO EXERCITO: EXPOSICAO DO MINISTRO DO EXERCITO AO SENADO FEDERAL. Rio de Janeiro: Imprensa do Exército, 1968.

159. ———. ESTATUTO DO CLUBE MILITAR. Rio de Janeiro: Imprensa do Exército, 1968.

160. ———. FATOR DE INTEGRACAO NACIONAL. Coronel Octávio Costa. Rio de Janeiro: Imprensa do Exército, 1967.

161. ———. INSTRUCOES PARA O CONCURSO DE ADMISSAO E MATRICULA NA ESCOLA PREPARATORIA DE CAMPINAS. São Paulo: n.p., 1968.

162. ———. OPERACOES EM LOCALIDADE CONTRA FORCAS IRREGULARES. Rio de Janeiro: EGGCF, 1967.

163. ———. O ORCAMENTO DO MINISTERIO DO EXERCITO. Rio de Janeiro: Imprensa do Exército, 1968.

164. ------. MANUAL DE CAMPANHA: GUERRA PSICOLOGICA. Rio de Janeiro: Estabelecimento General Gustavo Cordeiro de Farias, 1966.

165. ———. MANUAL DE CAMPANHA: POLICIA, DISTURBIOS CIVIS E CALAMIDADES PUBLICAS. Rio de Janeiro: Estabelecimento General Gustavo Cordeiro de Farias, 1967.

166. ———. 1930-1940: A REPUBLICA DOS ESTADOS UNIDOS BRASIL E O EXERCITO BRASILEIRO. Rio de Janeiro: Livraria José Olympio, 1941.

167. ———. PLANO GERAL DE CONVOCACAO PARA O SERVICO MILITAR EN 1961.

168. ———. O SERVICO MILITAR COMO ELEMENTO DE UMA POLITICA DE VALORIZACAO DO HOMEN BRASILEIRO. General Aurélio de Lyra Tavares. Rio de Janeiro: Imprensa do Exército, 1968.

169. ———. O SEU EXERCITO. Rio de Janeiro: Gráficos Block, n.d.

170. Brazil. Ministerio do Exército. Academia Militar das Agulhas Negras. AULA INAUGURAL ANO LETIVO DE 1968: NOVAS DIMENSOES DA PROFISSAO MILITAR, 1968.

171. ———. CONCURSO DE ADMISSAO: "QUESTOES PROPOSTAS." January 1966.

172. ——. DIREITO CONSTITUCIONAL. 1966.

173. ——. FORMANDO OFICIAIS PARA O EXERCITO DO BRASIL. n.d. [1967 or 1968].

174. ——. INSTRUCOES PARA O CONCURSO DE ADMISSAO E MATRICULA, n.d. [1967 or 1968].

175. ——. PERFIS DE CHEFIA MILITAR, 1968.

176. Brazil. Ministério da Guerra. O EXERCITO E O EXODO RURAL. Coronel Hygino de Barros Lemos. Rio de Janeiro: Biblioteca do Exército, 1959.

177. Brazil. Ministério da Marinha. ALMANAQUE. Annual.

178. ——. ALMIRANTE FRONTIN: CENTENARIO DO NASCIMENTO, 1867-1967. Rio de Janeiro: Ministério da Marinha, 1967.

179. ——. SUBSIDIOS PARA A HISTORIA MARITIMA DO BRASIL. Multi-volume.

180. Brazil. Ministério do Planejamento e Coordenação Econômica. BALANCO ORCAMENTARIO CONSOLIDADO DO GOVERNO FEDERAL, 1964. September 1964.

181. ——. CONSOLIDACAO ORCAMENTARIA DO GOVERNO FEDERAL, 1965. June 1965.

182. ——. PROGRAMA DE ACAO ECONOMICA DO GOVERNO, 1964-1966. 2d ed. Documentos EPEA, no. 1, May 1965.

183. Brazil. Ministério das Relações Exteriores. A POLITICA EXTERIOR DA REVOLUCAO BRASILEIRA. Rio de Janeiro: Ministério das Relações Exteriores, 1966.

184. ——. Discurso de Embaixador Juracy Magelhães em Washington, 16 de fevereiro de 1965. TEXTOS E DECLARACOES SOBRE POLITICA EXTERNA: PRIMEIRO ANIVERSARIO DE REVOLUCAO DE 31 DE MARCO DE 1964. 1965.

185. "Brésil, 1972-1973: Les deux dernières années de la Présidence Médici." NOTES ET ETUDES DOCUMENTAIRES 31 (1974): 1-71.

186. Brigagão, Clovis. O MERCADO DA SEGURANCA: ENSAIOS SOBRE ECONOMIA POLITICA DEFESA. Rio de Janeiro: Editôra Nova Fronteira, 1984.

187. Brooke, Jim. "Dateline Brazil: Southern Superpower." FOREIGN POLICY 44 (1981): 167-80.

188. Brossard, Paulo. E HORA DE MUDAR. Pôrto Alegre: L&PM Editôres, 1977.

189. Broucker, José de. DOM HELDER CAMARA: THE VIOLENCE OF A PEACEMAKER. Mary Knoll, NY: Orbis Books, 1970.

190. Brown, Michael P. AIR FORCES OF THE WORLD. Geneva: INTERAVIA, 1984.

191. Brune, Johannes Maria, ed. DIE PAPAGEIENSCHAUKEL: DIKTATUR UND FOLTER IN BRASILIEN; EINE DOKUMENTATION. Dusseldorf: Patmos, 1971.

192. Bruneau, Thomas C. THE POLITICAL TRANSFORMATION OF THE BRAZILIAN CATHOLIC CHURCH. London: Cambridge University Press, 1974.

193. Bruneau, Thomas C., and Philippe Faucher. AUTHORITARIAN CAPITALISM: BRAZIL'S CONTEMPORARY ECONOMIC AND POLITICAL DEVELOPMENT. Boulder: Westview Press, 1981.

194. Buchanan, Paul G., and David Pion-Berlin. "Civil-Military Relations and Democratic Consolidation in Argentina and Brazil." Paper presented at the annual meeting of the Rocky Mountain Council on Latin American Studies, Tucson, Arizona, April 1990.

195. Bueno, Clodoalo. "O rearmamento naval brasileiro e a rivalidade Brasil-Argentina em 1906-08." HISTORIA (Univ. Estadual Paulista, São Paulo) 1 (1982): 21-35.

196. Bulhões, Octavio Gouveia de. DOIS CONEITOS DE LUCRO.
      Rio de Janeiro: APEC Editôra, 1969.

197. Bunker, Stephen G. "Policy Implementation in an Authoritarian
      State: A Case from Brazil." LATIN AMERICAN RESEARCH
      REVIEW 18 (1983): 33-58.

198. Burgess, Mike, and Daniel Wolf. "Brasil: El concepto de poder
      en la Escuela Superior de Guerra." CUADERNOS POLITICOS
      20 (1979): 89-103.

199. Burns, E. Bradford. "O Barão do Rio Branco opina sobre o
      Marechal Deodoro." REVISTA DE HISTORIA 34 (1967): 545-
      50.

200. ———. A HISTORY OF BRAZIL 2d ed. New York: Columbia
      University Press, 1980.

201. ———. NATIONALISM IN BRAZIL. New York: Praeger
      Publishers, 1968.

202. ———. "A Working Bibliography for the Study of Brazilian
      History." THE AMERICAS 22 (1965): 54-88.

203. ———, ed. PERSPECTIVES ON BRAZILIAN HISTORY. New
      York: Columbia University Press, 1967.

204. Cabral, Castilho. TEMPOS DE JANIO E OUTROS TEMPOS.
      Rio de Janeiro: Civilização Brasileira, 1962.

205. Café Filho, João. DO SINDICATO AO CATETE: MEMORIAS
      POLITICAS E CONFISSOES HUMANAS. 2 vols. Rio de
      Janeiro: José Olympio Editôra, 1966.

206. Calasans, José. "A revolução de 1930 na Bahia." PORTO DE
      TODOS OS SANTOS (Bahia) 1 (1968): 5-17.

207. Caldas, Alvaro. TIRANDO O CAPUZ. Rio de Janeiro:
      CODECRI, 1981.

208. Callado, Antonio. TEMPO DE ARRAES: PADRES E
      COMUNISTAS NA REVOLUCAO SEM VIOLENCIA. Rio de
      Janeiro: José Alvaro Editor, 1964.

209. Calogeras, João Pandía. PROBLEMAS DE ADMINISTRACAO. 2d ed. São Paulo: Companhia Editôra Nacional, 1938.

210. ——. PROBLEMAS DE GOVERNO. 2d ed. São Paulo: Companhia Editôra Nacional, 1936.

211. Calvo, Roberto. LA DOCTRINA MILITAR DE LA SEGURIDAD NACIONAL: AUTORITARISMO POLITICO Y NEOLIBERALISMO ECONOMICO EN EL CONO SUR. Caracas: Universidad Católica Andrés Bello, 1979.

212. Câmara, Dom Helder. REVOLUTION THROUGH PEACE. New York: Harper and Row, 1971.

213. Câmara, Dom Helder, et al. EL GRITO DEL TERCER MUNDO EN UN PUEBLO MARGINADO: ¿MILAGRO BRASILENO?; TESTIMONIOS. Buenos Aires: Merayo Editor, 1974.

214. Camargo, Aspasia Alcántara de. "Authoritarianism and Populism: Bipolarity in the Brazilian Political System." In THE STRUCTURE OF BRAZILIAN DEVELOPMENT, 99-126. Edited by Neuma Aguiar. New Brunswick, NJ: Transaction Books, 1979.

215. Camargo, Aspasia Alcántara de, and Walder de Góes. MEIO SECULO DE COMBATE: DIALOGO COM CORDEIRO DE FARIAS. Rio de Janeiro: Editôra Nova Fronteira, 1981.

216. Camargo, Aureo de Almeida. "Roteiro de 32." REVISTA DE HISTORIA 45 (1972): 203-60.

217. Camargo, Cândido Procopio Ferreira de. SAO PAULO 1975: CRECIMENTO E POBREZA, São Paulo: Edições Loyola, 1976.

218. Caminha, João Carlos Gonçalves. DELINEAMENTOS DA STRATEGIA. 3 vols. Rio de Janeiro: Biblioteca do Exército, 1982-83.

219. Cammack, Paul. "Clientelism and Military Government in Brazil." In PRIVATE PATRONAGE AND PUBLIC POWER:

POLITICAL CLIENTELISM IN THE MODERN STATE, 53-75. Edited by Christopher Clapham. New York: St. Martin's Press, 1982.

220.	Campos, Roberto de Oliveira. O MUNDO QUE VEJO E NAO DESEJO. Rio de Janeiro: José Olympio Editôra, 1976.

221.	———. DO OUTRO LADO DA CERCA. Rio de Janeiro: APEC, 1967.

222.	———. TEMAS E SISTEMAS. Rio de Janeiro: APEC Editôra, 1969.

223.	Campos, Roberto de Oliveira, with Mario Henrique Simonsen. A NOVA ECONOMIA BRASILEIRA. Rio de Janeiro: Crown Editores Internacionais, 1974.

224.	Cão, José. DUTRA: O PRESIDENTE E A RESTAURACAO DEMOCRATICA. São Paulo: Instituto Progresso Editorial, 1949.

225.	Cardoso, Fernando Henrique. THE AUTHORITARIAN REGIME AT THE CROSSROADS: THE BRAZILIAN CASE. Washington: The Wilson Center, 1981.

226.	———. AUTORITARISMO E DEMOCRATIZATION. Rio de Janeiro: Paz e Terra, 1975.

227.	———. "La cuestión del estado en Brasil." REVISTA MEXICANA DE SOCIOLOGIA 37 (1975): 603-30.

228.	———. "Os impasses de regime autoritário: O caso brasileiro." ESTUDOS CEBRAP 26 (1980): 170-94.

229.	———. "O papel dos empresários no processo de transição: O caso brasileiro." DADOS 26 (1983): 9-27.

230.	———. "El régimen político brasileño." APORTES 25 (1972): 6-31.

231.	Cardoso, Fernando Henrique, and Geraldo Müller. AMAZONIA: EXPANSAO DO CAPITALISMO. São Paulo: Editôra Brasiliense, 1977.

232.	Carli, Gileno de. ANATOMIA DA RENUNCIA. Rio de Janeiro:

Edições O Cruzeiro, 1962.

233. Carneiro, Glauco. HISTORIA DAS REVOLUCOES BRASILEIRAS. 2 vols. Rio de Janeiro: Edições O Cruzeiro, 1965-67.

234. ———. LUSARDO: O ULTIMO CAUDILHO. Rio de Janeiro: Editôra Nova Fronteira, 1977.

235. ———. O REVOLUCIONARIO SIQUEIROS CAMPOS. 2 vols. Rio de Janeiro: Gráfica Record Editôra, 1966.

236. Carneiro, Virginia Thereza Diniz. HISTORICO: A PARTICIPACAO DO BRASIL NA 2a GUERRA MUNDIAL. Rio de Janeiro: Artes Gráficas Industrias Reunidas, 1947.

237. Carone, Edgard. O.P.C.B., 1964-1982. São Paulo: DIFEL, 1982.

238. ———. A PRIMEIRA REPUBLICA, 1889-1930. São Paulo: DIFEL 1969.

239. ———. A REPUBLICA VELHA: EVOLUCAO POLITICA. São Paulo: DIFEL, 1971.

240. ———. A REPUBLICA VELHA: INSTITUICOES E CLASSES SOCIAIS, 1922-1938. São Paulo: DIFEL, 1970.

241. ———. REVOLUCAO DO BRASIL CONTEMPORANEO, 1922-1938. São Paulo: Editôra São Paulo, 1975.

242. ———. A SEGUNDA REPUBLICA, 1930-1937. São Paulo: DIFEL, 1973.

243. ———. O TENENTISMO: ACONTECIMENTOS, PER-SONAGENS, PROGRAMAS. São Paulo: DIFEL, 1975.

244. ———. A TERCEIRA REPUBLICA, 1937-1945. São Paulo: DIFEL, 1976.

245. Carvalho, Estevão Leitão de. DEVER MILITAR E POLITICA PARTIDARIA. São Paulo: Companhia Editôra Nacional, 1959.

246. ———. MEMORIAS DE UM SOLDADO LEGALISTA. 2 vols. Rio de Janeiro: Imprensa do Exército, 1962.

247. ———. NA REVOLUCAO DE 30: A ATITUDE DO 80. R. I.; GUARNICAO DE PASSO FUNDO. Rio de Janeiro: Schmidt, 1933.

248. Carvalho, Fernando de. O ARRAIAL: SE A REVOLUCAO DE 1964 NAO TIVESSE VENCIDO. Rio de Janeiro: Guavira Editores, 1964.

249. Carvalho, José Murilo de. "Armed Forces and Politics in Brazil, 1930-45." HISPANIC AMERICAN HISTORICAL REVIEW 62 (1982): 193-223.

250. ———. A CONSTRUCAO DA ORDEM: A ELITE POLITICA IMPERIAL. Rio de Janeiro: Editôra Campus, 1980.

251. ———. "Elite and State Building in Imperial Brazil." Ph. D. dissertation, Stanford University, 1974.

252. ———. "As forças armadas na Primeira República: O poder desestabilizador." In HISTORIA GERAL DA CIVILIZACÃO BRASILEIRA, 2:183-234. Edited by Sergio Buarque de Holanda, et al. São Paulo: DIFEL, 1977.

253. ———. "Political Elites and State Building: The Case of Nineteenth-Century Brazil." COMPARATIVE STUDIES IN SOCIETY AND HISTORY 24 (1982): 378-99.

254. Carvalho, Livio de. "Brazilian Wage Policies, 1964-1981." BRAZILIAN ECONOMIC STUDIES 8 (1984): 109-41.

255. Carvalho, Septembrino de. MEMORIAS DADOS PARA A HISTORIA DO BRASIL. Rio de Janeiro: n.p., n.d.

256. Carvalho Filho, Milton X. AS CONFERENCIAS NAVAIS INTERAMERICANAS E A POSICAO BRASILEIRA. Brasília: Marinha do Brasil, 1983.

257. Caso, Antonio, ed. A ESQUERDA ARMADA NO BRASIL, 1967-1971. Lisbon: Morães, 1976.

258. Castellat, Bibiano Sergio Machado da Fontoura. "EXERCITO": LIBRO DE CENTENARIO, 1500-1900. 2 vols. Rio de Janeiro: n.p., 1901.

259. Castro, Jeanne Berrance de. "As milicias nacionais." REVISTA DE HISTORIA (São Paulo) 36 (1968): 377-89.

260. ———. "O negro na guarda nacional brasileira." ANAIS DO MUSEU PAULISTA 23 (1969): 149-72

261. Cavalcanti, Paulo. O CASO EU CONTO, COMO O CASO FOI. São Paulo: Alfa-Omega, 1978.

262. Cavalcanti, Pedro Celso Uchoa, and Jovelino Ramos. DE MUITOS CAMINHOS. São Paulo: Editôra e Livraria Livramento, 1978.

263. Cavalcanti, Pedro Celso Uchoa, et al. MEMORIAS DO EXILIO: BRASIL 1964-19??. Lisbon: Editôra Arcadia, 1976.

264. Ceasar, Afonso. POLITICA, CIFRAO E SANGUE: DOCUMENTARIO DO 24 DE AGOSTO. Rio de Janeiro: Editorial Andes, 1956.

265. Ceasar, Antonio José de Lima. "La lucha contra el fascismo en Brasil y la Segunda Guerra Mundial." AMERICA LATINA (Moscow) 2 (1975): 57-62.

266. Cehelsky, Marta. LAND REFORM IN BRAZIL: THE MANAGEMENT OF SOCIAL CHANGE. Boulder: Westview Press, 1978.

267. Centro de Pesquisa e Documentação de História Contemporânea do Brasil da Fundação Getúlio Vargas (CPDOC). A REVOLUCAO DE 30: SEMINARIO INTERNACIONAL. Brasília: Editôra Universidade de Brasília, 1982.

268. Cerqueira, Marcello. CADAVER BARATO: UM RETRATO DO TERRORISMO. Rio de Janeiro: Pallas, 1982.

269. Chacon, Vamireh. O DILEMA POLITICO BRASILEIRO. São Paulo: Editôra Convivio, 1978.

270. ———. ESTADO E POVO NO BRASIL: AS EXPERIENCIAS DO ESTADO NOVO E DA DEMOCRACIA POPULISTA, 1937-1964. Rio de Janeiro: José Olympio Editôra em convenio com a Câmara dos Deputados, 1977.

271. Chagas, Carlos. 113 DIAS DE ANGUSTIA: IMPEDIMENTO
      E MORTE DE UM PRESIDENTE. Pôrto Alegre: L&PM
      Editores, 1979.

272. ———. A GUERRA DAS ESTRELAS, 1964-1984: OS
      BASTIDORES DAS SUCESSOES PRESIDENCIAIS. Pôrto
      Alegre: L&PM Editores, 1985.

273. ———. A IMPRENSA NO PROCESSO DEMOCRATICO. Vol
      1. Pôrto Alegre: Assembleia Legislativa Estado Rio Grande do
      Sul, Diretoria de Anais, 1981.

274. Chalout, Yves. ESTADO, ACUMULACAO E
      COLONIALISMO INTERNO: CONTRADICOES
      NORDESTE/SUDESTE, 1960-1977. Petrópolis: Editôra Vozes,
      1978.

275. Chilcote, Ronald H. BRAZIL AND ITS RADICAL LEFT: AN
      ANNOTATED BIBLIOGRAPHY ON THE COMMUNIST
      MOVEMENT AND THE RISE OF MARXISM, 1922-1972.
      Milwood, NY: Kraus International Publications, 1980.

276. ———. THE BRAZILIAN COMMUNIST PARTY: CONFLICT
      AND INTEGRATION 1922-1972. New York: Oxford University
      Press, 1974.

277. ———. REVOLUTION AND STRUCTURAL CHANGE IN
      LATIN AMERICA: A BIBLIOGRAPHY ON IDEOLOGY,
      DEVELOPMENT AND THE RADICAL LEFT, 1930-1965. 2
      vols. Stanford: Hoover Institution on War, Revolution and Peace,
      1970.

278. ———, ed. PROTEST AND RESISTANCE IN ANGOLA AND
      BRAZIL: COMPARATIVE STUDIES. Berkeley: University of
      California Press, 1972.

279. Child, Jack. GEOPOLITICS AND CONFLICT IN SOUTH
      AMERICA: QUARRELS AMONG NEIGHBORS. New York:
      Praeger Publishers, 1984.

280. Child, John. UNEQUAL ALLIANCE: THE INTER-
      AMERICAN MILITARY SYSTEM, 1938-1978. Boulder:
      Westview Press, 1980.

281. Christo, Carlos Alberto Libanio.   DAS CATACUMBAS: CARTAS DA PRISAO, 1969-1971. Rio de Janeiro: Civilização Brasileira, 1978.

282. Cidade, Francisco de Paula. "Da missão militar francesa aos nossos dias." REVISTA MILITAR BRASILEIRA 42 (1954): 131-86.

283. Clements, Benedict J. FOREIGN TRADE STRATEGIES, EMPLOYMENT, AND INCOME DISTRIBUTION IN BRAZIL. New York: Praeger Publishers, 1988.

284. Coaracy, Vivaldo.   TODOS CONTAM SUA VIDA: MEMORIAS DE INFANCIA E ADOLESCENCIA. Rio de Janeiro: Editôra José Olympio, 1959.

285. Coelho, Edmundo Campos. EM BUSCA DE IDENTIDADE: O EXERCITO E A POLITICA NA SOCIEDADE BRASILEIRA. Rio de Janeiro: Editôra Forense Universitaria, 1976.

286. ———.   "A institução militar no Brasil." BOLETIM INFORMATIVO E BIBLIOGRAFICO CIENCIAS SOCIAIS 19 (1985): 5-19.

287. Coelho, José Saldanha. UM DEPUTADO NO EXILIO. Rio de Janeiro: Editôra Leitura, 1965.

288. Coelho, Maria Cella Nunes, and Raymundo Garcia Cota. "Grandes projetos, tecnologia e questão ambiental: Carajás e energia nuclear." VOZES 78:10 (1984): 5-15.

289. Collier, David, ed.   THE NEW AUTHORITARIANISM IN LATIN AMERICA. Princeton: Princeton University Press, 1979.

290. Colson, Frank. "On Expectations: Perspectives on the Crisis of 1889 in Brazil." JOURNAL OF LATIN AMERICAN STUDIES 13 (1981): 265-92.

291. Comblin, Joseph.   EL PODER MILITAR EN AMERICA LATINA. Salamanca: Ediciones Sequence, 1978.

292. Conniff, Michael L. "The Tenentes in Power: A New Perspective on the Brazilian Revolution of 1930." JOURNAL OF LATIN AMERICAN STUDIES 10 (1978): 61-82.

293. ———. URBAN POLITICS IN BRAZIL: THE RISE OF POPULISM, 1925-1945. Pittsburgh: University of Pittsburgh Press, 1981.

294. Corbett, Charles D. "Politics and Professionalism: The South American Military." ORBIS 26 (1973): 927-51.

295. Cordeiro, Daniel Rapaoso, et al., eds. A BIBLIOGRAPHY OF LATIN AMERICAN BIBLIOGRAPHIES: SOCIAL SCIENCES AND HUMANITIES. Metuchen: Scarecrow Press, 1979.

296. Correa, Anna Maria Martinez. A REBELIAO DE 1924 EM SAO PAULO. São Paulo: HUCITEC, 1976.

297. Correa, Carlos Humberto. CATALOGO DAS DISSERTACOES E TESES DOS CURSOS DE POS-GRADUACAO DE HISTORIA, 1973-1985. Florianópolis: Editôra da UFSC, 1987.

298. Correa, Marcos Sá. 1964: VISTO E COMENTADO PELA CASA BRANCA. Pôrto Alegre: L&PM, 1977.

299. Correa, Serzedello. UMA FIGURA DA REPUBLICA PAZINAS DO PASSADO. Rio de Janeiro: Freitas Bastos, 1959.

300. Cortés, Carlos E. GAUCHO POLITICS IN BRAZIL: THE POLITICS OF RIO GRANDE DO SUL, 1930-1964. Albuquerque: University of New Mexico Press, 1974.

301. Cortés Conde, Roberto, and Stanley J. Stein, eds. LATIN AMERICA: A GUIDE TO ECONOMIC HISTORY, 1830-1930. Berkeley: University of California Press, 1977.

302. Costa, Didio Iratim Afonso da. NORONHA. Rio de Janeiro: Serviço de Documentação da Marinha, 1944.

303. ———. SALDANHA. Rio de Janeiro: Serviço de Documentação da Marinha, 1944.

304. Costa, João Cruz. CONTRIBUICAO A HISTORIA DAS IDEIAS NO BRASIL. Rio de Janeiro: Civilização Brasileira, 1967.

305. ———. PEQUENA HISTORIA DA REPUBLICA. 2d ed. Rio de Janeiro: Civilização Brasileira, 1968.

306. Costa, Octavio. EXERCITO: FATOR DE INTEGRACAO NACIONAL. Rio de Janeiro: Imprensa do Exército, 1967.

307. Costa, Samuel Guimarães da. FORMACAO DEMOCRATICA DO EXERCITO BRASILEIRO. Rio de Janeiro: Biblioteca do Exército, 1957.

308. Costa, Sergio Correa da. A DIPLOMACIA DO MARECHAL: INTERVENCAO ESTRANGEIRA NA REVOLTA DA ARMADA. 2d ed. Rio de Janeiro: Tempo Brasileiro, 1979.

309. Couhat, Jean Labayle. COMBAT FLEETS OF THE WORLD, 1980-81: THE SHIPS, AIRCRAFT AND ARMAMENT. Annapolis: United States Naval Institute, 1980.

310. Coutinho, Lourival. O GENERAL GOES DEPOE .... Rio de Janeiro: Coelho Branco, 1955.

311. Cruz, Adelina Maria Alves Novães e., et al., eds. IMPASSE NA DEMOCRACIA BRASILEIRA 1951-1955: COLETANEA DE DOCUMENTOS. Rio de Janeiro: Editôra da Fundação Getúlio Vargas, 1983.

312. Cruz, Sebastião C. Velasco de, and Carlos Estevam Martins. "De Castello a Figueiredo: Uma incursão na pre-história da abertura." In SOCIEDADE E POLITICA NO BRASIL POS-64. Edited by Bernardo Sorj and Maria Herminia T. de Almeida. São Paulo: Brasiliense, 1983.

313. Cunha, Euclides da. REBELLION IN THE BACKLANDS. Chicago: University of Chicago Press, 1944.

314. D'Aguiar, Hernani. A REVOLUCAO POR DENTRO. Rio de Janeiro: Editôra Artenova, 1976.

315. Dallari, Dalmo de Abreu. "The *Força Pública* of São Paulo in State and National Politics." In PERSPECTIVES ON ARMED POLITICS IN BRAZIL, 79-111. Edited by Henry H. Keith and Robert A. Hayes. Tempe: Arizona State University Press, 1976.

316. Dantas, Francisco C. de San Tiago. DOIS MOMENTOS DE RUI BARBOSA: CONFERENCIAS. Rio de Janeiro: Casa de Rui Barbosa, 1949.

317. Dantas, José Ibare. O TENENTISMO EM SERGIPE: DA REVOLTA DE 1924 A REVOLUCAO DA 1930. Petrópolis: Editôra Vozes, 1974.

318. Dassin, Joan. "Cultural Policy and Practice in the Nova República." LATIN AMERICAN RESEARCH REVIEW 24 (1989): 115-23.

319. ———, ed. TORTURE IN BRAZIL: A REPORT BY THE ARCHDIOCESE OF SAO PAULO. New York: Vintage Books, 1986.

320. Davis, Shelton H. VICTIMS OF THE MIRACLE: DEVELOPMENT AND THE INDIANS OF BRAZIL. New York: Cambridge University Press, 1977.

321. Deal, Carl W., ed. LATIN AMERICA AND THE CARIBBEAN: A DISSERTATION BIBLIOGRAPHY. Ann Arbor: University Microfilms International, 1977.

322. OS DEBATES DOS JORNALISTAS BRASILEIROS, 1970-1982. Brasília: Federação Nacional dos Jornalistas Profissionais, 1983.

323. Deckes, Flavio. RADIOGRAFIA DO TERRORISMO NO BRASIL, 1966-1980. São Paulo: Icone, 1985.

324. Della Cava, Ralph. THE CHURCH IN THE NEWS: CATHOLICISM AND SOCIETY IN THE BRAZILIAN PRESS, 1964-1980. Rio de Janeiro: Editôra Mazza Zero, 1985.

325. ———. MIRACLE AT JOASEIRO. New York: Columbia University Press, 1970.

326. Delorme, Robert L. LATIN AMERICA, 1983-1987: A SOCIAL SCIENCE BIBLIOGRAPHY. Westport, CT: Greenwood Press, 1988.

327. ———. LATIN AMERICA, 1979-1983: A SOCIAL SCIENCE BIBLIOGRAPHY. Santa Barbara: ABC Clio Press, 1981.

328. ———. LATIN AMERICA: SOCIAL SCIENCES INFORMATION SOURCES, 1967-1979. Santa Barbara: ABC Clio Press, 1981.

329. Denevan, William M. "Development and the Imminent Demise of the Amazon Rain Forest." PROFESSIONAL GEOGRAPHER 25 (1973): 130-35.

330. Denys, Odylio. CICLO REVOLUCIONARIO BRASILEIRO: MEMORIAS, 5 JULHO DE 1922 A 31 DE MARCO DE 1964. Rio de Janeiro: Editôra Nova Frontiera, 1980.

331. Departamento Intersindical de Estatística e Estudos Socio-Econômicos (DIEESE). "Dez anos de política salarial." ESTUDOS SOCIOECONOMICOS 1 (1975).

332. Días David, Mauricio. "El control militar-corporativo en Brasil y Chile." DESARROLLO INDOAMERICANO 12 (1977): 29-35.

333. Dimas Filho, Nelson. COSTA E SILVA: O HOMEN E O LIDER. Rio de Janeiro: Edições O Cruzeiro, 1966.

334. Dimenstein, Gilberto, et al. O COMPLO QUE ELEGEU TANCREDO. Rio de Janeiro: Editôra JB, 1985.

335. Dines, Alberto, et al. OS IDOS DE MARCO E A QUEDA EM ABRIL. Rio de Janeiro: José Alvaro, 1964.

336. Diniz, Eli. "Maquina política e oposição: O MDB no Rio de Janeiro." DADOS 23 (1980): 335-61.

337. ———. VOTO E MAQUINA POLITICA. Rio de Janeiro: Paz e Terra, 1982.

338. Diniz, Eli, and Renato Boschi. EMPRESARIADO NACIONAL E ESTADO NO BRASIL. Rio de Janeiro: Editôra Forense Universitaria, 1978.

339. DISSERATION ABSTRACTS INTERNATIONAL. Ann Arbor: University Microfilms International, 1938-.

340. Dornas, João. SILVA JARDIM. São Paulo: Brasiliana, 1936.

341. Dos Santos, Theotonio. "Brazil: The Origins of a Crisis." In LATIN AMERICA: THE STRUGGLE WITH DEPENDENCY AND BEYOND, 415-90. Edited by Ronald H. Chilcote and Joel C. Edelstein. Cambridge, MA: Schenkman Publishing Company, 1974.

342. Dos Santos, Wanderley Guilherme. PODER E POLITICA: CRONICA DO AUTORITARISMO BRASILEIRO. Rio de Janeiro: Editôra Forense Universitaria, 1978.

343. Dreifuss, Rene Armand. 1964: A CONQUISTA DO ESTADO; ACAO POLITICA, PODER E GOLPE DE CLASSE. Petrópolis: Vozes, 1981.

344. Drosdoff, Daniel. LINHA DURA NO BRASIL: O GOVERNO MEDICI, 1969-1974. São Paulo: Global, 1986.

345. Duarte, Celina Rabello. "Imprensa e redemocratização no Brasil." DADOS 26 (1983): 181-95.

346. Duarte, Paulo de Queiroz. O NORDESTE NA II GUERRA MUNDIAL: ANTECEDENTES E OCUPACAO. Rio de Janeiro: Editôra Record, 1971.

347. Dudley, William S. "Institutional Sources of Officer Discontent in the Brazilian Army, 1870-1889." HISPANIC AMERICAN HISTORICAL REVIEW 55 (1975): 44-65.

348. ———. "Professionalization and Politicization as Motivational Factors in the Brazilian Army Coup of 15 November 1889." JOURNAL OF LATIN AMERICAN STUDIES 8 (1976): 100-25.

349. ———. "Reform and Radicalism in the Brazilian Army, 1870-1889." Ph.D. dissertation, Columbia University, 1972.

350. Duff, Ernest A. "Luis Carlos Prestes and the Revolution of 1924." LUSO-BRAZILIAN REVIEW 4 (1967): 3-16.

351. Dulles, John W. F. ANARCHISTS AND COMMUNISTS IN BRAZIL, 1900-1935. Austin: University of Texas Press, 1975.

352. ———. BRAZILIAN COMMUNISM, 1935-1945: REPRESSION DURING WORLD UPHEAVAL. Austin: University of Texas Press, 1983.

353. ———. CARLOS LACERDA, BRAZILIAN CRUSADER: THE YEARS 1914-1960. Vol 1. Austin: University of Texas Press, 1991.

354. ———. CASTELLO BRANCO: THE MAKING OF A BRAZILIAN PRESIDENT. College Station: Texas A & M University Press, 1978.

355. ———. PRESIDENT CASTELLO BRANCO, BRAZILIAN REFORMER. College Station: Texas A & M University Press, 1980.

356. ———. UNREST IN BRAZIL: POLITICAL-MILITARY CRISES, 1955-1964. Austin: University of Texas Press, 1970.

357. ———. VARGAS OF BRAZIL: A POLITICAL BIOGRAPHY. Austin: University of Texas Press, 1967.

358. Dunnigan, James F., and Austin Bay. A QUICK AND DIRTY GUIDE TO WAR: BRIEFINGS ON PRESENT AND POTENTIAL WARS. New York: William Morrow, 1985.

359. Dupuy, Trevor N., et al. THE ALMANAC OF WORLD MILITARY POWER. San Rafael, CA: Presidio Press, 1980.

360. Durandin, Catherine. "L'idéologie de la sécurité nationale au Brésil." NOTES ET ETUDES DOCUMENTAIRES 4391/4393 (1977): 5-18.

361. Dutra, Eurico Gaspar. O DEVER DA VERDADE. Rio de Janeiro: Editôra Nova Fronteira, 1983.

362. Dyer, Gwynne. "Brazil." In WORLD ARMIES, 77-95. Edited by John Keegan. New York: Facts on File, 1979.

363. Einaudi, Luigi, and Herbert Goldhamer. AN ANNOTATED BIBLIOGRAPHY OF LATIN AMERICAN MILITARY JOURNALS. Santa Monica: Rand Corporation, 1965.

364. Einaudi, Luigi, and Alfred C. Stepan. LATIN AMERICAN INSTITUTIONAL DEVELOPMENT: CHANGING MILITARY PERSPECTIVES IN PERU AND BRAZIL. Santa Monica: Rand Corporation, 1971.

365. EL EJERCITO Y LA SOCIEDAD. Moscow: Academia de Ciencias de la URSS, 1982.

366. Ellis, Howard S., ed. THE ECONOMY OF BRAZIL. Berkeley: University of California Press, 1969.

367. ENCONTRO NACIONAL PELA DEMOCRACIA. 3 vols. Rio de Janeiro: Editôra Avenir, 1979

368. English, Adrian J. ARMED FORCES OF LATIN AMERICA: THEIR HISTORIES, DEVELOPMENT, PRESENT STRENGTH, AND MILITARY POTENTIAL. London: Jane's Publishing, 1984.

369. Erickson, Kenneth Paul. THE BRAZILIAN CORPORATIVE STATE AND WORKING CLASS POLITICS. Berkeley: University of California Press, 1977.

370. Escobari Cusicanqui, Jorge. BRASIL Y EL PETROLEO BOLIVIANO: LOS ACUERDOS DE ROBORE; LA VENTA DEL GAS. 2d ed. La Paz: Librería Editorial "Juventud", 1986.

371. Escola Superior de Guerra. CICLO DE CONFERENCIAS SOBRE SEGURANCA NACIONAL E DESENVOLVIMENTO. 11 vols. Rio de Janeiro: Escola Superior de Guerra, 1971.

372. Esquenazi-Mayo, Roberto, and Michael C. Meyer, eds. LATIN AMERICAN SCHOLARSHIP SINCE WORLD WAR II. Lincoln: University of Nebraska Press, 1971.

373. Evans, Peter. DEPENDENT DEVELOPMENT: THE ALLIANCE OF MULTINATIONAL, STATE, AND LOCAL CAPITAL IN BRAZIL. Princeton: Princeton University Press, 1979.

374. ———. "The Military, the Multinationals and the 'Miracle': The Political Economy of the 'Brazilian Model' of Development." STUDIES IN COMPARATIVE INTERNATIONAL DEVELOPMENT 9 (1974): 26-45.

375. Fagundes, Coriolano de Loyola Cabral. CENSURA & LIBERDADE DE EXPRESSÃO. São Paulo: Brusco, 1975.

376. Fagundes, Seabra. AS FORCAS ARMADAS NA CONSTITUICAO. Rio de Janeiro: Biblioteca do Exército, 1955.

377. Falção, Oscar de Barros. "A revolução de 5 de julho de 1924." REVISTA MILITAR BRASILEIRA 84 (1961): 71-134.

378. Farah, Paulo Cesar. TENENTISMO: BIBLIOGRAFIA. Rio de Janeiro: CPDOC, 1978.

379. Faucher, Philippe. LE BRESIL DES MILITARES. Montréal: Les Presses de L'Université de Montréal, 1981.

380. ———. "La crise de croissance du régime autoritaire brésilien." NORTHSOUTH 6 (1981): 27-51.

381. Faust, Jean-Jacques. "La révolution devore ses présidents." PREUVES (Paris) 163 (1964): 17-34.

382. Fausto, Boris. A REVOLUCAO DE 1930: HISTORIOGRAFIA E HISTORIA. São Paulo: Editôra Brasiliense, 1970.

383. Fernandes, Floristan. REFLECTIONS ON THE BRAZILIAN COUNTER-REVOLUTION. Armonk, NY: M.E. Sharpe, 1981.

384. ———. A REVOLUCAO BURGUESA NO BRASIL: ENSAIO DE INTERPRETACAO SOCIOLOGICA. Rio de Janeiro: Zahar Editôres, 1975.

385. Fernandes, Heloisa Rodrigues. OS MILITARES COMO CATEGORIA SOCIAL. São Paulo: Global, 1978.

386. ———. POLITICA E SEGURANCA: FORCA PUBLICA DO ESTADO DE SAO PAULO; FUNDAMENTOS HISTORICO-SOCIAIS. São Paulo: Alfa-Omega, 1974.

387. Ferreira, Domingos P.C.B. THE NAVY OF BRAZIL: AN EMERGING POWER AT SEA. Washington: National Defense University Press, 1983.

388. Ferreira, Oliveiros S. AS FORCAS ARMADAS E O DESAFIO DA REVOLUCAO. Rio de Janeiro: Edições GRD, 1964.

389. ———. "La geopolítica y el ejército brasileño." APORTES 12 (1969): 111-32.

390. Ferreira Filho, Arthur. REVOLUCAO DE 1923. Pôrto Alegre: Imprensa Oficial do Estado, 1973.

391. Fialho, Anfrisio. HISTORIA DE FUNDACAO DE REPUBLICA NO BRAZIL. Rio de Janeiro: n.p., 1891.

392. Fiechter, Georges-André. BRAZIL SINCE 1964: MODERNIZATION UNDER A MILITARY REGIME. New York: Halstead Press, 1975.

393. Fields, Gary S. "Who Benefits from Economic Development?: A Reexamination of Brazilian Growth in the 1960s." AMERICAN ECONOMIC REVIEW 67 (1977): 570-82.

394. Figueiredo, Argelina Maria Cheibub. "Política governmental e funções sindicais." M.A. thesis, Universidade de São Paulo, 1975.

395. Figueiredo, Euclydes. CONTRIBUICAO PARA A HISTORIA DA REVOLUCAO CONSTITUCIONALISTA DE 1932. São Paulo: Livraria Martins, 1954.

396. Figueiredo, Marcus. "Movimento estudantil brasileiro, 1968: Sua luta interna." VOZES 62 (1968): 791-94.

397. Figueiredo, Marcus Faria. POLITICA DE COERCAO NO SISTEMA POLITICO BRASILEIRO. Rio de Janeiro: Comissão Nacional de Justiça e Paz, 1978.

398. Figueiredo, Marcus Faria, and José Antonio Borges Cheibub. "A abertura política de 1973 a 1981: Quem disse o que, quando; Inventário de um debate." BOLETIM INFORMATIVO E BIBLIOGRAFICO DE CIENCIAS SOCIAIS 14 (1982): 29-61.

399. Fleischer, David V. "Parties, Elections and *Abertura* in Brazil." In NEW MILITARY POLITICS IN LATIN AMERICA, 79-96. Edited by Robert Wesson. New York: Praeger Publishers, 1982.

400. Flores, Maria César, ed. PANORAMA DO PODER MARITIMO BRASILEIRO. Rio de Janeiro: Serviço do Documentação Geral da Marinha, 1972.

401. Flynn, Peter. BRAZIL: A POLITICAL ANALYSIS. Boulder: Westview Press, 1978.

402. ———. "Brazil: Authoritarianism and Class Control." JOURNAL OF LATIN AMERICAN STUDIES 6 (1974): 315-33.

403. ———. "The Brazilian Developmental Model: The Political Dimension." THE WORLD TODAY 29 (1973): 481-94.

404. Fon, Antonio Carlos. TORTURA: A HISTORIA DA REPRESSAO POLITICA NO BRASIL. São Paulo: Global, 1979.

405. Fontoura, João Neves da. MEMORIAS. 2 vols. Rio de Janeiro: Editôra Globo, 1958-63.

406. Forjaz, Maria Cecilia Spina. TENENTISMO E POLITICA: TENENTISMO E CAMADAS MEDIAS URBANAS NA CRISE DA PRIMEIRA REPUBLICA. Rio de Janeiro: Paz e Terra, 1977.

407. Forum sobre a Amazonia, II, Rio de Janeiro, 1968. PROBLEMATICA DA AMAZONIA. Rio de Janeiro: Editôra da Casa do Estudiante do Brasil, 1969.

408. Fragoso, Antonio, ed. BRASIL, ¿MILAGRO O ENGANO?: DOS GRAVES DENUNCIOS. Lima: Centro de Estudios y Publicaciones, 1973.

409. Fragoso, Augusto. "A Escola Superior de Guerra." PROBLEMAS BRASILEIROS (São Paulo) 8 (1970): 19-34.

410. Franco, Afonso Arinos de Mello. UM ESTADISTA DE REPUBLICA: AFRANIO DE MELLO E SEU TEMPO. 3 vols. Rio de Janeiro: José Olympio Editôra, 1955.

411. ———. MEMORIAS. 3 vols. Rio de Janeiro: José Olympio Editôra, 1928.

412. Franco, Sergio da Costa. "O sentido histórico da Revolução de 1893." In FUNDAMENTOS DA CULTURA RIOGRANDENSE, 5o. serie, 1:193-216. Pôrto Alegre: Universidade do Rio Grande do Sul, 1962.

413. Franco, Virgilio A. de Mello. OUTUBRO, 1930. 3d ed. Rio de Janeiro: Schmidt, 1931.

414. Frederico, Celso. CONSCIENCIA OPERARIA NO BRASIL. São Paulo: Editôra Atica, 1978.

415.   Freed, Kenneth. "Brazil: World's Fifth-Largest Arms Maker." LOS ANGELES TIMES, 15 November 1981.

416.   Freire, Marcos. EM DEFESA DO HOMEN E DO MEIO. 2 vols. Brasília: Senado Federal, Centro Gráfico, 1980.

417.   ———. NACAO OPRIMIDA. Rio de Janeiro: Paz e Terra, 1977.

418.   ———. ULTIMA PALAVRA. Brasília: Senado Federal, Centro Gráfico, 1982.

419.   Freyre, Gilberto. FORCAS ARMADAS E OUTRAS FORCAS. Recife: Imprensa Oficial, 1965.

420.   ———. NACAO E EXERCITO. Rio de Janeiro: José Olympio, 1949.

421.   ———. ORDER AND PROGRESS. New York: Knopf, 1970.

422.   Fundação Getúlio Vargas. GUIA DE PUBLICACOES DA FGV, 1944-1974. Rio de Janeiro: Fundação Getúlio Vargas, 1974.

423.   ———. A REVOLUCAO DE 30: SEMINARIO INTERNACIONAL. Brasília: Editôra Universidade de Brasilia, 1982.

424.   Fundação Instituto Brasileiro de Geografia e Estadística. PUBLICACOES EDITADAS PELO IBGE. 2 vols. Rio de Janeiro: Fundação IBGE, 1984-1985.

425.   Furtado, Celso. ANALISE DO "MODELO" BRASILEIRO. Rio de Janeiro: Civilização Brasileira, 1972.

426.   ———. O BRASIL POS-"MILAGRE." Rio de Janeiro: Paz e Terra, 1981

427.   ———. THE ECONOMIC GROWTH OF BRAZIL: A SURVEY FROM COLONIAL TO MODERN TIMES. Berkeley: University of California Press, 1963.

428.   Gabaglia, A.C. Raja. PODER MARITIMO NAS DUAS GUERRAS MUNDIAIS, 1914-1918--1939-1945. Rio de Janeiro: Imprensa Naval, 1953.

429. Gabaglia, Laurita Pessôa Raja. EPITACIO PESSOA, 1865-1942.
      2 vols. Rio de Janeiro: José Olympio Editôra, 1951.

430. Gabeira, Fernando. CARTA SOBRE A ANISTIA: A
      ENTREVISTA DO PASQUIM; CONVERSAO SOBRE 1968.
      Rio de Janeiro: CODECRI, 1979.

431. ———. O QUE E ISSO, COMPANHEIRO?: DEPOIMENTO.
      Rio de Janeiro: CODECRI, 1979.

432. Galeano, Eduardo. "Brazil: The Coup and After." STUDIES ON
      THE LEFT 4:4 (1964): 55-76

433. Gall, Norman. "Atoms for Brazil: Dangers for all." FOREIGN
      POLICY 23 (1976): 155-201.

434. ———. "In the Name of Democracy: Brazil's Presidential
      Succession." AMERICAN UNIVERSITIES FIELD STAFF
      REPORTS 3 (1978): 1-12.

435. Gallet, Paul. FREEDOM TO STARVE. London: Penguin
      Books, 1967.

436. Gama, Arthur Oscar Saldanha da. A MARINHA DO BRASIL
      NA SECUNDA GUERRA MUNDIAL. Rio de Janeiro:
      CAPEMI Editôra e Gráfica, 1982.

437. Gaspari, Elio. GEISEL E GOLBERY: O SACERDOTE E O
      FEITICEIRO. São Paulo: DIFEL, 1989.

438. Gasparian, Marcos. O INDUSTRIAL. São Paulo: Martins
      Editôra, 1973.

439. Geisel, Ernesto. DISCURSOS. 5 vols. Brasília: Assessoria de
      Imprensa e Relações Públicas da Presidencia da República, 1976.

440. ———. UM HOMEN CHAMADO GEISEL: HISTORIA DO
      BRASIL; FATOS, MENSAGENS, DISCURSOS, POLITICA
      INTERNA, FORCAS ARMADAS. Brasília: Horizonte Editôra,
      1978.

441. Gôes, Walder de. O BRASIL DO GENERAL GEISEL:
      ESTUDO DO PROCESSO DE TOMADA DE DECISAO NO

REGIME MILITAR-BUROCRATICO. Rio de Janeiro: Nova Fronteira, 1978.

442.   ———. "O novo papel das forças armadas do Brasil." Paper presented at the seventh annual meeting of ANPOCS, Aguas de São Pedro, São Paulo, October 1983.

443.   ———. "O novo regime militar no Brasil." DADOS 27 (1984): 361-75.

444.   Goldemberg, José. ENERGIA NUCLEAR NO BRASIL. São Paulo: HUCITEC, 1978.

445.   Goldman, Alberto. CAMINHOS DE LUTA: PERIPECIAS DE UM POLITICO NA DEMOCRACIA RELATIVA. São Paulo: Núcleo de Divulgação Editorial, 1978.

446.   Gomes, Luisa Maria Gaspar. "Cronologia do governo Castelo Branco." DADOS 2/3 (1967): 112-32.

447.   Gooch, Herbert E. THE MILITARY AN POLITICS IN LATIN AMERICA. Los Angeles: Latin American Studies Center, California State University, 1979.

448.   Goodland, Robert J. A., and H. S. Irwin. AMAZON JUNGLE: GREEN HELL TO RED DESERT?; AN ECOLOGICAL DISCUSSION OF THE ENVIRONMENTAL IMPACT OF THE HIGHWAY CONSTRUCTION PROGRAM IN THE AMAZON BASIN. Amsterdam: Elsevier Scientific Publications, 1975.

449.   Gott, Richard, ed. GUERRILLA MOVEMENTS IN LATIN AMERICA. Garden City, NY: Doubleday, 1971.

450.   Grabendorff, Wolf, and Manfred Nitsch. BRASILIEN: ENTWICKLUNGSMODELLUNDAUSSENPOLITIK.Munich: Wilhelm Verlag, 1977.

451.   Graeff, Eduardo P. PERSPECTIVAS: FERNANDO HENRIQUE CARDOSO; IDEIAS E ATUACAO POLITICA. Rio de Janeiro: Paz e Terra, 1983.

452. Grael, Dicksen M. AVENTURA, CORRUPCAO, E TERRORISMO: A SOMBRA DA IMPUNIDADE. Petrópolis: Editôra Vozes, 1985.

453. Graham, Douglas Hume. "The Growth, Change and Reform of Higher Education in Brazil: A Review and Commentary on Selected Problems and Issues." In BRAZIL IN THE SIXTIES, 275-324. Edited by Riordan Roett. Nashville: Vanderbilt University Press, 1972.

454. Graham, Richard. "Governmental Expenditures and Political Change in Brazil, 1880-1899: Who Got What." JOURNAL OF INTER-AMERICAN STUDIES AND WORLD AFFAIRS 19 (1977): 339-68

455. Granado-Díaz, Manuel. "Brazilian Participation in World War II: The Battle of Monte Castello." M.A. thesis, University of Florida, 1979.

456. Grande, Humberto. "A doutrina do pan-americanismo bélico e o Brasil." CULTURA POLITICA 5 (1945): 26-42.

457. Green, Jim. "Liberalization on Trial: The Workers Movement." NACLA, REPORT ON THE AMERICAS, May-June 1979, 14-25.

458. Greno Velasco, José Enrique. "El acuerdo Brasil-RFA y el principio de no-proliferación nuclear." REVISTA DE POLITICA INTERNACIONAL (Madrid) 154 (1977): 113-43.

459. Griffin, Charles 'C., and J. Benedict Warren, eds. LATIN AMERICA: A GUIDE TO THE HISTORICAL LITERATURE. Austin: University of Texas Press, 1971.

460. Gropp, Arthur E., ed. A BIBLIOGRAPHY OF LATIN AMERICAN BIBLIOGRAPHIES. Metuchen, NJ: Scarecrow Press, 1971.

461. ——, ed. A BIBLIOGRAPHY OF LATIN AMERICAN BIBLIOGRAPHIES PUBLISHED IN PERIODICALS. 2 vols. Metuchen, NJ: Scarecrow Press, 1976.

462. Grow, Michael. SCHOLARS' GUIDE TO WASHINGTON, DC: LATIN AMERICAN AND CARIBBEAN STUDIES. Washington: Smithsonian Institution, 1979.

463. Guedes, Carlos Luis. TINHA QUE SER MINAS. Rio de Janeiro: Editôra Nova Fronteira, 1979.

464. Guglialmelli, Juan E. ARGENTINA, BRASIL, Y LA BOMBA ATOMICA. Buenos Aires: Tierra Nueva, 1976.

465. ———. "¿Y si Brasil fabrica la bomba atómica?" ESTRATEGIA 34-35 (1975): 5-21.

466. ———. "¿Fabrica el Brasil una bomba atómica?" ESTRATEGIA 70 (1982): 5-12.

467. Guillobel, Renato de Almeida. MEMORIAS. Rio de Janeiro: Fundação IBGE, 1973.

468. Guimarães, Carlos Eugenio de Andrada. ARTHUR OSCAR: SOLDADO DO IMPERIO E DA REPUBLICA. Rio de Janerio: Biblioteca do Exército, 1965.

469. Guimarães, Manoel Luz Lima Salgado, et al., eds. A REVOLUCAO DE 30: TEXTOS E DOCUMENTOS. Brasília: Editôra Universidade de Brasília, 1982.

470. Gurgel, José Alfredo Amaral. SEGURANCA E DEMOCRACIA: UMA REFLEXAO POLITICA. Rio de Janeiro: José Olympio Editôra, 1975.

471. Hahner, June E. "The Brazilian Armed Forces and the Overthrow of the Monarchy: Another Perspective." THE AMERICAS 26 (1969): 171-82.

472. ———. CIVIL-MILITARY RELATIONS IN BRAZIL, 1889-1898. Columbia: University of South Carolina Press, 1969.

473. ———. "Floriano Peixoto: Brazil's 'Iron Marshal': A Re-Evaluation." THE AMERICAS 31 (1975): 252-71.

474. ———. "The Paulista's Rise to Power: A Civilian Group Ends Military Rule." HISPANIC AMERICAN HISTORICAL REVIEW 47 (1967): 149-65.

475. Haines, Gerald K. THE AMERICANIZATION OF BRAZIL: A STUDY OF U.S. COLD WAR DIPLOMACY IN THE THIRD WORLD, 1945-54. Wilmington: Scholarly Resources, 1989.

476. Hall, Lawrence Henry. "João Pandía Calogeras: Minister of War, 1919-1922; The role of a Civilian in the Development of the Brazilian Army." Ph.D. dissertation, New York University, 1984.

477. Halperin, Ernst. TERRORISM IN LATIN AMERICA. Beverly Hills: Sage Publications for Georgetown University, 1976.

478. THE HANDBOOK OF LATIN AMERICAN STUDIES. Cambridge: 1936-51; Gainesville: 1951-78; Austin: University of Texas Press, 1971-.

479. Harding, Timothy. "The Political History of Organized Labor in Brazil." Ph.D. dissertation, Stanford University, 1973.

480. ———. "Revolution Tomorrow: The Failure of the Left in Brazil." STUDIES ON THE LEFT 4:4 (1964): 30-54.

481. Harmon, Ronald M., and Bobby J. Chamberlain. BRAZIL: A WORKING BIBLIOGRAPHY IN LITERATURE, LINGUISTICS, HUMANITIES, AND SOCIAL SCIENCES. Tempe: Arizona State University Press, 1975.

482. Haussman, Fay, and Jerry Haar. EDUCATION IN BRAZIL. Hamden, CT: Archon Books, 1978.

483. Hayes, Robert A. THE ARMED NATION: THE BRAZILIAN CORPORATE MYSTIQUE. Tempe: Arizona State University Press, 1989.

484. ———. "The Formation of the Brazilian Army and Its Political Behavior, 1807-1930." Ph.D. dissertation, University of New Mexico, 1969.

485. ———. "The Military Club and National Politics in Brazil." In PERSPECTIVES ON ARMED POLITICS IN BRAZIL, 140-55. Edited by Henry H. Keith and Robert A. Hayes. Tempe: Arizona State University Press, 1976.

486.   ——. "The Tragedy of Marshal Deodoro da Fonseca: A Military Class Perspective." LUSO-BRAZILIAN REVIEW 14 (1977): 211-24.

487.   Heare, Gertrude E. TRENDS IN LATIN-AMERICAN MILITARY EXPENDITURES, 1940-1970: ARGENTINA, BRAZIL, CHILE, COLOMBIA, PERU, AND VENEZUELA. Washington: Dept. of State Pub. 8618, Inter-American Series, no. 99, 1971.

488.   Hennessy, Alistair. "Fascism and Populism in Latin America." In FASCISM: A READER'S GUIDE, ANALYSES, INTERPRETATIONS, BIBLIOGRAPHY, 255-94. Edited by Walter Laquer. Berkeley: University of California Press, 1976.

489.   Henriques, Affonso. ASSENSAO E QUEDA DE GETULIO VARGAS. 3 vols. Rio de Janeiro: Distribuidora Record, 1966.

490.   Henriques, Elber de Mello. A FEB DOZE ANOS DEPOIS. Rio de Janeiro: Biblioteca do Exército, 1959.

491.   Hewlett, Silvia Ann. THE CRUEL DILEMMAS OF DEVELOPMENT: TWENTIETH-CENTURY BRAZIL. New York: Basic Books, 1980.

492.   Hilton, Stanley E. "Ação Integralista Brasileira: Fascism in Brazil, 1932-1938." LUSO-BRAZILIAN REVIEW 9 (1972): 3-29.

493.   ——. "The Armed Forces and Industrialists in Modern Brazil: The Drive for Military Autonomy, 1889-1954." HISPANIC AMERICAN HISTORICAL REVIEW 62 (1982): 629-73.

494.   ——. O BRASIL E A CRISE INTERNACIONAL, 1930-1945. Rio de Janeiro: Civilização Brasileira, 1977.

495.   ——. BRAZIL AND THE GREAT POWERS, 1930-1939: THE POLITICS OF TRADE RIVALRY. Austin: University of Texas Press, 1975.

496.   ——. "Brazil and the Post-Versailles World: Elite Images and Foreign Policy Strategy, 1919-1929." JOURNAL OF LATIN AMERICAN STUDIES 12 (1980): 341-64.

497. ———. BRAZIL AND THE SOVIET CHALLENGE, 1917-1947. Austin: University of Texas Press, 1991.

498. ———. "Brazilian Diplomacy and the Washington-Rio de Janeiro 'Axis' during the World War II Era." HISPANIC AMERICAN HISTORICAL REVIEW 59 (1979): 201-31.

499. ———. "Brazil's International Economic Strategy, 1945-1960: Revival of the German Option." HISPANIC AMERICAN HISTORICAL REVIEW 66 (1986): 287-309.

500. ———. HITLER'S SECRET WAR IN SOUTH AMERICA, 1939-1945: GERMAN MILITARY ESPIONAGE AND ALLIED COUNTER ESPIONAGE IN BRAZIL. Baton Rouge: Louisiana State University Press, 1981.

501. ———. "Military Influence on Brazilian Economic Policy, 1930-1945: A Different View." HISPANIC AMERICAN HISTORICAL REVIEW 53 (1973): 71-94.

502. ———. "The Overthrow of Getúlio Vargas in 1945: Diplomatic Intervention, Defense of Democracy, or Political Retribution?" HISPANIC AMERICAN HISTORICAL REVIEW 67 (1987): 1-37.

503. Hippólito, Lucia. DE RAPOSAS E REFORMISTAS: O PSD E A EXPERIENCIA DEMOCRATICA BRASILEIRA, 1945-64. Rio de Janeiro: Paz e Terra, 1985.

504. HISPANIC AMERICAN PERIODICALS INDEX (HAPI). Los Angeles: Latin American Center, UCLA, 1970/74-.

505. HISTORIA DA UNE [I.E., UNIAO NACIONAL DOS ESTUDANTES]: DEPOIMENTOS DE EX-DIRIGENTES. São Paulo: Editorial Livramento, 1980.

506. Holanda, Sergio Buarque de, and Pedro Moacyr Campos, eds. HISTORIA GERAL DA CIVILIZACÃO BRASILEIRA. 4 vols. São Paulo: DIFEL, 1975-77.

507. Horowitz, Irving Louis. BEYOND EMPIRE AND REVOLUTION: MILITARIZATION AND CONSOLIDATION IN THE THIRD WORLD. New York: Oxford University Press, 1982.

508.   ——.   REVOLUTION IN BRAZIL. New York: Oxford University Press, 1964.

509.   ——. "Revolution in Brazil: The Counter-Revolutionary Phase." NEW POLITICS 3 (1964): 71-80.

510.   HUMAN RIGHTS IN LATIN AMERICA, 1964-1980: A SELECTIVE ANNOTATED BIBLIOGRAPHY COMPILED AND EDITED BY THE HISPANIC DIVISION. Washington: Library of Congress, 1983.

511.   Humphreys, R. A. LATIN AMERICA AND THE SECOND WORLD WAR, 1938-1942. Vol. 1. London: Athlone Press, University of London, 1981.

512.   ——, ed. LATIN AMERICAN HISTORY: A GUIDE TO THE LITERATURE IN ENGLISH. London: Oxford University Press, 1958.

513.   Ianni, Octavio. O COLAPSO DO POPULISMO NO BRASIL. Rio de Janeiro: Civilização Brasileira, 1968.

514.   Ingleton, Roy D. POLICE OF THE WORLD. New York: Charles Scribner's Sons, 1979.

515.   Inojosa, Joaquim. REPUBLICA DE PRINCESA: JOSE PEREIRA X JOAO PESSOA, 1930. Rio de Janeiro: Civilização Brasileira, 1980.

516.   Instituto de Direito Público e Ciencia Política (INDIPO), Centro de Pesquisa e Documentação de História Oral (CPDOC). Programa de História Oral, Fundação Getúlio Vargas. CATALOGO DE DEPOIMENTOS. Rio de Janeiro: Fundação Getúlio Vargas, 1981.

517.   Ireland, Rowan. CATHOLIC BASE COMMUNITIES, SPIRITIST GROUPS, AND THE DEEPENING OF DEMOCRACY IN BRAZIL. Washington: Wilson Center, 1983. Working Paper.

518.   Jackson, William V., comp. CATALOG OF BRAZILIAN ACQUISITIONS OF THE LIBRARY OF CONGRESS, 1964-1974. Boston: G.K. Hall, 1975.

519. ———. LIBRARY GUIDE FOR BRAZILIAN STUDIES. Pittsburgh: University of Pittsburgh Book Center, 1964.

520. Jaguaribe, Hélio. "A renuncia de Jânio Quadros e a crise política brasileira." REVISTA BRASILEIRA DE CIENCIAS SOCIAIS 1 (1961): 272-311.

521. Jakubs, Debra L. "Police Violence in Times of Political Tension: The Case of Brazil, 1968-1971." In POLICE AND SOCIETY, 85-106. Edited by David H Bayley. Beverly Hills: Sage Publications, 1977.

522. Jenkin, Serguei. "La insurrección tenentista en São Paulo." AMERICA LATINA (Moscow) 2 (1975): 156-76.

523. Jenks, Margaret Sarles. "Maintaining Political Control through Parties: The Brazilian Strategy." COMPARATIVE POLITICS 15 (1982): 41-72.

524. ———. "Political Parties in Authoritarian Brazil." Ph.D. dissertation, Duke University, 1979.

525. Johnson, John J. THE MILITARY AND SOCIETY IN LATIN AMERICA. Stanford: Stanford University Press, 1964.

526. Jordão, Fernando. DOSSIE HERZOG: PRISAO, TORTURA E MORTE NO BRASIL. São Paulo: Global Editôra, 1979.

527. Jorge, Fernando. AS DIRETRIZES GOVERNAMENTAIS DO PRESIDENTE ERNESTO GEISEL: SUBSIDIOS E DOCUMENTOS PARA A HISTORIA DO BRASIL CONTEMPORANEO. São Paulo: The author, 1976.

528. José, Elias. O GRITO DOS TORTUARADOS: CONTOS. Rio de Janeiro: Editôra Nova Fronteira, 1986.

529. José, Emiliano, and Oldack Miranda. LAMARCA: O CAPITAO DA GUERRILHA. São Paulo: Global Editôra, 1980.

530. Kalwa, Erich. "El tenientismo brasileño: Un estudio sobre el sentido político de la polémica actual." ISLAS 76 (1983): 127-41.

531. Keefe, Eugene K. "National Security." In BRAZIL: A COUNTRY STUDY, 289-334. Edited by Richard F. Nyrop. Washington: U.S. Government Printing Office, 1983.

532. Keegan, John, ed. WORLD ARMIES. 2d ed. Detroit: Gale Research, 1983.

533. Keith, Henry H. "Soldiers as Saviors: The Brazilian Military Revolts of 1922 and 1924 in Historical Perspective." Ph.D. dissertation, University of California, Berkeley, 1969.

534. Keith, Henry H., and Robert A. Hayes, eds. PERSPECTIVES ON ARMED POLITICS IN BRAZIL. Tempe: Arizona State University Press, 1976.

535. Kinzo, Maria D'Alva G. LEGAL OPPOSITION POLITICS UNDER AUTHORITARIAN RULE IN BRAZIL: THE CASE OF THE MDB, 1966-1979. New York: St. Martin's Press, 1988

536. Klinger, Bertholdo. NARRATIVAS AUTOBIOGRAFICAS. 6 vols. Rio de Janeiro: Editôra O Cruzeiro, 1946-53.

537. ———. PARADA E DESFILE DUMA VIDA DE VOLUNTARIO DO BRASIL NA PRIMEIRA METADE DO SECULO. Rio de Janeiro: Editôra O Cruzeiro, 1958.

538. Knight, Peter T. "Brazil: Deindexation and Economic Stabilization." Paper prepared at the World Bank, Washington, 2 December 1983.

539. Kohl, James, and John Litt, eds. URBAN GUERRILLA WARFARE IN LATIN AMERICA. Cambridge, MA: MIT Press, 1974.

540. Koral, Boris. A GRANDE REVOLUCAO DE OUTUBRO E A AMERICA LATINA. São Paulo: Alfa Omega, 1980.

541. Krane, Dale. "Opposition Strategy and Survival in Praetorian Brazil: 1964-79." JOURNAL OF POLITICS 45 (1983): 28-63.

542. Krieger, Daniel. DESDE AS MISSOES: SAUDADES, LETRAS, ESPERANCA. Rio de Janeiro: Editôra José Olympio, 1977.

543. Krischke, Paulo J. A IGREJA E AS CRISES POLITICAS NO BRASIL. Petrópolis: Editôra Vozes, 1979.

544. ——, ed. BRASIL: DO "MILAGRE" A "ABERTURA." São Paulo: Cortez Editôra, 1982.

545. Krischke, Paulo J., and Scott Mainwaring, eds. A IGREJA NAS BASES EM TEMPO DE TRANSICAO, 1974-1985. Pôrto Alegre: L&PM Editôra, 1986.

546. Kubitschek, Jucelino. MEU CAMINHO PARA BRASILIA. 3 vols. Rio de Janeiro: Bloch Editôres, 1974.

547. Kucinski, Bernardo. ABERTURA: A HISTORIA DE UMA CRISE. São Paulo: Editôra Brasil Debates, 1982.

548. ——. "Energía nuclear y democracia: Algunos aspectos políticos del acuerdo de cooperación entre los gobiernos de Brasil y la RFA." NUEVA SOCIEDAD 31-32 (1977): 111-25.

549. Lacerda, Carlos. DEPOIMENTO. Rio de Janeiro: Editôra Nova Fronteira, 1977.

550. ——. DISCURSOS PARLAMENTARES: SELETA. Rio de Janeiro: Editôra Nova Fronteira, 1982.

551. Lacerda, Mauricio de. ENTRE DUAS REVOLUCOES. Rio de Janeiro: Libraria Editôra, 1927.

552. Lacombe, Américo Jacobina. BRASIL: PERIODO NACIONAL. Mexico City: Instituto Panamericano de Geografía e História, Comisión de História, 1956.

553. ——. INTRODUCAO AO ESTUDO DA HISTORIA DO BRASIL. São Paulo: Companhia Editôra Nacional, 1974.

554. Lafayette, Pedro. SALDANHA DA GAMA. 2 vols. Rio de Janeiro: Editôra Souza, 1959.

555. ——. TRES PERFIS: SALDANHA DA GAMA, BARAO DE PENEDO, SILVEIRA MARTINS. Rio de Janeiro: Livraria Clássica Brasileira, 1955.

556. LaFeber, Walter. "United States Depression Diplomacy and the Brazilian Revolution, 1893-1894." HISPANIC AMERICAN HISTORICAL REVIEW 40 (1960): 107-18.

557. Lago, Laurencio. OS GENERAIS DO EXERCITO BRASILEIRO, 1865-1889. Rio de Janeiro: Imprensa Nacional, 1942.

558. Lagoa, Ana. SNI: COMO NASCEU, COMO FUNCIONA. São Paulo: Editôra Brasiliense, 1983.

559. Lamounier, Bolivar. "Apontamentos sobre a questão democrática brasileira." In COMO RENASCEM AS DEMOCRACIAS, 4-40. Edited by Alain Rouquié, Bolivar Lamournier, and Jorge Schvarzer. São Paulo: Editôra Brasiliense, 1985.

560. Lamounier, Bolivar, and José Eduardo Farias. O FUTURO DA ABERTURA: UM DEBATE. São Paulo: Cortez Editôra, 1981.

561. Langguth, A. J. HIDDEN TERRORS. New York: Pantheon Books, 1978.

562. Langoni, Carlos Geraldo. INCOME DISTRIBUTION AND ECONOMIC DEVELOPMENT IN BRAZIL. Rio de Janeiro: Banco Nacional da Habitação, 1973.

563. Lapa, José Roberto do Amaral. A HISTORIA EM QUESTAO. Petrópolis: Editôra Vozes, 1976.

564. Lavenère-Wanderley, Nelson Freire. HISTORIA DA FORCA AEREA BRASILEIRA. 2d ed. Rio de Janeiro: Ministério da Aeronáutica, 1975.

565. ———. "El pensamiento estratégico brasileño: El poder aeroespacial." ESTRATEGIA 63 (1980): 107-17.

566. Leal, Hamilton. A GRANDE LEGENDA: 5 DE JULHO. Rio de Janeiro: Livraria Agir Editôra, 1976.

567. Leal, Victor Nunes. CORONELISMO, ENXADA E VOTO: O MUNICIPIO E O REGIME REPRESENTATIVO NO BRASIL. 3d ed. São Paulo: Alfa Omega, 1976.

568. Leclerc, Max. CARTAS DO BRASIL. São Paulo: Editôra Nacional, 1942.

569. Le Doare, Hélène. "Le Brésil et le Cone Sud: Les conflits frontaliers; Bibliographie commentée." CAHIERS DES AMERIQUES LATINES 18 (1978): 215-25.

570. Leite, Aureliano. "Causas e objetivos da Revolução de 1932." REVISTA DE HISTORIA 25 (1962): 139-66.

571. ———. PAGINAS DE UMA LONGA VIDA. São Paulo: Livraria Martins Editôra, 1967.

572. Leonhart, William Kahn, ed. ESTRUCTURA MILITAR BRASILEIRA. Rio de Janeiro: n.p., 1972.

573. Leonzo, Nanci. "Um empresario nas milicias paulistas: O brigadeiro Luis Antonio de Souza." ANAIS DO MUSEU PAULISTA 30 (1980-81): 241-54.

574. Lernoux, Penny. CRY OF THE PEOPLE. Garden City, NY: Doubleday, 1980.

575. ———. PEOPLE OF GOD: THE STRUGGLE FOR WORLD CATHOLICISM. New York: Viking, 1989.

576. Levine, Robert M. BRAZIL, 1822-1930: AN ANNOTATED BIBLIOGRAPHY FOR SOCIAL HISTORIANS. New York: Garland Publishing, 1983.

577. ———. BRAZIL SINCE 1930: AN ANNOTATED BIBLIOGRAPHY FOR SOCIAL HISTORIANS. New York: Garland Publishing, 1980.

578. ———. HISTORICAL DICTIONARY OF BRAZIL. Metuchen, NJ: Scarecrow Press, 1979.

579. ———. "A Revolução de 1935." CADERNOS BRAZILEIROS 10 (1968): 47-59.

580. ———. THE VARGAS REGIME: THE CRITICAL YEARS, 1935-1938. New York: Columbia University Press, 1970.

581. Levy, Herbert V. A COLUNA INVICTA: ROMAO GOMES; UM CLASSICO DA REVOLUCAO CONSTITUCIONALISTA. 2d ed. São Paulo: Livraria Martins Editôra, 1967.

582. Lieuwen, Edwin. ARMS AND POLITICS IN LATIN AMERICA. New York: Praeger Publishers, 1960.

583. ———. PRESIDENTS VS GENERALS: NEOMILITARISM IN LATIN AMERICA. New York: Praeger Publishers, 1964.

584. Lima, Alceu Amoroso. A EXPERIENCIA REACCIONARIA. Rio de Janeiro: Edições Tempo Brasileiro, 1968.

585. ———. REVOLUCAO, REACAO OU REFORMA? Rio de Janeiro: Editôra Tempo Brasileiro, 1964.

586. Lima, Alexandre J. Barbosa. A VERDADE SOBRE A REVOLUCAO DE OUTUBRO. São Paulo: Alfa-Omega, 1975.

587. Lima, Lourenço M. A COLUNA PRESTES: MARCHAS E COMBATES. Rio de Janeiro: Editôra Brasiliense, 1951.

588. Lima, Luiz Gonzaga de Souza. EVOLUCAO POLITICA DOS CATOLICOS E DA IGREGA NO BRASIL. Petrópolis: Editôra Vozes, 1979.

589. Lima Júnior, Olavo Brasil de. "Electoral Participation in Brazil, 1945-1978." LUSO-BRAZILIAN REVIEW 20 (1983): 65-92.

590. A LINHA REVOLUCIONARIA DO PARTIDO COMUNISTA DO BRASIL. Rio de Janeiro: Edições Caramuru, 1971.

591. Lins, Maria de Lourdes Ferreira. A FORCA ESPEDICIONARIA BRASILEIRA: UMA TENTATIVA DE INTERPRETACAO NO 30 ANO DE PARTICIPACAO DO BRASIL NA II GRANDE GUERRA MUNDIAL. São Paulo: Editoras Unidas, 1975.

592. Linz, Juan J. "The Future of an Authoritarian Situation, or the Institutionalization of an Authoritarian Regime: The Case of Brazil." In AUTHORITARIAN BRAZIL: ORIGINS, POLICIES, AND FUTURE, 233-54. Edited by Alfred Stepan. New Haven: Yale University Press, 1973.

593. Lombardi, Mary. BRAZILIAN SERIAL DOCUMENTS: A SELECTIVE AND ANNOTATED GUIDE. Bloomington: Indiana University Press, 1974.

594. Lopes, Murilo Ribiero. RUI BARBOSA E A MARINHA. Rio de Janeiro: Casa de Rui Barbosa, 1953.

595. Lopes, Theodorico, and Gentil Torres. MINISTROS DA GUERRA DO BRASIL, 1808-1950. Rio de Janeiro: Borsoi, 1950.

596. Lorenzo-Fernandez, O. S. A EVOLUCAO DA ECONOMIA BRASILEIRA. Rio de Janeiro: Zahar Editôres, 1976.

597. Loureiro Júnior, José. O GOLPE DE NOVEMBRO. Rio de Janeiro: Livraria Clássica Brasileira, 1957.

598. Love, Joseph L. RIO GRANDE DO SUL AND BRAZILIAN REGIONALISM, 1882-1930. Stanford: Stanford University Press, 1971.

599. ———. SAO PAULO IN THE BRAZILIAN FEDERATION, 1889-1937. Stanford: Stanford University Press, 1980.

600. Loveman, Brian, and Thomas M. Davies, Jr. THE POLITICS OF ANTI-POLITICS: THE MILITARY IN LATIN AMERICA. 2d ed. Lincoln: University of Nebraska Press, 1989.

601. Lowenthal, A.F., ed. ARMIES AND POLITICS IN LATIN AMERICA. New York: Holmes and Meier Publishers, 1976.

602. Luddeman, Margarete K. NUCLEAR TECHNOLOGY FROM WEST GERMANY: A CASE OF DISHARMONY IN U.S.-BRAZILIAN RELATIONS. Washington: Latin American Studies Program, Georgetown University, 1978.

603. Luz, Nicia Vilela. "A década de 1920 e suas crises." REVISTA DO INSTITUTO DE ESTUDOS BRASILEIROS 6 (1969): 67-75.

604. Lyra, Heitor. HISTORIA DE QUEDA DO IMPERIO. 2 vols. São Paulo: Editôra Nacional, 1964.

605. McAlister, Lyle N. "Civil-Military Relations in Latin America." JOURNAL OF INTER-AMERICAN STUDIES 3 (1961): 341-50

606. ———. "Recent Research and Writing on the Role of the Military in Latin America." LATIN AMERICAN RESEARCH REVIEW 11 (1966): 5-36

607. Macaulay, Neill. THE PRESTES COLUMN: REVOLUTION IN BRAZIL. New York: New Viewpoints, 1974.

608. McCann, Frank D. "Aviation Diplomacy: The United States and Brazil, 1939-1941." INTER-AMERICAN ECONOMIC AFFAIRS 21 (1968): 35-50.

609. ———. "Brazil and the United States and the Coming of World War II, 1937-1942." Ph.D. dissertation, Indiana University, 1967.

610. ———. THE BRAZILIAN-AMERICAN ALLIANCE, 1937-1945. Princeton: Princeton University Press, 1973.

611. ———. "The Brazilian Army and the Problem of Mission, 1939-1964." JOURNAL OF LATIN AMERICAN STUDIES 12 (1980): 107-26.

612. ———. "The Brazilian Army and the Pursuit of Arms Independence, 1899-1979." In WAR, BUSINESS, AND WORLD MILITARY INDUSTRIAL COMPLEXES, 171-93. Edited by Benjamin Franklin Cooling. Port Washington, NY: Kennikat Press, 1981.

613. ———. "The Brazilian General Staff and Brazil's Military Situation, 1900-1945." JOURNAL OF INTER-AMERICAN STUDIES AND WORLD AFFAIRS 25 (1983): 299-324.

614. ———. "The Formative Period of Twentieth-Century Brazilian Army Thought, 1900-1922." HISPANIC AMERICAN HISTORICAL REVIEW 64 (1984): 739-65.

615. ———. A NACAO ARMADA: ENSAIOS SOBRE A HISTORIA DO EXERCITO BRASILEIRO. Recife: Editôra Guararapes, 1982.

616. ———. "The Nation in Arms: Obligatory Military Service during the Old Republic." In ESSAYS CONCERNING THE SOCIOECONOMIC HISTORY OF BRAZIL, 211-43. Edited by Dauril Alden and Warren Dean. Gainsville: University Presses of Florida, 1977.

617. ———. "Origins of the 'New Professionalism' of the Brazilian Military." JOURNAL OF INTER-AMERICAN STUDIES AND WORLD AFFAIRS 21 (1979): 505-22.

618. ———. "Vargas and the Destruction of the Brazilian Integralista and Nazi Parties." THE AMERICAS 26 (1969): 15-34.

619. McCloskey, Michael B. "The United States and the Brazilian Naval Revolt, 1893-1894." THE AMERICAS 2 (1948): 296-321.

620. McDonough, Peter. "Os limites da legitimidade autoritária no Brasil." DADOS 20 (1979): 91-121.

621. ———. "Mapping an Authoritarian Power Structure: Brazilian Elites during the Médici Regime." LATIN AMERICAN RESEARCH REVIEW 16 (1981): 79-106.

622. ———. POWER AND IDEOLOGY IN BRAZIL. Princeton: Princeton University Press, 1981.

623. Macedo, Ubiraten de. "Origens nacionais da doutrina da ESG." CONVIVIUM 22 (1979): 514-18.

624. Machado, F. Zenha. OS ULTIMOS DIAS DO GOVERNO DE VARGAS: A CRISE POLITICA DE AGOSTO DE 1954. Rio de Janeiro: Lux, 1955.

625. Magalhães, João Batista. A COMPREENSAO DA UNIDADE DO BRASIL. Rio de Janeiro: Biblioteca do Exército, 1956.

626. ———. A EVOLUCAO MILITAR DO BRASIL. Rio de Janeiro: Biblioteca do Exército, 1956.

627. Magalhães, José Vieira Couto de. DIARIO DO GENERAL COUTO DE MAGALHÃES, 1887-1890. São Paulo: n.p., 1974.

628. Magalhães, Juracy Montenegro. MINHAS MEMORIAS PREVISORIAS: DEPOIMENTO PRESTADO AO CPDOC. Rio de Janeiro: Civilização Brasileira, 1982.

629. Magalhães Júnior, Raymundo. DEODORO: A ESPADA CONTRA O IMPERIO. 2 vols. São Paulo: Companhia Editôra Nacional, 1957.

630. Magano, Octavio Bueno. ORGANIZACAO SINDICAL BRASILEIRA. São Paulo: Editôra Revista dos Tribunais, 1982.

631. Magnet, Alejandro. "Armamentismo y desarme en América Latina." POLIT 6 (1960): 56-73.

632. Mahar, Dennis J. FRONTIER DEVELOPMENT POLICY IN BRAZIL: A STUDY OF THE AMAZON EXPERIENCE. New York: Praeger Publishers, 1979.

633. Maia, João do Prado. "A epopeia das 'caças' na segunda guerra mundial." REVISTA DO INSTITUTO HISTORICO E GEOGRAFICO BRASILEIRO 306 (1975): 113-34.

634. Mainwaring, Scott. THE CATHOLIC CHURCH AND POLITICS IN BRAZIL, 1916-1985. Stanford: Stanford University Press, 1986.

635. ———. "The Transition to Democracy in Brazil." JOURNAL OF INTER-AMERICAN STUDIES AND WORLD AFFAIRS 28 (1986): 149-79.

636. Mainwaring, Scott, and Eduardo J. Viola. "Transition to Democracy: Brazil and Argentina in the 1980s." JOURNAL OF INTERNATIONAL AFFAIRS 38 (1985): 193-219.

637. Malloy, James M., and Mitchell A. Seligson, eds. AUTHORITARIANS AND DEMOCRATS: REGIME TRANSITION IN LATIN AMERICA. Pittsburgh: University of Pittsburgh Press, 1987.

638. Manchester, Alan K. "Brazil in Transition." SOUTH ATLANTIC QUARTERLY 54 (1955): 167-76.

639. Mangabeira, João. IDEIAS POLITICAS DE JOAO MANGABEIRA. 3 vols. Brasília: Senado Federal; Rio de Janeiro: Fundação Casa de Rui Barbosa, MEC, 1980.

640. Manor, Paul. "Un prolétariat en uniforme et une révolution 'honnete': Quelques considerations sur la rébellion des équipages de la flotte brasilienne de haute mer en novembre 1910." CARAVELLE 30 (1978): 63-108.

641. Manwaring, Max. "The Military in Brazilian Politics." Ph.D. dissertation, University of Illinois at Champaign-Urbana, 1968.

642. Marighela, Carlos. POR QUE RESISTI A PRISAO. São Paulo: Edições Contemporâneas, 1965.

643. Marighela, Carlos, et al. A QUESTAO AGRARIA NO BRASIL. São Paulo: Brasil Debates, 1980

644. Marini, Ruy Mauro, and Olga Pellicer de Brody. "Militarismo y desnuclearización en América Latina: El caso de Brasil." FORO INTERNACIONAL 8 (1967): 1-24.

645. Markoff, John, and Silvio R. Duncan Baretta. "Professional Ideology and Military Activism in Brazil: Critique of a Thesis of Alfred Stepan." COMPARATIVE POLITICS 17 (1985): 175-91.

646. Marotti, Giorgio. CANUDOS: STORIA DI UNA GUERRA. Rome: Bulzoni Editore, 1978.

647. Martin, Percy A. "Causes of the Collapse of the Brazilian Empire." HISPANIC AMERICAN HISTORICAL REVIEW 4 (1921): 4-48.

648. Martins, Carlos Estevam, et al. OS PARTIDOS E AS ELEICOES NO BRASIL. Rio de Janeiro: Paz e Terra, 1975

649. Martins, Heloisa Helena Teixeira de Souza. ESTADO E A BUROCRATIZACAO DO SINDICATO NO BRASIL. São Paulo: Editôra HUCITEC, 1979.

650. Martins, Luciano. "A Revolução de 1930 e seu significado político." In A REVOLUCAO DE 30: SEMINARIO INTERNACIONAL. Issued by the Centro de Pesquisa e Documentação de História Contemporânea do Brasil da Fundação Getúlio Vargas (CPDOC). Brasília: Editôra Universidade de Brasilia, 1982.

651. Martins, Mario. EM NOSSOS DIAS DE INTOLERANCIA. Rio de Janeiro: Edições Tempo Brasileiro, 1965.

652. Mattei, Georges M. BRESIL: POUVOIR ET LUTTE DES CLASSES. Paris: Editions Cujas, 1966.

653. Mattos, Carlos de Meira. BRASIL: GEOPOLITCA E DESTINO. Rio de Janeiro: José Olympio Editôra, 1975.

654. Maul, Carlos. "O almirante Jeronymo Gonçalves." MENSARIO 6 (1939): 879-84.

655. ———. O EXERCITO E A NACIONALIDADE. Rio de Janeiro: Biblioteca do Exército, 1950.

656. Maura, A. Lourival de. AS FORCAS ARMADAS E O DESTINO HISTORICO DO BRASIL. São Paulo: Companhia Editôra Nacional, 1937.

657. Medeiros, Ana Ligia Silva, and Monica Hirst. BIBLIOGRAFIA HISTORICA, 1930-45. Brasília: Editôra Universidade de Brasília, 1982.

658. Medeiros, Ana Ligia Silva, and Maria Celina Soares D'Araujo, eds. VARGAS E OS ANOS CINQUENTA: BIBLIOGRAFIA. Rio de Janeiro: Fundação Getúlio Vargas, 1983.

659. Medeiros, Jarbas. "Introdução ao estudo do pensamento político autoritario brasileiro, 1914/1945." REVISTA DE CIENCIA POLITICA 17:2 (1974).

660. Medina, José Maria F. "Argentina y Brazil: Redemocratización y poder militar." NUEVA SOCIEDAD 73 (1984): 135-44.

661. Mello, Alexandre, and Nilva R. Mello. O BRASIL E A BACIA DO PRATA. São Paulo: n.p., 1980.

662. Mello, Custódio José de. O GOVERNO PROVISORIO E A REVOLUCAO DE 1893. 2 vols. São Paulo: Companhia Editôra Nacional, 1938.

663. Mello, Jayme Portella de. A REVOLUCAO E O GOVERNO COSTA E SILVA. Rio de Janeiro: Guavira Editôres, 1979.

664. Mendes, Candido. "O governo Castelo Branco: Paradigma e prognose." DADOS 2-3 (1967): 63-111.

665. ———. "Sistema política e modelos de poder no Brasil." DADOS 1 (1966): 7-41.

666. Mendes, Evelyse Maria Freire. BIBLIOGRAFIA DO PENSAMENTO POLITICO REPUBLICANO, 1870-1970. Brasília: Editôra Universidade de Brasília, 1980.

667. Mendes, Raimundo Teixeira. BENJAMIN CONSTANT. Rio de Janeiro: Imprensa Nacional, 1936.

668. Mendoça, Rubens de. HISTORIA DAS REVOLUCOES EM MATO-GROSSO. Goiânia, Brazil: Editôra Rio Bonito, 1970.

669. Mercadante, Paulo. MILITARES E CIVIS: A ETICA E O COMPROMISSO. Rio de Janeiro: Zahar Editôres, 1978.

670. Mericle, Kenneth S. "Conflict Regulation in the Brazilian Industrial Relations System." Ph.D. dissertation, University of Wisconsin, 1974.

671. ———. "Corporatist Control of the Working Class: Authoritarian Brazil since 1964." In AUTHORITARIANISM AND CORPORATISM IN LATIN AMERICA, 303-38. Edited by James Malloy. Pittsburgh: University of Pittsburgh Press, 1977.

672. Merrick, Thomas W., and Douglas H. Graham, eds. OS MILITARES E A REVOLUCAO DE 30. Rio de Janeiro: Paz e Terra, 1979.

673. Meyer, Michael C. SUPPLEMENT TO A BIBLIOGRAPHY OF UNITED STATES-LATIN AMERICAN RELATIONS SINCE 1810. Linclon: University of Nebraska Press, 1979.

674. Meyers, David J. "Brazil: Reluctant Pursuit of the Nuclear Option." ORBIS 27 (1984): 881-911.

675. Mikkelsen, Vagn. "State and Military: Some Considerations on Latin America and the Brazilian Case." IBERO-AMERICANA 7 (1978): 77-88.

676. "Os militares." CADERNOS BRASILEIROS 38 (1966).

677. Miranda, Salim de. FLORIANO. Rio de Janeiro: Biblioteca do Exército, 1963.

678.   Mirow, Kurt Rudolf. LOCURA NUCLEAR: OS ENGANOS DO
       ACORDO BRASIL-ALEMANHA. Rio de Janeiro: Civilização
       Brasileira, 1979.

679.   Moises, José Alvaro, et al. ALTERNATIVAS POPULARES DE
       DEMOCRACIA: BRASIL, ANOS 80. Petrópolis: Editôra Vozes,
       1982.

680.   ———. LICOES DE LIBERDADE E DE OPRESSAO: OS
       TRABALHADORES E A LUTA PELA DEMOCRACIA. Rio
       de Janeiro: Paz e Terra, 1982.

681.   Moltmann, Bernard. "Die brasilianischen Streitkraefte, 1880-1910:
       Versuch einer politischen und sozialen Standortsbestimmung."
       JARHBUCH   FUR   GESCHICHTE   VON   STAAT,
       WIRTSCHAFT UND GESELLSCHAFT LATEINAMERIKAS
       16 (1979): 341-64.

682.   Moniz, Edmundo. A GUERRA SOCIAL DE CANUDOS. Rio
       de Janeiro: Civilização Brasileira, 1978.

683.   Monjardin, Adelpho Poli. O EXERCITO VISTO POR UM
       CIVIL. Rio de Janeiro: n.p., 1960.

684.   Monnet, Jean-Pierre. "L'Amazonie est á vendre." APONTA-
       MENTOS ARQUEOLOGICOS 172 (1974): 5-10.

685.   Monteiro, Duglas Teixeira. OS ERRANTES DO NOVO
       SECULO: UM ESTUDO SOBRE O SURTO MILENARISTA
       DO CONTESTADO. São Paulo: Duas Cidades, 1974.

686.   Monteiro, Frederico Mindello Carneiro. DEPOIMENTOS
       BIOGRAFICOS. Rio de Janeiro: Gráfica Olympica, 1977.

687.   Moore, John, ed. JANE'S FIGHTING SHIPS, 1981-82. New
       York: Jane's, 1981.

688.   Morães, Denis de, and Francisco Viana, eds. PRESTES: LUTAS
       E AUTOCRITICAS. Petrópolis: Editôra Vozes, 1982.

689.   Morães, Evaristo de. DA MONARCHIA PARA A
       REPUBLICA, 1870-1889. Rio de Janeiro: Athena Editôra, 1936.

690. Morães, João Baptista Mascarenhas de. THE BRAZILIAN EXPEDITIONARY FORCE BY ITS COMMANDER. Washington: U.S. Government Printing Office, 1965.

691. ———. A FEB PELO SEU COMMANDANTE. São Paulo: Instituto Progresso Editorial, 1947.

692. ———. MEMORIAS. 2 vols. Rio de Janeiro: Editôra José Olympio, 1969.

693. Morães, Rubens Borba de. BIBLIOGRAFIA BRASILIANA. 2 vols. Rev. and enl. ed. Los Angeles: Latin American Center, UCLA; Rio de Janeiro: Livraria Kosmos Editôra, 1983.

694. Morães, Rubens Borba de, and William Berrien, eds. MANUAL BIBLIOGRAFICO DE ESTUDOS BRASILEIROS. Rio de Janeiro: Gráfica Editôra Souza, 1949.

695. Morães, Walfrido. JAGUNCOS E HEROIS: A CIVILIZACÃO DO DIAMANTE NAS LAVRAS DA BAHIA. Rio de Janeiro: Civilização Brasileira, 1963.

696. Morães Filho, Evaristo de. O PROBLEMA DO SINDICATO UNICO NO BRASIL. Rio de Janeiro: Editôra A. Noite, 1952.

697. Moreira, Hilton Berutti Augusto. O BRASIL E SUAS RESPONSIBILIDADES NO ATLANTICO SUL. Brasília: Ministério da Marinha, Diretoria de Portos e Costas, 1972.

698. ———. "Transportes maritimos: Desenvolvimento e segurança nacional." REVISTA MARITIMA BRASILEIRA 91 (1971): 44-62.

699. Morel, Edmar. O GOLPE COMECOU EM WASHINGTON. Rio de Janeiro: Editôra Brasiliense, 1965.

700. ———. A REVOLTA DA CHIBATA. 2d ed. Rio de Janeiro: Editôra Letras e Artes, 1963.

701. Morley, Samuel A. LABOR MARKETS AND INEQUITABLE GROWTH: THE CASE OF AUTHORITARIAN CAPITALISM IN BRAZIL. New York: Cambridge University Press, 1982.

702. Morris, Michael A. INTERNATIONAL POLITICS AND THE SEA: THE CASE OF BRASIL. Boulder: Westview Press, 1979.

703. Mota, Carlos Guilherme. "A historiografia brasileira nos últimos quarenta anos: Tentativa de avaliação crítica." Paper read at the Primeira Encuentro de Historiadores Latinoamericanos, Mexico City, 1974.

704. Mourão, Milciades M. DUTRA: HISTORIA DE UM GOVERNO. Rio de Janeiro: n.p., 1955.

705. Mourão Filho, Olympio. MEMORIAS: A VERDADE DE UM REVOLUCIONARIO. Rio de Janeiro: L&PM Editores, 1978.

706. ———. "Relatório de revolução democrática iniciada pela 4a RME, 4a DI em 31 de março de 1964." COMMANDO DE 4A REGIAO MILITAR, 4A DIVISAO DE INFANTARIA E GUARNICAO DE JUIZ DE FORA, 9 May 1964.

707. Muricy, Antonio Carlos de Silva. PALAVRAS DE UM SOLDADO. Rio de Janeiro: Imprensa do Exército, 1971.

708. Muricy, José Cândido da Silva. A REVOLUCAO DE 93 NOS ESTADOS DE SANTA CATARINA E PARANA. Rio de Janeiro: Editorial Americana, 19??.

709. Nabuco, Joaquim. A INTERVENCAO ESTRANGEIRA DURANTE A REVOLTA DE 1893. 2d ed. São Paulo: Editôra Nacional, 1939.

710. NACLA, LATIN AMERICA AND EMPIRE REPORT. "Brazil: The Continental Strategy." May-June 1975, 1-32.

711. Naziazene, Ademar. POLICIA MILITAR DA PARAIBA: SUA HISTORIA DE 1831-1957. João Pessôa: Senado Federal, Centro Gráfico, 1972.

712. Neto, Elias Chaves. SENTIDO DINAMICO DE DEMOCRACIA. São Paulo: Editôra Brasiliense, 1982.

713. Netto, Antonio Delfim. A RECUPERACAO DA ECONOMIA EM 1980-1981. Brasília: Presidencia da República, Secretaria de Planejamento, 1981.

714. Netto, Bento Munhoz da Rocha. RADIOGRAFIA DE NOVEMBRO. 2d ed. Rio de Janeiro: Civilização Brasileira, 1961.

715. Netto, João Cândido Maia. LA CRISIS BRASILENA. Buenos Aires: Jorge Alvarez Editor, 1965.

716. Netto, José Antonio. MEMORIAS DO GENERAL ZECA NETTO. Pôrto Alegre: Martins Livreiro, 1983.

717. Neves, João. JOAO NEVES DA FONTOURA: DISCURSOS PARLAMENTARES. Brasília: Câmara dos Deputados, 1978.

718. Neves, Lucfilia de Almeida. O COMANDO GERAL DOS TRABLHADORES NO BRASIL, 1961-1964. Belo Horizonte: Editôra VEGA, 1981.

719. Nobrega, Vandick Londres da. 1964 (I.E. MIL NOVECENTOS E SESSENTA E QUATRO): SEGURANCA E DEFENSA DO BRASIL. Rio de Janeiro: Livraria Freitas Bastos, 1977.

720. Nogueira, Mario G. "Democracia participativa: Uma visão da abertura dos militares." REVISTA DE CIENCIA POLITICA 26 (1983): 58-68.

721. Nogueira Filho, Paulo. IDEAIS E LUTAS DE UM BURGUES PROGRESSISTA: A GUERRA CIVICA, 1932. 2 vols. Rio de Janeiro: Editôra José Olympio, 1965.

722. Novelli Júnior, Mauro Renault Leite e, and Luiz Gonzaga, eds. MARECHAL EURICO GASPAR DUTRA: O DEVER DA VERDADE. Rio de Janeiro: Editôra Nova Fronteira, 1983.

723. Nunes, Antonio Carlos Félix. FORA DE PAUTA: HISTORIAS E HISTORIA DO JORNALISMO NO BRASIL. São Paulo: Proposta Editorial, 1981.

724. Nunes, Carlos. BRASIL: SATELITE Y GENDARME. Montevideo: Aportes, 1969.

725. Nunes, Jorge Fischer. O RISO DOS TORTURADOS: ANEDOTARIO DE GUERRILHA URBANA. Pôrto Alegre: Proletra, 1982.

726.   Nunn, Frederick. "European Military Influence in South America: The Origins and Nature of Professional Militarism in Argentina, Brazil, Chile and Peru." JAHRBUCH FUR GESCHICHTE VON STAAT, WIRTSCHAFT UND GESSELSCHAFT LATEINAMERIKAS 12 (1975): 230-52.

727.   ——. "The Latin American Military Establishment: Some Thoughts on its Origins and an Illustrative Bibliographic Essay." THE AMERICAS 28 (1971): 135-51.

728.   ——. "Military Professionalism and Professional Militarism in Brazil, 1870-1970: Historical Perspectives and Political Implications." JOURNAL OF LATIN AMERICAN STUDIES 4 (1972): 29-54.

729.   ——. YESTERDAY'S SOLDIERS: EUROPEAN MILITARY PROFESSIONALISM IN SOUTH AMERICA, 1890-1940. Lincoln: University of Nebraska Press, 1983.

730.   Nyrop, Richard F. BRAZIL: A COUNTRY STUDY. 4th ed. Washington: Secretary of the Army, 1983.

731.   O'Brien, Philip, and Paul Cammack, eds. GENERALS IN RETREAT: THE CRISIS OF MILITARY RULE IN LATIN AMERICA. Dover, NH: Manchester University Press, 1985.

732.   O'Donnell, Guillermo. MODERNIZATION AND BUREAUCRATIC AUTHORITARIANISM. Berkeley: University of California Press, 1973.

733.   O'Donnell, Guillermo, Philippe C. Schmitter, and Lawrence Whitehead, eds. TRANSITION FROM AUTHORITARIAN RULE. Baltimore: Johns Hopkins University Press, 1986.

734.   Oliveira, Clovis de. A INDUSTRIA E A MOVIMENTO CONSTITUCIONALISTA DE 1932. São Paulo: Centro e Federação das Industrias do Estado de São Paulo, 1956.

735.   Oliveira, Eliézer Rizzo de. AS FORCAS ARMADAS: POLITICA E IDEOLOGIA NO BRASIL, 1964-1969. Petrópolis: Editôra Vozes, 1976.

736.   Oliveira, José Teixeira de, ed. O GOVERNO DUTRA. Rio de Janeiro: Civilização Brasileira, 1956.

737. Oliveira, Lucia Lippi. "Revolução de 1930: Uma bibliografia comentada." BOLETIM INFORMATIVO E BIBLIOGRAFICO DE CIENCIAS SOCIAIS 4 (1978): 8-18.

738. O'Reilly, Donald Francis. "Rondon: Biography of a Brazilian Republican Army Commander." Ph.D. dissertation, New York University, 1969.

739. Orico, Oswaldo. CONFISSOES DO EXILIO-J.K. Rio de Janeiro: F. Alves, 1977.

740. Ottoni, Carlos H.B. O ADVENTO DA REPUBLICA NO BRASIL. Rio de Janeiro: Typographia Perseverança, 1890.

741. Pacheco, José de Assis. REVIVENDO 32...EXUMACAO DE UM DIARIO DE GUERRA. São Paulo: n.p., 1954.

742. Pang, Eul-Soo. BAHIA IN THE FIRST BRAZILIAN REPUBLIC: CORONELISMO AND OLIGARCHIES, 1889-1934. Gainesville: University of Florida Press, 1979.

743. ———. "Coronelismo in Northeast Brazil." In THE CACIQUES: OLIGARCHICAL POLITICS AND THE SYSTEM OF CACIQUISMO IN THE LUSO-HISPANIC WORLD, 65-88. Edited by Robert Kern. Albuquerque: University of New Mexico Press, 1973.

744. ———. "The Darker Side of Brazil's Democracy." CURRENT HISTORY, January 1988, 21-24,40.

745. ———. "The Political Economy of the Brazilian Arms Industry." Paper presented at the annual meeting of the Rocky Mountain Council on Latin American Studies, Las Cruces, NM, February 1989.

746. Paredes, Maximiliano. ROBORE Y EL MILITARISMO BRASILENO. La Paz, Bolivia: Editorial Letras, 1960.

747. Parker, Phyllis R. BRAZIL AND THE QUIET INTERVENTION, 1964. Austin: University of Texas Press, 1979.

748. ———. 1964: O PAPEL DOS ESTADOS UNIDOS NO GOLPE DE ESTADO DE 31 DE MARCO. Rio de Janeiro: Editorial Civilização Brasileira, 1977.

749. Partido Comunista do Brasil. CINQUENTA ANOS DE LUTA. Lisbon: Edições Maria da Fonte, 1975.

750. ———. GUERRA POPULAR: CAMINHO DA LUTA ARMADA NO BRASIL. Lisbon: Edições Maria da Fonte, 1974.

751. ———. POLITICA E REVOLUCIONARIZACAO. Lisbon: Edições Maria da Fonte, 1977.

752. Paula, Euripedes Simões de. "A FEB: Tema para um historiador." REVISTA DO INSTITUTO HISTORICO E GEOGRAFICO BRASILEIRO 317 (1977): 77-91.

753. P.C.B: VINTE ANOS DE POLITICA, 1958-1979; DOCUMENTOS. São Paulo: Livraria Editôra Ciencias Humanas, 1980.

754. Pedreira, Fernando. MARCO 31: CIVIS E MILITARES NO PROCESSO DA CRISE BRASILEIRA. Rio de Janeiro: J. Alvaro, 1964.

755. Peixoto, Alzira Vargas do Amaral. GETULIO VARGAS: MEU PAI. 2d ed. Pôrto Alegre: Editôra Globo, 1960.

756. Peixoto, Artur Vieira, et al., eds. FLORIANO: MEMORIAS E DOCUMENTOS 6 vols. Rio de Janeiro: Ministério da Educação, 1939.

757. Penna, J.O. de Meira. POLITICA EXTERNA: SEGURANCA E DESENVOLVIMENTO. Rio de Janeiro: Livraria AGIR Editôra, 1967.

758. Perdigão, Luis F. MISSAO DE GUERRA: OS EXPEDICIONARIOS DA FAB NA GUERRA EUROPEIA. Rio de Janeiro: Gráfico de Luxo, 1958.

759. Peregrino, Umberto. HISTORIA E PROJECAO DAS INSTITUICOES CULTURAIS DO EXERCITO. Rio de Janeiro: Editôra José Olympio, 1967.

760. ———. "Projeção da cultura militar no secundo reinado." REVISTA DO INSTITUTO HISTORICO E GEOGRAFICO BRASILEIRO 314 (1977): 183-204.

761.   ———.   "OS SERTOES" COMO HISTORIA MILITAR. Rio de
        Janeiro: Biblioteca do Exército, 1956.

762.   Pereira, Antonio Carlos. FOLHA DOBRADA: DOCUMENTO
        E HISTORIA DO POVO PAULISTA EM 1932. São Paulo:
        Estado de São Paulo, 1982.

763.   Pereira, Luiz Carlos Bresser. DEVELOPMENT AND CRISIS
        IN BRAZIL, 1930-1983. Boulder: Westview Press, 1984.

764.   Pereira, Osny Duarte. LA SEUDORIVALIDAD ARGENTINO-
        BRASILENA: PRO Y CONTRA DE ITAIPU. Buenos Aires:
        Ediciones Corregidor, 1975.

765.   Pereira Júnior, Jesse Torres. "Os atos institucionais em face do
        direito administrativo." REVISTA BRASILEIRA DE ESTUDOS
        POLITICOS 47 (1978): 77-114.

766.   Perrin, Dimas. DEPOIMENTO DE UM TORTURADO. Rio
        de Janeiro: Nova Cultura Editôra, 1979.

767.   Perry, William. CONTEMPORARY BRAZILIAN FOREIGN
        POLICY: THE INTERNATIONAL STRATEGY OF AN
        EMERGING POWER. Beverly Hills: Sage Publications, 1976.

768.   Pesce, Eduardo Italo.   "The Brazilian Naval Modernization
        Program."   UNITED   STATES   NAVAL   INSTITUTE
        PROCEEDINGS 108 (1982): 145-48.

769.   Pessôa, Pantaleão. REMINISCENCIAS E IMPOSICOES DE
        UMA VIDA, 1885-1965. Rio de Janeiro: Gráfica Lux, 1972.

770.   Piazza, Walter Fernando.   SANTA   CATARINA: SUA
        HISTORIA. Florianópolis: Editorial da Universidade Federal de
        Santa Catarina, 1983.

771.   Piedracueva, Haydée.   A BIBLIOGRAPHY OF LATIN
        AMERICAN   BIBLIOGRAPHIES,   1975-1979:   SOCIAL
        SCIENCES AND HUMANITIES. Metuchen, NJ: Scarecrow
        Press, 1982.

772.   Pilla, Raul.   A REVOLUCAO JULGADA: A CRISE
        INSTITUCIONAL. Pôrto Alegre: Livraria Lina, 1969

773. Pillar, Olyntho. OS PATRONOS DAS FORCAS ARMADAS. Rio de Janeiro: n.p., 1966.

774. Pinheiro, José Juarez Bastos. A FORCA EXPEDICIONARIA BRASILEIRA NA SEGUNDA GUERRA MUNDIAL: RESUMO HISTORICO. Rio de Janeiro: Impressora Polar, 1976.

775. Pinheiro Filho, Celso, and Lina Celso Pinhiero. SOLDADOS DE TIRADENTES: HISTORIA DA POLICIA MILITAR DO PIAUI. Rio de Janeiro: Editôra Artenova, 1975.

776. Pinto, Bilac. GUERRA REVOLUCIONARIA. Rio de Janeiro: Forense de Artes Gráficas, 1965

777. Pires, Pandia. "PRETO 29": A VERDADE HISTORICA SOBRE OS ULTIMOS ACONTECIMENTOS DO BRASIL. Rio de Janeiro: n.p., 1946.

778. Placer, Xavier, and Nellie Figueira. PUBLICACOES DA BIBLIOTECA NACIONAL: CATALOGO, 1872-1974. Rio de Janeiro: Biblioteca Nacional, Divisão de Publicações, 1975.

779. Poerner, Arthur José. O PODER JOVEM: HISTORIA DE PARTICIPACAO POLITICA DOS ESTUDANTES BRASILEIROS. Rio de Janeiro: Editôra Civilização Brasileira, 1968.

780. Pomar, Pedro Estevam da Rocha. MASSACRE NA LAPA: COMO O EXERCITO LIQUIDOU O COMITE CENTRAL DO P.C. DO B. São Paulo: Busca Vida, 1987.

781. Poppino, Rollie E. "Brasil: Nôvo modelo para o desenvolvimento nacional." REVISTA BRASILEIRA DE ESTUDOS POLITICOS 36 (1973): 105-15.

782. ———. "Brazil after a Decade of Revolution." CURRENT HISTORY, January 1974, 1-5,35.

783. ———. BRAZIL: THE LAND AND PEOPLE. 2d ed. New York: Oxford University Press, 1973.

784. Portela, Fernando. GUERRA DE GUERRILHAS NO BRASIL. São Paulo: Global, 1979.

785. Portes, Alejandro. "Legitimacy, Co-optation, and the Authoritarian State: Comments on 'After the Miracle.'" LUSO-BRAZILIAN REVIEW 15 (1978): 302-07.

786. Pôrto, Angela, Lilian de A. Fritsch, and Sylvia F. Padilha. PROCESSO DE MODERNIZACAO DO BRASIL, 1850-1930: ECONOMIA E SOCIEDADE; UMA BIBLIOGRAFIA. Rio de Janeiro: Fundação Casa de Rui Barbosa, and Biblioteca CREFISUL, 1985.

787. Portocarrero, Nilza Pereira da Silva. VIDA DE UMA REPORTER: FATO E DEPOIMENTOS POLITICOS. Brasília: n.p., 1981.

788. Prado, Eduardo. FASTOS DA DITADURA MILITAR NO BRASIL. São Paulo: Escola Typ. Salesiana, 1902.

789. Prado Júnior, Caio. A REVOLUCAO BRASILEIRA 5th ed. São Paulo: Editôra Brasiliense, 1977.

790. Quartim, João. DICTATORSHIP AND ARMED STRUGGLE IN BRAZIL. New York: Monthly Review Press, 1971.

791. Queiroz, Mauricio Vinhas de. MESSIANISMO E CONFLITO SOCIAL: A GUERRA SERTANEJA DO CONTESTADO, 1913-1916. Rio de Janeiro: Civilização Brasileira, 1966.

792. Rabben, Linda. "Amazon Gold Rush: Brazil's Military Stakes Its Claim." THE NATION, 12 March 1990, 341-42.

793. Rachum, Ilan. "Nationalism and Revolution in Brazil, 1922-1930: A Study of Intellectual, Military and Political Protesters and of the Assault on the Old Republic." Ph.D. dissertation, Columbia University, 1970.

794. ———. "From Young Rebels to Brokers of National Politics: The Tenentes of Brazil, 1922-1967." BOLETIN DE ESTUDIOS LATINOAMERICANOS Y DEL CARIBE 23 (1977): 41-60.

795. Ramos, Guerreiro. A CRISE DO PODER NO BRASIL: PROBLEMAS DA REVOLUCAO NACIONAL BRASILEIRA. Rio de Janeiro: Zahar, 1961.

796. Rebello, Gilson. A GUERRILHA DE CAPARAO. São Paulo: Alfa-Omega, 1980.

797. Rebelo, Darino Castro. TRANSAMAZONICA: INTEGRACAO EM MARCHA. Rio de Janeiro: Ministério do Trabalho, Centro de Documentação e Publicações, 1973.

798. Rego, Orlando L.M. de Morães. HISTORIA DA MILICIA PARAENSE NA CAMPANHA DE CANUDOS. Belém: Imprensa Universitaria do Pará, 1967.

799. Reis, Edgardo Moutinho dos. EXERCITO DE PADIOLEIROS E BISTURIS. Rio de Janeiro: Mabri Livraria e Editôra, 1969.

800. Reis, Fabio Wanderley. "O eleitorado, os partidos e o regime autoritario brasileiro." In SOCIEDADE E POLITICA NO BRASIL POS-64. Edited by Bernado Sorg and Maria Herminia Távares de Almeida. São Paulo: Brasiliense, 1983.

801. ———, ed. OS PARTIDOS E O REGIME: A LOGICA DO PROCESSO ELEITORAL BRASILEIRO. São Paulo: Edições Símbolo, 1978.

802. Reis Filho, Daniel Aarão, and Jair Ferreira de Sá. IMAGENS DA REVOLUCAO: DOCUMENTOS POLITICOS DAS ORGANIZACOES CLANDESTINAS DE ESQUERDA DOS ANOS 1961-1971. Rio de Janeiro: Marco Zero, 1985.

803. Rengifo, Antonio. "New Institutional Ideology in Latin American Military Coups: Brazil and Peru." Ph.D. dissertation, Texas Christian University, 1979.

804. REPRESSION OF THE CHURCH IN BRAZIL: REFLECTION ON A SITUATION OF OPPRESSION, 1968-1978. Rio de Janeiro: Centro Ecumênico de Documentação e Informação, 1978.

805. REVISTA BRASILEIRA DE ESTUDOS POLITICOS 26 (1966). Volume on Brazilian national security.

806. REVISTA BRASILEIRA DE POLITICA INTERNACIONAL 9 (1967). Volume on debate over Brazilian nuclear energy policy.

807. Rodrigues, Eduardo Celestino. PROBLEMAS DO BRASIL POTENCIA. 3d ed. São Paulo: Editoras Unidas, 1973.

808. Rodrigues, José Honorio. "Brazilian Historiography: Present Trends and Research Requirements." In SOCIAL SCIENCE IN LATIN AMERICA, 231-57. Edited by Manuel Diegues Júnior and Bryce Wood. New York: Columbia University Press, 1967.

809. ———. THE BRAZILIANS: THEIR CHARACTER AND ASPIRATIONS. Austin: University of Texas Press, 1967.

810. ———. CONCILIACAO E REFORMA NO BRASIL: UM DESAFIO HISTORICO-CULTURAL. 2d ed. Rio de Janeiro: Editôra Nova Fronteira, 1982.

811. ———. INDEPENDENCIA, REVOLUCAO E CONTRA-REVOLUCAO. 5 vols. Rio de Janeiro: F. Alves Editôra, 1975-76.

812. ———. A PESQUISA HISTORICA NO BRASIL. 2d ed. São Paulo: Editôra Nacional, 1969.

813. Rodrigues, Leda Maria Pereira, "A questão militar e a propaganda republicana." REVISTA DE HISTORIA 3/4 (1965): 195-234.

814. Rodrigues, Leôncio Martins and Fabio Munhoz. "Bibliografia sobre trabalhadores e sindicatos no Brasil." ESTUDOS CEBRAP (1974).

815. Rodrigues, Raul Oliveira. UM MILITAR CONTRA O MILITARISMO: A VIDA DE SALDANHA DA GAMA. Rio de Janeiro: Edições O Cruzeiro, 1959.

816. Rodriguez, Inês Caminha Lopes. A REVOLTA DE PRINCESA: UMA CONTRIBUICAO AO ESTUDIO DO MANDONISMO LOCAL; PARAIBA, 1930. João Pessõa: Sec. da Educação e Cultura, Paraíba, 1978.

817. Roett, Riordan. BRAZIL: POLITICS IN A PATRIMONIAL SOCIETY. Boston: Allyn and Bacon, 1972.

818. ———. "Brazil's Transition to Democracy." CURRENT HISTORY, March 1989, 117-20, 49.

819. ——, ed. BRAZIL IN THE SIXTIES. Nashville: Vanderbilt University Press, 1972.

820. Romano, Robert. BRASIL: IGREJA CONTRA ESTADO; CRITICA AO POPULISMO CATOLICO. São Paulo: Kairos Livraria e Editôra, 1979.

821. Ronning, C. Neal. "The Military and the Formulation of Internal and External Policy in Brazil in the Twentieth Century." In PERSPECTIVES ON ARMED POLITICS IN BRAZIL, 207-24. Edited by Henry H. Keith and Robert A. Hayes. Tempe: Arizona State University Press, 1976.

822. Rosa, Virginio Santa. O SENTIDO DO TENENTISMO. Rio de Janeiro: Schmidt, 1933.

823. Rosenbaum, H. Jon. "Project Rondon: A Brazilian Experiment in Economic and Political Development." AMERICAN JOURNAL OF ECONOMICS AND SOCIOLOGY 30 (1971): 187-201.

824. Rossi, Waldemar. BRAZIL: STATE AND STRUGGLE. London: Latin American Bureau, 1982.

825. Rouquié, Alain. DEMILITARIZATION AND THE INSTITUTIONALIZATION OF MILITARY-DOMINATED POLICIES IN LATIN AMERICA. Washington: Wilson Center, 1982.

826. ——. L'ETAT MILITARE EN AMERIQUE LATINE. Paris: Editions du Seuil, 1982.

827. ——. LES PARTIS MILITARES AU BRESIL. Paris: Presses de la Fondation Nationale des Sciences Politiques, 1980.

828. Rouquié, Alain, Bolivar Lamournier, and Jorge Schvarzer, eds. COMO RENASCEM AS DEMOCRACIAS. São Paulo: Brasiliense, 1985.

829. Rowe, James. "Brazil Stops the Clock. Part 1, 'Democratic Formalism' before 1964 and in the Elections of 1966." AMERICAN UNIVERSITIES FIELD STAFF REPORTS, EAST COAST SOUTH AMERICA SERIES 13 (1967).

830. ———. "Brazil Stops the Clock. Part 2, The New Constitution and the New Model." AMERICAN UNIVERSITIES FIELD STAFF REPORTS, EAST COAST SOUTH AMERICAN SERIES 13 (1967).

831. ———. "The 'Revolution' and the 'System': Notes on Brazilian Politics." AMERICAN UNIVERSITIES FIELD STAFF REPORTS, EAST COAST SOUTH AMERICAN SERIES 12 (1966).

832. Russell, Charles A., James A. Miller, and Robert E. Hildner. "The Urban Guerrilla in Latin America: A Select Bibliography." LATIN AMERICAN RESEARCH REVIEW 9 (1974): 37-80.

833. Sábato, Jorge A. "El plan nuclear brasileño y la bomba atómica." ESTUDIOS INTERNACIONALES 11 (1978): 73-82.

834. Sães, Decio. O CIVILISMO DAS CAMADAS MEDIAS URBANAS NA PRIMEIRA REPUBLICA BRASILEIRA. Campinas, São Paulo: Universidad Estadual de Campinas, 1973.

835. ———. CLASE MEDIA E POLITICA NA PRIMEIRA REPUBLICA BRASILEIRA, 1889-1930. Petrópolis: Editôra Vozes, 1975.

836. Saint-Jean, Iberico Manuel. "Los ejércitos de Argentina y Brasil: Algunos aspectos comparativos." ESTRATEGIA 1 (1970): 97-107.

837. Sales, Júnior, A.C. de. O IDEALISMO REPUBLICANO DE CAMPOS SALES. Rio de Janeiro: Editôra Zelio Valverde, n.d.

838. Salgado, Plinio. OBRAS COMPLETAS. 20 vols. São Paulo: Editôra das Américas, 1954-56.

839. Salles, Antonio Pinheiro. CONFESSO QUE PEGUEI EM ARMAS. Belo Horizonte: Editôra Vega, 1979.

840. Salles, José Bento Teixeira de. MILTON CAMPOS: UMA VOCACAO LIBERAL. Belo Horizonte: Editôra Vega, 1975.

841. Sanders, Thomas G. "Institutionalizing Brazil's Conservative Revolution." AMERICAN UNIVERSITIES FIELD STAFF REPORT, EAST COAST SOUTH AMERICA 14 (1970): 1-17.

842. Santos, Francisco Agenor de Noronha. CENTENARIO DO NASCIMENTO DO ALMIRANTE JULIO CESAR DE NORONHA: ESBOCO BIOGRAFICO, 1845-1945. Rio de Janeiro: Editôra Zelio Valverde, 1945.

843. Santos, Francisco Ruas. COLECAO BIBLIOGRAFICA MILITAR. Rio de Janeiro: Biblioteca do Exército, 1960

844. ———. FONTES PARA A HISTORIA DA F.E.B. Rio de Janeiro: Biblioteca do Exército, 1958.

845. ———, ed. MARECHAL CASTELLO BRANCO: SEU PENSAMENTO MILITAR, 1946-1964. Rio de Janeiro: Imprensa do Exército, 1968.

846. Santos, Ralph G. "Brazilian Foreign Policy and the Dominican Crisis: The Impact of History on Events." THE AMERICAS 29 (1972): 62-77.

847. Santos, Wanderley Guilherme dos. "Autoritarismo e apos: Convergencias e divergencias entre Brasil e Chile." DADOS 25 (1982):151-63

848. ———. SESSENTA E QUATRO: ANATOMIA DA CRISE. São Paulo: Editôra Vértice, 1986.

849. Saunders, John V.D. "A Revolution of Agreement among Friends: The End of the Vargas Era." HISPANIC AMERICAN HISTORICAL REVIEW 44 (1964):197-213.

850. Scavarda, Levy. "O almirantado brasileiro: Esboço histórico." SUBSIDIOS PARA A HISTORIA MARITIMA DO BRASIL 20 (1963-64): 167-214.

851. Scheina, Robert L. LATIN AMERICA: A NAVAL HISTORY, 1810-1987. Annapolis, MD: Naval Institute Press, 1987.

852. Schmink, Marianne. "Land Conflicts in Amazonia." AMERICAN ETHNOLOGIST 9 (1982): 341-57.

853. Schneider, Ronald M. BRAZIL: FOREIGN POLICY OF A FUTURE WORLD POWER. Boulder: Westview Press, 1976.

854. ———. "The Brazilian Military in Politics." In NEW MILITARY POLITICS IN LATIN AMERICA, 52-75. Edited by Robert Wesson. New York: Praeger Publishers, 1982.

855. ———. THE POLITICAL SYSTEM OF BRAZIL: EMERGENCE OF A "MODERNIZING" AUTHORITARIAN REGIME, 1964-1970. New York: Columbia University Press, 1971.

856. Schooyans, Michel. DEMAIN LE BRESIL?: MILITARISME ET TECHNOCRATIE. Paris: Les Editions Du Cerf, 1977.

857. Schoultz, Lars. NATIONAL SECURITY AND UNITED STATES POLICY TOWARD LATIN AMERICA. Princeton: Princeton University Press, 1987.

858. Schulz, John Henry. "The Brazilian Army and Politics, 1850-1894." Ph.D. dissertation, Princeton University, 1973.

859. Seckinger, Ron, and F.W.O. Morton. "Social Science Libraries in Greater Rio de Janeiro." LATIN AMERICAN RESEARCH REVIEW 15 (1979): 180-201.

860. Seitenfus, Ricardo Antonio Silva. O BRASIL DE GETULIO VARGAS E A FORMACAO DOS BLOCOS, 1930-1942: O PROCESSO DO ENVOLVIMENTO BRASILEIRO NA II GUERRA MUNDIAL. São Paulo: Editôra Nacional, 1985.

861. ———. "Ideology and Diplomacy: Italian Fascism and Brazil, 1935-1938." HISPANIC AMERICAN HISTORICAL REVIEW 64 (1984): 503-34.

862. Selcher, Wayne A., ed. BRAZIL IN THE INTERNATIONAL SYSTEM: THE RISE OF A MIDDLE POWER. Boulder: Westview Press, 1981.

863. ———. POLITICAL LIBERALIZATION IN BRAZIL: DYNAMICS, DILEMMAS, AND FUTURE PROSPECTS. Boulder: Westview Press, 1985.

864. Silva, Augusto Carlos de Souza e. O ALMIRANTE SALDANHA E A REVOLTA DA ARMADA. Rio de Janeiro: Editôra José Olympio, 1936.

865. Silva, Cyro. FLORIANO PEIXOTO: O CONSOLIDADOR DA REPUBLICA. São Paulo: Editôra Edaglit, 1963.

866. Silva, Edmundo de Macedo Soares e. "Industria y seguridad nacional: El caso Brasil." In EJERCITO Y REVOLUCION INDUSTRIAL. Edited by Jean Cazenueve, et al. Buenos Aires: J. Alvarez, 1964.

867. Silva, Egydio Moreira de Castro e. A MARGEM DO MINISTERIO CALOGERAS: MEMORIAS. Vol. 1. Rio de Janeiro: Editôra Melso, 1962.

868. Silva, Golbery do Couto e. CONJUNTURA POLITICA NACIONAL: O PODER EXECUTIVO E GEOPOLITICA DO BRASIL. Rio de Janeiro: Editôra José Olympio, 1981.

869. ———. GEOPOLITICA DO BRASIL. Rio de Janeiro: Editôra José Olympio, 1967.

870. Silva, Hélio. 1930: A REVOLUCAO TRAIDA. Rio de Janeiro: Civilização Brasileira, 1966.

871. ———. 1933: O CONSTITUINTE. Rio de Janeiro: Civlização Brasileira, 1969.

872. ———. 1933: A CRISE DO TENENTISMO. Rio de Janeiro: Civilização Brasileira, 1968.

873. ———. 1922: SANGUE NA AREIA DE COPACABANA. Rio de Janeiro: Civilização Brasileira, 1964.

874. ———. 1926: A GRANDE MARCHE. Rio de Janeiro: Civilização Brasileira, 1965.

875. ———. 1889: A REPUBLICA NAO ESPEROU O AMANHECER. Rio de Janeiro: Civilização Brasileira, 1972.

876. Silva, Hélio, and Maria Cecilia Ribas Carnerio. OS GOVERNOS MILITARES, 1969-1974. São Paulo: Editôra Tres, 1975.

877. ———. 1945: POR QUE DEPUSERAM VARGAS. Rio de Janeiro: Civilização Brasileira, 1976.

878. ——. 1942: GUERRA NO CONTINENTE. Rio de Janeiro: Civilização Brasileira, 1972

879. ——. 1944: O BRASIL NA GUERRA. Rio de Janeiro: Civilização Brasileira, 1974.

880. ——. 1964: GOLPE OU CONTRAGOLPE? Rio de Janeiro: Civilização Brasileira, 1975.

881. Silva, José Calasans Brandão da. NO TEMPO DE ANTONIO CONSELHEIRO: FIGURAS E FATOS DA CAMPANHA DE CANUDOS. Salvador: Universidade da Bahia, 1959.

882. Silveira, Geraldo Tito. CRONICA DA POLICIA MILITAR DE MINAS. Belo Horizonte: Imprensa Oficial do Estado de Minas Gerais, 1966.

883. Simmons, Charles W. "Deodoro da Fonseca: Fate's Dictator." JOURNAL OF LATIN AMERICAN STUDIES 5 (1963):45-52.

884. ——. MARSHAL DEODORO AND THE FALL OF DOM PEDRO II. Durham: Duke University Press, 1966.

885. Simões, Solange de Deus. DEUS, PATRIA E FAMILIA: AS MULHERES NO GOLPE DE 1964. Petrópolis: Editôra Vozes, 1985.

886. Simon, David N., et al. ENERGIA NUCLEAR EM QUESTAO. Rio de Janeiro: Instituto Euvaldi Lodi, 1981.

887. Simonsen, Mário Henrique. NOVOS ASPECTOS DA INFLACAO BRASILEIRA. São Paulo: ANPES, 1970.

888. ——. PALESTRAS E CONFERENCIAS. 7 vols. Rio de Janeiro: Ministério da Fazenda, 1974-78.

889. Simonsen, Mário Henrique, and Roberto de Oliveira Campos. A NOVA ECONOMIA BRASILEIRA (THE NEW BRAZILIAN ECONOMY). Rio de Janeiro: Crown Editôra Internacionais, 1974.

890. Singer, Paul. REPARTICAO DA RENDA: POBRES SOB O REGIME MILITAR. Rio de Janeiro: Zahar, 1986.

891.	Skidmore, Thomas.	"Brazil's Slow Road to Democratization, 1974-1985." In DEMOCRATIZING BRAZIL: PROBLEMS OF TRANSITION AND CONSOLIDATION, 5-42. Edited by Alfred Stepan. New York: Oxford University Press, 1989.

892.	———. "The Historiography of Brazil, 1889-1964. Part 1." HISPANIC AMERICAN HISTORICAL REVIEW 55 (1975): 716-48.

893.	———. "The Historiography of Brazil, 1889-1964. Part 2." HISPANIC AMERICAN HISTORICAL REVIEW 56 (1976): 81-109.

894.	———. "The Political Economy of Policy-making in Authoritarian Brazil, 1967-1970." In GENERALS IN RETREAT: THE CRISIS OF MILITARY RULE IN LATIN AMERICA, 115-43. Edited by Philip O'Brien and Paul Cammack. Manchester, England: Manchester University Press, 1985.

895.	———. "Politics and Economic Policy Making in Authoritarian Brazil." In AUTHORITARIAN BRAZIL, 3-46. Edited by Alfred Stepan. New Haven: Yale University Press, 1973.

896.	———. POLITICS IN BRAZIL, 1930-1964: AN EXPERIMENT IN DEMOCRACY. New York: Oxford University Press, 1967.

897.	———. THE POLITICS OF MILITARY RULE IN BRAZIL, 1964-85. New York: Oxford University Press, 1988.

898.	———. "Workers and Soldiers: Urban Labor Movements and Elite Responses in Twentieth-Century Latin America." In ELITES, MASSES, AND MODERNIZATION IN LATIN AMERICA, 1850-1930. Edited by Virginia Bernard. Austin: University of Texas Press, 1979.

899.	———. "The Years between the Harvests: The Economies of the Castello Branco Presidency, 1964-1967." LUSO-BRAZILIAN REVIEW 15 (1978): 153-77.

900.	Smith, Joseph. "American Diplomacy and the Naval Mission to Brazil, 1917-1930." INTER-AMERICAN ECONOMIC AFFAIRS 35 (1981): 73-91.

901. ——. "Britain and the Brazilian Naval Revolt, 1893-4."
      JOURNAL OF LATIN AMERICAN STUDIES 2 (1970): 175-98.

902. ——. "United States Diplomacy toward Political Revolt in Brazil,
      1889-1930." INTER-AMERICAN ECONOMIC AFFAIRS 37
      (1983): 3-21.

903. Smith, Nigel J.H.   RAINFOREST CORRIDORS: THE
      TRANSAMAZON COLONIZATION SCHEME. Berkeley:
      University of California Press, 1982.

904. Smith, Peter Seaborn. "Góes Monteiro and the Role of the Army
      in Brazil." LATROBE UNIVERSITY INSTITUTE OF LATIN
      AMERICAN STUDIES OCCASIONAL PAPER SERIES, NO.
      2. Bundoora, Victoria, Australia, 1979.

905. ——. "The Góes Monteiro Papers." REVISTA DE HISTORIA
      55 (1977): 205-25.

906. ——. OIL AND POLITICS IN MODERN BRAZIL. Toronto:
      Maclean-Hunter Press, 1976.

907. Smith, William C. "The Political Transition in Brazil: From
      Authoritarian Liberalization and Elite Conciliation to
      Democratization." In COMPARING NEW DEMOCRACIES:
      TRANSITION AND CONSOLIDATION IN
      MEDITERRANEAN EUROPE AND THE SOUTHERN
      CONE, 179-240. Edited by Enrique Baloyra. Boulder: Westview
      Press, 1987.

908. Soares, Glaucio. "The Brazilian Political System: New Parties and
      Old Cleavages." LUSO-BRAZILIAN REVIEW 19 (1982): 39-66.

909. ——. "La cancelación de los mandatos de parlamentarios en
      Brasil."   REVISTA MEXICANA DE SOCIOLOGIA 42
      (1980):267-86.

910. ——. "Military Authoritarianism and Executive Absolutism in
      Brazil." STUDIES IN COMPARATIVE INTERNATIONAL
      DEVELOPMENT 14 (1979): 104-26.

911.	Sobrinho, J.F. Velho. DICIONARIO BIO-BIBLIOGRAFICO BRASILEIRO ILUSTRADO. 2 vols. Rio de Janeiro: Irmãos Pongetti, 1937-38.

912.	Sodré, Nelson Werneck. BRASIL: RADIOGRAFIA DE UM MODELO. Petrópolis: Editôra Vozes, 1974.

913.	———. A COLUNA PRESTES: ANALISE E DEPOIMENTOS. Rio de Janeiro: Civilização Brasileira, 1978.

914.	———. HISTORIA DA BURGUESIA BRASILEIRA. 2d ed. Rio de Janeiro: Civilização Brasileira, 1967.

915.	———. HISTORIA MILITAR DO BRASIL. Rio de Janeiro: Civilização Brasileira, 1965.

916.	———. INTRODUCAO A REVOLUCAO BRASILEIRA. Rio de Janeiro: Editôra José Olympio, 1958.

917.	———. MEMORIAS DE UM SOLDADO. Rio de Janeiro: Civilização Brasileira, 1967.

918.	———. O QUE SE DEVE LER PARA CONHECER O BRASIL. 5th ed. Rio de Janeiro: Civilização Brasileira, 1976.

919.	Sorj, Bernardo, and Maria Herminia T. de Almeida, eds. SOCIEDADE E POLITICA NO BRASIL POS-64. São Paulo: Brasiliense, 1983.

920.	Sosnovski, Anatoli. "Brasil: La evolución del régimen y el ejército." AMERICA LATINA (USSR) 1 (1982): 26-33.

921.	Souza, Amaury de. "Março ou abril?: Uma bibliografia comentada sobre o movimento político de 1964 no Brasil." DADOS 1/2 (1966): 160-75.

922.	Souza, Maria do Carmo Campello de. ESTADO E PARTIDOS POLITICOS NO BRASIL, 1930-1964. São Paulo: Alfa-Omega, 1976.

923.	Souza, Maria Inez Salgado de. OS EMPRESARIOS E A EDUCACAO: O IPES E A POLITICA EDUCACIONAL APOS 1964. Petrópolis: Editôra Vozes, 1981.

924. Stacchini, José. MARCO 64: MOBILIZACAO DA AUDACIA. São Paulo: Editôra Nacional, 1965.

925. Starling, Helosia Maria Murgel. OS SENHORES DAS GERAIS: OS NOVOS INCONFIDENTES E O GOLPE DE 1964. Petrópolis: Editôra Vozes, 1986.

926. Stauffer, David Hall. "Origem e fundação do Serviço de Proteção aos Indios." REVISTA DE HISTORIA 10 (1959): 73-95; 11 (1960): 435-53; 11 (1960): 165-83; 11 (1960): 427-50; 12 (1961): 413-33.

927. Stein, Stanley J. "The Historiography of Brazil, 1808-1889." HISPANIC AMERICAN HISTORICAL REVIEW 40 (1960): 234-78.

928. Stepan, Alfred C. OS MILITARES: DA ABERTURA A NOVA REPUBLICA. Rio de Janeiro: Paz e Terra, 1986.

929. ——. THE MILITARY IN POLITICS: CHANGING PATTERNS IN BRAZIL. Princeton: Princeton University Press, 1971.

930. ——. "Political Leadership and Regime Breakdown: Brazil." In THE BREAKDOWN OF DEMOCRATIC REGIMES: LATIN AMERICA, 110-37. Edited by Juan B. Linz and Alfred Stepan. Baltimore: Johns Hopkins University Press, 1978.

931. ——. RETHINKING MILITARY POLITICS: BRAZIL AND THE SOUTHERN CONE. Princeton: Princeton University Press, 1988.

932. ——. "State Power and the Strength of Civil Society in the Southern Cone of Latin America." In BRINGING THE STATE BACK IN, 317-43. Edited by P. Evans, Theda Skocpol, and D. Rueschemeyer. New York: Cambridge University Press, 1985.

933. ——, ed. AUTHORITARIAN BRAZIL: ORIGINS, POLICIES, AND FUTURE. New Haven: Yale University Press, 1973.

934. ——, ed. DEMOCRATIZING BRAZIL: PROBLEMS OF TRANSITION AND CONSOLIDATION. New York: Oxford University Press, 1989.

935.   Straubhaar, Joseph D. "Television and Video in the Transition from Military to Civilian Rule in Brazil." LATIN AMERICAN RESEARCH REVIEW 24 (1989): 140-55.

936.   Stumpf, André Gustavo, and Merval Pereira Filho. A SEGUNDA GUERRA: SUCESSAO DE GEISEL. São Paulo: Brasiliense, 1979.

937.   Syrkis, Alfredo. OS CARBONARIOS: MEMORIAS DA GUERRILHA PERDIDA. São Paulo: Global, 1980.

938.   Syvrud, Donald E. FOUNDATIONS OF BRAZILIAN ECONOMIC GROWTH. Stanford: Stanford University Press, 1974.

939.   Tambs, Lewis A. "Five Times against the System: Brazilian Foreign Military Expeditions and Their Effect on National Priorities." In PERSPECTIVES ON ARMED POLITICS IN BRAZIL, 117-205. Edited by Henry H. Keith and Robert A. Hayes. Tempe: Arizona State University Press, 1976.

940.   ———. "Rubber, Rebels, and Rio Branco: The Contest for the Acre." HISPANIC AMERICAN HISTORICAL REVIEW 46 (1966): 254-73.

941.   Tavares, Aurelio de Lyra. ASPECTOS CONJUNTARAIS DA FRANCA: VISITA DA ESCOLA SUPERIOR DE GUERRA A EMBAIXADA DO BRASIL EM PARIS, JUNHO 1973; EXPOSICAO DO EMBAIXADOR.... Paris: The author, 1973.

942.   ———. O BRASIL DA MINHA GERACAO. Rio de Janeiro: Biblioteca do Exército, 1977.

943.   ———. "El ejército brasileño y la actual coyuntura nacional." ESTRATEGIA 1 (1969): 43-56.

944.   ———. O EXERCITO BRASILEIRO VISTO PELO SEU MINISTRO. Recife: Universidade Federal de Pernambuco, 1968.

945.   ———. EXERCITO E NACAO. Recife: Universidade Federal de Pernambuco, 1965.

946.   ———. O EXERCITO NO GOVERNO COSTA E SILVA. N.p.: Imprensa Nacional, 1968.

947. ———. HISTORIA DA ARMA DE ENGENHARIA: CAPITULO DA FEB. João Pessoa: Universidade Federal de Paraíba, 1966.

948. ———. VILAGRAN CABRITA E A ENGENHARIA DE SEU TEMPO. Rio de Janeiro: Biblioteca do Exército, 1981.

949. Távora, Araken. O DIA EM QUE VARGAS MORREU. Rio de Janeiro: Editôra do Repórter, 1966.

950. ———. VOO REBELDE. Rio de Janeiro: Sociedade Gráfica Vida Doméstica, 1964?

951. Távora, Juarez. A GUISA DE DEPOIMENTO SOBRE A REVOLUCAO BRASILEIRA DE 1924. São Paulo: "O Combate," 1927.

952. ———. UMA VIDA E MUITAS LUTAS. Rio de Janeiro: Editôra José Olympio, 1973.

953. Taylor, John W.R., ed. JANE'S ALL THE WORLD'S AIRCRAFT, 1981-82. New York: Jane's, 1981.

954. Taylor, Lance, and Edmar L. Bacha. "The Unequalizing Spiral: A First Growth Model for Belinda." QUARTERLY JOURNAL OF ECONOMICS 90 (1976): 197-218.

955. Tellarolli, Rodolfo. PODER LOCAL NA REPUBLICA VELHA. São Paulo: Editôra Nacional, 1977.

956. Terra, Adamastor. BRASIL: LA GUERRILLA DE ARAGUAIA. Buenos aires: Nativa Libros, 1973.

957. Tiller, Ann Quiggins. "The Igniting Spark: Brazil, 1930." HISPANIC AMERICAN HISTORICAL REVIEW 45 (1965): 384-92.

958. Tocantins, Leandro. EUCLIDES DA CUNHA E O PARAISO PERDIDO. Rio de Janeiro: Gráfica Record Editôra, 1968.

959. ———. "The World of the Amazon Region." In MAN IN THE AMAZON, 21-32. Edited by Charles Wagley. Gainesville: University of Florida Presses, 1974.

960. Torres, Alberto. O PROBLEMA NACIONAL BRASILEIRO: INTRODUCAO A UM PROGRAMMA DE ORGANIZACAO NACIONAL. Rio de Janeiro: n.p., 1914.

961. Torres, João Camilo de Oliveira. "As forças armadas como força política." REVISTA BRASILEIRA DE ESTUDOS POLITICOS 20 (1966): 39-47.

962. "A tortura no Brasil." VOZES 77 (1983): 24-40.

963. Trask, David F., Michael C. Meyer, and Roger R. Trask, eds. A BIBLIOGRAPHY OF UNITED STATES-LATIN AMERICAN RELATIONS SINCE 1810. Lincoln: University of Nebraska Press, 1968.

964. Trevisan, Leonardo. O PENSAMENTO MILITAR BRASILEIRO. São Paulo: Editôra Global, 1985.

965. ———. O QUE TODO CIDADAO PRECISA SABER SOBRE INSTITUICAO MILITAR E ESTADO BRASILEIRO. São Paulo: Editôra Global, 1987.

966. ———. A REPUBLICA VELHA. São Paulo: Editôra Global, 1982.

967. Trindade, Hélio Henrique. INTEGRALISMO: O FASCISMO BRASILEIRO NA DECADA DE 30. São Paulo: DIFEL, 1974.

968. Troyano, Annez Andraus. ESTADO E SINDICALISMO. São Paulo: Edições Símbolo, 1978.

969. Tullis, F. LaMond. MODERNIZATION IN BRAZIL: A STORY OF POLITICAL DUELING AMONG POLITICIANS, CHARISMATIC LEADERS, AND MILITARY GUARDIANS. Provo, UT: Brigham Young University Press, 1973.

970. Ulibarri, George S., and John P. Harrison, eds. GUIDE TO MATERIALS ON LATIN AMERICA IN THE NATIONAL ARCHIVES OF THE UNITED STATES. Washington: National Archives and Records Service, 1974.

971. United States. Congress. House Committee on Foreign Affairs. Sub-committee on National Security Policy and Scientific Developments. REPORTS OF THE SPECIAL STUDY

MISSION TO LATIN AMERICA: PT. 1, MILITARY ASSISTANCE TRAINING. Washington: U.S. Government Printing Office, 1970.

972. United States. Department of State. FOREIGN RELATIONS OF THE UNITED STATES. "THE AMERICAN REPUBLICS." National Archives, Washington.

973. ———. POLITICAL AND MILITARY RECORDS RELATING TO INTERNAL AFFAIRS OF BRAZIL. Decimal Files, 1910-. National Archives, Washington.

974. University Microfilms International. LATIN AMERICA: A CATALOG OF SELECTED DOCTORAL DISSERTATION RESEARCH. Ann Arbor: University Microfilms International, 1984.

975. Uricoechea, Fernando. THE PATRIMONIAL FOUNDATIONS OF THE BRAZILIAN BUREAUCRATIC STATE. Berkeley: University of California Press, 1980.

976. Ustra, Carlos Alberto. ROMPENDO O SILENCIO: OBAN DOI/CODI, 29 SET 70-23 JAN 74. Brasília: Editerra Editorial, 1987.

977. Vale, Oswaldo. O GENERAL DUTRA E A REDEMOCRATIZACAO DE 1945. Rio de Janeiro: Civilização Brasileira, 1978.

978. Varas, Augusto. MILITARIZATION AND THE INTERNATIONAL ARMS RACE IN LATIN AMERICA. Boulder: Westview Press, 1985.

979. ———, ed. DEMOCRACY UNDER SIEGE: NEW MILITARY POWER IN LATIN AMERICA. Westport, CT: Greenwood Press, 1989.

980. Vargas, Indio. GUERRA E GUERRA, DIZIA O TORTURADOR. Rio de Janeiro: CODECRI, 1981.

981. Vasconcellos, Didi. 30 ANOS EM 4 ETAPAS. São Paulo: Editôra Obelisco, 1968.

982. Vasconcelos, Genserico de. HISTORIA MILITAR DO BRASIL. 2d ed. 2 vols. Rio de Janeiro: n.p., 1943.

983. Vasconcelos, Manuel Meira de. BRASIL: POTENCIA MILITAR. Rio de Janeiro: Editôra Zelio Valverde, 1945.

984. Velloso, João Paulo dos Reis. O ULTIMO TREM PARA PARIA: DE GETULIO A SARNEY; "MILAGRES," CHOQUES E CRISES DO BRASIL MODERNO. Rio de Janeiro: Editôra Nova Fronteira, 1986.

985. Venancio Filho, Alberto. NOTICIA HISTORICA DA ORDEM DOS ADVOGADOS DO BRASIL, 1930-1980. Rio de Janeiro: OAB, 1982.

986. Vergara, Luiz. FUI SECRETARIO DE GETULIO VARGAS: MEMORIAS DOS ANOS DE 1926-1954. Rio de Janeiro: Editôra Globo, 1960.

987. Viana Filho, Luis, ed. CASTELLO BRANCO: TESTAMUNHOS DE UMA EPOCA. Brasília: Universidade de Brasília, 1986.

988. ———. O GOVERNO DE CASTELLO BRANCO. 2d ed. Rio de Janeiro: Editôra José Olympio, 1975.

989. Vianna, Francisco J. de Oliveira. O OCASO DO IMPERIO. São Paulo: Companhia Melhoramentos de São Paulo, 1925.

990. Vianna, Hélio. "Atuais tendencias da historiografia brasileira." INTER-AMERICAN REVIEW OF BIBLIOGRAPHY 13 (1963): 30-59.

991. Vianna, Luiz Werneck. "Atualizando uma bibliografia: 'Nôvo sindicalismo,' cidadania e fábrica." BOLETIM INFORMATIVO E BIBLIOGRAFICO CIENCIAS SOCIAIS 17 (1984): 53-68.

992. ———. "Estudios sobre sindicalismo e movimento operario: Resenha de algumas tendencias." BOLETIM INFORMATIVO E BIBLIOGRAFICO CIENCIAS SOCIAIS 3 (1978): 9-24.

993. ———. LIBERALISMO E SINDICATO NO BRASIL. Rio de Janeiro: Paz e Terra, 1976.

994. Victor, Mario (pseud). CINCO ANOS QUE ABALARAM O
      BRASIL: DE JANIO QUADROS AO MARECHAL CASTELO
      BRANCO. Rio de Janeiro: Civilização Brasileira, 1965.

995. Vidigal, Armando A.F. A EVOLUCAO DE PENSAMENTO
      ESTRATEGICO NAVAL BRASILEIRO. Rio de Janeiro: n.p.,
      1982.

996. Vieira, Evaldo Amaro. ESTADO E MISERIA SOCIAL NO
      BRASIL: DE GETULIO A GEISEL, 1951-1978. São Paulo:
      Cortez Editôra, 1983.

997. Wallerstein, Michael. "The Collapse of Democracy in Brasil: Its
      Economic Determinants." LATIN AMERICAN RESEARCH
      REVIEW 15 (1980): 3-40

998. Walters, Marian C., ed.   LATIN AMERICA AND THE
      CARIBBEAN II: A DISSERTATION BIBLIOGRAPHY. Ann
      Arbor: University Microfilms International, 1980.

999. Walters, Vernon. SILENT MISSIONS. New York: Doubleday,
      1978.

1000. Wamberto, José.   CASTELO BRANCO: REVOLUCAO E
      DEMOCRACIA. Rio de Janeiro: n.p., 1970.

1001. Wedge, Bryant, "The Case Study of Student Political Violence:
      Brazil, 1964 and Dominican Republic, 1965." WORLD
      POLITICS 21 (1969): 183-206.

1002. Weffort, Francisco. "Clases populares y desarrollo social." In
      POPULISMO, MARGINALIZACION, Y DEPENDENCIA.
      Edited by Francisco Weffort and Aníbal Quijano. San José,
      Costa Rica: EDUCA, 1973.

1003. ———. "La crisis del populismo: Brasil, 1961-1964." REVISTA
      MEXICANA DE SOCIOLOGIA 41 (1979): 129-41.

1004. ———. O POPULISMO NA POLITICA BRASILEIRA. Rio de
      Janeiro: Paz e Terra, 1978.

1005. Weinstein, Barbara. THE AMAZON RUBBER BOOM, 1850-
      1920. Stanford: Stanford University Press, 1983.

1006.   Weschler, Lawrence. A MIRACLE, A UNIVERSE: SETTLING
        ACCOUNTS WITH TORTURERS. New York: Pantheon, 1990.

1007.   Wesson, Robert. NEW MILITARY POLITICS IN LATIN
        AMERICA. New York: Praeger Publishers, 1982.

1008.   ———. THE UNITED STATES AND BRAZIL: LIMITS OF
        INFLUENCE. New York: Praeger Publishers, 1981.

1009.   ———, ed. THE LATIN AMERICAN MILITARY
        INSTITUTION. New York: Praeger Publishers, 1986.

1010.   Wesson, Robert, and David V. Fleischer. BRAZIL IN
        TRANSITION. New York: Praeger Publishers, 1983.

1011.   Wilgus, A. Curtis, comp. LATIN AMERICA, SPAIN AND
        PORTUGAL: A SELECTED AND ANNOTATED
        BIBLIOGRAPHICAL GUIDE TO BOOKS PUBLISHED IN
        THE UNITED STATES, 1954-1974. Metuchen, NJ: Scarecrow
        Press, 1977.

1012.   Williams, John Hoyt. "Brazil: Giant of the Southern Hemisphere."
        NATIONAL DEFENSE 67 (1982): 40-43, 16-20.

1013.   ———. "The Undrawn Line: Three Centuries of Strife on the
        Paraguayan-Mato Grosso Frontier." LUSO-BRAZILIAN
        REVIEW 17 (1980): 17-40.

1014.   Wirth, John D. THE POLITICS OF BRAZILIAN
        DEVELOPMENT, 1930-1954. Stanford: Stanford University
        Press, 1970.

1015.   ———. "Tenentismo in the Brazilian Revolution of 1930."
        HISPANIC AMERICAN HISTORICAL REVIEW 44 (1964):
        161-79.

1016.   Wonder, Edward. "Nuclear Commerce and Nuclear Proliferation:
        Germany and Brazil, 1975." ORBIS, A JOURNAL OF WORLD
        AFFAIRS 21 (1977): 277-306.

1017.   Wood, David Lyle. "Abortive Panacea: Brazilian Military
        Settlements, 1850-1913." Ph.D. dissertation, University of Utah,
        1972.

1018. WORLD OF LEARNING. 41st ed. London: Europa Publications, 1991.

1019. Young, Jordan M. BRAZIL: EMERGING WORLD POWER. Malabar, FL: Robert E. Krieger, 1982.

1020. ———. THE BRAZILIAN REVOLUTION OF 1930 AND THE AFTERMATH. New Brunswick, NJ: Rutgers University Press, 1967.

1021. ———. "Military Aspects of the 1930 Brazilian Revolution." HISPANIC AMERICAN HISTORICAL REVIEW 44 (1964): 180-96.

PERIODICALS

1022. AIR POWER HISTORY, 1988-. (formerly AEROSPACE HISTORIAN, 1953-88.)

1023. ALMANAQUE DO EXERCITO.

1024. THE AMERICAS, 1944-.

1025. AMNESTY INTERNATIONAL REPORT.

1026. ANAIS DA BIBLIOTECA NACIONAL.

1027. A ANCORA, 1907-.

1028. AVIACAO E ASTRONAUTICA, 1938-.

1029. BIBLIOGRAFIA BRASILEIRA, 1983-. (formerly BOLETIM BIBLIOGRAFICO BRASILEIRO DA BIBLIOTECA NACIONAL, 1954-1983.)

1030. BOLETIM DA ASSOCIACAO DOS DIPLOMADOS DA ESCOLA SUPERIOR DE GUERRA, 1968-. (Formerly SEGURANCA E DESENVOLVIMENTO.)

1031. BOLETIM DA BIBLIEUX. (Biblioteca do Exército.)

1032. BOLETIM DA BIBLIOTECA DA CAMARA DOS DEPUTADOS.

1033. BOLETIM DO CLUBE NAVAL.

1034. BOLETIM DO EXERCITO.

1035. BOLETIM DO INSTITUTO DOS ECONOMISTAS DO ESTADO DO RIO DE JANEIRO (IERP), 1977-.

1036. BOLETIM INFORMATIVO. (Serviço Geográfico do Exército.)

1037. BOLETIM INFORMATIVO E BIBLIOGRAFICO CIENCIAS SOCIAIS.

1038. BOLETIM MENSAL DO ESTADO-MAIOR DO EXERCITO, 1911-23.

1039. BOLETIM PERIODICO DO CORPO DE OFICIAIS DA AERONAUTICA.

1040. BRAZIL WATCH.

1041. CADERNOS DO NOSSO TEMPO, 1953-56.

1042. DADOS.

1043. DEFEZA NACIONAL, 1913-.

1044. ECONOMIA: REVISTA DA ANPEC, 1977-.

1045. O ESTADO DE SAO PAULO.

1046. ESTRATEGIA, 1969-82. (Argentina.)

1047. ESTUDOS CEBRAP.

1048. ESTUDOS SOCIOECONOMICOS.

1049. FOLHA DE SAO PAULO.

1050. O GLOBO.

1051. HISPANIC AMERICAN HISTORICAL REVIEW, 1918-.

1052. ISTO E.

1053. JORNAL DA TARDE.

1054. JORNAL DO BRASIL.

1055. JOURNAL OF INTER-AMERICAN STUDIES AND WORLD AFFAIRS, 1959-.

1056. JOURNAL OF LATIN AMERICAN STUDIES, 1969-.

1057. JOURNAL OF MILITARY HISTORY, 1989-. (formerly MILITARY AFFAIRS, 1936-89.)

1058. LATIN AMERICAN PERSPECTIVES, 1974-.

1059. LATIN AMERICAN REPORTS.

1060. LATIN AMERICAN RESEARCH REVIEW, 1965-.

1061. LATIN AMERICAN WEEKLY REPORT, 1967-.

1062. LUSO-BRAZILIAN REVIEW.

1063. MANCHETE.

1064. A MARINHA EM REVISTA, 1947-.

1065. NACLA. REPORT ON THE AMERICAS, 1966-.

1066. NAVIGATOR.

1067. NOTES ET ETUDES DOCUMENTAIRES.

1068. NOTICIARIO DO EXERCITO, 1958-.

1069. OPINIAO.

1070. RESENHA DE POLITICA EXTERIOR DO BRASIL, 1974-.

1071. REVISTA BRASILEIRA DE ESTUDOS POLITICOS, 1945-. (Universidade Federal de Minas Gerais.)

1072. REVISTA CIVILIZACAO BRASILEIRA, 1965-.

1073. REVISTA DE AERONAUTICA, 1959-.

1074. REVISTA DE HISTORIA. (São Paulo.)

1075. REVISTA DE INTENDENCIA DA AERONAUTICA, 1952-.

1076. REVISTA DE INTENDENCIA DO EXERCITO BRASILEIRO, 1926-.

1077. REVISTA DE MEDICINA MILITAR, 1892-.

1078. REVISTA DO CIRCULO DE ENGENHARIA MILITAR, 1938-.

1079. REVISTA DO CLUBE MILITAR, 1926-.

1080. REVISTA DO INSTITUTO DE GEOGRAFIA E HISTORIA MILITAR DO BRASIL, 1936-.

1081. REVISTA DO INSTITUTO HISTORICO E GEOGRAFICO BRASILEIRO, 1839-.

1082. REVISTA DOS MILITARES.

1083. REVISTA INTERAMERICANA DE BIBLIOGRAFIA/ INTER-AMERICAN REVIEW OF BIBLIOGRAPHY, 1951-.

1084. REVISTA MARITIMA BRASILEIRA, 1880-.

1085. REVISTA MEXICANA DE SOCIOLOGIA, 1939-.

1086. REVISTA MILITAR, 1899-1910.

1087. REVISTA MILITAR BRASILEIRA, 1914-.

1088. STATISTICAL ABSTRACT OF LATIN AMERICA, 1955-.

1089. TECNOLOGIA MILITAR.

1090. VEJA.

1091. VISAO.

1092. VOZES, 1906-.

CHAPTER VIII

THE CARIBBEAN

Bruce J. Calder
University of Illinois at Chicago

INTRODUCTION

Since the arrival of European powers in the Caribbean in the late sixteenth century, the area has been a zone of military confrontation, at first between the Spanish and the indigenous Caribbean peoples and, after 1560, between the Spanish and competing European nations. While the activities of the non-Spanish interlopers, the English and then the Dutch and the French, were at first limited to harassing Spain's colonies and trade, after 1620 their efforts involved the seizure of smaller islands (such as Curaçao, Jamaica, Barbados, St. Kitts, Martinique, and Guadeloupe) and even parts of the mainland, areas that were weakly defended and of little importance relative to Spain's huge and lucrative empire.

The development of rival European bases in the Caribbean gave rise to considerable semi-official and extra-official warlike activity against Spain in the form of privateers and pirates, who plundered both trans-Atlantic trade routes and coastal cities and towns. Against these incursions Spain's defensive measures (including massive city walls and fortresses in such strategic places as Havana, Santo Domingo, and San Juan, plus naval squadrons and garrisons scattered throughout the region) offered only limited protection.

Of greater eventual importance than Spain's defenses were a series of seventeenth-century treaties by which Spain recognized the Dutch, British, and French Caribbean colonies. While these agreements ended the worst excesses of state-sponsored piracy, continued inter-colonial friction between Spain and her rivals over contraband and smuggling

485

eventually led to war on several occasions during the eighteenth century. As a result, England seized Havana briefly in 1762 and Trinidad permanently in 1797.

The late eighteenth-century rebellion in French Saint Domingue marked the beginning of the Latin American independence movements and brought both British and French armies to the island to wage war unsuccessfully against Haitian revolutionary commanders. For a variety of reasons, the Spanish possession of Santo Domingo (eastern Hispaniola, subsequently the Dominican Republic) was at first the only Caribbean colony to follow Haiti's example, although Cuba later fought three wars for independence before becoming a semi-independent protectorate of the United States in 1898; Puerto Rico experienced a small but unsuccessful armed uprising in the 1860s.

Once independent, Haiti and the Dominican Republic fought each other during the nineteenth century. Dominican troops also defeated a small Spanish army during an attempted recolonization in the 1860s. More important, however, were various internal wars caused by the presence of competing political and economic factions, whose forces were often led by regionally-based popular military leaders, known in Spanish as *caudillos*.

The history of Caribbean military affairs in the twentieth century, like that of the foregoing years, is exceedingly complex. It involves the military histories of the three republics, Cuba, the Dominican Republic, and Haiti, which have been at least nominally independent during the entire twentieth century, as well as those smaller entities which became independent states in the 1960s and 1970s or which in a few cases, remained colonies. But equally important, if not more so, than the histories of specific Caribbean nations is the military history of the Caribbean as a region. During the twentieth century, just as previously, it was a zone of confrontation among larger outside powers. While Spain is no longer a factor, a researcher must also consider the Caribbean aspects of the policies of the United States, Canada, and various European states including Great Britain, France, Germany, and the Soviet Union. United States and European commercial and military competition, in the form of intervention, two world wars, and the Cold War have all had direct and dramatic effects in the Caribbean area.

In order to cover the above-mentioned topics, this essay begins by noting the relatively few general works that deal with Caribbean military affairs on a regional basis. It then moves to a discussion of the strategic issue, beginning with the United States-European competition at the beginning of the twentieth century and ending with the efforts of the United States to maintain its control of the Caribbean area in the later part of that century. Then, after short sections on bibliographies, archival sources, and first-person accounts, the essay continues with a discussion of individual countries, first treating the history of military institutions and events in Cuba, the Dominican Republic, and Haiti. It also surveys the more limited literature on the military aspects of the history of the United States colony of Puerto Rico and of the recently independent British Caribbean states (particularly Jamaica, Trinidad and Tobago, Barbados, and Grenada). Also included is a brief discussion of military and police affairs in Guyana and Surinam, countries that are, informally if not technically, part of the Caribbean and are not covered in other chapters of this volume. Unfortunately, few sources could be found concerning military affairs in many of the small Caribbean states or in such colonies as Martinique and Guadeloupe.

This bibliography is intended to be thorough but is by no means exhaustive. It is meant to include most books, both scholarly and popular, which focus on the topics mentioned above. Booklets, scholarly articles, and government publications are included only when they seem particularly relevant and important. Newspaper and popular magazine articles, as well as unpublished government documents, are not included. For those who want to burrow more deeply into such sources, it is advisable to consult the footnotes and the often excellent bibliographies that are included in many of the works cited below.

GENERAL WORKS

The general reference works that treat the military from a global or Latin American perspective usually devote little attention to the militaries of the Caribbean. Two exceptions are the Jane's book on Latin America by English (141), and an encyclopedic volume by Keegan (242), both of which include many of the Caribbean states. Also neglectful of the region are the broad analyses of the Latin American military which have appeared during the past thirty years. This is true both of the older studies, such as those by Lieuwen (274), and Johnson (238), and of the newer efforts by such authors as Black (44), Varas (509), and Wesson (526), to mention only three examples of many books written on Latin American military affairs in the 1970s and 1980s. Only Rouquié (436), is somewhat better for his inclusion of the Caribbean.

The general works on military subjects that treat the Caribbean countries seriously are those which focus specifically on the area. In this category, one should first note an historiographical essay by Pérez (381), which surveys the literature on Caribbean armies in the twentieth century. Except for the Pérez work other literature on the military has a narrower chronological focus, beginning with the United States military interventions of the first third of the twentieth century. Aside from the many works that cover individual United States interventions and occupations, noted elsewhere by country, only a few treat these phenomena generally. Especially valuable on these topics are the two volumes by Munro (347, 348), who served in the State Department during the 1920s and 1930s, as well as books by Callcott (62), Langley (254, 255), Perkins (398), and Pratt (410), as well as a thesis by Auxier (24), and an article by Pérez (391). Also useful are Challener (72), who studies military influences on United States policy before 1914, and Tulchin (490), who traces United States actions in the Caribbean during and after World War I in part of a larger work. The termination of the last United States occupations in the 1930s seems to have produced a general lack of interest in Caribbean military matters until the advent of Fidel Castro and the Cuban Revolution in 1959. Among the few studies covering the intervening period is an article on United States strategic planning for Latin America between 1919 and 1945 by Child (76). There is as yet no study focused specifically on the Caribbean during World War II, which saw the establishment of a series of United States Caribbean bases, a campaign of German submarine warfare, and other military-related phenomena. But some information is available in general works on the United States military, particularly in books by Morison (338), Conn, Engleman, and Fairchild (84), and Conn and Fairchild (85). Goodhart (196), and Roskill (435), offer considerably less material on the Caribbean, but from a British point of view, and an article by Smith (460), treats the wartime situation in Martinique. Also useful are a 1940 American Geographical Society survey of the Caribbean islands (404), including their defenses, and the publications of the Anglo-American Caribbean Commission (14), created by the United States and Great Britain to assure the security of the Caribbean area and its full involvement in the Allied war effort.

Writers on military matters, both at the time and subsequently, have almost completely neglected the Caribbean during the period from 1945 to the late 1950s. Only the coming of revolution to Cuba changed this state of affairs. After that, the continuing existence of the Cuban revolutionary government since 1959 resulted in a voluminous literature on Cuba and in greater research interest on the Caribbean generally. More recently, the rise to power of several leftist Caribbean governments in the late 1970s and the advent of a more conservative administration in Washington seem to have prompted numerous studies of strategic and security issues. Written mostly by North Americans, these works often reflect strong points of view, with some writers supporting a cold war and a strong military position; others argue against the militarization of United States policy and point out its impact on the Caribbean region. Strategic and security questions have gained such prominence, in fact, that many writers on the contemporary

Caribbean, whatever the main focus of their work, deal extensively with these matters. This is clear in the recent general studies by Ambursley and Cohen (11), Barry, Wood, and Preusch (29), De Kadt (106), Heine and Manigat (217), Payne (376), Pearce (378), Pierre-Charles (402), Polanyi-Levitt (405), Schulz and Graham (448), and Sunshine (470). Strategic and security issues are even more central to the books and articles by Adelman and Reading (4), Domínguez (129), Erisman (145), Erisman and Martz (146), Fauriol (148), González (191), Greene and Scowcroft (199), Hayes (214), MacFarlane (290), Moorer and Fauriol (336), Moss (343), PACCA (406), Sims and Anderson (458), Stodder and McCarthy (467), Tardanico (477), and Varas (510). Finally, focused more directly on military affairs are works by the Caribbean Project for Peace and Justice (364), Cintron Tiryakian (80), Couteau-Begaire (89), Dixon (123), García Muñiz (173), Jaramillo Edwards (235), R. Kennedy, et al. (243), Klare and Aronson (246), Morris (340), Muller Rojas (345), Phillips (399), Ronfeldt (433), and Vego (516). Looking at the same questions from a Canadian point of view are Brian MacDonald (287), S. Neil MacFarlane (291), and Simmons (457).

A number of works have appeared in recent years focused on the Soviet presence in the Caribbean area. Analyses of this genre have been produced by Ashby (19), the Center for Strategic and International Studies of Georgetown University (464), Leiken (263), Roberts (425), Theberge (479, 480, 481), and the United States government (498).

BIBLIOGRAPHIES

Caribbean bibliography has not yet been well developed. Although there are an increasing number of good general bibliographies on the region and on individual nations, at best they include one or two entries on military affairs. The exception to this pattern is Cuba, where the revolution has provoked considerable scholarly and popular interest and thus bibliographies. Concerning the Dominican Republic, for example, the only formal bibliography on military affairs is by Mariñez (304), on United States interventions. In this case, as for other countries, the most productive strategy is to consult the bibliographies of the best existing scholarly works on military affairs, such as Atkins (21), on the Dominican Republic, Delince (108), on Haiti, and Phillips and Young (401), on the non-Hispanic Caribbean. There are several bibliographies on the United States military which contain sections on North American involvement in the Caribbean. Those by Beede (32), and Johnstone (239), focus on small wars, while another by Higham and Mrozek (224), is more general.

There are a number of excellent bibliographical sources on Cuba. On the military phase of the revolution, Pérez's THE CUBAN

REVOLUTIONARY WAR, 1953-1958 (388), with 2483 entries, is a required source. Other bibliographies focused on military themes are Gillingham and Roseman (185), on the missile crisis, Nodal (356), on Cuba in Africa, and an unsigned bibliography on Moncada (41). Also useful are the more general bibliographies by Czarnecki (97), on Cuba in Soviet writings, Lieuwen and Valdés (275), Peraza Sarausa (380), Pérez (390, 396), Suchlicki (469), and two bibliographical essays by Pérez (385, 387). In a class by itself is Ronald Chilcote's (75), massive two-volume work which contains 68,000 items and covers the years 1953 to 1978. Another important source is the semi-annual CUBAN STUDIES/ESTUDIOS CUBANOS (541), which provides the most up-to-date bibliographical information on Cuba.

ARCHIVAL GUIDES AND SOURCES

The main Caribbean archival holdings on twentieth-century military affairs, those of the national archives of Cuba, the Dominican Republic, and Haiti, are not generally open to scholars. Exceptions to this would be papers relating to military affairs of the latter two countries before the organization of modern military structures (the Garde d'Haiti, 1915, and the Guardia Nacional Dominicana, 1917), since these might be found in the personal papers of *caudillo* leaders rather than among strictly military documents.

Fortunately for researchers, there is an at least partly satisfactory way around lack of access to Caribbean military archives because of the intense involvement of the United States in Caribbean affairs. Various record groups in the United States National Archives hold Caribbean military records, particularly relating to the period of the United States occupations when the United States itself created, trained, and led the Cuban, Dominican, and Haitian armed forces. These record groups are clearly identified in the studies by Pérez (382), Calder (60), Healey (215, 216), Schmidt (445), and others. And since the United States maintained its dominant role in these nations even after the occupations ended, United States diplomatic and military documents, open except for recent years, continue to contain considerable information on military affairs.

Most of the twentieth-century military history of the non-Hispanic Caribbean is colonial history, and researchers would have to consult the archives of the European colonial powers, most of which are now open to about 1960 (as are those of the United States for Puerto Rico). The more contemporary military archives of the newly independent Caribbean states are not likely to be open to researchers, but since there are other equally viable ways to gather information on recent events, that should not prevent scholarly work.

MEMOIRS, JOURNALS, AND EYEWITNESS ACCOUNTS

Most of the first-hand accounts of Caribbean military history deal with Cuba. Consuegra (86), and Solano Alvarez (462), treat the revolution of 1917. Lima (277), reports on a failed 1931 uprising against Gerardo Machado, while Adam y Silva (3), Carrillo (65), Horacio Ferrer (156), and Lamar Schweyer (252), give personal accounts of the events of 1933, particularly the overthrow of Machado and the subsequent sergeants' rebellion which destroyed the old officers' corps and brought Fulgencio Batista to prominence. Fausel (149), reports on arms dealing with Batista in the 1930s.

A large number of works concern the Cuban revolution of 1952-58. Among the most famous of them is Che Guevara's PASAJES DE LA GUERRA REVOLUCIONARIA (204), which is also translated into English (205), and published in a much abbreviated version for youth (206). Fidel Castro's letters and speeches from the period of the military phase of the revolution are collected in Bonachea and Valdés (47). Also important are personal accounts by other individual revolutionaries, including Ameijeiras Delgado (12), Chomón (78), Cienfuegos (79, 58), Franqui (163, 164), Pardo Llada (373, 374), Pavón (375), Quevedo Pérez (416), Rojo del Río (432), and Macaulay (285), the last a North American. Dorschner and Fabricio (131), and McManus (293), present two sets of accounts by participants, including persons in the urban resistance as well as those in the Sierra Madre. Rubiera and Sierra (437), have collected the memoirs of those associated with Frank País, long the leader of the urban resistance. Bayó (30), relates how he became involved with Castro and the revolution during Castro's exile in Mexico. The revolutionary papers published by Desnoes (113), in 1961 include such documents as Raúl Castro's campaign diaries. Two books by Rosell Leyva (434), and Ventura Novo (519), ex-officers in Batista's army and national police, report on conditions during the last months of the revolution in 1958.

Of the specific military events of the Cuban revolution, the 1953 attack on the Moncada barracks is well documented by memoirs and eyewitness accounts, among them a book based on the recollections of the participants by Merle (318), a memoir by Santamaría (441), and two collections of interviews, letters, and other primary materials (487, 517). The 1961 Bay of Pigs invasion is also well documented, particularly by the two-volume collection entitled ASI SE DERROTO AL IMPERIALISMO (20), and by a published United States government report (358). Del Pino (110), remembers his days as a Cuban fighter pilot, while Eduardo Ferrer (155), relates the story of the air war from the exile side. An edited volume by Martínez (309), offers testimony and documents from the trials of the captured Bay of Pigs participants. Also, there are the recollections of members of the Kennedy administration, with Hillsman (225), Schlesinger (443), and Sorensen (463), providing the most detailed accounts. Hunt (229), provides the views of a CIA participant. On the 1962 missile crisis, Robert Kennedy (244), provides a memoir and documents; other members of the Kennedy administration are again useful.

Aside from the Cuban materials, the largest number of first-hand accounts of Caribbean military matters come from the Dominican Republic. The earliest Dominican event covered by a work of this kind is that of Gilbert (184), who briefly joined the peasant guerrilla struggle against the United States marines during the United States occupation of 1916-24. Arvelo (18), has recently written his memoirs of a 1949 expedition against Rafael Leonidas Trujillo. Other accounts relate to events in the turbulent period of the 1960s and 1970s. A brief guerrilla struggle that followed the 1963 coup is recorded in the published campaign diary of Manolo Tavárez (115). And from the 1965 intervention there are the books by General Bruce Palmer (371), commander of the invading United States forces, and by United States ambassador Martin (308), as well as the recollections of a leftist rebel, Raful (417). To understand the ultra-conservative views of one of the top Dominican army leaders of this period, General Elías Wessin y Wessin, see his 1965 testimony to the United States Senate Committee on the Judiciary (499). On the 1973 Caamañó Deñó invasion, an autobiographical history by Hermann (220), is available.

Memoirs that reveal episodes of Haitian military history are few. A traveler to Haiti in 1921, Kuser (251), recorded his personal impressions of the *cacos*, the peasant rebels fighting the United States marines, and two marines, Wise (531), and Wirkus (530), left behind sometimes fanciful accounts of their service in Haiti. Calixte (61), provides an autobiographical account of a political-military controversy which took place in the late 1930s.

From Puerto Rico there is a first-person chronicle of the Spanish American War written in the early twentieth century by Rivero Méndez (423), an artillery commander.

SPECIALIZED WORKS: CUBA

Cuba's military is the largest, most professional, and best studied in the Caribbean. It also has a rich and complex history, having been destroyed and begun anew three times between 1898 and 1959. By far the most important writer on this subject is Louis A. Pérez, Jr., whose ARMY POLITICS IN CUBA, 1898-1958 (382), shows the development of the Cuban military from 1898 to the moment of its defeat by Fidel Castro and his fellow revolutionaries. A second thorough study, by

Fermoselle (151), begins with the colonial period and ends with the situation as of 1986. Also important, and showing the other side of the institutional coin, are the studies by Barquín López (28), on Cuban guerrilla struggles from the colonial period to 1959 and by Pérez (393), on banditry and peasant protest. Other synthetic but narrower works on military history include articles on the Rural Guard between 1898 and 1911 by Allan Millett (327), and Pérez (395), a book by Chang (73), on the army between 1899 and 1933, a master's thesis by Regan (418), which covers the military from 1933 to 1959, and an article by Mateo (311), analyzing the army from 1925 to 1952. Other than these writers, most have dealt with individual events or more limited time periods. One should also note a general work, Hugh Thomas's monumental CUBA: THE PURSUIT OF FREEDOM (482), which covers everything from the wars for independence to the events of the 1953-59 revolution in considerable detail.

There is a huge literature on the three Cuban wars for independence which, however, fall outside the purview of this bibliography. Nonetheless it makes sense to mention several basic sources on the third and last of these wars, 1895-98, since it is so important to what follows. Philip S. Foner's two-volume work (158), is an excellent general study, while Marshall (307), focused on the military campaign of United States forces in 1898. A volume by Higham and Mrozek (224), indicates other sources on United States participation and shows how this episode fits into United States military history. The Cuban view of the war is ably presented in books by Guerra y Sánchez (202), and Roig de Leuchsenring (430). The United States naval base at Guantánamo, one of the spoils of this war, has received the attention of Reynolds (420), and Bender (38).

The aftermath of the Cuban War for independence became the first United States occupation, postponing independence until 1902. In terms of military history, this immediate post-war period is of great importance, since the Cuban army of independence was systematically marginalized and eventually destroyed by the occupiers, who then replaced it with a more pliable military institution controlled by Washington and the Cuban elite. The transformation of the military is best detailed in Pérez's work (382), on the Cuban army, while the occupation in general is detailed by Healey (216), and by Hitchman's (226), biography of General Leonard Wood. Also useful is Pérez's (384), broader history of Cuba between 1878 and 1902, which details the creation of the post-independence military in a later chapter.

Cuba's independent history was checkered with revolutions and United States military interventions until 1934, events charted in Montenegro González (334). The revolution of 1906, which brought the second United States intervention, is the subject of works by Collazo

(81), and Ibarra (230). The intervention itself is the subject of books by Lockmiller (279), and Allan Millett (326), and of articles by Millett (325), and Minger (331). These two events, as well as subsequent revolutions and United States involvement, are also covered in Pérez's analysis (386), of the years 1902 to 1934 and in articles by Smith (461), and Pino Santos (403).

Another contribution by Pérez (389), covers the years from 1909 to 1912, setting the stage for two studies of the Race War of 1912, a book by Fermoselle (152), and an article by Pérez (394). For the 1913 to 1921 period one again turns to Pérez (392), whose excellent study of these years pays considerable attention to internal political and military unrest and to the limited intervention response of the United States. Two older Cuban works by Navas (350), and Zamora y López (535), document the 1917 revolution.

Cuba's critical revolution of 1933, which in some ways was more political than military, is detailed by Aguilar (5), Franco Varona (161), Polish historian Kula (249), and Sarabia (442). But it had a tremendous impact on the Cuban army because post-revolutionary political turmoil inspired a successful rebellion by non-commissioned officers against the old officer corps. Its leader was Sergeant Fulgencio Batista. The subsequent regime of Sergeant, then General, Batista, though it relied heavily on armed forces' support, has provoked little analysis of military institutions, except for the aforementioned works of Pérez. Two Cuban booklets (300, 93), from the late 1930s, containing a debate between Mañach and Sosa de Quesada, raise the matter of the military's growing role in Cuban society under Batista, and a scholarly work by Gellman (181), illustrates elements of military cooperation between the United States and Cuba during the same period.

The Cuban Revolution, which displaced Batista and the Cuban army in January 1959, has inspired the writing of large numbers of works, many of them on military matters. Several of the best broad studies of the military phase of the revolution (1953-59) are Bonachea and San Martín (46), and Barquín López (28). Other works that devote sustained attention to the revolutionary war include Aaron (1), Arvelo (17), Giménez (187), González (192), Iglesias (231), Masetti (310), Mayo (313), Otero Echevarría (363), Taber (475), Hugh Thomas (482), and publications of the FAR (94, 95), the Cuban revolutionary armed forces. Most of these studies treat the military history of the revolution as a whole; several, however, focus on narrower topics, such as the opening of the fronts beyond the Sierra Maestra and the events of the final offensive in late 1958. One event in particular, the ill-fated attack on the Moncada barracks which began the revolution, has been much celebrated since 1959. The best account is Mencía's (317), two-volume work, while Merle (318), Rojas (431), a documentary collection (517), and a twentieth-anniversary book issued in 1973 by the Cuban government (332), offer other information. Also important on Moncada, as on the events of 1953 to 1959 in general, are the many memoirs of revolutionaries, noted in detail elsewhere. Like memoirs, biographies are another important source for the military history of the revolution. There are a number of biographies of the revolutionary leader, Fidel Castro, most of which treat the military aspects of his life. In this regard, one should consult Matthews's 1969 work (312), as well as two more recent studies by Bourne (50), and Szulc (474). Works on Camilo Cienfuegos by Gálvez (171), and Pérez Tarrau (397), also offer data on military events, as do Cienfuegos's (58), published letters and writings. There are two accounts of the life of Frank País, the leader of the revolutionary underground until he was assassinated by Batista's forces, by Malo de Molina (299), and Portuondo (409). Several other less notable figures in the 26th of July movement have been portrayed in short biographies by Barceló Fundora (27), and Fresnillo (166).

The military phase of the Cuban Revolution, as a successful guerrilla war against a professional army, was an inspiration to many Latin Americans who sought rapid change in their societies. Thus events in Cuba caused renewed interest in guerrilla wars, both by those who wanted to encourage revolution and those who wanted to prevent it. Among the works prompted by the tactics of the revolution are books by Taber (476), and Debray (104), and a study produced by American University (465). Also important is Guevara's (203), analysis of guerrilla war, which also appears in part in Mallin's (298), edited version.

A number of works have appeared on the nature and operations of the Cuban armed forces during the period since 1959. Among them are those by Benítez Manaut (39), Del Pino (111), Domínguez (125, 127), Fermoselle (150), Horowitz (228), Judson (240, 241), Leogrande (264, 267), Pérez (383), Suchlicki (468), Vellinga (518), and an exile group (165). The authors cover a broad range of topics, among them the internal politics of the army, the biographies of top generals, the nature of civil-military relations, the education and values of the military, the effect of the armed forces on the revolutionary political process, and the draft. The handbook (96), of the revolutionary militia is also published.

The first military test of the newly institutionalized revolutionary army took place at the Bay of Pigs/Playa Girón, where the Cuban government forces decisively defeated United States-supported exile invaders. The best and most thorough accounts of this event in English are those by Higgins (223), and Wyden (532), and, in Spanish, Otero's four-volume work (362), and the two-volume collection of documents titled ASI SE DERROTO AL IMPERIALISMO (20). Of varying usefulness are Alvarez (9), Castro (69), Enzenberger (142), Raúl González (195), Light and Marzani (276), Meyer and Szulc (320), and exile reports by Johnson (236), and Lazo (260). Also available is a photo essay by Corrales (88), documents and testimony from the trials of the invaders by the Cuban government (309), and a published version of a once secret United States government study (358), of the Bay of Pigs operation.

It is ironic that the most thoroughly covered military event of the Cuban revolution is the missile crisis of 1962, which hardly involved Cuba. Most accounts of the incident focus on the actions of the United States and Soviet leaders who controlled events, rather than on the Cubans, who reacted to them. Also, this was primarily a non-military confrontation, so most studies are as much or more concerned with diplomacy, decision making, law, geopolitics, and politics as they are with military actions. An early account by Abel (2), who interviewed most of the United States officials involved, remains very useful, as does that by Weintal and Bartlett (523). More recent works include those of Allison (8), Blight (45), Bonfonti (48), Brune (55), Chayes (74), Cook (87), Detzer (117), Dinerstein (122), Garthoff (178), Gillingham and Roseman (185), Leighton (261), Medland (316), and Pope (408). Earlier publications of varying quality and usefulness are those of Allison (7), the Foreign Policy Association (159), Horelick (227), James and Hubbell (234), Larson (258), and Pachter (366). Views from other nations include studies by Delmas (Belgium) (109), Gerosa (Italy) (182), Ghent (Canada) (183), Medina Peña (Mexico) (315), Robin (France) (426), Semidei (France) (453), Shkadova (USSR) (456), Statsenko (USSR) (466), and Manrara (a Cuban exile) (302).

As both the Bay of Pigs invasion and the missile crisis would suggest, the relationship between Cuba and the United States and that between Cuba and the Soviet Union are of great importance in military, diplomatic, and other affairs. A recent history of the relationship between the United States and Cuba, which puts the above-mentioned military confrontations into an overall context, is Morley's IMPERIAL STATE AND REVOLUTION: THE UNITED STATES AND CUBA, 1952-1986 (339). Other useful studies, most emphasizing security and strategic questions, are by Bender (37), Brenner (52), Crassweller (90), Erisman (144), Foner (157), Langley (256), Tokatlián (488), and Welch (524). For a contrasting view, two Russian works that analyze the United States-Cuban relationship are those of Grinevich (201), and Vladimirov (522).

Two general analyses of Cuban diplomatic and military policies abroad are a book by Robbins (424), who traces Cuban diplomatic and military ties from 1960 to the 1980s and examines Cuba's involvement in Latin America, the Caribbean, and Africa, and an article by Domínguez (124). Goldenberg (189), and Detrez (116), detail Cuban involvement in Latin America in the 1960s, and an edited volume by

Levine (269), examines Cuba's role, including its military aspects, in the contemporary Caribbean.

Most of what has been written about Cuban military operations abroad (both those involving formal commitments of troops and clandestine support of revolutionary movements), touches on the question of the nature of the relationship of Cuba to the Soviet Union. Partisans of the traditional Cold War school of analysis tend to view Cuba as a puppet of the Soviet Union, carrying out Soviet policies with Moscow's support and direction. Alternatively, other analysts stress the fact that the Cubans usually have their own motives for their operations abroad, which often, but not always, happen to coincide with the desires of the Soviets. Among the many studies that examine Cuba's foreign military involvements in terms of these several viewpoints are a work by Duncan (136), which explores contemporary Cuban and Soviet influence in Latin America and Africa, and edited volumes by Valenta and Ellison (508), and Larkin (257), which focus on Cuban and Soviet influence in revolutionary Grenada and Central America respectively. Studies emphasizing the Cuban and Soviet role in the Caribbean, Central America, and Latin America generally are Leiken (262), López Segrera (280), Jackson (232), Valdés Paz (505), and the hearings of the United States Senate (498), and House of Representatives (493, 496, 497). The Cuban-Soviet tie is also evident in the case of Africa, as various studies make clear. Books by LeoGrande (266), Luce (283), Mallin (297), Mesa-Lago and Belkin (319), and Samuels, et al. (439), present the issue from differing ideological perspectives, as do articles by Bender (36), Domínguez (126, 128), Durch (138), LeoGrande (265), Roca (427), Valdés (504), and Valenta (506).

Several publications examine the presence of Soviet troops and advisors in Cuba itself, including a book by Newsom (351), short studies by Duffy (134), Garthoff (177), and Harvey (213), a United States State Department report (501), and United States House of Representatives hearings (494, 495). To put these military connections in a broader context, see García and Mironchuk (172), Levesque (268), and Torres Ramírez (489), on Cuban-Soviet relations in general.

SPECIALIZED WORKS: DOMINICAN REPUBLIC

The most worthwhile book-length analysis of the Dominican military is Atkins's 1981 work (21). Other useful sources are books by Arciniegas (15), and Rivera Cuesta (422), and a lengthy article by Mariñez (304). Vega y Pagán's (513, 515), histories of the armed forces and the National Guard are little more than panegyric to Trujillo. Bell (33), Black (43), and Kryzanek and Wiarda (248), also offer chapter-length analyses of contemporary military affairs. Mariñez (306), provides information and analysis on popular armed uprisings, particularly those of the earlier twentieth century. Arciniegas (16), Gatón Richiez (179), and Peláez Ruíz (379), contain mainly technical and legal information on military affairs.

The United States has been heavily involved, often in a military sense, in Dominican affairs ever since the late nineteenth century. Two useful overviews of this relationship are by Welles (525), a United States diplomat, and MacMichael (295), both of whom include substantial information on United States military interventions in the first third of the twentieth century. By far the most important of the earlier incursions was that of 1916, which resulted in military occupation until 1924. The only recent general study of it is that of Calder (60), with Knight's older work (247), and a thesis by MacMichael (294), providing useful backups. All of these sources contain considerable data on military affairs. More limited general analyses can be found in short books by Alvarez Quiñones (10), and Castro García (70), and in articles by Castor (66), and Millett and Gaddy (329). Also limited in scope but focused more directly on military affairs, most of them on the initial Dominican resistance in 1916 or on the six-year war (1917-22) between the United States marines and Dominican peasants, are works by Beach (31), Calder (59), Condit and Turnbladh (83), Ducoudray (133), Fuller and Cosmas (167), Goldwert (190), and María Filomena González (193, 194).

Military politics (always an important ingredient in Dominican national politics) during the presidency of General Horacio Vásquez (1924-30) are best described in a general work on the period by Medina Benet (314). The upshot of these politics was the rise to power of General Rafael Trujillo (1930-61), whose regime depended heavily on military support. The general biographies of Trujillo, the best of them by Crassweller (91), Diederich (119), Espaillat (147), (Trujillo's Undersecretary of Defense and Secretary of State Security in the 1950s), De Galíndez (105), and Ornes (360), all include information on the Dominican military, as do the scholarly studies by Atkins and Wilson (22), and Wiarda (527, 528). Also useful is a book of documents edited by Vega (512), which focuses on the use of the military and the police for political repression. Vega y Pagán's books (513, 514), on military affairs under Trujillo are without merit as history but do offer some documents on the period. Two unsuccessful attempts to overthrow the Trujillo dictatorship occurred in 1949 and 1959. The first occasion is documented by a participant, Arvelo (18), and the second in books by Delancer (107), Hermann (221), and Vargas (511).

The assassination of Trujillo in 1961 led to a period of instability in the Dominican Republic in which the military assumed an even greater importance in national affairs. The period 1961-64 and the role of the military in it is the subject of a keen analysis by Juan Bosch (49), president from 1961 to 1963, when he was ousted by the Dominican armed forces. The supposed reasons for his demise are detailed in LIBRO BLANCO (130), issued by the military. A failed attempt to ignite a guerrilla war against the new regime in 1963 is documented in Despradel (115).

The eventual result of the 1963 coup was the nearly successful revolution begun in 1965 by pro-Bosch forces, an event that brought United States military intervention. This armed intrusion, as well as the 1963 coup and related political events, has been the subject of dozens of books and hundreds of articles, most of which are critical to one degree or another of United States actions. Among the better scholarly books on the intervention are those by Gleijeses (188), Lowenthal (281), Moreno (337), and Slater (459). Also useful are the critical analyses by United States writers Bracey (51), Draper (132), Kurzman (250), and Szulc (473); Dominicans Despradel (114), and Franco (160); Mexican writer Llano Montes (278); French reporter Niedergang (354); and Russian analysts Ananova (13), and Zhukov (536, 537). There are a number of edited works by Americans Carey (64), and Mansbach (303); by Dominicans Brugal Alfáu (54), Arlette Fernández (153), Guión Sierra (207), and Ricardi (421); and by an Argentine writer, Selser (452). Virtually the only outright defenses of Washington's action have come from Mallin (296), the Center for Strategic Studies at Georgetown University (71), and the OAS (359), which officially sponsored the invading force. Other valuable sources include the memoirs of the commander of United States forces, Palmer (371), of United States ambassador Martin (308), of the Brazilian general who commanded the Latin American forces, De Meira Mattos (112), and of leftist participant Raful (417), a biography of Francisco Caamañó Deñó by Hermann (222), and military analyses by Greenberg (197), and Yates (533). The events of 1965 have also spawned at least two dissertations, by Morris (341), and Schoonmaker (447). Among useful articles are those of Lambrecht (253), Lowenthal (282), Quello and Isa Conde (415), and Wilson (529).

The one military event of note since 1965, the failed invasion by leftist revolutionaries under Colonel Ernesto Francisco Caamañó Deñó in 1973, has been documented in books by Hermann (220), and Ovalles (365). This, as well as preceding events, is the subject of a well-written analysis by Latorre (259).

SPECIALIZED WORKS: HAITI

Just one book, by Delince (108), is dedicated in its entirety to an analysis of the Haitian military. Other than Delince, who focuses on the contemporary military, there is an anonymous booklet, NOTES HISTORIQUES: ARMEE D'HAITI (357), on the period 1915-50 and several books, noted below, on military affairs during the United States occupation of 1915-34. Limited information on the military is also contained in three general works. Nicholls's excellent analysis (352), portrays military affairs in the broader context of Haitian history and includes an outstanding bibliography. Robert and Nancy Heinl (219), have provided a second thorough study, while Leyburn's (273), famous 1941 book provides information on the role of the military in Haitian life in the late 1930s as well as a chapter on the United States occupation.

In Haiti, as in the other independent Caribbean republics, the United States has been heavily involved in internal affairs. The details of this relationship have been explored most fully by Montague (333). The most dramatic single episode of this relationship was the United States's long military occupation of Haiti from 1915 to 1934, which has been best treated in an excellent work by Schmidt (445). Other general studies of the occupation, including its military aspects, are an edited work by Balch (26), and books by Bellegarde (34), Castor (67), Lutskov (284), Millsbaugh (330), Nicolas (353), and Padmore (367). Healey (215), and Gaillard (169), concentrate on the opening three years of the United States presence.

Focused more purely on military matters are studies by Gaillard (168, 170), and Millet (324), of the guerrilla war that Haitian peasants, called *cacos*, fought against the United States Marines in two periods between 1915 and 1920. Franklyn (162), presents a fictionalized historical account of marine pilots in these episodes, while McCrocklin (286), records the history of the Garde d'Haiti, the Haitian puppet military originally begun by the marines to help combat the *caco* resistance. McCrocklin, later shown to have plagiarized much of his work, depended heavily on two studies by Hart (211, 212), which are available in the Breckenridge Library of the United States Marine Corps. Also useful are the chapters on Haiti in several histories of the United States Marines by Heinl (218), Allan Millett (328), and Moskin (342), and in the biographies of individual soldiers by Burke (56), Schmidt (444), Thomas (483), and Venzón (520). There are also several marine memoirs, noted elsewhere. Two histories of the Haitian resistance to the occupation, by Bellegarde (35), and Sylvain (472), tend to be more focused on elite political resistance than on the *caco* war.

The role of the military in Haitian politics after United States withdrawal in 1934 is the subject of a work by Calixte (61), the head of the Haitian military in that period, and is placed in a more general context in the previously noted book by Leyburn (273). A published United States document (503), recalls Haitian-United States cooperation during World War II; a thesis by Dumas-Pierre (135), illustrates the army's role in the political crisis of 1946; and a history by Auguste (23), reveals the army's major role in Haitian politics between 1946 and 1957, the beginning of the Duvalier regime. A biography of François Duvalier by Diederich and Burt (120), contains considerable information on the army and the other repressive forces which helped maintain Papa Doc's highly personal rule. Delince (108), noted above, provides a scholarly contemporary analysis.

SPECIALIZED WORKS: PUERTO RICO

There is a small literature on Puerto Rican military affairs. A work by Rivero Méndez (423), details the limited military actions that took place in Puerto Rico prior to and during the United States takeover in 1898 at the end of the Spanish American War; Berbusse (40), analyzes the first two years of occupation. A 1923 government report (414), details the implementation of the United States military draft after 1917, the year of the Jones Act, which forced United States citizenship on most Puerto Ricans and ended even the theoretical concept of an independent Puerto Rican military. Thereafter, Puerto Ricans have been represented in the United States armed forces in numbers increasingly disproportionate to their percentage of the United States population. Two works, by Muñoz Rivera (346), and Padrón (368), detail the experiences of the members of the 65th Infantry Regiment, a United States army unit made up of Puerto Ricans during World War II. Little else is available on Puerto Rican military affairs during the wartime period except for several publications of the government of Puerto Rico (82, 413, 539), one of which (539), lists all of the units and officers of the "State Guard" at that time. Another (82), explores the possible use of United States Navy lands on the island of Vieques for a resettlement project, an irony considering protests of the navy's lack of consideration for Vieques's Puerto Rican residents in later years.

More recent writings on Puerto Rican military affairs cover a variety of issues, many of them of particular interest to writers with a nationalistic perspective. An article by Darragh (102), studies the organization and structure of the Puerto Rican National Guard, while a series of short books and articles by Brown (53), Enders (140), Meyn (321), Meyn and Rodríguez (322), and Samoiloff (438), examine the United States military presence in Puerto Rico. Nationalists have various objections to the presence of United States forces, which are reviewed in a short work by the EPICA Task Force (143). One such objection, often symbolized by protests against the United States Navy's use of the island of Vieques as a bombing range despite the presence of a nearby Puerto Rican community, is that North American military reservations and installations occupy a large part of the island while producing little of benefit to Puerto Ricans. Another and more recent nationalistic objection, discussed in articles and booklets by Gautier Mayoral (180), Meyn and Rodríguez (323), and Rodríguez Beruff (428, 429), is to the use of Puerto Rico as a base for projecting United States military power in the Caribbean during the 1970s and 1980s. Finally, touching on a unique subject, Ronald Fernández (154), describes military aspects of the nationalist struggle for independence, but these have been of slight importance in the overall context of pro-independence politics.

The situation of the Virgin Islands, purchased by the United States from Denmark in 1917 for security reasons, has apparently failed to generate any single study of its place in United States strategic policy.

SPECIALIZED WORKS: THE NON-SPANISH CARIBBEAN

Only in recent years has a literature begun to appear on military affairs in the non-Spanish Caribbean. It has generally been focused on the larger English-speaking islands that became independent in the 1960s, 1970s, and 1980s. Jamaica, Trinidad and Tobago, and Barbados, as well as the smaller islands, have had very small armies which have generally been obedient to civilian authorities. In reality, they have had little or no ability to project their military power abroad, have a very limited defense capability, and thus have amounted to little more than national police and security forces. More recently, especially during the administration of United States President Ronald Reagan, there has been effort (directed from Washington) to strengthen these forces. While the increased effort is directed primarily against internal security threats (i.e., political forces advocating changes viewed negatively by local elites and by Washington), there has been some effort to create a regional security force, especially among the smaller states of the eastern Caribbean. The catalyst for most of these recent actions was the short-lived socialist revolution of Maurice Bishop and the New Jewel Movement on the island of Grenada, which was ended by a United States military intervention in 1983.

The literature on these subjects, except for the United States invasion of Grenada, is limited. There is virtually no historical writing except for work on the United States military presence in the English-speaking Caribbean during World War II by Palmer (369, 370), and Howard Johnson (237). The best overall work on contemporary matters is Phillips and Young, MILITARIZATION IN THE NON-HISPANIC CARIBBEAN (401), which contains both general essays and case studies of Grenada, Surinam, Guyana, and Belize. A second source of importance is the papers produced for the 1988

Conference on Peace and Development at the University of the West Indies in Mona, Jamaica. The papers, which treat the general theme of Caribbean militarization and specifically the countries of Barbados and Jamaica (as well as two Hispanic nations, Cuba and the Dominican Republic), are tentatively scheduled to be published as a book (39, 174, 304, 372, 400, 534). Also useful are the 1974 dissertation on "The Military in the Commonwealth Caribbean" by McFarlane (289), a booklet by the Resource Center (419), on United States policy in the Eastern Caribbean, and a series of related articles: George Black (42), and García Muñiz (175), focus on United Nations security policy in the English-speaking Caribbean under Reagan; Lewis (271), and Taylor (478), look at the recent attempts to create a regional security system in the eastern Caribbean; and Murray (349), and Preston (411), write on the Canadian military relationship, past and present, to the British Caribbean islands.

Aside from the sources mentioned above, relatively little is available on the militaries of the individual non-Hispanic nations except for Grenada, noted separately below, and Haiti. On Jamaica, two articles by García Muñiz (174, 176), are available; Shak (455), analyzes events involving the military of Trinidad and Tobago in 1970; and Alexis (6), discusses a brief British military intervention in St. Kitts in 1983. On Guyana there is a booklet on small state security issued by the Ministry of Foreign Affairs (208), and several publications by Danns (98, 99, 100, 101), on the military and the police. Danns's works, along with more on the same subject by Greene (198), and a recent general study by Baber and Henry (25), constitute one of the most thorough examinations to date of a Caribbean military/police force and clearly reveal the broad range of uses and misuses to which political authorities may direct them. This theme is also taken up in an article by Diederich (118). Studies of the regime of Surinam's General Desi Bouterse indicate similar tendencies there, with various authors reporting a general militarization of that society since the 1980 Sergeants' Coup that brought Bouterse to power. Books focused on these recent events in Surinam include those by Cárdenas (63), Chin and Buddingh (77), Haakmat (209), Polime and Thoden zan Velzen (407), and Verkey and Van Westerloo (521). A recent volume edited by Sedoc-Dahlberg (450), contains essays by Sedoc-Dahlberg (451), and Thorndike (486), which focus directly on military issues in Surinam. Other than the case of Surinam, there seem to be no other studies of military-related phenomena for either the Dutch or French speaking/controlled possessions in the Caribbean area (except, as previously noted, the literature on Haiti and the article by Smith (460), on Martinique during World War II).

SPECIALIZED WORKS: GRENADA

The one non-Hispanic nation associated with an extensive literature on military affairs is tiny Grenada. But this ironic situation, which clearly illustrates the fact that the relative importance assigned to individual Caribbean nations is decided by outside powers, has not long been the case. Grenada, owing to its diminutive size and its status as a British colony until 1974, was almost entirely ignored by writers until a socialist revolutionary group, the New Jewel Movement, carried out a popular coup against the government of Prime Minister Eric Gairy in 1979. That event and the 1983 demise of the revolution (when the United States invaded the island in order to oust the politically and militarily divided socialist government) catapulted Grenada into the world spotlight, resulting in an outpouring of books and articles.

A number of books provide intelligent overviews of recent Grenadan history, including the pre-revolutionary period, the revolution of 1979, the events of 1979-83 and the 1983 United States invasion. Among the best of these are Payne, Sutton, and Thorndike GRENADA: REVOLUTION AND INVASION (377), and works by Schoenhals and Melanson (446), Gordon Lewis (272), O'Shaughnessy (361), Thorndike (484, 485), Pryor (412), and the Latin American Bureau (200). Also useful are a book chapter by Manigat (301), books by Earle (139), and Khachaturov (245), and a dissertation by McIntire (292), on the strategic implications of the Grenadan revolution. Focused more centrally on the United States invasion are books by Burrowes (57), Gilmore (186), Nitoburg (355), Sandford and Vigilante (440), Sunshine and Wheaton (471), and Valenta (507), as well as edited works by Valenta and Ellison (508), and Dunn and Watson (137). Other reactions to the incursion have taken various forms, including a forceful condemnation by the leaders of Cuba (68); several studies of the event from the standpoint of international law by Davidson (103), Diéguez (121), Levitin (270), Moore (335), and Shahabuddeen (454); hearings by the United States House of Representatives (491, 492); and publication of selected captured documents (generally intended to show the Marxist-Leninist leanings of Grenada's revolutionary leaders) by the United States government (500), and privately by Seabury and McDougall (449), and Crozier (92). There are also several articles pertaining to Grenada which are of special interest: Jacquier (233), examines the intervention from a French military point of view; Halliday (210), analyzes the invasion with regard to its various aftereffects in Grenadan society; Motley (344), focuses on Grenada as an example of low-intensity conflict; and Scott MacDonald (288), examines the future of foreign aid to the Caribbean in light of the Grenadan experience.

PERIODICALS

There are relatively few periodicals produced by and for the Caribbean militaries. Two are available to researchers on the Cuban military, the BOLETIN DEL EJERCITO (540), issued from 1916 to 1933, and VERDE OLIVO (545), the official publication of the Cuban revolutionary army from 1959 to the present. Judson (240), offers an analysis of the content of VERDE OLIVO. On the Dominican Republic there are also two military periodicals available, the army's REVISTA DE LAS FUERZAS ARMADAS (543), published from 1966, and the air force's ALAS (538), issued since 1980. On Guyana, THE SCARLET BERET (544), is the Guyana defense force's official journal. Also available are scattered volumes of the annual reports for the *gendarmerie* or Garde d'Haiti, RAPORT (542), the predecessor institution of the present Haitian army, and for the Puerto Rican state guard (National Guard), ANNUAL REPORT (539).

Researchers have sometimes found military periodicals to be of limited use since they are internal publications that put forward a "party line" and often emphasize routine institutional matters. This being the case, an attractive alternative is some of the many journals and newsletters that focus on the Caribbean. These publications, which range from scholarly to popular, are aimed at a variety of different specialized audiences and cover a broad range of topics, including military (especially contemporary) affairs. Many of these publications are reviewed in the closing pages of the "Bibliographic Guide" in Heine and Manigat (217), or can be located through the standard Caribbean bibliographies.

FUTURE RESEARCH

The field of Caribbean military affairs is wide open for researchers and writers. Only Cuba's armed forces have begun to receive the attention that they deserve, while the military institutions of other countries, as well as other military related topics, have generally languished.

The two best studies of the armed forces in the Dominican Republic and Haiti, by Atkins (21), and Delince (108), are entirely oriented to the present. Thus the histories of the militaries of these two countries, where the institution has been of tremendous political importance, are almost entirely unwritten. The coverage of military affairs is episodic at best, treating important events such as the Dominican uprising of 1965 and ignoring the rest. For the remainder of the Caribbean's colonies and nations, there is very little published work on any aspect of military affairs. This is particularly true for the areas that remained colonies during the twentieth century (most of the Caribbean Islands until the 1960s), despite the fact that British, French, Dutch, and United States archives must contain considerable material germane to military matters. Concerning the military institutions of the newly independent nations, we have only slightly more information. While this might be excused because they have very short histories, these are still institutions of importance in the small countries that they serve. Generally we know little about their size and structure, their arms and training, the degree of their professionalization, their political orientation, or impact on politics. Neither do we have any idea how the military interacts with the broader economic and social structures of which it forms a part.

The last statement applies not only to the small, recently independent Caribbean states but even to the larger and better studied countries. Little or no research has been done which would help investigators understand the effect that militaries and militarization have on the Caribbean economy and society. It seems likely, for example, that military expenditures act as a drag on development, but no study exists that documents this phenomenon. Similarly, several scholars have observed in passing that military careers seem to offer a means of social and economic advancement in highly stratified societies, but no organized research exists on this topic for any Caribbean nation.

The recent interest in the Caribbean as a strategic matter notwithstanding, the history of the region as an arena of international confrontation has attracted little scholarly attention. Despite some attention to the Caribbean's strategic importance during the first quarter of the twentieth century by such previously mentioned authors as Challener (72), Munro (347, 348), and Tulchin (490), little has been written that focuses on military aspects of this international rivalry, including World War I, except for studies of individual United States interventions. Nor has a broad study been made concerning the tremendous impact of World War I on the economies of the Caribbean.

The United States clearly established military and economic hegemony in the Caribbean after World War I, but it was again challenged militarily in the 1940s. Just as for the earlier period, however, there are few studies of World War II and its considerable impact on the Caribbean. Except for a dissertation dealing with Trinidad and a small amount of research on Puerto Rico, the only Caribbean-focused studies of military planning, military actions (such as submarine warfare), military bases, or the war's considerable impact on the area's shipping and economic life are chapters in more general works.

The period between World War II and 1980 has also been ignored by military analysts except for the Cuban revolution and the several crises associated with it. Thus we know relatively little about the Cold

War and the impact of Cold War programs (such as military aid, training, and arms sales) in the Caribbean region. For this period as for earlier ones, much of what needs to be known about Caribbean military affairs awaits the attention of future authors.

BIBLIOGRAPHY: THE CARIBBEAN

1. Aaron, Harold R. "The Seizure of Political Power in Cuba, 1956-1959." Ph.D. dissertation, Georgetown University, 1964.

2. Abel, Elie. THE MISSILE CRISIS. Philadelphia: J. B. Lippincott, 1966. Also published as THE MISSILES OF OCTOBER. London: MacGibbon & Kee, 1969.

3. Adam y Silva, Ricardo. LA GRAN MENTIRA, 4 DE SEPTIEMBRE DE 1933. Havana: Editorial Lex, 1947.

4. Adelman, Alan, and Reid Reading, eds. CONFRONTATION IN THE CARIBBEAN BASIN: INTERNATIONAL PERSPECTIVES ON SECURITY, SOVEREIGNTY, AND SURVIVAL. Pittsburgh: Center for Latin American Studies, University of Pittsburgh, 1984.

5. Aguilar, Luis. CUBA, 1933: PROLOGUE TO REVOLUTION. Ithaca: Cornell University Press, 1972.

6. Alexis, Francis. "British Intervention in St. Kitts (Based on an Analysis of British Parliamentary Acts and Royal Orders Dealing with the Relationship between the Islands of St. Kitts, Nevis and Anguilla before St. Kitts and Nevis Gained Full Independence, Sept. 19, 1983)." NEW YORK UNIVERSITY JOURNAL OF INTERNATIONAL LAW AND POLITICS 16 (1984): 581-600.

7. Allison, Graham T. CONCEPTUAL MODELS AND THE CUBAN MISSILE CRISIS. Santa Monica: Rand Corporation, 1965.

8. ———. ESSENCE OF DECISION: EXPLAINING THE CUBAN MISSILE CRISIS. Boston: Little, Brown, 1971.

9. Alvarez, Justina. HEROES ETERNOS DE LA PATRIA. Havana: Ediciones Venceremos, 1964.

10. Alvarez Quiñones, Roberto. 1916: OCUPACION YANQUI DE LA REPUBLICA DOMINICANA. Havana: Casa de las Américas, 1975.

11. Ambursley, Fitzroy, and Robin Cohen. CRISIS IN THE CARIBBEAN. New York: Monthly Review Press, 1983.

12. Ameijeiras Delgado, Efigenio. MAS ALLA DE NOSOTROS: COLUMNA 6 "JUAN MANUEL AMEIJEIHAS," II FRENTE ORIENTAL "FRANK PAIS." Santiago de Cuba: Editorial Oriente, 1984.

13. Ananova, E. V. "Vooruzhennaia Interventiia Ssha v Dominikanskoi Respublike." Parts 1, 2. NOVAIA I NOVEISHAIA ISTORIIA (U.S.S.R.) 12 (1968): 42-57, 13(1969): 4-37.

14. Anglo-American Caribbean Commission. REPORT OF THE ANGLO-AMERICAN CARIBBEAN COMMISSION TO THE GOVERNMENTS OF THE UNITED STATES AND GREAT BRITAIN FOR THE YEARS 1942-1943. Washington: Anglo-American Caribbean Commission, 1943. Subsequent volumes published in 1944-45.

15. Arciniegas, Nelson Antonio. HISTORIA DE LA MARINA DE GUERRA. Santo Domingo: Editora Nivar, 1984.

16. ———. INSTRUCCION NAVAL MILITAR EN SANTO DOMINGO. Santo Domingo: Editora del Caribe, 1976.

17. Arvelo, Perina. REVOLUCION DE LOS BARBUDOS. Caracas: Editorial Landi, 1961.

18. Arvelo, Tulio H. CAYO CONFITE Y LUPERON: MEMORIAS DE UN EXPEDICIONARIO. Santo Domingo: Universidad Autónoma de Santo Domingo, 1982.

19. Ashby, Timothy. THE BEAR IN THE BACKYARD: MOSCOW'S CARIBBEAN STRATEGY. Lexington, Mass.: Lexington Books, 1987.

20. ASI SE DERROTO AL IMPERIALISMO. 2 vols. Mexico City: Siglo XXI Editores, 1978.

21. Atkins, G. Pope. ARMS AND POLITICS IN THE DOMINICAN REPUBLIC. Boulder: Westview Press, 1981.

22. Atkins, G. Pope, and Larman C. Wilson. THE UNITED STATES AND THE TRUJILLO REGIME. New Brunswick: Rutgers University Press, 1972.

23. Auguste, Maurepas. GENESE D'UNE REPUBLIQUE HEREDITAIRE: HAITI, 25 MAI 1957. Paris: La Pensée Universelle, 1974.

24. Auxier, George Washington. "The Military Aspects of the Foreign Policy of the United States with Respect to the Caribbean Sea." M.A. thesis, Miami University of Ohio, 1934.

25. Baber, Colin, and Jeffrey Henry. GUYANA: BEYOND THE BURNHAM ERA. New York: Columbia University Press, 1986.

26. Balch, Emily Greene. OCCUPIED HAITI. New York: Writers Publishing, 1927.

27. Barceló Fundora, Nereida. LYDIA: LA MENSAJERA. Santiago de Cuba: Editorial Oriente, 1980.

28. Barquín López, Ramón M. LAS LUCHAS GUERRILLERAS EN CUBA: DE LA COLONIA A LA SIERRA MAESTRA. Madrid: Playor, 1975.

29. Barry, Tom, Beth Wood, and Deb Preusch. THE OTHER SIDE OF PARADISE: FOREIGN CONTROL IN THE CARIBBEAN. New York: Grove Press, 1984.

30. Bayó, Alberto. MI APORTE A LA REVOLUCION CUBANA. Havana: Imprenta Ejército Rebelde, 1960.

31. Beach, Edward L. THE WRECK OF THE MEMPHIS. New York: n.p., 1966.

32. Beede, Benjamin R. INTERVENTION AND COUNTERINSURGENCY: AN ANNOTATED BIBLIOGRAPHY OF THE SMALL WARS OF THE UNITED STATES, 1898-1984. New York: Garland Publishing, 1985.

33. Bell, Ian. THE DOMINICAN REPUBLIC. Boulder: Westview Press, 1981.

34. Bellegarde, Dantes. L'OCCUPATION AMERICAINE D'HAITI: SES CONSEQUENCES MORALES ET ECONOMIQUES. Port-au-Prince: Imprimerie Cheraquit, 1928-29.

35. ———. LA RESISTANCE HAITIENNE. Port-au-Prince: Editions Beauchemin, 1937.

36. Bender, Gerald J. "Angola, the Cubans, and American Anxieties; Angola, Cuba, and the United States." FOREIGN POLICY 31 (1978): 3-30.

37. Bender, Lynn Darrell. CUBA VS. THE UNITED STATES: THE POLITICS OF HOSTILITY. 2d ed. San Juan: Interamerican University Press, 1981.

38. ———. "Guantánamo: Its Political, Military and Legal Status." CARIBBEAN QUARTERLY (Jamaica) 19(1973): 80-86.

39. Benítez Manaut, Raúl, et al. "Fuerzas armadas, sociedad y pueblo: Cuba y Nicaragua." Paper presented at the Conference on Peace and Development, University of the West Indies, Mona, Jamaica, May 1988.

40. Berbusse, Edward J. THE UNITED STATES IN PUERTO RICO, 1898-1900. Chapel Hill: University of North Carolina Press, 1966.

41. BIBLIOGRAFIA DEL ASALTO AL CUARTEL MONCADA. Havana: n.p., 1975.

42. Black, George. "Mare Nostrum: U.S. Security Policy in the English-Speaking Caribbean." NACLA REPORT ON THE AMERICAS, July-August 1985, 13-48.

43. Black, Jan Knippers. THE DOMINICAN REPUBLIC: POLITICS AND DEVELOPMENT IN AN UNSOVEREIGN STATE. Boston: Allen and Unwin, 1986.

44. ———. SENTINELS OF EMPIRE: THE UNITED STATES AND LATIN AMERICAN MILITARISM. Westport: Greenwood Press, 1986.

45. Blight, James G. ON THE BRINK. New York: Hill and Wang, 1989.

46. Bonachea, Ramón L., and Marta San Martín. THE CUBAN INSURRECTION, 1952-1959. New Brunswick: Transaction Books, 1974.

47. Bonachea, Rolando E., and Nelson P. Valdés, eds. REVOLUTIONARY STRUGGLE, 1947-1958, by Fidel Castro. Cambridge: MIT Press, 1972.

48. Bonfonti, Matthieu A. CONNIVENCE: L'AFFAIRE DE MISSILES DE CUBA: L'ENTENTE SECRETE LA PLUS EXTRAORDINAIRE. Paris: Editions Olivier Orban, 1977.

49. Bosch, Juan. THE UNFINISHED EXPERIMENT: DEMOCRACY IN THE DOMINICAN REPUBLIC. London: Pall Mall Press, 1965.

50. Bourne, Peter G. FIDEL: A BIOGRAPHY OF FIDEL CASTRO. New York: Dodd, Mead, 1986.

51. Bracey, Audrey. RESOLUTION OF THE DOMINICAN CRISIS OF 1965: A STUDY IN MEDIATION. Lanham, MD: University Press of America, 1980.

52. Brenner, Philip. FROM CONFRONTATION TO NEGOTIATION: U.S. RELATIONS WITH CUBA. Boulder: PACCA/Westview Press, 1988.

53. Brown, Peter. "U.S. Military Presence in Puerto Rico." Río Piedras: American Friends Service Committee, 1975. Unpublished.

54. Brugal Alfáu, Danilo. TRAGEDIA EN SANTO DOMINGO: DOCUMENTOS PARA LA HISTORIA. Santo Domingo: Editora del Caribe, 1966.

55. Brune, Lester H. THE MISSILE CRISIS OF OCTOBER, 1962: A REVIEW OF ISSUES AND REFERENCES. Claremont: Regina Books, 1985.

56. Burke, Davis. MARINE!: THE LIFE OF LT. GEN. LEWIS B. (CHESTY) PULLER USMC (RET.). Boston: Little, Brown, 1962.

57. Burrowes, Reynold A. REVOLUTION AND RESCUE IN GRENADA: AN ACCOUNT OF THE U.S. CARIBBEAN INVASION. Westport: Greenwood Press, 1988.

58. Cabrera Alvarez, Guillermo, ed. HABLAR DE CAMILO. Havana: Instituto del Libro, 1970.

59. Calder, Bruce J. "Caudillos and Gavilleros versus the United States Marines: Guerrilla Insurgency during the Dominican Intervention, 1916-1924." HISPANIC AMERICAN HISTORICAL REVIEW 58(1978): 649-75.

60. ———. THE IMPACT OF INTERVENTION: THE DOMINICAN REPUBLIC DURING THE U.S. OCCUPATION OF 1916-1924. Austin: University of Texas Press, 1984.

61. Calixte, D.P. HAITI: CALVARY OF A SOLDIER. New York: Negro Universities Press, 1969.

62. Callcott, Wilfrid Hardy. THE CARIBBEAN POLICY OF THE UNITED STATES, 1890-1920. New York: Octagon Books, 1966.

63. Cárdenas, Osvaldo. DE REVOLUTIE VAN SERGEANTEN. Nijmegen, Netherlands: University of Nijmegen, 1988.

64. Carey, John, ed. THE DOMINICAN REPUBLIC CRISIS, 1965. Dobbs Ferry, N.Y.: Oceana Publications, 1967.

65. Carrillo, Justo. CUBA 1933: ESTUDIANTES, YANQUIS Y SOLDADOS. Coral Gables: Research Institute for Cuban Studies, University of Miami, 1985.

66. Castor, Suzy. "The American Occupation of Haiti, 1915-1934, and the Dominican Republic, 1916-1924." MASSACHUSETTS REVIEW 15(1974): 253-75.

67. ———. LA OCUPACION NORTEAMERICANA DE HAITI Y SUS CONSEQUENCIAS, 1915-1934. Mexico City: Siglo XXI Editores, 1971.

68. Castro, Fidel. LA INVASION A GRANADA. Mexico City: Editorial Katún, 1983.

69. ———. PLAYA GIRON. Havana: Comisión Nacional del Monumento a los Caídos en Playa Girón, 1961.

70. Castro García, Teofilo. INTERVENCION YANQUI, 1916-1924. Santo Domingo: Editorial Taller, 1978.

71. Center for Strategic Studies. DOMINICAN ACTION, 1965. Washington: Georgetown University, 1966.

72. Challener, Richard D. ADMIRALS, GENERALS AND AMERICAN FOREIGN POLICY, 1898-1914. Princeton: Princeton University Press, 1973.

73. Chang, Federico. EL EJERCITO NACIONAL DE LA REPÚBLICA NEOCOLONIAL, 1899-1933. Havana: Editorial Ciencias Sociales, 1981.

74. Chayes, Abraham. THE CUBAN MISSILE CRISIS: INTERNATIONAL CRISES AND THE ROLE OF LAW. New York: Oxford University Press, 1974.

75. Chilcote, Ronald H., ed. CUBA, 1953-1978: A BIBLIOGRAPHIC GUIDE TO THE LITERATURE. 2 vols. White Plains: Kraus International, 1986.

76. Child, John. "From 'Color' to 'Rainbow': U.S. Strategic Planning for Latin America, 1919-1945." JOURNAL OF INTERAMERICAN STUDIES AND WORLD AFFAIRS 21 (1979): 233-59.

77. Chin, Henk E., and Hans Buddingh. SURINAM: POLITICS, ECONOMICS AND SOCIETY. London: Frances Pinter Publishers, 1987.

78. Chomón, Faure. LA VERDADERA HISTORIA DEL ASALTO AL PALACIO PRESIDENCIAL. Havana: Prensa Estudiantil, 1959.

79. Cienfuegos, Camilo. PAGINAS DEL DIARIO DE CAMPANA. Havana: Ministerio de Educación, 1962.

80. Cintron Tiryakian, Josefina. "The Military and Security Dimensions of U.S. Caribbean Policy." In THE CARIBBEAN CHALLENGE: U.S. POLICY IN A VOLATILE REGION, 48-71. Edited by H. Michael Erisman. Boulder: Westview Press, 1984.

81. Collazo, Enrique. LA REVOLUCION DE AGOSTO DE 1906. Havana: Imprenta C. Martínez, 1907.

82. Committee for the Investigation of Conditions in the Island of Vieques. REPORT ON THE POSSIBILITIES OF UTILIZING NAVY LANDS IN VIEQUES ISLAND FOR A RESETTLEMENT PROJECT. San Juan: n.p., 1943.

83. Condit, Kenneth W., and Edwin T. Turnbladh. HOLD HIGH THE TORCH: A HISTORY OF THE 4TH MARINES. Washington: U.S. Marine Corps, 1960.

84. Conn, Stetson, Rose C. Engelman, and Byron Fairchild. GUARDING THE UNITED STATES AND ITS OUTPOSTS. Vol. 12, part 2 of UNITED STATES ARMY IN WORLD WAR II: THE WESTERN HEMISPHERE. Washington: Department of the Army; U.S. Government Printing Office, 1964.

85. Conn, Stetson, and Byron Fairchild. THE FRAMEWORK OF HEMISPHERE DEFENCE. Vol. 12, part 1 of UNITED STATES ARMY IN WORLD WAR II: THE WESTERN HEMISPHERE. Washington: Department of the Army; U.S. Government Printing Office, 1960.

86. Consuegra, W.L. HECHOS Y COMENTARIOS: LA REVOLUCION DE FEBRERO DE 1917 EN LAS VILLAS. Havana: La Comercial, 1920.

87. Cook, Fred J. THE CUBAN MISSILE CRISIS, OCTOBER, 1962: THE U.S. AND RUSSIA FACE A NUCLEAR SHOWDOWN. New York: Franklin Watts, 1972.

88. Corrales, Raúl. PLAYA GIRON. Havana: Editorial Letras Cubanas, 1981.

89. Couteau-Begaire, Herve. GEOSTRATEGIE DE L'ATLANTIQUE SUD. Paris: Press Universitaires de France, 1985.

90. Crassweller, Robert D. CUBA AND THE UNITED STATES: THE TANGLED RELATIONSHIP. New York: Foreign Policy Association, 1971.

91. ———. TRUJILLO: THE LIFE AND TIMES OF A CARIBBEAN DICTATOR. New York: Macmillan, 1966.

92. Crozier, Brian, ed. THE GRENADA DOCUMENTS. Woodbury, N.J.: Sherwood Press, 1987.

93. Cuba. Consejo Corporativo de Educación, Sanidad y Beneficencia. MILITARISMO, ANTI-MILITARISMO, SEUDO-MILITARISMO, by Arístedes Sosa de Quesada. Havana: Instituto Cívico-Militar, 1939.

94. Cuba. Fuerzas Armadas Revolucionarias (FAR). Sección de Historia. DICIEMBRE DEL 58. Havana: Editorial de Ciencias Sociales, 1977.

95. ———. SEGUNDO FRENTE ORIENTAL "FRANK PAIS." Havana: Imprenta Federico Engels, 1976.

96. Cuba. Militia. MANUAL BASICO DEL MILICIANO DE TROPAS TERRITORIALES. Havana: Editorial Orbe, 1981.

97. Czarnecki, Jan. CUBA IN SOVIET WRITINGS, 1959-1972: AN ANNOTATED BIBLIOGRAPHY OF SOVIET PUBLICATIONS ON CUBA IN THE COLLECTION OF THE UNIVERSITY OF MIAMI. Coral Gables: University of Miami Press, 1977.

98. Danns, George K. "Decolonization and Militarization in the Caribbean: The Case of Guyana." In THE NEWER CARIBBEAN: DECOLONIZATION, DEMOCRACY, AND DEVELOPMENT, 63-94. Edited by Paget Henry and Carl Stone. Philadelphia: Institute for the Study of Human Issues, 1983.

99. ———. DOMINATION AND POWER IN GUYANA: A STUDY OF THE POLICE IN A THIRD WORLD CONTEXT. New Brunswick: Transaction Books, 1982.

100. ———. "Militarization and Development: An Experiment in Nation Building." TRANSITION 1(1978): 23-44.

101. ———. "The Role of the Military in the National Security of Guyana." BULLETIN OF EASTERN CARIBBEAN AFFAIRS (Barbados) 11 (1986): 23-44.

102. Darragh, Shaun M. "The Puerto Rican Military Forces." MILITARY REVIEW 58(1978): 46-53.

103. Davidson, Scott. GRENADA: A STUDY IN POLITICS AND THE LIMITS OF INTERNATIONAL LAW. Aldershot, England: Gower, 1987.

104. Debray, Régis. REVOLUTION IN THE REVOLUTION? New York: Grove Press, 1968.

105. De Galíndez, Jesús. THE ERA OF TRUJILLO: DOMINICAN DICTATOR. Tucson: University of Arizona Press, 1973.

106. De Kadt, Emanuel, ed. PATTERNS OF FOREIGN INFLUENCE IN THE CARIBBEAN. London: Oxford University Press for the Royal Institute of International Affairs, 1972.

107. Delancer, Juan. PRIMAVERA 1959: CONSTANZA, MAIMON Y ESTERO HONDO. Santo Domingo: Imprenta Amigo del Hogar, 1979.

108. Delince, Kern. ARMEE ET POLITIQUE EN HAITI. Paris: Editions L'Harmattan, 1979.

109. Delmas, Claude. CRISES A CUBA. Brussels: Editions Complex 1983.

110. Del Pino, Rafael. AMANECER EN GIRON. Havana: Instituto Cubano del Libro and Editorial de Arte y Literatura, 1969.

111. ———. GENERAL DEL PINO SPEAKS: AN INSIGHT INTO ELITE CORRUPTION AND MILITARY DISSENSION IN CASTRO'S CUBA. Washington: Cuban American National Foundation, 1987.

112. De Meira Mottos, Carlos. A EXPERIENCIA DO FAIBRAS NA REPUBLICA DOMICANA. Rio de Janeiro: Escola Superior de Guerra, 1967.

113. Desnoes, Edmundo. LA SIERRA Y EL LLANO. Havana: Casa de las Américas, 1961.

114. Despradel, Fidelio. HISTORIA GRAFICA DE LA GUERRA DE ABRIL. Santo Domingo: Editora Cosmos, 1975.

115. ——. MANOLO TAVAREZ EN SU JUSTA DIMENSION HISTORICA: LAS MANACLAS; DIARIO DE LA GUERRILLA. Santo Domingo: Editora Alfa y Omega, 1983.

116. Detrez, Conrad. LES MOUVEMENTS REVOLUTIONNAIRES EN AMERIQUE LATINE. Brussels: Editions Vie Ouvriere, 1972.

117. Detzer, David. THE BRINK: CUBAN MISSILE CRISIS, 1962. New York: Crowell, 1979.

118. Diederich, Bernard. "The End of West Indian Innocence: Arming the Police." CARIBBEAN REVIEW 13(1984): 10-13.

119. ——. TRUJILLO: THE DEATH OF THE GOAT. Boston: Little, Brown, 1978.

120. Diederich, Bernard, and Al Burt. PAPA DOC: THE TRUTH ABOUT HAITI TODAY. New York: McGraw-Hill, 1969.

121. Diéguez, Richard P. "The Grenada Intervention: 'Illegal' in Form, Sound as Policy." NEW YORK UNIVERSITY JOURNAL OF LAW AND POLITICS 16(1984): 1167-1204.

122. Dinerstein, Herbert S. THE MAKING OF A MISSILE CRISIS, OCTOBER 1962. Baltimore: Johns Hopkins University Press, 1976.

123. Dixon, Marlene. "Overview: Militarism as Foreign Policy; Reagan's Second Term." CONTEMPORARY MARXISM 10 (1985): i-xxiii.

124. Domínguez, Jorge I. "Armed Forces and Foreign Relations." In CUBA IN THE WORLD, 53-86. Edited by Cole Blasier and Carmelo Mesa-Lago. Pittsburgh: University of Pittsburgh Press, 1978.

125. ——. "The Civic-Soldier in Cuba." In POLITICAL-MILITARY SYSTEMS: COMPARATIVE PERSPECTIVES, 209-38. Edited by Catherine Kelleher. Newbury Park: Sage, 1974.

126. ——. "The Cuban Operations in Angola: Costs and Benefits for the Armed Forces." CUBAN STUDIES/ESTUDIOS CUBANOS 8 (1978): 10-21.

127. ——. "Institutionalization and Civil-Military Relations." CUBAN STUDIES/ESTUDIOS CUBANOS 6(1976): 39-65.

128. ——. "Political and Military Limitations and Consequences of Cuban Policies in Africa." CUBAN STUDIES/ESTUDIOS CUBANOS 10 (1980): 1-35.

129. ——. U.S. INTERESTS AND POLICIES IN THE CARIBBEAN AND CENTRAL AMERICA. Washington: American Enterprise Institute for Public Policy Research, 1982.

130. Dominican Republic. Centro de Enseñanza de las Fuerzas Armadas. LIBRO BLANCO DE LAS FUERZAS ARMADAS Y DE LA POLICIA NACIONAL DE LA REPUBLICA DOMINICANA: ESTUDIOS Y PRUEBAS DOCUMENTALES DE LAS CAUSAS DEL MOVIMENTO REIVINDICADOR DE 25 DE SEPTIEMBRE DE 1963. Santo Domingo: Editora del Caribe, 1964.

131. Dorschner, John, and Roberto Fabricio. THE WINDS OF DECEMBER. New York: Coward, McCann and Geoghegan, 1980.

132. Draper, Theodore. THE DOMINICAN REVOLT: A CASE STUDY IN AMERICAN POLICY. New York: Commentary, 1968.

133. Ducoudray, Félix Servio. LOS "GAVILLEROS" DEL ESTE: UNA EPOPEYA CALUMNIADA. Santo Domingo: Editora de la Universidad Autónoma de Santo Domingo, 1976.

134. Duffy, Gloria. "Crisis Management and the Cuba Brigade." INTERNATIONAL SECURITY 8(1983): 67-87.

135. Dumas-Pierre, Antonin. "La Garde d'Haiti et la conjoncture de 1946." M.A. thesis, University of Quebec, 1975.

136. Duncan, W. Raymond. THE SOVIET UNION AND CUBA: INTERESTS AND INFLUENCE. New York: Praeger Publishers, 1985.

137. Dunn, Peter, and Bruce W. Watson, eds. AMERICAN INTERVENTION IN GRENADA: THE IMPLICATIONS OF OPERATION URGENT FURY. Boulder: Westview Press, 1985.

138. Durch, William J. "The Cuban Military in Africa and the Middle East: From Algeria to Angola." STUDIES IN COMPARATIVE COMMUNISM 11 (1978): 34-74.

139. Earle, Stafford, ed. THE GRENADA MASSACRE. Jamaica: Earle Publishers, 1983.

140. Enders, John. LA PRESENCIA MILITAR NORTEAMERICANA EN PUERTO RICO. Río Piedras: Proyecto Caribeño de Justicia y Paz, 1979.

141. English, Adrian J. ARMED FORCES OF LATIN AMERICA: THEIR HISTORIES, DEVELOPMENT, PRESENT STRENGTH AND MILITARY POTENTIAL. London: Jane's Publishing, 1984.

142. Enzenberger, Hans M. THE HAVANA INQUIRY. New York: Holt, Rinehart, Winston, 1974.

143. EPICA Task Force. PUERTO RICO: A PEOPLE CHALLENGING COLONIALISM; A PEOPLE'S PRIMER. Washington: EPICA, 1976.

144. Erisman, H. Michael. CUBA'S INTERNATIONAL RELATIONS: THE ANATOMY OF A NATIONALISTIC FOREIGN POLICY. Boulder: Westview Press, 1985.

145. ———, ed. THE CARIBBEAN CHALLENGE: U.S. POLICY IN A VOLATILE REGION. Boulder: Westview Press, 1984.

146. Erisman, H. Michael, and John D. Martz, eds. COLOSSUS CHALLENGED: THE STRUGGLE FOR CARIBBEAN INFLUENCE. Boulder: Westview Press, 1982.

147. Espaillat, Arturo. TRUJILLO: THE LAST CAESAR. Chicago: Henry Regnery, 1964.

148. Fauriol, Georges. "The Caribbean Basin Environment." In STRATEGIC RESPONSES TO CONFLICT IN THE 1980'S. Edited by William J. Taylor, Jr., Steven Maaranen, and Gerrit W. Gong. Lexington, Mass.: Lexington Books, 1984.

149. Fausel, Robert W. "Selling Airplanes to Batista's Cuba." AEROSPACE HISTORIAN 32(1985): 82-99.

150. Fermoselle, Rafael. CUBAN LEADERSHIP AFTER CASTRO: BIOGRAPHIES OF CUBA'S TOP GENERALS. Coral Gables: Graduate School of International Studies, University of Miami, 1987.

151. ———. THE EVOLUTION OF THE CUBAN MILITARY, 1492-1986. Miami: Ediciones Universal, 1987.

152. ———. POLITICA Y COLOR EN CUBA: LA GUERRITA DE 1912. Montevideo: Ediciones Géminis, 1974.

153. Fernández, Arlette, ed. CORONEL FERNANDEZ DOMINGUEZ: FUNDADOR DEL MOVIMIENTO MILITAR CONSTITUCIONALISTA. Santo Domingo: Editora Cosmos, 1980.

154. Fernández, Ronald. LOS MACHETEROS: THE WELLS FARGO ROBBERY AND THE VIOLENT STRUGGLE FOR PUERTO RICAN INDEPENDENCE. New York: Prentice Hall, 1987.

155. Ferrer, Eduardo. OPERACION PUMA. N.p.: International Aviation Consultants, 1975.

156. Ferrer, Horacio. CON EL RIFLE AL HOMBRO. Havana: Imprenta El Siglo XX, 1950.

157. Foner, Philip S. A HISTORY OF CUBA AND ITS RELATIONS WITH THE UNITED STATES. 2 vols. New York: International Publishers, 1962-65.

158. ———. THE SPANISH-CUBAN-AMERICAN WAR AND THE BIRTH OF AMERICAN IMPERIALISM, 1895-1902. 2 vols. New York: Monthly Review Press, 1972.

159. Foreign Policy Association. THE CUBAN CRISIS: A DOCUMENTARY RECORD. New York: Foreign Policy Association, 1963.

160. Franco, Franklin. REPUBLICA DOMINICANA: CLASES, CRISIS Y COMANDOS. Havana: Casa de las Américas, 1966.

161. Franco Varona, M. LA REVOLUCION DEL 4 DE SEPTIEMBRE. Havana: n.p., 1934.

162. Franklyn, Irwin R. KNIGHTS IN THE COCKPIT: A ROMANTIC EPIC OF THE FLYING MARINES IN HAITI. New York: Dial Press, 1931.

163. Franqui, Carlos. DIARY OF THE CUBAN REVOLUTION. New York: Viking Press, 1980.

164. ———. EL LIBRO DE LOS DOCE. Mexico City: Ediciones Era, 1966.

165. Frente Obrero Revolucionario Democrático Cubano. SERVICIO MILITAR OBLIGATORIO EN CUBA ROJA. Miami: n.p., 1964.

166. Fresnillo, Estrella. NICO LOPEZ: SONADOR DE LIBERTADES. Havana: Editorial Gente Nueva, 1978.

167. Fuller, Stephen M., and Graham A. Cosmas. MARINES IN THE DOMINICAN REPUBLIC, 1916-1924. Washington: History and Museums Division, USMC, 1974.

168. Gaillard, Roger. LES BLANCS DEBARQUENT, 1918-1919: CHARLEMAGNE PERALTE; LE CACO. Port-au-Prince: Imprimerie Le Natal, 1982.

169. ———. LES BLANCS DEBARQUENT, 1914-1915: LES CENT-JOURS DE ROSALVO BOBO; OU UNE MISE A MORT POLITIQUE. N.p.: Press Nationales, 1973.

170. ———. LES BLANCS DEBARQUENT, 1915: PREMIER ECRASEMENT DU CACOISME. Port-au-Prince: Imprimerie Le Natal, 1981.

171. Gálvez, William. CAMILO: SENOR DE LA VANGUARDIA. Havana: Editorial de las Ciencias Sociales, 1979.

172. García, Angel, and Piotr Mironchuk. ESBOZO HISTORICO DE LAS RELACIONES ENTRE CUBA-RUSIA Y CUBA-USSR. Havana: Instituto Cubano del Libro, 1976.

173. García Muñiz, Humberto. BOOTS, BOOTS, BOOTS: INTERVENTION, REGIONAL SECURITY AND MILITARIZATION IN THE CARIBBEAN, 1979-1986. Río Piedras: Caribbean Project for Peace and Justice, 1986.

174. ———. "Defence Policy and Planning in the Caribbean: An Assessment of the Case of Jamaica on its 25th Independence Anniversary." Paper presented at the Conference on Peace and Development in the Caribbean, University of the West Indies, Mona, Jamaica, May 1988.

175. ———. "La estrategia militar en el Caribe angloparlante." EL CARIBE CONTEMPORANEO (Mexico) 17-43.

176. ———. "Jamaica: Las fuerzas de seguridad; Fiel de la balanza en el futuro?" SEQUENCIA: REVISTA AMERICANA DE CIENCIAS SOCIALES (Mexico) 6(1986): 118-50.

177. Garthoff, Raymond. "American Reaction to Soviet Aircraft in Cuba, 1962 and 1978." POLITICAL SCIENCE QUARTERLY 95 (1980): 427-39.

178. ———. REFLECTIONS ON THE CUBAN MISSILE CRISIS. Washington: Brookings Institution, 1987.

179. Gatón Richiez, Carlos. LEGISLACION MILITAR INTERIOR DEL EJERCITO NACIONAL: INDICE ANALITICO ALFABETICO..., 1917-1937. Santo Domingo: n.p., 1939.

180. Gautier Mayoral, Carmen. "Apuntes sobre la represión actual en Puerto Rico." CASA DE LAS AMERICAS (Cuba) 21(1980): 26-38.

181. Gellman, Irvin F. ROOSEVELT AND BATISTA: GOOD NEIGHBOR DIPLOMACY IN CUBA, 1933-1945. Albuquerque: University of New Mexico Press, 1973.

182. Gerosa, Guido, ed. I DOCUMENTI TERRIBLI: I MISSILI A CUBA. Milan: A. Mondadori Editore, 1974.

183. Ghent, Jocelyn Maynard. "Canada, the United States, and the Cuban Missile Crisis." PACIFIC HISTORICAL REVIEW 48 (1979): 159-84.

184. Gilbert, Gregorio Urbano. MI LUCHA CONTRA EL INVASOR YANQUI DE 1916. Santo Domingo: Editora de la Universidad Autónoma de Santo Domingo, 1975.

185. Gillingham, Arthur, and Barry Roseman. THE CUBAN MISSILE CRISIS. Los Angeles: Center for the Study of Armament and Disarmament, 1976.

186. Gilmore, William C. THE GRENADA INTERVENTION: ANALYSIS AND DOCUMENTATION. New York: Mansell Publications, Facts on File, 1984.

187. Giménez, Armando. SIERRA MAESTRA: LA REVOLUCION DE FIDEL CASTRO. Buenos Aires: Editorial Lautaro, 1959.

188. Gleijeses, Piero. THE DOMINICAN CRISIS: THE 1965 CONSTITUTIONALIST REVOLT AND AMERICAN INTERVENTION. Baltimore: Johns Hopkins University Press, 1978.

189. Goldenberg, Boris. THE CUBAN REVOLUTION AND LATIN AMERICA. New York: Praeger Publishers, 1965.

190. Goldwert, Marvin. THE CONSTABULARY IN THE DOMINICAN REPUBLIC AND NICARAGUA: PROGENY AND LEGACY OF U.S. INTERVENTION. Gainesville: University of Florida Press, 1962.

191. González, Edward. "U.S. Strategic Interest in the Caribbean." In THE CARIBBEAN AND WORLD POLITICS: CROSS CURRENTS AND CLEAVAGES. Edited by Jorge Heine and Leslie Manigat. New York: Holmes and Meier, 1988.

192. González, Emilio T. "The Development of the Cuban Army." MIILITARY REVIEW 61 (1981): 56-64.

193. González, María Filomena. LINEA NOROESTE: TESTIMONIO DEL PATRIOTISMO OLVIDADO. San Pedro de Macorís, Dominican Republic: Universidad Central del Este, 1985.

194. ———. "Las resistencias a la primera ocupación militar norteamericana, 1916-1924." Paper presented at the Conference on the Dominican Republic, Rutgers University, Newark, N.J., April 1986.

195. González, Raúl. GENTE DE PLAYA GIRON. Havana: Ediciones Venceremos, 1962.

196. Goodhart, Philip. FIFTY SHIPS THAT SAVED THE WORLD: THE FOUNDATIONS OF THE ANGLO-AMERICAN ALLIANCE. Garden City: Doubleday, 1965.

197. Greenberg, Lawrence M. UNITED STATES ARMY UNILATERAL AND COALITION OPERATIONS IN THE 1965 DOMINICAN REPUBLIC INTERVENTION. Washington: U.S. Army Center for Military History, 1987.

198. Greene, J. Edward. "Cooperativism, Militarism, Party Politics and Democracy in Guyana." In THE NEWER CARIBBEAN: DECOLONIZATION, DEMOCRACY, AND DEVELOPMENT, 257-80. Edited by Paget Henry and Carl Stone. Philadelphia: Institute for the Study of Human Issues, 1983.

199. Greene, James R., and Brent Scowcroft. WESTERN INTERESTS AND U.S. POLICY OPTIONS IN THE CARIBBEAN BASIN: REPORT OF THE ATLANTIC COUNCIL'S WORKING GROUP ON THE CARIBBEAN BASIN. Boston: Oelgeschlager, Gunn and Hain, 1984.

200. GRENADA: WHOSE FREEDOM? London: Latin American Bureau, 1984.

201. Grinevich, E.A. VASHINGTON PROTIV GAVANY: RUBINSKAYA REVOLUTSIIA I IMPERIALIZM. Moscow: Mezhdunar Otnosheniia, 1982.

202. Guerra y Sánchez, Ramiro. EN EL CAMINO DE LA INDEPENDENCIA. Havana: Editorial de Ciencias Sociales, 1974.

203. Guevara, Ernesto [Che]. LA GUERRA DE GUERRILLAS. Havana: Departamento de Instrucción de MINFAR, 1960.

204. ———. PASAJES DE LA GUERRA REVOLUCIONARIA. Medellín: Editorial Z, 1971.

205. ———. REMINISCENCES OF THE CUBAN REVOLU-TIONARY WAR. New York: Monthly Review Press, 1968.

206. ———. TRES COMBATES. Havana: Editora Juvenil, 1965.

207. Guión Sierra, Jimmy, et al. LA GUERRA DE ABRIL. Santo Domingo: Producciones la Causa, 1965.

208. Guyana. Ministry of Foreign Affairs. SAFEGUARDING THE SECURITY OF SMALL STATES. Georgetown: Ministry of Foreign Affairs, 1982.

209. Haakmat, Andre. DE REVOLUTIE UITGEGLEDEN. Amsterdam: Jan Mets, 1987.

210. Halliday, Fred. "An Ambiguous Turning Point: Grenada and Its Aftermath." NACLA REPORT ON THE AMERICAS, November-December 1984, 20-31.

211. Hart, Major Franklin A. (USMC). "A Critical Analysis of the Initiation, Organization, Operations and Policies of the Garde d'Haiti." Senior School Thesis, 1935. Breckenridge Library, USMC.

212. ———. THE HISTORY OF THE GARDE D'HAITI. Port-au-Prince: Headquarters, Garde d'Haiti, 1934. Breckenridge Library, USMC.

213. Harvey, Mose L. SOVIET COMBAT TROOPS IN CUBA: IMPLICATIONS OF THE CARTER SOLUTION FOR THE USSR. Coral Gables: Advanced International Studies Institute, University of Miami, 1979.

214. Hayes, Margaret Daly. LATIN AMERICA AND THE U.S. NATIONAL INTEREST: A BASIS FOR U.S. FOREIGN POLICY. Boulder: Westview Press, 1983.

215. Healey, David F. GUNBOAT DIPLOMACY IN THE WILSON ERA: THE U.S. NAVY IN HAITI, 1915-1916. Madison: University of Wisconsin Press, 1976.

216. ———. THE UNITED STATES IN CUBA, 1898-1902: GENERALS, POLITICIANS AND THE SEARCH FOR POLICY. Madison: University of Wisconsin Press, 1963.

217. Heine, Jorge, and Leslie Manigat, eds. THE CARIBBEAN AND WORLD POLITICS: CROSS CURRENTS AND CLEAVAGES. New York: Holmes and Meier, 1988.

218. Heinl, Robert Debs, Jr. SOLDIERS OF THE SEA: THE UNITED STATES MARINE CORPS, 1775-1962. Annapolis: United States Naval Institute, 1962.

219. Heinl, Robert Debs, Jr., and Nancy Gordon Heinl. WRITTEN IN BLOOD: THE STORY OF THE HAITIAN PEOPLE, 1492-1971. Boston: Houghton Mifflin, 1978.

220. Hermann, Hamlet. CARACOLES: LA GUERRILLA DE CAAMANO. Santo Domingo: Editora El País, 1980.

221. ———. DE HEROES, DE PUEBLOS. Santo Domingo: Editora Alfa y Omega, 1979.

222. ———. FRANCISCO CAAMANO. Santo Domingo: Editora Alfa y Omega, 1983.

223. Higgins, Trumbull. THE PERFECT FAILURE: KENNEDY, EISENHOWER, AND THE CIA AT THE BAY OF PIGS. New York: W.W. Norton, 1987.

224. Higham, Robin, and Donald J. Mrozek, eds. A GUIDE TO THE SOURCES OF UNITED STATES MILITARY HISTORY. Hamden, Conn.: Archon Books, 1975.

225. Hillsman, Roger. TO MOVE A NATION. Garden City: Doubleday, 1967.

226. Hitchman, James H. LEONARD WOOD AND CUBAN INDEPENDENCE, 1898-1902. The Hague: Martinus Nijhoff, 1971.

227. Horelick, Arnold Lawrence. THE CUBAN MISSILE CRISIS. Santa Monica: Rand Corporation, 1963.

228. Horowitz, Irving Louis. "Military Origins of the Cuban Revolution." ARMED FORCES AND SOCIETY 1(1975): 402-18.

229. Hunt, E. Howard. GIVE US THIS DAY. New Rochelle: Arlington House, 1973.

230. Ibarra, Jorge. "Agosto de 1906: Una intervención armada." REVISTA DE LA BIBLIOTECA NACIONAL JOSE MARTI (Cuba) 15(1973): 161-86.

231. Iglesias, Joel. DE LA SIERRA MAESTRA AL ESCAMBRAY. Havana: Editorial Letras Cubanas, 1979.

232. Jackson, D. Bruce. CASTRO, THE KREMLIN, AND COMMUNISM IN LATIN AMERICA. Baltimore: Johns Hopkins University Press, 1969.

233. Jacquier, B. "L'intervention des Etats-Unis a Grenade." ARES: DEFENSE ET SECURITE (France) (1984-85).

234. James, Daniel, and John G. Hubbell. STRIKE IN THE WEST: THE COMPLETE STORY OF THE CUBAN CRISIS. New York: Holt, Rinehart, and Winston, 1963.

235. Jaramillo Edwards, Isabel. LA ESTRATEGIA INTERVENCIONISTA ESTADOUNIDENSE HACIA EL MEDIO ORIENTE Y EN LA "CUENCA DEL CARIBE." Havana: Centro de Estudios Sobre el Caribe, 1983.

236. Johnson, Haynes Bonner. THE BAY OF PIGS: THE LEADERS' STORY OF BRIGADE 2506. New York: W.W. Norton, 1964.

237. Johnson, Howard. "The United States and the Establishment of the Anglo-American Caribbean Commission." JOURNAL OF CARIBBEAN HISTORY (Barbados) 19 (1984) 26-47.

238. Johnson, John J. THE MILITARY AND SOCIETY IN LATIN AMERICA. Stanford: Stanford University Press, 1964.

239. Johnstone, John H., comp. AN ANNOTATED BIBLIOGRAPHY OF THE UNITED STATES MARINES IN GUERRILLA, ANTI-GUERRILLA, AND SMALL WAR ACTIONS. Washington: U.S. Marine Corps Historical Branch, 1962.

240. Judson, C. Fred. "Continuity and Evolution of Revolutionary Symbolism in VERDE OLIVO, 233-50." In CUBA: TWENTY-FIVE YEARS OF REVOLUTION. Edited by Sandor Halebsky and John M. Kirk. New York: Praeger Publishers, 1985.

241. ———. CUBA AND THE REVOLUTIONARY MYTH: THE POLITICAL EDUCATION OF THE CUBAN REBEL ARMY, 1953-1963. Boulder: Westview Press, 1985.

242. Keegan, John, ed. WORLD ARMIES. New York: Facts on File, 1979.

243. Kennedy, R., et al. THE ROLE OF THE U.S. MILITARY: CARIBBEAN BASIN FINAL REPORT. Carlisle Barracks, Pa.: Strategic Studies Institute, U.S. Army War College, 1981.

244. Kennedy, Robert F. THIRTEEN DAYS: A MEMOIR OF THE CUBAN MISSILE CRISIS. New York: W.W. Norton, 1969.

245. Khachaturov, Karen Armenovich. BOL I GNEV GRENADY. Moscow: Sov. Rossiia, 1985.

246. Klare, Michael T., and Cynthia Aronson. SUPPLYING REPRESSION: U.S. SUPPORT FOR AUTHORITARIAN REGIMES ABROAD, 1977. Washington: Institute for Policy Studies, 1981.

247. Knight, Melvin M. THE AMERICANS IN SANTO DOMINGO. New York: Vanguard Press, 1928.

248. Kryzanek, Michael J., and Howard J. Wiarda. THE DOMINICAN REPUBLIC: A CARIBBEAN CRUCIBLE. Boulder: Westview Press, 1982.

249. Kula, Marcin. REVOLUCJA 1933 ROKU NA KUBIE. Warsaw: Zaklad Narodowy im. Ossaloinskich, 1978.

250. Kurzman, Dan. SANTO DOMINGO: REVOLT OF THE DAMNED. New York: Putnam, 1965.

251. Kuser, J. Dryden. HAITI: ITS DAWN OF PROGRESS AFTER YEARS IN A NIGHT OF REVOLUTION. Boston: R.G. Badger, 1921. Reprinted: Westport: Negro Universities Press, 1970.

252. Lamar Schweyer, Alberto. COMO CAYO EL PRESIDENTE MACHADO. Madrid: Espasa-Calpe, 1941.

253. Lambrecht, Rainer. "Prezedenfall fur 'Schnelles Eingreifen': Die militarische Intervention der USA in der Dominikanischen Republik, 1965-1966." MILITARGESCHICHTE (East Germany) 22 (1983): 413-24.

254. Langley, Lester D. THE BANANA WARS: AN INNER HISTORY OF AMERICAN EMPIRE, 1900-1934. Lexington: University of Kentucky Press, 1983.

255. ———. THE UNITED STATES AND THE CARIBBEAN IN THE TWENTIETH CENTURY. Athens: University of Georgia Press, 1982.

256. ———, ed. THE UNITED STATES, CUBA AND THE COLD WAR. Lexington, Mass.: D.C. Heath, 1970.

257. Larkin, Bruce D., ed. VITAL INTERESTS: THE SOVIET ISSUE IN U.S. CENTRAL AMERICAN POLICY. Boulder: Lynne Rienner Publishers, 1988.

258. Larson, David L., ed. THE CUBAN CRISIS OF 1962: SELECTED DOCUMENTS AND CHRONOLOGY. Boston: Houghton Mifflin, 1963.

259. Latorre, Eduardo. POLITICA DOMINICANA CONTEMPORANEA. Santo Domingo: Instituto Tecnológico de Santo Domingo, 1979.

260. Lazo, Mario. DAGGER IN THE HEART: AMERICAN POLICY FAILURES IN CUBA. New York: Funk and Wagnalls, 1968.

261. Leighton, Richard M. THE CUBAN MISSILE CRISIS OF 1962: A CASE IN NATIONAL SECURITY CRISIS MANAGEMENT. Washington: National Defense University, 1978.

262. Leiken, Robert S. "Soviet and Cuban Policy in the Caribbean Basin," 447-77. In REVOLUTION AND COUNTERREVOLUTION IN CENTRAL AMERICA AND THE CARIBBEAN. Edited by Donald E. Schulz and Douglas H. Graham. Boulder: Westview Press, 1984.

263. ———. SOVIET STRATEGY IN LATIN AMERICA. New York: Praeger Publishers, 1982. Published for the Center for Strategic and International Studies, Georgetown University, Washington, DC.

264. LeoGrande, William M. "Civil-Military Relations in Cuba: Party Control and Political Socialization." STUDIES IN COMPARATIVE COMMUNISM 11(1978): 278-91.

265. ———. "Cuban-Soviet Relations and Cuban Policy in Africa." CUBAN STUDIES/ESTUDIOS CUBANOS 10(1980): 1-37.

266. ———. CUBA'S POLICY IN AFRICA. Berkeley: Institute of International Studies, University of California, 1980.

267. ———. "The Politics of Revolutionary Development: Civil-Military Relations in Cuba, 1959-1976." JOURNAL OF STRATEGIC STUDIES 1(1978): 260-94.

268. Levesque, Jacques. THE U.S.S.R. AND THE CUBAN REVOLUTION. New York: Praeger Publishers, 1978.

269. Levine, Barry B., ed. THE NEW CUBAN PRESENCE IN THE CARIBBEAN. Boulder: Westview Press, 1983.

270. Levitin, M. J. "The Law of Force and the Force of Law: Grenada, the Falklands, and Humanitarian Intervention." HARVARD INTERNATIONAL LAW JOURNAL 27(1986): 621-57.

271. Lewis, Gary P. "Prospects for a Regional Security System in the Eastern Caribbean." MILLENIUM 15(1986): 73-90.

272. Lewis, Gordon K. GRENADA: THE JEWEL DESPOILED. Baltimore: Johns Hopkins University Press, 1987.

273. Leyburn, James G. THE HAITIAN PEOPLE. New Haven: Yale University Press, 1941.

274. Lieuwen, Edwin. GENERALS VS. PRESIDENTS: NEO-MILITARISM IN LATIN AMERICA. New York: Praeger Publishers, 1964.

275. Lieuwen, Edwin, and Nelson P. Valdés. THE CUBAN REVOLUTION: A RESEARCH GUIDE, 1959-1969. Albuquerque: University of New Mexico Press, 1971.

276. Light, Robert E., and Carl Marzani. CUBA VS. THE C.I.A. New York: Marzani and Munsell, 1961.

277. Lima, Alfredo. LA ODISEA DE RIO VERDE. Havana: Cultural, 1934.

278. Llano Montes, Antonio. SANTO DOMINGO: BARRICADAS DE ODIOS. Mexico City: Editores Mexicanos Unidos, 1966.

279. Lockmiller, David A. MAGOON IN CUBA: A HISTORY OF THE SECOND INTERVENTION, 1906-1909. Chapel Hill: University of North Carolina Press, 1938.

280. López Segrera, Francisco. EL CONFLICTO CUBA-ESTADOS UNIDOS Y LA CRISIS CENTROAMERICANA, 1959-1984. Mexico City: Editorial Nuestro Tiempo, 1985.

281. Lowenthal, Abraham F. THE DOMINICAN INTERVENTION. Cambridge: Harvard University Press, 1972.

282. ———. "The Political Role of the Dominican Armed Forces: A Note on the 1963 Overthrow of Juan Bosch and on the 1965 Dominican 'Revolution.' " JOURNAL OF INTER-AMERICAN STUDIES AND WORLD AFFAIRS 15(1973): 355-61.

283. Luce, Phillip A. THE NEW IMPERIALISM: CUBA AND THE SOVIETS IN AFRICA. Washington: Council for Inter-American Security, 1979.

284. Lutskov, N.D. OKKUPATSIIA GAITI SOEDINENNYMI SHTATAMI, 1915-1934. Moscow: n.p., 1981.

285. Macaulay, Neill. A REBEL IN CUBA: AN AMERICAN'S MEMOIR. Chicago: Quadrangle Books, 1970.

286. McCrocklin, James H. GARDE D'HAITI, 1915-1934: TWENTY YEARS OF ORGANIZATION AND TRAINING BY THE UNITED STATES MARINE CORPS. Annapolis: United States Naval Training Institute, 1956.

287. MacDonald, Brian. CANADA, THE CARIBBEAN, AND CENTRAL AMERICA. Toronto: Canadian Institute of Strategic Studies, 1986.

288. MacDonald, Scott B. "The Future of Foreign Aid in the Caribbean after Grenada: Finlandization and Confrontation in the

Eastern Tier." INTER-AMERICAN ECONOMIC AFFAIRS 38 (1985): 59-74.

289. McFarlane, Malcolm. "The Military in the Commonwealth Caribbean: A Study in Comparative Institutionalization." Ph.D. dissertation, University of Western Ontario, 1974.

290. MacFarlane, Neil. INTERVENTION AND REGIONAL SECURITY. London: International Institute for Strategic Studies, 1985.

291. MacFarlane, S. Neil. SUPERPOWER RIVALRY AND SOVIET POLICY IN THE CARIBBEAN BASIN. Ottawa: Canadian Institute for International Peace and Security, 1986.

292. McIntire, Alexander Haywood, Jr. "Revolution and Intervention in Grenada: Strategic and Geopolitical Implications." Ph.D. dissertation, University of Miami, 1984.

293. McManus, Jane, ed. FROM THE PALM TREE: VOICES FROM THE CUBAN REVOLUTION. Secaucus, N.J.: Lyle Stuart, 1983.

294. MacMichael, David C. "High Tide of Empire: The American Occupation of the Dominican Republic, 1916-1924." M.A. thesis, University of Oregon, 1960.

295. ———. "The United States and the Dominican Republic, 1871-1940: A Cycle in Caribbean Diplomacy." Ph.D. dissertation, University of Oregon, 1964.

296. Mallin, Jay. CARIBBEAN CRISIS. Garden City: Doubleday, 1965.

297. ———. CUBA IN ANGOLA. Coral Gables: Research Institute for Cuban Studies, University of Miami, 1987.

298. ———, ed. "CHE" GUEVARA ON REVOLUTION: A DOCUMENTARY OVERVIEW. Coral Gables: University of Miami Press, 1969.

299. Malo de Molina, Gustavo F. FRANK PAIS: APUNTES SOBRE UN LUCHADOR CLANDESTINO. Havana: Editorial Gente Nueva, 1979.

300. Mañach, Jorge. EL MILITARISMO EN CUBA. Havana: Seone, Fernández, 1939.

301. Manigat, Leslie. "Grenada: Revolutionary Shockwave, Crisis, and Intervention." In THE CARIBBEAN AND WORLD POLITICS: CROSS CURRENTS AND CLEAVAGES. Edited by Jorge Heine and Leslie Manigat. New York: Holmes and Meier, 1988.

302. Manrara, Louis V. BETRAYAL OPENED THE DOOR TO RUSSIAN MISSILES IN RED CUBA. Miami: Truth About Cuba Committee, 1968.

303. Mansbach, Richard W., ed. DOMINICAN CRISIS, 1965. New York: Facts on File, 1971.

304. Mariñez, Pablo A. "The Armed Forces in the Dominican Republic: Professionalization and Politicization." Paper presented at the Conference on Peace and Development in the Caribbean, University of the West Indies, Mona, Jamaica, May 1988.

305. ———. INJERENCIAS, AGRESIONES E INTERVENCIONES NORTEAMERICANAS EN LA REPUBLICA DOMINICANA: BIBLIOGRAFIA BASICA PARA SU ESTUDIO. Santo Domingo: Editorial Universitaria, 1985.

306. ———. RESISTENCIA CAMPESINA, IMPERIALISMO Y REFORMA AGRARIA EN LA REPUBLICA DOMINICANA, 1899-1978. Santo Domingo: Ediciones CEPAE, 1984.

307. Marshall, Samuel Lyman Atwood. THE WAR TO FREE CUBA: THE MILITARY HISTORY OF THE SPANISH-AMERICAN WAR. New York: Franklin Watts, 1966.

308. Martin, John Barlow. OVERTAKEN BY EVENTS: THE DOMINICAN CRISIS FROM THE FALL OF TRUJILLO TO THE CIVIL WAR. Garden City: Doubleday, 1966.

309. Martínez, Aurelio, ed. HISTORIA DE UNA AGRESION: DECLARACIONES Y DOCUMENTOS DEL JUICIO SEGUIDO A LA BRIGADA MERCENARIA ORGANIZADA POR LOS IMPERIALISTAS YANQUIS QUE INVADIO A CUBA EL 17 DE ABRIL DE 1961. Havana: Ediciones Venceremos, 1962.

310. Masetti, Jorge. LOS QUE LUCHAN Y LOS QUE LLORAN. Buenos Aires: Editorial Jorge Alvarez, 1969.

311. Mateo, Maricela. "El ejército oligárquico en la política neocolonial cubana, 1925-1952." SANTIAGO (Cuba) 22 (1976): 87-120.

312. Matthews, Herbert L. FIDEL CASTRO. New York: Simon and Schuster, 1969.

313. Mayo, José. LA GUERRILLA SE VISTIO DE YAREY. Havana: Editora Política, 1979.

314. Medina Benet, Víctor M. LOS RESPONSABLES: FRACASO DE LA TERCERA REPUBLICA. 2d ed. Santo Domingo: Amigo del Hogar, 1976.

315. Medina Peña, Luis. EL SISTEMA BIPOLAR EN TENSION: LA CRISIS DE OCTUBRE DE 1962. Mexico City: El Colegio de México, 1971.

316. Medland, William J. THE CUBAN MISSILE CRISIS OF 1962: NEEDLESS OR NECESSARY? New York: Praeger Publishers, 1988.

317. Mencía, Mario. EL GRITO DEL MONCADA. 2 vols. Havana: Editora Política, 1986.

318. Merle, Robert. MONCADA: PREMIER COMBAT DE FIDEL CASTRO, 26 JUILLET 1953. Paris: R. Laffont, 1965.

319. Mesa-Lago, Carmelo, and June S. Belkin, eds. CUBA IN AFRICA. Pittsburgh: University of Pittsburgh Press, 1982.

320. Meyer, Karl E., and Tad Szulc. THE CUBAN INVASION: THE CHRONICLE OF A DISASTER. New York: Praeger Publishers, 1962.

321. Meyn, Marianne. EL APARATO MILITAR NORTEAMERICANO EN PUERTO RICO. Santo Domingo: Ediciones EDOC, 1982.

322. Meyn, Marianne, and J. Rodríguez. "El aparato militar norteamericano en Puerto Rico." CASA DE LAS AMERICAS (Cuba) 21 (1980): 7-25.

323. ———. PUERTO RICO: VICTIMA DE LOS PLANES INTERVENCIONISTAS DE LOS ESTADOS UNIDOS EN EL CARIBE. Río Piedras: Consejo de la Paz de Puerto Rico, 1982.

324. Millet, Kethly. LES PAYSANS HAITIENS ET L'OCCUPATION AMERICAINE D'HAITI, 1915-1930. Montreal: Collectif Paroles, 1979.

325. Millett, Allan Reed. "The General Staff and the Cuban Intervention of 1906." MILITARY AFFAIRS 31(1967): 113-19.

326. ———. THE POLITICS OF INTERVENTION: THE MILITARY OCCUPATION OF CUBA, 1906-1909. Columbus: Ohio State University Press, 1968.

327. ———. "The Rise and Fall of the Cuban Rural Guard, 1898-1911." THE AMERICAS 29 (1972): 191-213.

328. ———. SEMPER FIDELIS: THE HISTORY OF THE UNITED STATES MARINE CORPS. New York: Macmillan, 1980.

329. Millett, Richard, and G. Dale Gaddy. "Administering the Protectorates: The U.S. Occupation of Haiti and the Dominican Republic." REVISTA/REVIEW INTERAMERICANA 6 (1976): 383-402.

330. Millsbaugh, Arthur Chester. HAITI UNDER AMERICAN CONTROL, 1915-1930. Boston: World Peace Foundation, 1931.

331. Minger, Ralph Eldin. "William H. Taft and the United States Intervention in Cuba in 1966." HISPANIC AMERICAN HISTORICAL REVIEW 41(1961): 75-89.

332. MONCADA: EDICION HOMENAJE AL VIGESIMO ANIVERSARIO DEL 26 DE JULIO DE 1953. Havana: Editorial de Ciencias Sociales del Instituto Cubano del Libro, 1973.

333. Montague, Ludwell Lee. HAITI AND THE UNITED STATES, 1714-1938. Durham: Duke University Press, 1940.

334. Montenegro González, Augusto. "Ejércitos, partidos e intervenciones norteamericanas en Cuba, 1899-1959." UNIVERSITAS HUMANISTICA (Colombia) 11(1982): 7-90.

335. Moore, John Norton. LAW AND THE GRENADA MISSION. Charlottesville: Center for Law and National Security, University of Virginia, 1984.

336. Moorer, Thomas H., and Georges A. Fauriol. CARIBBEAN BASIN SECURITY. New York: Praeger Publishers, 1984. Published for the Center for Strategic and International Studies, Georgetown University, Washington, DC.

337. Moreno, José Antonio, BARRIOS IN ARMS: REVOLUTION IN SANTO DOMINGO. Pittsburgh: University of Pittsburgh Press, 1970.

338. Morison, Samuel Eliot. HISTORY OF UNITED STATES NAVAL OPERATIONS IN WORLD WAR II. Vol. 10. Boston: Little, Brown, 1956.

339. Morley, Morris M. IMPERIAL STATE AND REVOLUTION: THE UNITED STATES AND CUBA, 1952-1986. New York: Cambridge University Press, 1987.

340. Morris, Curtis S., Jr. THE UNITED STATES-CARIBBEAN BASIN MILITARY CONNECTION: A PERSPECTIVE ON REGIONAL MILITARY-TO-MILITARY RELATIONSHIPS. Washington: American Enterprise Institute, 1983.

341. Morris, Michael Alan. "The Problem of Control of American Military Interventions: Vietnam and the Dominican Republic." Ph.D. dissertation, Johns Hopkins University, 1971.

342. Moskin, J. Robert. THE U.S. MARINE CORPS STORY. New York: McGraw-Hill, 1977.

343. Moss, Robert, ed. THE STABILITY OF THE CARIBBEAN: REPORT OF A SEMINAR HELD AT DITCHLEY PARK, OXFORDSHIRE, U.K., MAY 1973. Washington: Center for Strategic and International Studies, Georgetown University, 1973.

344. Motley, James Berry. "Grenada: Low-Intensity Conflict and the Use of U.S. Military Power." WORLD AFFAIRS 146(1983-84): 221-38.

345. Muller Rojas, Alberto A. "El armamentismo en el Caribe." In GEOPOLITICA DE LAS RELACIONES DE VENEZUELA CON EL CARIBE. Edited by Andrés Serbín. Caracas: Fundación Fondo Editorial, Acta Científica Venezolana, 1983.

346. Muñoz Rivera, Manuel. ¿HACIA DONDE, HEROES?: LA HISTORIA TRAGICOMICA BELICA EN ESTA SEGUNDA GUERRA MUNDIAL DE LOS SOLDADOS PUERTORRIQUENOS PERTENECIENTES AL REGIMIENTO REGULAR DE PUERTO RICO, 65 DE INFANTERIA. New York: Azteca Press, 1948.

347. Munro, Dana Gardner. INTERVENTION AND DOLLAR DIPLOMACY IN THE CARIBBEAN, 1900-1921. Princeton: Princeton University Press, 1964.

348. ———. THE UNITED STATES AND THE CARIBBEAN REPUBLICS, 1921-1933. Princeton: Princeton University Press, 1974.

349. Murray, David. "Garrisoning the Caribbean: A Chapter in Canadian Military History." REVISTA INTERAMERICANA (Puerto Rico) 7 (1977): 73-86.

350. Navas, José. LA CONVULSION DE FEBRERO. Matanzas, Cuba: Imprenta El Escritorio, 1917.

351. Newsom, David D. THE SOVIET BRIGADE IN CUBA: A STUDY IN POLITICAL DIPLOMACY. Bloomington: Indiana University Press, 1987.

352. Nicholls, David. FROM DESSALINES TO DUVALIER: RACE, COLOUR AND NATIONAL INDEPENDENCE IN HAITI. New York: Cambridge University Press, 1979.

353. Nicolas, Hogar. L'OCCUPATION AMERICIANE D'HAITI: LA REVANCHE DE L'HISTOIRE. Madrid: Industrias Gráficas España, n.d.

354. Niedergang, Marcel. LA REVOLUTION DE SAINT-DOMINGUE. Paris: Librairie PLON, 1966.

355. Nitoburg, E., A.S. Fetisov, and P.P. Iakovlev. TRAGEDIIA GRENADY. Moscow: "Mysl," 1984.

356. Nodal, Roberto. THE CUBAN PRESENCE IN AFRICA. Madison: University of Wisconsin Press, 1980.

357. NOTES HISTORIQUES: ARMEE D'HAITI, 1915-1950; PUBLIEES A L'OCCASION DU CENT-CINQUANTENAIRE DE L'INDEPENDENCE NATIONALE, 1ER JANVIER 1954. Port-au-Prince: n.p., 1953.

358. OPERATION ZAPATA: THE "ULTRASENSITIVE" REPORT AND TESTIMONY OF THE BOARD OF INQUIRY ON THE BAY OF PIGS. Frederick, Md.: University Publications of America, 1981.

359. Organization of American States. FUERZA INTERAMERICANA DE PAZ. Washington: Pan American Union, 1966.

360. Ornes, Germán E. TRUJILLO: LITTLE CAESAR OF THE CARIBBEAN. New York: Thomas Nelson and Sons, 1958.

361. O'Shaughnessy, Hugh. GRENADA: AN EYEWITNESS ACCOUNT OF THE U.S. INVASION AND THE CARIBBEAN HISTORY THAT PROVOKED IT. New York: Dodd, Mead Company, 1984.

362. Otero, Lisandro. PLAYA GIRON: DERROTA DEL IMPERIALISMO. 4 vols. Havana: Ediciones Venceremos, 1961-62.

363. Otero Echevarría, Rafael. REPORTAJE A UNA REVOLUCION: DE BATISTA A FIDEL CASTRO. 2d ed. Santiago, Chile: Editorial del Pacífico, 1959.

364. THE OTHER SIDE OF U.S. POLICY TOWARDS THE CARIBBEAN: RECOLONIZATION AND MILITARIZATION. Río Piedras: Caribbean Project for Peace and Justice, 1988.

365. Ovalles, Alejandro. CAAMANO: EL GOBIERNO Y LAS GUERRILLAS. Santo Domingo: n.p., 1973.

366. Pachter, Henry M. COLLISION COURSE: THE CUBAN MISSILE CRISIS AND COEXISTENCE. New York: Praeger Publishers, 1963.

367. Padmore, George. HAITI: AN AMERICAN SLAVE COLONY. Moscow: Centrizdat, 1931.

368. Padrón, Antonio E. El "65" EN REVISTA: DATOS HISTORICOS, RELATOS Y ANECDOTAS, TIPOS Y CUENTOS DEL REGIMIENTO. New York: Las Américas Publishing, 1961.

369. Palmer, Annette C., "Black American Soldiers in Trinidad, 1942-44: Wartime Politics in a Colonial Society." JOURNAL OF IMPERIAL AND COMMONWEALTH HISTORY (Great Britain) 14(1986): 203-18.

370. ———. "The United States and the Commonwealth Caribbean, 1940-1945." Ph.D. dissertation, Fordham University, 1979.

371. Palmer, Bruce. INTERVENTION IN THE CARIBBEAN: THE DOMINICAN CRISIS OF 1965. Lexington: University Press of Kentucky, 1989.

372. Pantojas García, Emilio. "Restoring Hegemony: The Complementarity of the Security, Economic and Political Components of U.S. Policy in the Caribbean Basin during the 1980s." Paper presented at the Conference on Peace and Development in the Caribbean, University of the West Indies, Mona, Jamaica, May 1988.

373. Pardo Llada, José. EL CHE QUE YO CONOCI. Medellín: n.p., 1970.

374. ———. MEMORIAS DE LA SIERRA MAESTRA. Havana: Editorial Tierra Nueva, 1960.

375. Pavón, Luís, ed. DIAS DEL COMBATE. Havana: Instituto del Libro, 1970.

376. Payne, Anthony J. THE INTERNATIONAL CRISIS IN THE CARIBBEAN. Baltimore: Johns Hopkins University Press, 1984.

377. Payne, Anthony J., Paul Sutton, and Tony Thorndike. GRENADA: REVOLUTION AND INVASION. New York: St. Martin's Press, 1984.

378. Pearce, Jenny. UNDER THE EAGLE: U.S. INTERVENTION IN CENTRAL AMERICA AND THE CARIBBEAN. Boston: South End Press, 1982.

379. Peláez Ruíz, Eugenio José. CODIGO DE JUSTICIA DE LAS FUERZAS ARMADAS. Santo Domingo: Editora Corripio, 1984.

380. Peraza Sarausa, Fermín, ed. REVOLUTIONARY CUBA: A BIBLIOGRAPHICAL GUIDE. 3 vols. Coral Gables: University of Miami Press, 1966-68.

381. Pérez, Louis A., Jr. "Armies of the Caribbean: Historical Perspectives, Historiographical Trends." LATIN AMERICAN PERSPECTIVES 14(1987): 490-507.

382. ———. ARMY POLITICS IN CUBA, 1898-1958. Pittsburgh: University of Pittsburgh Press, 1976.

383. ———. "Army Politics in Socialist Cuba." JOURNAL OF LATIN AMERICAN STUDIES 5(1976): 251-71.

384. ———. CUBA: BETWEEN EMPIRES, 1878-1902. Pittsburgh: University of Pittsburgh Press, 1983.

385. ———. CUBA: BETWEEN REFORM AND REVOLUTION. New York: Oxford University Press, 1988.

386. ———. CUBA UNDER THE PLATT AMENDMENT, 1902-1934. Pittsburgh: University of Pittsburgh Press, 1986.

387. ———. "The Cuban Revolution Twenty-Five Years Later: A Survey of Sources, Scholarship, and the State of the Literature." In CUBA: TWENTY-FIVE YEARS OF REVOLUTION, 1959-1984, 393-412. Edited by Sandor Halebsky and John M. Kirk. New York: Praeger Publishers, 1985.

388. ——. THE CUBAN REVOLUTIONARY WAR, 1953-1958. Metuchen, N.J.: Scarecrow Press, 1976.

389. ——. "Dollar Diplomacy, Preventative Intervention and the Platt Amendment in Cuba, 1909-1912." INTER-AMERICAN ECONOMIC AFFAIRS 38(1984): 22-44.

390. ——. HISTORIOGRAPHY IN THE REVOLUTION: A BIBLIOGRAPHY OF CUBAN SCHOLARSHIP, 1959-1979. New York: Garland Publishing, 1982.

391. ——. "Intervention, Hegemony, and Dependency: The United States in the Circum-Caribbean, 1898-1980." PACIFIC HISTORICAL REVIEW 51(1982): 165-94.

392. ——. INTERVENTION, REVOLUTION AND POLITICS IN CUBA, 1913-1921. Pittsburgh: University of Pittsburgh Press, 1978.

393. ——. LORDS OF THE MOUNTAIN: BANDITRY AND PEASANT PROTEST IN CUBA, 1878-1918. Pittsburgh: University of Pittsburgh Press, 1989.

394. ——. "Politics, Peasants, and People of Color: The 1912 Race War in Cuba Reconsidered." HISPANIC AMERICAN HISTORICAL REVIEW 60(1986): 509-39.

395. ——. "Supervision of a Protectorate: The United States and the Cuban Army, 1898-1908." HISPANIC AMERICAN HISTORICAL REVIEW 52 (1972): 250-71.

396. ——, ed. CUBA: AN ANNOTATED BIBLIOGRAPHY. Westport: Greenwood Press, 1988.

397. Pérez Tarrau, Gabriel. CRONOLOGIA DE UN HEROE. Havana: Gente Nueva, 1976.

398. Perkins, Whitney T. CONSTRAINTS OF EMPIRE: THE UNITED STATES AND CARIBBEAN INTERVENTIONS. Westport: Greenwood Press, 1981.

399. Phillips, Dion E. "Caribbean Militarization: A Response to the Crisis." CONTEMPORARY MARXISM 10 (1985): 92-109.

400. ———. "The Creation, Structure and Training of the Barbados Defense Force." Paper presented at the Conference on Peace and Development, University of the West Indies, Mona, Jamaica, May 1988.

401. Phillips, Dion E., and Alma H. Young. MILITARIZATION IN THE NON-HISPANIC CARIBBEAN. Boulder: Lynne Rienner Publishers, 1986.

402. Pierre-Charles, Gerard. EL CARIBE CONTEMPORANEO. Mexico City: Siglo XXI Editores, 1981.

403. Pino-Santos, Oscar. "Intervencionismo Yanqui en Cuba: De Magoon a Batista." CASA DE LAS AMERICAS (Cuba) 14 (1973): 48-61.

404. Platt, Raye R., et al. THE EUROPEAN POSSESSIONS IN THE CARIBBEAN AREA. New York: American Geographical Society, 1941.

405. Polanyi-Levitt, Kari. "The Origins and Implications of the Caribbean Basin Initiative: Mortgaging Sovereignty." INTERNATIONAL JOURNAL (Canada) 40 (1986) 229-81.

406. Policy Alternatives for the Caribbean and Central America (PACCA). CHANGING COURSE: A BLUEPRINT FOR PEACE IN CENTRAL AMERICA AND THE CARIBBEAN. 2d ed. Washington: Institute for Policy Studies, 1984.

407. Polime, T.S., and H.U.E. Thoden zan Velzen. VLUCHTELINGEN, OPSTANDELINGEN, EN ANDERE BOSNEGERS VAN OOST-SURINAME, 1986-1988. Utrecht: University of Utrecht, 1988.

408. Pope, Ronald R., ed. SOVIET VIEWS ON THE CUBAN MISSILE CRISIS: MYTH AND REALITY IN FOREIGN POLICY ANALYSIS. Washington: University Press of America, 1982.

409. Portuondo, Yolanda, comp. FRANK: SUS ULTIMOS TREINTA DIAS. Havana: Editorial Letras Cubanas, 1986.

410. Pratt, Julius W. AMERICA'S COLONIAL EXPERIMENT. New York: Prentice Hall, 1950.

411. Preston, Richard A. "Caribbean Defense and Security: A Study of the Implications of Canada's 'Special Relationship' with the Commonwealth West Indies." SOUTH ATLANTIC QUARTERLY 70(1971): 317-31.

412. Pryor, Frederic L. REVOLUTIONARY GRENADA: A STUDY IN POLITICAL ECONOMY. New York: Praeger Publishers, 1986.

413. Puerto Rico. Office of the Adjutant General. MANUAL DEL SOLDADO PUERTORRIQUENO. San Juan: Bureau of Supplies, Printing, and Transportation, 1939.

414. ———. REPORT OF THE ADJUTANT GENERAL TO THE GOVERNOR OF PUERTO RICO ON THE OPERATION OF THE MILITARY REGISTRATION AND SELECTIVE DRAFT IN PUERTO RICO. San Juan: Bureau of Supplies, Printing and Transportation, 1924.

415. Quello, J.I., and N. Isa Conde. "Revolutionary Struggle in the Dominican Republic and Its Lessons." WORLD MARXIST REVIEW 8(1965): 92-103, 9(1966): 53-56.

416. Quevedo Pérez, José. LA BATALLA DEL JIGUE. Havana: Instituto Cubano del Libro, 1973.

417. Raful, Tony. LA REVOLUCION DE ABRIL DE 1965. Santo Domingo: Editorial Santo Domingo, 1985.

418. Regan, John Carl. "The Armed Forces of Cuba, 1933-1959." M.A. thesis, University of Florida, 1970.

419. Resource Center. FOCUS ON THE EASTERN CARIBBEAN: BANANAS, BUCKS AND BOOTS. Albuquerque: Resource Center, 1984.

420. Reynolds, Bradley Michael. "Guantánamo Bay, Cuba: The History of an American Naval Base and Its Relationship to the Formulation of United States Foreign Policy and Military Strategy toward the Caribbean, 1895-1910." Ph.D. dissertation, University of Southern California, 1982.

421. Ricardi, Antonio, et al. LA REVOLUCION DOMINICANA DE ABRIL VISTA POR CUBA. Santo Domingo: Universidad Autónoma de Santo Domingo, 1974.

422. Rivera Cuesta, Marcos. LAS FUERZAS ARMADAS Y LA POLITICA DOMINICANA. Santo Domingo: Imprenta Talleres de Artes Gráficas "Luly," 1986.

423. Rivero Méndez, Angel. CRONICA DE LA GUERRA HISPANOAMERICANA EN PUERTO RICO. New York: Plus Ultra Educational Publishers, 1973.

424. Robbins, Carla Anne. THE CUBAN THREAT. New York: McGraw-Hill, 1983.

425. Roberts, Jack L. "The Growing Soviet Naval Presence in the Caribbean: Its Politico-Military Impact upon the United States." NAVAL WAR COLLEGE REVIEW 23(1971): 31-42.

426. Robin, Gabriel. LA CRISE DE CUBA, OCTOBRE 1962. Paris: Economica, 1984.

427. Roca, Sergio. "Economic Aspects of the Cuban Involvement in Africa." CUBAN STUDIES/ESTUDIOS CUBANOS 10 (1980): 55-90.

428. Rodríguez Beruff, Jorge. "El papel estratégico de Puerto Rico en el contexto de la nueva política de Reagan hacia el Caribe." CUADERNOS DE CEREP (Puerto Rico) 5 (1982): 1-16.

429. ———. "Puerto Rico and the Militarization of the Caribbean, 1979-1984." CONTEMPORARY MARXISM 10 (1985): 68-91.

430. Roig de Leuchsenring, Emilio. LA GUERRA LIBERTADORA CUBANA DE LOS TREINTA ANOS, 1868-1898: RAZON DE SU VICTORIA. Havana: n.p., 1952.

431. Rojas, Marta. LA GENERACION DEL CENTENARIO EN EL MONCADA. Havana: Ediciones R, 1964.

432. Rojo del Río, Manuel. LA HISTORIA CAMBIO EN LA SIERRA. San José, Costa Rica: Editorial Texto, 1981.

433. Ronfeldt, David. GEOPOLITICS, SECURITY, AND U.S. STRATEGY IN THE CARIBBEAN BASIN. Santa Monica: Rand Corporation, 1983.

434. Rosell Leyva, Florentino E. LA VERDAD. Miami: n.p., 1960.

435. Roskill, S.W. THE WAR AT SEA, 1939-1945. Vol. 2. London: HMSO, 1956.

436. Rouquié, Alain. L'ETAT MILITAIRE EN AMERIQUE LATINE. Paris: Editions du Seuil, 1982.

437. Rubiera, Daysi, and Miguel Sierra, comps. TESTIMONIOS SOBRE FRANK. Santiago de Cuba: Editorial Oriente, 1978.

438. Samoiloff, Louise Cripps. CALAMITY IN THE CARIBBEAN: PUERTO RICO AND THE BOMB. Cambridge: Schenkman, 1987.

439. Samuels, Michael A., et al. IMPLICATIONS OF SOVIET AND CUBAN ACTIVITIES IN AFRICA FOR UNITED STATES POLICY. Washington: Center for Strategic and International Studies, Georgetown University, 1979.

440. Sandford, Gregory W., and Richard Vigilante. GRENADA: THE UNTOLD STORY. Lanham, Md.: University Press of America, 1984.

441. Santamaría, Haydée. MONCADA. Secaucus, N.J.: Lyle Stuart, 1980.

442. Sarabia, Nydia. FLORO PEREZ. Havana: Editorial Gente Nueva, 1978.

443. Schlesinger, Arthur M., Jr. A THOUSAND DAYS: JOHN F. KENNEDY IN THE WHITE HOUSE. Boston: Houghton Mifflin, 1965.

444. Schmidt, Hans. MAVERICK MARINE: GENERAL SMEDLEY D. BUTLER AND THE CONTRADICTIONS OF AMERICAN MILITARY HISTORY. Lexington: University Press of Kentucky, 1987.

445. ———. THE UNITED STATES OCCUPATION OF HAITI, 1915- 1934. New Brunswick: Rutgers University Press, 1971.

446. Schoenhals, Kai P., and Richard A. Melanson. REVOLUTION AND INTERVENTION IN GRENADA: THE NEW JEWEL MOVEMENT, THE UNITED STATES AND THE CARIBBEAN. Boulder: Westview Press, 1985.

447. Schoonmaker, Herbert Garrettson. "United States Military Forces in the Dominican Crisis of 1965." Ph.D. dissertation, University of Georgia, 1977.

448. Schulz, Donald E., and Douglas H. Graham, eds. REVOLUTION AND COUNTERREVOLUTION IN CENTRAL AMERICA AND THE CARIBBEAN. Boulder: Westview Press, 1984.

449. Seabury, Paul, and Walter A. McDougall. THE GRENADA PAPERS. San Francisco: Institute for Contemporary Studies, 1984.

450. Sedoc-Dahlberg, Betty, ed. THE DUTCH CARIBBEAN: PROSPECTS FOR DEMOCRACY. New York: Gordon and Breach, 1990.

451. ———. "Suriname, 1975-1989: Domestic and Foreign Policies under Military and Civilian Rule." In THE DUTCH CARIBBEAN: PROSPECTS FOR DEMOCRACY. Edited by Betty Sedoc-Dahlberg. New York: Gordon and Breach, 1990.

452. Selser, Gregorio. ¡AQUI, SANTO DOMINGO!: LA TERCERA GUERRA SUCIA. Buenos Aires: Editorial Palestra, 1966.

453. Semidei, Manuela. KENNEDY ET LA REVOLUTION CUBAINE: UN APPRENTISSAGE POLITIQUE? Paris: Julliard, 1972.

454. Shahabuddeen, M. THE CONQUEST OF GRENADA: SOVEREIGNTY IN THE PERIPHERY. Georgetown: University of Guyana, 1986.

455. Shak, St. Raffique. "The Military Crisis in Trinidad and Tobago during 1970." In READINGS IN GOVERNMENT AND

POLITICS IN THE WEST INDIES. Edited by Trevor Munroe and Rupert Lewis. Mona, Jamaica: University of the West Indies, 1971.

456. Shkadova, I.N., et al. MUZHESTVO I BRATSTVO = VALENTIA Y FRATERNIDAD. Moscow: Voen, izd-vo Ministerstva Oborony SSSR, 1982.

457. Simmons, David A. "Militarization of the Caribbean: Concerns for National and Regional Security." INTERNATIONAL JOURNAL (Canada) 40 (1985): 348-76.

458. Sims, Richard, and James Anderson. "The Caribbean Strategic Vacuum." CONFLICT STUDIES 21(1980): 1-23.

459. Slater, Jerome. INTERVENTION AND NEGOTIATION: THE UNITED STATES AND THE DOMINICAN REVOLUTION. New York: Harper and Row, 1970.

460. Smith, C.A. "Martinique in World War II." U.S. NAVAL INSTITUTE PROCEEDINGS 81(1955): 169-74.

461. Smith, Robert Freeman. "Cuba: Laboratory for Dollar Diplomacy, 1898-1917." HISTORIAN 28 (1966): 586-609.

462. Solano Alvarez, Luís. MI ACTUACION MILITAR O APUNTES PARA LA HISTORIA DE LA REVOLUCION DE FEBRERO DE 1917. Havana: Imprenta El Siglo XX, 1920.

463. Sorensen, Theodore C. KENNEDY. New York: Harper and Row, 1965.

464. SOVIET SEAPOWER. Washington: Center for Strategic and International Studies, Georgetown University, 1969.

465. Special Operations Research Office. CASE STUDY IN INSURGENCY AND REVOLUTIONARY WARFARE: CUBA, 1953-1959. Washington: American University, 1963.

466. Statsenko, Igor. "Sobre algunos aspectos político-militares de la crisis del Caribe." AMERICA LATINA (USSR) 3 (1978): 140-50.

467. Stodder, Joseph H., and Kevin F. McCarthy. PROFILES OF THE CARIBBEAN BASIN IN 1950/1980: CHANGING

GEOPOLITICAL AND STRATEGIC DIMENSIONS. 2d ed. Santa Monica: Rand Corporation, 1986.

468. Suchlicki, Jaime. THE CUBAN MILITARY: STATUS AND OUTLOOKS. Coral Gables: Research Institute for Cuban Studies, University of Miami, 1988.

469. ———. THE CUBAN REVOLUTION: A DOCUMENTARY BIBLIOGRAPHY, 1952-1968. Coral Gables: University of Miami Press, 1968.

470. Sunshine, Catherine A. THE CARIBBEAN: SURVIVAL, STRUGGLE AND SOVEREIGNTY. Washington: Epica, 1985.

471. Sunshine, Catherine A., and Philip Wheaton. DEATH OF A REVOLUTION: AN ANALYSIS OF THE GRENADA TRAGEDY AND OF THE U.S. INVASION. Washington: Epica, 1983.

472. Sylvain, Georges. DIX ANNEES DE LUTTE POUR LA LIBERTE, 1915-1925. 2 vols. Port-au-Prince: Editions Henri Deschamps, n.d.

473. Szulc, Tad. DOMINICAN DIARY. New York: Delacorte Press, 1965.

474. ———. FIDEL: A CRITICAL PORTRAIT. New York: William Morrow, 1986.

475. Taber, Robert. M-26: BIOGRAPHY OF A REVOLUTION. New York: Lyle Stuart, 1961.

476. ———. THE WAR OF THE FLEAS: A STUDY OF GUERRILLA WARFARE; THEORY AND PRACTICE. New York: Lyle Stuart, 1965.

477. Tardanico, Richard, ed. CRISES IN THE CARIBBEAN BASIN. Beverly Hills: Sage Publications, 1987.

478. Taylor, Frank F. "Peacekeeping in Paradise: The Arming of the Eastern Caribbean." TRANSAFRICA FORUM 38 (1986): 59-74.

479. Theberge, James D. RUSSIA IN THE CARIBBEAN. 2 vols. Washington: Center for Strategic and International Studies, Georgetown University, 1973.

480. ———. THE SOVIET PRESENCE IN LATIN AMERICA. New York: Crane, Russak, 1974.

481. ———, ed. SOVIET SEAPOWER IN THE CARIBBEAN: POLITICAL AND STRATEGIC IMPLICATIONS. New York: Praeger Publishers, 1972.

482. Thomas, Hugh. CUBA: THE PURSUIT OF FREEDOM. New York: Harper and Row, 1971.

483. Thomas, Lowell. OLD GIMLET EYE: THE ADVENTURES OF SMEDLEY D. BUTLER AS TOLD TO LOWELL THOMAS. New York: Farrar and Rinehart, 1933.

484. Thorndike, Tony. GRENADA. New York: Columbia University Press, 1986.

485. ———. GRENADA: POLITICS, ECONOMICS, AND SOCIETY. Boulder: Lynne Rienner Publishers, 1985.

486. ———. "Suriname and the Military." In THE DUTCH CARIBBEAN: PROSPECTS FOR DEMOCRACY. Edited by Betty Sedoc-Dahlberg. New York: Gordon and Breach, 1990.

487. TODO EMPEZO EN EL MONCADA. Mexico City: Editorial Díogenes, 1973.

488. Tokatlián, Juan Gabriel, ed. CUBA Y ESTADOS UNIDOS: UN DEBATE PARA LA CONVIVENCIA. Buenos Aires: Grupo Editor Latinoamericano, 1984.

489. Torres Ramírez, Blanca. LAS RELACIONES CUBANO-SOVIETICAS. Mexico City: Institute for the Study of Human Issues, 1978.

490. Tulchin, Joseph S. THE AFTERMATH OF WAR: WORLD WAR I AND U.S. POLICY TOWARD LATIN AMERICA. New York: New York University Press, 1971.

491. United States. Congress. House. Committee on Armed Services. FULL COMMITTEE HEARING ON THE LESSONS LEARNED AS A RESULT OF THE U.S. MILITARY OPERATIONS IN GRENADA: HEARING, JANUARY 24, 1984. 98th Cong., 2d sess. Washington: U.S. Government Printing Office, 1984.

492. United States. Congress. House. Committee on Foreign Affairs. U.S. MILITARY ACTIONS IN GRENADA: IMPLICATIONS FOR U.S. POLICY IN THE EASTERN CARIBBEAN: HEARINGS, NOVEMBER 2-16, 1983, BEFORE THE SUBCOMMITTEES ON INTERNATIONAL SECURITY AND SCIENTIFIC AFFAIRS AND ON WESTERN HEMISPHERE AFFAIRS. 98th Cong., 1st sess. Washington: U.S. Government Printing Office, 1984.

493. United States. Congress. House. Committee on Foreign Affairs. Subcommittee on Inter-American Affairs. THE IMPACT OF CUBAN-SOVIET TIES IN THE WESTERN HEMISPHERE: HEARINGS, APRIL 25-26, 1979, AND MARCH 26-MAY 14, 1980. 96th Cong., 1st and 2d sess. Washington: U.S, Government Printing Office, 1979-80.

494. ———. SOVIET ACTIVITIES IN CUBA: HEARINGS; PARTS 4-5, OCTOBER 31, 1973, AND NOVEMBER 20-21, 1974. 93d Cong., 1st and 2d sess. Washington: U.S. Government Printing Office, 1974.

495. ———. SOVIET NAVAL ACTIVITIES IN CUBA: HEARINGS, SEPTEMBER 30-NOVEMBER 24, 1970, AND SEPTEMBER 28, 1971, BEFORE THE SUBCOMMITTEE ON INTER-AMERICAN AFFAIRS. 91st Cong., 2d sess., and 92d Cong., 1st sess. Washington: U.S. Government Printing Office, 1971.

496. United States. Congress. House. Committee on International Relations. Subcommittee on Inter-American Affairs. THE IMPACT OF CUBAN-SOVIET TIES IN THE WESTERN HEMISPHERE: HEARINGS, MARCH 14-APRIL 2, 1978. 95th Cong., 2d sess. Washington: U.S. Government Printing Office, 1978.

497. United States. Congress. House. Committee on International Relations. Subcommittee on International Political and Military Affairs. SOVIET ACTIVITIES IN CUBA: HEARINGS; PARTS

6-7, OCTOBER 7, 1975-SEPTEMBER 16, 1976. 94th Cong., 1st and 2d sess. Washington: U.S. Government Printing Office, 1976.

498. United States. Congress. Senate. Committee on the Judiciary. Subcommittee on the Internal Security Act. THE COMMUNIST THREAT TO THE U.S. THROUGH THE CARIBBEAN: HEARINGS, JULY 14, AUGUST 13, AND NOVEMBER 5, 1959. 86th Cong., 1st sess. Washington: U.S. Government Printing Office, 1959-60.

499. ———. HEARING BEFORE THE SUBCOMMITTEE TO INVESTIGATE THE ADMINISTRATION OF THE INTERNAL SECURITY ACT AND OTHER INTERNAL SECURITY LAWS: TESTIMONY OF BRIGADIER GENERAL ELIAS WESSIN Y WESSIN, OCTOBER 1, 1965. 89th Cong., 1st sess. Washington: U.S. Government Printing Office, 1965.

500. United States. Department of Defense, and Department of State. GRENADA DOCUMENTS: AN OVERVIEW AND SELECTION. Washington: U.S. Government Printing Office, 1984.

501. United States. Department of State. CUBAN ARMED FORCES AND THE SOVIET MILITARY PRESENCE. Washington: U.S. Government Printing Office, 1982.

502. United States. Department of State. U.S. Section of the Anglo-American Caribbean Commission. THE CARIBBEAN ISLANDS AND THE WAR: A RECORD OF PROGRESS IN FACING STERN REALITIES. Washington: U.S. Government Printing Office, 1943.

503. United States. Military Mission. AGREEMENT BETWEEN THE UNITED STATES OF AMERICA AND HAITI. Washington: U.S. Government Printing Office, 1941.

504. Valdés, Nelson P. "Cuban Involvement in the Horn of Africa: The Ethiopian-Somali War and the Eritrean Conflict." CUBAN STUDIES/ESTUDIOS CUBANOS 10(1980): 49-89.

505. Valdés Paz, Juan. "Cuba and the Crisis in Central America." CONTEMPORARY MARXISM 10(1985): 38-67.

506. Valenta, Jiri. "The Soviet-Cuban Intervention in Angola, 1975." STUDIES IN COMPARATIVE COMMUNISM 11 (1978): 3-33.

507. ———. SOVIET STRATEGY IN THE CARIBBEAN BASIN: THE GRENADA CASE STUDY. Washington: Kennan Institute for Advanced Russian Studies, Wilson Center, 1984.

508. Valenta, Jiri, and Herbert J. Ellison, eds. GRENADA AND SOVIET/CUBAN POLICY: INTERNAL CRISIS AND U.S./OECS INTERVENTION. Boulder: Westview Press, 1986.

509. Varas, Augusto. MILITARIZATION AND THE INTERNATIONAL ARMS RACE IN LATIN AMERICA. Boulder: Westview Press, 1985.

510. ———, ed. HEMISPHERIC SECURITY AND U.S. POLICY IN LATIN AMERICA. Boulder: Westview Press, 1989.

511. Vargas, Mayobanex. TESTIMONIO HISTORICO, JUNIO 1959. Santo Domingo: Editora Cosmos, 1981.

512. Vega, Bernardo, ed. CONTROL Y REPRESION EN LA DICTADURA TRUJILLISTA. Santo Domingo: Fundación Cultural Dominicana, 1986.

513. Vega y Pagán, Ernesto. HISTORIA DE LAS FUERZAS ARMADAS. Ciudad Trujillo: Impresora Dominicana, 1955. Vols. 16 and 17 of "La Era de Trujillo."

514. ———. MILITARY BIOGRAPHY OF GENERALISSIMO RAFAEL L. TRUJILLO MOLINA, COMMANDER IN CHIEF OF THE ARMED FORCES OF THE DOMINICAN REPUBLIC. Ciudad Trujillo: Editorial Atenas, 1956.

515. ———. SINTESIS HISTORICA DE LA GUARDIA NACIONAL DOMINICANA: GENESIS DEL ACTUAL EJERCITO NACIONAL. Ciudad Trujillo: Editorial Atenas, 1953.

516. Vego, Milan. "The Caribbean Navies." NAVAL FORCES 4 (1983): 26-36.

517. 26 [VEINTISEIS]. Havana: Editorial de Ciencias Sociales, 1971.

518. Vellinga, M. L. "The Military and the Dynamics of the Cuban Revolutionary Process." COMPARATIVE POLITICS 8 (1976): 245-71.

519. Ventura Novo, Esteban. MEMORIAS: MIAMI, NOVIEMBRE DE 1960. Mexico City: Imprenta M. León Sánchez, 1961.

520. Venzón, Anne Cipriano. "The Papers of General Smedley Darlington Butler, USMC, 1915-1918." Ph.D. dissertation, Princeton University, 1982.

521. Verkey, Elma, and Gerald van Westerloo. HET LLEGERGROENE SURINAME. Amsterdam: Vrij Nederland Press, 1983.

522. Vladimirov, Vladimir K. KUBA V MEZHAMERIKANSKIKH. Moscow: Mezhdunar Otnosheniia, 1984.

523. Weintal, Edward, and Charles Bartlett. FACING THE BRINK: AN INTIMATE STUDY OF CRISIS DIPLOMACY. New York: Scribner, 1967.

524. Welch, Richard E., Jr. RESPONSE TO REVOLUTION: THE UNITED STATES AND THE CUBAN REVOLUTION, 1959-1961. Chapel Hill: University of North Carolina Press, 1985.

525. Welles, Sumner. NABOTH'S VINEYARD: THE DOMINICAN REPUBLIC, 1844-1924. 2 vols. New York: Payson and Clarke, 1928.

526. Wesson, Robert, ed. THE LATIN AMERICAN MILITARY INSTITUTION. New York: Praeger Publishers, 1986.

527. Wiarda, Howard J. DICTATORSHIP AND DEVELOPMENT: THE METHODS OF CONTROL IN TRUJILLO'S DOMINICAN REPUBLIC. Gainesville: University of Florida Press, 1968.

528. ———. DICTATORSHIP, DEVELOPMENT AND DISINTE-GRATION: POLITICS AND SOCIAL CHANGE IN THE DOMINICAN REPUBLIC. 3 vols. Ann Arbor: University Microfilms International, 1975.

529. Wilson, Larman C. "La intervención de los Estados Unidos en el Caribe: La crisis de 1965 en la República Dominicana." REVISTA DE POLITICA INTERNACIONAL (Spain) 122 (1972): 37-82.

530. Wirkus, Faustin E., and Taney Dudley. THE WHITE KING OF LA GONAVE. Garden City: Garden City Publishing, 1931.

531. Wise, Frederick M., and Meigs O. Frost. A MARINE TELLS IT TO YOU. New York: J.H. Sears, 1929.

532. Wyden, Peter. BAY OF PIGS: THE UNTOLD STORY. New York: Simon and Schuster, 1979.

533. Yates, Lawrence A. POWER PACK: U.S. INTERVENTION IN THE DOMINICAN REPUBLIC, 1965-1966. Fort Leavenworth, Kans.: U.S. Army Command and General Staff College, 1988.

534. Young, Alma H. "Peace, Democracy and Security in the Caribbean." Paper presented at the Conference on Peace and Development in the Caribbean, University of the West Indies, Mona, Jamaica, May 1988.

535. Zamora y López, Juan Clemente. EL ESTADO Y EL EJERCITO. Havana: Imprenta de A. Miranda, 1917.

536. Zhukov, Vladimir Georgievich, and Vadim Vadimovich Listov. "BOL'SHAIA DUBINKA" NAD SANTO DOMINGO. Moscow: Mezdunar Otnosheniia, 1969.

537. ———. POLKOVNIK RID VOZVRASHCHAETSIA V SANTO DOMINGO. Moscow: Izd-vo Polit. Lit-ry, 1965.

PERIODICALS

538. ALAS: ORGANO DE LA FUERZA AEREA DOMINICANA, 1980-.

539. ANNUAL REPORT OF THE STATE GUARD OF PUERTO RICO.

540. BOLETIN DEL EJERCITO, 1916-33. (Cuba).

541. CUBAN STUDIES/ESTUDIOS CUBANOS, 1975-. Continues
     CUBAN STUDIES NEWSLETTER, 1970-74.

542. RAPORT, 1926/27-. (Haiti).

543. REVISTA DE LAS FUERZAS ARMADAS, 1966-. (Dominican
     Republic).

544. THE SCARLET BERET, 1971-. (Guyana).

545. VERDE OLIVO, 1959-. (Cuba).

CHAPTER IX

CENTRAL AMERICA

Stephen Webre
Louisiana Tech University

INTRODUCTION

The compiler of a bibliography on the military in twentieth-century Central America faces the same difficulty that confronts the student of religion in sixteenth-century Europe or of slavery in the antebellum United States: the institution is so central to society and its influence so pervasive that it touches virtually every aspect of life. The principle of selection employed here is based on a definition of "military history" as the history of armed institutions and their role in society as well as the history of armed conflict. Even so, the range of works included is quite broad and it should be said, in addition, that almost any contemporary work on Central America will have something significant to say about the military.

The core of the Central American region consists of the five "historic" republics of Guatemala, El Salvador, Honduras, Nicaragua, and Costa Rica. Collectively, these states formed the largest part of the Spanish *audiencia* of Guatemala in colonial times. Upon independence from Spain in 1821, they united briefly with Mexico but seceded two years later to form the United Provinces of Central America, a federal union governed under a constitution modeled loosely upon that of the United States.

Central Americans did not inherit a well-developed military tradition from the Spanish who had never maintained a large regular force in the colony, nor did they develop one for themselves during the great Latin American independence struggles of the early nineteenth century, which left the region largely untouched. After 1824, the federation government attempted to create a modern army, but resources were scarce and the

557

principles of federalism so deeply held that little came of it. In addition to the federal force, each state was allowed to maintain its own troops under its own commander. Not surprisingly, political rivalries quickly became military rivalries and the Central American union collapsed amid civil warfare by 1839.

The "armies" of the five states that emerged from the ruins of the federation tended to be small, fluid bodies held together by personal loyalty to certain popular commanders, or *caudillos*. Poorly trained and armed and always vulnerable to desertion, they were sometimes useful in the constant isthmian warfare that plagued the nineteenth century, but they were not reliable instruments of national policy.

The professionalization of Central American armed forces began in the late nineteenth century with the so-called "Liberal" dictatorships which sought to reform and strengthen the state apparatus in the service of a booming commodity export sector. Coffee, and later bananas, demanded infrastructural improvements, political stability, and domestic order. Modernization and the extension of control often went hand in hand. Railroads and telegraph systems could make small countries even smaller, and trained officers in command of troops armed with repeating rifles could overwhelm local resistance to state power.

El Salvador pioneered the process, importing South American, French, and Spanish officers to serve as instructors as early as the 1850s. Guatemala followed suit; its military academy, the Escuela Politécnica, established by Spanish officers in 1873, set the standard and came to train officers not only for the Guatemalan army but for other isthmian forces as well. Both of these countries eventually experienced a "Frankenstein" effect; in the twentieth century their armed forces ceased to be servants of the state and rather became its master. In El Salvador the army has ruled since 1931, in Guatemala since at least 1954.

Military modernization was a tardier process in the other Central American states. In Nicaragua, institutional development suffered from foreign intervention and its political consequences. It was not until the last decade of the nineteenth century that the country established a military academy staffed with German and Chilean officers. But its graduates had little beneficial impact on a ragged, venal force generally too quick to become involved in partisan squabbles. The United States suppressed the Nicaraguan army and replaced it with a "constabulary" of its own design during the long Marine intervention from 1912 to 1934.

In Honduras and Costa Rica, the first serious professionalization efforts came only at North American urging during World War II. In the latter country, the impact was short-lived. Costa Ricans, staunchly proud of their civilian tradition and customarily suspicious of standing forces, abolished their regular army in 1948. In Honduras, by contrast, the army has grown since the creation of its first permanent military academy in 1952 and is now a major player in national politics.

In addition to the five component states of the old Central American federation, we normally include Panama as well because of its size and location. Part of Colombia until 1903, Panama became independent as part of Theodore Roosevelt's power play to obtain a canal right-of-way. Because the United States guaranteed Panama's independence with its own forces, the new nation for decades had only a national police force. Since World War II, however, that force has evolved into a modern army, called the National Guard, which is heavily involved in politics.

A seventh and final Central American state is Belize, formerly British Honduras. Independent only since 1981, Belize had no military forces of its own until 1978 and even now it depends upon the protection of Great Britain and the United States. Its military history is negligible.

GENERAL WORKS

It is odd, given the importance of the subject, that there are few general works devoted specifically to the military in Central America as a whole. Those that do exist, such as the studies by José N. Rodríguez (150), and Pedro Zamora Castellanos (195), tend to be traditionalist in approach and in any case treat only the very early part of the twentieth century.

By contrast, there is a substantial bibliography on the history of the armed forces in the individual countries. For Guatemala, there is a dated survey by Pedro Zamora Castellanos (194), while Augusto Acuña (1), and Francisco Armando Samayoa Coronado (161), have both contributed traditionalist histories of the Escuela Politécnica. Since World War II, Guatemalan and North American social scientists have on several occasions turned their attention to the social composition and political behavior of the armed forces. Important studies include those by sociologist Mario Monteforte Toledo (120, 122, 123), anthropologist Richard N. Adams (3, 4), and political scientists Gabriel Aguilera Peralta (8), and Jerry L. Weaver (184, 185, 186, 187).

For neighboring El Salvador, the standard traditional history is that of Gregorio Bustamante Maceo (31), which covers only the early period of the century. The dissertations by Robert Elam (60), and Stephen Rozman (158), adopt a more sophisticated approach and carry the story through the 1960s. Like the Guatemalan military, the Salvadoran armed forces have dominated political life in their country for most of the century. But, unlike their Guatemalan peers, the Salvadoran officers have had at times a reputation as enlightened agents of change and development, if not always of social justice. The relationship between the Salvadoran military and political, economic, and social reform has been the subject of several studies, among them those of Charles W. Anderson (14), Harry Kantor (93), and Nicolás Mariscal (108).

The Salvadoran crisis and civil war of the 1980s have focused new attention on the country's military establishment and specially on the internal division between progressives and hardliners within the officer corps which has tended to paralyze the political process. The most significant recent studies include those by Carlos Andino Martínez (17), Shirley Christian (42), Rafael Guidos Véjar (79), and William LeoGrande and Carla Robbins (95).

Nicaragua has the distinction of having twice in this century scrapped its existing military establishment to build an entirely new one. On the first occasion, the Nicaraguan National Guard grew out of a constabulary force officered and trained by U.S. Marines. Traditional accounts of this period in Nicaraguan military history include those by Adolfo Reyes Huete (147), and Ildo Sol (174). Richard Millett (117), has written the standard modern history of the National Guard and the Somoza family dynasty which it helped to establish and maintain in power. Millett's work has largely superseded that by Marvin Goldwert (71). When the last Somoza fell in 1979, the National Guard collapsed and disintegrated. The victorious Sandinistas, with Soviet and Cuban assistance, have rebuilt the army on the base of their own guerrilla ranks and popular militias. The literature on the new Revolutionary Armed Forces is sparse, but Stephen M. Gorman's essay (74), is a place to begin.

In spite of their late development, the armies of both Honduras and Panama have played important, even dominant, roles in national politics and, perhaps significantly, have had a reputation as progressive and reformist. In neither case is the literature abundant but Steve C. Ropp (152), James A. Morris (126), Leticia Salamón (160), and Mario Posas and Rafael del Cid (141), have contributed importantly to our understanding of the Honduran army and its role in politics and society, while Ropp (153, 154), Larry Pippin (140), Robert Miller (115), George Priestley (142), and Ricardo Stevens (178), have produced significant studies on Panama.

It is surprising that so important a development in the Central American context as Costa Rica's dissolution of its army has attracted little study, but the essay by Tord Hoivik and Solveig Aas (82), is of interest. Costa Rica's admirers, both at home and abroad, routinely attribute the country's well-established tradition of democracy and civilian control to the absence of regular armed forces. Be that as it may, Costa Rica does have armed institutions and may not be immune to the temptations of militarism, as skeptics such as John Saxe-Fernández (164), have pointed out.

BIBLIOGRAPHIES

There is little in the way of published bibliographies on the Central American armed forces and military history; most of what is available, like that by Van L. Minor (119), is highly specialized. For general introductions to the literature, however, the reader will find the recent bibliographic essays by Ron Seckinger (165), and Neill Macaulay (100), to be of great value.

ARCHIVAL SOURCES

It is extremely unlikely in the foreseeable future that any serious scholar will gain more than superficial access to the papers of any Central American military institution. In most of the countries, the armed forces are jealous of their secrets and their prerogatives and, in any case, the history of national archival repositories has been uneven and unfortunate.

Only in Costa Rica is there a significant body of papers readily available to researchers. These materials in the Archivos Nacionales de Costa Rica in San José contain administrative records for the first half of the twentieth century and have been of use to local university students doing theses. At the other end of the isthmus, in Guatemala, there is a large number of bundles of Ministry of Defense records held in the storage area of the Archivo General de Centro América. Not even the archive's employees appear to know what they contain, but it is unlikely that there is anything there after 1944 and equally unlikely that they would be opened to a historian without ministry permission.

The Archivo Nacional de Honduras does contain military materials for the nineteenth century, but is weak on all kinds of documentation for the twentieth. Sadly, neither El Salvador nor Nicaragua has been even as fortunate as Honduras. The Salvadoran archives burned in 1889 and the present Archivo General de la Nación in San Salvador dates only from 1948. Technically, all ministries must deliver papers more than thirty years old to the archives, but even then they need not be open to the public. In Nicaragua, civil warfare, earthquakes, and fires have taken a heavy toll on the national archives. Since the Revolution of 1979, the Sandinista government has reorganized the archival service, but, in fact, holdings are sparse and do not go much beyond 1940 where they do exist.

Because of the important role played by foreign officers and governments in the development of the Central American military, it is

entirely possible that researchers will find useful materials in other
capitals. A good example is the early history of the Nicaraguan National
Guard, which, because of the role of the U.S. Marines, is well
documented in North American repositories. These sources are
described at length by Macaulay (101), and Millett (117).

MEMOIRS, JOURNALS, AND EYEWITNESS ACCOUNTS

The two great military episodes of Nicaraguan history, the guerrilla
war waged by Augusto César Sandino against the Marine occupation in
the 1920s and 1930s, and the successful insurrection led by latter-day
Sandinistas against the Somoza dictatorship in the 1970s, have produced
the richest legacy in published first-hand accounts. For military
operations and other details of Sandino's army and its campaigns, there
are the memoirs by Abelardo Cuadra (47), and Gregorio Gilbert (69).
Differing North American views are available in the reportage of radical
journalist Carleton Beals (24), and Marine officer Calvin Carter (39).
Retired General Vernon Megee's unpublished master's thesis (112), is
a rarity, a scholarly account by an eyewitness.

The failure of traditional Caribbean exile invasions, such as that
described by Luis Cardenal Argüello (36), to topple the Somozas, led
to the emergence of guerrilla movements in the hills and the creation
of the Sandinista National Liberation Front in the 1960s. The
subsequent long war came to its climax in the late 1970s and produced
reminiscences on both sides. For the victors, the personal account of
Omar Cabezas Lacayo (32, 33), has become an instant classic, while the
recollections of Humberto Ortega Saavedra (131, 132), and Henry Ruiz
(159), contribute to an understanding of Sandinista strategic thinking.
Pilar Arias (18), has gathered the accounts of a number of other
Sandinista combatants. With the help of a ghostwriter, Anastasio
Somoza Debayle (175), got in his last, bitter word shortly before his
assassination in Paraguay in 1980, while his crony and momentary
successor, Francisco Urcuyo Maliaño (181), has left an account of the
last days. Also of interest are the recollections of a National Guard
defector, José Antonio Robleto Siles (148).

The 1980s have witnessed a new war in Nicaragua, that of the U.S.
supported and financed Contras against the Sandinista government.
Journalist Christopher Dickey (52), accompanied Contra units on
incursions into Nicaraguan territory and has produced a vivid account.
Equally vivid is the testimony of the impact on the Nicaraguan populace
of the Contra war edited by Marlene Dixon (54). The published
testimony of Marine Lieutenant Colonel Oliver North (179), explains
how the United States continued to arm and finance the Contras, even
after Congress prohibited it.

For El Salvador, poet and revolutionary Roque Dalton (49), has recast the reminiscences of a participant in the peasant revolt of 1932, the bloody repression of which seated the military firmly in power for the next five decades. The four-day war with Honduras in 1969, sometimes trivialized as the "Football War," produced many contemporary accounts, notable among which is that of Luis Lovo Castelar (98). The crisis of the 1970s and 1980s has been less productive of readable accounts than in Nicaragua, but worth mentioning are the early political testament of the enigmatic guerrilla chieftain Salvador Cayetano Carpio (38), and the ghostwritten autobiography of civilian president José Napoleón Duarte (57). Among accounts by North American observers, the richest and most provocative is probably that by Charles Clements (44), a former Air Force pilot turned pacifist who served as a surgeon in guerrilla territory on the Guazapa front.

The events of the past two decades have called forth debate over the proper role of the armed forces in Salvadoran society. Army officers, retired as well as active, have from time to time joined in this discussion. Roberto López Trejo (97), takes a conventional, predictable view, while Mariano Castro Morán (41), pleads for change, and especially a greater concern for social justice.

For Guatemala, former CIA agent David Atlee Phillips (139), recalls his role in the shadow war which brought down the Arbenz regime in 1954; an old campaigner, General Miguel Ydígoras Fuentes (192), whose inability to control guerrilla activity led to his ouster as president in 1963, justifies his career and regime; former Roman Catholic missionaries Thomas and Marjorie Melville (114), explain their sympathy for the guerrillas of the 1960s; and a young guerrilla combatant, Mario Payeras (135, 136), evokes the difficult days of reforming in the hills between the savage repression of the late 1960s and the guerrilla resurgence of the late 1970s. An unusual recent work is retired infantry Colonel César Augusto Silva Girón's career autobiography (171), in which he recalls his days in Ubico's and later Arbenz's army and engages in critical reflection on the corrupt and abusive nature of military rule since then.

For other countries there is very little. In a class by itself is novelist Graham Greene's personal memoir (76), of his friendship with Panama's General Omar Torrijos.

SPECIALIZED WORKS

One of the most traditional approaches to military history, biography, has been largely neglected for Central America, although there are a few isolated studies worth noting. Augusto César Sandino has attracted many biographers, including favorable ones such as

Gustavo Alemán Bolaños (9, 10), and Gregorio Selser (166), and unfavorable ones such as his nemesis Anastasio Somoza García (176), whose work is nonetheless valuable for the documents it reproduces. Other rebel figures have received less attention, although there is a biography of Agustín Farabundo Martí, namesake of the current Salvadoran guerrilla front, by Jorge Arias Gómez (19), and an anonymous study of Guatemalan guerrilla leader Luis Turcios Lima (180).

Some of the famed military dictators of the early twentieth century have also been studied, but the quality of such works varies widely. For Nicaragua, there is an essay on José Santos Zelaya by Charles Stansifer (177), and studies on the elder Somoza by Ternot MacRenato (106), and Richard Millett (116). Kenneth J. Grieb (77), has written on Guatemala's Jorge Ubico and Gilberto González y Contreras (72), focuses on Honduras' Tiburcio Carías Andino. David Luna (99), Alberto Peña Kampy (137), and Everett A. Wilson (191), have all approached the regime of Maximiliano Hernández Martínez of El Salvador from quite different perspectives.

Hard to categorize works include journalist Hermann B. Deutsch's (50), account of soldier-of-fortune Lee Christmas and Manuel Octavio Zea Carrascosa's (196), compendium of biographical sketches of Guatemalan defense ministers. Finally, even the biographies of civilian antidictators can contribute to our understanding of the Central American military, as evidenced by the studies by Arturo Castro Esquivel (40), and Charles D. Ameringer (13), on Costa Rica's José Figueres and by Stephen Webre (189), on El Salvador's José Napoleón Duarte.

The most common approach to Central American military history has been the study of individual conflicts, the majority of which have been civil wars and insurrections, rather than wars between independent states.

The most conspicuous exception to the latter generalization is the so-called "Football War" between El Salvador and Honduras, July 14-18, 1969, which has produced a substantial bibliography. The standard survey account in English is by Thomas P. Anderson (16). Much of the literature, including the studies by Marco Virgilio Carías, et al. (37), William Durham (59), and Eddy Jiménez (90), concerns itself with the socioeconomic causes and consequences of the war, while other works, such as those of Mary Jeanne Reid Martz (110, 111), Franklin D. Parker (134), and Alain Rouquié (157), concentrate on the diplomatic process and other aspects of interstate relations. Purely military accounts include those by Luis Lovo Castelar (98), and José Luis González Sibrián (73), who tell the story from the point of view of

Salvadoran ground forces, and Orlando Henríquez (80), who provides an account of the performance of the Honduran Air Force.

As for civil wars and insurrections, those of Nicaragua have probably inspired the most studies. The standard work on Sandino's campaign against the Marines is still that of Neill Macaulay (101), while John Booth (27), Shirley Christian (43), and David Nolan (129), have all contributed readable and useful overviews of the war of the 1970s. On the Contra war of the 1980s, in addition to the book by Christopher Dickey (52), and the so-called CIA "assassination manual" (143), recent works by E. Bradford Burns (30), and Leslie Cockburn (45), also merit mention.

El Salvador's aborted peasant uprising of 1932, which ended in disaster but produced the heroes and symbols for the current guerrilla struggle in that country, is the subject of a thorough account by Thomas P. Anderson (15). The two best works on the crisis of the 1980s, those by Enrique A. Baloyra (22), and Tommie Sue Montgomery (124), both devote attention to the military organization of both sides, but neither is concerned with the description of combat. Two studies critical of the guerrillas, one from the right and one from the left, are by R. Bruce McColm (102), and Gabriel Zaid (193), respectively.

The role of the Guatemalan military in the movement which overthrew General Jorge Ubico in 1944 and in the reformist civilian government which succeeded him is the subject of studies by Kenneth J. Grieb (78), and Anita Frankel (66). Apart from these works, little attention has gone to anything except the guerrilla insurgency which broke out in the 1960s and was finally brutally suppressed by the early 1970s. Eduardo Galeano (67, 68), Adolfo Gilly (70), and especially Richard Gott (75), and Donn Munson (127), have all written about the guerrillas, while Gabriel Aguilera Peralta (5, 7), and John A. Booth (28), have concerned themselves with the campaign of state terror the insurgency provoked. Little is available on the guerrilla resurgence of the 1980s and the Guatemalan government's genocidal campaign against it, but the essay by Caesar D. Sereseres (167), is a helpful place to start.

As Rafael Obregón Loria (130), makes clear, even peaceful Costa Rica has had its problems. The civil war of 1948 which resulted in the abolition of the army is the subject of accounts by John Patrick Bell (25), and Miguel Acuña Valerio (2).The shadowy "Caribbean Legion" of armed exiles which triumphed in 1948 is demythologized in an excellent study by Charles D. Ameringer (12).

In Nicaragua early on, and in the rest of the region increasingly since World War II, the United States has been a major player in the development of the Central American armed forces. Although it is facile to blame Washington entirely for the militarization of isthmian societies, as many commentators do, the role of U.S. policy demands serious attention and receives it in such studies as those of Don L. Etchison (64), Brian Jenkins and Caesar D. Sereseres (87), and Richard Alan White (190).

PERIODICALS

Entries in the accompanying bibliography will suggest the wide variety of periodicals, academic and military, in which useful materials may be found. Beyond this, there are only a few specialized journals or magazines the researcher may wish to be aware of. Both the Guatemalan (200), and Salvadoran (197) armies have published (irregularly) magazines which at times have contained historical articles or other materials useful to the historian. In the United States, the MARINE CORPS GAZETTE (199), and LEATHERNECK (198), are predictably rich on the Marine role in Nicaragua in the 1920s and 1930s, while more recently SOLDIER OF FORTUNE (201), magazine not only has covered the Contra war there but also has been active in recruiting private support for it.

FUTURE RESEARCH

Central American military historiography is not highly developed for any century and the twentieth, in spite of all the attention drawn by the crises of the 1980s, is no exception. Good institutional histories are for the most part lacking. We could certainly use narrative accounts of the development of the military establishment in each of the isthmian states as a basis from which to address a whole range of questions which suggest themselves.

In the strictly martial sense, solid accounts of campaigns, battles, skirmishes, and so on, are few and far between for virtually all wars, internal or otherwise. Frequently, the mission of the armed forces, whether stated or not, has been not the defense of frontiers but the maintenance of domestic peace, i.e., the suppression of dissent. Even so, historians may question the adequacy of any Central American army as a fighting force. How have officers and men been trained and in what doctrines and theories? How have they been armed and how and by whom have the decisions been made to allocate resources to them? The experience of the Salvadoran army confronting the guerrillas in the 1980s has suggested that, as usual, the generals had been planning for the wrong war. An excellent topic for investigation would be the history of efforts by U.S. military advisors to convince them of that.

Along these lines, scholars should remain mindful of the important role played throughout the twentieth century by foreign military elites in the shaping of Central America's armed forces. The role of Spanish,

South American, and German officers in the early days may be accessible through archives in those countries. Although the Marine mission in Nicaragua has been well studied, less attention has been given to U.S. military missions beginning during World War II and continuing afterward. Certainly, the role of the U.S. Army's military assistance commands and of the School of the Americas, located until recently in the Panama Canal Zone, merits a history as does the more recent role of Israeli, Argentine, Cuban, and Soviet advisors on the isthmus.

Scholars have already gone beyond the military's purely warmaking role to such questions as military intervention in politics. The convenient umbrella concept of military rule needs definition and clarification, as it has clearly meant one thing in one time and place and something quite different in another. The transition from personal to corporate dictatorship in both Guatemala and El Salvador from the 1930s to the 1950s, for example, was a fact of great significance. The process found only pale reflection in Honduras and Panama. It was not replicated at all in Nicaragua, and it is at least possible that the persistence of personalist rule in that country made it more vulnerable to radical insurgency than its neighbors.

There is a fruitful area of investigation open here for scholars interested in comparative studies, who will wish to ask not only why the armed forces of some countries developed more slowly than others, but also how, why, and to what effect the emerging military elites interacted with their civilian counterparts in government, society, and the private sector. Of particular interest is an increasingly visible tendency in some countries for military officers to occupy roles previously reserved to civilian elites, particularly in technocratic functions such as as cabinet members and managers of state enterprises. Once trained only as engineers, officers now study economics and business administration and, on rare occasions, even humanities, and frequently they do so in universities rather than in military academies. When, in 1976, I asked Rubén Zamora, now a leader of the Salvadoran opposition, what effect this had had on the officers or on the universities, he replied that it was "a good question." It still is, and someone should look into it.

The social composition of the officer corps has received some attention in all the Central American countries, but no one has studied the origins, behavior, or expectations of enlisted men. In countries where soldiers are frequently called upon to shoot down their own compatriots and generally comply, this is a question of more than passing concern. We are fond of saying that Guatemalan commanders have recruited Indians to kill ladinos and vice versa or that in Somoza's Nicaragua the National Guard relied upon Mosquitos from the Caribbean coast to repress the Spanish-speaking highlanders, but how much of this is really true and what else of interest might we learn by studying the background, recruitment, and training of the enlisted ranks?

By no means exhaustive of the many possibilities for future research on the Central American military in the twentieth century, but of great importance, is the need for studies which transcend the bounds of formal military structures and examine official paramilitary organizations (police), quasi and extraofficial paramilitary organizations (peasant militias and "death squads," although the latter are unlikely to make their papers available or consent to oral interviews), and irregular military organizations (guerrilla forces). All of these have become extremely significant in Central America in recent decades, and no version of the region's history which fails to take them into account can be complete.

BIBLIOGRAPHY: CENTRAL AMERICA

1. Acuña G., Augusto. LA ESCUELA POLITECNICA Y SU PROXIMO CENTENARIO. Guatemala City: Tipografía Nacional, 1973.

2. Acuña Valerio, Miguel. EL 48. San José: Trejos Hermanos, 1975.

3. Adams, Richard N. CRUCIFIXION BY POWER: ESSAYS ON GUATEMALAN NATIONAL SOCIAL STRUCTURE, 1944-1966. Austin: University of Texas Press, 1970.

4. ———. "The Development of the Guatemalan Military." STUDIES IN COMPARATIVE INTERNATIONAL DEVELOPMENT 4 (1968-69): 91-109.

5. Aguilera Peralta, Gabriel. "El proceso de terror en Guatemala." APORTES 24 (1972): 116-36.

6. ———. "La dimensión militar en la crisis de Centroamérica." ANUARIO DE ESTUDIOS CENTROAMERICANOS 12 (1986): 25-40.

7. ———. LA VIOLENCIA EN GUATEMALA COMO FENOMENO POLITICO. Cuernavaca: Centro Intercultural de Documentación, 1971.

8. ———. "Le processus de militarisation de l'état guatemalteque." NS (Ottawa) 8 (1983): 59-81.

9. Alemán Bolaños, Gustavo. SANDINO, EL LIBERTADOR: LA EPOPEYA, LA PAZ, EL INVASOR, LA MUERTE. Mexico City: Ediciones del Caribe, 1952.

10. ———. SANDINO! ESTUDIO COMPLETO DEL HEROE DE LAS SEGOVIAS. Mexico City: Imprenta de la República, 1932.

11. American University. CASE STUDY IN INSURGENCY AND REVOLUTIONARY WARFARE: GUATEMALA 1944-1954. Washington, D.C.: Special Operations Research Office, 1964.

12. Ameringer, Charles D. THE DEMOCRATIC LEFT IN EXILE: THE ANTIDICTATORIAL STRUGGLE IN THE

CARIBBEAN, 1945-1959. Coral Gables: University of Miami Press, 1974.

13. ———. DON PEPE: A POLITICAL BIOGRAPHY OF JOSE FIGUERES. Albuquerque: University of New Mexico Press, 1978.

14. Anderson, Charles W. "El Salvador: The Army as Reformer." In POLITICAL SYSTEMS OF LATIN AMERICA, 53-72. Edited by Martin C. Needler. Princeton: Van Nostrand, 1964.

15. Anderson, Thomas P. MATANZA: EL SALVADOR'S COMMUNIST REVOLT OF 1932. Lincoln: University of Nebraska Press, 1971.

16. ———. THE WAR OF THE DISPOSSESSED: HONDURAS AND EL SALVADOR. Lincoln: University of Nebraska Press, 1981.

17. Andino Martínez, Carlos. "El estamento militar en El Salvador." ESTUDIOS CENTRO AMERICANOS 34 (1979): 615-30.

18. Arias, Pilar, ed. NICARAGUA: REVOLUCION; RELATOS DE COMBATIENTES DEL FRENTE SANDINISTA. Mexico City: Siglo XXI Editores, 1980.

19. Arias Gómez, Jorge. ESBOZO BIOGRAFICO: FARABUNDO MARTI. San José: Editorial Universitaria Centroamericana, 1972.

20. Arieh Gerstein, Jorge. "El conflicto entre Honduras y El Salvador: Análisis de sus causas." FORO INTERNACIONAL 11 (1971): 552-68.

21. Arnson, Cynthia. "In Salvadoran Military and Regime Transformation." POLITICAL CHANGE IN CENTRAL AMERICA: INTERNAL AND EXTERNAL DIMENSIONS, 97-113. Edited by Wolf Grabendorf, Heinrich-W. Krumweide, and Jörg Todt. Boulder: Westview Press, 1984.

22. Baloyra, Enrique A. EL SALVADOR IN TRANSITION. Chapel Hill: University of North Carolina Press, 1982.

23. Barry, Tom. GUATEMALA: THE POLITICS OF COUNTERINSURGENCY. Albuquerque: Inter-Hemispheric Education Resource Center, 1986.

24. Beals, Carleton. BANANA GOLD. Philadelphia: Lippincott, 1932.

25. Bell, John Patrick. CRISIS IN COSTA RICA: THE REVOLUTION OF 1948. Austin: University of Texas Press, 1971.

26. Bonner, Raymond. WEAKNESS AND DECEIT: U.S. POLICY AND EL SALVADOR. New York: Times Books, 1984.

27. Booth, John A. THE END AND THE BEGINNING: THE NICARAGUAN REVOLUTION. Boulder: Westview Press, 1982.

28. ———. "A Guatemalan Nightmare: Levels of Political Violence, 1966-72." JOURNAL OF INTERAMERICAN STUDIES AND WORLD AFFAIRS 22 (1980): 195-225.

29. BOLETIN DEL EJERCITO. San Salvador, 1949-

30. Burns, E. Bradford. AT WAR IN NICARAGUA: THE REAGAN DOCTRINE AND THE POLITICS OF NOSTALGIA. New York: Harper and Row, 1987.

31. Bustamante Maceo, Gregorio. HISTORIA MILITAR DE EL SALVADOR: DESDE LA EPOCA ANTERIOR A LA CONQUISTA, HASTA NUESTROS DIAS, 1821-1932. San Salvador: Talleres Gráficos Cisneros, 1935.

32. Cabezas Lacayo, Omar. FIRE FROM THE MOUNTAIN: THE MAKING OF A SANDINISTA. New York: Crown Publishers, 1985.

33. ———. LA MONTANA ES ALGO MAS QUE UNA INMENSA ESTEPA VERDE. Mexico City: Siglo XXI Editores, 1982.

34. Cable, Vincent. "The 'Football War' and the Central American Common Market." INTERNATIONAL AFFAIRS 45 (1969): 658-71.

35. Cáceres Prendes, Jorge Rafael. "Consideraciones sobre el discurso político de la Revolución de 1948 en El Salvador."

ANUARIO DE ESTUDIOS CENTROAMERICANOS 5 (1979): 33-52.

36. Cardenal Argüello, Luis G. MI REBELION: LA DICTADURA DE LOS SOMOZA. Mexico City: Ediciones Patria y Libertad, 1961.

37. Carías, Marco Virgilio, et al. LA GUERRA INUTIL: ANALISIS SOCIOECONOMICO DEL CONFLICTO ENTRE HONDURAS Y EL SALVADOR. San José: Editorial Universitaria Centroamericana, 1971.

38. Carpio, Salvador Cayetano. SECUESTRO Y CAPUCHA. 6th ed. San José: Editorial Universitaria Centroamericana, 1982.

39. Carter, Calvin B. "The Kentucky Feud in Nicaragua." WORLD'S WORK 54 (1927): 312-31.

40. Castro Esquivel, Arturo. JOSE FIGUERES FERRER. San José: Imprenta Tormo, 1955.

41. Castro Morán, Mariano. FUNCION POLITICA DEL EJERCITO SALVADORENO EN EL PRESENTE SIGLO. San Salvador: Universidad Centroamericana Editores, 1984.

42. Christian, Shirley. "El Salvador's Divided Military." THE ATLANTIC MONTHLY, 1983, 50-60.

43. ———. NICARAGUA: REVOLUTION IN THE FAMILY. New York: Random House, 1985.

44. Clements, Charles. WITNESS TO WAR: AN AMERICAN DOCTOR IN EL SALVADOR. New York: Bantam Books, 1984.

45. Cockburn, Leslie. OUT OF CONTROL: THE STORY OF THE REAGAN ADMINISTRATION'S SECRET WAR IN NICARAGUA, THE ILLEGAL ARMS PIPELINE, AND THE CONTRA DRUG CONNECTION. New York: Atlantic Monthly Press, 1987.

46. Crain, David A. "Guatemalan Revolutionaries and Havana's Ideological Offensive of 1966-1968." JOURNAL OF INTERAMERICAN STUDIES AND WORLD AFFAIRS 17 (1975): 175-205.

47. Cuadra, Abelardo. HOMBRE DEL CARIBE. Edited by Sergio Ramírez. San José: Editorial Universitaria Centroamericana, 1979.

48. Cunningham, Alden M. "U.S. Strategic Options in Nicaragua." PARAMETERS: JOURNAL OF THE U.S. ARMY WAR COLLEGE 18 (1988): 60-72.

49. Dalton, Roque. MIGUEL MARMOL: LOS SUCESOS DE 1932 EN EL SALVADOR. San José: Editorial Universitaria Centroamericana, 1972.

50. Deutsch, Hermann B. THE INCREDIBLE YANQUI: THE CAREER OF LEE CHRISTMAS. London: Longmans, Green, 1931.

51. Devine, Frank J. EL SALVADOR: EMBASSY UNDER ATTACK. New York: Vantage Press, 1981.

52. Dickey, Christopher. WITH THE CONTRAS: A REPORTER IN THE WILDS OF NICARAGUA. New York: Simon and Schuster, 1985.

53. Diederich, Bernard. SOMOZA AND THE LEGACY OF U.S. INVOLVEMENT IN CENTRAL AMERICA. New York: E. P. Dutton, 1981.

54. Dixon, Marlene, ed. ON TRIAL: REAGAN'S WAR AGAINST NICARAGUA; TESTIMONY OF THE PERMANENT PEOPLES' TRIBUNAL. San Francisco: Synthesis Publications, 1985.

55. ──, and Susanne Jonas, eds. REVOLUTION AND INTERVENTION IN CENTRAL AMERICA. San Francisco: Synthesis Publications, 1983.

56. Dodd, Thomas J., Jr. "La guerra de fútbol en Centroamérica." REVISTA CONSERVADORA DEL PENSAMIENTO CENTROAMERICANO 23 (1970): 30-32.

57. Duarte, José Napoleón, with Diana Page. DUARTE: MY STORY. New York: G. P. Putnam's Sons, 1986.

58. Dunkerley, James. THE LONG WAR: DICTATORSHIP AND REVOLUTION IN EL SALVADOR. London: Junction Books, 1982.

59. Durham, William. SCARCITY AND SURVIVAL IN CENTRAL AMERICA: ECOLOGICAL ORIGINS OF THE SOCCER WAR. Stanford: Stanford University Press, 1979.

60. Elam, Robert Varney. "Appeal to Arms: The Army and Politics in El Salvador, 1931-1964." Ph.D. dissertation, University of New Mexico, 1968.

61. EL SALVADOR: LA LARGA MARCHA DE UN PUEBLO, 1932-1982. Madrid: Editorial Revolución, 1982.

62. El Salvador. Ministerio de Defensa. LA BARBARIE HONDURENA Y LOS DERECHOS HUMANOS: PROCESO DE UNA AGRESION. San Salvador: Ministerio de Defensa, 1969.

63. El Salvador. Presidencia de la República. LA VERDAD SOBRE EL CONFLICTO BELICO ENTRE EL SALVADOR Y HONDURAS. San Salvador: Presidencia de la Republica, 1969.

64. Etchison, Don L. THE UNITED STATES AND MILITARISM IN CENTRAL AMERICA. New York: Praeger Publishers, 1975.

65. Evans, Ernest. "Revolutionary Movements in Central America: The Development of New Strategy." In RIFT AND REVOLUTION: THE CENTRAL AMERICAN IMBROGLIO, 167-93. Edited by Howard J. Wiarda. Washington: American Enterprise Institute for Public Policy Research, 1984.

66. Frankel, Anita. "Political Development in Guatemala, 1944-1954: The Impact of Foreign, Military, and Religious Elites." Ph.D. dissertation, University of Connecticut, 1969.

67. Galeano, Eduardo. GUATEMALA: OCCUPIED COUNTRY. New York: Monthly Review Press, 1969.

68. ———. "With the Guerrillas in Guatemala." In LATIN AMERICA: REFORM OR REVOLUTION, 370-80. Edited by James Petras and Maurice Zeitlin. Greenwich: Fawcett, 1968.

69. Gilbert, Gregorio U. JUNTO A SANDINO. Santo Domingo: Editora de la Universidad Autónoma de Santo Domingo, 1979.

70. Gilly, Adolfo. "The Guerrilla Movement in Guatemala." MONTHLY REVIEW 17 (1965): 9-40, and (1965): 7-41.

71. Goldwert, Marvin. THE CONSTABULARY IN THE DOMINICAN REPUBLIC AND NICARAGUA: PROGENY AND LEGACY OF UNITED STATES INTERVENTION. Gainesville: University of Florida Press, 1962.

72. González y Contreras, Gilberto. EL ULTIMO CAUDILLO: ENSAYO BIOGRAFICO. Mexico City: B. Costa-Amic, 1946.

73. González Sibrián, José Luis. LAS 100 HORAS: LA GUERRA DE LEGITIMA DEFENSA DE LA REPUBLICA DE EL SALVADOR. San Salvador: Tipografía Offset Central, n.d.

74. Gorman, Stephen M. "The Role of the Revolutionary Armed Forces." In NICARAGUA IN REVOLUTION, 115-32. Edited by Thomas W. Walker. New York: Praeger, 1982.

75. Gott, Richard. GUERRILLA MOVEMENTS IN LATIN AMERICA. Garden City: Doubleday, 1971.

76. Greene, Graham. GETTING TO KNOW THE GENERAL: THE STORY OF AN INVOLVEMENT. New York: Simon & Schuster, 1984.

77. Grieb, Kenneth J. GUATEMALAN CAUDILLO: THE REGIME OF JORGE UBICO, GUATEMALA, 1931-1944. Athens: Ohio University Press, 1979.

78. ———. "The Guatemalan Military and the Revolution of 1944." THE AMERICAS 32 (1976): 524-43.

79. Guidos Véjar, Rafael. EL ASCENSO DEL MILITARISMO EN EL SALVADOR. San Salvador: Universidad Centroamericana Editores, 1980.

80. Henríquez, Orlando. EN EL CIELO ESCRIBIERON HISTORIA. Tegucigalpa: Tipografía Nacional, 1972.

81. Hill, Roscoe R. "American Marines in Nicaragua, 1912-1925." In HISPANIC AMERICAN ESSAYS: A MEMORIAL TO JAMES ALEXANDER ROBERTSON, 341-60. Edited by A. Curtis Wilgus. Chapel Hill: University of North Carolina Press, 1942.

82. Hoivik, Tord, and Solveig Aas. "Demilitarization in Costa Rica: A Farewell to Arms?" JOURNAL OF PEACE RESEARCH 18 (1981): 333-51.

83. Howard, Alan. "With the Guerrillas in Guatemala." NEW YORK TIMES MAGAZINE, 26 June 1966, 8-24.

84. Ibarra Grijalva, Domingo. THE LAST NIGHT OF GENERAL AUGUSTO C. SANDINO. Trans. by Gloria Bonitz. New York: Vantage Books, 1973.

85. "Integrating the Big Guns: The Central American Defense Council." NACLA LATIN AMERICA & EMPIRE REPORT, 7 May-June 1973, 22-26.

86. Jamail, Milton Henry. "Guatemala 1944-1972: The Politics of Aborted Revolution." Ph.D. dissertation, University of Arizona, 1972.

87. Jenkins, Brian, and Caesar D. Sereseres. "U.S. Military Assistance and the Guatemalan Armed Forces." ARMED FORCES AND SOCIETY 3 (1977): 575-94.

88. Jennings, Kenneth A. "Sandino against the Marines: The Development of Air Power for Conducting Counterinsurgency Operations in Central America." AIR UNIVERSITY REVIEW 37 (1986): 85-95.

89. Jiménez, Carlos María. LA LEGION CARIBE. San José: Imprenta Borrasé, 1948.

90. Jiménez, Eddy. LA GUERRA NO FUE DE FUTBOL. Havana: Casa de las Américas, 1974.

91. Johnson, Kenneth F. "On the Guatemalan Political Violence." POLITICS AND SOCIETY 4 (1973): 55-82.

92. Jonas, Susanne. "CONDECA: Military Maneuvers." NACLA REPORT ON THE AMERICAS, March 1977, 38-39.

93. Kantor, Harry. PATTERNS OF POLITICS AND POLITICAL SYSTEMS IN LATIN AMERICA. Chicago: Rand McNally, 1969.

94. Langley, Lester D. THE BANANA WARS: AN INNER HISTORY OF AMERICAN EMPIRE, 1900-1934. Lexington: University Press of Kentucky, 1983.

95. LeoGrande, William, and Carla Robbins. "Oligarchs and Officers: The Crisis in El Salvador." FOREIGN AFFAIRS 58 (1980): 1084-103.

96. Leonard, Thomas M. U.S. POLICY AND ARMS LIMITATION IN CENTRAL AMERICA: THE WASHINGTON CONFERENCE OF 1923. Los Angeles: Center for the Study of Disarmament, California State University-Los Angeles, 1982.

97. López Trejo, Roberto. REALIDAD DRAMATICA DE LA REPUBLICA: 25 ANOS DE TRAICION A LA FUERZA ARMADA Y A LA PATRIA. San Salvador: Editorial Ahora, 1974.

98. Lovo Castelar, Luis. LA GUARDIA NACIONAL EN CAMPANA: RELATOS Y CRONICAS DE HONDURAS. San Salvador: Editorial Lea, 1971.

99. Luna, David. "Análisis de una dictadura fascista latinoamericana: Maximiliano Hernández Martínez, 1931-1944." LA UNIVERSIDAD 94 (1969): 38-130.

100. Macaulay, Neill. "Central America: Military History and Guerrilla Warfare." In RESEARCH GUIDE TO CENTRAL AMERICA AND THE CARIBBEAN, 96-105. Edited by Kenneth J. Grieb, et al. Madison: University of Wisconsin Press, 1985.

101. ———. THE SANDINO AFFAIR. Chicago: Quadrangle Books, 1967.

102. McColm, R. Bruce. "El Salvador's Guerrillas: Structure, Strategy and . . . Success?" FREEDOM AT ISSUE 74 (1983): 3-16.

103. McDonald, Ronald H. "Civil-Military Relations in Central America: The Dilemmas of Political Institutionalization." In RIFT AND REVOLUTION: THE CENTRAL AMERICAN

IMBROGLIO, 129-66. Edited by Howard J. Wiarda. Washington: American Enterprise Institute for Public Policy Research, 1984.

104. McDonald, Ronald H., and Nina Tamrowski. "Technology and Armed Conflict in Central America." JOURNAL OF INTERAMERICAN STUDIES AND WORLD AFFAIRS 29 (1987): 93-108.

105. MacRenato, Ternot. "Anastasio Somoza: A Nicaraguan Caudillo." M.A. thesis, University of San Francisco, 1974.

106. ———. "The Rise to Power of Anastasio Somoza Garcia." NEW SCHOLAR 8 (1982): 308-23.

107. Mallin, Jay. "Salvador-Honduras War, 1969: The 'Soccer War'." AIR UNIVERSITY REVIEW 21 (1970): 87-92.

108. Mariscal, Nicolás. "Militares y reformismo en El Salvador." ESTUDIOS CENTRO AMERICANOS 33 (1978): 9-29.

109. Marroquín Rojas, Clemente. LOS CADETES: HISTORIA DEL SEGUNDO ATENTADO CONTRA ESTRADA CABRERA. Guatemala City: Imprenta La Hora Dominical, n.d.

110. Martz, Mary Jeanne Reid. CENTRAL AMERICAN SOCCER WAR: HISTORICAL PATTERNS AND INTERNAL DYNAMICS OF OAS SETTLEMENT PROCEDURES. Athens: Ohio University Press, 1978.

111. ———. "OAS Settlement Procedures and the El Salvador-Honduras Conflict." SOUTH EASTERN LATIN AMERICANIST 19 (1975): 1-7.

112. Megee, Vernon E. "United States Military Intervention in Nicaragua." M.A. thesis, University of Texas, Austin, 1963.

113. Melville, Thomas, and Marjorie Melville. GUATEMALA: THE POLITICS OF LAND OWNERSHIP. New York: Free Press, 1971.

114. ———. WHOSE HEAVEN, WHOSE EARTH? New York: Alfred A. Knopf, 1971.

115. Miller, Robert Howard, Jr. "Military Government and Approaches to National Development: A Comparative Analysis of the Peruvian and Panamanian Experiences." Ph.D. dissertation, University of Miami, 1975.

116. Millett, Richard. "Anastasio Somoza García: Fundador de la dinastía Somoza en Nicaragua." ESTUDIOS CENTRO AMERICANOS 30 (1975): 725-41.

117. ———. GUARDIANS OF THE DYNASTY: A HISTORY OF THE U.S. CREATED GUARDIA NACIONAL DE NICARAGUA AND THE SOMOZA FAMILY. Maryknoll, NY: Orbis Books, 1977.

118. ———. "Praetorians or Patriots? The Central American Military." CENTRAL AMERICA: ANATOMY OF CONFLICT, 69-91. Edited by Robert S. Leiken. New York: Pergamon Press, 1984.

119. Minor, Van L. "A Brief Classified Bibliography Relating to United States Intervention in Nicaragua." HISPANIC AMERICAN HISTORICAL REVIEW 11 (1931): 261-77.

120. Monteforte Toledo, Mario. "El ejército." In GUATEMALA: MONOGRAFIA SOCIOLOGICA, 359-74. 2d ed. Mexico City: Instituto de Investigaciones Sociales, UNAM, 1965: 359-74.

121. ———. "La política militar de los Estados Unidos en Centroamérica." CUADERNOS AMERICANOS 162 (1969): 30-43.

122. ———. "La violencia." In CENTRO AMERICA: SUB-DESARROLLO Y DEPENDENCIA, 2: 253-82. Mexico City: Instituto de Investigaciones Sociales, UNAM, 1972.

123. ———. "Los militares." In CENTRO AMERICA: SUB-DESARROLLO Y DEPENDENCIA, 2: 177-220. Mexico City: Instituto de Investigaciones Sociales, UNAM, 1972.

124. Montgomery, Tommie Sue. REVOLUTION IN EL SALVADOR: ORIGINS AND EVOLUTION. Boulder: Westview Press, 1982.

125. Morales Molina, Manuel, comp. EL SALVADOR: UN PUEBLO QUE SE REBELA; CONFLICTO DE JULIO DE 1969. 2 vols. San Salvador: Tipografía Central, 1973-74.

126. Morris, James A. HONDURAS: CAUDILLO POLITICS AND MILITARY RULERS. Boulder: Westview Press, 1984.

127. Munson, Donn. ZACAPA: THE INSIDE STORY OF GUATEMALA'S COMMUNIST REVOLUTION. Canoga Park, CA: Challenge Books, 1967.

128. Nalty, Bernard C. THE UNITED STATES MARINES IN NICARAGUA. Rev. ed. Washington, D.C.: U.S. Marine Corps, 1962.

129. Nolan, David. "From *FOCO* to Insurrection: Sandinista Strategies of Revolution." AIR UNIVERSITY REVIEW 37 (1986): 71-84.

130. Obregón Loria, Rafael. CONFLICTOS MILITARES Y POLITICOS DE COSTA RICA. San José: Imprenta La Nación, 1951.

131. Ortega Saavedra, Humberto. 50 ANOS DE LUCHA SANDINISTA. Managua: Ministerio del Interior, 1979.

132. ———. "La insurrección nacional victoriosa." NICARAUAC 1 (1980): 25-57. Interview.

133. Palmer, David Scott. "Military Governments and U.S. Policy: General Concerns and Central American Cases." AEI FOREIGN POLICY AND DEFENSE REVIEW 4 (1982): 24-29.

134. Parker, Franklin D. "The *FUTBOL* Conflict and Central American Unity." ANNALS OF THE SOUTHEASTERN CONFERENCE ON LATIN AMERICAN STUDIES 3 (1972): 44-59.

135. Payeras, Mario. "Days of the Jungle: The Testimony of a Guatemalan Guerrillero, 1972-1976." MONTHLY REVIEW 35 (1983): 19-94.

136. ———. LOS DIAS DE LA SELVA. Havana: Casa de las Américas, 1980.

137. Peña Kampy, Alberto. EL GENERAL MARTINEZ: UN PATRIARCAL PRESIDENTE DICTADOR. San Salvador: Editorial Tipográfica Ramírez, n.d.

138. Petras, James. "Revolution and Guerrilla Movements in Latin America: Venezuela, Colombia, Guatemala, and Peru." LATIN AMERICA: REFORM OR REVOLUTION, 329-69. Edited by James Petras and Maurice Zeitlin. Greenwich: Fawcett, 1968.

139. Phillips, David Atlee. THE NIGHT WATCH: TWENTY-FIVE YEARS OF PECULIAR SERVICE. New York: Atheneum, 1977.

140. Pippin, Larry LaRae. THE REMON ERA: AN ANALYSIS OF A DECADE OF EVENTS IN PANAMA, 1947-1957. Stanford: Institute of Hispanic American and Luso-Brazilian Studies, Stanford University, 1964.

141. Posas, Mario, and Rafael del Cid. "Honduras: Los límites del reformismo castrense 1972-1979." REVISTA MEXICANA DE SOCIOLOGIA 42 (1981): 607-48.

142. Priestley, George. MILITARY GOVERNMENT AND POPULAR PARTICIPATION IN PANAMA: THE TORRIJOS REGIME, 1968-1975. Boulder: Westview Press, 1986.

143. PSYCHOLOGICAL OPERATIONS IN GUERRILLA WARFARE. With essays by Joanne Omang and Aryeh Neier. New York: Vintage Books, 1985.

144. Ramírez, Sergio, ed. AUGUSTO CESAR SANDINO. San José: Imprenta Nacional, 1978.

145. REPORT OF THE PRESIDENT'S NATIONAL BIPARTISAN COMMISSION ON CENTRAL AMERICA. New York: Macmillan, 1984.

146. REVISTA MILITAR. Guatemala, 1920-.

147. Reyes Huete, Adolfo, ed. ETAPAS DEL EJERCITO. Managua: Talleres Nacionales, n.d.

148. Robleto Siles, José Antonio. YO DESERTE DE LA GUARDIA NACIONAL DE NICARAGUA. San José: Editorial Universitaria Centroamericana, 1979.

149. Rodríguez, Abraham. "Actuación de la OEA en el conflicto." ESTUDIOS CENTRO AMERICANOS 24 (1969): 423-32.

150. Rodríguez, José N. ESTUDIOS DE HISTORIA MILITAR DE CENTRO AMERICA. Guatemala City: Tipografía Nacional, 1930.

151. Ropp, Steve C. "Goal Orientations of Nicaraguan Cadets: Some Applications for the Problem of Structural/Behavioral Projection in Researching the Latin American Military." JOURNAL OF COMPARATIVE ADMINISTRATION 4 (1972): 107-16.

152. ———. "The Honduran Army in the Socio-Political Evolution of the Honduran State." THE AMERICAS 30 (1974): 504-28.

153. ———. "Military Reformism in Panama: New Directions or Old Inclinations." CARIBBEAN STUDIES 12 (1972): 45-63.

154. ———. PANAMANIAN POLITICS: FROM GUARDED NATION TO NATIONAL GUARD. New York: Praeger, 1982.

155. ———, and James A. Morris, eds. CENTRAL AMERICA: CRISIS AND ADAPTATION. Albuquerque: University of New Mexico Press, 1984.

156. Rosenberg, Mark B. "Honduran Scorecard: Military and Democrats in Central America." CARIBBEAN REVIEW 12 (1983): 12-15, 40-42.

157. Rouquié, Alain. "Honduras-El Salvador: La guerre de cent heures; Un cas de 'désintégration' régionale." REVUE FRANCAISE DE SCIENCE POLITIQUE 21 (1971): 1290-316.

158. Rozman, Stephen L. "The Socialization of Military Rule in El Salvador." Ph.D. dissertation, University of Kansas, 1970.

159. Ruiz, Henry. "La montaña era como un crisol donde se forjaban los mejores cuadros." NICARAUAC 1 (1980): 8-24. Interview.

160. Salamón, Leticia. MILITARISMO Y REFORMISMO EN HONDURAS. Tegucigalpa: Editorial Guaymuras, 1982.

161. Samayoa Coronado, Francisco Armando. LA ESCUELA POLITECNICA ATRAVES DE SU HISTORIA. 2 vols. Guatemala City: Tipografía Nacional, 1964.

162. Saxe-Fernández, John. "El Consejo de Defensa Centroamericano y la Pax Americana." CUADERNOS AMERICANOS 150 (1967): 39-57.

163. ———. "The Central American Defense Council and Pax Americana." In LATIN AMERICAN RADICALISM, 75-101. Edited by Irving L. Horowitz, Josué de Castro, and John Gerassi. New York: Random House, 1969.

164. ———. "The Militarization of Costa Rica." MONTHLY REVIEW 24 (1972): 61-70.

165. Seckinger, Ron. "The Central American Militaries: A Survey of the Literature." LATIN AMERICAN RESEARCH REVIEW 16 (1981): 246-58.

166. Selser, Gregorio. SANDINO: GENERAL DE HOMBRES LIBRES. 2 vols. Buenos Aires: Editorial Triángulo, 1959.

167. Sereseres, Caesar D. "The Highland War in Guatemala." In LATIN AMERICAN INSURGENCIES, 97-130. Edited by Georges A. Fauriol. Washington: Center for Strategic and International Studies, Georgetown University, and National Defense University, 1985.

168. ———. "Military Development and the United States Military Assistance Program for Latin America: The Case of Guatemala, 1961-1969." Ph.D. dissertation, University of California, Riverside, 1971.

169. ———. "U.S. Military Aid, Authoritarian Rule and Military Politics in Central America." ARMED FORCES AND SOCIETY 5 (1979): 329-33.

170. Shugart, Matthew Soberg. "Thinking about the Next Revolution: Lessons from United States Policy in Nicaragua." JOURNAL OF

INTERAMERICAN STUDIES AND WORLD AFFAIRS 29 (1987): 73-92.

171. Silva Girón, César Augusto. CUANDO GOBIERNAN LAS ARMAS: GUATEMALA; 31 ANOS DE MISERIA. Guatemala City: Impreofset Oscar de León Palacios, 1987.

172. Smith, Julian C., et al. A REVIEW OF THE ORGANIZATION AND OPERATIONS OF THE GUARDIA NACIONAL DE NICARAGUA, BY DIRECTION OF THE MAJOR GENERAL COMMANDANT OF THE UNITED STATES MARINE CORPS. n.p., n.d.

173. Smith, Laun C., Jr. "Central American Defense Council: Some Problems and Achievements." AIR UNIVERSITY REVIEW (1969): 67-75.

174. Solórzano, Ildefonso [Ildo Sol]. LA GUARDIA NACIONAL DE NICARAGUA: SU TRAYECTORIA E INCOGNITA, 1927-1944. Granada: El Centro-Americano, 1944.

175. Somoza Debayle, Anastasio, and Jack Cox. NICARAGUA BETRAYED. Belmont, MA: Western Islands, 1980.

176. Somoza García, Anastasio. EL VERDADERO SANDINO, O EL CALVARIO DE LAS SEGOVIAS. Managua: Tipografía Robelo, 1936.

177. Stansifer, Charles L. "José Santos Zelaya: A New Look at Nicaragua's 'Liberal' Dictator." REVIEW/REVISTA INTERAMERICANA 7 (1977): 466-85.

178. Stevens, Ricardo. METAMORFOSIS DE LAS FUERZAS ARMADAS EN PANAMA, 1968-1986. Panama City: n.p., 1987.

179. TAKING THE STAND: THE TESTIMONY OF LIEUTENANT COLONEL OLIVER L. NORTH. New York: Pocket Books, 1987.

180. TURCIOS LIMA: BIOGRAFIA Y DOCUMENTOS. Montevideo: Ediciones de la Banda Oriental, 1969.

181. Urcuyo Maliaño, Francisco. SOLOS: LAS ULTIMAS 43 HORAS EN EL BUNKER DE SOMOZA. Guatemala City: Editorial Académica Centro América, 1979.

182. Villalobos, Joaquín. "Desarrollo militar y perspectiva insurreccional en El Salvador." AMERICA LATINA (Moscow) 11 (1982): 63-79.

183. Waghelstein, John D. "El Salvador and the Press: A Personal Account." PARAMETERS: JOURNAL OF THE U.S. ARMY WAR COLLEGE 15 (1985): 66-70.

184. Weaver, Jerry L. "Las fuerzas armadas guatemaltecas en la política." APORTES 22 (1969): 133-46.

185. ———. "The Military Elite and Political Control in Guatemala, 1963-1966." SOCIAL SCIENCE QUARTERLY 50 (1969): 127-35.

186. ———. "The Political Elite of a Military-Dominated Regime: The Guatemalan Example." JOURNAL OF DEVELOPING AREAS 3 (1969): 373-88.

187. ———. "Political Style of the Guatemalan Military Elite." STUDIES IN COMPARATIVE INTERNATIONAL DEVELOPMENT 5 (1969-70): 63-81.

188. Weaver, Kenneth Leroy. "Transnational Military Elites: The Central American Case." Ph.D. dissertation, University of Washington, 1973.

189. Webre, Stephen. JOSE NAPOLEON DUARTE AND THE CHRISTIAN DEMOCRATIC PARTY IN SALVADORAN POLITICS, 1960-1972. Baton Rouge: Louisiana State University Press, 1979.

190. White, Richard Alan. THE MORASS: UNITED STATES INTERVENTION IN CENTRAL AMERICA. New York: Harper and Row, 1984.

191. Wilson, Everett A. "The Crisis of National Integration in El Salvador, 1919-1935." Ph.D. dissertation, Stanford University, 1969.

192. Ydígoras Fuentes, Miguel. MY WAR WITH COMMUNISM. Englewood Cliffs: Prentice-Hall, 1963.

193. Zaid, Gabriel. "Enemy Colleagues: A Reading of the Salvadoran Tragedy." DISSENT 29 (1982): 13-40.

194. Zamora Castellanos, Pedro. NUESTROS CUARTELES. Guatemala: Tipografía Nacional, 1932.

195. ———. VIDA MILITAR DE CENTRO AMERICA. 2 vols. 2d ed. Guatemala City: Editorial del Ejército, 1966.

196. Zea Carrascosa, Manuel Octavio. SEMBLANZAS: MINISTROS DE LA GUERRA Y DE LA DEFENSA NACIONAL DE GUATEMALA. Guatemala City: Editorial del Ejército, 1971.

PERIODICALS

197. BOLETIN DEL EJERCITO, 1949-.

198. LEATHERNECK, 1917-.

199. MARINE CORPS GAZETTE, 1916-.

200. REVISTA MILITAR, 1920-.

201. SOLDIER OF FORTUNE, 1975-.

CHAPTER X

CHILE

Brian Loveman
San Diego State University

INTRODUCTION

Military institutions and operations have overwhelmingly influenced Chilean history in the nineteenth and twentieth centuries. The selected bibliographical references in this chapter provide a basic foundation for those interested in understanding the historical development and political role of the military in Chilean society.

From the time of Spanish conquest in the 1540s until the independence movement after 1810, Chile was essentially a military frontier of the Spanish empire. The highest-ranking Spanish official in the colony, the Captain General, exercised civilian and military command over a territory perpetually threatened by Indian warfare and piratical attacks by Spain's European rivals. The Chilean colony, from the early sixteenth century, represented a permanent drain on the Spanish and Peruvian treasuries for military subsidies and permanent garrisons in the south and south-central regions. For most of the colonial period the Spanish were unable to control the territory south of the Bío Bío River, leaving this region in the hands of the Araucanian Indians. However, the military budget represented a large part of colonial administrative costs, and the military, though usually no larger than 1,000-2,000 active-duty personnel, played a key role in colonial society.

With independence in 1818, the victorious armies of Argentine General José de San Martin and the Chilean Bernardo O'Higgins, became the foundations of political rule in Chile. Military forces continued their battle against isolated remnants of royalist forces,

587

bandits, and local *caudillos* into the late 1820s. Chilean army and naval forces (the latter under the command of a former British naval officer, Lord Cochrane) also contributed to the defeat of Spain and secured Peruvian independence in the mid-1820s. A partial legacy of these military campaigns would be the emergence of military leaders as Chilean presidents (General Joaquín Prieto and Manual Bulnes) in the key decades between 1830 and 1850 as Chile consolidated its national identity and established its new political system.

The Chilean military, thus, played a central role in the formation of the new nation. Wars with the Peru-Bolivia Confederation (1836-1839), civil wars in 1851 and 1859, and another conflict with Peru and Bolivia, the War of the Pacific (1879-1883), all contributed to the generation of a spirit of Chilean nationalism, suppression of regionalism, and expansion of national territory.

Development of military professionalism was slow, but a small number of officers studied in Europe. French influence was dominant in the army until the 1880s, and British influence prevailed in the navy. The navy intervened in minor ways in regional disputes involving Peru, Ecuador, and Colombia in the 1840s and 1850s, and also sought to protect Chilean boundary claims in the Patagonian region disputed by Argentina. The army remained relatively small, usually less than 3,000 troops, but was backed up by a militia or national guard numbering over 50,000; it had more political than military importance under most circumstances. Divisions within the army during the civil wars of 1851 and 1859 threatened the institution's professional development, but government victories in each case reaffirmed national control over the challenges from the provinces.

Ongoing efforts to pacify Indian territory and promote southernly colonization occupied army units from the 1850s onward. This meant that a legitimate military mission existed for the Chilean army on the southern frontier as well as in the protection of the country from potential threats from Peru, Bolivia, and Argentina. In the mid-1860s, a minor military engagement with Spain also added to the military's contributions to national defense and nationalistic spirit. Even so, the army's strength typically remained between 3,000 to 4,000 personnel until the 1880s.

In 1879, war broke out between Chile and its northern neighbors as a result of conflicts over resources in the Atacama desert. Simultaneously, a decision was made to pacify Indian territory to the south. The Chilean army dramatically expanded from its customary 3,000 to 4,000 troops to over 45,000, and major commitments of resources to purchase modern arms and naval vessels transformed the armed services. Military institutions would be from this time forward important elements in Chilean national politics. The influence of the armed forces in modern Chilean politics and society originated with consolidation of central government control throughout the century in the late nineteenth century, in the southern provinces through definitive subjugation of the Indian population in the 1880s and in the north as a result of defeat of the neighboring nations of Peru and Bolivia in the War of the Pacific (1879-83); see Gonzalo Bulnes (48). This victory increased Chilean territory by approximately one-third through the transfer of sparsely-settled, but mineral rich regions of southern Peru and Bolivia, to Chilean control. The spoils of military conquest have generated the revenues for the country's major export booms in the late nineteenth and much of the twentieth centuries. These monies financed public works, modernization of the country's transportation and communication network, and a significant share of public investment. The seacoasts of these mineral rich regions also include several of Chile's major ports and an important fishing industry. In these respects much of the economic foundation of modern Chile derives from its military feats in the late nineteenth century.

GENERAL WORKS

Despite the key role of military victories in Chilean history, there are few general works on the armed forces and their role in the socio-economic and political development of the nation. Nunn's excellent overview, YESTERDAY'S SOLDIERS (180), as well as another of his works, THE MILITARY IN CHILEAN HISTORY (177), are useful. Also, one should consult Joxe (132), Hillmon (124), Téllez Cárcamo (226), Barceló Lira (25), Rouquié (208), and some official histories (71, 97).

In addition to the small number of general historical works, each branch of the armed services has been the topic of specialized histories. López Rubio (144), deals with the army. The navy can be found in Langlois (139), López Urrutia (146), the text used at the Naval Academy by Novoa de la Fuente (171), and the volume of selected articles by Rodríguez (203). Flores Alvarez (102, 103), and selected articles in the FUERZA AEREA (269), contain information on the air force. The *carabineros* (national police) are treated in Zapata (266).

ARCHIVAL GUIDES AND SOURCES

Archival sources with useful material on the Chilean military include the more general holdings of the Biblioteca Nacional, the Biblioteca del

Congreso, and the documentary collections of the individual government ministries, such as those of the Ministry of Interior and the Ministry of Foreign Relations, as well as the more specialized holdings of the armed forces themselves. The latter, particularly for the twentieth century, are not as accessible as most other Chilean government depositories, and this situation is especially true for materials relating to the last quarter century.

Prior to the early 1970s, the most important source of archival materials on the military was found in the Biblioteca del Estado Mayor General del Ejército de Chile (BEMGE). Subsequently, these papers were transferred to the Biblioteca Central del Ejército, housed at the War Academy. This depository includes the libraries of the Ministry of Defense and the old War Academy. While scholars have made good use of these holdings for studies on the period prior to the mid-twentieth century, including such documents as officer rosters, training materials, annual reports, and military education papers, access to the collections is quite restricted. The political role of the armed forces since 1973 makes unlikely an easing of the tight controls over more recent material in the archives. Nevertheless, at some time in the future, these files will be invaluable sources for scholars attempting to interpret twentieth century civil-military relations in Chile.

Official and semi-official sources on the Chilean military, although not as abundant as other material, is available and can be useful in shedding light on its role in politics and society, and its aspirations; see, for example, Academia de Guerra (1, 2), CODIGO DE JUSTICIA MILITAR (68), Escuela Militar (96), HISTORIA DE LA ARTILLERIA DE CHILE (126), Ministerio de Guerra (157), and Ministerios de Guerra y Marina (159).

MEMOIRS, JOURNALS, AND EYEWITNESS ACCOUNTS

Officers of the armed forces have published a number of personal accounts, recollections, and memoirs describing their experiences and perceptions of military life and Chilean society. Most of these sources are specific accounts of historical incidents. Barros Ortiz (30), was highly critical of civilian politicians and emphasized the need to respond to social and economic challenges in ways consistent with Chilean nationalism. He also claimed that the army should save the country from further social disintegration through direct intervention in political life. This volume was reissued and distributed to Chilean officers after the coup of 1973. Bennett (33), was a member of the high command sympathetic to the 1924 coup by junior officers, with which Ahumada (5), and Blanche E. (39), also deal. Aldunate Phillips's (8), volume is a detailed account of civil-military relations from the coup of 1924 to 1927. Barros Merino (28), relates the experiences of a Chilean officer sent for training in Germany. Another officer, Walker Martínez (259), also underwent military instruction in Germany; in addition he reveals much about generational divisions within the Chilean army. Cabrera (54), provides impressions of the influence of the Chilean officers' diffusion of the German military tradition in Ecuador. Von Schroeders (258), looks at the 1931 naval mutiny.

More reflective analyses considering longer spans of time or broader themes relating to civil-military relations include Sáez Morales (210), which looks at the military and politics from the late nineteenth century until 1932, and Téllez Cárcamo (227).

For the most recent period of Chilean history several sources are of the utmost interest. Carlos Prats González's memoirs (197), are a detailed chronology and inside account of the Popular Unity period (1970-73). Prats served as the commander of the Estado Mayor de la Defensa Nacional; he was later assassinated in Buenos Aires. Augusto Pinochet's THE CRITICAL DAY (188), is a translation of EL DIA DECISIVO. In it he recalls his military career, gives his opinions of Marxism, and outlines the events leading up to the coup of 1973. Nathaniel Davis (79), served as the United States ambassador to Chile during the final two years of the Popular Unity administration.

SPECIALIZED WORKS:
POST-WAR OF THE PACIFIC, PROFESSIONALIZATION,
AND CIVIL WAR

The exploitation of the economic resources contained in the lands conquered by military force in the late nineteenth century created the roots of a militant labor movement which was forged in the nitrate fields, ports, and copper mines of the region. The workers in these places and their political participation in late nineteenth and early twentieth-century Chile gave rise to a number of confrontations with the nation's military.

The victorious armed forces that emerged from the War of the Pacific (1879-83) soon underwent reorganization and professionalization under the direction of German officers. In a sense these changes and their consequences for Chile's military and society are the beginning of the country's socio-economic and political history in the twentieth century, though the formative period in this process occurred in the 1880s. Prior to the War of the Pacific, Chile maintained an army of approximately 3,000-4,000 soldiers. The navy also experienced significant transformation during the same period, 1880-1900.

The strictly technical and organizational aspects of this professionalization were of less immediate importance than the dramatic political consequences. Nunn (173, 174, 177, 180), treats both issues in several books and articles. Especially useful is his YESTERDAY'S SOLDIERS (180), a wealth of research covering European military missions and the influence of their legacy in South America.

In addition to Nunn's works, memoirs, commentaries, and monographs by military officers have contributed insight into the impact of German missions and the subsequent professionalization of the Chilean armed forces; they include Arriagada Herrera (19), Barros Merino (28), a Chilean officer sent to Germany for training, Díaz Valderrama (89), Epstein (95), Lara (140), the Ministerio de Guerra whose MEMORIA (158), contains detailed information on the German missions and development within the armed forces in general, Sáez Morales (210), and Walker Martínez (259), who also traveled to Germany for military instruction.

In 1891 Emil Körner, the German officer entrusted with directing the professionalization (Prussianization) of the Chilean army, took sides with congressional forces in a civil war that ousted President Manuel Balmaceda. Körner masterminded the victorious opposition military campaign and then managed to purge the army of pro-Balmaceda elements, thus enhancing the careers of officers who had supported the insurrection. Hervey (123), served as a special correspondent for the TIMES of London on the civil war. United States naval officers, Sears and Wells (216), reported on the personnel, equipment, and growth of the Chilean armed forces of the time.

Afterward, the army continued its program of modernization, even sending instructors to Colombia, Ecuador, and El Salvador to diffuse the Prussian model of military organization and training; see Cabrera (54), Pérez (185). Also, Latin American officers from as far away as Costa Rica visited Chile to imbibe German ideology and skills as related in Zúñiga Montúfar (268). In the meantime, initial strides were made in the area of military aviation, and the Chilean navy also experienced a growing pride in its successful traditions.

Other issues, too, would emerge in the late nineteenth century and continue to have relevance for the future. One was the low salaries and poor promotion opportunities that constantly proved to be a source of discontent in the army; see Adán (4).

SPECIALIZED WORKS:
CIVIL-MILITARY RELATIONS, 1900-32

Although neither the army nor the navy had acted as a unified force in the civil war, the evolution of a self-conscious, proud, and Prussian-influenced officer corps permanently transformed Chilean civil-military relations after 1891. At the same time the pressures of socio-economic change and the challenges of working class and urban demands on the old order destabilized society. Information on defense-related institutions and civil-military relations from approximately the turn of the century until the early 1920s, as well as selected works describing the role of the armed forces as an instrument for securing internal order, can be found. The best general work is Nunn's CHILEAN POLITICS, 1920-1931 (173), a basic source for the role of the military in politics and institutional development in the first three decades of the twentieth century. Medina Franzani (153), is a plea for the Chilean government to dedicate more resources to the defense establishment and for more serious attention to be given to military education. It is a "benchmark" in the professional armed forces' dissatisfaction with civilian leadership and their aspirations for a more ample role in modernizing society. Other works worth consulting include Bari M. (26), Barros Ortiz (30), Boonen Rivera (40), Riquelme (201), and Viaux (254), all of which, too, urged that the army take a greater role in the socio-economic and political life of the nation.

By 1924, several of the Germans' star students would overturn the "parliamentary" system that Körner's armed victory had helped to create, and they would attempt to impose new directions on Chilean national life. A growing frustration with the perceived lack of resources and respect afforded the armed forces by the civilian sector and its leadership induced recurrent, if muffled, machinations within the military aimed at improving the status and role of officers in society.

Several works detail the institutional development and political involvement of the Chilean armed forces in the period 1924-32. Alessandri Palma (9), provides a political overview from 1920 to 1932. Donoso (90), and Strawbridge (223), are good sources for the pre-1924 evolution of discontent within the armed forces, while they, Ahumada (5), Aldunate Phillips (8), Bennett (33), Millar Carvacho (156), Monreal (161), and Prats González (197), all deal with the coup of 1924 and its aftermath. The important work of Heise González (122), examines the 1925 constitution and the politico-military context of the time. Ex-naval officer Contreras G. (74), and Vicuña F. (256), analyze the first administration of President Carlos Ibáñez del Campo (1927-31). Montero (162), offers an apology for Ibáñez and the military's role in politics. Cerda (60), examines the role of military officers in politics between 1927 and 1932. Grove (116), discusses the role of his brother, Marmaduke, in the short-lived "socialist republic" of 1932, while Aránguiz Latorre (16), President Juan Esteban Montero's (1931-32) private secretary, deals with the coup of 1932.

SPECIALIZED WORKS:
NATIONAL DEVELOPMENT, 1932-70

From 1932 to 1970, the visible role of the nation's armed forces in Chilean politics receded; Chileans and foreign observers alike generally accepted the view that the military had been "professionalized" and, therefore, depoliticized. One insight into Chilean politics between 1939 and 1953 with some useful information on the military of the time is by Claude Bowers (41), the United States ambassador.

In some ways this perception of a tamed military was true. For example, Tarr (224), examines civilian militias during the 1930s. In other ways, however, the Chilean armed forces had achieved, or had forced upon them, a certain contradictory role expansion that belied the image of a "nonpolitical," professionalized military force. In addition, a mounting frustration and resentment developed because of poor pay, low status, and civilian neglect of, or disdain for, the institution. Future President Allende (11), wrote about this situation as early as 1943. Hansen (119), in a study that caused great controversy in Chile regarding the role of the CIA in social science research, noted the alienation and frustration of military officers with their lack of status and economic opportunity in the 1950s and 1960s. In an important leftist study, Lechner (141), also assessed Chilean political polarization. Similar conclusions are also arrived at in the works by Frühling, Portales, and Varas (106), Joxe (132), and North (169).

Periodic coup plots and manueverings proved to be unsuccessful; see Nef (168). Nevertheless, a small number of officers continued to engage in provocative challenges to the Christian Democratic administration of President Eduardo Frei in the late 1960s as described in Bicheno (34), Garay Vera (108), Piacentini (187), Prats González (197), Valenzuela (241), Varas (248), and Viaux (255). A critique of the policies of the Frei administration with references to the military can also be found in Olvarría Bravo (181).

SPECIALIZED WORKS: POLITICS, 1970-73

Almost half a century after officers ended the parliamentary republic in the 1920s, the Chilean armed forces again directly intervened in the government, this time suppressing the Popular Unity government of socialist President Salvador Allende with a brutal coup in 1973. The three years of Popular Unity administration deserve close consideration precisely because of the important role played by the military institution in the political process during this era.

Accounts of the period are abundant; one should start with the following. Allende (12), writing early in his presidency, offers optimistic reflections on the role of the armed forces and *carabineros* in the Chilean road to socialism. Altamirano (13), a leading socialist politician, analyzed the failure of the Popular Unity government; chapter ten focuses especially on the armed forces. Arriagada Herrera (18), evaluates the role of the armed forces during the Allende presidency and the evolution of civil-military relations. The prologue to the same volume is written by Eduardo Frei in which the former president gives his interpretation of the events leading to the 1973 coup. Bitar (36), a prominent member of Allende's cabinet, examines in detail the Popular Unity program and the policy constraints it faced as well as a brief but insightful consideration of the military's role between 1970 and 1973. Popular Unity government supporters Castillo, Echeverría, and Larraín (59), study the possibilities of neutralizing the political role of the armed forces and avoiding a coup. CHILE: A COUNTRY STUDY (63), contains historical material on the 1970-73 years and data on national security and the armed forces plus a chronology of significant political and economic events. DeVylder (86), is perhaps the best single volume dealing with the political and economic policies of and constraints on the popular Unity administration. Garcés (109), a Spaniard and one of Allende's closest political advisors, gives a retrospective analysis. Joxe (133), looks at the military's consideration of placing constraints on the Popular Unity program. Moss (166), sharply criticizes the Allende government and examines military participation in the president's cabinet. Palacios (184), is a scathing leftist critique of the Communists' non-revolutionary tactics and lack of preparation for the coup plus a detailed account of United States plots and relationships with the Chilean military. Prats González (197), served as the commander of the Estado mayor de la Defensa Nacional during the Popular Unity period. Rojas (207), contains detailed information on the identities of military officers involved in the coup and troop deployment. It is also chronicles the application of the gun control law through military searches of factories. THE SCHNEIDER CASE (213), details the assassination of General René Schneider in an effort to prevent Allende from coming to office. Uribe (236), looks at the United States role and contacts with the military in the overthrow of Allende. Varas (248), in conversations with an opposition military commander, details the plots against the

Allende coalition by civilian leaders and armed forces officers. The WHITE BOOK (261), is the official military justification of the coup, along with allegations of a plan (Zeta) by the Allende government to execute military officers and seize power in a violent takeover.

SPECIALIZED WORKS: POLITICS SINCE 1973

Finally, from 1973 to 1990, a military junta, headed by General Augusto Pinochet Ugarte, governed Chile. It restructured and expanded the armed forces, greatly increased defense budgets, and profoundly transformed Chilean society through authoritarian politics and drastic economic initiatives. One of the best places to start is with Arriagada Herrera (19, 20, 21, 22, 23), who has written several books and articles on the Pinochet years. They include IDEOLOGIA POLITICA DE LOS MILITARES (19), which, among other things, treats the modern "national security" doctrine of the 1960s-80s, the principal philosophy of the Pinochet regime. The collection of essays FUERZAS ARMADAS Y SEGURIDAD NACIONAL (107), outlines the doctrine and its relationship to the national economy and society. Cortés Rencoret (77, 78), a former professor at the Academia de Guerra, also deals with the doctrine and how it was included in the military junta's vision of a new Chilean society. NUESTRO CAMINO (172), is a collection of essays by leading supporters of the military junta. LAS TRANSFORMACIONES EDUCACIONALES (235), studies the educational policies and changes introduced by the military government. Jarvis (130), offers an overview and analysis of the policies of the military government toward agriculture. Varas (246), presents a comprehensive treatment of the changes in military structure, budgets, and internal policies as well as of public policy and foreign relations after 1973. He also includes material on the emergence of the Chilean arms industry, as does Williams (264). Branch and Propper (42), detail the assassination of ex-Popular Unity official Orlando Letelier by Chilean agents in Washington, D.C., in 1976. Other works that also should be consulted for the post-1973 military regime include CHILE: THE PINOCHET DECADE (65), Correa, Sierra, and Subercaseaux (75), Frühling, Protales, and Varas (106), García (111), Huneeus (128), and Remmer (198, 199).

A voluminous literature has developed concerning the public policies and human rights record of the Chilean military junta and the government of General Pinochet since 1973. The selected references below include only a small number of works focusing on economic and human rights issues, but they have been chosen in an effort to provide the reader with basic sources which include further bibliographical references on these topics. MODELO ECONOMICO CHILENO (160), for example, is a collection of essays on the Chilean economic model after 1973 and is generally critical of the "neoliberal" policies adopted by the military government and its civilian advisers. Contrariwise, Walton (260), is a generally positive survey of the economic policies and performance in Chile from 1973 to the mid-1980s. Other works that also should be consulted are Bitar (37), Foxley (105), Levy (142), Schoultz (214, 215), Silva (218), Smith (222), and Valenzuela and Valenzuela (242).

PERIODICALS

Military journals, published first by the army and followed later by the navy, air force, and *carabineros*, have provided an important outlet for officers' intellectual endeavors which can be of value to the historian. Among the most useful are: FUERZA AEREA (269), edited by the general staff of the air force; MEMORIAL DEL EJERCITO DE CHILE (MECH) (270), the official publication of the general staff of the army; POLITICA Y GEOESTRATEGIA (271), which is published by the Academia Nacional de Estudios Políticos y Geoestratégicos (ANEPE); REVISTA ARMAS Y SERVICIOS DEL EJERCITO (272), a quarterly of popular, historical, and technical articles created after 1973 and directed toward non-commissioned officers and enlisted personnel; REVISTA DE MARINA (273), the official organ of the navy; REVISTA DEL SUBOFICIAL (274), produced by the army general staff for non-commissioned officers; and SEGURIDAD NACIONAL (275), the journal of the Academia Superior de Seguridad Nacional.

FUTURE RESEARCH

Considering the importance of military institutions in Chilean social, economic, and political development, there are surprisingly few systematic empirical studies of the evolution, role, and performance of the military services in the twentieth century. This is only partly due to the difficulty in obtaining access to archival sources and to official military documentary materials. The military coup of 1973 and the subsequent transformations within the Chilean armed forces and national police further inhibited most serious research, though at the same time it inspired both Chilean and foreign scholars to reconsider conventional views of civil-military relations.

Civil-military relations and more narrowly military and technical themes were neglected so long, both by Chilean and foreign scholars, that a number of important research opportunities exist. Among the most important of these would be recruitment, training, and political socialization within the three major service branches since the 1920s; interservice rivalries and congressional relations of the armed forces; the influence of foreign training missions and weapons procurement programs, especially since World War II; and the role expansion experienced by the armed forces prior to the 1973 military coup. Also of considerable interest would be the relationship between strategic planning for external contingencies and the political role of the armed forces since the 1960s. Examination of this role expansion should provide insight both into the diversification of technical expertise and specialization within the armed services and the relationship of this increasing specialization to the military's political and administrative role in Chilean society.

With time, the events of 1973 and the military regime that followed seem destined to engender a multifaceted research program that will both serve to provide a better understanding of Chilean history in the twentieth century more generally, and to enhance our understanding of the specific changes within the military institutions as a result of their increased role in politics. The impact upon the armed forces and *carabineros* of participation in national planning and internal administration since 1973 is also of immediate and long-term concern. The challenge of a research program that achieves these objectives requires the talents of a new generation of Chilean specialists and, in particular, of investigators with new, creative approaches to the study of the military institutions and civil-military relations. This challenge represents a difficult, but potentially fruitful agenda for future research as Chile makes the transition from military to civilian government in 1990.

BIBLIOGRAPHY: CHILE

1. Academia de Guerra. ACADEMIA DE GUERRA, 1886-1986. Santiago: n.p., 1986.

2. ——. RESENA HISTORICA DE LA ACADEMIA DE GUERRA, 1836-1936. Santiago: Instituto Geográfico Militar, 1936.

3. "La acción del ejército en la liberación de Chile." Unpublished ms. circulated informally by Chilean officers, n.d.

4. Adán, Aníbal Leonicio. "La disponibilidad en el ejército." REVISTA MILITAR 1 (1898).

5. Ahumada, General Arturo. EL EJERCITO Y LA REVOLUCION DE SEPTIEMBE DE 1924: REMINISCENCIAS. Santiago: La Tracción, 1931.

6. Alba, Victor. EL MILITARISMO. Mexico City, UNAM, 1959.

7. Aldona S., Colonel Guillermo. "El ejército: Escuela de civismo e instituciones de equilibrio social." MEMORIAL DEL EJERCITO DE CHILE, September-October 1940, 687-709.

8. Aldunate Phillips, Captain Raúl. LA REVOLUCION DE LOS TENIETES. Santiago: La Gratitud Nacional, n.d.

9. Alessandri Palma, Arturo. RECUERDOS DE GOBIERNO. 3 vols. Santiago: Editorial Nascimento, 1967.

10. Alexander, Robert. THE TRAGEDY OF CHILE. Westport: Greenwood Press, 1978.

11. Allende, Salvador. LA CONTRADICCION DE CHILE. Santiago: Socialist Party of Chile, 1943.

12. ——. "Fuerzas armadas y carabineros." In NUESTRO CAMINO AL SOCIALISMO: LA VIA CHILENA, 128. Buenos Aires: Ediciones Papiro, 1971: 128.

13. Altamirano, Carlos. DIALECTICA DE UNA DERROTA. Mexico City: Siglo XXI Editores, 1977.

14. Alvarez, Lieutenant Carlos Soto. EDUCACION E INSTRUCCION MILITAR. Santiago: n.p., 1905.

15. Anguita, Bernabé F., comp. LA ESCUELA NAVAL DE CHILE. Valparaíso: Talleres Tipográficos de la Armada, 1902.

16. Aránguiz Latorre, Manuel. EL 4 DE JUNIO. Santiago: Zig Zag, 1933.

17. Arce Fernández, Horacio. "La fuerza armada y la seguridad nacional," prologue. In ESTATUTO JURIDICO DE LAS FUERZAS ARMADAS. Santiago: n.p., 1957.

18. Arriagada Herrera, Genaro. DE LA VIA CHILENA A LA VIA INSURRECCIONAL. Santiago: Editorial del Pacífico, 1974.

19. ———. IDEOLOGIA POLITICA DE LOS MILITARES. Santiago: ICHEH, 1981.

20. ———. "The Legal and Institutional Framework of the Armed Forces in Chile." In MILITARY RULE IN CHILE: DICTATORSHIP AND OPPOSITIONS, 117-43. Edited by J. Samuel Valenzuela and Arturo Valenzuela. Baltimore: Johns Hopkins University Press, 1986.

21. ———. EL PENSAMIENTO POLITICO DE LOS MILITARES. Santiago: Centro de Investigaciones Socioeconómicas, 1981.

22. ———. PINOCHET: THE POLITICS OF POWER. Translated by Nancy Morris. Boston: Unwin Hyman, 1988.

23. ———. LA POLITICA MILITAR DE PINOCHET. Santiago: ICHEH, 1986.

24. Balart Contreras, René. "Las fuerzas armadas y la historia política chilena." PUNTO FINAL, 3 July 1973.

25. Barceló Lira, José M. "La evolución del ejército desde la ocupación del territorio araucano (1859-1879) hasta nuestros días." MEMORIAL DEL EJERCITO DE CHILE, March-April 1935, 199-218.

26. Bari M., Captain David. EL EJERCITO ANTE LAS NUEVAS DOCTRINAS SOCIALES. Santiago: n.p., 1922.

27. Barrientos, Carlos. CARABINEROS DE CHILE ANTE EL DERECHO Y LA JURISPRUDENCIA. Santiago: Editorial Universitaria, 1962.

28. Barros Merino, Tobías. LA VIDA MILITAR EN ALEMANIA. Santiago: n.p., 1890.

29. Barros Ortiz, Tobías. RECOGIENDO LOS PASOS. 2 vols. Santiago: Planeta, 1984-88.

30. ———. VIGILIA DE ARMAS: CHARLAS SOBRE LA VIDA MILITAR. Santiago: Estado Mayor del Ejército, 1920.

31. Bello Codesido, Emilio. RECUERDOS POLITICOS: LA JUNTA DE GOBIERNO DE 1925; SU ORIGEN Y RELACION CON LA REFORMA DEL REGIMEN CONSTITUCIONAL. Santiago: Editorial Nascimento 1954.

32. Benedicto, Colonel Agustín. "El ejército en el estado moderno." MEMORIAL DEL EJERCITO DE CHILE, February 1929.

33. Bennett, General Juan P. LA REVOLUCION DEL 5 DE SEPTIEMBRE DE 1924. Santiago: Balcells, 1925.

34. Bicheno, H.E. "Las fuerzas armadas en el sistema político chileno." MEMORIAL DEL EJERCITO DE CHILE, May-June 1972, 26-37.

35. Birn, Laurence, ed. THE END OF CHILEAN DEMOCRACY. New York: Seabury Press, 1973.

36. Bitar, Sergio. CHILE: EXPERIMENT IN DEMOCRACY. Philadelphia: Institute for the Study of Human Issues, 1986.

37. ———, comp. CHILE: LIBERALISMO ECONOMICO Y DICTADURA POLITICA. Lima: Instituto de Estudios Peruanos, 1980.

38. Blakemore, Harold. "The Chilean Revolution of 1891 and its Historiography." HISPANIC AMERICAN HISTORICAL REVIEW 45 (1965): 393-421.

39. Blanche E., Colonel Bartolomé. HERIDAS ABIERTAS. Santiago: n.p., 1924.

40. Boonen Rivera, Jorge. PARTICIPACION DEL EJERCITO EN EL DESARROLLO Y PROGRESO DEL PAIS. Santiago: Imprenta del Globo, 1917.

41. Bowers, Claude. CHILE THROUGH EMBASSY WINDOWS, 1939-1953. New York: Simon and Schuster, 1958.

42. Branch, Taylor, and Eugene M. Propper. LABYRINTH. New York: Viking Press, 1982.

43. Bravo, Alfredo Guillermo. EL 4 DE JUNIO: EL FESTIN DE LOS AUDACES. Santiago: Editorial Universitaria, 1955.

44. Bravo, R. Leonidas. LO QUE SUPO UN AUDITOR DE GUERRA. Santiago: Editorial del Pacífico, 1955.

45. Bravo Lavín, Mario. CHILE FRENTE AL SOCIALISMO Y AL COMUNISMO. Santiago: Editorial Ercilla, 1934.

46. Bray, Donald W. "Chilean Politics During the Second Ibáñez Administration (1952-58)." Ph.D. dissertation, Stanford University, 1961.

47. Brieba A., Luis. ACTUACION DEL EJERCITO EN LAS ELECCIONES DE 1924. Santiago: n.p., 1927.

48. Bulnes, Gonzalo. GUERRA DEL PACIFICO. 3 vols. Valparaíso: Sociedad Imprenta y Litografía Universo, 1912-19.

49. Burnett, Ben G. POLITICAL GROUPS IN CHILE. Austin: University of Texas Press, 1970.

50. Burr, Robert N. BY REASON OR FORCE: CHILE AND THE BALANCING OF POWER IN SOUTH AMERICA, 1830-1905. Berkeley: University of California Press, 1965.

51. Bustos, Montaldo. "Ningún cuerpo armado puede deliberar." MEMORIAL DEL EJERCITO DE CHILE, July-August 1953, 79-84.

52. Cabero, Alberto. CHILE Y LOS CHILENOS. 3rd ed. Santiago: Editorial Lyceum, 1948.

53. ———. RECUERDOS DE DON PEDRO AGUIRRE CERDA. Santiago: Imprenta Nascimento, 1948.

54. Cabrera, Luis, et al. MISION MILITAR CHILENA EN EL ECUADOR. Quito: Imprenta del Ejército, 1902.

55. Cáceres, Juan. "Comentario sabatino." ZIG ZAG 13 (1924).

56. Canessa Robert, Lieutenant Julio. "El ejército garantiza el cumplimiento de su misión." REVISTA ARMAS Y SERVICIOS DEL EJERCITO 28 (1983).

57. Carranza Ríos, Ignacio. CHILE 80: EL PRINCIPIO DEL FIN. Caracas: Servicio Gráfico Editorial, 1980.

58. Carrasco, C. Arnaldo. "Aviación militar." MEMORIAL DEL EJERCITO DE CHILE, April 1917, 581-85.

59. Castillo, Fernando, Rafael Echeverría, and Jorge Larraín. "Las masas, el estado y el problema del poder en Chile." CUADERNOS DE LA REALIDAD NACIONAL 16 (1973): 3-70.

60. Cerda, José M. RELACION HISTORICA DE LA REVOLUCION DE LA ARMADA DE CHILE. Concepción: n.p., 1934.

61. Charlin, Carlos. DEL AVION ROJO A LA REPUBLICA SOCIALISTA. Santiago: Editorial Quimantú, 1972.

62. Chavkin, Samuel. THE MURDER OF CHILE. New York: Everest, 1982.

63. CHILE: A COUNTRY STUDY. Washington: U.S. Government Printing Office, 1985.

64. "Chile: Beyond the Darkest Decade." NACLA REPORT ON THE AMERICAS, September-October 1983, 2-41.

65. CHILE: THE PINOCHET DECADE. London: Latin American Bureau, 1983.

66. CHILE UNDER MILITARY RULE. New York: IDOC/North America, 1974.

67. Cleven, N.A.N. "Suppression of Opposition in Chile." NEW YORK TIMES CURRENT HISTORY MAGAZINE, February 1928, 732-33.

68. CODIGO DE JUSTICIA MILITAR. 2d ed. Santiago: n.p., 1944.

69. Colby, William E. HONORABLE MEN: MY LIFE IN THE CIA. New York: Simon and Schuster, 1978.

70. Collings, H.T. "Chile's New Anti-Bolshevist Government." NEW YORK TIMES CURRENT HISTORY MAGAZINE, July 1927, 639-40.

71. Comité de Historia Militar del Ejército. HISTORIA MILITAR DE CHILE. 3 vols. Santiago: Estado Mayor, 1969.

72. CONSTITUCION POLITICA DE CHILE. 1980.

73. Contreras G., Víctor. "Balance aeronáutico de 1921." MEMORIAL DEL EJERCITO DE CHILE, April 1922, 568-71.

74. ———. BITACORA DE LA DICTADURA: ADMINISTRACION IBANEZ 1927-1931. Santiago: Imprenta Cultura, 1942.

75. Correa, Raquel, Malu Sierra, and Elizabeth Subercaseaux. LOS GENERALES DEL REGIMEN. Santiago: Editorial Aconcagua, 1983.

76. Correa Prieto, Luis. EL PRESIDENTE IBANEZ: LA POLITICA Y LOS POLITICOS; APUNTES PARA LA HISTORIA. Santiago: Orbe, 1962.

77. Cortés Rencoret, Colonel Gerardo. INTRODUCCION A LA SEGURIDAD NACIONAL. Santiago: Instituto de Ciencia Política, Universidad Católica de Chile, 1976.

78. ———. "La seguridad nacional como objetivo de gobierno." In NUESTRO CAMINO. Santiago: Ediciones Encina, 1976.

79. Davis, Nathaniel. THE LAST TWO YEARS OF SALVADOR ALLENDE. Ithaca: Cornell University Press, 1985.

80. De Riz, Liliana. SOCIEDAD Y POLITICA EN CHILE: DE PORTALES A PINOCHET. Mexico City: UNAM, 1979.

81. Délano, Manuel. "Lo que cuestan las FF.AA." [Fuerzas Armadas]." HOY (Santiago), 3-9 September 1984, 29-31.

82. ———. "¿Cuánto gana un general?" ANALISIS (Santiago), 11-17 February 1986.

83. Departamento de Orden y Seguridad. MONOGRAFIA DE CARABINEROS DE CHILE. Santiago: Imprenta de Carabineros, 1969.

84. Depuis, Colonel Gustavo. "Realidad nacional permite visualizar el futuro del Ejército." EL MERCURIO (Santiago), 14 September 1986, C3.

85. "La dernier campagne au Chile." REVUE MILITAIRE DE L'ETRANGER, April 1892, 304-30.

86. DeVylder, Stefan. ALLENDE'S CHILE: THE POLITICAL ECONOMY OF THE RISE AND FALL OF THE UNIDAD POPULAR. Cambridge: Cambridge University Press, 1976.

87. Díaz, Francisco J. "Instituciones armadas y vida nacional." REVISTA CHILENA, October 1917, 113-29.

88. Díaz Feliú, Gustavo A. "El soldado alemán: El ejército chileno debe conservar su tradición prusiana," MEMORIAL DEL EJERCITO DE CHILE, May-June 1971, 126-27.

89. Díaz Valderrama, Francisco Javier. CUARENTA ANOS DE INSTRUCCION MILITAR ALEMAN EN CHILE. Santiago: Imprenta Jeneral Díaz, 1926.

90. Donoso, Ricardo. ALESSANDRI: AGITADOR Y DEMOLEDOR; CINCUENTA ANOS DE HISTORIA POLITICA DE CHILE. 2 vols. Mexico City: Fondo de Cultura Económica, 1952.

91. ———. DESARROLLO POLITICO Y SOCIAL DE CHILE DESDE LA CONSTITUCION DE 1833. 2d ed. Santiago: Imprenta Universitaria, 1942.

92. Donoso Loero, Teresa, ed. BREVE HISTORIA DE LA UNIDAD POPULAR. Santiago: EL MERCURIO, 1974.

93. English, Adrian J. ARMED FORCES OF LATIN AMERICA. London: Jane's Publishing Co., 1984.

94. ———. "The Chilean Navy." NAVY INTERNATIONAL 87 (1983).

95. Epstein, Fritz. "European Military Influence in Latin America." Washington: Library of Congress, 1941. Unpublished ms.

96. Escuela Militar. ESCUELA MILITAR DE CHILE. Santiago: n.p., 1903.

97. Estado Mayor del Ejército. HISTORIA MILITAR DE CHILE. 3 vols. Santiago: Biblioteca del Oficial, 1984.

98. ———. "La seguridad nacional: Función de Gobierno." MEMORIAL DEL EJERCITO DE CHILE, May-June 1949.

99. Estado Mayor General. LA GUERRA CIVIL DE 1891: RELACION HISTORIA MILITAR. Santiago: n.p., 1917.

100. Fenner Marín, Oscar. OBSERVACIONES SOBRE LA LABOR QUE CORRESPONDERA A LA COMISION REVISORA DE LAS LEYES DE JUSTICIA MILITAR. Santiago: Imprenta del Ministerio de Guerra, 1925.

101. Figueroa, Pedro Pablo. ALBUM MILITAR DE CHILE, 1810-1879. Santiago: Imprenta i Encua dernación Barcelona, 1898.

102. Flores Alvarez, Enrique. "Historia de nuestra aviación." REVISTA DE LA FUERZA AEREA 1-2 (1941-42).

103. ———. HISTORIA DE LA AVIACION EN CHILE. Santiago: Imprenta Rapid, 1933.

104. Fontaine, Arturo Aldunate, and Cristián Zegers A. "Cómo llegaron las fuerzas armadas a la acción del 11 de septiembre de 1973." EL MERCURIO (Santiago), 11 September 1974, separata.

105. Foxley, Alejandro. LATIN AMERICAN EXPERIMENTS IN NEO-CONSERVATIVE ECONOMICS. Berkeley: University of California Press, 1983.

106. Frühling, Hugo, Carlos Portales, and Augusto Varas. ESTADO Y FUERZAS ARMADAS EN EL PROCESO POLITICO CHILENO. Santiago: FLACSO, 1982.

107. FUERZAS ARMADAS Y SEGURIDAD NACIONAL. Santiago: Ediciones Portada, 1973.

108. Garay Vera, Cristián. "Doctrina Schneider-Prats: La crisis del sistema político y la participación militar, 1969-1973." REVISTA POLITICA DEL INSTITUTO DE CIENCIA POLITICA DE LA UNIVERSIDAD DE CHILE 10 (1986).

109. Garcés, Joan. ALLENDE Y LA EXPERIENCIA CHILENA, Barcelona: Editorial Ariel, 1976.

110. ———. REVOLUCION, CONGRESO Y CONSTITUCION: EL CASO TOHA: Santiago: Editorial Quimantú, 1972.

111. García, Pío, comp. LAS FUERZAS ARMADAS Y EL GOLPE DEL ESTADO EN CHILE. Mexico City: Siglo XXI Editores, 1976.

112. Garretón, Manuel Antonio. EL PROCESO POLITICO CHILENO. Santiago: FLACSO, 1983.

113. Gazmuri, Cristían. "Las armas chilenas: 1973-1984." DEFENSA Y DESARME, September-December 1985.

114. Gil, Federico G. THE POLITICAL SYSTEM OF CHILE. Boston: Houghton Mifflin, 1966.

115. Gil, Federico G., Ricardo Lagos, and Henry Landsberger, eds. CHILE AT THE TURNING POINT: LESSONS OF THE SOCIALIST YEARS, 1970-1973. Translated by John S. Gitlitz. Philadelphia: Institute for the Study of Human Issues, 1979.

116. Grove, Jorge V. DESCORRIENDO EL VELO: EPISODIO DE LOS DOCE DIAS DE LA REPUBLICA SOCIALISTA. Valparaíso: Imprenta Aurora de Chile, 1933.

117. Guillard Marinot, General Roberto. "La intervención del ejército en los acontecimientos del presente siglo: Clase magistral...con motivo del 101 aniversario de la creación de la Academia de Guerra del Ejército." La Reina: Comando de Institutos Militares, 1987. Mimeo.

118. Guzmán, Leonardo. UN EPISODIO DE LA HISTORIA NACIONAL: JULIO-NOVIEMBRE DE 1931. Santiago, n.p., 1966.

119. Hansen, Roy A. "Military Culture and Organizational Decline: A Study of the Chilean Army." Ph.D. dissertation, University of California, Los Angeles, 1967.

120. Haring, C.H. "Chilean Politics, 1920-1928." HISPANIC AMERICAN HISTORICAL REVIEW 11 (1931): 1-26.

121. ———. "The Chilean Revolution of 1931." HISPANIC AMERICAN HISTORICAL REVIEW 13 (1933): 197-203.

122. Heise González, Julio. LA CONSTITUCION DE 1925 Y LAS NUEVAS TENDENCIAS SOCIALES. Santiago: Editorial Universitaria, 1951.

123. Hervey, Maurice H. DARK DAYS IN CHILE. London: n.p., 1892. Reprinted by the Institute for the Study of Human Issues, Philadelphia, 1979. Special correspondent for the TIMES of London on the civil war of 1891.

124. Hillmon, Tommie Junior. "A History of the Armed Forces of Chile from Independence to 1920." Ph.D. dissertation, Syracuse University, 1963.

125. Hiriart Laval, Hernán. "La política militar y la opinión pública." MEMORIAL DEL EJERCITO DE CHILE, May-June 1964, 15-19.

126. HISTORIA DE LA ARTILLERIA DE CHILE. Santiago: Instituto Geográfico Militar, 1946.

127. Hojman, David E., ed. CHILE AFTER 1973: ELEMENTS FOR THE ANALYSIS OF MILITARY RULE. Liverpool: Centre for Latin American Studies, University of Liverpool, 1985.

128. Huneeus, Carlos. EL EJERCITO Y LA POLITICA EN EL CHILE DE PINOCHET: SU MAGNITUD Y ALCANCES. Santiago: CERC, 1988.

129. ———, and Jorge Olave. AUTORITARISMO, MILITARES Y TRANSICION A LA DEMOCRACIA: CHILE EN UNA PERSPECTIVA COMPARADA. Santiago: CERC, 1986.

130. Jarvis, Lovell S. CHILEAN AGRICULTURE UNDER MILITARY RULE: Berkeley: Institute of International Studies, University of California, 1985.

131. Johnson, John J. THE MILITARY AND SOCIETY IN LATIN AMERICA. Stanford: Stanford University Press, 1964.

132. Joxe, Alain. LAS FUERZAS ARMADAS EN EL SISTEMA POLITICO DE CHILE. Santiago: Editorial Universitaria, 1970.

133. ———. "Is the 'Chilean Road to Socialism' Blocked?" In THE CHILEAN ROAD TO SOCIALISM. 223-51. Edited by J. Ann Zammit. Austin: University of Texas Press, 1973.

134. Kaplan Cojano, Oscar. DICCIONARIO MILITAR. Santiago: Instituto Geográfico Militar, 1944.

135. Keegan, John. "Chile." In WORLD ARMIES, 126-30. Edited by John Keegan. New York: Facts on File, 1979.

136. Keller R., Carlos. LA ETERNA CRISIS CHILENA. Santiago: Editorial Nascimento, 1931.

137. Kissinger, Henry. YEARS OF UPHEAVAL. Boston: Little Brown, 1982.

138. Körner, Emil. "Militarische Nachrichten aus Chile." MILITAR WOCHENBLATT 11 (1890): 117-19.

139. Langlois, Luis. INFLUENCIA DEL PODER NAVAL EN LA HISTORIA DE CHILE DESDE 1810 A 1910. Valparaíso: Imprenta de la Armada, 1911.

140. Lara, Alberto. LOS OFICIALES ALEMANES EN CHILE. Santiago: n.p., 1929.

141. Lechner, Norbert. LA DEMOCRACIA EN CHILE. Buenos Aires: Ediciones Signos, 1970.

142. Levy, Fred D., et al. CHILE: AN ECONOMY IN TRANSITION. Washington: World Bank, 1980.

143. Lieuwen, Edwin. ARMS AND POLITICS IN LATIN AMERICA. New York: Frederick A. Praeger Publishers, 1961.

144. López Rubio, Lieutenant Colonel Sergio E. HISTORIA DEL EJERCITO. Santiago: Editorial Quimantú, 1973.

145. López Silva, Major Claudio. "Las fuerzas armadas en el tercer mundo." MEMORIAL DEL EJERCITO DE CHILE, July-August 1970, 11-51.

146. López Urrutia, Carlos. HISTORIA DE LA MARINA DE CHILE. Santiago: Editorial Andrés Bello, 1969.

147. Loveman, Brian. CHILE: THE LEGACY OF HISPANIC CAPITALISM. 2d ed. New York: Oxford University Press, 1988.

148. MacEoin, Gary. NO PEACEFUL WAY. New York: Sheed and Ward, 1974.

149. Manns, Patricio. REVOLUCION DE LA ESCUADRA. Santiago: Ediciones Universitarias de Valparaíso, 1972.

150. Marín Balmaceda, Raúl. LA CAIDA DE UN REGIMEN: JULIO DE 1931. Santiago: Imprenta Universitaria, 1933.

151. ———. 4 DE JUNIO DE 1932. Santiago: Imprenta Universitaria, 1933.

152. Medina Fraguela, General Ernesto. NUESTRA DEFENSA NACIONAL FRENTE A LA OPINION PUBLICA. Santiago: Imprenta Benapres y Fernández, 1941.

153. Medina Franzani, Ernesto. EL PROBLEMA MILITAR DE CHILE. Leipzig: C.C. Roder, 1912.

154. Medina Lois, Captain Alejandro. "Seguridad nacional: Un concepto que debe difundirse." MEMORIAL DEL EJERCITO DE CHILE, September 1966.

155. MEMORANDUM DE LA GUERRA CIVIL DE 1891. Santiago: n.p., 1892.

156. Millar Carvacho, René. "Significado y antecedentes del movimiento militar de 1924." REVISTA HISTORIA 11 (1972-73).

157. Ministerio de Guerra. ALBUM GRAFICO DEL EJERCITO: CENTENARIO DE LA INDEPENDENCIA DE CHILE. Santiago: n.p., 1910.

158. ———. MEMORIA DEL MINISTERIO DE GUERRA PRESENTADA AL CONGRESO NACIONAL, (selected years). Santiago.

159. Ministerios de Guerra y Marina. ALBUM HISTORICO. Santiago: Editora "Atenas," 1928.

160. MODELO ECONOMICO CHILENO: TRAYECTORIA DE UNA CRITICA. Santiago: Editorial Aconcagua, 1982.

161. Monreal, Enrique. CHILE ANTE EL NUEVO REGIMEN. Santiago: n.p., 1928.

162. Montero, René. LA VERDAD SOBRE IBANEZ. Santiago: n.p., 1952.

163. Montero Moreno, René. ORIGENES DEL PROBLEMA SOCIAL EN CHILE: TEMA DEL INVIERNO. Santiago: N. Avaria, 1926.

164. Moore, General Manuel. INSTRUCCIONES PARA EL DESARROLLO DE LAS VIRTUDES MILITARES DEL CUERPO DE OFICIALES DE LA IV DIVISION DEL EJERCITO. Valdivia: Central, 1917.

165. Morley, Morris, and Steven Smith. "Imperial 'Reach': U.S. Policy and the CIA in Chile." JOURNAL OF POLITICAL AND MILITARY SOCIOLOGY 5 (1977): 203-16.

166. Moss, Robert. CHILE'S MARXIST EXPERIMENT. Newton Abbot, England: David and Charles, 1973.

167. Muñoz, Heraldo. LAS RELACIONES EXTERIORES DEL GOBIERNO MILITAR CHILENO. Santiago: Prospel-CERC, Ediciones del Omitorrinco, 1986.

168. Nef, Jorge. "The Politics of Repression: The Social Pathology of the Chilean Military." LATIN AMERICAN PERSPECTIVES 1 (1974): 58-77.

169. North, Liisa. CIVIL-MILITARY RELATIONS IN ARGENTINA, CHILE, AND PERU. Berkeley: Institute of International Studies, University of California, 1966.

170. ———. "The Military in Chilean Politics." STUDIES IN COMPARATIVE INTERNATIONAL DEVELOPMENT 11 (1976): 73-106.

171. Novoa de la Fuente, Luis. HISTORIA NAVAL DE CHILE. Valparaíso: Imprenta de la Armada, 1944.

172. NUESTRO CAMINO. Santiago: Ediciones Encina, 1976.

173. Nunn, Frederick M. CHILEAN POLITICS 1920-1931: THE HONORABLE MISSION OF THE ARMED FORCES. Albuquerque: University of New Mexico Press, 1970.

174. ———. "Emil Körner and the Prussianization of the Chilean Army: Origins, Process, and Consequences, 1885-1920." HISPANIC AMERICAN HISTORICAL REVIEW 50 (1970): 300-22.

175. ———. "Latin American State within the State: The Politics of the Chilean Army, 1924-1927." AMERICAS 27 (1970): 40-55.

176. ———. "Military-Civilian Relations in Chile: The Legacy of the Golpe of 1973." INTER-AMERICAN ECONOMIC AFFAIRS 29 (1975): 43-58.

177. ———. THE MILITARY IN CHILEAN HISTORY: ESSAYS ON CIVIL-MILITARY RELATIONS, 1810-1973. Albuquerque: University of New Mexico Press, 1976.

178. ———. "Military Rule in Chile: The Revolutions of September 5, 1924 and January 23, 1925." HISPANIC AMERICAN HISTORICAL REVIEW 47 (1967): 1-21.

179. ———. "New Thoughts on Military Intervention in Latin American Politics: The Chilean Case, 1973." JOURNAL OF LATIN AMERICAN STUDIES 7 (1975): 271-304.

180. ———. YESTERDAY'S SOLDIERS: EUROPEAN MILITARY PROFESSIONALISM IN SOUTH AMERICA, 1890-1940. Lincoln: University of Nebraska Press, 1983.

181. Olvarría Bravo, Arturo. CHILE BAJO LA DEMOCRACIA CRISTIANA. 6 vols. Santiago: n.p., 1965-70.

182. ———. CHILE ENTRE DOS ALESSANDRI. 4 vols. Santiago, n.p., 1962.

183. Orrego Vicuña, Francisco, ed. CHILE: THE BALANCED VIEW. Santiago: Institute of International Studies, University of Chile, 1975.

184. Palacios, Jorge. CHILE: AN ATTEMPT AT 'HISTORIC COMPROMISE'; THE REAL STUDY OF THE ALLENDE YEARS. Chicago: Banner Press, 1979.

185. Pérez, Enrique. "Chile y la cultura militar en la América Hispana." HISPANIA (London), 1 (1912).

186. Petras, James, and Morris Morley. THE UNITED STATES AND CHILE: IMPERIALISM AND THE ALLENDE GOVERNMENT. New York: Monthly Review Press, 1975.

187. Piacentini, Pablo. "La doctrina Schneider-Prats y el gobierno de la Unidad Popular." ESTRATEGIA (Buenos Aires) 3 (1972): 24-28.

188. Pinochet, General Augusto. THE CRUCIAL DAY. Santiago: Editorial Renacimiento, 1982.

189. "Pinochet's Plebiscite: Choice with No Options." NACLA REPORT ON THE AMERICAS, March-April 1988, 13-40.

190. Pinto Durán, Carlos. LA REVOLUCION CHILENA. Santiago: Valiente, 1925.

191. Polloni R., Lieutenant Colonel Alberto. LAS FUERZAS ARMADAS DE CHILE: COMPENDIO CIVICO MILITAR. Santiago: Editorial Andrés Bello, 1972.

192. Portales, Carlos. "Militarization and Political Institutions in Chile." In GLOBAL MILITARIZATION, 123-44. Edited by Peter Wallensteen, John Galtung, and Carlos Portales. Boulder: Westview Press, 1985.

193. Portales, Carlos, and Augusto Varas. "Gasto militar en Chile, 1952-1980." Santiago: FLACSO, 1981.

194. ———. "The Role of Military Expenditure in the Development Process: Chile 1952-1973 and 1973-1980; Two Contrasting Cases." IBERO AMERICANA (Stockholm) 12 (1983): 21-50.

195. Powers, Thomas. THE MAN WHO KEPT THE SECRETS: RICHARD HELMS AND THE CIA. New York: Knopf, 1979.

196. Prado Vásquez, Colonel Guillermo. LA CARRERA DE OFICIAL: LO QUE ES Y LO QUE DEBE SER. Santiago: n.p., 1952.

197. Prats González, General Carlos. MEMORIAS. Santiago: Editorial Antártica, 1985.

198. Remmer, Karen L. "Public Policy and Regime Consolidation: The First Five Years of the Chilean Junta." JOURNAL OF DEVELOPING AREAS 13 (1979): 441-61.

199. ———. "Political Demobilization in Chile, 1973-1978." COMPARATIVE POLITICS 12 (1980): 275-301.

200. República Socialista. PROGRAMA DE ACCION INMEDIATA DE LA REPUBLICA SOCIALISTA. Concepción: n.p., 1932.

201. Riquelme, Aníbal. "Relación que debe existir entre la política de un estado y el alto comando del ejército." MEMORIAL DEL EJERCITO DE CHILE, September 1914, 638-50.

202. Rivas Sánchez, Fernando, and Elisabeth Reiman Weigert. LAS FUERZAS ARMADAS DE CHILE: UN CASO DE PENETRACION IMPERIALISTA. Mexico City: n.p., 1976.

203. Rodríguez, Juan Agustín. CRONICAS NACIONALES Y NAVALES. Valparaíso: Imprenta de la Armada, 1953.

204. Rodríguez Mendoza, Emilio. COMO SI FUERA AHORA. Santiago: Editorial Nascimento, 1929.

205. ———. EL GOLPE DE ESTADO DE 1924: AMBIENTE Y ACTORES. Santiago: Ediciones Ercilla, 1938.

206. Rojas, Robinson. "The Chilean Armed Forces: The Role of the Military in the Popular Unity Government." In THE CHILEAN ROAD TO SOCIALISM, 310-22. Edited by Dale L. Johnson. New York: Doubleday, 1973.

207. ———. THE MURDER OF ALLENDE. New York: Harper and Row, 1976. Translation of ESTOS MATARON A ALLENDE (Barcelona: Ediciones Martínez Roca, 1974.

208. Rouquié, Alain. EL ESTADO MILITAR EN AMERICA LATINA. Mexico City: Siglo XXI Editores, 1984.

209. Roxborough, Ian, Philip O'Brien, and Jackie Roddick. CHILE: THE STATE AND REVOLUTION. New York: Holmes and Meier, 1977.

210. Sáez Morales, Carlos. RECUERDOS DE UN SOLDADO. 3 vols. Santiago: Editorial Ercilla, 1933-34.

211. Salcedo, Colonel Carlos. "La política y la preparación militar de un país." MEMORIAL DEL EJERCITO DE CHILE, June 1926.

212. Santillana, Pablo. CHILE: ANALISIS DE UN ANO DE GOBIERNO MILITAR. Buenos Aires: Prensa LatinoAmericana, 1974.

213. THE SCHNEIDER CASE: OPERATION ALPHA. Santiago: Editorial Quimantú, 1972.

214. Schoultz, Lars. HUMAN RIGHTS AND UNITED STATES POLICY TOWARD LATIN AMERICA. Princeton: Princeton University Press, 1981.

215. ———. NATIONAL SECURITY AND UNITED STATES POLICY TOWARD LATIN AMERICA. Princeton: Princeton University Press, 1987.

216. Sears, Lieutenant James H. (U.S.N.), and Ensign B.W. Wells, Jr. THE CHILEAN REVOLUTION OF 1891. Washington: U.S. Government Printing Office, 1893.

217. Sigmund, Paul. THE OVERTHROW OF ALLENDE AND THE POLITICS OF CHILE, 1964-1976. Pittsburgh: University of Pittsburgh Press, 1977.

218. Silva, Patricio. ESTADO, NEOLIBERALISMO Y POLITICA AGRARIA EN CHILE, 1973-1981. Dordrecht, The Netherlands: Foris Publications, 1987.

219. Silva Maturana, Raúl. CAMINO AL ABISMO: LO QUE NO SE HA DICHO SOBRE EL PROCESO DE LA LINEA RECTA. Santiago: Editorial Universitaria, 1955.

220. Silva Solar, Julio. "El integrismo católico-fascista en la ideología de la junta militar." CHILE-AMERICA (Rome) 2 (1975): 1-13.

221. Smirnow, Gabriel. LA REVOLUCION DESARMADA: CHILE, 1970-1973. Mexico City: Ediciones ERA, 1977.

222. Smith, Brian H. THE CHURCH AND POLITICS IN CHILE. Princeton: Princeton University Press, 1982.

223. Strawbridge, George Jr. "Militarism and Nationalism in Chile, 1920-1932." Ph.D. dissertation, University of Pennsylvania, 1968.

224. Tarr, Terrence S. "Military Intervention and Civilian Reaction in Chile." Ph.D. dissertation, University of Florida, 1967.

225. Taufic, Camilo. CHILE EN LA HOGUERA. Buenos Aires: Corregidor, 1974.

226. Téllez Cárcamo, Indalicio. HISTORIA MILITAR DE CHILE. Santiago: Instituto Geográfico Militar, 1925.

227. ———. RECUERDOS MILITARES. Santiago: Instituto Geográfico Militar, 1945.

228. Terán, Captain Domingo L. TEMA MILITAR. Santiago: n.p., 1917.

229. Thomas, Jack Ray. "The Evolution of a Chilean Socialist: Marmaduke Grove." HISPANIC AMERICAN HISTORICAL REVIEW 47 (1967): 22-37.

230. ———. "Marmaduke Grove: a Political Biography." Ph.D. dissertation, Ohio State University, 1962.

231. ———. "The Socialist Republic of Chile." JOURNAL OF INTER-AMERICAN STUDIES 6 (1964): 203-20.

232. Timossi, Jorge. GRANDES ALAMEDAS: EL COMBATE DEL PRESIDENTE ALLENDE. Havana: Editorial de Ciencias Sociales, 1974.

233. Toro Dávila, Agustín. SINTESIS HISTORICO-MILITAR DE CHILE. Santiago: Editorial Universitaria, 1976.

234. Torres, Major L. Leiva. "La nacionalidad y la patria frente al anarquismo y al antimilitarismo." MEMORIAL DEL EJERCITO DE CHILE, June 1926.

235. LAS TRANSFORMACIONES EDUCACIONALES BAJO EL REGIMEN MILITAR. 2 vols. Santiago: PIIE, 1984.

236. Uribe, Armando. THE BLACK BOOK OF AMERICAN INTERVENTION. Boston: Beacon Press, 1975.

237. United States. Congress. House. Committee on Foreign Affairs. Subcommittee on Inter-American Affairs. UNITED STATES-CHILEAN RELATIONS. 93d Cong., 1st sess., 1973.

238. ———. Senate. Select Committee to Study Governmental Operations with Respect to Intelligence Activities. ALLEGED ASSASSINATION PLOTS INVOLVING FOREIGN LEADERS. 94th Cong., 1st sess., 1975.

239. ———. Senate. Select Committee to Study Governmental Operations with Respect to Intelligence Activities. COVERT ACTION IN CHILE, 1963-1973. 94th Cong., 1st sess., 1975 Committee Print.

240. Valdivieso Ariztia, Rafael. CRONICA DE UN RESCATE: CHILE, 1973-1988. Santiago: Editorial Andrés Bello, 1988.

241. Valenzuela, Arturo. THE BREAKDOWN OF DEMOCRATIC REGIMES: CHILE. Baltimore: Johns Hopkins University Press, 1978.

242. Valenzuela, Arturo, and J. Samuel Valenzuela, eds. MILITARY RULE IN CHILE: DICTATORSHIP AND OPPOSITIONS. Baltimore: Johns Hopkins University Press, 1986.

243. Valenzuela, María Elena. LA MUJER EN EL CHILE MILITAR. Santiago: Ediciones Chile y América, 1987.

244. Valenzuela Reyes, Major Luis. "Misión de la fuerzas armadas y su participación en el desenvolvimiento normal de nuestra vida democrática." MEMORIAL DEL EJERCITO DE CHILE, May-June 1958, 22-29.

245. Varas, Augusto. "La intervención civil de las fuerzas armadas." In ESTADO Y FUERZAS ARMADAS, 59-81. Edited by Hugo Frühling, Carlos Portales, and Augusto Varas. Santiago: El Gráfico, 1982.

246. ——. LOS MILITARES EN EL PODER: REGIMEN Y GOBIERNO MILITAR EN CHILE, 1973-1986. Santiago: FLACSO/Pehuén, 1987.

247. Varas, Augusto, and Felipe Aguero. EL PROYECTO POLITICO MILITAR. Santiago: FLACSO, 1984.

248. Varas, Florencia. CONVERSACIONES CON VIAUX. Santiago: Impresiones Eire, 1972.

249. ——. GUSTAVO LEIGH: EL GENERAL DISIDENTE. Santiago: Editorial Aconcagua, 1979.

250. Varas, José Miguel. IBANEZ EL HOMBRE: BIOGRAFIA HISTORICA CRITICA. Santiago: Imparcial, 1953.

251. Vergara, Pilar. AUGE Y CAIDA DEL NEOLIBERALISMO EN CHILE: UN ESTUDIO SOBRE LA EVOLUCION IDEOLOGICA DEL REGIMEN MILITAR. Santiago: FLACSO, 1985.

252. Vergara Montero, Ramón. POR RUTAS EXTRAVIADAS. Santiago: Imprenta Universitaria, 1933.

253. Vial Correa, Gonzalo. "Decadencia, consensus y unidad nacional en 1973." POLITICA Y GEOESTRATEGIA (Santiago) 36 (1985): 5-35.

254. Viaux, Major Ambrosio. "La política y la guerra," MEMORIAL DEL EJERCITO DE CHILE, March 1921.

255. Viaux, General Roberto. "Carta del General Roberto Viaux al Presidente Eduardo Frei." EL DIARIO ILUSTRADO (Santiago), 27 October 1969.

256. Vicuña F., Carlos. LA TIRANIA EN CHILE. 2 vols. Santiago: Imprenta Universo, 1938-39.

257. Videla V., Benjamín. "La intervención del ejército en obras de beneficio público." MEMORIAL DEL EJERCITO DE CHILE, September-October 1947, 64-80.

258. Von Schroeders, Admiral Edgardo. EL DELEGADO DEL GOBIERNO Y EL MOTIN DE LA ESCUADRA. Santiago: Imprenta Universo, 1933.

259. Walker Martínez, Gustavo. ESTUDIOS MILITARES. Santiago: Imprenta Barcelona, 1901.

260. Walton, Gary M., ed. THE NATIONAL ECONOMIC POLICIES OF CHILE. Greenwich, CT: JAI Press, 1985.

261. WHITE BOOK OF THE CHANGE OF GOVERNMENT IN CHILE. Santiago: Editora Nacional Gabriela Mistral, 1973.

262. Whitehead, Laurence. "The Chilean Dictatorship." WORLD TODAY (London) 32 (1976): 366-76.

263. Wilhelmy von Wolff, Manfred. "Hacia un análisis de la política exterior chilena contemporánea." ESTUDIOS INTER-NACIONALES 12 (1979): 440-71.

264. Williams, John H. "The Emergence of the Chilean Arms Industry." THE RETIRED OFFICER 4 (1986).

265. Würth Rojas, Ernesto. IBANEZ: CAUDILLO ENIGMATICO. Santiago: Editorial del Pacífico, 1958.

266. Zapata, Silva F. CARABINEROS DE CHILE: RESENA HISTORICA, 1541-1944. Santiago: Imprenta Universo, 1944.

267. Zegers Ariztia, Cristián. "The Armed Forces: Support of a Democratic Institutionality." In CHILE: A CRITICAL SURVEY, 311-24. Santiago: Institute of General Studies, 1972.

268. Zúñiga Montúfar, Gerardo. EL EJERCITO DE CHILE: IMPRESIONES Y APUNTES. Santiago: Imprenta Universo, 1904.

PERIODICALS

269. FUERZA AEREA, 1941. (Formerly REVISTA DE LA FUERZA AEREA.)

270. MEMORIAL DEL EJERCITO DE CHILE (MECH).

271. POLITICA Y GEOSTRATEGIA. (Formerly SEGURIDAD NACIONAL).

272. REVISTA ARMAS Y SERVICIOS DEL EJERCITO.

273. REVISTA DE MARINA, 1885-.

274. REVISTA DEL SUBOFICIAL.

275. SEGURIDAD NACIONAL.

CHAPTER XI

COLOMBIA AND VENEZUELA

Winfield J. Burggraaff
University of Missouri-Columbia

INTRODUCTION

In the twentieth century the Colombian and Venezuelan military establishments have been a study in contrasts. The Colombian armed forces generally have been one of the politically weakest in South America. They have been subordinated to Colombia' s powerful civilian elites, in particular the two traditional political parties--the Conservatives and the Liberals. On only two occasions in this century has the military deposed a constitutionally elected civilian president. The quasi-military government of General Gustavo Rojas Pinilla (1953-57) ultimately was regarded as a disaster by almost all political forces as well as by important elements in the officer corps. In the mid-l960s, when armed forces commander Alberto Ruíz Novoa was perceived to have become too outspoken in his advocacy of populist reforms, President Guillermo León Valencia easily dismissed him. The same fate subsequently awaited two controversial army commanders, General Guillermo Pinzón Caicedo in 1969 and General Alvaro Valencia Tobar in 1975. Despite decades of internal insurgency and serious security problems the Colombian armed forces have remained subservient to civilian leadership. It would probably take a combination of stepped-up guerrilla pressures, an unacceptable increase in illegal narcotics operations, and the beginning of the disintegration of establishment political party cooperation for the military directly to attempt to take national power.

During much of the twentieth century the political role of the Venezuelan military has been strikingly different from that of the

Colombian armed forces. The Venezuelan army totally dominated the country from 1899 to 1958 with the exception of the Acción Democrática-dominated *trienio*, 1945-48. A succession of four army generals from the Andean state of Táchira wielded power during those years, although the regimes of Generals Eleazar López Contreras (1935-41) and Isaías Medina Angarita (1941-45) were quasi-democratic. Since 1959, however, the Venezuelan armed forces, for a variety of reasons, have cooperated amicably with the civilian democratic leadership.

In general there is, as one might imagine, more scholarly and polemical work on the Venezuelan than on the Colombian armed forces. Much of the most detached and analytical secondary literature has been done by scholars outside the two countries under review, especially by North Americans, although Colombian and Venezuelan scholars have made significant contributions as well. This essay intends to be representative of the extant literature, but by no means is exhaustive.

GENERAL WORKS

Several general reference works on the military from an international or regional perspective include succinct information on both the Colombian and Venezuelan armed forces. One of the most detailed is English, ARMED FORCES OF LATIN AMERICA (67), but two briefer sketches are also useful: Dupuy, et al., THE ALMANAC OF WORLD MILITARY POWER (61), and Keegan, WORLD ARMIES (96). Heare (89), studies military expenditures over a thirty-year period. THE POLITICAL AND SOCIO-ECONOMIC ROLE (139), includes useful material on the military in both countries as does Wesson's more recent THE LATIN AMERICAN MILITARY INSTITUTION (205), which contains a section on the political role of the military. Colombia and Venezuela are two of the nine countries used as case studies. Peeler (130), analyzes the democratic process in Colombia, Venezuela, and Costa Rica, but devotes only a brief section to the role of the military. Varas (195), briefly examines the nature of the defense and security strategy of the two countries.

COLOMBIA

No all-inclusive single- or multi-volume work exists on the overall history of the Colombian armed forces, which perhaps is a reflection of their limited political and social influence. A brief work that presents an overview of the development of the armed institution in Colombia is by J. León Helguera (90), who wrote shortly after the restitution of civilian government following the fall of Rojas Pinilla. Anthony Maingot's incisive essay (113), provides a fairly detailed history of the armed forces with focus on the status of the officer corps. A Colombian perspective was provided at the same time by Francisco Leal Buitrago (103). Two works by Robert H. Dix (58, 59) provide a thoughtful political science perspective on the military as an actor on the Colombian political stage and stress the low self-esteem of army officers and the persistent loyalty of civilians to the two traditional parties. Valencia Tovar (192), among other things, underscores the importance of the *reforma militar* of President Rafael Reyes (1904-09) that, in effect, created a professional national army for the first time. The early part of the century is covered by Rueda Vargas (160).

One of the leading students of the Colombian military is J. Mark Ruhl, whose brief monograph (162), and essays (161, 163) offer keen insights into the political role of the armed forces. He argues that, although the military has become larger, stronger, and more professional in recent decades, the strength and resilience of the civilian political elites have inhibited the armed forces from uniting behind a military solution to political crises. Two doctoral dissertations from the mid-1970s, one by Robert W. Studer (177), and another by J. O. Icenhour (95), also shed valuable light on civil-military relations in this century. A brief analysis of military politics is found in Corr (56). Durán (62), a retired general, provides a narrowly institutional approach of only limited value. Echeverri (64), writing in the late 1970s, worried that Colombian society was becoming militarized.

VENEZUELA

Indispensible background to twentieth-century military developments in Venezuela is found in Gilmore (82). The creation of a semi-professionalized military institution during the long Juan Vicente Gómez dictatorship is studied by Ziems (208), who places the evolution of a permanent national army within a broad national and international socio-economic context. Burggraaff (31), studies chronologically the changing political role of the armed forces from the death of Gómez in 1935 to the beginnings of the modern democratic state in 1959. An army general, García Villasmil (79), provides a brief sketch of the development of the Venezuelan armed forces from Gómez's time to the 1960s, with emphasis on institutional progress. COPEI (Christian Democratic party) leader La Riva (99), one of the party's military specialists, presents a thumbnail sketch of Venezuelan military history and the changing constitutional status of the armed forces, and deals with related issues that in his country are frequently regarded as "taboo." Finally, Blutstein, et al., AREA HANDBOOK FOR VENEZUELA (21), includes a section on national security that contains much useful information on the military establishment in particular and security affairs in general.

BIBLIOGRAPHIES

Full-scale bibliographies on either the Colombian or Venezuelan armed forces are lacking; much work needs to be done. This essay is an attempt to help rectify this unfortunate omission.

Some useful information on the Colombian military, however, is found in three works on La Violencia (1946-65). Two are by Russell W. Ramsey, SURVEY AND BIBLIOGRAPHY OF LA VIOLENCIA IN COLOMBIA (148), and "Critical Bibliography on La Violencia in Colombia" (145). Gonzalo Sánchez, "La Violencia in Colombia: New Research, New Questions" (167), calls for more rigorous study of the relationship between the army and La Violencia. More generally, the Instituto Caro y Cuervo has published the ANUARIO BIBLIOGRAFICO COLOMBIANO (2), which includes brief sections on politics and the military.

Little bibliographical work has been done on the Venezuelan military per se, although Lombardi, et al., VENEZUELAN HISTORY: A COMPREHENSIVE WORKING BIBLIOGRAPHY (106), contains sections on general history that include numerous items related to twentieth-century military affairs. The bibliography in Ziems (208), is helpful for the Andean dictatorial regimes as is Burggraaff's (31), for the entire period to 1959. A general and very comprehensive bibliography for the Castro years is Sullivan's BIBLIOGRAFIA COMENTADA DE LA ERA DE CIPRIANO CASTRO (180). Cárdenas (40), is useful for research on Táchira, the state that dominated the military and national politics beginning in 1899.

ARCHIVAL GUIDES AND SOURCES

Owing to the extremely sensitive nature of civil-military relations in both Colombia and Venezuela, most defense-related records are kept confidential. Access to archives or depositories that contain important documents relating to the armed forces in recent decades is highly restricted.

Nonetheless, one valuable archival source is the United States Department of State decimal files in the National Archives (188, 189), which provide valuable intelligence on key military personnel and civil-military crises. As of this writing these documents are open in most cases until the mid-1950s. There is more material on the Venezuelan than on the Colombian military. In Bogotá the Archivo Nacional de Colombia and the archive of the Academia Colombiana de Historia include records from the early years of this century that may be pertinent to the role of the military in public life. The archive of the Colombian Defense Ministry, also in Bogotá, includes in its holdings voluminous documentation on the War of a Thousand Days (1899-1902).

One important exception to the dearth of accessible archival sources for Venezuela is the BOLETIN DEL ARCHIVO HISTORICO DE MIRAFLORES (22). Largely the creation of the distinguished historian Ramón J. Velásquez, this periodical, which was founded in 1959, has published thousands of documents from the Castro-Gómez era. Many of these papers from the Venezuelan presidential archive deal with the developing national army as well as with major revolutions and minor military and regional revolts. Thus far 124 volumes have been published. The section on La República (1830 to present day) in the Archivo General de la Nación (Caracas) should also be consulted.

PUBLISHED DOCUMENTS

In both Colombia and Venezuela an important source of information on the formal workings of the armed forces is the annual reports that each defense ministry submits to congress (48, 198). Also useful for both countries are United States State Department documents collected in the FOREIGN RELATIONS OF THE UNITED STATES series (187). For Colombia there are a few scattered works such as COMPILACION DE LAS DISPOSICIONES QUE REGLAMENTAN EL SERVICIO MILITAR OBLIGATORIO (51), and EL GOBIERNO, EL EJERCITO, Y LAS MEDIDAS DEL ESTADO DE SITIO (50).

Venezuelan historiography is somewhat better off than Colombian in terms of collected documents. For the Castro period a six-volume collection, DOCUMENTOS DEL GENERAL CIPRIANO CASTRO (44), is available as well as CASTRO: EPISTOLARIO PRESIDENCIAL (43), and León, HONOR Y PATRIOTISMO (105). For the Gómez regime, the most comprehensive collection is Correa, EL GENERAL J. V. GOMEZ: DOCUMENTOS PARA LA

HISTORIA DE SU GOBIERNO (57). The military justification for its 1948 *golpe* against President Gallegos is found in DOCUMENTOS OFICIALES RELATIVOS AL MOVIMIENTO MILITAR DEL 24 DE NOVIEMBRE DE 1948 (199). An unofficial collection appeared more recently, EL GOLPE CONTRA EL PRESIDENTE GALLEGOS: DOCUMENTOS PARA LA HISTORIA (83). As president, Colonel (later General) Pérez Jiménez published collections of his speeches and pronouncements. Examples are PENSAMIENTO POLITICO DEL PRESIDENTE DE VENEZUELA (136), and a series of volumes titled VENEZUELA BAJO EL NUEVO IDEAL NACIONAL (201, 202, 203). Examples of anti-Pérez Jiménez documentary collections are DOCUMENTOS PARA LA HISTORIA: LA DENUNCIA, CRIMENES, Y TORTURAS EN EL REGIMEN DE PEREZ JIMENEZ (46), and ASI SE FRAGUO LA INSURRECCION (4). Civil-military relations in the post-Pérez Jiménez period are the theme of a collection of speeches by former President Carlos Andrés Pérez (134). More generally, the multi-volume EL PENSAMIENTO POLITICO VENEZOLANO DEL SIGLO XX (197), under the direction of Ramón J. Velásquez, contains some important documents bearing on the military's role in public life as does volume two of DOCUMENTOS QUE HICIERON HISTORIA (200). Finally, Rivas Rivas's three-volume HISTORIA GRAFICA DE VENEZUELA (155), is a collection of newspaper accounts of the political history of Venezuela from 1935 to 1959. In it the 1945, 1948, and 1958 upheavals receive extensive coverage.

MEMOIRS, JOURNALS, AND EYEWITNESS ACCOUNTS

COLOMBIA

In this category Colombia is less fortunate than Venezuela; the literature is sparse and scattered. An early memoir from the 1899-1902 civil war is Lucas Caballero's MEMORIAS DE LA GUERRA DE LOS MIL DIAS (33). Caballero, secretary general of the Supreme Directorate of War, went on various campaigns and traveled abroad to purchase war supplies. Valencia Tovar's ARMAS E HISTORIA (192), is an interesting collection of lectures and speeches by a controversial army commander who was forced into retirement in the 1970s for allegedly interfering in civilian politics. A unique memoir is that of Buitrago Salazar, translated into English as ZARPAZO THE BANDIT (27). Buitrago was an army sergeant who infiltrated important guerrilla bands that operated in western Colombia in the 1960s and successfully led them to their own destruction. Also of importance is Sierra Ochoa (172). An army colonel who fought guerrilla forces in eastern Colombia, Sierra offers not only military solutions to the problem of populist insurgency but also preventive socio-economic solutions as well.

VENEZUELA

We are fortunate to have a considerable number of personal recollections by major and minor participants in Venezuelan civil-military affairs. Pocaterra, for example, provides a slashing indictment of the despotic regimes of Cipriano Castro (1899-1908) and Juan Vicente Gómez (1908-35) in his MEMORIAS DE UN VENEZOLANO DE LA DECADENCIA (137). The Gómez years and the transition to democracy are an important period in Venezuelan politico-military history. Indispensible to understanding the thinking of the man who led the transition from brutal dictatorship to paternalistic democracy is General López Contreras's, own analysis of the changing role of the military as presented in PAGINAS PARA LA HISTORIA MILITAR (109), and PROCESO POLITICO-SOCIAL (110). He also discusses the development of the armed forces during his presidency in GOBIERNO Y ADMINISTRACION (108). General Medina Angarita, who succeeded López Contreras, defends his wide-open regime in CUATRO ANOS DE DEMOCRACIA (120); he takes credit for the growing professionalism of the officer corps. Acción Democrática (AD) leader Rómulo Betancourt (9, 10, 11) explains his party's decision to join junior officers in an armed rebellion against Medina. The ten-year military dictatorship that followed the AD *trienio* has been justified by the powerful interior minister of the period, Laureano Vallenilla Lanz, in ESCRITO DE MEMORIA (194). The military dictator, General Marcos Pérez Jiménez, defends his regime and attacks his critics in FRENTE A LA INFAMIA (135). More general reminiscences are found in Moya Martínez (121), while General López Contreras looks back at the entire 1899-1941 period in the previously cited PAGINAS (109). Betancourt, a political enemy of López, Medina, and Pérez Jiménez, covers the sweep of the twentieth century in his classic VENEZUELA: POLITICA Y PETROLEO (11). Finally, Edito Ramírez, the author of EL 18 DE OCTUBRE (144), is a retired colonel who participated in the 1945 revolution and many subsequent events in Venezuelan politico-military history.

SPECIALIZED WORKS

COLOMBIA

Owing to the secondary role played by the military institution in national life, especially during the first fifty years of this century, specialized works are scarce. Even the War of a Thousand Days (1899-1902) was not so much a conflict involving a professional military establishment as it was a struggle between rival armed political bands led by civilian leaders who gave themselves the title of general. The best account of the origins, conduct, and aftermath of the civil war is Charles Bergquist, COFFEE AND CONFLICT IN COLOMBIA (8). The story of the 1903 Panamanian revolution, including the activities of Colombian troops, is told well by McCullough in THE PATH BETWEEN THE SEAS (111). The most useful study of the controversial regime of General Rafael Reyes (1904-09) is Lemaitre (104). The crucial period from the 1930s to the 1950s is studied by Fluharty in DANCE OF THE MILLIONS (71). Having published the work before the overthrow of General Rojas, he is less critical of the dictator than most other observers who wrote subsequently, such as Martz (118). Quintero (143), provides an account of an abortive military coup against President Alfonso López Pumarejo in 1944. General Ruíz Novoa's EL BATALLON COLOMBIA EN KOREA (164), is written from the standpoint of a former battalion commander in Korea.

The most dramatic exception to the tradition of civilian supremacy was the authoritarian regime of Rojas Pinilla. Canal Ramírez (37), contends that Rojas had been unequaled in gaining the fierce loyalty of his subordinates in the officer ranks. Yet he acknowledges that, by the end of the dictatorship, many of these men had shifted their primary allegiance from the increasingly heavy-handed autocrat to the overall welfare of the nation. In another volume (38) the same author, an admitted admirer of the armed forces, reaches the debatable conclusion that the military had been the only serious institution in the country in the last forty years. A clearly anti-Rojas work is Urán Rojas, ROJAS Y LA MANIPULACION DEL PODER (190). The transition from authoritarian to democratic systems, a concept being widely explored in the 1980s, is studied in the context of Colombia in Hartlyn, "Military Governments and the Transition to Civilian Rule: The Colombian Experience of 1957-1958" (88).

The most tragic episode in modern Colombian history was the phenomenon of La Violencia which racked large portions of the country from approximately 1946 to 1965. La Violencia had many manifestations and many actors, the military being only one of them. Nevertheless, a number of works either directly treat the military role or are useful to some extent in helping us understand the position of the army vis-a-vis La Violencia. One of the key studies of military politics from the beginning of La Violencia to the early 1970s is Maullin, SOLDIERS, GUERRILLAS, AND POLITICS (119). The author first traces the rise of military professionalism throughout the twentieth century and then assesses the impact of a sustained guerrilla threat on the professionalism and political role of the armed forces. He argues, in essence, that the professionalism and clearly developed doctrine of national security of the armed forces caused them to adopt a partisan position and to assume an increased political influence. Indeed, from the early 1960s on, the military, according to Maullin, became the guardians of a semi-closed political order and ideological allies of the National Front political elites as they joined forces to suppress the extreme-left insurgents.

Other studies that treat the military's role in suppressing the political violence include Gilhodes, "El ejército analiza La Violencia" (81), Guzmán Campos, et al., LA VIOLENCIA EN COLOMBIA (84), Henderson, WHEN COLOMBIA BLED (91), Oquist (125), and Sánchez (167). Ramsey (147), argues that the professionalism of the Colombian military contributed significantly to the prevention of total anarchy. Several of the works cited above hold the army responsible for excessive use of force and intimidation at various times during the period, but tend to be even more critical of the top civilian leadership. General Landazábal Reyes's FACTORES DE VIOLENCIA (101), illustrates the evolution of national security doctrine by the military in the 1970s.

VENEZUELA

Surprisingly little has been written on the Venezuelan armed forces themselves as organizations. Two brief works deal with the early years of the Guardia Nacional (later renamed the Fuerzas Armadas de Cooperación FAC), Aguirre Rojas (1), and Navarro Cárdenas (123). A history of the military school was written by a one-time director of the Escuela Militar, General García Villasmil (80).

The regimes of the *andino* generals have drawn the attention of many writers, although much of the literature is more polemical and anecdotal than analytical. The most thorough and balanced study of the Castro regime, including military affairs, is Sullivan (180). Ziems (208), already cited, is important for both the Castro and Gómez governments.

More has been written on Gómez than Castro, yet no single work stands out. Marxist polemicist and historian Rangel (149, 150), offers provocative interpretations of a period still not sufficiently understood. Also of value is a more recent work by Segnini (171). Some merit can also be found in works by Rourke (159), Lavin (102), Fernández (70), Cordero Velásquez (55), and Gallegos Ortíz (74).

Sanin [Tarre Murzi] (168), sheds considerable light on the post-Gómez transition to democracy in his sympathetic study of General López Contreras. The best work yet to appear on General Medina Angarita is Bustamante (32), who likewise is sympathetic to her subject. Cordero Velásquez (54), provides a wealth of information on the background to the 1945 civil-military conspiracy and fall of Medina.

The Pérez Jiménez military dictatorship has attracted considerable attention, much of it polemical in tone. Capriles Ayala's biography (39), is a loosely organized attempt to relate Pérez Jiménez's career to the broader Venezuelan panorama. The second of the two volumes published thus far ends, however, in 1948. During his regime flatterers such as Tarnoi (183), and Landaeta (100), painted highly sympathetic portraits while political enemies such as Betancourt (11), Valmore Rodríguez (156), and a host of others savagely attacked the regime for its repression and corruption. Two recent works that partially revise the totally negative view of the dictatorship espoused by exiles and members of the clandestine opposition are Avendaño Lugo (5), and Rincón Noriega (154), the latter of whom portrays Pérez Jiménez as a staunch nationalist and astute geopolitician. The dictator defends his regime in a book-length interview in Blanco Muñoz (18).

The fall of the dictatorship on 23 January 1958 and the tumultuous shift to civilian rule are told in exhaustive detail by Doyle (60). Among other works that examine the process of the 1958 revolution are Taylor (184), Umaña Bernal (186), which includes some key documents and detailed chronology, Rangel (151), ENERO 23 DE 1958 (66), and Brett Smith (25). Ortega Díaz (126), provides a brief account from a Communist party perspective. Ewell (69), offers a balanced analysis of the unprecedented extradition and trial of the ex-dictator. Between January 1958 and the early 1960s a number of military conspiracies and revolts, from the left as well as from the right, threatened to undermine the country's incipient democratic system. Among the works that treat these events are Trejo (185), Blanco Muñoz (17), and Brett Martínez (24).

The political comportment and attitudes of the military institution within the current democratic system are carefully analyzed by Gene Bigler (14, 15, 16), a specialist on Venezuelan military politics. Romero,

SEGURIDAD, DEFENSA, Y DEMOCRACIA (158), is the product of a 1979 conference that includes presentations on national security philosophy from left-wing politicians to the highest-level military brass. Schaposnik (170), an Argentine academic exiled in Venezuela, studies the democratization of the armed forces in fairly general terms, but stresses the professional, apolitical role that they have played since 1959.

PERIODICALS

The Colombian and Venezuelan armed forces have published a variety of journals and magazines over the course of this century, primarily aimed at a military audience. Especially in the last few decades, however, important periodicals such as Colombia's REVISTA DE LAS FUERZAS ARMADAS (214), and REVISTA DEL EJERCITO (215), and Venezuela's FUERZAS ARMADAS DE VENEZUELA (formerly REVISTA DE LAS FUERZAS ARMADAS) (220), have included material that deals with broader issues such as socio-economic development, national security doctrine, and the role of military professionals in a civilian democracy.

Inasmuch as so many military publications have come and gone or have altered titles and subtitles or have changed their frequency of publication, it is difficult to provide an accurate, comprehensive, and up-to-date compilation. However, a list of titles of some of the major journals appears at the end of the bibliography.

FUTURE RESEARCH

In general the existing scholarly literature has made huge strides in the study of the Colombian and Venezuelan military in comparison with the state of the art twenty-five years ago. Nevertheless, a number of areas need to be addressed or more thoroughly researched. For both countries comprehensive histories of the separate branches of the armed forces would be valuable to scholars. Little has been done as well on the impact on the cadets of their experience at the respective military school of each country. For example, does anything approaching a *tanda* (intense loyalty to members of one's class) exist as has occurred at the Salvadoran military school? Similarly, it would be helpful to know more about officer experiences in foreign, mainly United States, military schools throughout the century in terms of the formation of attitudes toward development, democracy, professionalism, and political involvement. Also, although some valuable work has been done already, more study needs to be undertaken on the making of military budgets and decision-making regarding defense expenditures and foreign arms purchases. For example, to what extent do inter-service and intra-service rivalries influence this process? An area about which little is known is the impact of military service on the conscripts who comprise the bulk of the manpower of the national armies; what is the influence of army duty on their post-military experience in the work force and society?

Turning to Colombia, inasmuch as it was the only Latin American country to send troops to Korea to fight with United Nations forces, a thorough study of the Colombian infantry's participation in the war would make an important contribution, especially if it sheds light on future career patterns and political attitudes of officers who served there. Although much has been written on the Rojas Pinilla dictatorship, a book-length, balanced study of his authoritarian-populist regime is still lacking. More needs to be known, too, about the impact on military thinking of decades of domestic violence and insurgency and threats from abroad. Is the armed forces' primary mission containing Marxist insurgency, cooperating with the United States in isolating Cuba and Nicaragua in the Caribbean Basin, or defending the nation's sovereignty, honor, and borders in potentially explosive territorial disputes with Venezuela and Nicaragua?

Many aspects of the public role of the Venezuelan military have already been explored, but preliminary work in some areas could be further developed and refined. More precise study needs to be done on the regional origins of the officer corps both during and after the era of *andino* dominance. In the contemporary period a politically significant question to explore is the level of autonomy that the armed forces enjoy. How independent are they of the two establishment political parties and the economic elites? How would greater or lesser autonomy affect the stability of a democratic system that is seeing its legitimacy and credibility slowly erode? Finally, although some stimulating work has been done recently on Venezuela's geopolitical concerns and on its role as a middle-range power in the Caribbean Basin, a closer examination needs to be made of the attitudes of military officers toward the appropriate means of resolving long-standing border disputes with Colombia and Guyana.

BIBLIOGRAPHY: COLOMBIA AND VENEZUELA

1. Aguirre Rojas, Alberto. LA GUARDIA NACIONAL DE VENEZUELA. Caracas: Tipografía La Nación, 1952.

2. ANUARIO BIBLIOGRAFICO COLOMBIANO. Bogotá: Instituto Caro y Cuervo, 1951.

3. Arbeláez, Tulio. EPISODIOS DE LA GUERRA DE 1899 A 1903. 2d ed. Bogotá: Imprenta Nacional, 1936.

4. ASI SE FRAGUO LA INSURRECCION: LOS DOCUMENTOS DE LA CLANDESTINIDAD, 1956-1958. Caracas: Ediciones de la Revista Cruz del Sur, 1958.

5. Avendaño Lugo, José R. EL MILITARISMO EN VENEZUELA: LA DICTADURA DE PEREZ JIMENEZ. Caracas: Ediciones Centauro, 1982.

6. Beltrán, César David. "The Violent Tradition: Caudillism and Militarism in Venezuela." M.A. thesis, George Washington University, 1971.

7. Beltrán, Virgilio R. EL PAPEL POLITICO Y SOCIAL DE LAS FUERZAS ARMADAS EN AMERICA LATINA: ENSAYOS. Caracas: Monte Avila, 1970.

8. Bergquist, Charles W. COFFEE AND CONFLICT IN COLOMBIA, 1886-1910. Durham: Duke University Press, 1978.

9. Betancourt, Rómulo. EL 18 DE OCTUBRE DE 1945: GENESIS Y REALIZACIONES DE UNA REVOLUCION DEMOCRATICA. Barcelona and Caracas: Seix Barral, 1979.

10. ———. LA REVOLUCION DE OCTUBRE 1945. Caracas: Centauro, 1987.

11. ———. VENEZUELA: POLITICA Y PETROLEO. Barcelona and Caracas: Seix Barral, 1978.

12. ———, et al. EL CUARTELAZO DEL 24 DE NOVIEMBRE 1948. Caracas: Acción Democrática, 1980.

13. Betancourt Sosa, Francisco. PUEBLO EN REBELDIA: RELATO HISTORICO DE LA SUBLEVACION MILITAR DEL 7 DE ABRIL DE 1928. Caracas: Ediciones Garrido, 1959.

14. Bigler, Gene E. "The Armed Forces and Patterns of Civil-Military Relations." In VENEZUELA: THE DEMOCRATIC EXPERIENCE, 113-33. Edited by John D. Martz and David J. Myers. New York: Praeger Publishers, 1977.

15. ———. "Political Restraint and Military Professionalization in Venezuela." Caracas: Instituto de Estudios Superiores de Administración (IESA), 1981.

16. ———. "Professional Soldiers and Restrained Politics in Venezuela." In NEW MILITARY POLITICS IN LATIN AMERICA, 175-97. Edited by Robert Wesson. New York: Praeger Publishers, 1982.

17. Blanco Muñoz, Agustín. LA CONSPIRACION CIVICO-MILITAR: GUAIRAZO, BARCELONAZO, CARUPANAZO, PORTENAZO. Caracas: Universidad Central de Venezuela, 1981.

18. ———. HABLA EL GENERAL MARCOS PEREZ JIMENEZ. Caracas: Editorial José Martí, 1983.

19. ———. EL 23 DE ENERO: HABLA LA CONSPIRACION. Caracas: Editorial Ateneo de Caracas, 1980.

20. Blutstein, Howard I., et al. AREA HANDBOOK FOR COLOMBIA. 3d ed. Washington: U.S. Government Printing Office, 1977.

21. ———. AREA HANDBOOK FOR VENEZUELA. 3d ed. Washington: U.S. Government Printing Office, 1977.

22. BOLETIN DEL ARCHIVO HISTORICO DE MIRAFLORES. Caracas: Presidencia de la República, 1959-.

23. Brandt, Carlos. BAJO LA TIRANIA DE CIPRIANO CASTRO. Caracas: Tipografía Vargas, 1952.

24. Brett Martínez, Alí. EL PORTENAZO: HISTORIA DE UNA REBELION. Caracas: Ediciones Adaro, 1970.

25. Brett Smith, Italo. LA GUARDIA NACIONAL EN EL 23 DE ENERO DE 1958. Caracas: Garza Impresores, 1980.

26. Briceño Ayestarán, Santiago. MEMORIAS DE SU VIDA MILITAR Y POLITICA. Caracas: Tipografía Americana, 1949.

27. Buitrago Salazar, Evelio. ZARPAZO THE BANDIT: MEMOIRS OF AN UNDERCOVER AGENT OF THE COLOMBIAN ARMY. University: University of Alabama Press, 1977.

28. Burggraaff, Winfield J. "Andeanism and Anti-Andeanism in Twentieth-Century Venezuela." THE AMERICAS 32 (1975): 1-12.

29. ———. "Las fuerzas armadas de Venezuela en transición: El período de López Contreras." BOLETIN HISTORICO 17 (1968): 184-201.

30. ———. "The Military Origins of Venezuela's 1945 Revolution." CARIBBEAN STUDIES 11 (1971): 35-54.

31. ———. THE VENEZUELAN ARMED FORCES IN POLITICS, 1935-1959. Columbia: University of Missouri Press, 1972.

32. Bustamante, Nora. ISAIAS MEDINA ANGARITA: ASPECTOS HISTORICOS DE SU GOBIERNO. Caracas: Fondo Editorial Lola de Fuenmayor, 1985.

33. Caballero, Lucas. MEMORIAS DE LA GUERRA DE LOS MIL DIAS. Bogotá: Editorial Aguila Negra, 1939.

34. Caicedo Montua, Francisco A. BANZAY: DIARIO EN LAS TRINCHERAS COREANAS. Bogotá: Imprenta y Publicaciones de las Fuerzas Armadas, 1961.

35. Calcaño Herrera, Julio. BOSQUEJO HISTORICO DE LA REVOLUCION LIBERTADORA, 1902-1903. Caracas: Litografía del Comercio, 1944.

36. Callanan, Edward F. "Terror in Venezuela." MILITARY REVIEW 49 (1969): 49-56.

37. Canal Ramírez, Gonzalo. DEL 13 DE JUNIO AL 10 DE MAYO EN LAS FUERZAS ARMADAS. Bogotá: Ediciones Documentos Colombianos, 1958.

38. ———. El 13 DE JUNIO EN 33 NUMEROS DE YA. Bogotá: Antares, 1954.

39. Capriles Ayala, Carlos. PEREZ JIMENEZ Y SU TIEMPO. 2 vols. Caracas: Editorial Dusa, 1986-87.

40. Cárdenas, Horacio. BIBLIOGRAFIA TACHIRENSE. Caracas: Editorial Arte, 1964.

41. Carrizales, Luisa Amelia, and Morris Sierralta. DEFENSA DEL GENERAL JESUS MARIA CASTRO LEON: EL ANTEJUICIO MILITAR. Maracay: Tipografía Violeta, 1963.

42. Castrillón, Alberto. 120 DIAS BAJO EL TERROR MILITAR. Bogotá: Tercer Mundo, 1973.

43. Castro, Cipriano. CASTRO: EPISTOLARIO PRESIDENCIAL, 1899-1908. Caracas: Universidad Central de Venezuela, 1974.

44. ———. DOCUMENTOS DEL GENERAL CIPRIANO CASTRO. 6 vols. Caracas: Herrera Irigoyen, 1903-08.

45. CASTRO-COMMUNIST INSURGENCY IN VENEZUELA: A STUDY OF INSURGENCY AND COUNTERINSURGENCY OPERATIONS AND TECHNIQUES IN VENEZUELA, 1960-1964. Alexandria, VA: Atlantic Research Corp., 1964.

46. Catalá, José A. DOCUMENTOS PARA LA HISTORIA: LA DENUNCIA, CRIMENES, Y TORTURAS EN EL REGIMEN DE PEREZ JIMENEZ. Caracas: n.p., 1969.

47. ———. LAS MASCARAS DEL DICTADOR PEREZ JIMENEZ. Caracas: Ediciones Centauro, 1984.

48. Colombia. Ministerio de Defensa Nacional (formerly Ministerio de Guerra). MEMORIA AL CONGRESO. Bogotá. Annual report.

49. ———. MINISTERIO DE DEFENSA, 1974-1978. Bogotá: El Ministerio, 1978.

50. Colombia. Ministerio de Gobierno. EL GOBIERNO, EL EJERCITO, Y LAS MEDIDAS DEL ESTADO DE SITIO. Bogotá: Imprenta Nacional, 1944.

51. Colombia. Ministerio de Guerra. COMPILACION DE LAS DISPOSICIONES QUE REGLAMENTAN EL SERVICIO MILITAR OBLIGATORIO. Bogotá: Imprenta Nacional, 1915.

52. Comité de Solidaridad con los Presos Políticos. EL LIBRO NEGRO DE LA REPRESION: FRENTE NACIONAL, 1958-1974. Bogotá: Comité de Solidaridad con los Presos Políticos, 1974.

53. Coniglio, James V. "The Nationalization of the Colombian Army: La reforma militar." M.A. thesis, University of Florida, 1970.

54. Cordero Velásquez, Luis. BETANCOURT Y LA CONJURA MILITAR DEL 45. Caracas: n.p., 1978.

55. ———. GOMEZ Y LAS FUERZAS VIVAS. Caracas: Editorial DON EME, 1971.

56. Corr, Edwin G. THE POLITICAL PROCESS IN COLOMBIA. Denver: Graduate School of International Studies, University of Denver, 1972.

57. Correa, Luis, ed. EL GENERAL J.V. GOMEZ: DOCUMENTOS PARA LA HISTORIA DE SU GOBIERNO. Caracas: Litografía del Comercio, 1925.

58. Dix, Robert H. COLOMBIA: THE POLITICAL DIMENSIONS OF CHANGE. New Haven: Yale University Press, 1967.

59. ———. THE POLITICS OF COLOMBIA. New York: Praeger Publishers, 1987.

60. Doyle, Joseph J. "Venezuela 1958: Transition from Dictatorship to Democracy." Ph.D. dissertation, George Washington University, 1967.

61. Dupuy, Trevor N., et al. THE ALMANAC OF WORLD MILITARY POWER. 4th ed. San Rafael, CA: Presidio Press, 1980.

62. Durán, Jaime. "Fuerzas armadas." In ENCICLOPEDIA DE COLOMBIA, 4:421-42. Edited by Lucas Morán Arce. N.p.: Editorial Nueva Granada, 1977.

63. ———. "Las fuerzas armadas respetan las instituciones democráticas." REVISTA DEL EJERCITO 12 (1971): 13-14.

64. Echeverri, Alvaro. EL PODER Y LOS MILITARES: UN ANALISIS DE LOS EJERCITOS DEL CONTINENTE Y COLOMBIA. Bogotá: Fondo Editorial Suramérica, 1978.

65. Ellner, Steve. "Venezuelans Reflect on the Meaning of the 23 de enero." LATIN AMERICAN RESEARCH REVIEW 20 (1985): 244-56.

66. ENERO 23 DE 1958: RECONQUISTA DE LA LIBERTAD POR ACCION DEL PUEBLO Y DE LAS FUERZAS ARMADAS. Caracas: Ediciones Centauro, 1982.

67. English, Adrian J. ARMED FORCES OF LATIN AMERICA: THEIR HISTORIES, DEVELOPMENT, PRESENT STRENGTH, AND MILITARY POTENTIAL. London: Jane's, 1984.

68. Estados Unidos de Venezuela. SUMARIO DEL JUICIO SEGUIDO A LAS PERSONAS INDICIADAS DE HABER COMETIDO EL ASESINATO DEL CORONEL CARLOS DELGADO CHALBAUD, PRESIDENTE DE LA JUNTA MILITAR DE GOBIERNO. Caracas: Oficina Nacional de Información y Publicaciones, 1951.

69. Ewell, Judith. THE INDICTMENT OF A DICTATOR: THE EXTRADITION AND TRIAL OF MARCOS PEREZ JIMENEZ. College Station: Texas A&M University Press, 1981.

70. Fernández, Pablo Emilio. GOMEZ: EL REHABILITADOR. Caracas: Jaime Villegas Editor, 1956.

71. Fluharty, Vernon L. DANCE OF THE MILLIONS: MILITARY RULE AND THE SOCIAL REVOLUTION IN COLOMBIA, 1930-1956. Pittsburgh: University of Pittsburgh Press, 1957.

72. Fonseca F., Jaime. EL MILITAR: PENSAMIENTO Y ACCION. Caracas: n.p., 1973.

73. Forero Manzano, Eloísa, and Federico Alamo Fuentes. PEREZ JIMENEZ HABLA DE LA CONSPIRACION. Caracas: n.p., 1960.

74. Gallegos Ortíz, Rafael. EL CACHORRO JUAN VICENTE GOMEZ. Caracas: Editorial Fuentes, 1976.

75. Gallón Giraldo, Gustavo. QUINCE ANOS DE ESTADO DE SITIO EN COLOMBIA, 1958-1978. Bogotá: Librería y Editorial América Latina, 1979.

76. García Gil, Pedro. CUARENTA Y CINCO ANOS DE UNIFORME: MEMORIAS, 1901-1945. Caracas: Editorial Bolívar, 1947.

77. García Ponce, Guillermo, and Francisco Camacho Barrios. DIARIO DE LA RESISTENCIA Y LA DICTADURA, 1948-1958. Caracas: Ediciones Centauro, 1982.

78. García Villasmil, Martín. ANTE LA OPINION: ARTICULOS Y ENTREVISTAS. Caracas: Ediciones Políticas "Equilibrio," 1973.

79. ———. 40 ANOS DE EVOLUCION EN LAS FUERZAS ARMADAS. Caracas: Oficina Técnica MINDEFENSA, 1966.

80. ———. ESCUELAS PARA FORMACION DE OFICIALES DEL EJERCITO: ORIGEN Y EVOLUCION DE LA ESCUELA MILITAR, 1810-1964. Caracas: MINDEFENSA, 1964.

81. Gilhodes, Pierre. "El ejército analiza La Violencia." Paper presented at the Primer Simposio Internacional sobre La Violencia en Colombia, Bogotá, June 1984.

82. Gilmore, Robert L. CAUDILLISM AND MILITARISM IN VENEZUELA, 1810-1910. Athens: Ohio University Press, 1964.

83. EL GOLPE CONTRA EL PRESIDENTE GALLEGOS: DOCUMENTOS PARA LA HISTORIA. Caracas: Ediciones Centauro, 1982.

84. Guzmán Campos, Germán, et al. LA VIOLENCIA EN COLOMBIA: ESTUDIO DE UN PROCESO SOCIAL. 2d ed. Bogotá: Ediciones Tercer Mundo, 1962.

85. Guzmán Pérez, José E. LOPEZ CONTRERAS: EL ULTIMO GENERAL. Caracas: Gobernación del Distrito Federal, 1983.

86. ———. LA REVOLUCION ANDINA. Caracas: Espasande Editores, 1986.

87. Guzmán Pérez, José E., ed. ISAIAS MEDINA ANGARITA: DEMOCRACIA Y NEGOCIACION. Caracas: Espasande Editores, 1985.

88. Hartlyn, Jonathan. "Military Governments and the Transition to Civilian Rule: The Colombian Experience of 1957-1958." JOURNAL OF INTER-AMERICAN STUDIES AND WORLD AFFAIRS 16 (1984): 245-81.

89. Heare, G.E. TRENDS IN LATIN AMERICAN MILITARY EXENDITURES, 1940-1970. Washington: U.S. Department of State, 1971.

90. Helguera, J. León. "The Changing Role of the Military in Colombia." JOURNAL OF INTER-AMERICAN STUDIES 3 (1961): 351-58.

91. Henderson, James D. WHEN COLOMBIA BLED: A HISTORY OF THE VIOLENCIA IN TOLIMA. University: University of Alabama Press, 1985.

92. Heredia, Cipriano. EL AÑO 29: RECUENTO DE LA LUCHA ARMADA. Caracas: Ediciones Centauro, 1974.

93. Herrera Campins, Luis. FRENTE A 1958. Caracas: Presidencia de la República, 1984.

94. Herwig, Holger H. GERMANY'S VISION OF EMPIRE IN VENEZUELA, 1871-1914. Princeton: Princeton University Press, 1986.

95. Icenhour, J.O. "The Military in Colombian Politics." Ph.D. dissertation, George Washington University, 1976.

96. Keegan, John. WORLD ARMIES. 2d ed. Detroit: Gale Research, 1983.

97. Kolb, Glen L. DEMOCRACY AND DICTATORSHIP IN VENEZUELA, 1945-1958. New London: Connecticut College Press, 1974.

98. Kosolchyk, Boris. LEGAL FOUNDATIONS OF MILITARY LIFE IN COLOMBIA. Santa Monica: Rand Corporation, 1967.

99. La Riva, Edecio. LOS FUSILES DE LA PAZ. Caracas: Tipografía Remar, 1968.

100. Landaeta, Federico. MI GENERAL: BREVE BIOGRAFIA DEL GENERAL MARCOS PEREZ JIMENEZ. La Coruña, Spain: n.p., 1957.

101. Landazábal Reyes, Fernando. FACTORES DE VIOLENCIA. Bogotá: Ediciones Tercer Mundo, 1975.

102. Lavin, John. A HALO FOR GOMEZ. New York: Pageant Press, 1954.

103. Leal Buitrago, Francisco. "Política e intervención militar en Colombia." REVISTA MEXICANA DE SOCIOLOGIA 32 (1970): 491-538.

104. Lemaitre, Eduardo. RAFAEL REYES: BIOGRAFIA DE UN GRAN COLOMBIANO. Bogotá: Banco de la República, 1981.

105. León, César A., ed. HONOR Y PATRIOTISMO: INTERESANTES DOCUMENTOS PARA LA HISTORIA DE VENEZUELA. Caracas: Herrera Irigoyen, 1906.

106. Lombardi, John V., et al. VENEZUELAN HISTORY: A COMPREHENSIVE WORKING BIBLIOGRAPHY. Boston: G.K. Hall, 1977.

107. Looney, Robert E. THE POLITICAL ECONOMY OF LATIN AMERICAN DEFENSE EXPENDITURES: CASE STUDIES OF VENEZUELA AND ARGENTINA. Lexington, MA: Lexington Books, 1986.

108. López Contreras, Eleazar. GOBIERNO Y ADMINISTRACION, 1936-1941. Caracas: Editorial Arte, 1966.

109. ———. PAGINAS PARA LA HISTORIA MILITAR DE VENEZUELA. Caracas: Tipografía Americana, 1944.

110. ———. PROCESO POLITICO-SOCIAL, 1928-1936. Caracas: Editorial Ancora, 1955.

111. McCullough, David. THE PATH BETWEEN THE SEAS: THE CREATION OF THE PANAMA CANAL, 1870-1914. New York: Simon & Schuster, 1977.

112. Machillanda Pinto, José. "Poder político y poder militar en Venezuela durante la democracia, 1958-1986." Post-graduate thesis, Universidad Simón Bolívar, 1987.

113. Maingot, Anthony. "Colombia." In THE MILITARY IN LATIN AMERICAN SOCIOPOLITICAL EVOLUTION: FOUR CASE STUDIES, 127-95. Edited by Lyle N. McAlister, et al. Washington: Center for Research in Social Systems, American University, 1970.

114. ———. "Colombia: Civil-Military Relations in a Political Culture of Conflict." Ph.D. dissertation, University of Florida, 1967.

115. Mancera Galletti, Angel. CIVILISMO Y MILITARISMO. Caracas: n.p., 1960.

116. Márquez Bustillos, V. LA REFORMA MILITAR VENEZOLANA. Caracas: Lit. y Tip. del Comercio, 1917.

117. Martínez Landínez, Jorge. HISTORIA MILITAR DE COLOMBIA: LA GUERRA DE LOS MIL DIAS. Bogotá: n.p., 1956.

118. Martz, John D. COLOMBIA: A CONTEMPORARY POLITICAL SURVEY. Chapel Hill: University of North Carolina Press, 1962.

119. Maullin, Richard L. SOLDIERS, GUERRILLAS, AND POLITICS IN COLOMBIA. Lexington, MA: Lexington Books, 1973.

120. Medina Angarita, Isaías. CUATRO ANOS DE DEMOCRACIA. Caracas: Pensamiento Vivo, 1963.

121. Moya Martínez, Francisco A. LA HEGEMONIA ANDINA: REMINISCENCIAS POLITICO-ADMINISTRATIVAS DE LOS GOBIERNOS DE LOS GENERALES CASTRO, GOMEZ, LOPEZ CONTRERAS, Y MEDINA ANGARITA. Medellín: Editorial Bedout, 1977.

122. Muller Rojas, Alberto. "Equipamiento militar, política de defensa, y política exterior: El caso venezolano." POLITICA INTERNACIONAL 2 (1986): 22-33.

123. Navarro Cárdenas, Pedro A. LOS PIONEROS: DATOS SOBRE LA CREACION DE LA GUARDIA NACIONAL. Caracas: Guardia Nacional, 1967.

124. Núñez, Enrique B. EL HOMBRE DE LA LEVITA GRIS: LOS ANOS DE LA RESTAURACION LIBERAL. Caracas: Ediciones Edime, 1953.

125. Oquist, Paul. VIOLENCE, CONFLICT, AND POLITICS IN COLOMBIA. New York: Academic Press, 1980.

126. Ortega Díaz, Pedro. VEINTITRES DE ENERO Y OTRAS NOTAS DE HISTORIA. 2d ed. Caracas: Ediciones La Muralla, 1978.

127. Pacheco, Emilio. DE CASTRO A LOPEZ CONTRERAS. Caracas: Editorial Domingo Fuentes, 1984.

128. Paredes, Antonio. COMO LLEGO CIPRIANO CASTRO AL PODER: MEMORIAS CONTEMPORANEAS. 2d ed. Caracas: Ediciones Garrido, 1954.

129. Payne, James L. PATTERNS OF CONFLICT IN COLOMBIA. New Haven: Yale University Press, 1968.

130. Peeler, John A. LATIN AMERICAN DEMOCRACIES: COLOMBIA, COSTA RICA, VENEZUELA. Chapel Hill: University of North Carolina Press, 1985.

131. Peña, Alfredo. DEMOCRACIA Y GOLPE MILITAR. Caracas: Editorial Ateneo de Caracas, 1979.

132. Peralto Ortíz, Bernardo E. "El militar y los delitos políticos." Ph.D. dissertation, Pontificia Universidad Javeriana, 1959.

133. Pérez, Ana Mercedes. LA VERDAD INEDITA: HISTORIA DE LA REVOLUCION DE OCTUBRE REVELADA POR SUS DIRIGENTES MILITARES. 2d ed. Buenos Aires: Editorial Colombo, 1953.

134. Pérez, Carlos Andrés. DISCURSOS MILITARES, 1974-1979. Caracas: Ministerio de la Defensa, 1979.

135. Pérez Jiménez, Marcos. FRENTE A LA INFAMIA. 2d ed. Caracas: Ediciones Garrido, 1968.

136. ———. PENSAMIENTO POLITICO DEL PRESIDENTE DE VENEZUELA. Caracas: Imprenta Nacional, 1954.

137. Pocaterra, José Rafael. MEMORIAS DE UN VENEZOLANO DE LA DECADENCIA. 4 vols. Caracas: Ediciones Edime, 1966.

138. Polanco Alcántara, Tomás. EL GENERAL DE TRES SOLES: BIOGRAFIA DE ELEAZAR LOPEZ CONTRERAS. Caracas: Editorial Arte, 1985.

139. THE POLITICAL AND SOCIO-ECONOMIC ROLE OF THE MILITARY IN LATIN AMERICA. Miami: Center for Advanced International Studies, University of Miami, 1972.

140. Premo, Daniel L. "The Colombian Armed Forces in Search of a Mission." In NEW MILITARY POLITICS IN LATIN AMERICA, 151-73. Edited by Robert Wesson. New York: Praeger Publishers, 1982.

141. Prieto Silva, Enrique A. GUARDIA NACIONAL: DESARROLLO, SEGURIDAD, Y DEFENSA. Caracas: Ministerio de la Defensa, 1985.

142. PROCESO A UN EX-DICTADOR: JUICIO AL GENERAL (R) MARCOS PEREZ JIMENEZ. 2 vols. Caracas: J.A. Catalá, 1969.

143. Quintero, José Gregorio. EL GOLPE MILITAR CONTRA LOPEZ. Cali: n.p., 1977.

144. Ramírez R., Edito J. EL 18 DE OCTUBRE Y LA PROBLEMATICA VENEZOLANA ACTUAL, 1945-1979. Caracas: Avila Arte, 1981.

145. Ramsey, Russell W. "Critical Bibliography on La Violencia in Colombia." LATIN AMERICAN RESEARCH REVIEW 8 (1973): 3-44.

146. ———. GUERRILLEROS Y SOLDADOS. Bogotá: Ediciones Tercer Mundo, 1981.

147. ———. "The modern violencia in Colombia, 1946-1965." Ph.D. dissertation, University of Florida, 1970.

148. ———. SURVEY AND BIBLIOGRAPHY OF LA VIOLENCIA IN COLOMBIA. Gainesville: University of Florida Libraries, 1974.

149. Rangel, Domingo Alberto. LOS ANDINOS EN EL PODER: BALANCE DE UNA HEGEMONIA, 1899-1945. Caracas: n.p., 1964.

150. ———. GOMEZ: EL AMO DEL PODER. Valencia, Venezuela: Vadell Hermanos, 1975.

151. ———. LA REVOLUCION DE LAS FANTASIAS. Caracas: Ediciones OFIDI, 1966.

152. Rangel, José Vicente, et al. MILITARES Y POLITICA: UNA POLEMICA INCONCLUSA. Caracas: Ediciones Centauro, 1976.

153. Riascos Grueso, Eduardo. GEOGRAFIA GUERRERA DE COLOMBIA. Cali: Imprenta Bolivariana, 1949.

154. Rincón Noriega, Fredy. EL NUEVO IDEAL NACIONAL Y LOS PLANES ECONOMICO-MILITARES DE PEREZ JIMENEZ, 1952-1957. Caracas: Ediciones Centauro, 1982.

155. Rivas Rivas, José, comp. HISTORIA GRAFICA DE VENEZUELA. 3 vols. Caracas: Pensamiento Vivo, 1961-63.

156. Rodríguez, Valmore. BAYONETAS SOBRE VENEZUELA. Mexico City: Editores B. de Silva, 1950.

157. Romero, Aníbal. LA MISERIA DEL POPULISMO: MITOS Y REALIDADES DE LA DEMOCRACIA EN VENEZUELA. Caracas: Ediciones Centauro, 1986.

158. ———, ed. SEGURIDAD, DEFENSA, Y DEMOCRACIA EN VENEZUELA. Caracas: Editorial Equinoccio, 1980.

159. Rourke, Thomas [Daniel Joseph Clinton]. GOMEZ: TYRANT OF THE ANDES. New York: Greenwood Press, 1969.

160. Rueda Vargas, Tomás. EL EJERCITO NACIONAL. Bogotá: Librería Colombiana, Camacho Roldán, 1944.

161. Ruhl, J. Mark. "Civil-Military Relations in Colombia: A Societal Explanation." JOURNAL OF INTER-AMERICAN STUDIES AND WORLD AFFAIRS 23 (1981): 123-46.

162. ———. COLOMBIA: ARMED FORCES AND SOCIETY. Syracuse: Syracuse University Press, 1980.

163. ———. "The Military." In POLITICS OF COMPROMISE: COALITION GOVERNMENT IN COLOMBIA, 181-206. Edited by R. Albert Berry, et al. New Brunswick, NJ: Transaction Books, 1980.

164. Ruíz Novoa, Alberto. EL BATALLON COLOMBIA EN KOREA. Bogotá: Imprenta Nacional de Publicaciones, 1956.

165. ———. EL GRAN DESAFIO. Bogotá: Ediciones Tercer Mundo, 1965.

166. Salazar, Víctor M. MEMORIAS DE LA GUERRA, 1899-1902. Bogotá: Editorial ABC, 1943.

167. Sánchez, Gonzalo. "La Violencia in Colombia: New Research, New Questions." HISPANIC AMERICAN HISTORICAL REVIEW 65 (1985): 789-807.

168. Sanin [Alfredo Tarre Murzi]. LOPEZ CONTRERAS: DE LA TIRANIA A LA LIBERTAD. Caracas: Editorial Ateneo de Caracas, 1982.

169. Santana, Arturo. MANUAL DEL SOLDADO. Caracas: Imprenta Nacional, 1916.

170. Schaposnik, Eduardo C. LA DEMOCRATIZACION DE LAS FUERZAS ARMADAS VENEZOLANAS. Caracas: Fundación Nacional Gonzalo Barrios/ILDIS, 1985.

171. Segnini, Yolanda. LA CONSOLIDACION DEL REGIMEN DE JUAN VICENTE GOMEZ. Caracas: Academia Nacional de la Historia, 1982.

172. Sierra Ochoa, Gustavo. LAS GUERRILLAS EN LOS LLANOS ORIENTALES. Manizales, Colombia: n.p., 1954.

173. ———. TIERRA, EJERCITO, COLONIZACION. Manizales, Colombia: n.p., 1950.

174. Siso, Carlos. CASTRO Y GOMEZ. Caracas: Prensas Venezolanas de Editorial Arte, 1985.

175. Springer, P.B. "Social Sources of Political Behavior of Venezuelan Military Officers: An Exploratory Analysis." POLITICO 30 (1965): 348-55.

176. Stambouli, Andrés. CRISIS POLITICA: VENEZUELA, 1945-1958. Caracas: Editorial Ateneo de Caracas, 1980.

177. Studer, Robert W. "The Colombian Army: Political Aspects of Its Role." Ph.D. dissertation, University of Southern California, 1975.

178. Suárez, Santiago Gerardo. EL REGIMEN DE LOPEZ CONTRERAS. Caracas: Editorial Arte, 1965.

179. ———. TEMAS MILITARES. Caracas: n.p., 1970.

180. Sullivan, William M. BIBLIOGRAFIA COMENTADA DE LA ERA DE CIPRIANO CASTRO, 1899-1908. Caracas: Imprenta Nacional, Oficina Central de Información, 1977.

181. ———. "The Rise of Despotism in Venezuela: Cipriano Castro, 1899-1908." Ph.D. dissertation, University of New Mexico, 1974.

182. Tamayo Suárez, Oscar. DE FRENTE A LA REALIDAD VENEZOLANA. Limoges, France: n.p., 1963.

183. Tarnoi, Ladislao. EL NUEVO IDEAL NACIONAL DE VENEZUELA: VIDA Y OBRA DE MARCOS PEREZ JIMENEZ. Madrid: Ediciones Verdad, 1954.

184. Taylor, Philip B., Jr. THE VENEZUELAN GOLPE DE ESTADO OF 1958: THE FALL OF MARCOS PEREZ JIMENEZ. Washington: Institute for the Comparative Study of Politicll Systems, 1968.

185. Trejo, Hugo. LA REVOLUCION NO HA TERMINADO. Valencia, Venezuela: Vadell Hermanos, 1977.

186. Umaña Bernal, José, ed. TESTIMONIO DE LA REVOLUCION EN VENEZUELA: 1 DE ENERO-23 DE JULIO, 1958. Caracas: Tipografía Vargas, 1958.

187. United States. Department of State. FOREIGN RELATIONS OF THE UNITED STATES. Volumes on THE AMERICAN REPUBLICS, 1900-. Washington: U.S. Government Printing Office.

188. ———. Political and Military Records Relating to Internal Affairs of Colombia. Decimal Files, 1910-. National Archives, Washington.

189. ———. Political and Military Records Relating to Internal Affairs of Venezuela. Decimal Files, 1910-. National Archives, Washington.

190. Urán Rojas, Carlos H. ROJAS Y LA MANIPULACION DEL PODER. Bogotá: C. Valencia Editores, 1983.

191. Urueta, Carlos Adolfo. DOCUMENTOS MILITARES Y POLITICOS RELATIVOS A LA CAMPANA DEL GENERAL RAFAEL URIBE URIBE. Bogotá: Imprenta del Vapor, 1904.

192. Valencia Tovar, Alvaro. ARMAS E HISTORIA. Bucaramanga, Colombia: Imprenta del Departamento, 1970.

193. ———. UISHEDA: VIOLENCIA EN EL LLANO. Bogotá: Canal Ramírez, 1969.

194. Vallenilla Lanz, Laureano. ESCRITO DE MEMORIA. Mexico City: Editorial Mazatlán, 1961.

195. Varas, Augusto. MILITARIZATION AND THE INTERNATIONAL ARMS RACE IN LATIN AMERICA. Boulder: Westview Press, 1985.

196. Velásquez, Ramón J., et al. VENEZUELA MODERNA: MEDIO SIGLO DE HISTORIA, 1926-1976. 2d ed. Caracas: Fundación Eugenio Mendoza and Editorial Arte, 1979.

197. ———, eds. EL PENSAMIENTO POLITICO VENEZOLANO DEL SIGLO XX: DOCUMENTOS PARA SU ESTUDIO. 16 vols. Caracas: Congreso de la República, 1983.

198. Venezuela. Ministerio de Defensa Nacional. MEMORIA AL CONGRESO. Annual report.

199. Venezuela. Oficina Nacional de Información y Publicaciones. DOCUMENTOS OFICIALES RELATIVOS AL MOVIMIENTO MILITAR DEL 24 DE NOVIEMBRE DE 1948. Caracas: Oficina Nacional de Información y Publicaciones, 1949.

200. Venezuela. Presidencia de la República. DOCUMENTOS QUE HICIERON HISTORIA: SIGLO Y MEDIO DE VIDA REPUBLICANA,1810-1961.Caracas:EdicionesConmemorativas del Sesquicentenario de la Independencia, 1962.

201. ———. VENEZUELA BAJO EL NUEVO IDEAL NACIONAL: REALIZACIONES DURANTE EL SEGUNDO ANO DE GOBIERNO DEL GENERAL MARCOS PEREZ JIMENEZ. Caracas: Imprenta Nacional, 1955.

202. ———. VENEZUELA BAJO EL NUEVO IDEAL NACIONAL: REALIZACIONES DURANTE EL TERCER ANO DE GOBIERNO DEL GENERAL MARCOS PEREZ JIMENEZ. Caracas: Imprenta Nacional, 1956.

203. Venezuela. Servicio Informativo Venezolano. VENEZUELA BAJO EL NUEVO IDEAL NACIONAL: REALIZACIONES DURANTE EL PRIMER ANO DE GOBIERNO DEL CORONEL MARCOS PEREZ JIMENEZ. Caracas: Servicio Informativo Venezolano, 1954.

204. Villar Borda, Carlos J. ROJAS PINILLA: EL PRESIDENTE LIBERTADOR. Bogotá: Editorial Iqueima, 1953.

205. Wesson, Robert, ed. THE LATIN AMERICAN MILITARY INSTITUTION. New York: Praeger Publishers, 1986.

206. Wilde, A.W. "Conversations among Gentlemen: Oligarchical Democracy in Colombia." In THE BREAKDOWN OF DEMOCRATIC REGIMES: LATIN AMERICA, 28-81. Edited by J.J. Linz and A. Stepan. Baltimore: Johns Hopkins University Press, 1978.

207. WILFRIDO OMANA: CAPITAN DEL EJERCITO VENEZOLANO, ASESINADO EN CARACAS; LOS CRIMENES DE PEREZ JIMENEZ. Caracas: Ediciones Centauro, 1971.

208. Ziems, Angel. EL GOMECISMO Y LA FORMACION DEL EJERCITO NACIONAL. Caracas: Editorial Ateneo de Caracas, 1979.

PERIODICALS

Columbia

209. BOLETIN. Ministerio de Guerra.

210. BOLETIN MILITAR DE COLOMBIA.

211. COLOMBIA AERONAUTICA.

212. EJERCITO.

213. REVISTA DE LA INFANTERIA.

214. REVISTA DE LAS FUERZAS ARMADAS.

215. REVISTA DEL EJERCITO.

216. REVISTA POLICIA NACIONAL DE COLOMBIA.

Venezuela

217. AEROSPACIO.

218. BOLETIN DEL ARCHIVO HISTORICO DE MIRAFLORES.

219. BOLETIN MILITAR.

220. FUERZAS ARMADAS DE VENEZUELA. Formerly REVISTA DE LAS FUERZAS ARMADAS.

221. GUARDIA NACIONAL.

222. EL INGENIERO: REVISTA DE LA INGENIERIA MILITAR.

223. REVISTA DE LA ESCUELA SUPERIOR.

224. REVISTA DE LAS FUERZAS AEREAS.

225. REVISTA DEL EJERCITO.

226. REVISTA DEL EJERCITO, MARINA, Y AERONAUTICA.

227. REVISTA GUARDIA NACIONAL.

228. SIEMPRE FIRMES.

CHAPTER XII

MEXICO

David G. LaFrance
Oregon State University

INTRODUCTION

Although large, the historiography on the Mexican military does not
make up in numbers for what it lacks in quality. Volume after volume
deals with combat and biography, but few go beyond the obvious to
explore widely the socio-economic as well as the political implications
of this all-important institution. Admittedly, particularly for foreigners,
the Mexican armed forces in the twentieth century have not been nearly
as enticing to investigate as their more interventionist-minded Latin
American counterparts in countries such as Argentina, Brazil, Chile,
and Peru. Also, Mexico's military as well as civilian leadership is quite
close-mouthed and does not readily provide the scholar with
information about its activities whether in regard to the present or the
past.

Nevertheless, in recent years this situation has been changing as
scholars of Mexico have begun to probe the complexities of this topic,
but much still needs to be done. As such, this chapter reviews the
existent literature on the Mexican military from the latter half of the
nineteenth century to the present with the purpose of orienting the
prospective researcher to the field.

Many students of the Mexican armed forces, such as Jorge Alberto
Lozoya (234) and Jean Meyer (276), argue that it was not until after
Benito Juárez returned to the presidency in 1867 after defeating
Maxmilian and the French army, see Dabbs (113), that the country
developed a full-fledged professional military institution. Before that
time Mexico's armies consisted of irregular, rag-tag groups with little or
no organization, training, or discipline, and standardized chains of

command. Oftentimes, they fought mostly as guerrilla units, especially during the independence period (1810-21), the War of the Reform (1858-61), and the French Intervention (1862-67). Even during the war with the United States, the Mexicans only briefly, and early in the conflict, fielded what might be considered a conventional fighting machine. Between 1867 and the outbreak of the revolution in 1910, the period of the so-called Restored Republic and the Porfiriato, the army, as a cohesive institution harnessed by strong and astute leaders, played a key role in the economic and political changes taking place in the nation. It helped to maintain domestic law and order and to centralize power in the federal government, all in a bid to stimulate economic development through the encouragement of mainly foreign investment. In 1911, the Porfirian federal army proved incapable of dealing with the guerrilla warfare unleashed by revolutionary leader Francisco I. Madero, but it remained virtually intact until the overthrow of Madero's successor, Victoriano Huerta, in 1914. As a result of specific policies undertaken by the victorious Carrancista coalition and the ensuing civil war, the national military disintegrated leaving Mexico in the control of dozens of local and regional revolutionary leaders who, at most, paid mere lip service to the weakened central government.

Slowly, but surely, from the late 1910s to the 1930s a new national and largely depoliticized military was forged. The gradual strengthening of the central government, the elimination of older officers, the recruitment of newly trained younger professional soldiers, and the brief incorporation of the armed forces into the newly formed official party all served to bring about this result.

Despite the suppression of labor and students and other evidence of meddling in politics, the Mexican army since World War II has continued to have a reputation as an apolitical professional institution dedicated to serving the nation and its civilian leadership. This perception is reinforced by the military's low official budgets, relatively few men in uniform, and a reluctance openly to intervene in the civilian-controlled decision-making process in contrast to many of its Latin American counterparts.

GENERAL WORKS

General works dealing with the Mexican military fall into two broad categories, reference sources that provide information on the contemporary armed forces and histories that trace their development over time.

For basic information on today's institution, such as budgets, equipment and weapons, personnel, and organization, one can consult Trevor Dupuy (130), John Keegan (213), Michael Brown (62), Adrián

English (135), Phyllis Greene Walker (445), and STATISTICAL ABSTRACT OF LATIN AMERICA published annually by U.C.L.A.'s Latin American Center (388). The available syntheses of the history of the military since independence are few and leave much to be desired. The difficulty of doing in-depth research on the subject plus the emphasis on combat mean that most works are poorly documented, seldom analytical, and highly subjective. Nevertheless, a small number of recent works show promise, and a perusal of them can be of value.

Echenique (131) and Castillo Negrete (88) deal with the major military events of the nineteenth century, and Cota Soto (104) provides a chronology by state from 1808 to 1945. More useful, but written for the Secretaría de la Defensa Nacional, is Jesús de León Toral's recent official history of the army (226). In her general history, journalist Gloria Fuentes (147) includes sections on the development of such important topics as the military educational system, aviation, and industry. She concludes by examining the relationship between the armed forces and the civilian sector, particularly in light of the economic crisis of the 1980s, and remains confident of the army's continued subordinate role. In his more thoroughly researched work, Jorge Alberto Lozoya (233) has written a brief history of the army that deals mostly with the question of politics. He comes to the conclusion that a military caste system was never able to develop in the nineteenth century which was a key factor in the depolitization of the armed forces in the twentieth century. Guillermo Boils (51) traces the history of the institution from 1915 to the 1970s, and, like Lozoya, focuses most of his attention on the question of the political role of the military. Boils, however, concentrates on the the years following 1968.

The Mexican navy receives some attention in Robert Scheina's (374) general work on Latin American naval history. Juan de Dios Bonilla's HISTORIA MARITIMA DE MEXICO (126) surveys the navy from the conquest to the 1960s and calls for further improvements in it and in the merchant marine. Carlos Bosch García's (55) history starts with the conquest and ends with the 1920s; he urges traditionally land-bound Mexico to pay more attention to and take advantage of its marine resources. Raziel García Arroyo (150) covers colonial times to the 1950s, but he is even less analytical.

One general work on the Mexican air force that merits mention is José Villela (443). It deals with aviation in both thought and action from the pre-conquest to the present and focuses on the development of military and civilian air power in the twentieth century.

BIBLIOGRAPHIES

Bibliographic guides and other finding aids for Mexican history are fairly extensive although few deal exclusively with the military. Nevertheless, time spent perusing this general material will yield many dividends. The standard bibliography of bibliographies for Latin America is Arthur Gropp (174) (175) whose volume published in 1968 covers monographs through 1964 while his 1971 follow-up deals with the period 1965-69. Subsequent complements to Gropp have been compiled by Daniel Cordeiro (98) and then Haydée Piedracueva (325). Gropp also produced a bibliography of bibliographies published in periodicals which goes through the year 1965 (176). Barnard and Rasmussen have a recent one for Mexico alone (34).

The best general source for both articles and monographs continues to be the HANDBOOK OF LATIN AMERICAN STUDIES (186) now published at the University of Texas. For articles alone, one must consult the HISPANIC AMERICAN PERIODICALS INDEX (HAPI) (196). Another important source is the BIBLIOGRAPHIC GUIDE TO LATIN AMERICAN STUDIES (46) which is a compilation of the acquisitions of the Library of Congress and the University of Texas. The annual BIBLIOGRAFIA HISTORICA MEXICANA (44) is the best bibliography currently produced in Mexico while BIBLIOGRAFIA MEXICANA (45) will also be of value. Each issue of the journal INTER-AMERICAN REVIEW OF BIBLIOGRAPHY/REVISTA INTERAMERICANA DE BIBLIOGRAFIA (480) contains sections on recently published articles and completed doctoral dissertations. One older but still somewhat useful work is Griffin (173).

In terms of more specialized material, one will find the following worth consulting: The most complete listing of theses written in the United States is DISSERTATION ABSTRACTS INTERNATIONAL (127). Its publisher, University Microfilms International (U.M.I.), has also issued LATIN AMERICA AND THE CARIBBEAN: A DISSERTATION BIBLIOGRAPHY (116), edited by Carl W. Deal, with two supplements by Walters (446) and U.M.I. (423). The nearly infathomable world of Mexican government publications still needs a good bibliography, but Ker (216) who covers the period 1821 to 1936 and Fernández de Zamora (142) who deals with 1937 to 1970 are a modest beginning. The Trask, Meyer, and Trask (407) volume, supplemented by Meyer (284), is the best bibliography on United States-Latin American relations. Two often overlooked sources for material on the military are travelers' accounts and fiction. Garold Cole (97) deals with Americans who wrote about their trips to Mexico between 1821 and 1972. Although not strictly a bibliography, John

Brushwood's (63) survey of the Mexican novel serves as a very useful reference guide while Moore (291) and Rutherford (358) have compiled works that treat fictionalized accounts of one of Mexico's most violent and studied periods, the Revolution of 1910.

The revolution also has other bibliographies dedicated exclusively to it. They include the three volumes of Roberto Ramos (337) which have recently been brought up to date by Dirk Raat (335). Two other very useful sources for material on the revolutionary period in general (from the Porfiriato to about 1940) is González y González (169) and Ross (356). Since newspaper and magazine publishers in Mexico seldom compile cumulative indices, the latter work is of particular importance.

As for the military itself, the Secretaría de Guerra y Marina (264) has published one bibliography which deals with the period 1536 to 1936 and the Secretaría de la Defensa Nacional (256) a second one. A more recent and useful effort is an article by Olguin Pérez (307).

Finally, there exists a large number of other types of finding aids beside bibliographies that will prove useful to the student of the Mexican military. For specific names, dates, places, and events, for example, one should start with the ENCICLOPEDIA DE MEXICO (134) and the DICCIONARIO PORRUA (122). Given the large number of revolutionary officers who later became politicians, Camp's (75) compilation of political biographies also can be useful. Several bi-lingual dictionaries dealing with military terms and subjects are available; they include Mangold (236), Merino (251), and the United States Department of the Army (421).

ARCHIVAL GUIDES AND SOURCES

Although the number of archives and collections on nineteenth- and twentieth-century Mexican history is expanding rapidly, published catalogs, guides, and indices to the holdings still lag far behind. In many cases, the researcher must work without their assistance, but invariably the extra effort is worth it.

For general guides to the archives and libraries of Mexico City one should start with the still useful Greenleaf and Meyer (170) volume and a more recent work compiled by the Universidad Iberoamericana's Department of History (420). Michael Grow's SCHOLARS' GUIDE TO WASHINGTON, D.C., FOR LATIN AMERICAN AND CARIBBEAN STUDIES (177) is also a good reference tool for the person undertaking research in the capital city of the United States.

Without doubt, the best source for primary material on the Mexican military is the Archivo Histórico de Defensa Nacional located in Mexico City. Along with its library, the "Defensa" contains the most complete holdings dealing with the country's armed forces since independence. Nevertheless, entrance can be difficult to arrange, especially for foreigners, and the more contemporary the topic, the less the chance of gaining such permission. At least two guides to portions of the collection exist. The secretariat itself issued one catalog which covers the period 1821 to 1847 (258). The second, which is untitled and unpublished, deals with the first decade of the revolution, 1910-1920, and was compiled by Luis Muro of the Colegio de México. It is available for consultation at that institution's Centro de Estudios Históricos.

Another must for the researcher is Mexico's Archivo General de la Nación (A.G.N.) which has a very active publishing program. It has issued the GUIA GENERAL... (23) and produces its own BOLETIN (465) which attempts to keep its patrons abreast of the latest acquisitions and other activities. Among the A.G.N.'s catalogs that directly relate to the military are its GUIA DEL RAMO, TITULOS Y DESPACHOS DE GUERRA (22), its ARCHIVO DE GUERRA (20), and the papers of presidents Alvaro Obregón (1924-28) and Plutarco Elías Calles (1924-28) dealing with defense and security matters (21). Other revolutionary figures whose collections are also indexed and published are Alfredo Robles Domínguez (18) and Genovevo de la O (19). These collections do not begin to exhaust the holdings of the A.G.N., however; one must make a personal visit to ascertain the extent of this vast repository.

The Instituto de Investigaciones Históricas of Mexico's National Autonomous University, the U.N.A.M., also is actively collecting in the area of military history and has published guides to two of its holdings, the papers of revolutionary generals Amado Aguirre (155) and Jacinto Treviño (419).

The Centro de Estudios de Historia de México (Condumex), also located in Mexico City, has a guide to its archive of Jenaro Amezcua (322) who served as a general in the Zapatista army. The Condumex also contains a number of other important materials, including a large pamphlet collection on the nineteenth century and the papers of Venustiano Carranza, Manuel W. González, and Felix Díaz, but most do not yet have published indices.

The large and still little-consulted Porfirio Díaz collection boasts one published guide and another in progress. Laurens Perry (323) has compiled an inventory of the microfilmed version which is located at the Universidad de las Américas in Cholula, Puebla. The Universidad Iberoamericana in Mexico City, which holds the original manuscripts, is in the process of issuing detailed catalogues of the collection, but thus far only a small portion of the entire archive has been indexed.

Another still largely untapped archival source, photographs, is now made much more easy to consult by the recent appearance of Martha Davidson's (114) comprehensive and valuable guide to picture sources. She describes the collections in literally dozens of archives, libraries, museums, governmental and private institutions, and universities. Among them, the researcher should be aware of two especially comprehensive holdings, each of which contains material useful to the military historian. One is the Fondo Casasola located in the Instituto Nacional de Antropología e Historia's (I.N.A.H.) Fonoteca in Pachuca which boasts nearly 500,000 photos and negatives taken by Casasola and others between 1890 and 1960. The second is the Hermanos Mayo collection which is housed in the A.G.N. and consists of 4.5 million negatives that cover the period 1940-82.

In addition to the archival sources mentioned above, many other possibilities exist for the researcher despite the fact that most still do not have published guides. In some cases, the depositories will have internal indices or other finding aides that the investigator will be able to consult on the premises. In Mexico City one also will want to explore the manuscript holdings of the Biblioteca Nacional, the Museo Nacional de Antropología e Historia, the Secretaría de Relaciones Exteriores, and El Colegio de México. In addition, the opportunities for work in state and municipal archives on military topics are nearly limitless.

As for other countries' documentation of Mexican history, one should begin with the consular and embassy reports of the major foreign nations with interests in Mexico. A good place to start is the Despatches from United States Ministers to Mexico, 1823-1906; the Records of the Department of State Relating to the Internal Affairs of Mexico, 1910-; the Despatches from United States Consuls; the Records of the Foreign Service Posts of the Department of State; and United States Military Intelligence Reports, Mexico. All these collections are in the National Archives in Washington, D.C., and Ulibarri and Harrison (416) should be referred to for a guide to the Latin American materials located there. Most of this and other related material also can be obtained on microfilm from Scholarly Resources in Wilmington, Delaware, and University Publications of America in Bethesda, Maryland. For Britain, one can consult Foreign Office Records, General Correspondence-Political-Mexico, which is found in the Public Record Office in London and also microfilmed.

PUBLISHED DOCUMENTS

Except for governmental reports, published documentary sources for the study of the military in Mexico are very limited, and most of what exists pertains to the Revolution of 1910.

As for governmental publications, both the Secretaría de la Defensa Nacional and the Secretaría de Marina (combined in the Secretaría de Guerra y Marina, 1835-1937), publish a wide variety of material. The most important are the periodic INFORMES (259) (270) and MEMORIAS (261) (268). These reports generally go into great detail about the activities and makeup of each secretariat. Also of value are the many published laws, decrees, regulations, manuals, and other official edicts (260) (266) (271).

Other branches of the Mexican government, too, publish documents that are of use to the military historian. The Secretaría de Hacienda y Crédito Público has a volume (269) on the Pani-De la Huerta controversy that led to the latter's rebellion against the central government in 1923-24. The Senate also (273) issued a series dealing with the constitutional history of the armed forces.

Of the non-governmental sources, the most valuable is the twenty-one volume series by Fabela and Fabela (139) which deals with the revolution from 1910 to 1920. Although mostly political in nature, the collection can reveal much about the military. EL EJERCITO CAMPESINO DEL SUR (133) contains documents on the Zapatistas taken from the Jenaro Amezcua collection in the Condumex and the Gildardo Magaña papers at the UNAM. Other published documents that pertain to the revolution include Sierra and Yáñez (380) on Madero, Hanrahan (187), who has taken material from the United States National Archives on the early period of the upheaval, and González Ramírez (168). Papers dealing with one revolutionary officer, Felipe Angeles (15), are also in print.

MEMOIRS, JOURNALS, AND EYEWITNESS ACCOUNTS

Again, like so many of the other types of sources that treat the Mexican military, personal observations of the topic are concentrated on the Revolution of 1910 and its immediate aftermath.

Before 1910, Balbontín (32) outlines the career of an artillery officer from the late 1840s to the time he served in the war ministry in the late 1870s under Díaz. BARBAROUS MEXICO (414), by John Kenneth Turner, a United States socialist whose observations of Porfirian Mexico in 1908-09, including its armed forces, proved very important in exposing the repressive nature of the Díaz regime.

Many foreigners who resided in or visited Mexico during the revolution recorded their experiences. Among them are the Englishwoman, Rosa King (217), who owned a hotel in Cuernavaca from where she observed the Zapatistas. John Reed (341), an American journalist, traveled with Pancho Villa in northern Mexico. I. Thord-Gray (397), a British officer, fought in the Constitutionalist army. Harry

Toulmin (406) served in Pershing's expedition to Mexico to capture Villa in 1916-17. In 1919-20 Senator Albert Bacon Fall (422) held a series of hearings to investigate the Mexican revolution. Several dozen United States citizens who had been south of the border testified, many of whom had had contact with the military. Rosalie Evans (138) owned a hacienda in the state of Puebla and died at the hands of revolutionists in the early 1920s.

Personal accounts of civilians who participated as combatants in the revolution are numerous. A recent work edited by Oscar Martínez (243) contains the testimonies of a cross-section of people who experienced the upheaval along the Mexican-United States border. It was not unusual for some of these relatively obscure individuals to take advantage of the revolution to forge for themselves successful military and eventually civilian careers. Two examples are Donato Bravo Izquierdo (60) and Porfirio del Castillo (118), who became the governors of Puebla and Tlaxcala, respectively.

Autobiographies, diaries, and other first-hand renditions of the careers and revolutionary participation of other military figures include Victoriano Huerta (201), Alvaro Obregón (304), Pancho Villa (182), Emilio Portes Gil (331), Francisco Múgica (296), Amado Aguirre (5), José Luis Amezcua (13), Gabriel Gavira (156), and Luis Alamillo Flores (8). Torrea (400) and Urquizo (426) reflect on their experiences during the *decena trágica*. Barragán (35), Carranza's chief of staff, has written a history of the Constitutionalist army, and the Aguirre Benavides (6) talk about their participation in Villa's División del Norte.

Several works deal with the 1926-29 Cristero movement and the closely related Escobar rebellion against the central government. They are Degollado Guizar (117), Rivero del Val (348), Santibáñez (370), and Calles (69).

Finally, for the post-revolutionary period, Menéndez González (250) provides us with an interesting look at the daily experiences of an infantry corporal who served in the army's sanitary corps in 1945 and 1946. Mancisidor (235), a naval captain, offers an account of his career between 1930 and 1960.

Other particularized accounts of Mexican history that the military historian should consider in his quest for material include photographs, film, *corridos*, and novels. All four, when used imaginatively, can provide insights unobtainable from, and which complement, ordinary written material.

One of the most important photographers and collectors of photographs on Mexican history was Gustavo Casasola. He personally participated in and recorded the revolution, while others' work has also been added to supplement his multi-volume published histories. One should start by consulting his series on the military from 1810 to 1980

(83) and the revolution from 1900 to 1960 (84). Brenner (61) also contains many good shots of the revolution.

Another source of visual documentation that has hardly been tapped is the picture postcard. Paul Vanderwood and Frank Samponaro (437) explore this alternative and use it to examine the Mexican revolution and the United States's military reaction to events along the border between 1910 and 1917.

Motion picture and video film is an additional possiblity that, too, has been only little explored. Although Mexico's National Film Archive, the Cineteca Nacional, was mostly destroyed by fire in the early 1980s, much footage containing scenes of the military still exists. A good example is "The Ragged Revolution: The Romance and the Reality of the Mexican Revolution, 1910-1920," released by Document Associates.

The Mexican *corrido*, a type of folk song, is a form of oral history depicting life in Mexico from amorous exploits to military adventures. Merle Simmons (382) has written the best work exploring this music as a source to study Mexico. María y Campos (241), Moreno (293), and Razo Oliva (339) take a closer look at it during the revolution.

The Mexican novel, too, says much about the history of the nation. Many writers participated personally in the events that they have set to fiction. As mentioned above, the best general guide to the topic is Brushwood (63). Those novels that deal mostly with military-related subjects, like so much of the historiography discussed in this chapter, focus on the revolution. Indeed, the novel of the revolution has become a special sub-genre of Mexican literature, and several works have been dedicated to its study. They include Castro Leal (90), Dessau (119), Hernández (191), and Morton (294).

While all of the individual works of fiction that one can consult are too numerous to include here, at least five deserve mention. In TOMOCHIC (146), Heriberto Frías criticizes the ruthlessness of the Porfirian army in putting down an Indian rebellion in Chihuahua. Francisco Urquizo (429) relates the story of a common soldier who makes the transition from serving in the Porfirian army to become a revolutionary. Mariano Azuela's LOS DE ABAJO (29), perhaps the most famous of the revolutionary novels, traces the life of a peasant forced to side with the rebels in order to save his family. Muñoz (297) offers vignettes of Villa's men and why they were attracted to the revolutionary leader. In MI GENERAL (231), López y Fuentes deals with a humble man who rose to the rank of general but could find no position in society once the fighting was over.

SPECIALIZED WORKS: RESTORED REPUBLIC
AND PORFIRIATO

Works dealing with the Mexican military between Juárez's return to power in 1867 and the outbreak of the revolution in 1910 have tended to focus on a small number of themes including biography, the armed forces' military and political roles in the creation and consolidation of the Juárez and Díaz regimes, the professionalization of the officer corps, peasant and Indian rebellions, and the Rurales.

Only Gutiérrez Santos (180) has written a general military history of the period (in this case 1876-1914), but several good general works exist which, although not focused principally on the military, do have important things to say about it as well as treating other subjects. The most comprehensive is Daniel Cosío Villegas's multi-volume HISTORIA MODERNA DE MEXICO (102) which covers the politics, economics, society, and foreign relations of the whole period. Scholes (377) and Sinkin (383) deal mainly with politics and the development of liberal governmental institutions under Juárez while Knapp (218) does the same for Juárez's successor, Sebastián Lerdo de Tejada. Perry (324) shows how Juárez and Lerdo used the military, among other means, to subvert liberal ideals and to create the basis of a monolithic centralized state against which Díaz revolted successfully but then used and perfected once in power. Coerver (96) takes a close look at the generally ignored Manuel González regime, 1880-1884, and Guerra (178) employs a sophisticated posopographical approach to examine the nature of the conflict between tradition and modernization in the nineteenth century and to trace the Díaz regime to its downfall.

Biographical works include Garfias M. (154) and Sánchez Lamego (364) who offer sketches of nineteenth-century generals. Díaz's military career is dealt with in Cantón (79), Cosío Villegas (103), Escudero (136), Miller (285), and Perry (324). Niemeyer (303) looks at one of Díaz's principal collaborators, General Bernardo Reyes, who served as zone commander, war minister, and governor of Nuevo León. Smith (385) has written a biography of Emilio Kosterlitzky, a Russian navy deserter who joined the Porfirian army and became the head of the Rurales.

As for the political role of the military in the Porfiriato, Alexius (10) demonstrates how Díaz used the armed forces to consolidate his power. Nonetheless, by keeping the army small (so as not to pose a threat to himself), allowing his officers to enrich themselves through corruption, and resorting to the levy, Díaz weakened the institution and alienated large sectors of the populace. In a similar vein, Vanderwood (437) claims that Díaz was well-versed in guerrilla warfare theory and attempted to apply it to meet the challenge of the revolutionaries, but corruption and personalism had eroded the army while three decades of accumulated grievances undermined his political base. Didapp (123) examines the Científico-Reyes rift and the relation of the armed forces to it.

The professionalization of the officer corps, particularly through the importation of foreign methodology and personnel, and its impact on the military are still a topic of much debate even for today's Latin American armed forces. Kelley (214) (215) claims that, using the French system, Díaz greatly improved Mexico's Colegio Militar and produced a number of well-trained officers. Nevertheless, when faced with the challenge of the Revolution of 1910, these men found themselves helplessly caught between a demoralized army of forced conscripts and high-ranking officers of the old tradition who failed to respond adequately to the crisis. Schiff (375) examines Germany's efforts to supplant the French as the principal outside influence on Mexico's army, but says it failed because of many Mexican officers' suspicion of Germany, the language barrier, and Berlin's unwillingness to alienate the United States by meddling south of the border.

While the post-1867 Juárez and Díaz regimes faced no significant foreign threats and fought no wars with outside powers, they did have to deal with a large number of internal problems such as filibusterers, bandits, smugglers, cattle rustlers, Indian uprisings, and agrarian revolts. Gregg (171) looks at how several of these issues affected United States-Mexican relations, particularly in view of the fact that many elements used the northern side of the international border as a sanctuary from Mexican officials. Jean Meyer (279) and Reina (343) outline the many peasant rebellions of the nineteenth century while Tutino (415) carries the analysis much further by placing rural discontent into a new and provocative theoretical framework.

Juárez and Díaz inherited two especially vexatious Indian insurgencies, both prompted by changing economic circumstances. The first, that of the Mayas of Yucatán, whose greatest insurgency came at mid-century, are examined in detail by González Navarro (166), Lapointe (223), and Reed (342). The second, the Mayos and Yaquis of Sonora, whose anti-government activities dated back to the colonial era, have also received a great deal of attention. Troncoso (410) and the state government of Sonora (109) have published chronicles of the conflict while Balbás (31) focused on the campaigns between 1899 and 1901. The best work on the topic has been done by Evelyn Hu-DeHart whose latest book (200) and an article (199) argue that the natives faced their greatest challenge under Díaz. During his dictatorship, as the capitalistic forces of nineteenth-century Mexico evolved, Yaqui lands became more valuable than their labor, and, in response to their attempts to defend it from appropriation by government-supported landowners, the dictator sanctioned the Indians' deportation to Yucatán to work as near slaves on the henequen plantations.

Finally, although strictly speaking not part of the military, the rural forces or Rurales played a key role in maintaining domestic law and order thereby enhancing the prestige of the Díaz regime. The best work on the subject has been done by Vanderwood (432) (433) (434) (435) who shows that the Rurales were created not by Díaz but as early as 1861 in the government's effort to eliminate rural banditry. Juárez, Lerdo, and then Díaz perfected and used them to their advantage.

SPECIALIZED WORKS: REVOLUTION

The revolution, 1910-1940, arguably the most important period in Mexican history since the Spanish conquest in the sixteenth century, has received the most attention from scholars, including those interested in military topics. Combat accounts, biography, and foreign intervention, mainly North American, traditionally have dominated the existent historiography. In recent years, however, another area of inquiry, the creation of a professional national army following the violent decade of 1910-20, has also received growing attention. Another important field of investigation, the armed forces' socio-economic impact on the life of the nation, has only barely been touched upon.

Several general histories of the period provide political and socio-economic background as well as some military-related material. A must is the multi-volume work HISTORIA DE LA REVOLUCION MEXICANA (197) which is published by El Colegio de México and covers up to 1960. New and important histories by John Hart (189), Alan Knight (219), and Ramón Eduardo Ruíz (357) focus on the late Porfiriato to the early 1920s. Cumberland's (111) study of the Constitutionalist years is still useful, and Quirk (334) succinctly and clearly deals with the complex political and military events of 1914-15. Dulles (129) remains a good narrative outline of the 1920s and 1930s while Bailey (30) and Jean Meyer (274) (275) provide the best accounts of the church-state conflict culminating in the Cristero rebellion, 1926-29.

Regional histories of the revolutionary period have come into their own in recent years, and many of them, too, can offer much to the researcher of the military. They include Aguilar Camín (2) on Sonora, Ankerson (16) and Falcón (140) on San Luis Potosí, Beezley (38) on Chihuahua, Benjamin (41) on Chiapas, Buve (65) on Tlaxcala, Jacobs (207) on Guerrero, Joseph (209) and Wells (447) on Yucatán, LaFrance (220) on Puebla, and Schryer (379) on Hidalgo.

Works that deal specifically with the armed action of the revolution are numerous, but vary greatly in usefulness and often take a highly partisan point-of-view. General histories of the violent 1910-20 decade include the official account by Luis Garfias M. (153), the detailed chronicle approach of Miguel A. Sánchez Lamego (367), and Dávila (115). In more focused studies of the period, Sanchez Lamego (368) deals with the Madero years, while he (366) (369), González (164), Coutiño M. (105), and Vigil and Híjar y Haro (441) all examine the war between Huerta and his opponents. The Villista war machine, its rivaly with Carranza's, and its eventual demise receive attention from Langle Ramírez (221), González (165), Calzadíaz Barrera (72), and Naylor (299).

For the 1920s and 1930s, the De la Huerta revolt of 1923-24 has only received limited attention including the works of Bravo Izquierdo (59) and Monroy Durán (290), while the Gómez and Serrano movement of 1927 has been virtually ignored. More sources exist, however, for the Cristero rebellion of 1926-29 and the allied insurrection led by J. Gonzalo Escobar in 1929. Portions of Jean Meyer (274) (275), as well as Moctezuma (287) and Olivera Sedano (308), deal directly with the fighting between federal and religious forces. Tuck (412) does the same from a narrower regional perspective, the Los Altos area of Jalisco. León de Garay (224) (225) outlines the action in the North surrounding the suppression of the Escobar rebellion. Except for small parts of Ankerson (16) and Falcón (140), the last significant armed challenge to the central government, that of Saturnino Cedillo in 1938, has also been largely overlooked.

In addition to combat accounts of the revolutionary years, biographies of participants in the upheavals of the 1910s and beyond are also plentiful. In most cases, these works assume an approach that might be characterized as one of "the man and his times" and therefore often include useful information beyond that of the individual's particular activities. To start, the inveterate chronicler of the military, Sánchez Lamego (365), has compiled brief biographical sketches of a number of revolutionary generals. Madero, although not a professional soldier, took part in combat on his own behalf, and both Cumberland (112) and Ross (355) deal with him. Madero's ally and later opponent, Pascual Orozco, is written about by Michael Meyer (282). Meyer (281) has also given Huerta comprehensive treatment, while Langle Ramírez (222) and Rausch (338) are more interested in his career before heading the country. Womack (453) has produced a classic on Zapata and his movement. Richmond (347) looks at the career of Carranza, Hall (185) and Alessio Robles (9) at Obregón up to his assumption of the presidency in 1920, Campobello (76) at Villa, and Manjarrez and Ortiz (237) at Cárdenas the soldier.

Many other biographies of revolutionary officers also exist. Among them are two that have been written on Lucio Blanco, by María y Campos (242) and Sapia-Bosch (373). Felipe Angeles boasts five: Calzadíaz Barrera (73), Cervantes M. (91), Jackson (206), Mena Brito (249), and Slattery (384). Pablo González is dealt with by Morales Hesse (292), Francisco Múgica by María y Campos (240), Saturnino Cedillo by Ankerson (16), Cándido Aguilar by Corzo Ramírez, González Sierra, and Skerritt (101), and Manuel García Vigil by Rojas (352). Miguel Ramos (336) offers a useful glimpse of José Refugio Velasco, a federal general who served Huerta.

Foreign military participation in Mexico, particularly between 1910 and 1920, was at times extensive and helped to determine the course of the revolution. Most intervention came from north of the border, but European meddling also occurred. Diplomatic accounts of Mexico's relations with other nations are numerous, and many deal in part with outsiders' impact on the country's armed forces. Katz (212) approaches the topic from a broad multi-national perspective, but focuses mostly on the European powers. Gilderhus (157), Grieb (172), and Haley (184) look at the United States and Calvert (70) at Britain. Ulloa Ortiz (418) takes the Mexican point of view.

Most of the literature dealing directly with foreign military intervention emphasizes the United States, Mexico's nearest powerful neighbor and the one country actually to invade and occupy Mexican territory on two different occasions in the 1910s. Clendenen (94) and Batchelder (36) examine the tensions and conflict between the two countries along their common frontier. Taylor (394) traces the activities of some of the soldiers of fortune who crossed the border to fight in Mexico. Arms sales to Mexico by the United States, always a complex and controversial issue, receive the attention of Holcombe (198) and Ulloa Ortiz (417). Quirk (333) and Sweetman (392) recount the United States occupation of Veracruz in 1914 while Woodbury (454) analyzes the historiography of the event. Several works look at Villa, the Columbus raid, and Pershing's punitive expedition into Mexico in 1916-17. They include Braddy (56) (57) and semi-official versions by Thomas and Allen (396) and Tompkins (399). Salinas Carranza (360) provides a Mexican point of view, and Katz (211) offers a new and convincing argument of why Villa attacked Columbus. Finally, Andrews (14) explores the role the United States played in helping the Obregón government to suppress the De la Huerta rebellion in the 1920s.

In recent years, many scholars, Mexicans and foreigners alike, have begun to examine more than the combat role of the armed forces during the revolution. One central line of inquiry is how and why the decentralized strong-man-led forces of the 1910s and 1920s became a national army by the 1930s with only a limited political role to play.

Lieuwen (226) (227) pioneered the research in this area and showed how astute policies taken by presidents from Carranza to Cárdenas along with the cooperation of key officers like Joaquín Amaro enabled the federal government to professionalize the institution and bring it under civilian control.

Various aspects of this same theme have been explored by many others. Schloming (376) looks at the relationship between revolution, military intervention, and party rule and comes to the conclusion that Mexico deviates from the norm in which the armed forces generally are a nation-destroyer, not a builder. Matute (245) demonstrates how, in his opinion, the army became a professional one in the decade 1914-24. Hansis (188) studies the military reforms of Obregón, and Haberman (183) concentrates on a key aspect of the president's program, the military colony. Likewise, several people have examined Cárdenas's role in this same process of taming (some would say manipulating) the army and making it loyal to civilian control, especially to himself in his conflict with Calles. They include Hernández Chávez (193), Wilkie (449), and Aguilar Oceguera (4). Cardenas had to back down under military pressure, however, when he proposed to distribute arms to campesinos and workers; see Alvarez y Alvarez (12).

Other issues, too, in addition to the military-political relatonship have been dealt with, but much more work needs to be done in these and other related areas. Michael Meyer (283) shows how Huerta militarized the society in his effort to defeat Carranza early in the revolution. Jean Meyer (278) examines the role of workers' batallions in Carranza's ranks and, after studying the federal army (277), claims that its internal makeup and functioning changed little from 1910 to 1930. Hernández Chávez (192) looks at the resistance to the First Chief's troops on the part of coffee barons in Chiapas and in a second article (194) shows how officers entered business in order to help finance their military activities thus preventing the rise of a capitalist class. Tobler (398) refutes the idea that the army was a progressive institution, claiming that it actually retarded agrarian reform; Katz (210) concurs, saying that despite the destruction of the old federal army between 1910 and 1920, real social change did not come about until the 1930s.

SPECIALIZED WORKS: POST-REVOLUTION

While one of the principal areas of inquiry regarding the Mexican military during the 1910-40 period was its taming, institutionalization, and depoliticization, post-1940 study has concentrated on why this pattern of non-interference in the governmental process, unlike so many of its Latin American counterparts, still exists and what the prospects are that it will continue. Other, although less developed, areas of research have dealt with World War II, the armed forces' relation to the United States, its potential for an expanded role in the Caribbean Basin, and civic action (mainly drug eradication) and internal security operations.

Most observers of the post-1940 Mexican military agreed, until at least the early 1970s, that it was nearly totally removed from exercising any direct influence on the political system from the 1940s to 1968. Medina (246) shows how the continuing efforts on the part of presidents following Cárdenas, such as Manuel Avila Camacho and Miguel Alemán, to professionalize and politically to isolate the armed forces, plus the cooptive measures enhanced by the economic growth enjoyed by Mexico after World War II, kept its governmental role to a minimum (one major exception was the use of troops to deal with the 1958-59 railroad strike). Turner (413), Lozoya (232) (233), and Margiotta (238) (239), writing in the late 1960s and early 1970s, all took this basic position; Lozoya even claimed that the participation of the military in civil conflicts was due to civilian pressure, not by the army's choice. These assertions were underpinned by studies like Heare (190) and Wilkie (450) which claimed a pattern of declining defense expenditures making Mexico's military budget one of the lowest of any Latin American nation.

The army's intervention in the 1968 protest movement ending in the Tlatelolco killings, however, marked a turning point in how the armed forces political role was perceived. This change was then reinforced over the next two decades by several additional developments involving the military such as the armed campaign against drugs and guerrillas and rumors and official denials of interference in the civilian government sector and of special economic treatment meted out to officers in the wake of the economic crises of 1976-77 and again after 1981. Other developments included the militarization of the Southeast following the discovery of large petroleum deposits in the region combined with the unstable situation in nearby Central America, an accelerated program of weapons modernization, and, finally, the rise to positions of influence in the institution of a new generation of national security-minded, highly trained, professional officers with little or no connection to the ideals of civilian political control that came out of the Revolution of 1910.

Debate since the mid-1970s, then, has focused mainly upon the degree to which the military has reentered the political arena and what this development means for the future of the nation. Nevertheless, few serious observers claim that the armed forces are soon about to carry out a coup d'état against the government. Most still see the army as a subtle behind-the-scenes actor whose role potentially is enhanced with each succeeding crisis.

While Wager (444) outlines many of the changes in the military that took place in the decade after 1968, Boils (51) takes a close look at the years 1968 to 1974. He comes to the conclusion that the military is not isolated from, but has always been an integral part of, the political system. As such it influences but does not direct the decision-making of the state. Ronfeldt (353) reiterated and gave further weight to this contention that the military might actually be exerting more influence on the government than was generally conceded thus raising the uneasy proposition that perhaps Mexico's officers are not so different from their Latin American counterparts. Subsequently, Piñeyro (327) and Williams (451) have both further refined the idea of the military as a part of the state apparatus, not an apolitical outsider, and one with limited direct influence on what still remains a civilian-dominated decision-making structure. In a later article published in 1985, Boils (50), specifically addressing the possibilities for a coup, concludes that despite a growing national security mentality on the part of the military and pressures from a deteriorating economy, Central America, and the United States, the civilian leadership has been able to hold its own, and the armed forces show no real disposition to take political control. Ronfeldt's (354) recent anthology on the Mexican military affirms many of these same views.

Except for an air squadron sent to the Philippines in 1945 to battle the Japanese, no Mexican fighting unit took a direct overseas combat role in World War II. Nevertheless, some six thousand Mexican citizens voluntarily joined the United States armed forces and the government, despite some internal opposition, cooperated closely with its northern neighbor during the war both militarily and economically. For overviews of war-time Mexico one should consult Torres Ramírez (404) and Cárdenas de la Peña (81). President Manuel Avila Camacho (27) (28) reflects the official position regarding Mexico's participation in the war effort. Prewett (332) wrote about the makeup of the Mexican army in 1941, and Santoro (372) and Gómez Arnau (161) examine Unites States-Mexican relations and collaboration on defense matters.

The military's more contemporary external relations have also received some attention. Although Mexico's armed forces since the end of World War II have been less closely linked to the United States military than many other Latin American nations, this connection has been the object of study by individuals such as Piñeyro (330) and the researchers at NACLA (298). Others, like Williams (452), look at the institution's potential for the projection of its influence into the Caribbean Basin, particularly as it justifies the militarization of oil-producing southeastern Mexico and the purchase of sophisticated offensive weapons by pointing out the need to defend the petroleum fields from instability in Central America.

Some work exists on the army's domestic activities, particularly the battle against drugs and subversion, but much more investigation in this area needs to be undertaken. Redick (340) looks at the military potential of the country's nuclear energy program and feels that the Treaty of Tlatelolco will be able to control the spread of nuclear weapons in the region. Craig (106) (107) has concentrated on the anti-drug campaign and suggests that human rights abuses are being committed. NACLA (298) claims that the marijuana and poppy eradication effort is used by the United States clandestinely to funnel war material to Mexico and to suppress legitimate political dissent. Rural and urban guerrilla activity reached a peak in the mid-1970s, and the army was called in to combat the threat. For overviews of the subject see Chaib (92) and López (230). At least three works, Bonilla Machorro (53), Castro (89), and Suárez (389), have focused on the best known of the anti-government leaders, Lucio Cabañas, who led a significant force in the mountains of Guerrero, one of Mexico's poorest states.

JOURNALS

When searching for information on the Mexican military in journal sources, one must consider two types: those that deal with Latin American and Mexican history in general and those dedicated wholly to the nation's armed forces, most of which are published by the various service branches themselves.

The bibliography at the end of this essay lists only the major journals that deal with Latin American and Mexican history in Mexico, Canada, the United States, and Western Europe such as HISTORIA MEXICANA (476), the CANADIAN JOURNAL OF LATIN AMERICAN AND CARIBBEAN STUDIES (472), the HISPANIC AMERICAN HISTORICAL REVIEW (475), the JOURNAL OF LATIN AMERICAN STUDIES (482), IBERO- AMERIKANISCHES ARCHIV (479), and CAHIERS DU MONDE HISPANIQUE ET LUSO-BRESILIEN (CARAVELLE) (471). Other countries, including several in Latin America, Eastern Europe, the Soviet Union, and Japan also publish periodical literature dedicated to the history of the region. Probably the best current listing of journals dealing with Latin America can be found in the HISPANIC AMERICAN PERIODICALS INDEX (HAPI) (196).

As for those journals included in the bibliography that deal specifically with the Mexican military, the list is representative, not comprehensive. Their dates, given the ephemerality and frequent name changes of many of these publications, are, in some cases, not definitive.

When dealing with the Mexican armed forces, one should not overlook current news sources such as newspapers and magazines. When read carefully, the country's press can reveal a great deal about the military and its role in society. Of special value in recent years has been PROCESO (489), a weekly that tends to probe more deeply into controversial and sensitive issues than most other publications. The best single depository for Mexican periodical publications is the Hemeroteca Nacional located in Mexico City.

FUTURE RESEARCH

Save for combat operations, biography, and now to a lesser extent the political role of the armed forces, little is still known about most aspects of the Mexican military from the Restored Republic to the present. Potential researchers in the field can hardly "miss" no matter what topic is chosen. As is the case in any investigative endeavor, however, one's access to materials greatly determines the feasibility of any given project. Consequently, until the Mexican military becomes more forthcoming, many areas of inquiry will remain virtually impossible to explore, and scholars will continue to nibble around the edges of important themes. Nevertheless, with persistence, imagination, and a bit of luck, one can expect to make significant contributions to the body of knowledge about this important institution.

In general terms, a good analytical survey of the armed forces for the entire nineteenth and twentieth centuries is needed. Also, in-depth syntheses would be useful for more focused chrolonogical periods such as the Restored Republic, the Porfiriato, and others in the twentieth century. The navy and, even more so, the air force demand much more than the inadequate attention that they thus far have received.

In addition to the general overview, three major areas merit the researcher's consideration. The first is the armed forces' external relations with other countries. Some work has been done on foreign arms sales, the use of outsiders and their methods in the effort to professionalize the Mexican soldier, and the connection to the United States, particularly since World War II. These and other topics still require further investigation. For example, what has been the impact of other nation's armed forces on the Mexican army's view of itself, and how has its reactions to this outlook changed over time? More specifically, for the post-war period, what impact has United States national security policy and the exchange of personnel had on the perceived role of the military and its educational programs? More analysis should also be focused on the impact of Mexico's assumption of the status of a mid-sized regional power and economic and political developments in the Caribbean Basin.

The domestic political, and especially economic and social, role of the military over time deserves more attention. What makes the Mexican situation so different, if it actually is, from other Latin American nations in which the armed forces regularly and openly interfere in government? Despite a significant amount of investigation, it is still not well understood exactly how the armed forces have wielded their influence in the decision-making processes of the country. The nature of civil-military relations at the local and state levels is also obscure. Moreover, little has been done on civic action programs from agricultural colonies established in the 1920s and 1930s, to road building in the 1960s and 1970s and drug enforcement in the 1980s. A penetrating analysis of even "hotter" topics including armed revolts of the 1920s and 1930s and the repression of labor and students and especially guerrillas is still lacking. Little light has been shed upon the military's connection to contraband, terrorism, death squads, torture, and other illegal activities. Finally, the economic role of the institution deserves a close look; what has been its financial impact on the nation; does it literally operate as an independent economic entity in and of itself like the militaries in many other Latin American countries; what are its connections to Mexico's still small, but growing, defense industry?

A third general area of inquiry is the internal makeup and nature of the institution. The origin, recruitment, training, and career patterns of personnel of all ranks over time are only slightly understood. Other topics for investigation and analysis include organization, reserve units, interservice relations, ideology and doctrine, and education. Corruption, too, merits consideration; it is common knowledge, for example, that officers often collect paychecks from other ministries (so-called *aviadores*) and that those in the quartermaster corps live especially well. These subterfuges and others (such as the transferral of equipment by the United States under the guise of drug eradication), may belie the contention of low military budgets and provide even more evidence that the armed forces actually play a more important role in the society than is often asserted.

BIBLIOGRAPHY: MEXICO

1. Acosta, Emilio N. HISTORIA DE LA CAMPANA DE LA COLUMNA EXPEDICIONARIA DEL NORTE, MARZO 4-MAYO 17, 1929. Mexico City: Imprenta Azteca, 1930.

2. Aguilar Camín, Héctor. LA FRONTERA NOMADA: SONORA Y LA REVOLUCION MEXICANA. Mexico City: Siglo XXI Editores, 1977.

3. Aguilar del Sordo, María Teresa, and María Cristina del Arenal Mitolo. "El general Manuel Peláez G.: Su actuación política y militar en las Huastecas." Lic. thesis, Universidad Nacional Autónoma de México, 1983.

4. Aguilar, Oceguera, Francisco Javier. "El papel de los militares en la etapa cardenista." Lic. thesis, Universidad Nacional Autónoma de México, 1973.

5. Aguirre, Amado. MIS MEMORIAS DE CAMPANA: APUNTES PARA LA HISTORIA; ESTAMPAS DE LA REVOLUCION MEXICANA. N.p.: n.p., 1953.

6. Aguirre Benavides, Luis, and Adrián Aguirre Benavides. LAS GRANDES BATALLAS DE LA DIVISION DEL NORTE AL MANDO DEL GENERAL FRANCISCO VILLA. Mexico City: Editorial Diana, 1964.

7. Alamillo Flores, Luis. DOCTRINA MEXICANA DE GUERRA. Mexico City: Talleres de Costa, 1943.

8. ———. MEMORIAS: LUCHADORES IGNORADOS AL LADO DE LOS GRANDES JEFES DE LA REVOLUCION MEXICANA. Mexico City: Editorial Extemporáneos, 1976.

9. Alessio Robles, Miguel. OBREGON COMO MILITAR. Mexico City:. Editorial Cultura, 1935.

10. Alexius Robert Martin. "The Army and Politics in Porfirian Mexico." Ph.D. dissertation, University of Texas, Austin, 1976.

11. Alvarez José María. ANORANZAS: EL MEXICO QUE FUE; MI COLEGIO MILITAR. 2 vols. Mexico City: Imprenta Ocampo, 1948-49.

12. Alvarez Y Alvarez de la Cadena, José. EL EJERCITO NACIONAL ANTE LA MILITARIZACION DE OBREROS Y CAMPESINOS. Mexico City: American Press, 1938.

13. Amezcua, José Luis. MEMORIAS DE UNA CAMPANA. Mexico City: Talleres Gráficos de la Nación, 1924.

14. Andrews, Gregory. "The Decisive Role of the United States in Suppressing the De la Huerta Rebellion in Mexico, 1923-1924." M.A. thesis, Northeast Missouri State University, 1979.

15. Angeles, Felipe. DOCUMENTOS RELATIVOS AL GENERAL FELIPE ANGELES. Mexico City: Domés, 1982.

16. Ankerson, Dudley. AGRARIAN WARLORD: SATURNINO CEDILLO AND THE MEXICAN REVOLUTION IN SAN LUIS POTOSI. DeKalb: Northern Illinois University Press, 1984.

17. Aragón, Alfredo. EL DESARME DEL EJERCITO FEDERAL POR LA REVOLUCION DE 1913. Paris: Welhoffet Roche, 1915.

18. Archivo General de la Nación. ARCHIVO DE ALFREDO ROBLES DOMINGUEZ. 2 vols. Mexico City: A.G.N., 1981.

19. ———. ARCHIVO DE GENOVEVO DE LA O. Mexico City: A.G.N., 1980.

20. ———. ARCHIVO DE GUERRA. 2 vols. Mexico City: A.G.N., 1982.

21. ———. CATALOGO DE LA SERIE ARMAS: FONDO PRESIDENTES ALVARO OBREGON, PLUTARCO ELIAS CALLES, 1920-1928. Mexico City: A.G.N., 1980.

22. ———. GUIA DEL RAMO TITULOS Y DESPACHOS DE GUERRA: COPIAS. 2d ed. Mexico City: A.G.N., 1980.

23. ———. GUIA GENERAL DE LOS FONDOS QUE CONTIENE EL ARCHIVO GENERAL DE LA NACION. Mexico City: A.G.N., 1981.

24. Arenas, Guzmán. LOS TRATADOS DE TEOLOYUCAN Y LA DISOLUCION DEL EJERCITO FEDERAL. Mexico City: Sec. de Gobernación, 1964.

25. Arías Arredondo, Juan. MANUAL DE INSTRUCCION MILITAR. Mexico City: n.p., 1942.

26. Asprey, Robert S. "Las fuerzas armadas de México." MARINE CORPS GAZETTE 50 (1966): 40-42.

27. Avila Camacho, Manuel. MEXICO COOPERA CON LAS NACIONES ALIADAS: NUESTRA BANDERA ONDEA EN LOS CAMPOS DE LA LUCHA. Mexico City: Sec. de Gobernación, 1944.

28. ———. EL SOLDADO MEXICANO Y LOS DESTINOS DE AMERICA. Mexico City: Sec. de Relaciones Exteriores, 1941.

29. Azuela, Mariano. LOS DE ABAJO. El Paso: El Paso del Norte, 1916.

30. Bailey, David C. ¡VIVA CRISTO REY!: THE CRISTERO REBELLION AND THE CHURCH-STATE CONFLICT IN MEXICO. Austin: University of Texas Press, 1974.

31. Balbás, Manuel. RECUERDOS DEL YAQUI: PRINCIPALES EPISODIOS DURANTE LA CAMPANA DE 1899 A 1901. Mexico City: Sociedad de Edición y Librería Franco Americana, 1927.

32. Balbontín, Manuel. MEMORIAS DEL CORONEL MANUEL BALBONTIN. Mexico City: Editorial Elede, 1958.

33. Banco Nacional Hipotecario Urbano Y de Obras Públicas. CASAS PARA GENERALES, JEFES Y OFICIALES DEL EJERCITO: [Various States]. Mexico City: Editorial Stylo, 1961-64.

34. Barnard, Joseph D., and Randall Rasmussen. "A Bibliography of Bibliographies for the History of Mexico." LATIN AMERICAN RESEARCH REVIEW 13(1978): 229-35.

35. Barragán Rodríquez, Juan B. HISTORIA DEL EJERCITO Y DE LA REVOLUCION CONSTITUCIONALISTA. 2 vols. Mexico City: Editorial Stylo, 1945.

36. Batchelder, Roger. WATCHING AND WAITING ON THE BORDER. Boston: Houghton Mifflin, 1917.

37. Bautista Rojas, Ramiro J. "El ejército en el México actual: Misión y perspectivas." Lic. thesis, Universidad Nacional Autónoma de México, 1976.

38. Beezley, William H. INSURGENT GOVERNOR: ABRAHAM GONZALEZ AND THE MEXICAN REVOLUTION IN CHIHUAHUA. Lincoln: University of Nebraska Press, 1973.

39. Bellemare, Louis de. ESCENAS DE LA VIDA MILITAR EN MEXICO. Mexico City: Vda. de Ch. Bouret, 1909.

40. Beltrán, Joaquín. LA TOMA DE LA PLAZA H. VERACRUZ EL 23 DE OCTUBRE DE 1912 Y LA INTROMISION YANQUI: OBRA ESCRITA; INCLUYENDO LOS DOCUMENTOS OFICIALES Y PARTICULARES CORRESPONDIENTES. Mexico City: Herrero Hnos., 1930.

41. Benjamin, Thomas. "Passages to Leviathan: Chiapas and the Mexican State, 1891-1947. Ph.D. dissertation, Michigan State University, 1981.

42. Bermúdez Flores, Renato de Jesús. "La justicia en la armada de México." Lic. thesis, Universidad Nacional Autónoma de México, 1963.

43. Beteta, Ignacio M. MENSAJE AL EJERCITO NACIONAL. Mexico City: D.A.P.P., 1937.

44. BIBLIOGRAFIA HISTORICA MEXICANA. Mexico City: El Colegio de México, 1967-.

45. BIBLIOGRAFIA MEXICANA. Mexico City: Biblioteca Nacional, 1967-.

46. BIBLIOGRAPHIC GUIDE TO LATIN AMERICAN STUDIES. Boston: G.K. Hall, 1978-.

47. Blanco, Santiago. EL PROYECTO DE ORDENANZA PARA EL EJERCITO DE LA REPUBLICA: ARTICULOS PUBLICADOS EN EL "SIGLO XIX." Mexico City: I. Cumplido, 1882.

48. Blasco Ibáñez, Vicente. EL MILITARISMO MEJICANO: ESTUDIOS PUBLICADOS EN LOS PRINCIPALES DIARIOS DE LOS ESTADOS UNIDOS. Valencia: Prometeo, 1920.

49. Boils Morales, Guillermo. "Fuerzas armadas y armamentismo en México." NUEVA POLITICA 2 (1977): 353-58.

50. ———. "Los militares en México, 1965-1985." REVISTA MEXICANA DE SOCIOLOGIA 47 (1985): 169-85.

51. ———. LOS MILITARES Y LA POLITICA EN MEXICO, 1915-1974. Mexico City: Ediciones "El Caballito," 1975.

52. Bonilla, Julio. APUNTES HISTORICOS SOBRE EL ORIGEN DEL COLEGIO MILITAR DE LA REPUBLICA. Mexico City: Gonzalo A. Esteva, 1884.

53. Bonilla Machorro, Carlos. EJERCICIO DE GUERRILLERO. 2d ed. Mexico City: Grupo Editorial Gaceta, 1983.

54. Bosch, Wilfredo. "El general Urguizo y la tropa de la revolución." REVISTA COAHUILENSE DE HISTORIA 13 (1980): 70-87.

55. Bosch García Carlos. MEXICO FRENTE EL MAR: EL CONFLICTO HISTORICO ENTRE LA NOVEDAD MARINERA Y LA TRADICION TERRESTRE. Mexico City: U.N.A.M., 1981.

56. Braddy, Haldeen. PANCHO VILLA AT COLUMBUS: THE RAID OF 1916 RESTUDIED. El Paso: Texas Western College Press, 1965.

57. ———. PERSHING'S MISSION IN MEXICO. El Paso: Texas Western College Press, 1966.

58. Brading D.A., ed. CAUDILLO AND PEASANT IN THE MEXICAN REVOLUTION. Cambridge: Cambridge University Press, 1980.

59. Bravo Izquierdo, Donato. LEALTAD MILITAR: CAMPANA
     EN EL ESTADO DE CHIAPAS E ISTMO DE
     TEHUANTEPEC, 1923-1924. Mexico City: n.p., 1948.

60. ———. UN SOLDADO DEL PUEBLO. Puebla: Editorial
     Periodística e Impresora, 1964.

61. Brenner, Anita. THE WIND THAT SWEPT MEXICO: THE
     HISTORY OF THE MEXICAN REVOLUTION, 1910-1942.
     Austin: University of Texas Press, 1943.

62. Brown, Michael P. AIR FORCES OF THE WORLD. Geneva:
     INTERAVIA, 1984.

63. Brushwood, John S. MEXICO IN ITS NOVEL: A NATION'S
     SEARCH FOR IDENTITY. Austin: University of Texas Press,
     1966.

64. Bulnes Galván, Carlos. "La guerra y el derecho castrense." Lic.
     thesis, Universidad Nacional Autónoma de México, 1961.

65. Buve, Raymond Th. J. "Peasant Movements, Caudillos and Land
     Reform During the Revolution, 1910-1917, in Tlaxcala, Mexico."
     BOLETIN DE ESTUDIOS LATINOAMERICANOS Y DEL
     CARIBE 18(1975): 112-52.

66. Calderón Gómez, René. "Régimen jurídico de las colonias
     agrícolas militares." Lic. thesis, Universidad Nacional Autónoma
     de México, 1966.

67. Calderón Serrano, Ricardo. "Derecho penal militar." Lic. thesis,
     Universidad Nacional Autónoma de México, 1944.

68. Calles, Plutarco Elías. LA ESCUELA SUPERIOR DE
     GUERRA Y PRINCIPIOS DE DOCTRINA PARA LA
     ORGANIZACION DEL EJERCITO DE MEXICO:
     CONFERENCIA PRONUNCIADA EN LA ESCUELA
     SUPERIOR DE GUERRA EL DIA PRIMERO DE FEBRERO
     DE 1934. Mexico City: Sec. de Relaciones Exteriores, 1934.

69. ———. PARTE GENERAL DE LAS OPERACIONES
     MILITARES DESARROLLADAS EN LOS ESTADOS DE
     VERACRUZ, ZACATECAS, DURANGO, COAHUILA,
     NUEVO LEON, CHIHUAHUA, SINALOA Y SONORA, BAJO

LA DIRECCION DEL C. GRAL. DE DIVISION PLUTARCO ELIAS CALLES DEL 3 DE MARZO AL 3 DE MAYO DE 1929. Mexico City: n.p., 1929.

70. Calvert Peter. THE MEXICAN REVOLUTION, 1910-1914: THE DIPLOMACY OF ANGLO-AMERICAN CONFLICT. Cambridge: Cambridge University Press, 1968.

71. Calzadíaz Barrera, Alberto. ANATOMIA DE UN GUERRERO: EL GENERAL MARTIN LOPEZ; HIJO MILITAR DE PANCHO VILLA. Mexico City: Editores Mexicanos Unidos, 1968.

72. ———. HECHOS REALES DE LA REVOLUCION: EL FIN DE LA DIVISION DEL NORTE. Mexico City: Editorial Patria, 1972.

73. ———. HECHOS REALES DE LA REVOLUCION: GENERAL FELIPE ANGELES. México: Editorial Patria, 1982.

74. Camp, Roderic A. "Mexican Military Leadership in Statistical Perspective since the 1930s." STATISTICAL ABSTRACT OF LATIN AMERICA 20(1980): 596-606.

75. ———. MEXICAN POLITICAL BIOGRAPHIES, 1935-1981. 2d ed. Tucson: University of Arizona Press, 1982.

76. Campobello, Nellie. APUNTES SOBRE LA VIDA MILITAR DE FRANCISCO VILLA. Mexico City: EDIAPSA, 1940.

77. Canales Montejano, Guillermo. HISTORIA MILITAR DE MEXICO: DIEZ CASOS CONCRETOS. Mexico City: Ediciones Ateneo, 1940.

78. Cañas Salazar, Rolando. "Sistema penitenciario en el fuero de guerra." Lic. thesis, Universidad Nacional Autónoma de México, 1967.

79. Cantón, Wilberto L. PORFIRIO DIAZ: SOLDADO DE LA REPUBLICA. Mexico City: Sec. de Educación Pública, 1966.

80. Cárdenas de la Peña, Enrique. EDUCACION NAVAL EN MEXICO. Mexico City: Sec. de Marina, 1967.

81. ———. GESTA EN EL GOLFO: LA SEGUNDA GUERRA MUNDIAL Y MEXICO. Mexico City: Editorial Primicias, 1966.

82. Carreño, Alberto María. "El Colegio Militar de Chapultepec, 1847-1947." BOLETIN DE LA SOCIEDAD MEXICANA DE FIA Y GEOGRA ESTADISTICA 66 (1948): 25-92.

83. Casasola, Gustavo. ANALES GRAFICOS DE LA HISTORIA MILITAR DE MEXICO, 1810-1980. 6 vols. Mexico City: Editorial G. Casasola, 1980.

84. ———. HISTORIA GRAFICA DE LA REVOLUCION MEXICANA, 1900-1960. 10 vols. Mexico City: Editorial F. Trillas, 1960-70.

85. Caso Gutiérrez, José Antonio. LA SELECCION Y CLASIFICACION DEL ELEMENTO HOMBRE EN EL EJERCITO MEXICANO. Mexico City: Ortega, 1951.

86. Castaños Dorador, Salvador. DEPURACION DEL EJERCITO NACIONAL: A LOS QUE LES VENGA AL SACO. N.p.: n.p., 1914.

87. Castellanos Alonso, Herberto. "La jurisdicción militar y el amparo: Sala Militar en la H. Suprema Corte." Lic. thesis, Universidad Nacional Autónoma de México, 1965.

88. Castillo Negrete, Emiliano de. HISTORIA MILITAR DE MEXICO EN EL SIGLO XIX. 2 vols. Mexico City: Antonio Rosas, 1883.

89. Castro, Simón Hipólito. GUERRERO: AMNISTIA Y REPRESION. Mexico City: Editorial Grijalbo, 1982.

90. Castro Leal, Antonio. LA NOVELA DE LA REVOLUCION MEXICANA. 2 vols. Mexico City: Aguilar, 1958-60.

91. Cervantes M., Federico. FELIPE ANGELES EN LA REVOLUCION: BIOGRAFIA, 1869-1919. Mexico City: Ediciones Botas, 1964.

92. Chaib, Alejandro Rafael. "Terrorist and Guerrilla Violence in Mexico, 1965-1978." M.A. thesis, University of Texas, Austin, 1984.

93. Chávarri, Juan N. EL HEROICO COLEGIO MILITAR EN LA HISTORIA DE MEXICO. Mexico City: Libro Mex Editores, 1960.

94. Clendenen, Clarence C. BLOOD ON THE BORDER: THE UNITED STATES ARMY AND THE MEXICAN IRREGULARS. New York: Macmillan, 1969.

95. Coello Ochoa, Carlos. "Sobre la situación de los marineros auxiliares en la armada de México." Lic. thesis, Universidad Nacional Autónoma de México, 1962.

96. Coerver, Don. THE PORFIRIAN INTERREGNUM: THE PRESIDENCY OF MANUEL GONZALEZ OF MEXICO, 1880-1884. Fort Worth: Texas Christian University Press, 1979.

97. Cole, Garold. AMERICAN TRAVELERS TO MEXICO, 1821-1972: A DESCRIPTIVE BIBLIOGRAPHY. Troy, N.Y.: Whitston Publishing Co., 1978.

98. Cordeiro, Daniel Rapaoso, ed. A BIBLIOGRAPHY OF LATIN AMERICAN BIBLIOGRAPHIES: SOCIAL SCIENCES AND HUMANITIES. Metuchen: Scarecrow Press, 1979.

99. Cordero, Dolores. "El ejército mexicano." REVISTA DE REVISTAS, 12 September 1973, 3-11.

100. Coronado Barajas, Rafael. "De las limitaciones impuestas al militar para actuar en política." Lic. thesis, Universidad Nacional Autónoma de México, 1949.

101. Corzo Ramírez, Ricardo, José G. González Sierra, and David A. Skerritt. NUNCA UN DESLEAL: CANDIDO AGUILAR, 1889-1960. Mexico City: El Colegio de México, 1986.

102. Cosío Villegas, Daniel, ed. HISTORIA MODERNA DE MEXICO. 10 vols. Mexico City: Editorial Hermes, 1955-72.

103. ———. PORFIRIO DIAZ EN LA REVUELTA DE LA NORIA. Mexico City: Editorial Hermes, 1953.

104. Cota Soto, Guillermo. HISTORIA MILITAR DE MEXICO: ENSAYO. Mexico City: Talleres Gráficos de la Nación, 1947.

105. Coutiño M., Ezequiel. REVOLUCION MEXICANA: LA LUCHA ARMADA, 1913-1914. Mexico City: Talleres Gráficos de la Nación, 1968.

106. Craig, Richard B. "La Campaña Permanente: Mexico's Antidrug Campaign." JOURNAL OF INTER-AMERICAN STUDIES AND WORLD AFFAIRS 20 (1978): 107-31.

107. ———. "Operation Condor: Mexico's Antidrug Campaign Enters a New Era." JOURNAL OF INTER-AMERICAN STUDIES AND WORLD AFFAIRS 22 (1980): 345-63.

108. Cravioto, Adrián. EL LIBRO DEL SOLDADO DE CABALLERIA. Mexico City: Caballero Hnos., 1936.

109. CRONICAS DE LA GUERRA DEL YAQUI. Hermosillo: Gobierno del Estado de Sonora, 1985.

110. Cruz, Roberto. ROBERTO CRUZ EN LA REVOLUCION MEXICANA. Mexico City: Editorial Diana, 1976.

111. Cumberland, Charles C. MEXICAN REVOLUTION: THE CONSTITUTIONALIST YEARS. Austin: University of Texas Press, 1972.

112. ———. MEXICAN REVOLUTION: GENESIS UNDER MADERO. Austin: University of Texas Press, 1952.

113. Dabbs, Jack Aubrey. THE FRENCH ARMY IN MEXICO, 1861-1867. The Hague: Mouton and Co., 1963.

114. Davidson, Martha, ed. PICTURE COLLECTIONS: MEXICO; A GUIDE TO PICTURE SOURCES IN THE UNITED MEXICAN STATES. Metuchen: Scarecrow Press, 1988.

115. Dávila, José María. EL EJERCITO DE LA REVOLUCION: CONTRIBUCION HISTORICA DEL EJERCITO MEXICANO. N.p.: n.p., 1938.

116. Deal, Carl W., ed. LATIN AMERICA AND THE CARIBBEAN: A DISSERTATION BIBLIOGRAPHY. Ann Arbor: University Microfilms International, 1977.

117. Degollado Guízar, Jesús. MEMORIAS DE JESUS DEGOLLADO GUIZAR: ULTIMO GENERAL EN JEFE DEL EJERCITO CRISTERO. Mexico City: Editorial Jus, 1957.

118. Del Castillo, Porfirio. PUEBLA Y TLAXCALA EN LOS DIAS DE LA REVOLUCION. Mexico City: Zavala, 1953.

119. Dessau, Adalbert. LA NOVELA DE LA REVOLUCION MEXICANA. Mexico City: Fondo de Cultura Económica, 1972.

120. Díaz Ordaz, Gustavo. EL IDEARIO DE MEXICO: SEGUIDO DE UN CAPITULO QUE TRATA DE LA APLICACIÓN HECHA POR EL SENOR ALMIRANTE DN. ANTONIO VAZQUEZ DEL MERCADO DE PENSAMIENTO MARITIMO DEL C. JEFE DEL EJECUTIVO. Mexico City: Sec. de Marina, 1969.

121. Díaz Reyes Retara, Fernando. VIDA MILITAR Y POLITICA DEL SR. GENERAL DE DIVISION DON LEONARDO MARQUEZ ARAUJO. Querétaro: n.p., 1978.

122. DICCIONARIO PORRUA DE HISTORIA, BIOGRAFIA Y GEOGRAFIA DE MEXICO. 2 vols. 4th ed. Mexico City: Editorial Porrúa, 1976.

123. Didapp, Juan Pedro. GOBIERNOS MILITARES DE MEXICO: LOS ATAQUES AL EJERCITO Y LAS MAQUINACIONES POLITICAS DEL PARTIDO CIENTIFICO PARA REGIR LOS DESTINOS NACIONALES. Mexico City: J.I. Guerrero, 1904.

124. Dillon, E.J. "Alvaro Obregón: As Military Organizer." SATURDAY EVENING POST, 4 Dec. 1920, 12, 61-74.

125. Dios Bonilla, Juan de. APUNTES PARA LA HISTORIA DE LA MARINA NACIONAL. Mexico City: n.p., 1946.

126. ———. HISTORIA MARITIMA DE MEXICO. 2d ed. Mexico City: Editorial Litoral, 1962.

127. DISSERTATION ABSTRACTS INTERNATIONAL. Ann Arbor: University Microfilms International, 1938-.

128. Domínquez, Zeferino. EL SERVICIO MILITAR AGRARIO Y LA PEQUENA PROPIEDAD. Mexico City: La Helvetia, 1913.

129. Dulles, John W. YESTERDAY IN MEXICO: A CHRONICLE OF THE REVOLUTION, 1919-1936. Austin: University of Texas Press, 1961.

130. Dupuy, Trevor N., et al. THE ALMANAC OF WORLD MILITARY POWER. 4th ed. San Rafael, Calif.: Presidio Press, 1980.

131. Echenique, Rafael. CATALOGO ALFABETICO Y CRONOLOGICO DE LOS HECHOS DE ARMAS QUE HAN TENIDO LUGAR EN LA REPUBLICA MEXICANA DESDE SU INDEPENDENCIA HASTA NUESTROS DIAS. Mexico City: Sec. de Fomento, 1894.

132. Einaudi, Luigi, and Herbert Goldhamer. AN ANNOTATED BIBLIOGRAPHY OF LATIN AMERICAN MILITARY JOURNALS. Santa Monica: Rand Corporation, 1965.

133. EL EJERCITO CAMPESINO DEL SUR: IDEOLOGIA, ORGANIZACION Y PROGRAMA. Mexico City: Centro de Estudios Históricos del Agrarismo en México, 1982.

134. ENCYCLOPEDIA DE MEXICO. 12 vols. 4th ed. Mexico City: Enciclopedia de México, 1978.

135. English, Adrián J. THE ARMED FORCES OF LATIN AMERICA: THEIR HISTORIES, DEVELOPMENT, PRESENT STRENGTH, AND MILITARY POTENTIAL. London: Jane's, 1984.

136. Escudero, Ignacio M. APUNTES HISTORICAS DE LA CARRERA MILITAR DEL SENOR GENERAL PORFIRIO DIAZ, PRESIDENTE DE LA REPUBLICA. Mexico: Cosmos, 1975. [Originally published in 1889.]

137. Espinosa de los Monteros Bretón, Leonardo. "La defensa del derecho como única finalidad del ejército." Lic. thesis, Universidad Nacional Autónoma de México, 1963.

138. Evans, Rosalie. THE ROSALIE EVANS LETTERS FROM MEXICO. Indianapolis: Bobbs-Merrill Co., 1926.

139. Fabela, Isidro, and Josefina E. de Fabela, eds. DOCUMENTOS HISTORICOS DE LA REVOLUCION MEXICANA. 27 vols. Mexico City: Editorial Jus and Fondo de Cultura Económica, 1960-73.

140. Falcón, Romana. REVOLUCION Y CACIQUISMO EN SAN LUIS POTOSI, 1910-1938. Mexico City: El Colegio de México, 1984.

141. Fernández de Lara Quiroga, César. "La armada en la Constitución de 1917." Lic. thesis, Universidad Nacional Autónoma de México, 1964.

142. Fernández de Zamora, Rosa María. LAS PUBLICACIONES OFICIALES DE MEXICO: GUIA DE PUBLICACIONES PERIODICAS Y SERIADAS, 1937-1970. Mexico City: U.N.A.M., 1977.

143. Fierro Villalobos, Roberto. ESTA ES MI VIDA. Mexico City: n.p., 1964.

144. Franco, Luis G. GLOSA DEL PERIODO DE GOBIERNO DEL C. GRAL. E ING. PASCUAL ORTIZ RUBIO, 1930-1932: TRES ANOS DE HISTORIA DEL EJERCITO DE MEXICO. Mexico City: n.p., 1946.

145. Franco González Salas, Teresa. "José González Salas: Ministro de la Guerra." Lic. thesis, Universidad Iberoamericana, 1979.

146. Frías, Heriberto. TOMOCHIC. 4th ed. Mexico City: Editorial Porrúa, 1979. [Originally published 1893-95.]

147. Fuentes, Gloria. EL EJERCITO MEXICANO. Mexico City: Editorial Grijalbo, 1983.

148. Galván Cantú, José E. CURSO DE HISTORIA MILITAR: PRIMER ANO, SEGUNDA ANTIGUEDAD. Mexico City: Escuela Superior de Guerra, 1933.

149. García, Rubén. EL SABER Y LOS MILITARES. Mexico City: Talleres Gráficos de la Nación, 1934.

150. García Arroyo, Raziel. BIOGRAFIA DE LA MARINA MEXICANA: SEMBLANZAS HISTORICAS. Mexico City: Sec. de Marina, 1960.

151. García Segura, José Jesús. "El ejército, el militar y la política." Lic. thesis, Universidad Nacional Autónoma de México, 1961.

152. García Vázquez, Carlos. "La jurisdicción militar." Lic. thesis, Universidad Nacional Autónoma de México, 1962.

153. Garfias M., Luis. BREVE HISTORIA MILITAR DE LA REVOLUCION MEXICANA. Mexico City: Sec. de Defensa Nacional, 1981.

154. ———. GENERALES MEXICANOS DEL SIGLO XIX. Mexico City: Sec. de Defensa Nacional, 1980.

155. Garritz, Amaya, ed. GUIA DEL ARCHIVO AMADO AGUIRRE. Mexico City: U.N.A.M., 1982.

156. Gavira, Gabriel. GENERAL DE BRIGADA GABRIEL GAVIRA: SU ACTUACION POLITICO-MILITAR REVOLUCIONARIA. Mexico City: Talleres Tipográficos de A. del Bosque, 1933.

157. Gilderhus, Mark T. DIPLOMACY AND REVOLUTION: U.S.-MEXICAN RELATIONS UNDER WILSON AND CARRANZA. Tucson: University of Arizona Press, 1977.

158. Gillingham, Harrold Edgar. MEXICAN DECORATIONS OF HONOUR. New York: American Numismatic Society, 1940.

159. Gómez, Arnulfo R. EL CENTINELA. Mexico City: n.p., 1924.

160. ———. ESTUDIOS MILITARES. Mexico City: n.p., 1926.

161. Gómez Arnau, Remedios. "Mexico y la Organización Norteamericana de la Defensa Hemisférica, 1938-1945." Lic. thesis, El Colegio de México, 1979.

162. Gómez Maqueo, Roberto. MEXICO PUEDE Y DEBE DESARROLLAR SUS MARINAS. 2d ed. Mexico City: México-Marítimo, 1954.

163. González, Manuel. ORDENANZA GENERAL PARA EL EJERCITO DE LA REPUBLICA MEXICANA. 2 vols. Mexico City: I. Cumplido, 1882,1886.

164. González, Manuel W. CON CARRANZA: EDISODIOS DE LA REVOLUCION CONSTITUCIONALISTA, 1913-1914. Mexico City: J. Cantú Leal, 1933-34.

165. ———. CONTRA VILLA: RELATOS DE LA CAMPANA, 1914-1915. Mexico City: Ediciones Botas, 1935.

166. González Navarro, Moisés. RAZA Y TIERRA: LA GUERRA DE CASTAS Y EL HENEQUEN. Mexico City: El Colegio de México, 1970.

167. González Ramírez, Manuel. LA CAPITULACION DEL EJERCITO DE LA DICTADURA ANTE CARRANZA Y OBREGON. Mexico City: Patronato de la Historia de Sonora, 1964.

168. ———, ed. FUENTES PARA LA HISTORIA DE LA REVOLUCION MEXICANA. 5 vols. Mexico City: Fondo de Cultura Económica 1954-57.

169. González y González, Luis, ed. FUENTES DE LA HISTORIA CONTEMPORANEA DE MEXICO: LIBROS Y FOLLETOS. 3 vols. Mexico City: El Colegio de México, 1961-62.

170. Greenleaf, Richard E., and Michael C. Meyer, eds. RESEARCH IN MEXICAN HISTORY: TOPICS, METHODOLOGY, SOURCES, AND A PRACTICAL GUIDE TO FIELD RESEARCH. Lincoln: University of Nebraska Press, 1973.

171. Gregg, Robert Danforth. THE INFLUENCE OF BORDER TROUBLES ON RELATIONS BETWEEN THE UNITED STATES AND MEXICO, 1876-1910. Baltimore: Johns Hopkins University Press, 1937.

172. Grieb, Kenneth J. THE UNITED STATES AND HUERTA. Lincoln: University of Nebraska Press, 1969.

173. Griffin, Charles C., ed. LATIN AMERICA: A GUIDE TO THE HISTORICAL LITERATURE. Austin: University of Texas Press, 1971.

174. Gropp, Arthur E., ed. A BIBLIOGRAPHY OF LATIN AMERICAN BIBLIOGRAPHIES. Metuchen: Scarecrow Press, 1968.

175. ———., ed. A BIBLIOGRAPHY OF LATIN AMERICAN BIBLIOGRAPHIES: SUPPLEMENT. Metuchen: Scarecrow Press, 1971.

176. ———, ed. A BIBLIOGRAPHY OF LATIN AMERICAN BIBLIOGRAPHIES PUBLISHED IN PERIODICALS. 2 vols. Metuchen: Scarecrow Press, 1976.

177. Grow, Michael. SCHOLARS' GUIDE TO WASHINGTON, D.C., FOR LATIN AMERICAN AND CARIBBEAN STUDIES. Washington: Smithsonian Institution Press, 1979.

178. Guerra, François-Xavier. LE MEXIQUE DE L'ANCIEN REGIME A LA REVOLUTION. 2 vols. Paris: L'Harmattan, Publications de la Sorbonne, 1985.

179. Gutiérrez Iturria, Jaime. MEXICO EN GUERRA. Mexico City: n.p., 1942.

180. Gutiérrez Santos, Daniel. HISTORIA MILITAR DE MEXICO, 1876-1914. Mexico City: Ediciones Ateneo, 1955.

181. Gutiérrez Soriano, Alfonso. "Algunos aspectos del fuero de guerra." Lic. thesis, Universidad Nacional Autónoma de México, 1952.

182. Guzmán, Martín Luis. MEMOIRS OF PANCHO VILLA. Austin: University of Texas Press, 1965.

183. Haberman, Roberto. "Bandit Colonies." THE SURVEY, 1 May 1924, 147-48, 196.

184. Haley, P. Edward. REVOLUTION AND INTERVENTION: THE DIPLOMACY OF TAFT AND WILSON WITH MEXICO, 1910-1917. Cambridge: M.I.T. Press, 1970.

185. Hall, Linda B. ALVARO OBREGON: POWER AND REVOLUTION IN MEXICO, 1911-1920. College Station: Texas A & M University Press, 1981.

186. HANDBOOK OF LATIN AMERICAN STUDIES. 1935-.

187. Hanrahan, Gene Z., ed. DOCUMENTS ON THE MEXICAN REVOLUTION. 9 vols. Chapel Hill, N.C.: Documentary Publications, 1976-85.

188. Hansis, Randall George. "The Political Strategy of Military Reform: Obregón and Revolutionary Mexico, 1920-1924." THE AMERICAS 36(1979): 199-233.

189. Hart, John Mason. REVOLUTIONARY MEXICO: THE COMING AND PROCESS OF THE MEXICAN REVOLUTION. Berkeley: University of California Press, 1987.

190. Heare, G.E. TRENDS IN LATIN AMERICAN MILITARY EXPENDITURES, 1940-1970. Washington: U.S. Department of State, 1971.

191. Hernández, Julia. NOVELISTAS Y CUENTISTAS DE LA REVOLUCION. Mexico City: Unidad Mexicana de Editores, 1960.

192. Hernández Chávez, Alicia. "La defensa de los finqueros en Chiapas, 1915-1920." HISTORIA MEXICANA 28 (1979): 335-69.

193. ———. LA MECANICA CARDENISTA. Mexico City: El Colegio de Mexico, 1980.

194. ———. "Militares y negocios en la revolución mexicana." HISTORIA MEXICANA 34(1984): 181-212.

195. Hernández Cruz, Arsenio. "La situación del ejército conforme al derecho constitucional." Lic. thesis, Universidad Nacional Autónoma de México, 1956.

196. HISPANIC AMERICAN PERIODICALS INDEX. Los Angeles: U.C.L.A. Latin American Center, 1970/74-.

197. HISTORIA DE LA REVOLUCION MEXICANA. 20 vols. Mexico City: El Colegio de México, 1977-83.

198. Holcombe, Harold Eugene. "United States Arms Control and the Mexican Revolution, 1910-1924." Ph.D. dissertation, University of Alabama, 1968.

199. Hu-DeHart, Evelyn. "Pacification of the Yaquis in the Late Porfiriato: Development and Implications." HISPANIC AMERICAN HISTORICAL REVIEW 54 (1974): 72-93.

200. ———. YAQUI RESISTANCE AND SURVIVAL: THE STRUGGLE FOR LAND AND AUTONOMY, 1821-1910. Madison: University of Wisconsin Press, 1984.

201. Huerta, Victoriano. MEMORIAS. Mexico City: Editiones Vertice, 1957.

202. Hughes, James B., Jr. MEXICAN MILITARY ARMS: THE CARTRIDGE PERIOD, 1866-1967. Houston: Deep River Armory, 1968.

203. Iglesias Calderón, Fernando. UN LIBRO DEL GENERAL EX-MINISTRO DE LA GUERRA: ERRORES MULTIPLES Y OMISIONES EXTRANAS. 2d ed. Mexico City: Editorial Mata, 1910.

204. Infante Miranda, Otilio. "La seguridad social en las fuerzas armadas de México." Lic. thesis, Universidad Nacional Autónoma de México, 1963.

205. Izazola Valdez, César. "El ejército y las situaciones de emergencia." Lic. thesis, Universidad Nacional Autónoma de México, 1958.

206. Jackson, Byron L. "The Political and Military Role of General Felipe Angeles in the Mexican Revolution, 1914-1915." Ph.D. dissertation, Georgetown University, 1976.

207. Jacobs, Ian. RANCHERO REVOLT: THE MEXICAN REVOLUTION IN GUERRERO. Austin: University of Texas Press, 1982.

208. Jiménez Carrasco, Jorge. "La noción de delito en el fuero de guerra." Lic. thesis, Universidad Nacional Autónoma de México, 1962.

209. Joseph, Gilbert M. REVOLUTION FROM WITHOUT: YUCATAN, MEXICO, AND THE UNITED STATES, 1880-1924. Cambridge: Cambridge University Press, 1982.

210. Katz, Friedrich. "Innen- und Aussenpolitische Ursachen des mexicanische Revolutionsverlaufs." JAHRBUCH FUR GESCHICHTE VON STAAT, WIRTSCHAFT UND GESELLSCHAFT LATEINAMERIKAS 15 (1978): 95-101.

211. ———. "Pancho Villa and the Attack on Columbus New Mexico." AMERICAN HISTORICAL REVIEW 83 (1979): 101-30.

212. ———. THE SECRET WAR IN MEXICO: EUROPE, THE UNITED STATES AND THE MEXICAN REVOLUTION. Chicago: University of Chicago Press, 1981.

213. Keegan, John. WORLD ARMIES. 2d ed. Detroit: Gale Research Co., 1983.

214. Kelley, James R. "The Education and Training of Porfirian Officers: Success or Failure?" MILITARY AFFAIRS 39 (1975): 124-28.

215. Kelley, James Richard. "Professionalism in the Porfirian Army Officer Corps." Ph.D. dissertation, Tulane University, 1970.

216. Ker, Annita Melville. MEXICAN GOVERNMENT PUBLICATIONS: A GUIDE TO THE MORE IMPORTANT PUBLICATIONS OF THE NATIONAL GOVERNMENT, 1821-1936. Washington: U.S. Government Printing Office, 1940.

217. King, Rosa E. TEMPEST OVER MEXICO: A PERSONAL CHRONICLE. Boston: Little, Brown, and Co. 1935.

218. Knapp, Frank Averill, Jr. THE LIFE OF SEBASTIAN LERDO DE TEJADA, 1823-1889. Austin: University of Texas Press, 1951.

219. Knight, Alan. THE MEXICAN REVOLUTION. 2 vols. Cambridge: Cambridge University Press, 1986.

220. LaFrance, David G. FRANCISCO I. MADERO Y LA REVOLUCION MEXICANA EN PUEBLA. Puebla: Universidad Autónoma de Puebla, 1987.

221. Langle Ramírez, Arturo. EL EJERCITO VILLISTA. Mexico City: Instituto Nacional de Antropología e Historia, 1961.

222. ———. EL MILITARISMO DE VICTORIANO HUERTA. Mexico City: U.N.A.M., 1976.

223. Lapointe, Marie. LOS MAYAS REBELDES DE YUCATAN. Zamora: El Colegio de Michoacán, 1983.

224. León de Garay, Alfonso. EL FINAL DE LA CAMPANA: LA VERDAD SOBRE LAS OPERACIONES MILITARES QUE ACABARON CON LA ASONADA DE 1929 Y CON LOS PRONUNCIAMIENTOS DE VERACRUZ, DURANGO, COAHUILA, CHIHUAHUA Y SONORA. Puebla: Guadalupana, [1929].

225. ———. EL PALPITAR DE LA CASTA: CRONICAS MILITARES SOBRE LA CAMPANA DEL NORTE CONTRA LOS PRONUNCIADOS DE DURANGO, NUEVO LEON Y COAHUILA, HASTA LA TOMA DE TORREON. Puebla: Guadalupana, 1929.

226. León Toral, Jesús de, et al. EL EJERCITO MEXICANO. Mexico City: Sec. de Defensa Nacional, 1979.

227. Lieuwen, Edwin. "Curbing Militarism in Mexico." NEW MEXICO HISTORICAL REVIEW 33 (1958): 257-76.

228. ———. MEXICAN MILITARISM: THE POLITICAL RISE AND FALL OF THE REVOLUTIONARY ARMY, 1910-1940. Albuquerque: University of New Mexico Press, 1968.

229. Lizárraga, Francisco. DICCIONARIO TECNICO INGLES-ESPANOL Y ESPANOL-INGLES PARA USO DE LOS EJERCITOS DE TIERRA, MAR Y AIRE. Madrid: Bibliográfica Española, 1953.

230. López, Jaime. DIEZ ANOS DE GUERRILLAS EN MEXICO, 1964-1974. Mexico City: Editorial Posada, 1974.

231. López y Fuentes, Gregorio. MI GENERAL. Mexico City: Ediciones Botas, 1943. [Originally published 1934.]

232. Lozoya, Jorge Alberto. "Breve historia del ejército mexicano." APORTES 20 (1971): 113-31.

233. ——. EL EJERCITO MEXICANO. 3d ed. Mexico City: El Colegio de México, 1984.

234. ——. "Un guión para el estudio de los ejércitos mexicanos en el siglo diecinueve." HISTORIA MEXICANA 17 (1968): 553-68.

235. Mancisidor, Francisco. MEXICO Y SU REVOLUCION MARITIMA: CONTRIBUCION A LA HISTORIA PATRIA. Mexico City: Imprenta Juan Pablos, 1960.

236. Mangold, Walter. THE POCKET MANUAL OF MILITARY TERMINOLOGY ARRANGED IN SECTIONS ACCORDING TO SERVICES AND SUBJECT: SPANISH-ENGLISH, ENGLISH-SPANISH. Madrid: Ed. Mangold, 1955.

237. Manjarrez, Froylán C., and Hernán Gustavo Ortiz. LAZARO CARDENAS: I. SOLDADO, II. GOBERNANTE, III. POLITICO NACIONAL. Mexico City: Editorial Patria, 1933.

238. Margiotta, Franklin D. "Civilian Control and the Mexican Military: Changing Patterns of Political Influence." In CIVILIAN CONTROL OF THE MILITARY: THEORY AND CASES FROM DEVELOPING COUNTRIES, 213-53. Edited by Claude E. Welch, Jr. Albany: State University of New York Press, 1976.

239. ——. "The Mexican Military: A Case Study in Nonintervention." M.A. thesis, Georgetown University, 1968.

240. María y Campos, Armando de. MUGICA: CRONICA BIOGRAFICA. Mexico City: Ediciones Populares, 1939.

241. ——. LA REVOLUCION MEXICANA A TRAVES DE LOS CORRIDOS POPULARES. 2 vols. Mexico City: Instituto Nacional de Estudios Históricos de la Revolución Mexicana, 1962.

242. ——. LA VIDA DEL GENERAL LUCIO BLANCO. Mexico City: Instituto Nacional de Estudios Históricos de la Revolución Mexicana, 1963.

243. Martínez, Oscar. FRAGMENTS OF THE MEXICAN REVOLUTION: PERSONAL ACCOUNTS FROM THE BORDER. Albuquerque: University of New Mexico Press, 1983.

244. Martínez Carazo, Leopoldo. LA CABALLERIA EN MEXICO. Mexico City: Sec. de Defensa Nacional, 1980.

245. Matute, Alvaro. "Del ejército constitucionalista al ejército nacional." ESTUDIOS DE HISTORIA MODERNA Y CONTEMPORANEA DE MEXICO 6(1977): 153-83.

246. Medina, Luis. CIVILISMO Y MODERNIZACION DEL AUTORITARISMO. Mexico City: El Colegio de México, 1979.

247. Medina Neri, Héctor. GUSTAVO BAZ: GUERRILLO DE EMILIANO ZAPATA. Ciudad Satélite, México: H. Medina Neri, 1979.

248. Mejía Peralta, Ignacio Agustín. "Retiros y pensiones militares." Lic. thesis, Universidad Nacional Autónoma de México, 1963.

249. Mena Brito, Bernardino. FELIPE ANGELES: FEDERAL. Mexico City: Publicaciones Herrerías, 1936.

250. Menéndez González, Antonio. EL DIARIO DE UN CONSCRIPTO. Mexico City: Colonial, 1946.

251. Merino, José. DICCIONARIO MILITAR-TECNICO: ESPANOL-INGLES, INGLES-ESPANOL. Madrid: n.p., 1953.

252. Mex Canto, Rafael. "Comentarios a la Ley de Seguridad Social para las Fuerzas Armadas (LSSFA)." Lic. thesis, Universidad Nacional Autónoma de México, 1963.

253. Mexico. Ejército Constitucionalista. APUNTES PARA UN PROYECTO DE ORGANIZACION DEL EJERCITO MEXICANO. San Juan Bautista: Imprenta del Gobierno, 1914.

254. ———. DECRETOS Y DEMAS DISPOSICIONES DEL EJERCITO CONSTITUCIONALISTA, FEBRERO 19 DE 1913 A ABRIL 30 DE 1914. Chihuahua: Imprenta del Gobierno, 1914.

255. ———. PARTES OFICIALES DE LA CAMPANA DE SONORA. Mexico City: Talleres Gráficos de la Nación, 1932.

256. Mexico. Sec. de Defensa Nacional. ALGUNAS FICHAS PARA UNA BIBLIOGRAFIA GENERAL DE LA SEC. DE LA DEFENSA NACIONAL. Mexico City: Nigromante, 1943.

257. ———. DEPARTAMENTO DE LA INDUSTRIA MILITAR, 1946-1952. Mexico City: n.p., 1952.

258. ———. GUIA DEL ARCHIVO HISTORICO MILITAR DE MEXICO. Mexico City: n.p., 1948.

259. ———. INFORME DEL C. SECRETARIO DE LA DEFENSA NACIONAL.

260. ———. LEYES, DECRETOS, REGLAMENTOS, MANUALES, etc.

261. ———. MEMORIA.

262. ———. PLAN DE GUADALUPE: HOMENAJE DEL EJERCITO MEXICANO; CINCUENTENARIO, 1913-1963. Mexico City: Sec. de Defensa Nacional, 1963.

263. Mexico. Sec. de Guerra y Marina. LOS ALOJAMIENTOS MILITARES EN LA REPUBLICA. Mexico City: Talleres Gráficos de la Nación, 1921.

264. ———. APUNTES PARA UNA BIBLIOGRAFIA MILITAR DE MEXICO, 1536-1936. Mexico City: Talleres Gráficos de la Nación, 1937.

265. ———. CAMPANA DE 1910 A 1911. Mexico City: Depto. de Estado Mayor, 1913.

266. ———. LEYES, DECRETOS, REGLAMENTOS, MANUALES, etc.

267. ———. LISTA OFICIAL DE LOS BUQUES DE GUERRA Y MERCANTES DE LA MARINA MEXICANA Y LAS SENALES DISTINTIVAS QUE LES CORRESPONDEN. Mexico City: Sec. de Guerra y Marina, 1909.

268. ———. MEMORIA.

269. Mexico. Sec. de Hacienda y Crédito Público. LA CONTROVERSIA PANI-DE LA HUERTA: DOCUMENTOS PARA LA HISTORIA DE LA ULTIMA ASONADA MILITAR. Mexico City: Sec. de Hacienda y Crédito Público, 1924.

270. Mexico. Sec. de Marina. INFORME.

271. ———. LEYES, DECRETOS, REGLAMENTOS, MANUALES, etc.

272. ———. MARINA DE MEXICO. Mexico City: Montauriol, 1967.

273. Mexico. Senado. DOCUMENTOS HISTORICOS CONSTITUCIONALES DE LAS FUERZAS ARMADAS MEXICANAS. 4 vols. Mexico City: Senado, 1965-66.

274. Meyer, Jean A. THE CRISTERO REBELLION: THE MEXICAN PEOPLE BETWEEN CHURCH AND STATE, 1926-1929. Cambridge: Cambridge University Press, 1976.

275. ———. LA CRISTIADA. 3 vols. Mexico City: Siglo XXI Editores, 1973-74.

276. ———. "El ejército mexicano en el siglo xix." VUELTA, February 1981, 28-30.

277. ———. "Grandes compañías, ejércitos populares y ejército estatal en la revolución mexicana, 1910-1930." ANUARIO DE ESTUDIOS AMERICANOS 31 (1974): 1005-30.

278. ———. "Los obreros en la revolución mexicana: Los batallones rojos." HISTORIA MEXICANA 21(1971): 1-37.

279. ———. PROBLEMAS CAMPESINOS Y REVUELTAS AGRARIAS, 1821-1910. Mexico City: SepSetentas, 1973.

280. ———, Enrique Krauze, and Cayetano Reyes. ESTADO Y SOCIEDAD CON CALLES. Mexico City: El Colegio de México, 1977.

281. Meyer, Michael C. HUERTA: A POLITICAL PORTRAIT. Lincoln: University of Nebraska Press, 1972.

282. ———. MEXICAN REBEL: PASCUAL OROZCO AND THE MEXICAN REVOLUTION 1910-1915. Lincoln: University of Nebraska Press, 1967.

283. ———. "The Militarization of Mexico, 1913-1914." THE AMERICAS 27 (1971): 293-306.

284. ———. SUPPLEMENT TO A BIBLIOGRAPHY OF UNITED STATES-LATIN AMERICAN RELATIONS SINCE 1810. Lincoln: University of Nebraska Press, 1979.

285. Miller, David Lynn. "Porfirio Díaz and the Army of the East." Ph.D. dissertation, University of Michigan, 1960.

286. Miranda del Raso, Mario. "El ejército nacional: Sus fines, la jurisdicción castrense, preceptos legales que lo rigen." Lic. thesis, Universidad Nacional Autónoma de México, 1958.

287. Moctezuma, Aquiles P. EL CONFLICTO RELIGIOSO DE 1926: SUS ORIGENES, SU DESARROLLO, SU SOLUCION. Mexico City: n.p., 1929.

288. Mondragón, Manuel. PROYECTO DE ORGANIZACION DEL EJERCITO SOBRE LA BASE DEL SERVICIO OBLIGATORIO. Mexico City: Mercantil, 1910.

289. Mondragón Murillo, Eduardo. "Convenios militares entre jefes militares." Lic. thesis, Universidad Nacional Autónoma de México, 1968.

290. Monroy Durán, Luis. EL ULTIMO CAUDILLO: APUNTES PARA LA HISTORIA DE MEXICO ACERCA DEL MOVIMIENTO ARMADO DE 1923 EN CONTRA DEL GOBIERNO CONSTITUIDO. Mexico City: J.S. Rodríguez, 1924.

291. Moore, Ernest Richard. BIBLIOGRAFIA DE NOVELISTAS DE LA REVOLUCION MEXICANA. Mexico City: n.p., 1941.

292. Morales Hesse, José. EL GENERAL PABLO GONZALEZ: DATOS PARA LA HISTORIA, 1910-1916. Mexico City: n.p., 1916.

293. Moreno, Daniel, ed. BATALLAS DE LA REVOLUCION Y SUS CORRIDOS. Mexico City: Editorial Porrúa, 1978.

294. Morton, F. Rand. LOS NOVELISTAS DE LA REVOLUCION MEXICANA. Mexico City: Editorial Cultura, 1949.

295. Mota, Gonzalo. EL GENERAL ESTEBAN BACA CALDERON: SUS RASGOS BIOGRAFICOS, SU ACTUACION REVOLUCIONARIA. Guadalajara: n.p., 1917.

296. Múgica Velázquez, Francisco José. DIARIO DE CAMPANA DEL GRAL. FRANCISCO J. MUGICA. Villahermosa: Universidad Juárez Autónoma de Tabasco, 1984.

297. Muñoz, Rafael F. ¡VAMANOS CON PANCHO VILLA! 5th ed. Mexico City: Escasa-Calpe Mexicana, 1984. [Originally published in 1931.]

298. NACLA-West Mexico Project. "United States-Mexico: Military Build-up." NACLA REPORT ON THE AMERICAS, March-April 1978, 40-42.

299. Naylor Thomas H. "Massacre at San Pedro de la Cueva: The Significance of Pancho Villa's Disastrous Sonora Campaign." WESTERN HISTORICAL QUARTERLY 8 (1977): 125-50.

300. Negrete Doroteo. LA VERDAD ANTE LA FIGURA MILITAR DE DON MIGUEL NEGRETE. Puebla: La Enseñanza, 1935.

301. Neri Rodríguez, Silvestre. "Nuevo reglamento para el Servicio de Sanidad Militar y las relaciones jurídicas que fundan y norman su aplicación." Lic. thesis, Universidad Nacional Autónoma de México, 1963.

302. Neve, Carlos D. HISTORIA GRAFICA DEL EJERCITO MEXICANO. Cuernavaca: M. Quesada Brandi, 1967.

303. Niemeyer, E.V., Jr. EL GENERAL BERNARDO REYES. Monterrey: Universidad de Nuevo León, 1966.

304. Obregón, Alvaro. OCHO MIL KILOMETROS EN CAMPANA. Mexico City: Fondo de Cultura Económica, 1959. [Originally published in 1917.]

305. O'Farrill Rómulo. ALBUM HISTORICO DEL EJERCITO MEXICANO: DEDICADO AL SENOR GENERAL DE DIVISION IGNACIO M. ESCUDERO. Mexico City: n.p., 1896.

306. Ojeda Mestre, Ramón. "Nota sobre armamentismo." NUEVA POLITICA 2 (1977): 359-62.

307. Olguín Pérez, Palmira. "Los militares en México: Bibliografía introductoria." REVISTA MEXICANA DE SOCIOLOGIA 38 (1976): 453-90.

308. Olivera Sedano, Alicia. ASPECTOS DEL CONFLICTO RELIGIOSO DE 1926 A 1929: SUS ANTECEDENTES Y CONSECUENCIAS. Mexico City: Instituto Nacional de Antropología e Historia, 1966.

309. Olvera Guillén, Herón. APUNTES DE HISTORIA MILITAR: ARREGLO DESTINADO A LOS ALUMNOS DE ESTE PLANTEL. Guadalajara: Escuela Militar de Aviación, n.d.

310. Orozco, Fernando. NARRACIONES MILITARES MEXICANOS. Mexico City: Sec. de Defensa Nacional, 1983.

311. Ortiz, Orlando. LOS DORADOS: PANCHO VILLA Y LA DIVISION DEL NORTE. Mexico City: Sec. de Educación Pública, 1982.

312. Palomares, Justino N., and Francisco Múzquiz. LAS CAMPANAS DEL NORTE (SANGRE Y HEROES): NARRACION DE LOS SUCESOS MAS CULMINANTES REGISTRADOS EN LAS BATALLAS DE TORREON, DURANGO, GOMEZ PALACIO Y SAN PEDRO. Mexico City: Andrés Botas, n.d.

313. Pavia, Lázaro. EL EJERCITO Y LA POLITICA. Mexico City: Sec. de Guerra y Marina, 1909.

314. Paz, Eduardo. A DONDE DEBEMOS LLEGAR: ESTUDIO SOCIOLOGICO MILITAR. Mexico City: Tipografía Mercantil, 1910.

315. ———. LA DEFENSA NACIONAL: ESTUDIO MILITAR. Mexico City: Carlos Paz, n.d.

316. ———. EL NUEVO PROJECTO DE LA LEY PARA EL SERVICIO MILITAR OBLIGATORIO. Mexico City: Tipografía Mercantil, 1912.

317. ———. RESENA HISTORICA DEL ESTADO MAYOR DEL EJERCITO MEXICANO. Mexico City: Depto. del Estado Mayor, 1911.

318. ———. EL SERVICIO MILITAR OBLIGATORIO A LA
     NACION MEXICANA Y AL EJERCITO. Mexico City: Depto.
     del Estado Mayor, 1908.

319. Peña y Troncoso, Gonzalo. EL LECTOR MILITAR
     MEXICANO: ESCRITO EXPRESAMENTE PARA LAS
     ESCUELAS PRIMARIAS MILITARES. Mexico City: I. Paz,
     1905.

320. Pereyra González, Pedro. "Pueblo y ejército." Lic. thesis,
     Universidad Nacional Autónoma de México, 1963.

321. Pérez-Maldonado Carlos. CONDECORACIONES MEXICANAS
     Y SU HISTORIA. Monterrey: n.p., 1942.

322. Pérez Montfort, Ricardo. GUIA DEL ARCHIVO DEL
     GENERAL JENARO AMEZCUA, 1909-1947. Mexico City:
     Condumex, 1982.

323. Perry, Laurens Ballard. INVENTARIO Y GUIA DE LA
     COLECCION GENERAL PORFIRIO DIAZ. Mexico City:
     Universidad de las Américas, 1969.

324. ———. JUAREZ AND DIAZ: MACHINE POLITICS IN
     MEXICO. DeKalb: Northern Illinois University Press, 1978.

325. Piedracueva, Haydée. A BIBLIOGRAPHY OF LATIN
     AMERICAN BIBLIOGRAPHIES, 1975-1979: SOCIAL
     SCIENCES AND HUMANITIES. Metuchen: Scarecrow Press,
     1982.

326. Pierres Maldonado, Rodolfo. "El militar ante los derechos de
     escalafón: Análisis critico y jurídico de un aspecto del derecho
     administrativo militar mexicano." Lic. thesis, Universidad Nacional
     Autónoma de México, 1940.

327. Piñeyro, José Luis. EJERCITO Y SOCIEDAD EN MEXICO:
     PASADO Y PRESENTE. Mexico City: Universidad Autónoma
     Metropolitana-Azcapotzalco and Puebla: Universidad Autónoma
     de Puebla, 1985.

328. ———. "The Mexican Army and the State: Historical and Political
     Perspectives." REVUE INTERNATIONALE DE SOCIOLOGIE
     14 (1978).

329. ———. "El potencial político del ejército mexicano." HISTORIA Y SOCIEDAD 19 (1978).

330. ———. "El profesional ejército mexicano y la asistencia militar de Estados Unidos, 1965-1975." Lic. thesis, El Colegio de México, 1976.

331. Portes Gil, Emilio. AUTOBIOGRAFIA DE LA REVOLUCION MEXICANA: UN TRATADO DE INTERPRETACION HISTORICA. Mexico City: Instituto Mexicano de Cultura, 1964.

332. Prewett, Virginia. "The Mexican Army." FOREIGN AFFAIRS 19 (1941): 609-20.

333. Quirk, Robert E. AN AFFAIR OF HONOR: WOODROW WILSON AND THE OCCUPATION OF VERACRUZ. Lexington: University of Kentucky Press, 1962.

334. ———. THE MEXICAN REVOLUTION, 1914-1915: THE CONVENTION OF AGUASCALIENTES. Bloomington: Indiana University Press, 1960.

335. Raat, W. Dirk. THE MEXICAN REVOLUTION: AN ANNOTATED GUIDE TO RECENT SCHOLARSHIP. Boston: G.K. Hall, 1982.

336. Ramos, Miguel S. UN SOLDADO: GRAL. JOSE REFUGIO VELASCO. Mexico City: Ediciones Oasis, 1960.

337. Ramos, Roberto. BIBLIOGRAFIA DE LA REVOLUCION MEXICANA. 3 vols. 2d ed. Mexico City: Instituto Nacional de Estudios Históricos de la Revolución Mexicana, 1959-60. [Originally published 1931-40.]

338. Rausch, George. "The Early Career of Victoriano Huerta." THE AMERICAS 21 (1964): 136-45.

339. Razo Oliva, Juan Diego. REBELDES POPULARES DEL BAJIO: HAZANAS, TRAGEDIAS Y CORRIDOS, 1910-1927. Mexico City: Editorial Katún, 1983.

340. Redick, John R. MILITARY POTENTIAL OF LATIN AMERICAN NUCLEAR ENERGY PROGRAMS. Beverly Hills: Sage Publications, 1972.

341. Reed, John. INSURGENT MEXICO. New York: D. Appleton and Co., 1914.

342. Reed, Nelson. THE CASTE WAR OF YUCATAN. Stanford: Stanford University Press, 1964.

343. Reina, Leticia. LAS REBELIONES CAMPESINAS EN MEXICO, 1819-1906. Mexico City: Siglo XXI Editores, 1980.

344. Reyes, Bernardo. CONVERSACIONES MILITARES ESCRITAS PARA LAS ACADEMIAS DEL SEXTO REGIMIENTO DE CABALLERIA PERMANENTE. San Luis Potosí: Bruno E. García, 1879.

345. ———. EL EJERCITO MEXICANO. Mexico City: J. Ballesca Sucesor, 1901.

346. ———. ENSAYO SOBRE UN NUEVO SISTEMA DE RECLUTAMIENTO PARA EL EJERCITO Y ORGANIZACION DE LA GUARDIA NACIONAL. San Luis Potosí: Dávalos, 1885.

347. Richmond, Douglas W. VENUSTIANO CARRANZA'S NATIONALIST STRUGGLE, 1893-1920. Lincoln: University of Nebraska Press, 1983.

348. Rivero del Val, Luis. ENTRE LAS PATAS DE LOS CABALLOS: DIARIO DE UN CRISTERO. Mexico City: Editorial Jus, 1953.

349. Rocha, Sóstenes. ENQUIRIDION PARA LOS SARGENTOS Y CABOS DEL EJERCITO MEXICANO. Mexico City: El Combate, 1887.

350. Rodríquez Meléndez, Alejandro. "La defensa nacional y su proyección en el derecho administrativo." Lic. thesis, Universidad Nacional Autónoma de México, 1965.

351. Rodríguez Ramírez, Eliseo. VESTUARIO Y EQUIPO DEL EJERCITO MEXICANO. Mexico City: Ediciones Ateneo, 1953.

352. Rojas, Basilio. UN GRAN REBELDE: MANUEL GARCIA VIGIL. Mexico City: Luz, 1965.

353. Ronfeldt, David F. "The Mexican Army and Political Order Since 1940." In ARMIES AND POLITICS IN LATIN AMERICA, 291-312. Edited by Abraham F. Lowenthal. New York: Holmes and Meier Publishers, 1976.

354. ———, ed. THE MODERN MEXICAN MILITARY: A REASSESSMENT. La Jolla: Center for United States-Mexican Studies, University of California, San Diego, 1984.

355. Ross, Stanley R. FRANCISCO I. MADERO: APOSTLE OF MEXICAN DEMOCRACY. New York: Columbia University Press, 1955.

356. ———, ed. FUENTES DE LA HISTORIA CONTEMPORANEA DE MEXICO: PERIODICOS Y REVISTAS. 4 vols. Mexico City: El Colegio de México and U.N.A.M., 1965-76.

357. Ruíz, Ramón Eduardo. THE GREAT REBELLION IN MEXICO, 1905-1924. New York: W.W. Norton and Co., 1980.

358. Rutherford, John David. AN ANNOTATED BIBLIOGRAPHY OF THE NOVELS OF THE MEXICAN REVOLUTION OF 1910-1917. Troy, N.Y.: Whitston Publishing Co., 1972.

359. Sáenz, Aarón. LOS HISTORICOS TRATADOS DE TEOLOYUCAN: DISOLUCION DEL EJERCITO FEDERAL Y CAPITULACION DE LA CIUDAD DE MEXICO, 13 DE AGOSTO DE 1914. Mexico City: Patronato de la Historia de Sonora, 1964.

359a. Salas, Elizabeth. "*Soldaderas* in the Mexican Military: Myth and Mythology." Ph.D. dissertation, University of California, Los Angeles, 1987.

360. Salinas Carranza, Alberto. LA EXPEDICION PUNITIVA. Mexico City: Ediciones Botas, 1936.

361. Sámano Piña, Oscar. "Bases para la modificación del Código de Justicia Militar." Lic. thesis, Universidad Nacional Autónoma de México, 1965.

362. Sánchez Lamego, Miguel A. APUNTES PARA LA HISTORIA DEL ARMA DE INGENIEROS EN MEXICO: HISTORIA

DEL BATALLON DE ZAPADORES. 5 vols. Mexico City: Sec.
de Defensa Nacional, 1943-49.

363. ———. CUERPO NACIONAL DE INGENIEROS MILITARES,
1827-1930. Mexico City: H. Barrales, 1931.

364. ———. GENERALES DE INGENIEROS DEL EJERCITO
MEXICANO, 1821-1914. Mexico City: n.p., 1952.

365. ———. GENERALES DE LA REVOLUCION: BIOGRAFIAS.
2 vols. Mexico City: Instituto Nacional de Estudios Históricos de
la Revolución Mexicana, 1979-81.

366. ———. HISTORIA MILITAR DE LA REVOLUCION
CONSTITUCIONALISTA. 3 vols. Mexico City: Talleres Gráficos
de la Nación, 1956-66.

367. ———. HISTORIA MILITAR DE LA REVOLUCION
MEXICANA. 3 vols. Mexico City: Instituto Nacional de Estudios
Históricos de la Revolución Mexicana, 1976-77.

368. ———. HISTORIA MILITAR DE LA REVOLUCION
MEXICANA EN LA EPOCA MADERISTA. 2 vols. Mexico
City: Instituto Nacional de Estudios Históricos de la Revolución
Mexicana, 1976.

369. ———. HISTORIA MILITAR DE LA REVOLUCION
ZAPATISTA BAJO EL REGIMEN HUERTISTA. Mexico City:
Instituto Nacional de Estudios Históricos de la Revolución
Mexicana, 1979.

370. Santibáñez, Enrique. REBELION MILITAR CONTRA EL
GOBIERNO LEGITIMO DEL SENOR PRESIDENTE DE LA
REPUBLICA LIC. D. EMILIO PORTES GIL: DESCRITA Y
COMENTADA POR UN OBSERVADOR. San Antonio: n.p.,
n.d.

371. Santibáñez, Manuel. RESENA HISTORICA DEL CUERPO
DEL EJERCITO DE ORIENTE. Mexico City: Tipografía de la
Oficina Impresora del Timbre, 1892.

372. Santoro, Carmela Elvira. "United States and Mexican Relations
During World War II." Ph.D. dissertation, Syracuse University,
1967.

373. Sapia-Bosch, Alfonso F. "The Role of General Lucio Blanco in the Mexican Revolution, 1913-1922." Ph.D. dissertation, Georgetown University 1977.

374. Scheina, Robert L. LATIN AMERICA: A NAVAL HISTORY, 1910-1987. Annapolis: Naval Institute Press, 1987.

375. Schiff, Warren. "German Military Penetration into Mexico during the Late Díaz Period." HISPANIC AMERICAN HISTORICAL REVIEW 39 (1959): 568-79.

376. Schloming, Gordon Clark. "Civil-Military Relations in Mexico, 1910-1940: A Case Study." Ph.D. dissertation, Columbia University, 1974.

377. Scholes, Walter V. MEXICAN POLITICS DURING THE JUAREZ REGIME, 1855-1872. Columbia: University of Missouri Press, 1957.

378. Schroeder, Francisco Arturo. "Concepto y contenido del derecho militar: Sustantividad del derecho penal castrense y sus diferencias con el derecho criminal común." Lic. thesis, Universidad Nacional Autónoma de México, 1965.

379. Schryer, Frans J. THE RANCHEROS OF PISAFLORES: THE HISTORY OF A PEASANT BOURGEOISIE IN TWENTIETH-CENTURY MEXICO. Toronto: University of Toronto Press, 1980.

380. Sierra, Catalina, and Agustín Yáñez, eds. ARCHIVO DE DON FRANCISCO I. MADERO. 3 vols. Mexico City: Sec. de Hacienda y Crédito Público, 1960.

381. Siliceo Castillo, Fernando. "El procesado militar y las garantías individuales." Lic. thesis, Universidad Nacional Autónoma de México, 1965.

382. Simmons, Merle E. THE MEXICAN CORRIDO AS A SOURCE OF INTERPRETIVE STUDY OF MODERN MEXICO, 1870-1950. Bloomington: Indiana University Press, 1957.

383. Sinkin, Richard N. THE MEXICAN REFORM, 1855-1876: A STUDY IN LIBERAL NATION-BUILDING. Austin: University of Texas Press, 1979.

384. Slattery, Matthew T. FELIPE ANGELES AND THE MEXICAN REVOLUTION. Parma Heights, Oh.: Greenbriar Books, n.d.

385. Smith, Cornelius Cole, Jr. EMILIO KOSTERLITZKY: EAGLE OF SONORA AND THE SOUTHWEST BORDER. Glendale, Calif.: Arthur H. Clark Co., 1970.

386. Sordo Noriega Murguía, Alonso. AZUETA. Mexico City: Asociación de la Heróica Escuela Naval Militar, 1979.

387. Souza, Francisco S. GUIA PRACTICA DEL PAGADOR DE MARINA. Mexico City: Morelos, 1922.

388. STATISTICAL ABSTRACT OF LATIN AMERICA. Los Angeles: U.C.L.A. Latin American Center, 1955-.

389. Suárez, Luis. LUCIO CABANAS: EL GUERRILLERO SIN ESPERANZA. 5th ed. Mexico City: Roca, 1976.

390. Suárez Farías, Francisco J. FUERZAS ARMADAS Y ESTADO EN AMERICA LATINA: EL CASO DE MEXICO; ANALISIS POLITICO DE RELACIONES ENTRE GOBIERNO CIVIL Y EJERCITO. Mexico City: Universidad Autónoma Metropolitana-Xochimilco, 1978.

391. Suárez Suárez, Rosendo. BREVE HISTORIA DEL EJERCITO MEXICANO. Mexico City: Anáhuac, 1938.

392. Sweetman, Jack. THE LANDING AT VERACRUZ, 1914. Annapolis: Naval Institute Press, 1968.

393. Tamayo, J.A. EL GRAL. OBREGON Y LA GUERRA. Tampico: El Mundo, 1922.

394. Taylor, Lawrence D. "Bums or Heroes: Soldiers of Fortune in the Mexican Revolution 1911-1916." In CHANGE AND PERSPECTIVE IN LATIN AMERICA: PROCEEDINGS OF THE 1982 MEETING OF THE ROCKY MOUNTAIN

COUNCIL ON LATIN AMERICAN STUDIES, 362-84. Edited by C. Richard Bath. El Paso: Center for Inter-American and Border Studies, University of Texas, 1982.

395. Terrazas Cervera, Salvador. "El ejército y la justicia castrense." Lic. thesis, Universidad de Coahuila, 1973.

396. Thomas, Robert S., and Inez V. Allen. THE MEXICAN PUNITIVE EXPEDITION UNDER BRIGADIER GENERAL JOHN J. PERSHING, 1916-1917. Washington: U.S. Dept. of the Army, 1954.

397. Thord-Gray, I. GRINGO REBEL: MEXICO, 1913-1914. Coral Gables: University of Miami, 1960.

398. Tobler, Hans W. "Las paradojas del ejército revolucionario: Su papel social en la reforma agraria mexicana, 1920-1935." HISTORIA MEXICANA 21 (1971): 38-79.

399. Tompkins, Frank. CHASING VILLA: THE STORY BEHIND THE STORY OF PERSHING'S EXPEDITION INTO MEXICO. Harrisburg: Military Service Publishing Co., 1934.

400. Torrea, Juan Manuel. LA DECENA TRAGICA: APUNTES PARA LA HISTORIA DEL EJERCITO MEXICANO; LA ASONADA MILITAR DE 1913. 2 vols. Mexico City: Ediciones Joloco and Academia Nacional de Historia y Geografía, 1939-60.

401. ———. LA LEALTAD EN EL EJERCITO MEXICANO: APUNTES PARA LA HISTORIA. Mexico City: n.p., 1939.

402. ———. LA VIDA DE UNA INSTITUCION GLORIOSA: EL COLEGIO MILITAR, 1821-1930. Mexico City: Talleres Tip. Centenario, 1931.

403. Torres Bravo, Camilo. "El crédito a los miembros del ejército a la armada." Lic. thesis, Universidad Nacional Autónoma de México, 1964.

404. Torres Ramírez, Blanca. MEXICO EN LA SEGUNDA GUERRA MUNDIAL. Mexico City: El Colegio de México, 1979.

405. Toscano y García de Quevedo, Juan Miguel. "El Artículo 13 de la constitución y los fueros militares." Lic. thesis, Universidad Autónoma de Guadalajara, 1975.

406. Toulmin, Harry Aubrey. WITH PERSHING IN MEXICO. Harrisburg: Military Service Publishing Co., 1935.

407. Trask, David F., Michael C. Meyer, and Roger R. Trask, eds. A BIBLIOGRAPHY OF UNITED STATES-LATIN AMERICAN RELATIONS SINCE 1810. Lincoln: University of Nebraska Press, 1968.

408. Treviño, Jacinto B. PARTE OFICIAL RENDIDO AL C. VENUSTIANO CARRANZA, PRIMER JEFE DEL EJERCITO CONSTITUCIONAL, CON MOTIVO DE LAS OPERACIONES LLEVADAS A CABO POR LA TERCERA DIVISION DEL CUERPO DE EJERCITO DEL NORESTE, DEL 21 DE MARZO AL 31 DE MAYO DE 1915, EN EL EBANO, SLP. Monterrey: El Constitucional, 1915.

409. Treviño, Pedro. FORMULARIO DE ACTUACIONES JUDICIALES MILITARES. Mexico City: José R. O'Farrill, 1902.

410. Troncoso, Francisco P. LAS GUERRAS CON LAS TRIBUS YAQUI Y MAYO DEL ESTADO DE SONORA. Mexico City: Depto. de Estado Mayor, 1905.

411. Trueba Barrera, Alberto, and Jorge Trueba Barrera. LEGISLACION FEDERAL DEL TRABAJO BUROCRATICO: COMENTARIOS Y JURISPRUDENCIA; DISPOSICIONES COMPLEMENTARIOS; LEGISLACION DE SEGURIDAD SOCIAL PARA LAS FUERZAS ARMADAS. 6th ed. Mexico City: Editorial Porrúa, 1975.

412. Tuck, Jim. THE HOLY WAR IN LOS ALTOS: A REGIONAL ANALYSIS OF MEXICO'S CRISTERO REBELLION. Tucson: University of Arizona Press, 1982.

413. Turner, Frederick C. "Mexico: Las causas de la limitación militar." APORTES 6 (1967): 57-65.

414. Turner, John Kenneth. BARBAROUS MEXICO. Austin: University of Texas Press, 1969. [Originally published 1909-10.]

415. Tutino, John. FROM INSURRECTION TO REVOLUTION IN MEXICO: SOCIAL BASES OF AGRARIAN VIOLENCE, 1750-1940. Princeton: Princeton University Press, 1986.

416. Ulibarri George S., and John P. Harrison, eds. GUIDE TO MATERIALS ON LATIN AMERICA IN THE NATIONAL ARCHIVES OF THE UNITED STATES. Washington: National Archives and Records Service, 1974.

417. Ulloa Ortiz, Berta. "Carranza y el armamento norteamericano." HISTORIA MEXICANA 17 (1967): 253-62.

418. ———. LA REVOLUCION INTERVENIDA: RELACIONES DIPLOMATICAS ENTRE MEXICO Y ESTADOS UNIDOS, 1910-1914. Mexico City: El Colegio de México, 1971.

419. Universidad Nacional Autónoma de México. Archivo Histórico. CATALOGO DEL ARCHIVO JACINTO B. TREVINO. Mexico City: U.N.A.M., 1984.

420. Universidad Iberoamericana. Departamento de Historia. GUIA DE ARCHIVOS Y BIBLIOTECAS. Mexico City: Ediciones El Caballito, 1984.

421. United States. Department of the Army. SPANISH MILITARY DICTIONARY: ENGLISH-SPANISH, SPANISH-ENGLISH. Washington: U.S. Government Printing Office, 1950.

422. United States. Senate. INVESTIGATION OF MEXICAN AFFAIRS: REPORT AND HEARINGS BEFORE A SUBCOMMITTEE OF THE COMMITTEE ON FOREIGN RELATIONS. 2 vols. 66th Cong., lst sess. Washington: U.S. Government Printing Office, 1920.

423. University Microfilms International. LATIN AMERICA: A CATALOG OF SELECTED DOCTORAL DISSERTATION RESEARCH. Ann Arbor: University Microfilms International, 1984.

424. Urquizo, Francisco L. ALMANAQUE MILITAR. Mexico City: Talleres Gráficos de la Nación, 1919.

425. ———. A UN JOVEN MILITAR MEXICANO. Mexico City: Empresas Editoriales, 1967.

426. ——. LA CIUDADELA QUEDO ATRAS: ESCENAS VIVIDAS DE LA DECENA TRAGICA. Mexico City: B. Costa-Amic, 1965.

427. ——. DE LA VIDA MILITAR MEXICANA. Mexico City: Herrero Hnos., 1930.

428. ——. FUI SOLDADO DE LEVITA DE ESOS DE CABALLERIA. Mexico City: Fondo de Cultura Económica, 1967.

429. ——. TROPA VIEJA. Mexico City: Populibros "La Prensa," 1974. [Originally published in 1943.]

430. Unión de Militares de Origen Revolucionario, 1910-1913. ESTATUTOS. Mexico City: n.p., 1923.

431. Valadés, José C. RAFAEL BUELNA: LAS CABALLERIAS DE LA REVOLUCION. Mexico City: Leega-Júcar, 1984.

432. Vanderwood Paul J. DISORDER AND PROGRESS: BANDITS, POLICE, AND MEXICAN DEVELOPMENT. Lincoln: University of Nebraska Press, 1981.

433. ——. "Genesis of the Rurales: Mexico's Early Struggle for Public Security." HISPANIC AMERICAN HISTORICAL REVIEW 50 (1970): 323-44.

434. ——. LOS RURALES MEXICANOS. Mexico City: Fondo de Cultura Económica, 1982.

435. ——. "Los rurales: Producto de una necesidad social." HISTORIA MEXICANA 22 (1972): 34-51.

436. ——. "Response to Revolt: The Counter-Guerrilla Strategy of Porfirio Díaz." HISPANIC AMERICAN HISTORICAL REVIEW 56 (1976): 551-79.

437. ——, and Frank N. Samponaro. BORDER FURY: A PICTURE POSTCARD RECORD OF MEXICO'S REVOLUTION AND U.S. WAR PREPAREDNESS, 1910-1917. Albuquerque: University of New Mexico Press, 1988.

438. Vargas Machuca, Rafael. "El ejército como un servicio público: Algunos aspectos del derecho administrativo militar." Lic. thesis, Universidad Nacional Autónoma de México, 1940.

439. Vela Fuentes, Roberto, ed. AGENDA MILITAR PARA USO DE LOS OFICIALES DEL EJERCITO MEXICANO. Mexico City: American Book and Printing Co., 1928.

440. Vega Hurtado, Pedro. "El servicio militar mexicano." Lic. thesis, Universidad Nacional Autónoma de México, 1963.

441. Vigil, José María, and Juan B. Híjar y Haro. ENSAYO HISTORICO DEL EJERCITO DE OCCIDENTE. 3 vols. Guadalajara: Seminario de Cultura Mexicana, 1970-72.

442. Villegas Torres, José. "El delite en el derecho militar." Lic. thesis, Universidad Nacional Autónoma de México, 1964.

443. Villela, José. PIONEROS DE LA AVIACION MEXICANA. Mexico City: Ediciones Colofón, 1964.

444. Wager, Stephen J. "The Mexican Military, 1968-1978: A Decade of Change." M.A. thesis, Stanford University, 1979.

445. Walker, Phyllis Greene. "National Security." In MEXICO: A COUNTRY STUDY, 315-73. Edited by James D. Rudolph. Washington: U.S. Government Printing Office, 1985.

446. Walters, Marian C., ed. LATIN AMERICA AND THE CARIBBEAN II: A DISSERTATION BIBLIOGRAPHY. Ann Arbor: University Microfilms International, 1980.

447. Wells, Allen. YUCATAN'S GILDED AGE: HACIENDAS, HENEQUEN, AND INTERNATIONAL HARVESTER, 1860-1915. Albuquerque: University of New Mexico Press, 1985.

448. Wesson, Robert, ed. THE LATIN AMERICAN MILITARY INSTITUTION. New York: Praeger Publishers, 1986.

449. Wilkie, James W. "El complejo militar-industrial en México durante la década de 1930: Diálogo con el General Juan Andreu Almazán." REVISTA MEXICANA DE CIENCIA POLITICA 20 (1974): 59-65.

450. ———. THE MEXICAN REVOLUTION: FEDERAL EXPENDITURE AND SOCIAL CHANGE SINCE 1910. 2d ed. Berkeley: University of California Press, 1972.

451. Williams, Edward J. "The Evolution of the Mexican Military and Its Implications for Civil-Military Relations." In MEXICO'S POLITICAL STABILITY: THE NEXT FIVE YEARS, 143-58. Edited by Roderic A. Camp. Boulder: Westview Press, 1986.

452. ———. "Mexico's Modern Military: Implications for the Region." CARIBBEAN REVIEW 10 (1981): 12-13, 45.

453. Womack, John, Jr. ZAPATA AND THE MEXICAN REVOLUTION. New York: Random House, 1968.

454. Woodbury, Ronald G. "Wilson y la intervención de Veracruz: Análisis historiográfico." HISTORIA MEXICANA 17 (1967): 263-92.

PERIODICALS

455. ALMANAQUE NAUTICO, 1967-.

456. THE AMERICAS, 1944-.

457. ANAHUAC, 1961-. [Fuerza Aérea.]

458. AVISOS A LOS MARINOS, 1962-.

459. BOLETIN, 1951-58. [Depto. Cartográfico Militar.]

460. BOLETIN BIBLIOGRAFICO MEXICANO, 1940-.

461. BOLETIN DE ESTUDIOS LATINOAMERICANOS Y DEL CARIBE, 1965-.

462. BOLETIN DE INFORMACION. [Sec. de Defensa Nacional.]

463. BOLETIN DE INGENIEROS, 1910-18.

464. BOLETIN DE SANIDAD MILITAR, 1948-54.

465. BOLETIN DEL ARCHIVO GENERAL DE LA NACION, 1930-.

466. BOLETIN JURIDICO MILITAR, 1935-55.

467. BOLETIN MILITAR, 1914-. [Ejército Constitucionalista.]

468. BOLETIN TECNICO, 1965-66.

469. BULLETIN OF LATIN AMERICAN RESEARCH, 1981-.

470. EL CABALLO, 1938-39.

471. CAHIERS DU MONDE HISPANIQUE ET LUSO-BRESILIEN (CARAVELLE), 1963-.

472. CANADIAN JOURNAL OF LATIN AMERICAN AND CARIBBEAN STUDIES, 1976-.

473. DEFENSA, 1941-.

474. GACETA MEDICO MILITAR, 1930-35.

475. HISPANIC AMERICAN HISTORICAL REVIEW, 1918-.

476. HISTORIA MEXICANA, 1951-.

477. HISTORIAS, 1982-.

478. HOSPITAL CENTRAL MILITAR, 1953-55.

479. IBERO-AMERIKANISCHES ARCHIV, 1975-.

480. INTER-AMERICAN REVIEW OF BIBLIOGRAPHY/REVISTA INTERAMERICANA DE BIBLIOGRAFIA, 1951-.

481. JAHRBUCH FUR GESCHICHTE VON STAAT, WIRTSCHAFT UND GESELLSCHAFT LATEINAMERIKAS, 1964-.

482. JOURNAL OF LATIN AMERICAN STUDIES, 1969-.

483. LATIN AMERICAN PERSPECTIVES, 1974-.

484. LATIN AMERICAN RESEARCH REVIEW, 1965-.

485. LATIN AMERICAN WEEKLY REPORT, 1967-.

486. EL LEGIONARIO, 1951-.

487. MEXICAN STUDIES/ESTUDIOS MEXICANOS, 1985-.

488. NACLA REPORT ON THE AMERICAS, 1966-.

489. ONDA CORTA, 1932-54.

490. PROCESO, 1976-.

491. REVISTA AEREA.

492. REVISTA DE LA ESCUELA MEDICO MILITAR, 1942-44.

493. REVISTA DE SANIDAD MILITAR,
1948-.

494. REVISTA DE MARINA, 1965-.

495. REVISTA DEL COLEGIO MILITAR, 192?-27.

496. REVISTA DEL EJERCITO Y DE LA MARINA, 1926-.

497. REVISTA DEL EJERCITO, 1906-.

498. REVISTA DEL HEROICO COLEGIO MILITAR, 1939-52.

499. REVISTA ECUESTRE MILITAR, 1960-63.

500. REVISTA GENERAL DE LA ARMADA DE MEXICO,
1960-64.

501. REVISTA GENERAL DE MARINA, 1940-.

502. REVISTA MEDICA, 1955-. [Marina Naval.]

503. REVISTA MEDICA MILITAR, 1938-40.

504. REVISTA MEXICANA DE CIENCIAS POLITICAS Y
SOCIALES, 1955-.

505. REVISTA MEXICANA DE SOCIOLOGIA, 1939-.

506. REVISTA MILITAR DE MEXICO.

507. REVISTA MILITAR DEPORTIVA, 1930-31.

508. REVISTA NAVAL MILITAR, 1936-39.

509. REVISTA TECNICA OBRAS MARITIMAS, 1956-61.

510. EL SOLDADO, 1925-46.

511. TOHTLI: REVISTA DE AERONAUTICA MILITAR, 1916-39.

512. TRANSMISIONES, 1946-.

CHAPTER XIII

PARAGUAY AND URUGUAY

John Hoyt Williams
Indiana State University

INTRODUCTION

Historically, and that is abundantly clear in the nations' twentieth-century historiography, Paraguay and Uruguay are so dissimilar that only the last four letters of their names are in common.

In the twentieth century Paraguay fought one of its two major wars (the Chaco War, 1932-35), emerging victorious over Bolivia, albeit at tremendous human and financial costs. Even more than the War of the Triple Alliance (1864-70), the Chaco War sprinkled heroes across the land (one of them, General Alfredo Stroessner, ruled Paraguay from 1954 to 1989), and cast something of a halo about the nation's military services. Always a highly politicized military (read army) machine, Paraguay's armed forces have often intervened in the civilian political arena. They have, however, by and large escaped opprobrium doing so, thanks to their image as a patriotic bulwark against foreign threat. On the other hand, the Uruguayan military had a firm reputation as a highly professional and apolitical force, protectors of the civilian political scene. Having fought no war against another country in this century (Uruguay did get around to declaring war on the Axis until February 1945), and having acted only briefly in two internal revolutions (1903-04, 1935), the Uruguayan armed forces customarily fought only tedium. This remained the case until the rise of the Tupamaro urban revolutionary movement in the late 1960s. That recrudescence of New Left violence and terror forced the military (which includes a national police force as large as the 22,220-man regular army) to exert increasing influence over an impotent civilian regime. By 1973 the military dominated politics and was waging a ruthless and utterly savage "dirty war" against real and suspected guerrillas in which Uruguay suffered greater proportional civilian losses than did Argentina in that nation's more publicized similar conflict. As in Argentina, the Uruguayan military won by extirpating the radicals, but it emerged with a soiled reputation at best.

Historiographically, we find an outpouring of literature in Paraguay concerning the Chaco War, albeit of greatly varying quality, but little in the way of studies of the armed forces during other epochs of the century. Work on the Uruguayan military is almost nonexistent, in part due to the absence of foreign enemies and also because the "dirty war," waged against its own people, constitutes its major twentieth-century activity; no one is proud of this fact.

PARAGUAY

Oddly, there are no major works by foreigners on the Paraguayan military or even on the Chaco War per se. David Zook's THE CONDUCT OF THE CHACO WAR (65), was a promising beginning, but only that. In fact, almost all the reputable historical studies by foreigners on Paraguay deal with the nineteenth century; the twentieth century has been avoided, especially by scholars interested in the armed forces. This is in large part due to the scarcity of historical documentation, for any part of the century and any subject within it, and the reluctance of Paraguayan military figures to grant frank interviews. Further, most of the studies written by Paraguayans on the Chaco War or other twentieth-century events related to the armed forces are highly polemical, politicized, self-serving, or "philosophical" in nature. Paraguayans have contributed significantly to what we know about the military of their country, but their various writings have been selective.

GENERAL WORKS

The beginner is forced to start with several odd works in the English language. These are the chapter on Paraguay in Adrian J. English, THE ARMED FORCES OF LATIN AMERICA (18), a largely historical treatment of imperfect accuracy; Charles Kolinski, HISTORICAL DICTIONARY OF PARAGUAY (32), useful for those seeking military tidbits; and, for a more recent overview, relevant sections of George Philip, THE MILITARY IN SOUTH AMERICAN POLITICS (42). Portions of César Caviedes's work on the military governments of the Southern Cone (13), can also be of value to the researcher. One Paraguayan book must be mentioned here as well; Colonel Luis Vittone, LAS FUERZAS ARMADAS PARAGUAYAS EN SUS

DISTINTAS EPOCAS (60), is a rather disjointed compendium which traces the Paraguayan armed forces from its creation to modern times. Vittone, in fact, might well be the most professional of Paraguayan military historians. Less global in scope, but still "general," are two treatments of the air force. Leandro Aponte's work (2), traces the military air arm from its beginnings to 1957, while Georg von Rauch's FUERZA AEREA DEL PARAGUAY (62), deals with the more recent epoch.

PUBLISHED DOCUMENTS

Aside from the works discussed below in the section on specialized works, many of which have primary source material in the text or appendices, and a few basically diplomatic studies, there is no collection of printed documents concerning the Paraguayan military in any epoch. The closest approximation is the ALBUM GRAFICO (16), published first by the Argentine Círculo Militar in 1938 and reissued in 1985 by a commission in Asunción called the Cincuentenario de la Defensa del Chaco (15). This is the only photographic history of the Chaco War, and the new edition has reproduced the pictures far more clearly than the poorly-printed Argentine original. This volume permits one to develop a true feeling for the harshness of conditions and combat in the Chaco.

MEMOIRS, JOURNALS, AND BIOGRAPHIES

In this category the historiography basically restricts one to the era of the Chaco War. In fact, there is some overlap with many of the works noted below, for, as in the case of the book by Antonio E. González (25), there is a fine line between the history he wrote and the history he lived.

Among those works deserving mention are several by Arturo Bray. Most notable are his two-volume HOMBRES Y EPOCAS DEL PARAGUAY (9), a collection of short biographies of Paraguayans of all periods, many of whom figured prominently in twentieth-century military affairs, such as Eligio Ayala and Manuel Gondra. Bray has also put to paper his own martial experiences in the very · valuable ARMAS Y LETRAS: MEMORIAS (10). His description of garrison duty in the Chaco before the war is unusually good, and the memoirs trace his career in uniform to 1939. Also focusing on the pre-war period is Alfredo L. Jaeggli's ALBINO JARA (30), a biography of a career officer who rose to become minister of war and (briefly) president of the republic (1911). In the former position he is credited with reorganizing the Paraguayan army and laying the basis for its professionalization.

As one might expect, the bulk of biographies and memoirs relate specifically to the Chaco War. Among the best are several treatments of the maximum Paraguayan hero, Mariscal Estigarribia (who later became president). Perhaps the best is his autobiography, carefully edited and translated by Pablo Max Ynsfrán as JOSE FELIX ESTIGARRIBIA: THE EPIC OF THE CHACO (64). This is one of the premier sources for the war years. Two biographies of the marshal are also worth consultation. The study by Justo Pastor Benítez (8), stresses the role of Estigarribia in the conflict, while that of Alfredo M. Seiferhead (52), uses a longer time frame and tends to stress the influence of the marshal (and the army) in Paraguayan politics. The much shorter biography in Vittone's work (61), is also worth a perusal.

Also related to the war is the biography by Leandro Aponte of Colonel Eugenio Garay (3), one of the marshal's most trusted lieutenants, who figured prominently in almost every major battle of the conflict. So lustrous was Garay's reputation that he was promoted to the rank of general after his death, and there is more than a little hero worship in this volume. General Juan B. Ayala, (4), the man who commanded the successful Paraguayan forces at the major victory of Toledo (February 1933), has left an interesting account of the first year or so of the war. Finally, Ernesto Pérez Acosta (41), wrote a valuable account of his experiences in the Chaco as well.

The Bolivians have contributed a great deal to this genre, too. Among the most reliable are General Félix Tabera R., APUNTES PARA LA HISTORIA DE LA GUERRA DEL CHACO: PICUIBA (55), which treats at length the organization and state of readiness of both armies on the eve of the war and in many of the early battles. Colonel David Toro Ruilova (56), Bolivia's most successful commander in the latter stages of the conflict, has left us his own (not entirely self-serving) memoirs, as has Lieutenant Colonel Oscar Moscoso (38), who precipitated the hostilities by leading Bolivian troops in the capture of Pitiantutá in June 1932. Demetrio Canelas has produced a biography of Bolivia's wartime president, SALAMANCA (11). Manuel María Oliver, an Argentine who was on the front lines as an observer, wrote an engaging and highly readable book, LA GUERRA EN EL CHACO BOREAL (40).

SPECIALIZED WORKS: THE CHACO WAR

While most treatments of the Chaco War include a good deal of information relevant to the early years of the century, the conflict itself, which has generated a vast literature, can be considered as a separate category of historiography. In addition to the Zook study (65), among the best accounts is Carlos J. Fernández's massive six-volume GUERRA DEL CHACO (20), in many ways the "standard" opus on the conflict. While not an official history in the customary sense, this work profits mightily from the author's extremely well-placed sources. If any author had carte blanche for researching the war, it was Fernández, and he used it well. Also of importance is General Vicente Machuca's LA GUERRA DEL CHACO DESDE LA TERMINACION DEL ARMISTICIO HASTA EL FIN DE LA CONTIENDA (35), which is especially strong on the early phases of the war. It contains a wealth of organizational data and reasonably good maps. Another general, Raimundo Rolón, has produced a solid treatment, LA GUERRA DEL CHACO (50), in two volumes. This account does not get too bogged down in operational detail. It is also among the most readable studies (which is not saying a great deal). Included among the better works on the war is Roberto Querejazu C.'s MASAMACLAY (43), a highly readable treatment from the Bolivian point of view. The title translates as "place without water," which is exceedingly apt, for the sere Chaco region demanded of the combatants that they focus on water wells rather than on roads and towns. The hydrographic nature of the conflict is also emphasized in the blunt title of another Bolivian contribution, Saturnino Rodríguez's FUE LA SED [IT WAS THE THIRST] (49). The Querejazu book is far more thorough and rewarding than that of Rodríguez, but the latter is worth consultation.

Also of note is Antonio E. González, PREPARACION DEL PARAGUAY PARA LA GUERRA DEL CHACO (25), which, despite the title, treats the entire course of the conflict. It is especially strong on Paraguay's acquisition of war materiel (a mean trick in itself), and the organization of the army before and at the outbreak of hostilities. The author was a high-level artillery commander in the struggle, but the work goes far beyond personal experience. One should also include Colonel Pedro P. Medina's LA GUERRA DEL CHACO (37), published in 1985. It covers the bulk of the conflict and includes good maps, which is important given the average person's ignorance of the Chaco.

Then, still dealing with the war, there are some works of more limited scope, but nevertheless of value. Among these one must mention two studies of the role of the navy; Juan Speratti, HISTORIA DE LA ARMADA NACIONAL, 1925-1937 (54), is a solid account, and Rodolfo Dávalos ACTUACION DE LA MARINA EN LA GUERRA DEL CHACO (17), has written specifically on the navy in the war itself. Sergio Recalde A. has produced a useful treatment of the role of the military medical corps in the conflict, LA SANIDAD EN LA GUERRA

DEL CHACO Y EL DOCTOR JUAN FRANCISCO RECALDE V. (45), something of a paean of praise to his physician father.

A few other treatments, none of them outstanding but all useful, should be mentioned. Julio Díaz Arguedas wrote the first official Bolivian history of the war in 1940, published by the Army Press, LA GUERRA CON EL PARAGUAY. Another Bolivian, Colonel Francisco Barrero U., produced CONDUCCION POLITICO-DIPLOMATICA DE LA GUERRA CON PARAGUAY (5), a book strong on logistics for both countries, the war on the home fronts, Argentina's (exaggerated) aid to Paraguay, and the "modern" nature of this conflict. Paraguayan Sindulfo Barreto, in PORQUE NO PASARON: REVELACIONES DIPLOMATICAS Y MILITARES (6), covers only the pre-war years, but it is strong on Paraguayan preparations for the struggle. Ricardo Mujía's BOLIVIA-PARAGUAY (39), in five volumes, is an excellent source on the background to the war, while the study by General Angel Rodríguez, AUTOPSIA DE UNA GUERRA (47), is a sober examination of the strategy implemented by both nations. Chilean Colonel Aquiles Vergara Vicuña, who served with the Bolivian army, has produced a sweeping, seven-volume treatment, which attempts (somewhat unsuccessfully) to assess the military strengths and weaknesses of the two countries, HISTORIA DE LA GUERRA DEL CHACO (57). Also from the Bolivian side is Jorge Antezana Villagrán's LA GUERRA DEL CHACO: HASTA CAMPO VIA (59), a thoughtful, critical treatment of a great battle lost by Bolivia in late 1933. In it he draws upon much material from the Paraguayan side and realistically assesses Bolivian weaknesses and mistakes (especially of command). Last in this section, but hardly least, are the observations of Colonel Luis Vittone in his TRES GUERRAS, DOS MARISCALES, DOCE BATALLAS (61), a book filled with organizational details and maps and especially astute in its treatment of the war's first year.

There are a host of small-unit operational histories which lie outside the purview of this essay, but in addition to the ALBUM GRAFICO (15), one should consult Emilio Chilavert, LA DICTADURA LIBERAL Y EL EJERCITO (14), for a jaundiced, partisan, but useful look at the military before the Chaco War. Also, related to the conflict are a number of other recommended studies including that of Leslie B. Rout, Jr. (51), on the mechanics of the peace conference and treaty and the role of a number of outside nations in both the war and the peace; Michael Grow's work on authoritarian regimes in Paraguay in the 1934-45 period (26); and Alfredo M. Seiferheld's excellent treatment of Nazi influence in Paraguay, and, especially, in the military, on the eve of World War II (53). For information on more recent decades one must turn to Paul W. Lewis's semi-biographical PARAGUAY UNDER STROESSNER (33), which covers the 1954-80 era.

PERIODICALS

Paraguay is not a nation rich in periodical literature on any subject. The military is virtually a taboo subject for serious publications, but one can turn up the occasional article of interest in HISTORIA PARAGUAYA (66), an annual published (irregularly) since 1956. The only other source is the sporadic REVISTA DE LAS FF AA DE LA NACION (67), published by the army itself since approximately 1961. While this magazine can be helpful, it is often a vehicle for patriotic dross.

FUTURE RESEARCH

Granted that this category is open-ended because so much needs to be done, it must be said that not a great deal will be accomplished. The Paraguayan military, while not a large establishment during peacetime, always has been respected by the public and continually has had a major political input. This should make the institution a prime candidate for serious scholarly attention. However, primary documentation on most aspects of the armed forces in the twentieth century (as very distinct from the nineteenth) virtually is nonexistent. The Archivo Nacional in Asunción holds no post-1900 material on any subject, and, in theory, public papers are held in the files of the ministry which generated them. In reality, documents of the Ministry of Defense do not exist, at least for research purposes. Likewise, interviews, save those dealing with the Chaco War, are almost impossible to get by either foreign or domestic scholars. It would be lovely to write a history of the military's role in the fearsome Civil War of 1947-48, for instance, but the lack of documentation, dearth of interviews, and absence of even basic bibliographic guides makes this impossible. If one ever is written, it will be a polemic done by someone with a political ax to grind.

Still, there are some practicable subjects which can and should be tackled. Most of these, of course, deal with the Chaco War. There has as yet been no *cartografía militar* (military cartography) of the war, and, without such, the conflict will never adequately be understood. On a broader scale, a sweeping history of the struggle itself, written by an objective foreign scholar, is both feasible, needed, and worthwhile. Since Paraguayans in general, and the government and army as well, are all proud of their nation's largely unexpected victory, the researcher openly can ask questions and will have access to a wider range of sources than for any other twentieth-century topic.

The only other subject of importance within the realm of possibility for the serious scholar is a broader study of the role of the military in the Chaco (as distinct from the war itself). The army has been active there since well before 1900 (predating civilian settlement), and was responsible for fighting Indians, mapping, surveying, building roads, running ranches and farms, staking Paraguay's claim to the region, and protecting immigrant settlements such as those of the Mennonites, who began arriving in significant numbers in 1926. Sadly, other military-related topics are unlikely to be realized even though Stroessner has left office.

URUGUAY

A book on the military historiography of twentieth-century Uruguay would be a shorter book than one on the history of crime in Switzerland. The case of the nineteenth century, more "removed" and far more turbulent, is quite the opposite. This brief discussion of sources dealing with the post-1900 Uruguayan armed forces will encompass a few studies treating the late nineteenth-century background and the first years of the twentieth (basically, up to the Revolution of 1904), and then the period before and during the Tupamaro upheaval, or "dirty war" of the 1960s and 1970s. Almost all of the work on the latter verges on the near hysterical in tone, but many treatments contain at least some worthwhile material on the modern Uruguayan military, which is to say, as in the case of Paraguay, the army.

GENERAL WORKS

On the general level there is precious little. The chapter in Adrian J. English's (19), treatment of the Latin American military is adequate, if brief. One should also consult the relevant portions of George Philip's (42), book on the armed forces' role in South American politics in recent times, as well as César Caviedes's (13), volume dealing with the authoritarian state in the Southern Cone region. Perhaps more rewarding, however, is the very cogent, seventy-page section devoted to Uruguay in the anthology edited by Howard Handelman and Thomas Sanders, MILITARY GOVERNMENT AND THE MOVEMENT TOWARD DEMOCRACY IN SOUTH AMERICA (29). Written by Handelman, it is far less adversarial than most.

SPECIALIZED WORKS:
NINETEENTH TO EARLY TWENTIETH-CENTURY

Dealing with the turn-of-the-century era, only five books stand out clearly as having relevance to this essay. Javier de Viana's CRONICAS DE LA REVOLUCION DEL QUEBRACHO (58), treats military issues related to the major internal upheaval of 1886. J. Ariel Madeiro López's, LA REVOLUCION DE 1897 (36), has a great deal of information with a good chapter on military developments following the last revolution of the nineteenth century. Manuel E. Fonseca's (21), biography of Gumersindo Saravía takes the reader only to 1894, but includes much material on both the Uruguayan army and navy in a critical period when the bedrock of professionalization was being laid. It is particularly strong on foreign influences in that process, influences that remained important well into this century. At times a bit syrupy, but still of value, is Arturo Rodríguez's BIOGRAFIA DEL CORONEL MANUEL M. RODRIGUEZ (48); it traces the life and times of a famous Uruguayan hero of the Paraguayan War (1864-70) and founder of the Colorado party, one of the nation's two traditional political factions. This volume includes considerable information on the army in the 1890s to 1904 and its involvement in the revolution of the latter year. Finally, Alfredo R. Castellanos (12), in his treatment of Aparicio Saravía and his epoch, presents a wealth of material relating to the military in the chaotic 1893-1904 period.

One book bridges the large gap between the early years of the century and the Tupamaro crisis. Adolfo Aguirre González's LA REVOLUCION DE 1935 (24), which covers more than the title would indicate, is a very good study, and chapters six to eight are especially germane. It is noteworthy that airpower was used effectively against the revolutionaries in this upheaval.

SPECIALIZED WORKS: THE TUPAMARO YEARS

Most of the literature on this period is shrill, strident, and partisan but even the shrillest, carefully gleaned, can yield solid information on the Uruguayan armed forces (and police), as well as the organization, strategy, and tactics of the left-wing guerrillas. With the revolutionaries in full hue and cry, Gabriel Ramírez wrote a thoughtful work, LAS FUERZAS ARMADAS URUGUAYAS EN LA CRISIS CONTINENTAL (44), which deals at length with the position of the military within Uruguayan society and the rising pressures on it to come to the rescue of a frightened middle class. Also to be noted is Edy Kaufman, URUGUAY IN TRANSITION FROM CIVILIAN TO MILITARY RULE (31), which, like the above work, attempts to place the armed forces and their political interference in a societal perspective.

On the guerrillas themselves, perhaps the best-known work is that of shrill María Esther Gilio, LA GUERRILLA TUPAMARA (22), published from exile in Argentina in 1970. Anne Edmundson translated the volume into English that same year as THE TUPAMARO GUERRILLAS (23), with a cogent introduction (much-needed) by Latin Americanist Robert J. Alexander, a specialist on left-wing politics. This study was written in the heyday of the terrorist (and military counter-terrorist) campaign, when young people were "disappearing" on a daily basis, and bomb blasts punctuated traffic noises in Montevideo. Once one shakes off the romantic rhetoric, one can proceed. While Gilio characterizes the Uruguayan government as the "Sadistic Father," she does at least define it and its organs of repression. In a similar vein, José Guerrero Martín's LOS TUPAMAROS: SEGUNDO PODER DE URUGUAY (27), can be mined for data on the tactics of both the Tupamaros and their uniformed enemies. The same can be said for the anonymous ACTAS TUPAMARAS (1), which at least has the advantage of a decade of reflection. Finally, Mario Benedetti, in his CRONICAS DEL 71 (7), presents a more ambivalent examination of the rebels and their foes.

There are also three articles which merit attention for the Tupamaro period. Carlos Bañales Guimaraes, in his "Las fuerzas armadas en la crisis uruguaya" (28), focuses on the societal pressures which impelled the army and police to act against the guerrillas in both the military and political spheres. Liliana de Riz (46), treats the same issues in her 1970 article, albeit with less sympathy. Finally, one should peruse Ronald McDonald's "The Rise of Military Politics in Uruguay" (34), for a relatively dispassionate account of the issue.

FUTURE RESEARCH

Research on twentieth-century military topics in Uruguay is exceedingly difficult, especially since there is not even a single general history of the nation's armed forces which merits mention. Despite the fact that some data for the period prior to World War II can be found in the somewhat disorganized Archivo General de la Nación, the infrastructure, including focused bibliographic guides, is nonexistent. A general account of the institution desperately is needed and perhaps could be written, but the period of the "dirty war" is so touchy that information is available only from the guerrilla side of the issue.

Information exists on the rest of the century, and because there has been no tradition of censorship or control of the media in Uruguay unlike Paraguay, again, with the exception of the Tupamaro period, public records can be found. Also, since the Uruguayan military has never had the patriotic halo which hovers above its Paraguayan counterpart, it is not so sacrosanct that it cannot be researched frankly, again, with the 1968-80 exception. Uruguayans, both civilian and military, are also quite open to interviews. Future scholars may well find a fertile field in Uruguay.

BIBLIOGRAPHY:
PARAGUAY AND URUGUAY

1. ACTAS TUPAMARAS: UNA EXPERIENCIA DE GUERRILLA URBANA. Madrid: Revolución, 1981.

2. Aponte, Leandro. CINCUENTA ANOS DE AERONAUTICA EN EL PARAGUAY. Asunción: El Arte, 1957.

3. ———. CORONEL EUGENIO A. GARAY: HEROE DEL CHACO. Asunción: Imp. Militar del E.M.G. 1944.

4. Ayala, Juan B. LAS BATALLAS DEL CHACO A LA LUZ DE LOS PRINCIPIOS DE GUERRA. Asunción: El Lector, 1985.

5. Barrero U., Francisco. CONDUCCION POLITICO-DIPLOMATICA DE LA GUERRA CON PARAGUAY. La Paz: Editorial "El Siglo," 1979.

6. Barreto, Sindulfo. PORQUE NO PASARON: REVELACIONES DIPLOMATICAS Y MILITARES. Asunción: Editorial El Gráfico, 1969.

7. Benedetti, Mario. CRONICAS DEL 71. Montevideo: ARCA, 1972.

8. Benítez, Justo Pastor. ESTIGARRIBIA: EL SOLDADO DEL CHACO. 2d ed. Buenos Aires: Ediciones Nizza, 1958.

9. Bray, Arturo. HOMBRES Y EPOCAS DEL PARAGUAY. 2 vols. 3d ed. Buenos Aires: Ediciones Nizza, 1957.

10. ———. ARMAS Y LETRAS: MEMORIAS. 3 vols. Asunción: Editorial El Gráfico, 1981.

11. Canelas, Demetrio. SALAMANCA. Cochabamba: n.p., 1937.

12. Castellanos, Alfredo R. APARICIO SARAVIA: EL CAUDILLO Y SU TIEMPO. Montevideo: ARCA, 1975.

13. Caviedes, César. THE SOUTHERN CONE: REALITIES OF THE AUTHORITARIAN STATE IN SOUTH AMERICA. Totowa, NJ: Rowman and Allanheld, 1984.

14. Chilavert, Emilio. LA DICTADURA LIBERAL Y EL EJERCITO. Asunción: "La Opinión," 1928.

15. Cincuentenario de la Defensa del Chaco. ALBUM GRAFICO. Asunción: Cincuentenario de la Defensa del Chaco, 1985.

16. Círculo Militar. ALBUM GRAFICO. Buenos Aires: Círculo Militar, 1938.

17. Dávalos, Rodolfo. ACTUACION DE LA MARINA EN LA GUERRA DEL CHACO. Asunción: El Reconstructor, 1974.

18. Díaz Arguedas, Julio. LA GUERRA CON EL PARAGUAY. La Paz: Imprenta del Ejército, 1940.

19. English, Adrian J. THE ARMED FORCES OF LATIN AMERICA. London: Jane's, 1984.

20. Fernández, Carlos J. GUERRA DEL CHACO. 6 vols. Buenos Aires: Imprenta Militar, 1956-76.

21. Fonseca, Manuel E. GUMERSINDO SARAVIA: EL GENERAL DE LA LIBERTAD. Montevideo: Florensa y Lafón, 1957.

22. Gilio, María Esther. LA GUERRILLA TUPAMARA. Buenos Aires: Ediciones de la Flor, 1970.

23. ———. THE TUPAMARO GUERRILLAS. New York: Saturday Review Press, 1970.

24. González, Adolfo Aguirre. LA REVOLUCION DE 1935. Montevideo: Librosur, 1985.

25. González, Antonio E. PREPARACION DEL PARAGUAY PARA LA GUERRA DEL CHACO. 2 vols. Asunción: Editorial El Gráfico, 1957.

26. Grow, Michael. THE GOOD NEIGHBOR POLICY AND AUTHORITARIANISM IN PARAGUAY. Lawrence: The Regents Press of Kansas, 1981.

27. Guerrero Martín, José. LOS TUPAMAROS: SEGUNDO PODER DE URUGUAY. Buenos Aires: Clio, 1972.

28. Guimaraes, Carlos Bañales. "Las fuerzas armadas en la crisis uruguaya." APORTES (Paris) 9 (1968): 26-57.

29. Handelman, Howard, and Thomas Sanders, eds. MILITARY GOVERNMENT AND THE MOVEMENT TOWARD DEMOCRACY IN SOUTH AMERICA. Bloomington: Indiana University Press, 1981.

30. Jaeggli, Alfredo L. ALBINO JARA: UN VARON METEORICO. Buenos Aires: Ediciones Nizza, 1963.

31. Kaufman, Edy. URUGUAY IN TRANSITION FROM CIVILIAN TO MILITARY RULE. New Brunswick: Transaction Books, 1979.

32. Kolinski, Charles. HISTORICAL DICTIONARY OF PARAGUAY. Metuchen, NJ: Scarecrow Press, 1973.

33. Lewis, Paul. PARAGUAY UNDER STROESSNER. Chapel Hill: University of North Carolina Press, 1980.

34. McDonald, Ronald. "The Rise of Military Politics in Uruguay." INTER-AMERICAN ECONOMIC AFFAIRS 28 (1975): 32-51.

35. Machuca, Vicente. LA GUERRA DEL CHACO DESDE LA TERMINACION DEL ARMISTICIO HASTA EL FIN DE LA CONTIENDA. Asunción: NAPA, 1983.

36. Madeiro López, J. Ariel. LA REVOLUCION DE 1897. Montevideo: Banda Oriental, 1980.

37. Medina, Pedro P. LA GUERRA DEL CHACO: SUS ANTECEDENTES Y SUS CAMPANAS. Asunción: NAPA, 1985.

38. Moscoso, Oscar. RECUERDOS DE LA GUERRA DEL CHACO. Sucre: Escuela Tip. Salesiana, 1939.

39. Mujía, Ricardo. BOLIVIA-PARAGUAY. 5 vols. La Paz: Editora de "El Tiempo," 1914-16.

40. Oliver, Manuel María. LA GUERRA EN EL CHACO BOREAL: COMO SE DEFIENDE EL PARAGUAY;

CRONICAS DE LA LINEA DE FUEGO. Buenos Aires: Roldán, 1935.

41. Pérez Acosta, Ernesto. LA CONTIENDA DEL CHACO. Asunción: n.p., 1962.

42. Philip, George D.E. THE MILITARY IN SOUTH AMERICAN POLITICS. London: Croom Helm, 1985.

43. Querejazu C., Roberto. MASAMACLAY. La Paz: Novedades, 1964.

44. Ramírez, Gabriel. LAS FUERZAS ARMADAS URUGUAYAS EN LA CRISIS CONTINENTAL. Montevideo: Tierra Nueva, 1971.

45. Recalde A., Sergio. LA SANIDAD EN LA GUERRA DEL CHACO Y EL DOCTOR JUAN FRANCISCO RECALDE V. Asunción: Toledo, 1985.

46. Riz, Liliana de. "Ejército y política en Uruguay." REVISTA LATINOAMERICANA DE SOCIOLOGIA (Buenos Aires) 6 (1970): 420-42.

47. Rodríguez, Angel. AUTOPSIA DE UNA GUERRA: CAMPANA DEL CHACO. Santiago: Ediciones Ercilla, 1940.

48. Rodríguez, Arturo. BIOGRAFIA DEL CORONEL MANUEL M. RODRIGUEZ. Montevideo: n.p., 1979.

49. Rodríguez, Saturnino. FUE LA SED. La Paz: n.p., 1959.

50. Rolón, Raimundo. LA GUERRA DEL CHACO. 2 vols. Asunción: n.p., 1951-63.

51. Rout, Leslie B., Jr. THE POLITICS OF THE CHACO PEACE CONFERENCE, 1935-1939. Austin: University of Texas Press, 1970.

52. Seiferheld, Alfredo M. ESTIGARRIBIA: VEINTE ANOS DE POLITICA PARAGUAYA. Asunción: NAPA, 1984.

53. ———. NAZISMO Y FASCISMO EN EL PARAGUAY: VISPERAS DE LA II GUERRA MUNDIAL; GOBIERNOS DE

RAFAEL FRANCO Y FELIX PAIVA, 1936-1939. Asunción: Editorial Histórica, 1985.

54. Speratti, Juan. HISTORIA DE LA ARMADA NACIONAL EN EL PERIODO 1925-1937. Asunción: Talleres Gráficos de la Escuela Técnica Salesiana, 1972.

55. Tabera R., Félix. APUNTES PARA LA HISTORIA DE LA GUERRA DEL CHACO: PICUIBA. 2d ed. La Paz: n.p., 1978.

56. Toro Ruilova, David. MI ACTUACION EN LA GUERRA DEL CHACO: LA RETIRADA DE PICUIBA. La Paz: Editorial Renacimiento, 1941.

57. Vergara Vicuña, Aquiles. HISTORIA DE LA GUERRA DEL CHACO. 7 vols. La Paz: Lit. e Imp. Unidas, 1940-44.

58. Viana, Javier de. CRONICAS DE LA REVOLUCION DEL QUEBRACHO. Montevideo: ARCA, 1979.

59. Villagrán, Jorge Antezana. LA GUERRA DEL CHACO: HASTA CAMPO VIA; ANALISIS Y CRITICA SOBRE LA CONDUCCION MILITAR. La Paz: Librería Los Amigos Del Libro, 1979.

60. Vittone, Luis. LAS FUERZAS ARMADAS DE LA NACION EN SUS DISTINTAS EPOCAS. Asunción: Editorial El Gráfico, 1959.

61. ———. TRES GUERRAS, DOS MARISCALES, DOCE BATALLAS. Asunción: Editorial El Gráfico, 1967.

62. Von Rauch, Georg. FUERZA AEREA DEL PARAGUAY. Genoa: Aviazione e Marina, 1972.

63. Weschler, Lawrence. A MIRACLE, A UNIVERSE: SETTLING ACCOUNTS WITH TORTURES. New York: Pantheon Books, 1990.

64. Ynsfrán, Pablo Max, ed. JOSE FELIX ESTIGARRIBIA: THE EPIC OF THE CHACO. Austin: University of Texas Press, 1952.

65. Zook, David. THE CONDUCT OF THE CHACO WAR. New York: Bookman Associates, 1960.

PERIODICALS

66. HISTORIA PARAGUAYA. 1956-.

67. REVISTA DE LAS FF AA DE LA NACION. 1961-.